T0292807

Capitalist Peace

Capitalist Peace

A History of American Free-Trade Internationalism

THOMAS W. ZEILER

OXFORD
UNIVERSITY PRESS

OXFORD
UNIVERSITY PRESS

Oxford University Press is a department of the University of Oxford. It furthers the University's objective of excellence in research, scholarship, and education by publishing worldwide. Oxford is a registered trade mark of Oxford University Press in the UK and certain other countries.

Published in the United States of America by Oxford University Press
198 Madison Avenue, New York, NY 10016, United States of America.

© Oxford University Press 2022

All rights reserved. No part of this publication may be reproduced, stored in a retrieval system, or transmitted, in any form or by any means, without the prior permission in writing of Oxford University Press, or as expressly permitted by law, by license, or under terms agreed with the appropriate reproduction rights organization. Inquiries concerning reproduction outside the scope of the above should be sent to the Rights Department, Oxford University Press, at the address above.

You must not circulate this work in any other form
and you must impose this same condition on any acquirer.

Library of Congress Control Number: 2022941525

ISBN 978–0–19–762136–3

DOI: 10.1093/oso/9780197621363.001.0001

1 3 5 7 9 8 6 4 2

Printed by Sheridan Books, Inc., United States of America

CONTENTS

ACKNOWLEDGMENTS

Over the half-dozen or so years of conceptualizing, researching, writing, and editing this book, I incurred huge debts that I can only partly repay by acknowledging them. Thanks to the University of Colorado Boulder for research leave and, on behalf of the Arts and Humanities, the beautiful flat in London. Thanks also to my numerous colleagues in the Department of History and the Program in International Affairs, as well as my dean buddies, David Brown and Jim White, and especially Jackie Rodgers (Lamaire) in the Program in International Affairs. Funding and archival assistance came from many sources, including the Hoover, Roosevelt, Truman, Eisenhower, Johnson, and Ford Presidential Libraries; the Hoover Institution, the Hagley Museum and Library, the Rockefeller Archives Center, the Bentley Library, the Seeley Mudd Library at Princeton University, and the Parliamentary Archives in London. I must single out Lisa Sullivan of the Harry S Truman Library Institute, who steered me to the wonderful Truman Scholar Award, as well as resources in Independence, Missouri, including Clifton Truman Daniel—the president's grandson–from whom I learned a lot over barbecue one night. Lisa and I commiserated over politics, and then, at long last, exalted over them, even in the pandemic, and I cherish her friendship.

Kathleen Kearns proved to be an editor extraordinaire in the final stages of the manuscript, improving and shortening the whole thing. Historians already know what a godsend Susan Ferber has been for years as a shrewd and supportive editor, and I also appreciate her longtime friendship as well. My colleague Bob Ferry is special to me for a lot of reasons, and one is his son, Danny Ferry, a graphic designer who provided draft after draft of the cover art. I'm proud to have friends, colleagues, and relatives who advised me, dished it out, and took a lot more from me along the way: Ted Alden, Bob Brigham, David Brown, Olivier Costa, Isabelle Davion, Mario Del Pero (and his students and colleagues at Sciences Po Paris), Fred Dessberg, Al Eckes, David Ekbladh, Jeff Engel and Katie Carte, Marc Gallicchio, Shon Howard, Richard Immerman (and Marion), Akira Iriye, Marc Jackson, the Kilbergs (Jay, Gina, Esta, Sam, and grandchildren) whom I have known seemingly forever, Diane Labrosse, David Leblang, Zach Levey, Maureen McElharen, James McAllister, Francine McKenzie, Bob McMahon, Jason Parker, Trudy Peterson, Andrew Preston, Kathy Rasmussen, Marc Selverstone, Katie Sibley, Jim Small, Jess Strum, Jeremi Suri, and Phil Weinstock. Anonymous reviewers proved invaluable to improving the manuscript. Thanks also to Chris, Dan, Michael, Sarah, Andrew, Nathan, Kevin, Alex, Keith, Ben, Doug, the late Jessica Martin, Gerritt, and Rob—doctoral students who endured my demands to include economics; they have always been interested and are interesting themselves, and I am proud to have helped in their educational missions.

Archives, and especially archivists, were simply essential. Special thanks to David Langbart at the National Archives and Records Administration, whom I count also as a good friend and unrivaled Civil War battlefield guide. My gratitude goes out also to Patrick Kerwin, Courtney Matthews in images, and other archivists at the Library of Congress, Michelle Bogart, Bob Holzweiss, and Zach Roberts at the George H.W. Bush Library, Lucas Clawson and Carol Lockman at Hagley, Paul Thomas and Sarah Patton at the Hoover Institution; Kevin Bailey and Marty Burtzloff at Eisenhower, William Baehr and David Woolner of the FDR Library, Emily Mathay and my old friends going back to my grad years, now Senior Archivist Maura Porter and the best reference technician around, Mike Desmond; Jennifer Cuddeback at the LBJ Library, Spencer Howard at the Herbert Hoover Library; Dorissa Martinez and Ryan Pettigrew of the Nixon Library; Jennifer Newby and Steve Branch in images of the Reagan Library; Jason Kaplan and Herbert Ragan of the Clinton Library; Randy Sowell, David Clark, and Jim Armistead at Truman; Donna Lehman and James Neal at the Gerald Ford Library; Bethany Antos at the Rockefeller Archive; Rebecca Baker at the University of Washington; Thomas Hayes in images at the Obama Library; Virginia Butler at the George W. Bush Archives; the Getty Images archives; and Sarah Alex of the Herb Block Foundation.

Family is the key to my work – they have been so patient and permissive! And nobody has endured me and my research more than Rocio, whom I have loved for over four decades and who shouldered many burdens. In that time came two wonderful kids, Jackson and Ella, whom I have adored well into three decades. My late father would have read this book with a discerning eye, and I wish he could have seen the end product as the creative and determined academic that he was, and my mom remains my source of interest in history as well as a rock of support, good cheer, and political rectitude. Siblings Doug, Jeanie, and Diana, and their spouses Rachel, Ralf, and Howie and kids Ryan, Nina, Alex, Maddie, Eli, and Aden—some more expert than others as body surfers at the Outer Banks or as fun gamers and partiers at night—but all a lot of fun, and smart to boot, who put a good perspective on research and writing.

ABBREVIATIONS

AFL-CIO	American Federation of Labor-Congress of Industrial Organizations
APEC	Asia-Pacific Economic Cooperation
ASEAN	Association of Southeast Asian Nations
CAFTA-DR	Central American Free Trade Agreement and Dominican Republic
CAP	Common Agricultural Policy
CIA	Central Intelligence Agency
COCOM	Coordinating Committee for Multilateral Export Controls
EC	European Community
ECOSOC	United Nations Economic and Social Council
EU	European Union
EEC	European Economic Community
FTA	Free Trade Agreement
FTAA	Free Trade Area of the Americas
GATT	General Agreement on Tariffs and Trade
ITO	International Trade Organization
MEFTA	U.S.-Middle East Free Trade Area
MITI	Ministry of International Trade and Industry (Japan)
MTN	Multilateral Trade Negotiations
NATO	North Atlantic Treaty Organization
NAFTA	North American Free Trade Agreement
OECD	Organization for Economic Cooperation and Development
OPEC	Organization of the Petroleum Exporting Countries
OTC	Organization for Trade Cooperation
PNTR	Permanent Normal Trade Relations
RTAA	Reciprocal Trade Agreements Act
STR	Special Trade Representative

TEA	Trade Expansion Act
TPP	Trans-Pacific Partnership
TTIP	Transatlantic Trade and Investment Partnership
UN	United Nations
UNCTAD	United Nations Conference on Trade andDevelopment
USMCA	U.S.-Mexico-Canada Agreement
USSR	Union of Soviet Socialist Republics (Soviet Union)
USTR	U.S. Trade Representative

Capitalist Peace

Introduction

The United States pursued free trade from the Great Depression onward, oftentimes at a cost to its own producers and workers. These sacrifices served the purpose of grand strategy, the coordination of the nation's resources and policies to achieve long-term diplomatic objectives. That is, exports and imports, tariffs and quotas, and trade deficits and surpluses were portraits drawn on a larger canvas of international affairs. Ever since Franklin D. Roosevelt's administration, which launched a trade policy steeped in Woodrow Wilson's liberal internationalist worldview, the United States linked trade to diplomatic objectives. Washington, DC, saw free trade as underscoring its international leadership and as instrumental to global prosperity, to winning wars and peace, and to shaping the liberal internationalist world order. Free trade, in short, was a cornerstone of an ideology of "capitalist peace."

That concept placed trade liberalization in service to political internationalism. In other words, by pursuing freer commercial exchanges, capitalist peace ideology knitted trade to national security imperatives and political causes. To be sure, capitalists sought a particular type of global trade, just like communists did and fascists before them. While these two ideologies relied on the state for guidance, capitalists harnessed the market through free trade. Leaders believed that free trade advanced private enterprise and thus the cause of capitalist peace, which, in turn, promoted prosperity, democracy, security, and attendant byproducts like development, cooperation, integration, and human rights. In so doing, the capitalist peace paradigm—with a core of liberal internationalist principles but ever changing to meet new circumstances and pressures—projected US power, interests, and values into the international arena even as capitalism brought both positive and negative results to the global order.

The capitalist peace concept and its impact were both embraced and disputed. Business people, producers, and consumers certainly sought profits. Like most citizens, they shared the vaguest of notions that foreign relations mattered to the national interest. For their part, protectionists and realists ridiculed the argument

Capitalist Peace. Thomas W. Zeiler, Oxford University Press. © Oxford University Press 2022.
DOI: 10.1093/oso/9780197621363.003.0001

that free trade augmented peace-making, even security. This book shows that free-trade internationalism has always been contested and that the capitalist peace paradigm shifted according to the desires of politicians and policymakers. Yet even the skeptics acknowledged the force of capitalist peace thinking. So, too, did trade partners in the developed world and many in the global South as well. Market capitalism, through free trade, was the carrier of the capitalist peace compact; neither mercantilism nor protectionism prevailed, although they were a constant in policymaking through most of the twentieth century.

Americans devised liberal trade policy using an ideological lens defined by the needs, aims, and strengths of the capitalist and democratic world. To be sure, outcries of exploitation and imperialism abroad, and of job losses and bankruptcy at home, grew more common after World War II. But while Washington debated and modified them, it always acknowledged the internationalist objectives of the capitalist peace paradigm—that is, until they came under attack during the Trump administration. This book explores chronologically, from 1930 to 2021, how free-trade internationalism, expressed in rhetoric and in the barometers of trade legislation, international tariff negotiations, foreign policy events, and domestic political change, revealed the persistence of (and pressures on) the capitalist peace in American foreign relations.

Historians have certainly touched on the capitalist peace doctrine, but they have not put sustained emphasis on this combination of trade, ideology, and diplomacy. During the Great Depression, US trade liberalism addressed, but failed to stop, fascist dictators and militarists. Trade liberalization—the reduction or elimination of tariffs and other barriers—became a key American aim in World War II and in planning for the peace. During the forty-five-year Cold War, the capitalist peace idea transformed into a more specific agenda applied to Free World defense. That is, it shed its universal peace intentions, the brainchild of secretary of state and free-trade acolyte Cordell Hull. Communism was, obviously, outside of the capitalist and democratic orbit, so implementing a worldwide collective vision of peace was impossible. Nonetheless, the united drive of internationalism and security within the Free World kept liberal trade at the center of foreign policy. In the era of globalization and renewed nationalism after the Cold War, universal trade liberalism returned for a decade or so as the United States enjoyed unrivaled dominance. Recurrent crises followed, and free trade became more contested.

In contemporary times, free-trade internationalism has been on the defensive. Capitalist peace ideology has desperately clung to the past as a rationale for free trade. Progressives have raised alarms about the market itself, some even arguing that US history has been a battle to be liberated from, rather than by, free markets. The old guard left—and the new left inspired by the classic works of William Appleman Williams, Thomas McCormick, Lloyd Gardner, and Walter LaFeber—seeded this critique by arguing that the United States exerted itself in the world not in rational response to geopolitical perils but on behalf of predatory American capital and multinational corporations as well as to rid the country of surplus goods that caused gluts on the market and thereby dropped prices and profits. This view led to a large segment of research on the history of capitalism, which excoriates globalization, neoliberalism, and capitalism itself as regressive, and which considers notions like capitalist peace (and free trade) to propagate inequalities and hardship in the United States and the world.[1]

Unlike Trump nationalists, however, the contemporary left supported internationalism even as their scholarship and political views misportrayed the intentions behind the American trade agenda. Indeed, scholars who have revised their thinking on internationalism have found they can weave into that topic the global capitalism influences of pacifism, socialism, culture, and justice movements.[2] That fight will only intensify as progressives and populists question free trade, a core of capitalist peace thought. Even those in the middle ask if capitalism and free trade brings peace; the Russian invasion of neighboring trade partner Ukraine in 2022, for instance, led many to doubt the linkage. But while the progressive scholars were right to focus on the economic aspects of foreign relations and to demonstrate that business influenced policy, this book also considers free trade's strategic, humanitarian, and even idealistic considerations. Whether the principle of capitalist peace, and its implementation under free-trade internationalist policy, will continue to guide grand strategy is not certain, but that does not alter the premise of *Capitalist Peace*, that it was a powerful and constructive vision for US foreign policy.

Throughout modern US history, protectionists questioned capitalist peace ideology. Like the politically laden term isolationism, protectionism is a misunderstood, ill-defined phenomenon; it has extreme forms but free traders unfairly characterized it as a bogeyman to good sense and national interests.[3] Many forms of protectionism abounded across the political spectrum. There were crackpots, but most sought to restrain trade liberalization out of concern for domestic economic welfare. Furthermore, protectionists and free traders shared similar goals, such as promoting national security, free enterprise, freedom, and human rights. They just interpreted these goals differently and disagreed about how to achieve them. In fact, the United States has never practiced strict free trade or protectionism. Rather, political scientist John Ruggie aptly termed US policies as "embedded liberalism," or the pursuit of trade liberalization but with allowances for regulations (including protective tariffs and other devices) to limit the unemployment that often results from free trade. Embedded liberalism was a compromise between free trade and protectionism that moderated both in the interest of domestic welfare.[4]

Without the compromise, politicians would have never moved toward free-trade internationalism to attain the aims of the capitalist peace in foreign policy. During the later Cold War, the nation leaned toward fair, rather than free, trade. This allowed sanctions against culprits (like Japan) that had effectively constrained free-market practices, leading to job losses and industrial decline in the United States. After the Cold War, the so-called Washington Consensus of neo-liberalism and globalization dismantled some of the embedded liberal state, provoking outcries from populists and progressives that resonate today. The point is that even when trade liberalization advanced, political pressures constantly bore down to moderate and modify it.

Thus, the Trump administration easily exploited the tension between free trade and protectionism—perhaps this tension represented the culmination of years of domestic backlash against the burdens of the capitalist peace that internationalists had trouble containing. It was not that Donald Trump and his trade advisor, Peter Navarro, were outliers as protectionist challengers to capitalist peace ideology; the dissent had long existed and had intensified by the time they took office, at a point when American decline seemed more apparent. Rather, the administration deviated from nearly nine decades of liberal leadership of the world order; the executive branch had never before abandoned Wilsonian ideals. That was jarring, but non-believers in capitalist peace have always existed. At around the same time as Ruggie's embedded liberal theory emerged, for instance, international relations scholar Susan Strange debunked the notion that protectionism threatened the world trade system or peace or that it had been the harbinger of the Great Depression. These ideas were largely myth-making propagated by liberal internationalists, she noted.[5] That critique was valid, though it missed the larger point about grand strategy and, above all, the success of the capitalist peace paradigm in promoting US global objectives. Trump's tariff wars not only proved to be feckless but questioned America's traditional and successful connection of trade to internationalism. Still, Trump got experts wondering about whether free trade fosters peace and democracy, not to mention prosperity, a drum that protectionists had beaten for decades.

Capitalist Peace will not address several issues trade histories generally grapple with. For example, it will not test the notion that laissez-faire is a myth because, as noted, protectionism has always been embedded in America's political economy and has long modified trade liberalism.[6] Nor, for that matter, will the book delve too deeply into the nuts and bolts of trade policy formulation, myriad trade practices and barriers, individual commodities and other goods, negotiations, institutions, trade patterns, and outcomes, from either a national or international perspective. This study does not attempt an international history of trade. Suffice to say that Washington forged an alliance of like-minded countries that accepted capitalist terms and the capitalist peace in general. They embraced the American drive for free-trade internationalism for reasons of prosperity, security, and political stability, following in the wake of the American hegemon. Furthermore, perhaps there was a communist peace doctrine under the Soviet Union, represented more recently by the People's Republic of China, but exploring those ideologies is beyond the reach of this study. *Capitalist Peace* does, indeed, touch on all of these key features, and related ones such as monetary, fiscal, investment, and foreign assistance. Suffice to say, moreover, that excellent comprehensive trade histories already exist.[7]

Rather, this book is about ideology, beliefs, and perceptions and their effect on foreign policy—and on history itself. It explores, in short, the resilience of the capitalist peace as the United States transformed from hegemon to unipolar power to a power that is possibly in decline and that certainly has rivals to its throne. It is intended to serve as a reminder that US leadership in the trade order made possible a prosperous, democratic, and secure internationalist world order. This is especially important when the democracies faced mercantilist challenges from fascists and their autarchical policies, from allies in the form of British imperialism and Soviet statism, and more recently from China's brand of aggressive, closed capitalism. This book argues that the historical alternatives to free-trade internationalism, such as neo-colonialism, were deplorable for the world and that whatever privileges and profits free trade conferred on the United States appear less egregious when the other possibilities are considered. The dangers these other options represent have been and are worth assessing in light of the recurrent call for Washington to turn away from global responsibilities.

Policymakers *believed* in the capitalist peace—it was an article of faith that built on the empirical data of historical relations among nations. From these experiences and perceptions, policy followed accordingly. Because they deemed the nationalists, populists, protectionists, and globalization skeptics who opposed them to be parochial, marginalized groups contemptuous of modernity and global involvement, free-trade advocates sought to lift policy beyond the singular focus on import competition. Instead, they had broad, internationalist political, economic, and social objectives in mind.[8]

Regardless of significant and growing protectionist pressures during the period of this book, the United States conceived of market capitalism as a peaceful influence in global affairs. Staunch free-trade advocates like nineteenth-century British businessman Richard Cobden decreed that "free trade is the international law of God."[9] Such hyperbole derived from political need, devised for an era in British history that hotly contested protectionism as the country transformed to free trade. For the free-trade internationalists, though, as for today's neo-liberals, the ultimate mission of trade policy was, indeed, to mitigate conflict and promote democracy. That was a tall, idealistic order—and the targets shifted and evolved over time, with full employment, establishing durable peacetime institutions, preventing war, and countering communism giving way to hardened conceptions of national security as well as various interpretations of human rights and democracy promotion. Capitalist peace ideology required faith shaped by real-world objectives embedded in internationalist thought.

Because officials dedicated themselves to the internationalist ideas and hopes behind capitalist peace ideology, elaboration and definition are necessary. In short, capitalist peace sought an internationalist world, and free trade (also referred to in this book as free trade internationalism) was the means to that end. The capitalist peace concept emerged from a philosophy that humans were capable of cooperation as much as war. Viable, stable, growing, and mutually prosperous economies were the fundamental building blocks of international relations; they undergirded security, democracy, liberty, and, ultimately, peace. These goals were often in tension. For instance, promotion of national security could clash with democracy and even peace. But they all reflected American power and the country's interest in using open and accessible commerce as a means to erect and preserve the capitalist peace.

Inequality would remain and grow, at home and abroad, and the notion of universalism that emerged during World War II would retreat in the Cold War and return after it, but the capitalist peace orchestrated general cooperation among like-minded nations that brought security for individual countries through alliances of sound, mutually prosperous economies—a long peace, as it were. Prosperity encouraged democracy, undermined the appeal of autocrats, and lifted all economic boats, including in the global South, and certainly among allies and others engaged in the capitalist world economy. The core values of the capitalist peace paradigm—promotion of private enterprise, freedom, security, and cooperation—remained constant but also adapted to new issues, circumstances, and leaders as they came along. Such a capitalist peace, anchored in liberal internationalist principles, had long been a dream of Wilsonian internationalists.

Free-trade internationalism mediated these ideals embedded in grand strategy. That is, free trade used a host of measures to achieve the capitalist peace. This book zeroes in primarily on multilateral trade liberalization among nations as the key approach to explain the capitalist peace concept. American diplomacy sought to open doors to trade in markets both abroad and at home by lowering US trade barriers through legislation and international negotiations. The General Agreement on Tariffs and Trade (GATT), followed by the World Trade Organization (WTO), became the chief mechanisms for pursuing the liberalization of barriers through periodic multilateral meetings of nations, called negotiating "rounds." These forums were masterminded by the United States and its closest trade allies, particularly, at first, Great Britain, but they also sought to shape the behavior of both friends and foes toward capitalist peace norms. Thus, even East-West (communist-capitalist) trade arrangements were predicated on trade liberalization and the expansion of market access in some form. Added to trade liberalization were financial, aid, and development policies that coalesced under the one roof of free-trade internationalist policy.

For the most part, this cause and effect—the conceptualization of the capitalist peace and the way free-trade internationalist policies put the concept into practice—worked. The point is worth elaboration because there is a debate over whether trade brings peace or fosters conflict. There is also a question of whether capitalism is essential at all to peace; a contingent of scholars privilege democracy over capitalism.[10] This point of view is important, but this book sides with the capitalist cause—that peace (and security) depend on a faith in liberal internationalism based, in large part, on free trade.

But is there, indeed, a capitalist peace? Skeptics abound who question whether the commercial exchanges that may exist among people, nations, and empires who have shared a mutual dependence have necessarily led to peace. Such suspicion was commonplace in the writings of Aristotle, Plato, and other ancient philosophers. Mercantilists ruled in medieval and Renaissance Europe, China, and India. In addition, a preoccupation with security (rather than peace) also provoked realists—modern-day mercantilists focused on trade as a tool in power politics—to demand more sober views of trade's effect on international relations. Historian John Gaddis, for instance, queried globalization enthusiast Thomas Friedman's Golden Arches theory. Friedman proclaimed that no two market-capitalist countries with McDonald's restaurants have ever gone to war—in his view because they exchanged goods. Gaddis replied that such arguments were "pleasant things to believe" but unsubstantiated by the historical record.[11]

Add to the doubters Karl Marx and others who have decried capitalism, including free trade, for causing a myriad of problems in the world. In the Marxist view, industrialization and development, abetted by free trade, exacerbated class conflict. Psychologist Stephen Pinker rightly notes that associating capitalism with peace is heretical to many progressives who note that free-trading business interests have profited from war as "merchants of death." There is certainly evidence to back up this claim, as there is reason to criticize free-market policies for underpinning the darker sides of hegemony. These include support for dictators, exploitation of peoples abroad, and a neo-liberal neglect of inequality at home. To be sure, free trade (and finance) often led to US dominance over foreign markets and consequently to impoverishment of the people in those markets. Free trade and globalization also yanked Americans into the international economy and out of their domestic way of life, causing them to lose autonomy.[12] Anti-capitalist protest, as a form of protectionism, surfaces in this book to challenge the capitalist peace adherents, who have believed for years that American leaders care much more about the "capitalist" part of the term than the "peace." And it is true that policymakers have spoken a lot about peace yet instigated deadly operations throughout the world. As historian Melvyn Leffler has argued, the postwar order reflected the goal not of peace but of safeguarding democratic capitalism by elevating geo-strategic concerns over economics.[13]

Both the progressive and realist views are borne out by history, as nations and peoples engaged in armed conflict regardless of how much they traded with each other. Consider World War I, a war supposedly fought to end all wars. That tragic conflict ended up dashing the hopes of internationalists who claimed that economically integrated societies would not fight each other. To be sure, conflict might ensue from the most open and intimate of commercial relations (see, for example, the close trade relations of arch-enemies France and Germany). Nationalists argue, moreover, that greater interdependence leads to greater dependence and thus to clashes over resources. The capitalist peace theory itself suffers from modeling errors and selection bias.[14] There are also variations in time periods that reveal the waxing and waning influence of trade on politics and on peaceful trends.

Deliberately setting aside fine points of theory, models, and even the historical record, this book explores the crucial issue of capitalist peace policymakers' internationalist *intentions*. The ideology resulted in the establishment of norms and institutions that prevented a major world war, boosted cooperation among friends and allies, and tried—though it did not always succeed—to foster more prosperity, democracy, freedom, and human rights in the world. Free-trade internationalism represented the best potential to accomplish these things, believed American foreign policy leaders. While the capitalist peace could not mitigate all conflict, poverty, and unfairness, it did serve an intellectual organizing purpose in grand strategy. Thus, as one scholar has noted, "capitalism's policemen"—the GATT, the International Monetary Fund (IMF) and World Bank, the Marshall Plan, and aid programs—resisted the economic nationalism of the Great Depression that had led to world war.[15] In foreign policy analyst Michael Mandelbaum's double negative phrasing, history "does not prove that international commerce can never exert a pacifying influence anywhere."[16] *Capitalist Peace* validates that view. Though not perfect by any means, the capitalist peace paradigm instilled internationalist values, practices, and institutions into the global, post–World War II order. Peace and democratic stability, through mutual prosperity and free enterprise, were the general results.

Pushed by the capitalist peace, free trade built coalitions of peace advocates. As theorist William Domke concluded three decades ago after crunching the data on trade and conflict, interdependence between national trading sectors bred more and stronger domestic groups that wished to avoid war. For most of the modern industrial era, this held true. Others, like international relations theorist Patrick McDonald, argued that private property and a competitive market, that is, liberal economic institutions, sowed peace between nations to the extent that capitalism has been historically a stronger influence on peace than democracy. These findings supported the hypothesis that, as Domke notes, "national governments that are more involved in trade are less inclined to make decisions for war."[17]

No matter how credible, neither realists nor socialists nor progressives offered persuasive evidence to change the minds of those who faithfully believed in economic liberalism as a means to avoid war and promote equity and democracy. Thus, variants of the capitalist peace dominated the literature, the commons, and the halls of government. Liberal regime theorists adhere to it. Peace theorists like Bruce Russet and John Oneal propose a "triangulating peace" model (institutions and law, democracy, and commercial integration) to illustrate the pacifying effects of trade, or at least the notion that violence among economically interdependent nations has costs.[18] That is, a combination of trade, democracy, and institutions enhances peace. Some scholars stress that liberal economics alone at least creates these conditions. In this view, an open and free capitalist economy allows democracy to flourish, and democracies are mostly peaceful.[19]

This idea arose from the Enlightenment's belief in human progress. François Quesnay and the French Physiocrats, classical liberal economists in Britain Adam Smith, David Ricardo, John Stuart Mill, and their followers in the Manchester School, led by Richard Cobden and John Bright, and Thomas Paine in the United States, as well as the Baron de Montesquieu and others before them, held that commerce naturally fostered peaceful relations among nations by evoking mutual needs and, therefore, encouragement to cooperate. Wrote Smith in 1776, in *The Wealth of Nations*, the road to commercial prosperity ran through free trade rather than through war and self-interested mercantilism.[20] Eighty years later, John Stuart Mill echoed that it was "commerce which is rapidly rendering war obsolete" and that, without exaggeration, international trade "in being the principal guarantee of the peace of the world, is the great permanent security for the uninterrupted progress . . . of the human race."[21] In short, capitalism and peace merged with views that the modern world was accelerating its interdependence through technology, travel, and the like. This was the bright side of modernization that saw globalized capitalism as the engine of integrated, peaceful societies, a perspective that persists today in neo-liberal circles.

The promotion of commerce to capitalist peace ideology followed logically. Liberal crusader Richard Cobden joined socialist Charles Russell, from the opposite end of the political spectrum, to embrace capitalist peace. For Cobden, free trade reinforced the peace movement, much like disarmament did. Free trade, he wrote in 1843, broke "down the barriers that separate nations; those barriers behind which nestle the feelings of pride, revenge, hatred and jealousy, which every now and then break their bonds and deluge whole countries with their blood."[22] That is, free exchanges of goods created mutual dependencies that built wealth, national power, and cultural ties. Britain's free trade within its empire was a good case. Free trade or, in actuality, the capitalist peace refrain, Cobden concluded, "arms its votaries by its own pacific nature, in that eternal truth—the more any nation traffics abroad upon free and honest principles, the less it will be in danger of wars."[23] American free-trade evangelist Cordell Hull—the "Tennessee Cobden"—took up the cause of capitalist peace when he became secretary of state in 1933.[24]

Democracy was pivotal to this view. From the Great Depression through the Cold War and the era of modern-day globalization to the 2016 election, the capitalist peace tied a free-trade agenda to the US alliance with democracies. The pursuit of democracy and security merged with the free-enterprise system into the capitalist peace model. Internationalists even believed that trade could transform the most undemocratic authoritarian regimes into peaceful democracies, writes political scientist Katherine Barbieri, and could serve as "the panacea for the earth's scourges, ranging from the distasteful characteristics of human nature to poverty and war."[25] It is true that democracies tend to trade with each other, even if they compete fiercely in the open market. While democracy and economic interdependence through freer trade might not depend on one other, both influence nations toward peaceful outcomes. Democracy and trade appeared so fused that Nobel Peace Prize–winning journalist Norman Angell claimed in his 1909 book, *The Great Illusion*, that free trade preceded political freedom which, in turn, brought peace. World War I broke out five years after the book's publication, giving the lie to this opinion, but that horrifying conflict justified the cause of capitalist peace and motivated its followers even more.[26]

A transformative shift from a century and a half of protectionism and tariff debates occurred in the United States by the mid-1930s. To be sure, from its beginnings, the nation sought commercial involvement as well as territorial expansion across the continent and beyond and even a crusading zeal for democracy in the world. But trade and financial activism abroad, on behalf of merchants and bankers, did not translate into strategic engagement until after the Spanish–American War of 1898. Actually, it took Woodrow Wilson to begin codifying a foreign policy agenda of internationalism during the First World War. Before the income tax was established around that time, the tariff—the government's main source of revenue—was naturally the subject of intense political and party conflict. Trade and diplomacy were linked, but from the late eighteenth to the early twentieth centuries tariff policy was not intended to serve both goals. The world's leading industrial nation and the major exporter of manufactured goods by the beginning of the twentieth century, the United States did not espouse a free-trade policy commensurate with its role as an economic powerhouse and rising global leader. Tariffs on imports remained high, driven by traditional Republican protectionism. Battles over the height of duties continued to consume Washington much as they had throughout the nineteenth century. Seeking to boost agricultural exports by coaxing foreigners to open their markets to US goods, the Democrats labored, vainly for the most part, to lower tariffs in return for a reciprocal decrease in protectionism abroad. Despite pressures to end special-interest influence over the tariff, and regardless of Wilson's brief success in cutting duties, protectionism ruled. Wilson set out to alter the tariff debate, namely, by trade liberalization. He injected this goal into his ultimate quest for a world of cooperation, peace, and security through mutual prosperity among nations. That effort of liberal internationalism bereft of realism came up short until put in the shrewder hands of Franklin Roosevelt.[27]

Still, it is worth noting that regardless of the aborted internationalism and the subsequent isolationist backlash of the 1920s and 1930s, the messianic Wilson made the first significant stab at expressing the capitalist peace paradigm. At the peace conference after World War I, Wilson pushed for free trade, equitable treatment for commerce, and principles of non-discrimination to combat preferential imperial systems abroad that closed their markets to outsiders. He hoped his brainchild, the League of Nations, would adopt his goals. Concrete steps toward free-trade internationalism were hard to come by in the 1920s, however, especially when Congress refused to ratify American participation in the League. Furthermore, Republicans ascended to the presidency from 1921 to 1933, injecting protectionism in trade law by increasing tariffs.[28]

Led by the Department of State, however, Republican diplomats did adopt the unconditional most-favored-nation principle. This automatically granted the same, reciprocal tariff concessions negotiated between the United States and another nation to third countries, without requiring compensation from the beneficiary. By ensuring such equality of treatment in commerce, policymakers in the State Department believed they could better avoid diplomatic misunderstandings and conflict. Most-favored-nation status had existed in treaties for decades. Still, it remained a rather vague norm that allowed nations to continue to discriminate against others, whether through customs unions or other preferential systems. Neither World War I nor the Republican State Department changed those facts, particularly in the application of trade law. To be sure, unconditional most-favored-nation treatment was a decisive shift in policy that led to the later reciprocal trade agreements program. Yet it did not effectively pry open markets overseas for US exporters, especially when it came to opening the British imperial system. Nonetheless, the principle of equality of treatment put even the Republicans, including President Herbert Hoover, on record as supporting free-trade internationalism.[29]

Setting the internationalist agenda, Woodrow Wilson had shunned protectionism, even as he tempered his free=trade campaign during the World War I emergency, as it was inimical to the capitalist peace design to counter economic nationalism and the political isolationism that followed. His Fourteen Points spelled out his desire for freedom of navigation and the removal of trade barriers under the rule of equality of commercial conditions. Thus, his postwar plans set a course of enshrining capitalist peace theory through the unconditional most-favored-nation principle, which became the guiding rule of US trade policy when the Republicans put it into place a few years later. The GOP, however, the party of business and industry that sought a home market protected from outside competition, had long privileged the domestic economics of trade over diplomatic objectives. Protectionist Republicans remained skeptical of the link between peace and low tariffs.

A strident internationalist, Herbert Hoover did not agree with such views in his own party. A Quaker steeped in peace ideology, the former darling of progressives was a fierce advocate of aid and trade abroad, of intervention on behalf of human rights, and of capitalist peace and democracy. He had shown his stripes as a mastermind of food relief during World War I. Hoover buckled, however, under GOP protectionist political pressure. He also welcomed the internationalist logic that the emerging Great Depression and the precipitous fall in world trade could be solved only by stabilizing exchange rates at the international level, rather than lowering tariffs at home. With the country descending into the Depression by late 1929, Republicans turned to even more protectionism, under the Hawley Smoot Tariff Act, as the means to protect farmers as well as manufacturers.[30] They stuck their heads in the sands of isolationism, passing the most controversial tariff law in over a century, perhaps in history.

The Democrats did not embrace classical liberalism and free trade, either. Certainly Franklin Roosevelt, taking the presidency in March 1933, did not. He brought a clear realism to Wilsonian foreign policy, prioritizing solutions to economic problems on the home front with his New Deal program of government activism. The Democrats did accept internationalism in foreign affairs, however, shaped by engagement through trade liberalization. To be sure, exports and imports fostered profits and prosperity. But the trade balance also lay at the heart of diplomacy as a peace and security instrument. Still, free-trade internationalism came second to the economy, at least for the moment, because isolationism remained a potent force. As international affairs expert Charles Kupchan has noted, one of Roosevelt's gifts was to make liberal internationalism appeal to both idealists and realists alike, as well as build a consensus of Americans from both political parties and from experts, business, and labor.[31] Trade policy evolved into a geo-strategic tool under the principled capitalist peace compact, as the democracies reeled toward conflict prodded by vicious fascist, communist, and militarist ideologies, while the Depression naggingly weakened them. This tumultuous and dangerous time serves as the starting point for this history of the capitalist peace.

Out of these cathartic crisis years, the view that trade relations were a basic form of human interaction, built good or ill feelings among people, and boosted the economic and political stability of nations further entrenched capitalist peace ideology. Its application through free-trade internationalism—partnerships shaped by American power, multilateral institutions and trade agreements, and a democratizing mission—did not save the paradigm from failure. Free-trade internationalism definitely exacerbated some problems, such as structural inequality, that led to conflict. It still does. But the starting point for the capitalist peace concept, and one of the cardinal purposes of economic liberalism for that matter, was the cooperation among democracies to prevent war. When it came to trade policy, there was a much larger agenda at stake—peace, security, human rights, and democracy.

This is a study of those free-trade perspectives—the hopes that shaped the foreign relations of the United States during its decades of predominance. It is also a history of how well capitalist peace worked in building a world made relatively safe for democracy. This was by no means a perfect world. For those in government and beyond, however, it was the safest and most prosperous way to run US foreign policy and the world order. Considering the horrors of war that preceded the so-called American Century, the world needed internationalism. The perception, and reality, of capitalist peace was instrumental in shaping American history and most of it for the better.

1

Depression, 1930–1935

In mid-January 1933, six weeks before Franklin D. Roosevelt moved into the White House, Nicholas Murray Butler, president of Columbia University, gave a speech to the League of Nations Association. Because of the Great Depression, he warned, "The modern world is in the gravest crisis of its history." Not only were disarmament treaties being whittled away, but an equally dire threat had also arisen from the "relentless international war now going on in the field of economics and finance, with the result that the trade of the world is strangulated and is sick unto death." Protectionism had so dissipated world trade that "each separate and isolated nation will be left to a quiet economic death in its own lonely bed." High tariffs were "quite as destructive of peace and human happiness as are battleships and guns, airships and poison-gas." Among other internationalist measures, Butler urged nations to remove barriers to trade that so choked the lifeblood of producers and workers that they embraced political extremists out of desperation. Economic liberalism, carried by free-trade internationalism, would "protect the peace of the world" by ameliorating the fear and distress that the Depression was causing.[1] Roosevelt and Secretary of State Cordell Hull labored over the fallout over protectionism by asserting the capitalist peace through a new trade law.

The infamous Hawley-Smoot Tariff and Roosevelt's jettisoning of the London Economic Conference of 1932–1933 have been seen as setbacks for capitalist peace, while the free-trade advocacy of Cordell Hull, the patron saint of the capitalist peace paradigm in the prewar years, as well as the advent of the Reciprocal Trade Agreements Act, set the United States on a course of bilateral, then multilateral, tariff liberalization efforts. These developments aimed to end the Depression, help US agriculture, labor, investment, consumer spending, and currencies recover, as well as curb the log-rolling politics of protectionism inherent in tariff legislation. But when it comes to Hawley-Smoot, for instance,

Capitalist Peace. Thomas W. Zeiler, Oxford University Press. © Oxford University Press 2022.
DOI: 10.1093/oso/9780197621363.003.0002

emphasis has focused on whether the law worsened the Depression by jacking tariffs to their highest relative levels rather than on grand strategy and internationalism.[2] Notably, when 1,028 university and private sector economists signed a May 4, 1930, letter to President Herbert Hoover protesting the pending Hawley-Smoot Tariff, they revealed concerns the tariff would undercut foreign policy interests.

Their petition showed that the economists clearly believed the bill would have terrible economic and political consequences, halting trade during the greatest economic slide in American history.[3] In contrast, protectionists predicted better economic times under the tariff, and legislators felt politically obligated to support it. A conspiratorial, somewhat paranoid, perspective held that Europe had joined to conquer the American market. But most protectionists were pragmatic, seeking simply to protect the home market from perceived unfair import competition. Hawley-Smoot's impact on the international arena was then, and is today, a matter of dispute.

Historian Alfred Eckes Jr. has argued that trade partners did not issue formal protests about the law or threaten to retaliate with their own tariff increases, while other scholars have claimed that the act was to blame for retaliation against US exports in at least several countries within months after its passage. Hawley-Smoot certainly deserves some blame for the rise of trade barriers worldwide, including the restrictive British Empire's Ottawa Agreement of 1932 that gave preferential treatment to British and Commonwealth producers at the expense of outsiders. At minimum, the last eight months of debate over Hawley-Smoot in 1929 and 1930 added to global financial insecurities that resulted in two stock market crashes. Europe's World War I debts could not be repaid, as trade revenue abroad had dried up. Monetary stability lay in ruins, especially in the farm sector so prominent in most states at the time; Hawley-Smoot devastated American farmers, already weak from a decade of falling prices, because they relied on exports. The Tariff Act affected only a fraction of world trade but the markets, and the voters, got the message. As American exports plunged from $5.16 billion to $1.65 billion over Hoover's term in office, the Republicans lost seats in Congress. Roosevelt trounced Hoover in the 1932 election, citing Hawley-Smoot's ruinous effects on producers and the incitement of a trade war abroad.[4]

In fairness, Herbert Hoover backed the capitalist peace concept. He had warned about the consequences of looking at trade and finance strictly in terms of bookkeeping rather than foreign policy. In his capacity as secretary of commerce in the 1920s, he had advocated expanding foreign trade after World War I, acknowledging America's growing dependence on imports of raw materials and semi-manufactured goods. As president, he said international trade was more than "the noisy dickering of merchants and bankers—it is the lifeblood of modern civilization."[5] Importers recognized Hoover as "a man who is internationally minded, who has at interest, not only the welfare of the people of the United States, but that of the entire human race," and thus they believed he would prevent the tariff bill wending its way through Congress from being drastically protectionist.[6] As a creditor nation, the United States could not avoid close ties to the international economy, Hoover believed, and since commerce and prosperity interlocked with peace, there could be no self-interest in an interdependent world in which the pursuit of markets blended with politics and pacifism.

The seeds of international acrimony, such as protectionism and indebtedness, could not be allowed to germinate, Hoover thought. Sounding like the ideal free-trade internationalist, he noted in 1925 that "the terminology of trade has been so infected by military terms" as to perpetrate the notion that commerce was a win-lose prospect. Protectionists feared losing. Only through mutual trade expansion could the world economy grow, however, and the prospects for world peace improve. Like his diplomats, Hoover understood Hawley-Smoot's dangers, yet the domestic economy dictated that he privilege Republican politics over internationalism. This defied the League of Nations, which encouraged multilateral free trade, and twenty-three nations made fifty-nine protests to the State Department as Congress debated Hawley-Smoot in 1929. Two dozen more joined in later. Europe disapproved, although major nations like Britain and Germany generally refused to retaliate, leaving smaller countries like Spain and Switzerland to take direct action against US protectionism. In Asia, the Japanese resorted to militarism to achieve economic ends by pursuing their Great East Asia Co-Prosperity Sphere. Their first move, in 1931, was to invade Manchuria for raw materials and trade.[7]

The response from America's closest friends was just as ominous. In Canada, the decidedly pro-British Conservative Party won election in July 1930 by, in part, pledging a nationalistic response toward the United States. Canada bought nearly 20 percent of US exports and sent 43 percent of its own to America. But under the enhanced imperial trade preference system set up in Ottawa in 1932, it cut duties on goods imported from the British Empire and raised them on nearly a third of American exports. In Britain, Canadian émigré and newspaper magnate Max Aitkin (Lord Beaverbrook) made imperial preferences a project. A conservative powerbroker, he lobbied for tariff discrimination toward nations outside of the British trading zone through his widely circulating *Daily Mail* and the Empire Crusade organization, which secured the allegiance of farmers and industry to protectionism. In a twist on internationalism, Beaverbrook conceived of tariffs as promoting Britain's "splendid" isolation through "Empire free trade" while at the same time the Commonwealth cooperated with the United States on security issues.[8]

The political effects of Hawley-Smoot were not lost on close trade partners in the Anglophone world. British Liberal Party leader David Lloyd George recognized in 1940 that the "main effects of Tariff [*sic*] are political as much as economic," including stimulating movement for a unified empire, an effort that sowed international economic distrust. The Beaverbrook crusade for empire only added to world enmity; the race for higher tariffs reached fever pitch, like a build-up to war. Lloyd George was already worried about the capitalist peace in the midst of the Great Depression due to rising nationalism, oppression of minorities, and the shadow of fascism across Europe and Asia. Hawley-Smoot propagated "ill-will" among nations, he warned.[9]

In the context of a global banking crisis and currency devaluations, Hawley-Smoot led to the breakdown of the world trade system—and peaceful politics with it. It did so by fostering a "beggar thy neighbor" cycle, notes trade historian Douglas Irwin, that diplomats failed to prevent.[10] A large number of newspaper editors and industrial, labor, and agricultural associations across the country despised this vicious turn in trade; not one important businessman expressed clear support for Hawley-Smoot because the economics did not add up and the diplomatic effects promised to worsen things even more through mutual retaliation. Rexford Tugwell, a signatory to the economist's letter to Hoover, summed up this consternation: "The world moves into the new decade bristling with mutual jealousies and fears, unwilling to cooperate, armed to the teeth, burdened with debt and sunk in the worst depression in history."[11] In other words, Hawley-Smoot undermined capitalist peace principles of trade liberalism, security, and international comity.

The dismay among internationalists was significant. Pleading with Hoover to veto the bill, a voter claimed that the world was watching. "Is it not better to have the whole world as friends instead of losing our export trade and have bitter feeling against the USA[?]"[12] Hoover himself had just returned from a goodwill mission to Latin America, but the tariff legislation, wrote the chairman of a pan-American group, provoked such "agitation for trade reprisals, boycotts, etc." that "anti-United States comment" was more widespread than at any time since President Theodore Roosevelt's "coup d'état" in Panama in 1903.[13] Religious leaders conceded that there were other ways to destroy a nation besides an arms race. "It might even be more merciful to shoot all the poor of any nation than to subject them to starvation," which was what they charged "a tariff wall of unprecedented height and thickness" would do. For an "American who is also a Christian the tariff is the one vital religious and ethical issue now before us."[14]

Academics supplemented their petition to Hoover by imploring him to block the legislation. If it passed, warned Irving Fisher of Yale University, "we shall become far more than we already are 'the most hated nation on earth,' which fact would be sure to prejudice your foreign policy, especially as to world peace and disarmament."[15] With nations refusing to cooperate to alleviate the war debt burden, warned a Harvard University professor of government, W.Y. Elliott, the stagnation of international trade might become permanent. In "our nationalistic world, bent upon self-sufficient systems mutually exclusive of all profitable exchange of goods," he predicted, the system might "first disintegrate into wars, or involve itself in suicidal class struggles."[16] When Hoover signed the Tariff Act on June 17, 1930, criticism from scholars erupted. Urging him to call a tariff conference to consider the matter of protectionism, two professors noted that the Pacific Institute of Relations had just closed its sessions in Berkeley, California with a feeling of doom. "We cannot but feel that the work of this and all similar groups will be rendered impotent and meaningless in the face of a world of hatred engendered by an unwise tariff." The recent Naval Limitations Treaty boosted peace through arms control, but "we cannot but feel that this great good will be nullified unless the trouble is attacked at its root, and this, as you yourself so well know, is mainly economic."[17] But domestic politics trumped diplomacy.

Franklin Roosevelt looked inward to solve America's Great Depression, not to capitalist peace through free trade. But he was an internationalist, particularly in trade. While he despised Hawley-Smoot, on the campaign trail he opposed a trade conference that might suck the United States into European political controversies through the League of Nations. Roosevelt had endorsed the League in 1920 as a means to prevent another world war, but he placed blame for the world debt problem, overspending on armaments, and commercial restrictions at the feet of America's allies. He simply advocated "economic cooperation" so that the country "can revive the trade of the world as well as trade within our own borders" and "maintain our international freedom and at the same time offer leadership to a sorely tried humanity."[18] Roosevelt backed reciprocal tariff deals, but not protectionism, to restart the wheels of industry and agriculture. The obtuse Democrat thus had it both ways. Not surprisingly, a frustrated Hoover called him "a chameleon on plaid" and "wobbly" on whether tariffs were too high or not. Hoover's staff found the Democratic candidate's utterances on the tariff to be so ambiguous that it was unclear what he would do on tariff rates if elected. According to Hoover, Roosevelt was either ignorant or trying to fool the people.[19] Both were likely, but soft-pedaling liberal trade in a depression was a winning ticket to the presidency.

Given his solid record of foreign involvement, Hoover was irritated when he met considerable resistance to Hawley-Smoot during the campaign, particularly from internationalists who favored Roosevelt. The Women's International League for Peace and Freedom admonished in August 1932, "we cannot develop international confidence, which is the basis for permanent peace and world disarmament, if we continue to preach a doctrine of economic isolation that means economic warfare" through high tariffs.[20] Reflecting this view, the Democratic platform blamed the president for worsening the Depression and international tensions by signing the Hawley-Smoot Act. That accusation sent him into fits of anger as he predicted Roosevelt would give away the store by lowering tariffs in conference with foreign friends. The GOP platform mentioned world peace but tied tariffs and trade agreement reciprocity mainly to economic health.[21]

For their part, the Democrats blended trade (and finance) into the larger context of the capitalist peace. Their platform declared, "In a nation's foreign policy is bound up two great essentials of human relations: spiritual and economic," including trade, which "has been the forerunner of international acquaintanceship" since merchants crossed the deserts and seas. While religion and territorial conquest dictated human history, "trade relations between nations have been the paramount concern that lay at the basis of foreign policy." The world had entered a "period of inter-dependency" that had more "to do with human rights not measured by the yardstick of trade [but] recognized by civilized nations." Candidate Roosevelt added that the tariff "cannot be separated from our other relations with foreign countries; the whole thing ties up together." If elected, his administration would adhere to "new principles of a higher law, a newer and better standard of international relations" through reciprocal cooperation with others.[22]

Despite that rhetoric, once elected, Roosevelt prioritized the domestic over the international, even though he referred to foreign trade as frozen in his inaugural address of March 4, 1933. Despite the utmost importance of US trade relations and the capitalist peace, they came second to reestablishing a sound national economy. International agreements would restore world trade, he explained, "but the emergency at home cannot wait on that accomplishment."[23] This stance brought him awfully close to backing protectionism, yet his "Brain Trust" counseled nationalistic remedies to the Depression, too.

Among this group of brilliant liberal advisors was economist Rexford Tugwell, now of the Department of Agriculture, who firmly believed in economic planning. Free traders and protectionists alike, he charged, were beholden to unfettered and selfish capitalist enterprise and class warfare. Sounding like a modern-day anti-globalizer, Tugwell argued that trade corruptly or naively served the interests of privileged corporations and politically connected producers. By their greed and monopolistic leanings, the laissez-faire free traders actually provoked the very protectionism that had ruined world trade, undercut exports, and emasculated international cooperation. Trade was never free, wrote Tugwell, but subject to "sinister private controls" that hindered recovery through cutthroat relations among nations. Careful trade restrictions were in order, because the United States was "entitled to autonomy" in its quest to right the domestic economy. Tugwell's logic spoke to the essence of the inward-turned New Deal and Roosevelt. Once it had solved the American crisis, government could then address international economic restrictions that provided "a richer soil for the development of fear, of envy, and of hatred," he advised.[24]

That sounded Wilsonian enough for Roosevelt; trade was not solely about economics, at least in rhetoric. He agreed with former French Prime Minister Edouard Herriot that peace depended on "progressive and simultaneous economic disarmament," including ways "of promoting rather than restricting international trade" by limiting barriers to commerce such as tariffs, quotas, and exchange restrictions.[25] Roosevelt also grasped capitalist peace theory. He noted in a joint statement with visiting Japanese dignitaries in May 1933, despite Japan's recent aggression in Manchuria, "that economic stability and political tranquility are complementary essentials to a sound basis for peace; that neither of these can be achieved without the other; and that both economic and military disarmament are needed for their attainment."[26] Still, this seemed rather boilerplate. He issued similar statements after visits with Nazi officials, such as Hjalmar Schacht, the mercantilist head of the Reichsbank.[27]

Nonetheless, aggression and militarization in the early 1930s intensified this capitalist peace perspective. Japan's invasion and occupation of Manchuria in 1931, Tokyo's predatory insistence on a trade expansion of cheap goods that punished British Commonwealth and US producers, the failure of the Geneva Disarmament Conference in 1932, and the advent of the Nazi dictatorship in Germany in 1933 terrified the internationalists. Latin America experienced the vicious Chaco War between Bolivia and Paraguay. Another border war brewed between Colombia and Peru, while Cubans, Mexicans, and Haitians protested heavy-handed US military interventions. On the diplomatic front, the outlook looked dim.

Secretary of State Cordell Hull stepped in. It was Hull who really took up the peace-through-trade banner that Roosevelt approved but did not wave vigorously. To be sure, Hull backed low tariffs to boost exports for farmers in his home state and minimize the prices of manufactured goods they needed. That was the classic free-trade approach. But the horror of World War I had "enlarged [his] views on trade and tariffs from the national to the international theater." Realizing that "wars were often largely caused by economic rivalry conducted unfairly," in 1916 Hull merged war with the aggressive imperialist competition that helped cause it. He referenced nineteenth-century French economist Frederic Bastiat, wrongly credited with free trade's famous aphorism that "when goods cannot cross borders, armies will." Hull summed up that "unhampered trade dovetailed with peace; high tariffs, trade barriers and unfair economic competition with war." With less trade obstruction, national jealousies would dissipate, living standards for all would rise, and then the "economic dissatisfaction that breeds war" could be eliminated, giving the world "a reasonable chance for lasting peace."[28]

Hull had long called for an international trade conference to establish a permanent congress designed to promote fair and friendly global trade. This endorsed the third point of President Woodrow Wilson's Fourteen Points, which called for the elimination of trade barriers and equality of trade as a means of preventing "international quarrels, the arousing of the war spirit, increased armaments, militarism, and, ultimately, war."[29] This conference would seek the universal adoption of the unconditional most-favored-nation principle (equality in trade treatment), in which a nation applied the same tariff regulations to all others, without discrimination, as long as other nations did the same. The participants would pursue an end to retaliation, boycotts, and domestic subsidies that allowed producers to undersell in international markets, and honor neutral maritime

Fig. 1.1 Cordell Hull, the patron saint of capitalist peace, signs a reciprocal trade agreement with Brazilian officials in 1935. Library of Congress, Prints & Photographs Division, Harris & Ewing.

rights to keep trade routes open. Hull came down hard against closed colonial systems that allowed the mother country to discriminate in favor of its empire, at the expense of outsiders.[30] Hoover, however, vetoed a world trade congress in 1932. Then he, alongside Congressman Willis Hawley and Senator Reed Smoot, went down in electoral defeat.

Hull got the last word when Roosevelt named him secretary of state. American history's leading disciple of free-trade internationalism devised a simple formulation: economic nationalism led to conflict. Trade brought higher living standards and thus contentment, leaving the rantings of despots to fall on deaf ears. In addition, democracy itself depended on the preservation of individual liberties; political freedom could not exist without protections for private enterprise from such government controls as tariffs, exchange restrictions, and subsidies. The capitalist peace logic was clear. "The truth is universally recognized," said Hull, "that trade between nations is the greatest peacemaker and civilizer within human experience."[31] This perceived linkage of trade to peace, internationalism, and national security provided a paradigm for US foreign policy for the next three-quarters of a century.

By 1933, Hull walked in step with expert opinion throughout the world, and particularly in the League of Nations, which convened planning groups for a London monetary and economic conference intended to combat the Great Depression by stabilizing exchange rates. One draft agenda in January 1933 warned that the quest for self-sufficiency through protectionism, barter, boycotts, and exchange controls would lower world standards of living to the point that democratic society itself would perish. This came down to "the failure of human will and intelligence to devise the necessary guarantees of political and economic international order," wrote one committee. Governments had to act, according to Hullian capitalist peace, by replacing the economic balance of power and military alliances with universal rules for a harmonious world order.[32]

Wisdom and determination were in order at the London Economic Conference, where America's Western European trade partners hoped for relief from their crushing World War I debts. The United States held the cards because Britain, France, Italy, and Germany owed it money. Due to domestic banking, political, and voter pressures, Roosevelt refused to back down, however. Like other statesmen, Hull had hoped that London would put in place an elaborate agenda of broad tariff and financial adjustments, in line with his trade and peace congress idea from 1916. He urged the continuation of the tariff truce, reductions on certain items or classes of goods, and no new tariffs or quotas under the most-favored-nation rule. Roosevelt would not tip his hand on trade barrier liberalization. Great Britain, frustrated that the United States appeared committed to its nationalistic high tariffs and restrictive debt policies despite the world economic crisis, pledged reciprocal nationalism in return.[33]

Indeed, the US delegation chairman, Bernard Child, discovered the Europeans to be as paralyzed by protectionism as the Americans. Dozens of officials, industrialists, and journalists confessed that while military matters scared them, the "fear of competition in the economic field" had not changed since the eighteenth century. Resentful of the Versailles Peace treaty and its impossible financial terms, the Germans had turned from liberalism to Nazi regimentation. France could precipitate a war just by imposing more sanctions or simply because it feared a German invasion. Benito Mussolini claimed that time had run out on international cooperation. The British and others criticized Japan for closing the open door to trade in Asia, and the Americans characterized Tokyo as the predatory "Yellow Peril" at every turn. Nations balked at solutions to trade problems, withdrawing "their paws like cats who have tread on water," wrote Child. The result was the "building of great walls" for the reason of "self-protection" of home markets, he added. Child noted that the world looked to Washington to lead it from the abyss, but that was a futile hope.[34] The New Deal's brand of economic nationalism shaped Roosevelt's response to the conferees. Hull warned him from London that "both economic and military disarmament are at present hanging in the balance," under assault from extreme protectionist forces. He got a tariff truce, and eventually sixty-one countries representing 90 percent of the world's trade acceded to it, a significant step forward. But reprisals, bilateral discrimination, and embargoes prevented a halt in tariff hikes.[35] Hull's internationalist vision was stymied.

The London Conference failed when Roosevelt did not come through, yet he also threw out a life preserver to drowning free-trade internationalists. He ended the gold standard to inflate the economy through New Deal spending, and he insisted on war debt repayment. Humiliatingly for Hull, he even announced a delay in sending a reciprocal trade bill to Congress. This left the Europeans with even more reason to be skeptical about expressions of the capitalist peace from the most protectionist nation on earth. Nonetheless, Roosevelt agreed with Hull "that most modern military conflicts and other serious international controversies are rooted in economic conditions, and that economic rivalries are in most modern instances the prelude to the actual wars that have occurred."[36] The conference failed to provide international solutions to the Depression, but all was not lost. Roosevelt held out a glimmer of hope to Hull, agreeing to discuss tariff reductions if they were global. Hull seized the lifeline and became ascendant over economic diplomacy.[37]

At the Pan American Conference in Montevideo at the end of 1933, Hull traded reciprocal trade agreements for a pledge the United States would never intervene in the Western Hemisphere, a deal that neatly expressed his belief in capitalist peace.[38] Building on his success in Latin America, Hull returned home to urge Roosevelt and Congress to reform trade policy. "To me," wrote Hull, "it seemed virtually impossible to develop friendly relations with other nations in the political sphere so long as we provoked their animosity in the economic sphere. How could we promote peace with them while waging war on them commercially?"[39]

In 1934, Congress fulfilled Hull's dream of an internationalist turn in trade legislation by passing the Reciprocal Trade Agreements Act (RTAA). Rather than focus on imports, the bill tied domestic recovery to trade by seeking to restore export markets. Because Roosevelt had not sent the bill to Congress during the London Conference, Hull had not been able to attest to other nations there that Washington was willing to dismantle its high-tariff system, but this was proof for all to see. The RTAA authorized the president to engage in cautious bilateral talks without having to submit each agreement to the Senate for ratification, which avoided direct protectionist pressures on and from Congress. Log-rolling would occur at renewals of the legislation rather than at tariff negotiations with other countries. The RTAA required tariff reductions on an unconditional most-favored-nation basis, which meant US exporters benefited from agreements third countries had forged. Roosevelt did not mention the peace dividends from reciprocal trade when he proposed the bill to Congress, nor did either the House or Senate (or Hull in his testimony to them) allude to capitalist peace much in the spring 1934 hearings on the act. The administration focused on alleviating the Depression. But the objectives and bureaucratic transformation in the legislation signaled a significant shift away from protectionist dominance of the policy process. In essence, the RTAA was a revolutionary first step in a decades-long victory for internationalists.[40]

Unsurprisingly, Republicans, protectionists, and isolationists vehemently opposed the legislation as a usurpation of congressional authority by "dictatorial" and unconstitutional executive power. They claimed it further evidenced the dangerous statism of the New Deal, and business voiced concerns about big government inroads on private enterprise. Protectionists called the RTAA a sellout of industry, labor, and especially farmers to a flood of imports, while isolationists pushed for separating the economy from other nations as a means of safeguarding livelihoods. Congressional power that restrained internationalism was critical to this goal of "America Self Contained," noted Samuel Crowther to the House Ways and Means Committee as it deliberated on the bill. Legal scholars defended the constitutionality of presidential authority in trade agreements.[41] On June 12, 1934, Roosevelt signed the landmark RTAA, which became—and remains—the basis for US trade policy.

Hull deemed the doctrine of equality of treatment, or non-discrimination, essential to US leadership over free-trade internationalism and the capitalist peace ideology. The assistant secretary of state, law professor Francis Sayre Sr., Woodrow Wilson's son-in law, argued that the principle encouraged "international trade and economic peace." Its contrary rule was "disequilibrium and economic war."[42] To be sure, Hull, and Roosevelt acknowledged that reciprocal trade agreements did not prevent fascist aggression. In 1934, Adolf Hitler was rearming, Mussolini eyed Ethiopia, and Japan readied to withdraw from the major naval limitation treaty. But the RTAA—"an indispensable cornerstone for the edifice of peace"—would offer an alternative to hostility.

For the moment, the economic distress of the Great Depression prevented the RTAA from overhauling the world trade system. By 1936, only three major trade partners (Canada, France, and the Netherlands) had signed reciprocal agreements. Talks were aborted with Germany and Italy, while Japan, Argentina, and Australia refused them entirely. Roosevelt's newly appointed foreign trade advisor, George Peek, saw protectionism and exchange controls as permanent fixtures in the world economy and thought the United States should likewise use them.[43] The president shared such realism and favored bilateralism. But Hull parried the Germans when they asked for special barter arrangements, calling their mercantilist policies, which in his view choked off trade and promoted chaos in Europe, "short-sighted and suicidal."[44]

Peek (and Roosevelt initially) approved of the barter agreement with Germany, which would discriminate against other nations and allow the Nazis to purchase 800,000 bales of American cotton at a time when Berlin had defaulted on $2 billion it owed the United States. Hull told the president that other cotton exporters, such as Brazil, would suffer and that giving Germany special advantages would toss aside the notion of equal treatment in commerce. Roosevelt backed away. Peek, however, continued to argue that trade objectives should "be based upon commercial and financial considerations as distinguished from diplomatic and political considerations."[45] He advocated two measures to prioritize the domestic economy: a foreign trade board to elevate legislative (protectionist) authority over the executive branch's free-trade leanings; and a return to the conditional most-favored-nation treatment of fifteen years earlier.[46] Hull persuaded the president to reject both ideas, and by mid-1935, Peek had resigned from the administration, to the great pleasure of the internationalists.[47] Nevertheless, he had voiced a line of thinking that never entirely retreated from American politics, namely, that capitalist peace theory did not hold up in the hard-bitten arena of international affairs.

Regardless of isolationist skepticism, Hull worked in 1935 to put reciprocity into effect by forging bilateral agreements that could be broadened on an unconditional most-favored-nation basis. Latin America was his initial focus. Because these nations usually traded a single or a few main commodities, an outcry at home was less likely. He then moved on to Belgium, targeting its auto market as a way to expand exports. Much anguish accompanied the agreement as both sides withdrew concessions. Roosevelt blew cold on granting unconditional equal treatment because it was unpopular with vocal import-competing voters who could punish him in the looming 1936 presidential election. Applying most-favored-nation treatment grew even more complicated. Democratic friends—namely, Canada, France, and Britain—had no such relationship with the United States, and thus they did not enjoy third-party benefits from the deals with Belgium and Brazil. Ironically, Nazi Germany did qualify for most-favored-nation status under a commercial agreement dating back ten years.[48]

The British Commonwealth now sought bilateral trade agreements with the United States. Britain seemed more interested in wielding its imperial power than in building a free-trade alliance to confront Nazism. War debts still overshadowed relations, as did the sterling bloc that privileged financial exchanges within the empire. As well, by 1932, a quarter of Britain's imports were duty free for the dominions, under the new Ottawa system of imperial preferences, but not for disadvantaged outsiders. In September 1934, Washington heard from the British ambassador, Sir Ronald Lindsay, that London sought a reciprocal trade agreement but preferred to wait until currency arrangements had been worked out. The Americans shot back that imperial preferences stood in the way of such a deal. Hull had initially approached Canada to dismantle the Ottawa system. The lure of the huge and adjoining US market led to an agreement that formed the largest two-way trade relationship in the world. It also built North American political unity. Hull and Prime Minister Mackenzie King, both free-trade visionaries, mingled trade and peace under the United States-Canadian trade pact of January 1936.[49]

Notably, war did not break out between the United States and any trade agreement country in the 1930s; in fact, almost all signatories to an RTAA deal ended up being allies in World War II. "The political line-up followed the economic line-up," Hull famously concluded.[50] However, the reciprocal trade treaties signed by the eve of the Second World War were reached with a select group of nations, mostly Latin American countries already under the powerful influence of the United States. Russia and China and other countries had not signed on to Hull's program by 1939 but ended up being allies anyway. Still, Hull's vision mattered. On one side were the Nazis and fascist Italy, warmongers voicing state-mandated economic theories. On the other side, Hull told Roosevelt, were "anglo-saxon conceptions, ideals, and training over many centuries" of freedom and individualism that were "deeply rooted in their minds and hearts."[51] One commentator on the RTAA, Charles T. Crowell, had said in 1935 that the State Department aimed for treaties "with nations utterly devoted to a policy of peace, in the same spirit as our national policy. What we are doing is creating a new bloc in the family of nations: a peace bloc."[52]

To the acclaim of exporters, twenty-one agreements resulted from the RTAA by the eve of World War II. At annual conventions, the peak American international commercial association, the National Foreign Trade Council, endorsed the legislation because it bolstered the free-enterprise system so critical not only to prosperity but also to the defense of democracy. The "fears of isolationists" had no place, proclaimed the Council. It had convened binational councils with Japan and China, among others, to overcome nationalist challenges to free trade. Protectionism threatened the United States with "a deadening system of bureaucratic control" that weakened the Constitution and the country's defense "against counter-revolutions which in their consequences must prove fatal to established order." In an era when the state ruled the economies in Italy, Germany, and the Soviet Union, and dominated even in Great Britain, the RTAA protected democracy, freedom, and, ultimately, peace.[53]

More business leaders came around to the capitalist peace argument. Thomas Watson of International Business Machines, who had attended the International Chamber of Commerce meetings in Paris in July 1935, recounted the complaints of German industrialists about US trade barriers. Watson sympathized, but decided solutions depended on "the interdependence of all civilized nations." Nations with common interests would help each other toward "a sounder material life, a better standard of living and a higher cultural and spiritual existence for the world as a whole."[54] Gerard Swope, president of the General Electric Company, noted in a radio address sponsored by the World Peace Foundation that trade arose through such cooperation. "Peace is fundamental of neighborly trade, domestic trade or world trade," he added, although militarism currently undermined that notion.[55]

Under the RTAA, exports and imports rose, even with a modest number of nations involved, yet Hull had grander designs. In 1935, he proudly noted that trade agreements had at least inspired hope that "the world can shortly expect a general movement in the direction of international economic sanity."[56] Hull also pursued "triangular, four-cornered, and multilateral trading" under the unconditional most-favored-nation principle, even though nations were doing their best at the moment to prevent the distribution of goods by discriminating against imports. Nonetheless, he persistently campaigned against narrow isolationism and rejoiced when the League of Nations, in September 1935, endorsed general principles for trade and currency liberalization.[57]

By this time, though, observers saw war in Europe as imminent. Britain and France differed too much to hold Hitler or Mussolini in check. Indeed, Italy attacked Ethiopia in October 1935. The response from Washington was outrage without teeth—a moral embargo that included a list of supplies, namely, oil, to be denied to Italy. Meanwhile, Japan consolidated power in Manchuria and eyed the rest of China. Tokyo demanded parity in the number of warships allowed under treaties rather than the smaller ratio of battleships and cruisers that it had previously accepted. And Roosevelt encountered growing isolationist sentiment at home. At hearings that indicted the munitions industry for pushing the United States into war in 1917, Congress legislated strict neutrality laws beginning in 1935 that hurt friends contending against the dictators by denying them arms and supplies. As militarists occupied Europe, Africa, and Asia, Roosevelt surveyed persistent discriminatory trade practices around the world. He noted to Eugene Thomas of the National Foreign Trade Council that his reciprocal trade agreements law stood out as "a definitely constructive program designed to combat" the tendency toward isolationism. As 1936 loomed, that was much optimistic bluster unmoored from the dangerous reality of mounting aggression in the world.[58]

2

Dictators, 1936–1940

The democracies soon failed their first tests against aggressors. After fascist Italy overran Ethiopia in 1936, the League of Nations condemned the attack, which did not stop Benito Mussolini. Worried about driving him into German hands, Britain and France feebly attempted to mediate and then imposed an ineffective embargo on Italy. Germany and Japan recognized the conquest. Meanwhile, Adolf Hitler violated post–World War I treaties by rebuilding his military and by reoccupying the Rhineland. Mussolini's dream of empire bore fruit, and Hitler's was on the way to reality. The United States condemned both Italy and the crypto-fascists in Spain, who Francisco Franco led into civil war against the Republican government in Madrid just months after Addis Ababa fell. Washington issued more indictments a year later when Japan attacked China, launching World War II in Asia. Franklin Roosevelt acknowledged the threat from the dictators, including the communist Josef Stalin in the Soviet Union, but neutrality legislation tied his hands. That is, except in trade policy; he trained the RTAA on bolstering the enfeebled democracies, namely, France and Britain. As war threatened and erupted, the capitalist peace paradigm went from theory to being put practice.

Cordell Hull ceased negotiating new trade agreements for most of 1936 because in an election year, protectionists would hound the president. Senators William Borah and Arthur Vandenberg, both GOP presidential aspirants, were among those who claimed the State Department gave away business in RTAA deals, while the centralization of power under a supposedly "dictatorial" executive branch horrified them. Their charge that the executive had unconstitutionally usurped legislative authority over commerce gained gravity when the Supreme Court in January 1936 struck down the Agricultural Adjustment Act as an overreach of power. Protectionists in general also ridiculed Hull's capitalist peace view, noting that, in actuality, "disturbed world conditions have constantly

Capitalist Peace. Thomas W. Zeiler, Oxford University Press. © Oxford University Press 2022.
DOI: 10.1093/oso/9780197621363.003.0003

increased in intensity" during the three years since the RTAA's inception.[1] Roosevelt also felt the heat from progressives. "These low-tariff policies are an integral part of a still more ominous policy of internationalism which is threatening the integrity and unity of the New Deal on every side," wrote his former confidant, Raymond Moley.[2] The Democratic platform deleted Hull's mention of peace aims in the tariff plank and favored the nationalists who sought to "give adequate protection" to producers at home.[3]

Nevertheless, Hull's lobbying yielded endorsements for the RTAA. Tariff walls could not be built around the United States without hurting growth, because America was the world's biggest exporter and second ranked importer, some two hundred businessmen argued. Thus, the program pushed other nations to remove their commercial barriers. Most journalists backed liberalization, some actually criticizing Hull's timidity for not using the RTAA more vigorously to open up trade partnerships. Although they appreciated his devotion to economic instruments as a means to promote peace, which later won him the Nobel Peace Prize, they lavished most of their attention on solving the Depression rather than diplomacy. The Republican presidential nominee, Alf Landon, who had opposed the Hawley-Smoot Tariff years before, preferred the approach of limited reciprocal trade pushed by his nationalistic advisor, George Peek, rather than unconditional most-favored-nation treatment. Hull confronted Landon. Instrumental to recovery, the RTAA, above all, fulfilled Wilsonian ideas about peace and legalism regarding the sanctity of treaties.[4]

Hull and Roosevelt adopted the capitalist peace mission on the campaign trail when electoral victory seemed likely. Preceding the president's appearance in Minneapolis in early October 1936, the secretary of state warned that economic distress opens the way "for the demagogue and the agitator, foments internal strife, and frequently leads to the supplanting of orderly democratic government." Fascist aggression proved that downward slide to authoritarianism and war.[5] Roosevelt agreed. In his famous Chautauqua speech in August, he did not claim that tariff reductions would stop war, "but we do feel that without a more liberal international trade war is a natural sequence."[6] Contented people were prone to peacefulness.[7]

Regarding that interconnection, however, the public also took cues from isolationists in Congress who placed strictures on trade under the Neutrality Act. This prohibitive legislation prevented normal application of capitalist peace ideas. The RTAA, shipping, aeronautics, and banking laws actually opened more commercial outlets than in any time previously, but Americans agreed that the Neutrality Act must apply to all belligerents, friends or not. The administration chafed at this thinking, warning that a general war was a distinct possibility and friends needed aid. Still, neutrality got more exacting; in 1937, Congress forbade credits to belligerents for normal business purposes. Congress would not allow Roosevelt to drag the country into war with an insistence on neutral rights, as Woodrow Wilson had in 1917. The neutrality handcuff on the executive branch concerned merchant groups like the National Foreign Trade Council.[8]

Isolationist policy virtually clamped a trade embargo on nations at war, friends or foe, which Hull feared weakened the democracies. Yet the internationalist cause grew even weaker. Those disillusioned by the League of Nation's inability to stop Italian, Japanese, and German advances added to the dissent. The only discretion Roosevelt possessed was to decide to apply a moral, arms, or economic embargo if a state of war was in effect. That was the case with Italy's aggression in Ethiopia. The State Department refused to renew a commercial treaty with Rome that stretched back to 1871. When Emperor Haile Selassie fled Addis Ababa in May 1936, the United States lifted its moral embargo on Italy because the war was over, and the League ended its sanctions. Neutrality law did not honor the spirit of the capitalist peace paradigm. Not only that, but the lifting of sanctions heartened the dictators, who moved toward total rearmament and territorial expansion. The Nazi regime subsidized its exports by altering the value of the German mark, which prompted the United States Treasury Department to retaliate with countervailing duties. Protests from Berlin, trade partners, and US business poured into Hull's office, resulting in the removal of the American duties in August 1936. The League of Nations' Economic Committee warned a month later that such restrictive commercial policies sowed the seeds of international conflict.[9]

As war clouds gathered, the State Department lamented the global cynicism about the prospects for peace. Assistant Secretary Sayre worried over the "prairie fire" of nationalism. Every new restriction to defend a nation, he warned, became a new weapon that made the economic struggle ever more deadly. If orderly trade exchanges and raw material procurement processes broke down, then "only force remains. Imperialistic expansion, whether in pursuit of markets or raw materials sources, cannot mean other than perpetual conflict." On the other hand, intelligent and cooperative trade agreements could build a substructure of prosperity and peace.[10] Neither he nor Hull held out much hope for that course at the moment.

Trade policy did not stop the fascist tide, but with Hull's guidance the United States signaled its opposition to aggressors. He got tougher on the Nazis, refusing Germany's request to buy war materiel rather than pay down its debt. As well, the State Department vigorously opposed Nazi mercantilist attempts to bring southeastern Europe—the Danube and the Balkan states of Austria, Bulgaria, Greece, and Yugoslavia—under economic control by barter, bilateral trade, and financial policies. After Italy invaded Ethiopia, Hull resisted Italian trade expansion, though the administration had not halted Italian imports.[11]

Japan got no such consideration. Hull deemed Tokyo a natural beneficiary of free trade, owing to its resource scarcities and rising standard of living, and he remained hostile to the seeming Japanese preference for militarism rather than capitalist peace. He rejected Tokyo's demand for naval parity with the United States and Britain at the 1936 Second London Naval Conference, considering it a risk to national security, but Japan abandoned the treaty limits anyway, began building its navy without restrictions, and started to fortify its possessions in the Pacific. The London talks ended in March, around the time Hitler took the Rhineland. Hull hoped for a rapprochement, but terms for trade peace were as challenging as arms control. In reality, he was hypocritical toward Japan, as he stomached American protectionism that pushed Tokyo into a corner: Either Japan could join the Western powers in granting equal trade treatment—and limit its exports—or it could go to war for markets. Tokyo protested that trade agreements with Latin American nations had actually cut its exports. New Deal recovery also depended, in part, on limiting imports from the competitive Japanese. The pressures of the 1936 election compelled Hull to demand "voluntary" export controls, but those restrictions only convinced the Japanese to look elsewhere for resources, pointing them ever more toward China. Hull could only lament that Japanese trade policies were "crushing China to her knees."[12]

The same happened to democracy in Europe. From 1936 to 1939, Spain's civil war sowed appalling destruction, revealing the democracies' feebleness in the face of fascism. Roosevelt invoked the Neutrality Act, and France and Britain embargoed both sides in Spain. In contrast, the dictators sent in their militaries. Hull could only fall back on vague idealism, such as a hope for more contact among peoples of the world, better education, and more international conferences to bring peace. Words did not stop the aggressors, of course. By October, Black and Brown Shirts initiated their Rome-Berlin Axis, an alliance that Japan joined as well. All the while, Britain and France vacillated in the face of Hitler's violations of pact after pact. Washington remained stuck "in a concrete mold of isolation," moaned Hull.[13]

Even the Western Hemisphere was at risk. German trade policies sought to lock down Latin American exports by demanding payment in special marks. This risked replacing US markets with discriminatory, yet lucrative, bilateral arrangements that strengthened the Nazi economy. Hull told the Germans he would not permit bilateralism, which he saw as part of the twisted logic of fascism, because they intended it to finance the Nazi war machine. Roosevelt visited Buenos Aires in December 1936, warning pan-American delegates not to fall into the fascist trap. Harking back to the Montevideo meeting that had endorsed the RTAA, he said that such trade deals "will be a notable contribution to the cause of peace."[14] Hull followed up in Argentina with an eight-point "pillars of peace" that included "commercial policies to bring each prosperity upon which enduring peace is founded." A "good neighbor" resolution followed, requiring hemispheric consultation if war threatened the region, and the Senate ratified it five months later.[15]

Meanwhile, the British Commonwealth's discriminatory imperial preference system was poisoning relations among the Western democracies. The United States saw these preferences, like fascist demands, as a foreign policy crisis. Canada was a member of the Ottawa system, but Hull's real target was Britain. The British still resented Roosevelt's scuttling of the 1933 London Economic Conference, however, and their leaders were split. The Treasury and Board of Trade hoped to separate political and economic relationships with the United States and thus embraced preferences. Most diplomats in the Foreign Office joined the capitalist peace camp, seeking trade cooperation to counter fascism. As Hull noted to British ambassador Ronald Lindsay, freer trade through the unconditional most-favored-nation process (rather than the discriminatory imperial trade and exchange control system) might determine war and peace in Europe. Hull worried that almost overnight, Mussolini and Hitler could convince some 35 million Italians and 65 million Germans to "arise the next morning and insist on being sent to the first-line trenches without delay." But if those people were employed, he argued, "they [would] have no disposition to follow agitators and to enthrone dictators."[16] Nevertheless, with New Deal nationalism protecting US markets and the war debt issue still outstanding, the British were not swayed by the capitalist peace perspective. They considered unequal, bilateral treatment through empire preferences the better course than hoping American trade policy would lead to lower tariffs.

The secretary of state so single-mindedly pleaded with the British against such thinking that his capitalist peace campaign dominated the Anglo-American relationship. Hull's principles followed a logical sequence, as he told the French, with whom the United States signed a reciprocal trade accord in May 1936: "(1) The restoration of international commerce, tending to stabilize relations among nations; (2) The re-employment of millions of unemployed persons throughout the world; and (3) The establishment of a sound foundation for building a permanent structure of world peace."[17] If nations had adopted trade liberalization over the past half-decade, he reasoned, the resulting prosperity might have coaxed Italy from Africa, Japan from China, Germany from the Rhineland, and Turkey from fortifying the Dardanelles. Trade reform might, quite simply, determine war and peace. The "size of armies, navies, and air forces and the killing power of these forces are being increased steadily," wrote Hull, while economies grew more intimately connected through military establishments. As a consequence, attention centered increasingly on "the dictators that head governments and the vast forces they command." Rather than trying to solve the Depression through an arms build-up, Hull argued, London must reject discriminatory agreements while Washington worked on lowering its high tariffs.[18]

For London, things were more multifaceted. Financial, imperial, tariff, and European diplomatic policies entwined in intricate complexity. Foreign Secretary Anthony Eden privately sympathized with Hull's stance, and even the export/import-oriented Board of Trade's Sir Walter Runciman shared the general view on capitalist peace. But Britain held its ground, blaming the Hawley-Smoot Tariff for the impasse and not budging on imperial preferences. British domestic politics stymied progress. The empire preference group lobbied vigorously, hardening London's position on protectionism. Conservative Neville Chamberlain, whom Hull labeled an empire reactionary, ousted the Labor Party's Stanley Baldwin as prime minister in the spring of 1937, in part by supporting protectionism and financial controls. Hull groaned that Chamberlain was "wedded to a static policy of high tariffs and armaments for self-defense without an immediate disposition to move at once in concert with other countries to the attack on excessive trade barriers and obstructions."[19] But to London, Hull sounded noble—and idealistic. The dire threat of war required empire unity around tariff preferences, not freer trade. This was no time for applying universal principles. If Hull could not provide assurances of massive tariff concessions by the United States, Britain would continue to look to its own empire for relief and rescue.[20]

That reasonable British and Commonwealth leaders resisted free trade irritated Hull. There was hope for change, however. For instance, Japan's threat to retaliate against protectionist Australia's wool exports caused Canberra to consider that a trade war with Tokyo might force Australia to stop discriminating against the United States. Still, Canberra refused to apply most-favored-nation treatment to American goods. Australia was a surplus-producing country but, wrote a frustrated Hull, it was helping drive "the world straight to an unprecedented, uneconomic condition, with the inevitable disastrous effects upon peoples, their welfare, and their civilization."[21] In short, Hull understood the need for imperial preferences but demanded that members of the Commonwealth not discriminate against outsiders to artificially divert trade from a foreign (the United States) to an empire source. In this vein, he saw the recent trade reciprocal trade agreement with Canada as a step toward a comprehensive accord with Britain, and thus the entire Commonwealth. The urgency hinged not just on economics. Canada had also recently made a trade deal with Nazi Germany, which frightened Hull because it helped fund Hitler's military. Prime Minister Mackenzie King, too, understood that the trade agreement was a better "substitute for militarism and big armaments and possible war" and thus endorsed the accord with his neighbor to the south.[22]

In early 1937, Hull accused the British and Canadians of forging a new discriminatory trade agreement that embraced economic nationalism at a perilous time. London and Ottawa disagreed, claiming their pact did not mean more discrimination because it reduced the number of goods granted margins of preferences. The Board of Trade noted that Britain still wanted a reciprocal trade agreement with the United States, even if it simply conventionalized current rates. Hull retorted that the next months would "determine the course of international peace and economic rehabilitation."[23]

Before formally engaging the British, Hull first had housekeeping to do—renewing tariff negotiating authority under the Reciprocal Trade Agreements Act that would expire in 1937. Extending the RTAA would not be automatic, however, with Congress inclined to turn inward. The Senate, for instance, had recently blocked the administration's request to join the World Court. Isolationist hysteria peaked as the Neutrality Act also came up for renewal. The new version made non-intervention permanent, though Roosevelt got some discretion to help democracies through the "cash and carry" provision that required nations to pay directly for US goods (thus avoiding the World War I debt scenario) and transport them on their own ships so as not to risk the lives of American seamen. This procedure perversely hurt the republican Spanish government's defense against Franco because an attachment to the bill prohibited selling arms to Spain. Germany and Italy faced no such limits. Stubbornly high levels of domestic unemployment added to the gloomy context of anti-internationalist sentiment as the RTAA campaign got under way. Hull argued for jobs but, considering an increasingly dismal international arena, he pushed for capitalist peace. As he noted later, "While striving to prevent the political fabric of the world from being rent completely to bits, I kept hammering home the economic side of international relations as the major possibility for averting the catastrophe" through the reciprocal trade program.[24]

During the 1936 election, isolationists had targeted the RTAA, and the administration expected strong opposition. Thus, instead of insisting on permanent legislation, Roosevelt compromised with another three-year term. He also injected capitalist peace ideology into the effort. To the House Ways and Means chairman, he wrote that reducing trade barriers "serves to strengthen the foundations of world peace" even in this "present unfortunate state of world affairs."[25] It was a tough sell. A National Peace Conference of three dozen religious, academic, and pacifist organizations endorsed the RTAA as part of a program of economic and military disarmament, even though protectionists argued that greater prosperity through freer trade, ironically, might be the safer bet by providing more finances for armaments. Still, the conference urged Roosevelt to call a global meeting for economic and military disarmament, because, in general, "as peace-time satisfactions increase, people are less willing to surrender them and thus less susceptible to war appeals."[26]

At House hearings in January 1937 and in a statement to the Senate Finance Committee in February, the State Department vigorously added the capitalist peace argument to the president's message. Hull struck at the protectionists, who had come up with no alternative to free-trade internationalism but instead depended on mercantilist-fed animosity. His lieutenant, Francis Sayre, warned that the "modern dragon of war" could only be defeated by acknowledging "that no nation through isolation can avoid the consequences of a major war." History showed, said Sayre, that "men will fight before they starve."[27]

RTAA opponents, less vocal than in 1934, zeroed in on this foreign policy argument. Francis Culkin, a House Republican from New York, accused Sayre of being an "ardent internationalist" to whom "any treaty is a good one, provided the other country is happy." Both he and Hull "fanatically believe that if we will blend our economic destinies with all of the other nations of the world, war will cease to be and the lion will lie down with the lamb." Placing the RTAA under Hull, "a mystic and a dreamer" on trade, was "like giving command of the army to an avowed pacifist or giving a Quaker the command of the navy."[28] Roy Woodruff, a Progressive turned Republican from Michigan, could not square capitalist peace theory with current affairs, which appeared to feature the worst bellicosity he could remember. It was a valid point; the capitalist peace was mere "hope" in these fraught times.[29] Yet the critics were overwhelmed by the large Democratic majority that saw no reason to junk the trade agreements program or abandon the New Deal. The House renewed the RTAA overwhelmingly, 284–100.[30]

The administration got a similar result in the Senate after a campaign by Hull and Sayre and criticism from the protectionists. As Hull noted to the Committee on Finance chairman, Pat Harrison of Mississippi, even if the nation avoided hostilities, "the profound economic upheaval which must inevitably accompany a widespread military conflict anywhere in the world" would hit American shores.[31] The Senate hearings, like those in the House, were jammed thick with testimony from industries protesting imports, charges of unconstitutional seizure by executive power, and trade partners who, like the British, supposedly plotted to trick Washington into canceling World War I debts. Facing the skeptics, the free traders turned to internationalism. Businessman and former government official Lewis Douglas put it simply that to "avoid war there must first be economic peace." The past half-decade had borne out that sad truism.[32] With Senate approval by a 58–24 vote, the RTAA was renewed in March 1937.

With the RTAA authority to negotiate down tariffs in hand, Washington turned to Great Britain. Building an open trading world and secure peace depended on Britain, which, said Hull, stood at the "apex of the arch" of trade and diplomacy.[33] Roosevelt told radio listeners in October 1937 that behind an Anglo-American trade accord was capitalist peace. Brain Truster Adolf Berle added to nodding bankers, investors, and exporters that if they wanted profits, then peace was imperative. Although it seemed "a far cry from a group of business men talking over their policy about a tariff act, a trade treaty, or a proceeding before the tariff commission, to a Bilbao capture or a clash on the Amur River," the democratic world was "looking straight down the gunbarrel" in Spain, China, and elsewhere.[34]

Hull and British ambassador Ronald Lindsay continued to talk. Lindsay confessed that Britain's sole objective was to rearm against the fascist threat. While Hull agreed on rearmament for the democracies, "a positive program for cooperation—namely, our trade agreements" would serve security as well. If both sides wanted peace, an Anglo-American trade deal would be a way to avert war rather than rely on a military build-up that would guarantee one.[35] Prime Minister Chamberlain quietly acquiesced to discussions, including modification of the Ottawa system, in the interests of "world economic stability and peace."[36] Hull believed an accord would inspire democracies and rally dozens of cowering nations against the militarists because both Britain and America carried tremendous economic and moral influence. Perhaps if even the dictators linked trade to foreign policy, "the gate would be wide open for a discussion of political problems."[37]

Idealistic as this was, US neutrality and determined fascist expansion gave the democracies little else to fall back on. John Foster Dulles, a prominent Republican lawyer and leading Christian voice for world comity, concluded, "Once the issues of international trade, stable exchanges, colonies, etc. are seen in their true significance, we will have gone far to assure progress towards a warless world."[38] Raymond Buell of the Foreign Policy Association deepened this argument by focusing on the dangers oppressive totalitarian state control represented to democracy, world stability, and capitalism. An Anglo-American reciprocal trade agreement was "the one concrete effort now being made in the whole field of international relations" to thwart "Fascist dictatorship."[39] The RTAA sought to convince the "overcrowded nations" of Japan, Germany, and Italy that, through the free exchanges of privately traded goods, their regimented economies that supported dictatorships could return to market practices conducive to democracy.[40] Yet for the time being, a deal between Britain and America was a more realistic hope for the capitalist peace.

Even with the internationalist rationale, reaching that agreement tested both sides. The Board of Trade continued to roll out statistics exemplifying low British tariff rates, a worsening balance of trade, and a preference system unprejudicial to world trade. London started to bend, however, fearing a collapse in Europe as 2 million Germans rearmed. The world heard "more distinctly the roar of the military Niagara," reported Canada's Mackenzie King to Hull before heading to London for the Imperial Conference in May 1937. An Anglo-American agreement was on the discussion agenda.[41] In London, King pushed for most-favored-nation treatment for trade partners to weaken economic nationalism. He even considered terminating the Ottawa agreement with Britain. Believing that Washington's tough stance on preferences was a bluff, Australia blocked Canada's intentions. Yet the Board of Trade's assurance that Roosevelt did not seek a complete abandonment of imperial preferences helped counter Australia's diffidence. In the meantime, a trilateral Anglo-American-Canadian agreement lowered some tariffs but did not impinge on the Ottawa system. Hull held out hope amid intensifying global chaos.[42]

To the dismay of the Americans, London's inability to see the bigger context of fascist depredations meant the talks dragged on through 1937 and well into the following year. With Italy and Germany threatening the Mediterranean and the Sino-Japanese War having just broken out, Hull was disappointed that "small groups of embargo-tariff people and their lobbies in the British Empire might be able to obstruct and delay this necessary action" for peace. Britain could no longer rely on the Royal Navy to keep trade channels open, either in Europe or in the Pacific. Relenting to this logic, and to pressure from France and Canada, the British agreed to negotiate a trade agreement in earnest. But they still resisted reducing preferences on competitive goods such as rice, lumber, and motion pictures. The new ambassador to Britain, Joseph Kennedy, cautioned in late July 1938 that unless Chamberlain "approach[es] this problem on a broader front, it might well be charged in Germany, Italy, Japan, and other countries" that the two democracies were "utterly incapable of sitting down and making simply, mutually profitable trade arrangements with each other." If Britain persisted in granting only "paltry concessions that spurned equality of treatment, Americans would turn more definitively toward isolationism as London seemingly denied any connection to "the philosophy and the spirit and the letter of this wholesome peace-making program of trade restoration" regardless of "the growing world dangers" at present.[43]

In early September 1938, the two sides finally reached a deal, even though Hull despaired over Britain's obsession over every duty reduction and the dollars to be gained while "the extremely dangerous hair-trigger European situation" persisted.[44] Avoiding pettiness was even more pressing as Czechoslovakia, at Hitler's behest, was dismembered in the Munich Pact of September 30, and then Hungary and Poland separated ethnic territories from the Czechs in early November. A stunned but impotent United States stood by as France and Britain submitted to totalitarian expansion in Europe. Hull agreed to a weaker Anglo-American trade agreement because none at all would abet the sad Munich storyline of democratic appeasement. Hull dismissed the expected protectionist outrage at home, just as he did the selfish empire isolationists on the other side. On November 17, 1938, after Canadian mediation, Ambassador Lindsay, Hull, and Prime Minister King signed both the British-American reciprocal trade accord and also a new US-Canada trade agreement at the White House. These reduced the percentage of duties in the United Kingdom, the United States, and Canada. British reluctance aside, the agreement signaled the tightening bonds between two key democracies, Roosevelt's willingness to intervene in Europe however he could, and the coming wartime Grand Alliance.[45]

Signed just eight months before Hitler invaded Poland, the trade pact came too late to verify capitalist peace theory. Indeed, as columnist Walter Lippmann admitted, further progress on Hull's trade program was unlikely with the "whole of Europe east of the Rhine to the Russian frontier, and from there across Asia to the Pacific Ocean" fallen in "the orbit of militarized totalitarian states" with centrally managed economies "as instruments of military power." Still, the

Fig. 2.1 British Ambassador Ronald Lindsay, Board of Trade President Walter Runciman, and Cordell Hull meet to sign the Anglo-American Trade Agreement of 1938, as trade merges with anti-fascist diplomacy. Library of Congress, Prints & Photographs Division, Harris & Ewing.

trade agreement veered Britain away from harm's way and toward unity with the Western Hemisphere. In sum, noted Lippmann, freer trade might not bring prosperity but could encourage solidarity.[46] Both Roosevelt and Hull knew, as well, that a world order based on trade internationalism would most certainly be postponed to a postwar era.[47]

From 1938 onward, mayhem erupted in the international arena. Because Japan called its ruthless invasion of China a punitive expedition and not a war, Roosevelt could not apply the Neutrality Act, which meant he could not compel the empire to pay cash and carry away American goods in its own ships, which might have depleted its military effort in Asia. Washington did denounce the indiscriminate bombing of Chinese civilians. And when Japanese planes sank the US gunboat *Panay* in December 1937 on the Yangtze River, killing three Americans and destroying three Standard Oil Company tankers, war was averted only by swift apologies and compensation from the Japanese. There was talk of the United States imposing economic sanctions on Tokyo, but business leaders wished to trade with Japan while others worried that involvement in China would drag the United States into war in Asia and take its eyes off Europe. On that continent, in 1939, Hitler took Austria and swallowed Czechoslovakia. Francisco Franco triumphed in the civil war that year, too, ushering in a dictatorship in Spain that would last four decades. The Roosevelt administration pushed vigorously for rearmament even as isolationists reared up against commitments beyond American shores. German encroachment in Latin America, including trade deals, was also concerning. In Lima, Cordell Hull declared pan-American solidarity against fascism and reasserted the Good Neighbor policy, even settling a bitter issue over Mexico expropriating US and European investments. The president pledged to avoid conflict by all means; Hull encouraged merchants to keep engaging in world commerce.[48]

But war, indeed, was imminent. In February 1939, London gave France a security guarantee in the event of a German or Italian attack. In April, Mussolini entered Albania. Roosevelt followed up with capitalist peace appeals to Hitler and Mussolini, hoping to discuss "opening up avenues of international trade to the end that every Nation of the earth may be enabled to buy and sell on equal terms in the world market as well as to possess assurance of obtaining the materials and products of peaceful economic life."[49] The dictators scoffed at such platitudes about trade and peace, which were all Roosevelt had in his arsenal, given isolationist constraints. Secret word came that Hermann Göring, director of the German economy and Hitler's chief deputy, would consider more liberal trade policies, and that the führer might even moderate his racial policy. But the Nazis could be trusted to change course neither on mercantilism nor in their treatment of the Jews. They also turned the tables, claiming democracies victimized them by denying them trade deals. In June, the House modified the arms embargo provision to tie the president's hands more than before. Pacifists scrambled to convene security and economic conferences to preserve the fading peace.[50]

These efforts failed. The führer turned to Poland, which readied for the Nazi attack, as did France and Britain, which gave guarantees of security to the Poles. When the war began on September 1, 1939, the United States woke up from its isolationist slumber by acknowledging that tariff walls had brought the world to this point by boosting autarchy that fueled militarism and undermined democratic solidarity. The war's outbreak relegated observers on both sides of the Atlantic to talking about postwar reconstruction of a prosperous and peaceful economic system. All that was left was the hope of better things to come. The United States would never again insulate itself from leadership, and it would shoulder much of the burden to reconstruct a new order. First, though, totalitarianism had to be defeated.[51] Roosevelt cleverly bypassed much of the Neutrality Act's restrictions through Lend-Lease aid to help Britain, while Washington watched the dictators overrun Western Europe and the Soviet tyrant, Stalin, subdue Estonia, Lithuania, Latvia, and Finland.

Hanging on to a semblance of internationalism, the administration asked for renewal of the Reciprocal Trade Agreements Act before it expired in June 1940. Hull took advantage of the war context, counseling Roosevelt that the need for the legislation was "more acute than ever" because the RTAA was "an emergency program to meet emergency conditions."[52] But protectionists also saw an opportunity. They lobbied for repeal or suspension of the twenty-one bilateral accords to date, which amounted to 60 percent of total US commerce, on the basis that the war had dislocated international trade and that high tariffs would guard producers from aggressors. They generally denounced Hull's sermons that liberal trade engendered peace. After all, war had come despite the trade program, with France, Britain, and many neutrals imposing restrictions so they could import only vital war goods. The United States should do the same. Hull called such thinking a return to "suicidal economic nationalism" inimical to the cause of democratic unity.[53]

Most business voices agreed that special trade controls—blocked exchanges, barter agreements, embargoes, blockades, and discriminatory bilateralism—led to undemocratic, and ultimately unpeaceful, policies. Economic warfare, in short, promoted military warfare. According to the Business Advisory Council of the Department of Commerce, reciprocal trade agreements "have contributed to international good will, even if they had been reduced to mere principles and not practice during wartime."[54] Cutting tariffs would reduce spending on arms, wrote Clarence Streit, an internationalist advocate of an Atlantic union of democracies. Influential columnist Dorothy Thompson elaborated on how war arose from unemployment and its resulting unrest and dictatorship as nations tried to "shut themselves up in geographical compartments," separated from others by protective tariffs and financial controls.[55]

More than at any other point of the RTAA's existence, Roosevelt mimicked his secretary of state's capitalist peace approach because current events were so gloomy. So, he looked to the future. As he proclaimed to Congress on January 3, 1940, the RTAA gave the United States a leadership role "when the time comes for a renewal of world peace." To be sure, that future lay far in the distance; this realist knew that mere trade agreements would not defeat fascism.[56] Thus, rearmament took precedence over trade to maintain a free society in the face of Nazi regimentation and enslavement. Nonetheless, trade was one of the "tools of democracy to make our economic system more efficient, to preserve our freedom, and to keep away even from any talk of dictatorship."[57] As France and Britain eyed Germany in the "phony war" that was ending in spring 1940, Hull followed with testimony to the House Ways and Means Committee that nations, particularly the totalitarians, had chosen their paths of self-containment. "When the peace conference meets," he explained, nations could choose instead the opposite direction of liberalism, expansion, and openness to provide jobs for the 80 million men now under arms.[58] To be sure, confessed the new assistant secretary of state, Henry Grady, the RTAA had not succeeded in averting war, but only because the fascists had already made so much headway across Europe and Asia. When those forces met defeat, however, "commercial peace and cooperation will be an absolute condition of peace."[59]

Opponents mocked these contentions, and they were further angered by administration implications that Hawley-Smoot had helped launch World War II. Noted Congressman Allen Treadway, this was a serious accusation that ignored the Versailles Treaty as a root cause of the war. That British Commonwealth trade would remain confined within the discriminatory imperial preference bloc was a given for the postwar era, so there would still be animosity. Senator Henry Cabot Lodge, Republican from Massachusetts, wondered why, if trade promoted peace, imperialist Great Britain was always among the first to go to war. The capitalist peace perspective was simply not "intellectually respectable" because free-trade imperialism clearly caused wars.[60] Internationalists dismissed such Anglophobic anti-imperialism. The progressive Henry Wallace, secretary of agriculture, patiently doubted that free trade explained why London was at war. Besides, added Grady, in light of the Ottawa system of preferences, Britain was no model of free trade.[61]

Regardless, a majority of Congress believed this was no time to debate imperialism and voted for the RTAA. The House passed the legislation, though the Senate approved it by a margin of only five votes. Fifteen Democrats crossed the aisle to suspend the legislation for the duration of the war until there was more clarity in trade relations. Retorted Hull, "I think if Moses had kept secret from his followers what a wonderful place there was over beyond that big mountain, they never would have been interested in crossing the Red Sea." In this case, the Promised Land was a postwar world in which millions of people worked through gainful, non-military employment furthered by trade expansion.[62] Roosevelt signed the RTAA of 1940 in mid-April, noting that this "powerful instrument" would help in "strengthening the foundations of stable peace."[63] A month later, the Nazis attacked France.

Capitalist peace theory remained academic as Hitler struck westward, overrunning the Low Countries and, with Mussolini's complicity, forcing the shocking surrender of France. By July 1940, with the democracies at bay, the only practicable measures available to the United States were to shore up hemispheric defenses, discourage Latin Americans from handing over European assets to the Axis powers, and encourage solidarity through trade deals. American neutrality, at least its advocacy in principle, had ended. Roosevelt proclaimed the famous "Four Freedoms," freedom of religion and expression and freedom from fear and want. When asked if "free trade, opening up trade" might be a fifth, the president confessed he had forgotten that one. He likened it to freedom from want—"in other words, the removal of certain barriers between nations, cultural in the first place and commercial in the second place. That is the fifth, very definitely."[64]

Roosevelt naturally had military matters on his mind. He acquiesced to sinking the French fleet docked in North Africa, which the British carried out despite recrimination by France, but he maintained relations with the collaborationist Vichy government for the moment as he cultivated the resistance leader, Charles de Gaulle. In September 1940, Roosevelt acceded to the wishes of the new British prime minister, Winston Churchill, for military aid. Skirting the Neutrality Act, he swapped fifty supposedly obsolete destroyers to Britain for Commonwealth holdings in the Western Hemisphere. The deal kept isolationists quiet and the Royal Navy afloat in the face of German attacks around the British Isles. The Soviet Union also warmed to the West, as Josef Stalin grew uneasy with Germany's rapid military advances. Russian diplomats complained about American trade discrimination. Hull countered that the United States had slowed trade because of Moscow's insidious pact with the Nazis in 1939 and its cruel Winter War with Finland that ended in Soviet victory in March 1940. In response, the United States had issued a "moral embargo" on such war goods as airplanes, aviation fuel, tin, and rubber. Washington also considered not renewing the most-favored-nation trade treaty with the Russians, although it was extended as a diplomatic olive branch despite the fact that American-Soviet trade was minuscule.[65] But the communist Stalin kept a firm grip on the Baltic states and Finland, readying his defenses for an expected German attack and shunning talk of a capitalist peace.

All the while, Roosevelt campaigned for reelection. The renewal of the RTAA of 1940 became an issue for Democratic electoral prospects, as protectionists railed against the program, but Republican candidate Wendell Willkie did not differ from Roosevelt on trade. He did question Hull's export and import figures as a way to gain votes and claimed that the war necessitated suspending the RTAA for the duration. But like the Democrats, Willkie advocated capitalist peace ideology and its eventual implementation through free-trade internationalism. Thus, the Democratic platform kept liberal trade principles paramount, "especially for the purpose of dealing with the conditions of the post-war period, as offering the only practicable path towards peaceful international relations."[66] In the midst of a deteriorating war for the democracies, Roosevelt was reelected to a third term in November. Italy invaded Greece just a week before his reelection, putting millions more under fascist oppression.

Washington also watched Tokyo, which capitalized on the European war by moving assertively in Asia. Japanese nationalists were angry that the United States-Japan trade treaty from 1911 would not be renewed and that Washington reacted hysterically to the Japan-led Co-Prosperity Sphere, including occupation of China. Showing forbearance, Roosevelt honored the most-favored-nation clause of the treaty for a few months before changing course. By fall 1940, Tokyo put into effect its militarist New Order by seizing parts of the Dutch East Indies and French Indochina. The United States readied embargoes on exports to Japan. American citizens were advised to withdraw from most of Asia, while the military prepared to reinforce the Philippines. Roosevelt also sent additional credits to the Nationalist Chinese government in its fight against the Imperial Army. The United States entered its last year of peace more alert to the dictators than ever before. Americans hoped "to keep alive basic ideas, formulas and programs relating to a sound and stable international relationship after the war," including liberal trade policy, Hull wrote his minister in occupied Holland.[67] The wartime dictators, however, were not listening to such overtures.

3

Universalism, 1941–1945

In September 1940, Japan signed the Tripartite Pact, a ten-year alliance with Italy and Germany that solidified the fascist juggernaut. Failing to defeat Britain, Hitler would launch a vicious war on the Soviet Union. The stalwart Russians would halt the Nazis and roll them back through Eastern Europe to Berlin. In 1944, American, British, and Canadian troops would invade the Third Reich through France as Nazism succumbed to an Allied pincer. In a parallel war without mercy, Japan would seize territories in impressive victories in 1942 and 1943. The United States would then brutally pry back Imperial forces toward Tokyo in a multi-pronged land, sea, and air counter-offensive across the Pacific. Japan would surrender in 1945 after an exhaustive blockade and bombings, the threat of invasion from the Soviet Union, and two atomic bombs. In 1940, however, the Roosevelt administration was looking for ways to contain Axis power by aiding Britain and Russia and undermining Japan's war machine. Liberal trade policy was not a war priority, though Cordell Hull's vision did not wait for peace to be declared. The United States' entry into war in December 1941 ended its isolationism. The Pearl Harbor attack also mobilized the American economy, leading to relief for domestic producers from foreign competition. As protectionism abated in the emergency, plans went forth for a universal postwar capitalist peace.

As Franklin Roosevelt promised in the annual address to Congress in January 1941, the United States was determined to defend itself, insulate the hemisphere from war, and refuse a peace dictated by the fascists. The freedom of Britain and its Commonwealth to secure trade routes in the Atlantic and Pacific and protect shipping was critical to these goals. The Americans put teeth in their pledges by using the US Navy to escort merchant ships carrying Lend-Lease supplies across the Atlantic to the allies. Lend-Lease passed Congress in March 1941 after Hitler overran southeastern Europe, occupied Norway and France, and sent the British

Capitalist Peace. Thomas W. Zeiler, Oxford University Press. © Oxford University Press 2022.
DOI: 10.1093/oso/9780197621363.003.0004

reeling westward across North Africa toward the empire's supply lifeline, the Suez Canal. When Japan continued to maraud in China and Southeast Asia, the administration began to embargo aircraft, credits, and, eventually, oil from Japan and terminated the 1911 commercial treaty. The Axis enemies advanced nonetheless. At least the United States had a clear mission to help those fighting Nazism. Roosevelt included freer trade in his arsenal as he railed against "a Nazi wall" of tariffs that Americans erroneously thought would keep them out of war.[1]

The administration looked past the disastrous military situation to push the capitalist peace paradigm for the future. Proclaiming the principles to guide a just peace, Hull prioritized non-discrimination in world commerce to grow trade and assure access to raw materials for all. Mutual prosperity, required for universal peace, meant tamping down economic nationalism. He had an audience. The National Foreign Trade Council urged more trade agreements that contributed "to the success of a broad program of peaceful cooperation among nations which will be indispensable if the objectives of enduring peace and of economic advancement are to be attained in the post-war world."[2] The Federal Council of Churches of Christ, an ecumenical association of Protestants, was just one civic group aiming for a "permanent peace" following the hostilities. Economic injustices spawned by protectionism and exclusionary trade and currency restrictions—which "no less than cannon and bombing planes, are potential instruments of war"—must be renounced, it declared. As the council concluded in May 1941, it called on the regenerating spirit of Jesus to validate the "interdependent economic order in which we now live."[3]

Many experts planned urgently for the postwar period to come, eager to avoid the abandonment of the capitalist peace that had occurred after the last war. Planning in trade hinged on Anglo-American relations. By mid-1941, consultations on preparatory action for the postwar period launched talks on security, politics, and economic reconstruction. Officials publicized these discussions to bring voters along. At one meeting at Oxford University in July 1941, British and American academics agreed that Washington's major contribution to peace lay in the economic realm, specifically in relieving the trade and financial pressures that made leaders reluctant to engage in the world.[4] For the United States, planning focused on ending discriminatory trade patterns, namely, imperial preferences.

Much has been written about how Lend-Lease became a lever for prying open the Ottawa imperial arrangement. Like expelling German diplomats, the peacetime draft, and US Navy efforts to keep sea lanes open, Lend-Lease was part of a huge military effort costing $50.1 billion (about $560 billion today, a whopping 17 percent of the total American World War II expenditure) to bring aid to Britain, Russia, France, China, and other allies. Because of the Neutrality Act, the president could not send direct military aid to Britain or to the Soviet Union once Hitler had invaded. Lend-Lease was a clever way to allow loans of equipment to the allies, who would repay after the war, without violating restrictions or burdening the already over-taxed British. Compensation could come in the form of territory turned over to the United States or, as Hull preferred, through dismantling the imperial trade system. In other words, Lend-Lease repayment demanded sacrifices by the Commonwealth.[5]

From the time Roosevelt signed Lend-Lease legislation in March 1941, the United States and Britain entered into intense negotiations over British compensation, which led to the Anglo-American Mutual Aid Agreement of 1942. The Agreement had a large reach. At its heart it called for an open, non-discriminatory, multilateral trade and payments system. Washington wanted preferential (unequal) treatment removed as quickly as possible while Commonwealth nationalists preferred the status quo of economic blocs surrounded by tariffs. Even socialists guarded the trade balance through discriminatory preferences that might be cautiously and gradually phased out. Wary of the still-beating heart of isolationism, London insisted that the United States shoulder the burden of war by granting loans on liberal terms and lowering its own high tariffs without requiring others to do so until postwar reconstruction had brought them back to health. As a result of London's anxiety, the State Department and the president refused the US Treasury's bookkeeper approach of keeping a ledger of what was owed. They opted for vague language that permitted repayment "by any other direct or indirect benefit" the president allowed. Hull jumped at this "Consideration" as an end to imperial preferences in future, not current, trade agreements, but the British saw a devious trick. What an irony, lectured a British newspaper, "if the lifeline thrown to us in 1941 served only to strangle us in 1944 and 1945."[6]

There was room for compromise. Hull represented the Americans while the influential economist John Maynard Keynes came from England to work out the aid agreement. Hull would not insist on a unilateral obligation to end preferences if the British pledged not to return to prewar protectionism. But Keynes expressed doubts that Britain could simply junk preferences or exchange controls without an imperial conference. After the war, he argued, Britain would need large imports of raw materials, food, and machinery for rehabilitation but would lack the means to pay for them because the war would have depleted its investments, destroyed its merchant fleet, and ruined its export trade (and much of its production at home). Meanwhile the United States would enjoy an excess of exports, so the burden of adjustment in trade must fall on Washington. Compelling Britain to commit to liberalizing trade barriers was simply unworkable for the foreseeable future.[7]

The Great Depression had moved Keynes away from trade liberalism toward national self-sufficiency, a shift that smacked into Hull's free-trade

Fig. 3.1 American machine guns just arrived in England in 1941 under the Lend-Lease program. The merchandise flowed across the Atlantic, but the Anglo-American negotiations over the tariff and trade principles and policies governing the aid was far from cooperative. Franklin D. Roosevelt Presidential Library and Museum, Photo ID: 65694(15).

internationalism. Actually, leaders from Churchill to Lord Halifax, ambassador to the United States, preached equal access, economic cooperation, and the "peaceful brotherhood of nations" through unselfish trade policies.[8] That is, they agreed to the capitalist peace, just not on how to get there. Like Keynes, they also weighed Britain's postwar plight as well as the unlikelihood that Roosevelt could maintain a liberal international approach in Congress or even remain in office. Like many in British industrial circles, Keynes was dubious that protectionism had been driven from the American chapel. As for the capitalist peace, said the protective Keynes, "the age of economic internationalism was not particularly successful in avoiding war."[9] He agreed with the New Dealers that unemployment, not tariffs, was the biggest postwar threat. However crude, tariffs were one method to boost jobs by blocking destructive laissez-faire practices.

Keynes was no protectionist, but he certainly sounded like one. He did not use the word "discrimination," he said, because he thought Hull misinterpreted it, in "the old bad sense of that word" rather than with an eye to "mak[ing] something new and better of the postwar world" by allowing Britain to survive. This was obfuscation, for Keynes admitted that imperial preferences aimed to insulate

Britain from world market forces. That was perfectly fine with him; the most-favored-nation principle "was a notorious failure and made such a hash of the old world" by its insistence on laissez-faire principles. In short, the free market had failed in the Great Depression.[10] Hull held an outdated view of trade, Keynes said, and governments required trade controls to ensure stability. The Americans countered that Keynes misunderstood the idea behind non-discrimination. This was not "a philosophical concept but rather a matter involving considerations of practical politics and economics." That is, discriminatory tariffs "aroused resentment" that had dashed aside the capitalist peace formula and resulted in the current war.[11]

Keynes argued that Britain must control its trade to guard its shrunken resources and increase sources of income through cautious preferential treatment in the Commonwealth. Britain was in survival mode. Keynes's draft agreement, presented to Assistant Secretary of State Dean Acheson, called for returning armaments under Lend-Lease and continued discussions on the "Consideration," with no obligation to end imperial tariff discrimination against the United States.[12]

That vagueness enraged both Acheson and Hull, and in response, the State Department prepared Article VII in the Mutual Aid Agreement. This rather anodyne provision called for Lend-Lease compensation through "mutually advantageous economic relations" followed by a pledge not to discriminate against goods originating from Britain or the United States.[13] Article VII arose from alarm over Keynes's economic nationalism, however justified, rather than capitalist peace concerns. "If our post-war economic relations with the United Kingdom should consist of trade warfare involving a contest for markets with no holds barred," Harry Hawkins, chief of the State Department's Trade Agreements Division, informed his bosses Hull, Acheson, and Undersecretary of State Sumner Welles, "such bitterness would be created as to make very difficult, if not wholly impossible, the collaboration in the economic and other fields which is so essential to the reconstruction of the world on a peaceful basis." A non-discriminatory trade regime was the "sine qua non to any post-war system" of prosperity, peace, and security.[14] This was sheer dogmatism to Keynes so he turned to Churchill for help. The prime minister met with Roosevelt off the coast of Newfoundland in August 1941 to draw up a declaration of war aims and postwar peace plans. Preferences were on the agenda.[15]

The resulting Atlantic Charter contained principles to ensure a better world after the war, among them territorial, political, social, and security guarantees. It also called for equal access to trade opportunities, markets, and resources. That demand turned out to be a most troublesome issue because imperial preferences denied equality in trade. Churchill defended them, though, as a foundation of British imperialism. He also wondered why high US tariffs were not on the table.

Roosevelt pushed for an end to discriminatory "artificial barriers" in commerce and he struck directly at Churchill's empire by denouncing colonialism, too. He pointed to tariff preferences as a root cause of poverty among colonial subjects in the Middle East, Africa, and Asia. Roosevelt did not seek the financial collapse of the British Empire; Washington would do everything in its power to prevent Britain's bankruptcy. But he considered imperial discrimination against trade partners—allies in the war, no less—unconscionable. The president could not "believe that we can fight a war against fascist slavery, and at the same time not work to free people all over the world from a backward colonial policy" based on unfair protectionism.[16] After all, they were engaged in an existential fight for democracy. The RTAA promoted free markets for free men, while the Ottawa system gave little hope for independence to the colonies. Churchill retorted that he would not permit any "tampering with the Empire's economic agreements" so fundamental to "our greatness."[17] He sounded like Lord Beaverbrook, the empire crusader, who hinged peace on Britain's freedom to practice protectionism. The United States was not going to knock Britain from its imperial perch. This would remain the basic British position well into the Cold War, as the empire stood its ground on its preferential trade network.[18]

In the end, Britain needed aid and Roosevelt wanted to release the Atlantic Charter quickly for public relations reasons. A compromise was reached that defied State Department demands to eliminate preferences. There was no uniform formula for eliminating imperial discrimination, though preferences remained on the table for future consultation once the war emergency was over. Thus, the Atlantic Charter's fourth principle merely pledged both sides to trade on "equal terms" (rather than end discrimination) and "with due respect for their existing obligations"—a loophole that kept alive the Ottawa system.[19] Experts knew, as economist J. B. Condliffe noted in a planning agenda for the postwar world, that this loophole signaled a return to bad habits of discriminatory protectionism, counter to the most-favored-nation principle of equality of treatment in trade relations. Roosevelt agreed. "In a truly free world all men and all people must have certain rights," including producing what they best could, which meant "equality of access to materials and to capital." He had in mind the fascists and militarists aiming to enslave the world but the British made him look hypocritical by deviating from free-trade internationalism in the Commonwealth as well. This was just plain old evil imperialism, noted the American ambassador in Britain, John Winant, and not what America was fighting for.[20]

The president faced a similar challenge convincing Americans that the capitalist peace required expanded trade competition at home. Public approval of internationalism certainly trended upward during the Mutual Aid talks with Britain. Members of the Council on Foreign Relations urged a surrender of sovereignty, for instance, to break the cycle of nationalism that led to self-impoverishment before the war. But they also turned Keynes on his head, noting that British economic desperation was all the more reason to seek open commercial policies. But the Providence, Rhode Island, chapter of the council saw a strong likelihood of postwar retreat to isolationism due to war-weariness and political disillusionment. Nearly a quarter of Americans were skeptical about the benefits of world commerce, 8 percent sought no trade with any other nations whatsoever, and over half sought trade protected by tariffs. Only 12 percent favored free trade. Many feared that "free trade absolutism" would alienate poor nations eager to develop but faced with rich countries' predatory exports and investments. They also worried over the chaos that import expansion might cause in the domestic economy. In the industrial and agricultural heartland of the Midwest, isolationism was dwindling, but many manufacturers, farmers, and workers still believed that trade internationalism would lower living standards and thus destroy "the American way" of life and democracy.[21]

In the end, Cordell Hull blamed the British, not Americans, for terms that neither changed the preference regime nor bound either country to lower commercial barriers. Churchill scored another victory when Article VII of the Mutual Aid agreement, modified according to his imperial wishes, was signed on February 23, 1942. During debate over Article VII, the State Department agreed to carry over the vague Atlantic Charter loophole on preferences by requesting an end to forms of discriminatory treatment in trade but not singling out the Ottawa system for reform. Hull interpreted Article VII as eventually ending imperial discrimination. London saw no such commitment, short of promising to discuss preferences. Roosevelt weakened Hull's crusade, writing Churchill to "make it perfectly clear to you that it is the furthest thing from my mind that we are attempting in any way to ask you to trade the principle of imperial preference as a consideration for Lend-Lease." All the president asked for was an openness on Britain's part to talk about economic policy. Churchill happily obliged.[22] Putting aside his irritation toward the British, Hull spun the deal as the fulfillment of his dream to establish a foundation for postwar liberal trade principles. Yet divergence on Article VII colored schemes to build a monetary system at Bretton Woods in 1944 and to construct the trade system in the years after that, as well as provisions of the large US loan of $3.75 billion in December 1945. Britain would not relinquish its empire. Although terms of the financial and trade agreements got Hull farther down the road toward instituting capitalist peace ideology, they did not attain his key objective of terminating imperial preferences.[23]

Because the military situation did not look secure, it took until September 1943—over a year and a half from the Article VII agreement—for a British delegation to arrive in Washington to talk about preferences. By that time, Allied forces had landed in North Africa and pushed eastward against German and Italian forces. The Soviets reversed their fortunes on the eastern front, winning the devastating battle at Stalingrad and then a series of victories topped by the massive tank battle of Kursk in summer 1943. The Japanese reached their limits in the Pacific by November 1943; the Americans prepared a counter-assault in three theaters pointed toward Tokyo. The war had turned decidedly in the favor of the United Nations (UN) by the time the British delegation arrived in Washington. A series of heated meetings in Casablanca, Quebec, Moscow, and Teheran addressed postwar territorial settlements and principles to govern the world. The Americans insisted on honoring the Atlantic Charter, the Four Freedoms, and the recent United Nations Declaration of basic principles by guaranteeing the security and political, economic, and social welfare of people around the world. In that visionary context, Washington downplayed narrow economic dealings at new negotiations on Lend-Lease and Article VII. The Roosevelt administration stressed instead, wrote a diplomat in London, principles "that will appeal to the imagination of the world, serve as a stimulus to all the forces fighting aggression and provide an answer to the question: 'What are we fighting for?' "[24] Hull answered that the allies aimed for a durable international foundation based on the capitalist peace paradigm. If trade and financial issues were excluded, "the same conditions of unemployment, distress and privation would arise in many parts of the world just as it did following the last World War, with the result that agitators, revolutionists and dictators would promptly make their appearance."[25]

Anglo-American trade talks were led by British economists James Meade and Lionel Robins, and trade specialist Harry Hawkins from the State Department, all of whom deliberated on ways to reduce trade barriers. Ironically, despite his peace vision, Hull's tariff-cutting plan was quite conservative out of fear of protectionist pressures at home. It sought bilateral selective product-by-product reductions, as the Reciprocal Trade Agreements Act called for. Britain preferred sweeping multilateral tariff cuts across entire sectors to free up trade to a maximum, especially by slashing US tariffs. Hawkins agreed but he did not want to jeopardize the 1943 renewal of the RTAA in Congress. For that reason, Meade and Robbins set aside the multilateral approach, but they also postponed a deal on preferences, sardonically throwing the capitalist peace argument back at the Americans. They warned that nations could not return to the prewar trade barriers because of the high risk of "the political insecurity which would result from such chaos."[26] The two sides decided to talk later about relaxing controls to expand trade as a boost to full employment and preventing war.[27]

Trade planning did not go entirely dormant for a year after these meetings, but the Allied focus on financial affairs at Bretton Woods and on a security organization, the United Nations, in 1944 slowed talks on Article VII. Both efforts embedded a multilateral system of governance that proved crucial to postwar trade and diplomatic agendas. Officials forged the Bretton Woods financial agreement to ensure prosperity, peace, and free societies through sound currencies, accessible credit, and less discriminatory exchange controls, all essential to a healthy world trade system and to avoiding another depression. As Assistant Secretary of State Acheson noted, the evil "tricks of economic warfare" would return after the war without the "economic collective security" of the International Monetary Fund (IMF) and World Bank. Without these vital institutions, added Treasury Secretary Henry Morgenthau Jr, a lack of "effective international economic cooperation" would undermine the United Nations security system being planned at Dumbarton Oaks.[28]

Americans at least also linked trade and peace. Avoiding the "exaggerated protectionism" of the interwar period, cautioned State Department planner Leo Pasvolsky, would also prevent "lower standards of living at home and . . . world misery, unrest and, ultimately, war."[29] But the British, despite their poking at Hull, stressed living standards, not foreign policy. A postwar American depression would undermine purchasing power, thus curbing imports and British economic reconstruction, including a workmen's compensation fund and a national medical service. London also feared that if Roosevelt lost his reelection bid in November 1944, the United States might not willingly enter into multilateral talks to reduce trade barriers. Retaining privileged access to Commonwealth markets was the best insurance against a reversal in American fortunes. This approach disregarded Hullian internationalism for domestic economic health in Great Britain.[30]

Acknowledging the need for a transitional period in the postwar era in which Britain must protect its markets, Hull chafed that British policy ran counter to the objectives of the United Nations, the interests of small nations, and free-trade internationalism in general. Jousting over preferences had gotten him nowhere, though. He tried another method to usher in capitalist peace universalism: create an organization responsible for global commercial policy. Working alongside the IMF and World Bank, a world trade body might reorder the trade system and bring about the capitalist peace. Such an organization could be negotiated simultaneously with Article VII. In fact, it might even absorb the issue of imperial preferences and American protectionism in its charge.[31]

As the British and Americans tangled over Article VII in 1943, after the accord had been signed, the RTAA came up for renewal once again. No trade agreements were then being negotiated as it was wartime, but *Business Week* and other internationalist voices perceived the renewal legislation as the opening salvo of the postwar planning for the peace. The chairman of the Chamber of Commerce of New York claimed at the House Ways and Means Committee hearings in April that the free countries had placed their faith in America's promise to promote internationalism and free trade after the war. "Are we going to keep faith with these nations, or are we going to repudiate our promises?" he asked.[32] Nelson Rockefeller, coordinator of inter-American affairs at State, testified that Nazi propagandists wanted nothing more than to see Allied policies disrupt unity among friends in the Western Hemisphere. The renewal aimed to establish "liberal enlightened world collaboration," said Clare Booth Luce, an anti–New Dealer but a booster of the United States' world leadership.[33]

Yet when Hull asked for a simple renewal of the authority to cut tariffs by up to 50 percent of their 1934 levels, protectionists pounced. They confronted his "myth" that trade agreements had profited the United States. In reality, the economic gains had been meager, unlike during the decades of protectionist Republican rule. Opponents also did not believe that "everyone is going to be happy and friendly" in a free-trading world, said Congressman Daniel Reed of New York. Sayre's remarks had "touched his heart," derided Minnesota Republican Harold Knutson, but he did not think on "a high altruistic plane." The political extremists appeared as well. Tom Linder, Georgia's commissioner of agriculture, labeled internationalists "great traitors and saboteurs of American liberties and American rights" who were trying to destroy the Constitution and substitute it with world government or dictatorship or empire.[34] Signs of what would later be right-wing red scare tactics were already present, unfairly tarring legitimate protectionists as extremists.

Even though the administration sloughed off this criticism, caution prevailed. In the House, the president accepted an amendment to extend the bill for two, rather than three, years. The GOP minority report then tried to save face, endorsing reciprocity as its historic stance. Isolationism was waning, however, as the RTAA's easy passage in the House (343–65) revealed. that Senate resistance had also declined. A longtime opponent, Senator Arthur Vandenberg, for instance, favored the legislation so as not to disrupt Allied unity, though he also claimed that, while the RTAA did some good in helping other countries, the "attempt to build it up to the paramount sanctity of the very Ark of The Covenant, is to ridicule its realities." The RTAA was "a pygmy in the presence of war," he said, and Roosevelt would do better to remember that his first duty was to the welfare of Americans.[35] Despite his misgivings, Vandenberg joined a bipartisan effort to beat back potentially crippling amendments, which House Speaker Sam Rayburn also counseled against, arguing that they signaled that at war's end, Americans would "stick our heads in the sand, and not do a man's part of the world's great work." The Senate agreed, passing the bill in a bipartisan manner,

59–23, with a majority (18–13) of Republicans in favor. Internationalism was burying isolationism.[36]

Nationalism and parochialism would never die, however, so the debate over free trade persisted. A majority of Americans welcomed a generosity toward others after the war, but only on a temporary basis and on the vague grounds that peace was good. They were not far off the Republican viewpoint of trade as an economic, not diplomatic, concern. Thus, in January 1943, only 40 percent approved of reducing trade barriers after the war and 44 percent opposed doing so. A vociferous nationalistic minority welcomed high-tariff protectionism. By June, the opponents of trade internationalism had expanded to 53 percent, falling to a still substantial 46 percent by the end of the year. As the Office of War Information explained, a large percentage of Americans believed that they could remain aloof from the world, with nearly half holding that the home economy was autonomous and an even larger number fearful that an influx of imports and immigrants would jeopardize their standard of living. A sizable number rejected "even verbally the principle of international collaboration" when it came to tariff reductions. The RTAA renewal showed that old opinions died hard.[37]

As the Allies rolled back fascism in 1944, bringing national policies in line with a cooperative world community—the intention of capitalist peace ideology—became the task of the United Nations. Roosevelt beat the drum for "like-minded nations in setting up a sound and equitable system of commercial and economic relationships" after the conflict.[38] But London and Washington were at odds within the broad framework of the capitalist peace agenda. Hull railed at Churchill's determination to hold on to imperial preferences, no matter the pledge to abandon them after the war, because Article VII was so flexible. Not keeping to his word might provoke a protectionist backlash in the United States. Yet in July 1944, Richard Law, British parliamentary under secretary for state for foreign affairs, requested a postponement of Article VII due to economic difficulties. Hull refused; the allies had come too far since Hawley-Smoot to undermine coordination of material and political solidarity so essential to a just peace. Otto Mallery, a Philadelphia business proponent of a transatlantic, free-trading union after the war, argued that the "have-nots" would not stand by and starve as Britain protected its empire.[39] The United States frowned equally on British imperialism and British socialism, and it believed that preferences supported both to the detriment of the rest of the world.

Trade planning was stymied by this standoff. Negotiations in early 1945 for a $3.75 billion ($58 billion today) loan, leading to the Anglo-American Financial Agreement the next year, coaxed the desperate British to promise to discuss curbs on preferences at a United Nations planning conference for an international commercial body. Preparing for this meeting, the State Department inserted into its "Proposals for Expansion of World Trade and Employment" a call to end imperial preferences alongside a pledge for steep US tariff reductions. That gave the British a way out if they deemed the American cuts inadequate. It also left the mistaken impression that the Ottawa system's days were numbered.[40]

Perhaps planning for a world trade organization would solve the impasse by injecting trade into grand strategy. Percy Bidwell, an economist at the Council on Foreign Relations, proposed a commission to administer reductions in tariffs on a most-favored-nation basis and other onerous barriers. The idea behind this body "goes much deeper" than trade or finance, he wrote. It placed economics squarely in the capitalist peace model "in the maintenance of peace among the nations and in the preservation in this country of democratic institutions." Americans had a "double responsibility," admonished Bidwell, to shape "not only their destiny but that of millions beyond their boundaries" through new rules for "international living consonant with twentieth century conditions."[41] This was the logic behind the discussions Hull oversaw at Dumbarton Oaks that led to the establishment of the United Nations and behind specialized agencies like the Food and Agriculture Organization, as well as the Four Freedoms, Atlantic Charter, and Mutual Aid Agreement. Mordecai Ezekiel of the Department of Agriculture declared that "the great conference to plan the freer and vaster world trade of the future has not yet been called," but these institutions, including Bidwell's commission, paved the way.[42]

Indeed, the business community in particular called for a world trade conference to go hand in hand with the United Nations security organization. Winthrop Aldrich, chairman of Chase National Bank and president of the International Chamber of Commerce, suggested that the United States take the initiative for a program that would reduce trade barriers, oppose cartel and commodity regulations, provide constructive foreign lending policies, and stabilize exchange rates. To get results and demonstrate leadership, Washington must offer substantial tariff concessions to elicit similar sacrifices from other nations. The Committee for Economic Development, a business forum on public policy born in 1942, extended this argument to the capitalist peace. In "a world where distance no longer is a barrier to intercourse between peoples, the new and more intimate relations engendered of constant inter-mingling may well be one of the most significant social phenomena of the years ahead" through free and expanded international trade.[43]

It was fitting for the imminent transformation in trade ideology, from universalism to a national interest-based security, that the capitalist peace champion, Cordell Hull, would depart from the internationalist effort. He submitted his resignation for health reasons in late 1944, after the Dumbarton Oaks conference that formulated the United Nations. Not a member of the White House's inner circle, Hull howled with capitalist peace fanaticism, oftentimes into the wilderness. In reality, Roosevelt never elevated the RTAA beyond a general disposition for freer trade and internationalism, not ranking it at the same level as military or financial issues. Such inattention gave Hull more latitude to make policy, but the president's political savvy, such as a willingness to accept some high tariffs, overmatched the nagging secretary's doctrinaire approach on free trade. Still, Hull rightly crowed that his discretionary influence yielded twenty-eight reciprocal trade agreements during the longest tenure in history of a secretary of state. Tariff rates fell an average of nearly 60 percent from Hawley-Smoot to 1945. During this time, moreover, most Republicans came around to the RTAA, while nations embraced the idea of unconditional most-favored-nation treatment under a multilateral trade system. The trade-peace nexus was idealistic, but Hull had pragmatically embedded capitalist peace ideology in the trade program.[44]

The year 1945 brought changes at the top. Reelected to a fourth term, Roosevelt died in April, months after Hull had retired. By then, both had marched the Allies toward victory in the war and toward planning for a durable peace. Hull doubted that Americans had fully learned the capitalist peace lesson because protectionists shunned foreign relations. Nevertheless, it was time to bury isolationism as a tradition; it had no more place in the nation than "the covered wagon." Living in a nation entangled in the global order, Americans may have different customs than others, he concluded, "but we have the same interest in public welfare, peace, and international trade."[45] His intellectual successor, Assistant Secretary of State Will Clayton, took up the capitalist peace mantle. He wrote his first letter on State Department stationery to Hull as recognition that "your foreign policy is so thoroughly ingrained in my system that I shall always work and fight for it."[46]

As the world's single biggest cotton merchant, Clayton opposed protectionism as an exporter, but as the Great Depression wore on, he also became more interested in peace. By 1938, the Texan had adopted Hullian logic that "dictatorships have been born of economic crises," and it was America's responsibility to prevent another systemic threat to democracy.[47] With the new president, Harry Truman, Clayton set out to wield free-trade internationalism, led by businessmen as well as government. A staunch New Dealer, Truman had long advocated tariff cuts, though he accepted restrictions on competitive imports. He took his cues from Clayton, Dean Acheson, and business advocates of capitalist peace.[48]

Shaping this faith in trade internationalism was an evolving focus on national security and defense rather than on Hull's vision of universal peace. This proved to be the most significant transformation in capitalist peace ideology in history. The term "economic security" applied to the domestic welfare but it became

Fig. 3.2 Economic diplomats plan the postwar peace at the US State Department, September 11, 1945: Leo Crowley, US Foreign Economic Administration; British Ambassador to the United States, Lord Halifax; American Assistant Secretary of State William Clayton; British Treasury advisor John Maynard Keynes; and US Secretary of Commerce Henry Wallace. Harris & Ewing. Harry S. Truman Library and Museum.

a watchword for trade as foreign economic policy became a weapon in grand strategy, particularly as Western policymakers perceived a bipolar split in which the Soviet Union resisted plans for freedom, democracy, and free enterprise. Josef Stalin and his successors actually hoped to participate in the world market economy, including the Bretton Woods monetary regime and, ostensibly, the international trade order.[49] But in the confusion and chaos at the end of the war and in experimental planning for the postwar era, perceptions—driven by fear and uncertainty on America's part—were everything. The Soviets were deemed a threat. Geopolitics had always been fused to capitalist peace objectives. Officials gave national security concerns increasing prominence as they overcame isolationism and adopted a leadership role in the postwar world. As the State Department put it in 1944, the "development of sound international economic relations is closely related to the problem of security." The term could be interpreted widely, but the hope was that a workable United Nations would provide universal security. If that did not work—and it did not as the Cold

War emerged—then free trade as a security tool for a certain bloc of nations would replace worldwide initiatives for peace, elevated in foreign policy to attain American interests.[50]

This became clear in the battle for the Reciprocal Trade Agreements Act in 1945, just before Roosevelt's death. As the president readied his postwar program for Congress, his tone was decidedly grim. Presenting the Bretton Woods accords to Congress in February, he warned of a return to economic warfare. The United States had the choice to determine "the kind of lives our grandchildren can live" by deciding on "shared prosperity" rather than "competing economic blocs."[51] This message was really no different from that of prior admonitions, but the British imperial system of trade and Soviet defiance over territorial domination gave it a sense of urgency. On March 26, Roosevelt requested that Congress steer away from a world economy based on "guns instead of butter" by extending the RTAA. He lauded Hull's capitalist peace universalism, but this realist was also frustrated about the prospects for international cooperation with the inflexible Stalin. Two weeks later, Roosevelt was dead.[52]

In order to support postwar national security, Truman did not change his predecessor's request to Congress, requesting a three-year extension and additional authority to lower tariffs. Previous bills allowed for 50 percent tariff reductions from 1930 levels. This legislation sought to halve the duties in effect in 1945, a sizable drop to below the rates of the Wilson administration three decades earlier. More audacious, the State Department sought across-the-board, multilateral cuts in tariffs rather than the bilateral, item-by-item approach followed since the start of the reciprocal trade program in 1934. They detected that the war had put the Republican Party (GOP) on board the capitalist peace train after the renewal of 1943; the party's platform in 1944 had endorsed the RTAA and avoidance of economic warfare, and Republican nominee Wendell Willkie had remained a free trader in the mold of Cordell Hull. But protectionists were still strong, even among Democrats, and a majority of Americans still opposed more imports. As always, isolationist sentiment existed side by side with internationalism. That led the Roosevelt and then the Truman administrations to tie trade ever more intimately to the United Nations, due to convene in May. Assistant Secretary of State Archibald MacLeish, sitting with Acheson and Clayton in a radio broadcast, equated reciprocal trade agreements with the security agendas of the United Nations and Bretton Woods. Writing to Congress, Edward Stettinius, the new secretary of state, noted that "we and the other United Nations will undertake to set up a framework of security within which countries can abandon the harmful economic practices into which they were led by the fear of aggression."[53] The RTAA served as a powerful reinforcement of that goal.

Appearing on behalf of Stettinius, Clayton based much of his testimony on the capitalist peace. The horrors "of the last 6 years have worked profound changes in the minds and spirits of people in every corner of the world. The people are sick of war and sick of the narrow economic practices which undermine material well-being, generate international friction, and set the stage for war." As nations looked to the United States for aid in reconstructing the world, the administration knew of no better way to lead than by reducing restrictive trade barriers. Trade and finance comprised a column of the arch of peace, the other pillar being security. Should one column fall, the entire structure would collapse.[54]

Yet partisanship flared in the RTAA debate because the stakes were high, as the bill provided the legal basis for the first postwar tariff negotiations. When Stettinius did not show up at the Ways and Means hearings due to pressing duties elsewhere, his absence was interpreted as his lacking Hull's passion on free-trade internationalism. Outraged protectionists pounced, led by the ranking Republican, Harold Knutson of Minnesota. He turned the logic of the capitalist peace doctrine on its head. If the Fordney-McCumber Tariff had been so protectionist, then why had war not broken out in the 1920s? Not only must the domestic economy come before foreign policy in trade matters, they argued, but Republicans rejected the isolationist label, charging instead that British preferences, Moscow's closed state-trading regime, and French imperialism amounted to isolationism in trade. The administration was being duped, said Knutson, by "the soft talk of world planners and globocrats who, we believe, would put the American worker, the American farmer, and the American businessman on the international auction block."[55]

Such views initially put the RTAA at risk in Congress but Democrats mustered enough support to defeat a host of protectionist amendments. The bill exited the Ways and Means Committee by a narrow 14–11 tally. Three days of debate on the House floor caused more amendments to be rejected, but not by much. A timely letter from President Truman to Rayburn tipped the scales, as the Speaker reminded Republicans and errant Democrats that "world order and peace and commerce" would be impeded without the RTAA. The House passed it comfortably, 239–153, with thirty-three GOP members voting for it.[56] In the Senate, where Truman, a former senator, presumably had influence, the Finance Committee nearly killed the bill. Isolationist Robert Taft, who held that free trade just as easily promoted war as peace by encouraging cutthroat competition, proposed an amendment to extend the legislation but with no new authority to cut tariffs. That prohibitive measure passed 10–9, with three Democrats in support. His brother, Charles Taft, a Republican internationalist who worked in the State Department, testified in opposition. Democrats mobilized in a weeklong debate in the Senate that quashed the amendment. The bill then passed 54–21, with five Democrats siding with opponents but fifteen Republicans crossing over. State Department negotiators had won authority to lower Hawley-Smoot tariff rates by up to 75 percent, but it had been a close call.[57]

Capitalist peace advocates were relieved. Acting Secretary of State Joseph Grew explained that approval of the RTAA without amendments meant that the United States could exercise its leadership for the common good. American economic power was "distrusted and even feared abroad," but it was the administration's intention "to dispel those fears not by statements of good intentions but by concrete examples of cooperation." At least Congress had helped relieve "irrational trade fears," wrote the *New York Times*, on the part of nations "still suffering from a species of economic shell-shock" from the Great Depression and world war.[58] Indeed, the war had eased passage, pointing opinion toward larger concerns of prosperity, peace, and diplomacy. An American soldier in Italy wrote during the Senate battle that the RTAA was a must because "the fight we have won and the fights we are winning" dictated that the United States, a creditor, be generous with impoverished, devastated nations that needed to sell their goods to the United States in order to survive.[59]

The diplomats moved ahead after the troubling win on the RTAA. By July 1945, experts had devised an International Trade Organization which, by November, was formalized by "Proposals for Consideration by an International Conference on Trade and Employment." The body would foster cooperation through a code of rules to remove barriers to trade and honor the spirit, if not the letter, of the Atlantic Charter and Article VII. The inclusion of employment revealed the still-exposed fissures between the Anglo-American powers, however. Commonwealth nations continued to insist that collaboration hinged on recognizing Franklin Roosevelt's fourth Freedom: from want. "There is a wide recognition of the fact," noted Australian minister Frederic Eggleston, "that in most countries of the world that object can be achieved only by maintaining a high level of employment."[60] The Americans countered that mixing employment with exchange and trade issues would encourage "uneconomic production or the imposition of positive barriers to international commerce," and thus political friction. To be clear, Washington welcomed talks on employment; employment would be included in the talks but always with trade expansion and the capitalist peace, in mind. Stettinius explained that jobs depended on "general international agreement to remove the excessive barriers and prevent the discriminatory practices which have restricted world trade in the past."[61]

The State Department's Office of International Trade Policy drafted steps to remove or reduce restrictions on trade, work that would be influenced by several considerations, including politics. The trade code must outlaw high tariffs, quota systems, and discriminatory preferences; forbid subsidies and cartels; and stabilize primary production from wild swings in prices. By December 1945, invitations to convene meetings to discuss "Proposals for the Expansion of World Trade and Employment" the following year went out initially to Western European nations represented by the United Kingdom, France, the Netherlands, and Luxembourg (and then Norway); the USSR and Czechoslovakia in the East; the British Dominions and India in the Anglo sphere; and Brazil and China. The American "Proposals" insisted that nations report to an International Trade Organization to bring policies in line with others under most-favored-nation treatment. This would ensure, wrote the Office's Joseph Coppock to chief trade planner Clair Wilcox, a "favorable international political environment" for success. Coppock warned that nations were still geared up for economic warfare. None of the big powers "have to learn this game; we know how to play it; we are organized to play it" and increased "economic distress, suspicion and recrimination can perpetuate it." The codes would restrain the United States, Britain, and the Soviet Union especially from creating exclusionary trade blocs through bribery, threats, and discriminatory deals that undermined trade liberalism.[62]

There was a big exception to the trade organization's mandate, one that shaped the next half-century of history. No nation was more at odds with free-trade internationalism than the Soviet Union, though the exhausted country was happy to restore trade and fair markets if it meant a faster and more secure recovery. While the Americans shipped huge supplies of Lend-Lease goods to fuel Stalin's monumental effort against Nazism during the war, the dictator was secretive and stubborn about cooperating on postwar territorial and political settlements. Westerners thought such behavior would carry over into the economic arena. Treasury Secretary Henry Morgenthau, therefore, believed the Russians might collaborate in trade and finance as long as the United States insisted on good conduct from them. Harry Truman tended to agree. Other less realist observers, such as advisor Harry Hopkins, hoped that Moscow would join the multilateral capitalist global system as an "equal partner" if the United States continued to cooperate on military deals and, after the war, provided reconstruction aid.[63]

But in trade relations, Hopkins was naive. Stalin had never responded to invitations to join in Article VII discussions and likely would not participate at the Employment and Trade conference because he naturally shunned capitalism. Unilateral trade deals let the Soviets dominate surrounding countries, pointed out Ambassador Averell Harriman; mercantilism kept fellow communists in line and served as a political weapon against the capitalist world. To be sure, the Soviets required imports for reconstruction. But while they might enter into commercial agreements on specific products, there was no indication they would refrain from discrimination, accept trade based on commercial considerations, or deviate from their state monopoly system. It dawned on Washington that the capitalist peace paradigm, while in theory universal, did not apply to the USSR.[64]

The two budding superpowers may have split regardless of any entreaties, but clearly their alliance was a marriage of convenience to defeat Nazism. They had long been at odds ideologically, and now strategic calculations separated them. Stalin's paranoia, stoked by what he saw as a delayed second front in France to relieve pressure on his beleaguered country, lent ammunition to his worldview that the capitalists wished the communists to exhaust themselves so they couldn't dictate postwar plans. Politically, Stalin also sought spheres of influence, a desire inimical to the American concept of an open world safeguarded by the collective security of the United Nations. At Yalta in February 1945, the dictator refused an open door in Eastern Europe, particularly Poland, because the Russians required a buffer zone between them and the West to thwart another invasion. Ethnic Eastern European voters in the United States, in particular, were embittered by Stalin's betrayal of self-determination and democracy. The refusal to grant the Soviets a loan, and then the sudden cut-off of Lend-Lease aid to Russia in May 1945, made anti-communists applaud, realists cringe, and Stalin double down on his obsessive suspicion of Western encirclement.

Fig. 3.3 The Big Three (Stalin, Truman, and Churchill) discuss communist, capitalist, and imperialist peace at the Potsdam Conference, July 17, 1945. United States Bureau of Aeronautics, Harry S. Truman Library and Museum.

The Cold War had not begun, but its outline emerged in a way that forced the United States to realize there was no return to isolationism. Coming out of the war, Washington pushed forward with the UN security system (headquartered in New York City), the shift to creditor status under the Bretton Woods institutions (housed in Washington, DC), and a liberal, multilateral trade order. With little competition from imports because nations lay prostrate and unproductive, the United States could ignore domestic interests for the moment. But leaders planned to open the domestic market to spur the recovery of its friends and allies. This design, part of an activist foreign policy of leadership over the world economy, did not emerge from generosity toward foreigners or neglect of American producers but from strategic calculations. It involved the evolution of internationalism—in a few years labeled the Marshall Plan perspective—into interventionist leadership around the world. Sheer US power, bolstered by unmatched productive capacity, control of global financial assets, and a predominant share of world trade—all coalescing to confront Stalin—changed the concept of capitalist peace from peace idealism to an alliance of self-sustaining, anti-communist trade partners. Before long, America anchored former enemies West Germany and Japan in a coalition to limit communist access to trade, finance, and technology. In sum, before 1945, internationalists had been certain that a non-discriminatory, multilateral global economic system would secure prosperity and peace for all. By the end of 1945, that view was a pacifist illusion. Geopolitical transformations shaped by war and stimulated by postwar tensions signaled a new era rooted in security (a common term by the late 1940s) and realpolitik.[65]

The security argument, ironically, also gave new life to protectionists. Although they were fairly quiescent just after the war, protectionists pointed to the military in World War II to rationalize protection of certain industries. Thus, they deemed watch manufacturing—essential to the technology of bombing sights in airplanes, the operation of landing craft, and precision timing devices—a national defense industry that had replaced Swiss imports during wartime. Industries lined up other products for tariff protection by citing the security imperative, such as rayon (the stand-in for silk during the war); minerals such as oil, zinc, and lead; blown glassware (for radar tubes), and organic chemicals. All were critical to the military; all must be protected.[66]

Until the end of the Second World War, the enemy of trade internationalists had been the forces of economic nationalism, manifested by protectionism, imperialism, discrimination, and dictatorship. The fear of nationalism did not evaporate but it blended into the pursuit of free enterprise and anti-communist democracy that lay at the heart of the United States' response in the nascent Cold

War. Realism, not universalism, that is, redefined the capitalist peace. American foreign policy, including trade policy, was designed to prevent the horror of communist takeover, just as it had combated the nightmare of fascism.[67] Experts talked of a cold war of opposing ideologies. Free-trade internationalism was in the thick of it.

4

Security, 1946–1950

Surveying the state of the union in January 1946, President Harry Truman spoke of the United States having "become a land of great responsibilities to all of the world" and of the United Nations as "the representative of the world as one society." But when it came to foreign economic policy, he deviated from such universalism, pointing out that though a "vast majority of the nations of the world have chosen to work together to achieve, on a cooperative basis, world security and world prosperity," this was not true of the Soviet Union. He announced a mid-year conference on world trade and employment to expand global commerce and to eliminate "unchecked economic rivalry and economic warfare." Truman knew it was needlessly provocative to single out the emerging rupture with the Soviets.[1] But he did so to underline his intention to defend free-enterprise capitalism, a bastion of democracy itself, through the power and hegemony of the United States in the world arena. The capitalist peace now meant capitalist security, and this transformation greatly affected the trade agenda.

Of the fifteen major trading nations, only the Soviets ignored a State Department invitation to the trade conference Truman announced. These core "nuclear" countries would prepare for a larger international meeting to establish a multilateral postwar trade system, replete with a code of principles and rules. The challenge for the United States, as the system's leader, was to set an example by sweeping away tariff protection. Although limited by the item-by-item method reciprocal trade law required, the State Department leaned toward a Canadian suggestion that the nuclear group, which represented two-thirds of world trade, make multilateral cuts in tariffs. Concessions would then be generalized under the cherished most-favored-nation rule, granting partners equal treatment for their goods. The Americans reinterpreted the Reciprocal Trade Agreements Act to allow wide-ranging duty reductions, which became the basis of negotiations under the General Agreement on Tariffs and Trade (GATT), beginning in 1947.

Capitalist Peace. Thomas W. Zeiler, Oxford University Press. © Oxford University Press 2022.
DOI: 10.1093/oso/9780197621363.003.0005

The process of reducing tariffs and other barriers was codified in the comprehensive International Trade Organization (ITO). Moscow was invited to participate in these seminal forums as well as in the Bretton Woods financial, aviation, labor, and Marshall Plan aid projects. When Stalin refused, Washington proceeded to build a Free World security system based on free-trade internationalism within the capitalist democracies.

The Soviets went their own way. Trade between the United States and the Soviet Union had never been significant. American exports to the USSR reached their peak in 1938, at $70 million, or 2.3 percent of US total exports, and imports from Russia to the United States were even more paltry. Lend-Lease goods had jacked up exports, however, and American businessmen hoped to continue this upward trajectory. They were bound to be disappointed. By the late 1940s, the Russians imposed their own trade system on Eastern Europe while Stalin also refused the multilateral trade regime of the West. The United States responded to Soviet state trading, bilateralism with satellites, and the use of economics to assert political hegemony by sanctioning a system of export controls to deny strategic goods to the communist bloc. In essence, export controls lifted trade from the economic realm and squarely placed it in the diplomatic one. The controls soon applied to the People's Republic of China and North Korea, and Washington demanded that Western European allies put them in place as well. Restrictions on East-West trade may have slowed Western European recovery by cutting off traditional trade ties. However, they played into the strategy of containing international communism as well as the domestic politics of the Red Scare, which further divided the world into two ideological camps.[2] Export controls revealed how embedded security and acceptance of a divided world had become in shaping capitalist peace ideology.

Business hopes for more trade with the communist side seemed quaint by 1946. The chargé d'affaires in Moscow, George Kennan, scheduled a meeting with Foreign Trade Commissar Anastas Mikoyan in January 1946 to extend an invitation to attend the trade conferences and discuss commercial practices. He anticipated the answer. Stalin preferred working in the UN Economic and Social Council—"so often political and tactical in nature," reported Kennan—in which his economic aims could be achieved, rather than "enforce general and permanent principles" in an International Trade Organization. Kennan exaggerated Soviet resistance, but he was correct that Moscow's "instincts are autarchic" in trade, a means of increasing "strategic economic strength and achieving economic independence." Besides, Stalin would never admit to a problem with employment or that more trade with capitalist nations was desirable. Russia also sought total freedom to purchase worldwide through its trade monopoly, not caring at all about foreign tariff levels (so negotiations were pointless) because its trade was not on a market basis. Thus, the Soviets evaded the most-favored-nation principle. In the end, Moscow stayed out of planning for the international trade system and ordered its satellites like Bulgaria to do so as well.[3]

The advent of the Cold War doomed trade cooperation with Stalin. He announced his hostility to capitalism in February 1946, and then Kennan enunciated the containment doctrine as the means of combating international communism by political and economic means. Trade became an instrument of containment, furthering the division of the world into factions. The Truman Doctrine, Marshall Plan, integration of Japan into the West's security system, and a new focus on development for poor nations consolidated the Free World. In 1949, Chinese communists won power, the United States orchestrated the NATO alliance, a crisis over rights in Berlin—like Germany itself, divided by communism and capitalism—came close to military conflict, and the Soviets detonated an atomic bomb. The outbreak of war in Korea the following year rationalized a vast expansion of the containment doctrine across the globe under the top-secret National Security Council policy paper known as NSC-68. Economic diplomacy, specifically free-trade internationalism for capitalist nations, became a key tool in America's Cold War kit.[4]

At the same time that Kennan's long telegram explaining Soviet behavior arrived on Truman's desk, in February 1946, the State Department's Commercial Policy Division under Winthrop Brown outlined a code of commercial conduct to guide the core nations in all areas related to trade, such as commodity agreements, state trade barriers, and tariff reductions. This became the framework that linked trade to employment in a larger convention—a Charter for an International Trade Organization—to manage trade relations. Tariff negotiations, under the General Agreement on Tariffs and Trade, were separated from ITO deliberations. GATT rules bound duty reductions made at negotiations against future increases and mandated that negotiations follow non-discriminatory and multilateral principles. In the expectation that crafting the ITO Charter would take time, GATT tariff concessions would come into force once the nuclear nations had negotiated them.

This two-track approach proved wise. The ITO Charter underwent numerous revisions over the next three years, from Washington proposals to modifications in London, Geneva, and in the final drafting in Havana in 1948. Ideological differences bogged down progress. Big business interests in the United States and Europe pushed for rules that restricted cartels, import and exchange controls, subsidies, and state trading. These were all elements of a perceived anti-free-enterprise position held by developing nations in the global South, as well as the new Soviet enemy. A properly conceived ITO, with market capitalism at its foundation, would quarantine communism and, in the words of William Jackson, president of the US Chamber of Commerce, confront its totalitarian bid "for territory, economies, and the mind and soul of humankind everywhere."[5]

Indeed, there were high hopes for the ITO, especially among liberal integrationists in the one-world crowd—a dying breed of universalist capitalist peace supporters. Otto Tod Mallery was one. This erstwhile campaigner for European union, world federation, and free trade held that the ITO's wide-ranging codes, empowered by the United Nations, would provide for "fair trade [as] the economic basis of the peace." Although the Cold War might be dividing Europe, he had faith that both sides could lift up devastated countries throughout the region by cooperation under the Charter. For idealists like Mallery, fear and power-mongering were standing in the way of cooperation in trade, as well as capitalist peace. The United States must disprove Karl Marx's prediction that capitalist democracy would self-destruct by greed and rivalry. The Charter, a "Magna Carta of economic peace," would demonstrate that bourgeois governments could prevent a return to the protectionist 1930s.[6]

Mallery and the employment-focused progressives occupied one end of the free-trade spectrum, with corporate market purists at the other. In the internationalist middle, citizens' groups advocating for the United Nations chafed at the delays in tariff negotiations and the formulation of the ITO Charter.[7] Free-enterprise conservative purists who questioned the ITO countered that peace and full employment were ultimate goals, but they were more focused on statist threats to capitalism. Even some in the Truman administration, and certainly in Congress, feared the ITO might promote socialism by regulating trade and investments. That proved too much in a Cold War climate in which defending free trade from regimentation and loss of opportunities and profits was imperative. Corporate critics pointed to government-mandated controls in trade, finance, industry, and agriculture all over the world. The National Foreign Trade Council insisted that free enterprise afforded assurances of competitive, efficient, non-discriminatory, and non-political international commerce. With those elements intact, the capitalist peace would be assured. But socialist and poor nations seemed to seek more trade restrictions and less freedom.[8] This ideological divide engaged ITO drafters for years.

The debate began at a United Nations preparatory committee for the ITO in London in October 1946. As usual, the Americans pushed for commitments to expand trade by reducing barriers and discrimination, under a Suggested Charter of the ITO, which pushed for trade liberalization on a multilateral basis. Negotiators hammered out the specifics, but under duress. Australia and India demanded the chair of the American delegation, Clair Wilcox, acknowledge the special needs of developing and poor nations. This meant regulation over trade to promote industrialization. By 1947, over six hundred amendments were inserted in the Charter by developing nations, led by Mexico and Chile. Most of them were unacceptable to the US delegation as violations of free enterprise and freer trade. The British publicly backed the Americans, though they sympathized with their imperial subjects. The Bank of England privately worried that the Suggested Charter made "the world, and particularly the British Empire, free for U.S. trade."[9]

American business was on guard. The National Foreign Trade Council closed its October 1947 meeting by issuing a "Program for Action" that included endorsement of the ITO as part of an agenda to promote US economic ties with Western Europe, including western Germany. Certainly, security and principles were at stake. A close reading showed these businessmen to be concerned with the survival of social, moral, and spiritual values "in which free institutions can survive and flourish." Noted the Council, these were "vital to our own security and to the preservation of our institutions, for if the freedoms we cherish for ourselves are lost to the rest of the world, we may be very sure that they will be lost also to us."[10] Such talk hinted of the capitalist peace platform's merger with the Cold War, to the detriment of a progressive, universalist ITO Charter.

Criticism from free-trade allies made Truman officials cringe at the prospect of failure for the ITO because it represented a leg of foreign policy. Wilcox published an entire book on the ITO—the administration's main campaign tool—reminding readers what was at stake. It was a matter of honoring the promise that the United States would restore a freer trading system and make good on the billions of dollars spent on foreign policy programs like Lend-Lease, loans, and the Marshall Plan. Since the ITO was "recognized everywhere as an American project," rejection risked undermining US leadership in international affairs. Protectionists looked at this as "mere sentimentality" and preferred to appraise the ITO only from the standpoint of domestic economic interests. So be it, exclaimed Wilcox. From "the purely selfish point of view of the United States," the Charter also made sense because Americans needed more imports and exports to maintain their standard of living. Freer trade would also answer free-enterprise purists' discomforts because trade barriers tied up foreign trade in a maze of controls run by huge bureaucracies. The administration sought to negotiate away such regimentation. Tariffs, for starters, were also the crudest instruments for protecting a nation's security.[11]

Thinking on national security reconceptualized capitalist peace ideology for the trade agenda, including the Charter. Security had previously meant stable welfare for Americans. By the end of World War II, it more commonly referred to national defense. For Cold Warriors, national security meant a tough combination of realism and internationalism, and the capitalist peace reflected this assertive application to the defense of the Free World. The challenge was clear in that context. State Department planners warned that without the ITO and freer trade, the "non-Russian world would be without a rudder in the international economic sea," with such disunity scoring propaganda points for the Soviets.[12] More generally, Truman worried that democracy would fail if capitalism brought only poverty and distress. Thus, he proclaimed that "part of our strategy of peace" was to "encourage a quick revival" of trade in the Free World.[13] The ITO would make that lucrative trade permanent, but as it integrated the regulatory state into its code in 1947, critics continued to mobilize against it.

Domestic opponents also looked on the GATT tariff negotiations with suspicion. That worried the politically astute secretary of state, James Byrnes, a former senator. The November 1946 midterm elections, in which Republicans took control of both chambers of Congress by, in part, criticizing tariff concessions that hurt producers and workers, were an obstacle to trade liberalization. Byrnes thus convinced Truman to block Will Clayton's request to publish US tariff offers prepared for the first GATT round. His sober advice drew on polling conducted by the World Trade Foundation of America, a new educational alliance of internationalist businessmen, academics, and civic groups. Its research showed a substantial majority of Americans in favor of export expansion under the reciprocal trade agreements program but a large number just as opposed to import competition. Typical was New Brunswick, New Jersey, where respondents stressed higher employment through exports while imports meant job loss. Internationalist sentiment was decidedly lacking as well. A large percentage did not know about the effects of trade on diplomacy (or on the economy, for that matter), although those with higher educational levels and a stake in trade understood the connection. Thus, in "our national scene the American citizen who engages in foreign trade is the natural leader in determining our international policies, conduct and action," responded an importer. Twice as many foreign-born as native-born respondents, the former cognizant of world affairs and the influence of American power, thought world trade aided peace. On the whole, the World Trade Foundation discovered a clear provincialism. A nation sequestered between two oceans still thought that geography isolated it from the global economic problems. Protectionism retained influence in a country emerging from depression, war, and isolationism.[14]

Truman postponed publicizing the potential list of concessions, but it was too late because the GOP took Congress, in part, by using free trade as a foil. Protectionists complained even more about the upcoming GATT talks. Truman pushed forward with them anyway, even as Republicans threatened to take away his negotiating authority by junking the RTAA. The Cold War—the capitalist peace/security nexus—saved his trade agenda. Republican interventionists worried that a resurgence of economic nationalism would weaken the response to Stalin as well as vitiate the attack on Britain's imperial trade preferences with its commonwealth and colonies that still motivated opposition to London in US policy. GOP moderates agreed with the president that if the United States failed to take the initiative in the GATT and the ITO, others would break the world into trading blocs that "could have profound effects upon world politics and the prospects for an enduring peace."[15] The earlier embrace by Congress of the Truman Doctrine to aid nations resisting communism had outlined a Cold War consensus in Washington. That sketch also included a rebranding of the capitalist peace paradigm to place trade liberalization in service to the national security state.

But drawing on anti-communist ideology could also backfire, as protectionists used this highly politicized version of the capitalist peace to excoriate freer trade. Republican propagators of the second Red Scare, three years before McCarthyism rose to infamy, leveled charges of communist subversion at the administration. Staunch protectionist Daniel Reed of New York charged Clayton's trade team with being communist sympathizers who required investigation. He railed at the secrecy of the looming GATT and ITO talks, hinting at a diabolic conspiracy. The State Department, he charged, was split "between Americanism and communism" at these trade conferences. Congressman Bertrand Gearhart of California assaulted Truman's general foreign policy, claiming that the "super-duper propaganda" of internationalism pushed by the "silk-hatted diplomatic brigade of the State Department" gave away the American store to foreigners through imports.[16] These were fanatics who sounded like Senator Joe McCarthy, but the GATT delegation feared their deleterious effect. For instance, American negotiators decided against tariff concessions for Czechoslovakia, a country sliding under Soviet control, because they might profit the communists. If similar restrictions occurred, a domino effect could unravel plans to provide massive aid under the Marshall Plan and embolden communist parties in Italy and other Free World nations teetering on insolvency and political instability to seize power. In any case, State Department diplomats made clear that the GATT did not serve as a bridge between East and West so as not to provoke extremists on the populist right.[17]

Conservatives in the United States and Europe sided with Truman's foreign policy, however. They blew the clarion against socialism and New Deal statism they witnessed at the ITO Charter negotiations. Trade policy influenced their general critiques of the threats to a free society. Academics gathered at Mont Pelerin, Switzerland, at the beginning of April 1947, at the same time the GATT convened fifty-five miles away across Lake Leman in Geneva, "to discuss the crisis of our times." These cerebral conservatives saw freedom of thought and expression, the rule of law, and private property and a competitive market—"central values of civilization"—menaced by destructive "creeds" like communism and its arbitrary wielding of power.[18] This sounded like capitalist peace dialogue. Indeed, the Austrian thinker and father of these neo-liberals, Frederick von Hayek, had written in his seminal *The Road to Serfdom* that neither order nor peace could endure if nationalistic intervention in the world economy persisted. Economic relations must be based on exchanges between individuals and companies for trade blocs "inevitably become the source of friction and envy between whole nations."[19] Voicing this capitalist peace logic, conservatives gave ideological cover to an administration often condemned by the radical right and left, as well as protectionists.

In agreement with the Mont Pelerin activists, Republican internationalists worked to block the extremists by offering the administration a compromise. They would let the RTAA run until its expiration in 1948, which would permit the GATT negotiations to proceed. In exchange, they wanted tariff concession offers submitted to the domestic-minded Tariff Commission to determine whether they imperiled American producers and workers and, if so, the point at which they did. Truman refused this "peril point" procedure, which gave protectionists leverage. In February 1947, he did issue an executive order that attached to all trade agreements an "escape clause" that could modify or cancel import tariff concessions deemed injurious to a producer at home. Cordell Hull had allowed a general escape clause provision in 1942, but under this proposal by Vandenberg and Eugene Milliken of Colorado, the Tariff Commission would shape negotiations alongside the State Department. But this was protectionism. According to the angry British, the escape clause laid to rest the wartime fiction that the United States would adjust to its creditor position by opening its economy to competition. The *London Times* argued that the Vandenberg-Millikin compromise also questioned the ITO's aspirations to solve disputes by the neutral arbitration procedures of the ITO Charter rather than by politically charged national measures of protection. Truman conceded the point, but he had a bigger one in mind: the capitalist peace. The escape clause recognized, he exclaimed, "that bipartisan support of our foreign economic policy, as well as of our foreign policy in general, is essential."[20] The GOP mainstream was in accord with the Democrats.

Trade internationalism, tightly tied to foreign policy under the securitized version of the capitalist peace, became the basic rationale for liberalizing tariffs and other barriers. Under Secretary of State for Economic Affairs Will Clayton barely veiled the Cold War rhetoric. He told the House Ways and Means Committee in spring 1947 that without a multilateral trade system, "we are going to leave a vacuum into which, inevitably, will move an economic system based on principles alien to our ideas, injurious to our interests, and highly restrictive on the volume of world trade."[21] The president summed up the situation in a major speech on foreign economic policy at Baylor University in Texas on

March 6. The liberal trade regime was critical because "foreign relations, political and economic, are indivisible." With a code like the ITO and tariff cuts in the GATT, discriminatory trade practices and regulations so essential to statism would not be allowed to sweep away private enterprise. The Charter and the GATT paved the way for "world freedom," he argued.[22]

President Truman played the Cold War card for political reasons, not just ideological ones. When protectionist Harold Knutson, the new chairman of the Ways and Means Committee, and his Republican colleague Joseph Martin, the new Speaker of the House, sought to dilute the RTAA and limit tariff concessions at the GATT negotiations, internationalists referred to the American foreign policy agenda. The announcement of the Marshall Plan deepened this trade-security argument. Truman told the Canadian parliament in June 1947 that the GATT and the ITO were more than commercial agreements. Both pursued, above all, "'the trade of free men.'" He reflected on the record flow of goods across the border. The resulting high standard of living was "a practical demonstration of the benefits of the democratic way of life and a free economy."[23] The argument worked. Surfacing from a brutal winter, Western Europe suffered such economic distress that communist parties had great leverage in the body politic. The Republicans, even die-hard protectionists like Robert Taft, conceded that the State Department must set tariff policy to engage in free-trade internationalism and activate the capitalist peace aspect of the containment doctrine. On the other side, the liberal Cold Warriors of the Americans for Democratic Action, created in January 1947, heeded the call to confront the Soviets by a vigorous internationalism. These realist centrists, disenchanted by pacifism, determined to strike "a heavy blow to the Leninist certitudes" through free trade and rising living standards.[24]

In this Cold War context and amid GOP warnings that it would scrutinize every tariff concession, the GATT round of talks convened at the Palais des Nations in Geneva in April 1947. The outlook was dim. The ambiguity of "mutually advantageous" terms of trade in Article VII, which dealt with imperial preferences, hovered over the negotiations. America's list of concessions was impressive, moreover, risking Republican outrage by maximizing the number and percentage (in terms of total imports) of concessions. The list covered over 93 percent of the imports into the United States from core nations on a most-favored-nation basis and entailed tariff cuts that would drop its high duties to pre–World War I levels. Despite their inaction on cutting imperial preferences, the British were given an even better offer, and to inspire and assure London, the Americans offered to terminate their preferences with Cuba. But in comparison, the Commonwealth, apart from Canada, insisted on retaining preferences (though they would not impose new ones) and put forth feeble tariff concessions offers. They wanted even more American concessions; Britain, a debtor and trade-deficit nation with a devastated economy, needed the United States, the world's creditor, to step up. The British would not let Washington destroy the Ottawa system of imperial preferences before America sacrificed its own interests through large tariff concessions to right the trade deficit and the lack of purchasing power—the dollar gap –the Europeans suffered. This argument climaxed in a fight over wool that nearly ended the GATT talks. When American wool producers sought protection from southern wool exports through an import fee, Australia and New Zealand demanded freer entry into the United States, the world's largest wool market. Without more US concessions on wool (and other commodities), preferences would remain in force, and the Commonwealth would walk out of the Geneva talks, to the delight of the Soviets, who would ridicule the tenuous capitalist peace.[25]

That is, the wool issue transcended trade relations. Washington sought a naval base on Manus Island, claimed by Australia, and the wool fee toughened Canberra on the issue. The British Board of Trade warned that should the wool bill become law, it would jeopardize relations cultivated since the Atlantic Charter in 1941. Foreign policy trumped protectionism; Truman promptly vetoed the import fee legislation in June, replacing it with a domestic subsidy. The Republican Congress, led by Vandenberg internationalists, accepted the deal after the president noted that the bill "contains features which would have an adverse effect on our international relations" while it did not really help domestic growers.[26] Australia remained at Geneva because of Truman's exercise of free-trade internationalism.

This deal did not close out the GATT negotiations, however, because the British held on to imperial preferences that discriminated against nations outside the Commonwealth. Indeed, in light of what Keynes called Britain's "financial Dunkirk" that led to the near collapse of the pound and drained reserves, London sought release from the obligation of non-discrimination in trade under Article VII and the loan agreement of July 1946. Will Clayton, the US delegation chief at the GATT talks, was enraged. He insisted that Britain honor Article VII or America would quit at Geneva, thereby aborting the GATT itself. That turned out to be sheer bluster. It may be that London's callous insistence on discrimination risked the entire capitalist peace agenda, but ironically, it was this very paradigm that prevented a collapse in Geneva. Breaking off talks with the United Kingdom would make America "appear to the world as Uncle Shylock" exacting "our pound of flesh" in preferences, wrote trade diplomat Harry Hawkins from London. Such a drastic move would halt tariff reductions covering three-quarters of world trade, expose the weakened empire to extremists at home, and inflame Anglo-American relations. On the flipside, ending the GATT meetings "in at atmosphere of success and good will, with the U.S. recognized as having been constructive, generous and understanding" would boost the ITO negotiations and provide "an objective towards which the Marshall Plan can work" by shoring up Free World economies. In short, cautioned Hawkins, failure would "provide the Russians with just the propaganda material they need" and end "a joint effort with our best friends in bitterness and disillusionment."[27]

The British won, again. In September 1947, they negotiated a deal to phase out preferences over the next ten years. By October, Clayton backed away even further by abandoning this gradual elimination of the Ottawa system, though London still cried foul. The eventual Anglo-American bilateral GATT deal called only for narrowing, not eliminating, preference margins after a three-year grace period. Free trade was supplanted by foreign policy concerns, namely, propping up an essential ally. Other core GATT nations, called "contracting parties," fell in line. Knowing the administration faced charges of appeasement from the Republican Congress, the aging Clayton tendered his resignation and became a special advisor on the ITO Charter. That the capitalist peace subsumed domestic interests was apparent when, as expected, protectionists erupted. Business critics, furthermore, did not like the coddling of socialized regulation in Britain and state trading activities, not to mention discriminatory trade practices that threatened the free-enterprise system. Truman glossed over the one-sided American concessions, however, calling the GATT a "landmark in the history of international economic relations," which it was.[28] Just in the sheer number of negotiations—fifteen with the United States alone and over ninety between other pairs of countries—Geneva represented "the most extensive action ever taken for the reduction of barriers to trade," exclaimed Undersecretary Robert Lovett of the State Department.[29]

The GATT became an informal negotiating forum that facilitated foreign policy aims, namely, recovering, stabilizing, and integrating the Free World. In the embedded liberal compromise that acknowledged protectionism but expedited domestic approval, nations could walk away or inject safeguards without fear of violating any rules. Agreements did not require ratification by legislatures, making the GATT a pliable tool of domestic politics and the containment doctrine. Trade historian Douglas Irwin adds that "foreign policy was arguably a crucial factor behind the political support for the postwar trade agreements program" but in fact foreign policy was *the* crucial factor. In his Marshall Plan announcement to Congress in December, Truman alluded numerous times to confronting the totalitarian USSR, which questioned whether democratic governments could prevent the collapse of capitalism. The dramatic battle for the mastery of Europe and Asia had begun, and democracy—even Western civilization—was at stake. Concerted foreign economic tools—the GATT, Bretton Woods institutions, the Marshall Plan, and the ITO—promoted the resuscitation of intra-European trade and thus full production for hundreds of millions of allies, including former enemies Germany and Japan, and their integration into a democratic capitalist economic bloc. In sum, through American leadership that hinged on admitting more imports in GATT accords, acting like a creditor, and otherwise fixing the world's payments imbalance to fund recovery, these four economic legs of containment bolstered the Cold War capitalist peace.[30]

No matter how persuasive, such Cold War internationalism faced obstacles in the capitalist world. Protectionism and socialism, that is, intervention by the state, were rooted in people's minds as the only routes to full employment, welfare, and equality. *The Communist Manifesto* said so. As the arduous GATT round and negotiations for the ITO Charter showed, however, exceptions persisted to the free-enterprise system so crucial to freedom and democracy. Price controls, government surplus disposal programs, quotas for development, and opt-outs of agreements to form discriminatory customs unions might ultimately doom this effort. The "ITO-IMF pattern of international economic relations" required a permanent non-discriminatory, multilateral trade system, reminded State Department advisor Joseph Coppock.[31]

By early 1948, the Truman administration had its trade agenda trifecta. The ITO, the first GATT round, and the RTAA backed up its capitalist peace words with deeds. All three faced opposition. The ITO Charter, signed by over fifty nations, showed that countries could work together to solve the historically contentious issue of trade organization, but it was far from a done deal. The GATT round was in the bag, though Britain had exposed the administration to protectionists at home. Likewise, renewing the RTAA, which was essential to future GATT talks, put protectionists on guard. On March 1, 1948, Truman announced his intention to send renewal legislation to Congress with the escape clause that permitted withdrawal or modification of tariff concessions. That, he hoped, would appease the protectionists.[32]

The Charter for an International Trade Organization, finalized in Havana, Cuba, in 1948, had opponents at the other end of the spectrum. Once the trade code was completed, this opposition—free-trading internationalists in tune with the administration—came out in force. Market capitalist purists in the big business community identified the statist ITO as an enemy of the private sector, democracy, and the containment doctrine, but the administration had long warned them that rejection of the Charter would emasculate their own goals for a healthy free-enterprise system. The consequences would redound on the United Nations, where the initial preparatory discussions for the Charter had been the first act of the Economic and Social Council (ECOSOC). The purists risked a capitalist world of economic warfare, to Stalin's delight, if the Havana Charter were not ratified because, as Coppock noted, it was "the very embodiment of economic liberalism in the international realm" and a counter to socialism. Government controls would spread and "free institutions generally" would weaken "because of the close affiliation of capitalistic economic arrangements and political and civil liberties." At a practical level, bankers would have trouble making loans and investments abroad. More generally, internationalism and the military strength of the Free World would suffer. Business free traders must discard their qualms and embrace the capitalist peace under the ITO.[33]

Ironically, the same Cold War atmosphere that had catalyzed a conclusion of the Geneva GATT round gave credence to the business purists on the ITO. Their leader was Philip Cortney, an early neo-liberal who cautioned against a "drift into Communism and finally to war" by an ITO that encouraged discrimination, protectionism, and "socialism the world over." Contrary to its original intention, claimed the U.S. Council of the International Chamber of Commerce, the Havana Charter was so hedged by qualifications to market principles as to render it ineffectual in liberalizing commercial exchanges. It "jeopardizes the free-enterprise system by giving priority to centralized national governmental planning of foreign trade" while allowing for nationalism, discrimination, and state planning for full employment.[34] The National Foreign Trade Council was more gentle, advocating the far less intrusive GATT instead. Even this reliable ally grumbled that the ITO lacked shields for investments and services like banking and shipping. The Charter was, simply, a threat to "our free society."[35] In sum, the ITO was obtuse, bureaucratically deficient, and so interventionist as to undermine capitalist, free-enterprise peace.[36]

They had good reason to worry. Wilcox, the delegation chief who had taken over from Clayton, allowed a group of developing nations led by Latin Americans to compromise the market principles of the Charter. These countries believed that the rich industrialized nations violated the national sovereignty of the poor by insisting on free trade and investment, thus preventing the development of infant industries through protectionism necessary for them to thrive. American negotiators were as appalled as the business purists by this nationalist bias, voiced by Argentina, Bolivia, Uruguay, and Venezuela. They lacked the votes to trash the Charter, even with the addition of the Arab League, China, Ceylon, and a few others, but they modified it because the Americans feared that an open break with the developing world would have far-reaching political consequences. Warned Albert Nufer, a career diplomat serving as the political advisor to the US delegation at Havana in 1948, a walkout would "inevitably be exploited by the Soviet Union and by the Communist groups and opposition parties in the several Latin American countries, as well as other parts of the world" by convincing people that the big capitalists were overwhelming small nations "in order to keep them in a semi-colonial state and to prevent them from industrializing."[37] Wilcox gave a bit, allowing regulations on investments and trade in the Havana Charter.

The administration tried to explain the foreign policy dilemma to the business purists, but to no avail. Remember Franklin Roosevelt's dashing of European hopes at the London Economic Conference in 1933 and how it soured future allies on the United States, wrote foreign policy advisor John Foster Dulles. Remember the battle against imperial preferences; the Havana Charter would help get rid of them. There was also the Marshall Plan. Philip D. Reed, chairman of the board of General Electric, warned that the European Recovery Program "would be left hanging in the air" if Congress rejected the Charter.[38] Purists were versed in all of these arguments against nationalism, protectionism, and communism, and they endorsed American leadership and a multilateral trade policy. But nations faced a choice, noted the chairman of the National Foreign Trade Council, Robert Loree. One was "freedom, with its reliance upon free, private, competitive enterprise" and the "recognition of the dignity and worth of the individual as inherent in political democracy and in the spiritual concept of freedom itself." The other was "economic regimentation, with its invitation, under socialism, to the materialistic concept that the individual is the servant of the State and a cog in the collectivist machine, and its subversion not only of economic freedom but of political freedom as well." The purists backed a truly *capitalist* peace, not the ITO.[39] They awaited the ratification process in Congress, when they would launch their final lobbying campaign against the code.

Sensing the split in free-trade forces, the Republicans rose up against the Reciprocal Trade Agreements Act. The RTAA was a linchpin of the ITO Charter and Truman's trade policy as he headed into the 1948 election campaign that he was predicted to lose. When asked by reporters in April whether Republican obstructionism, including on confirmations of civil servants, was a concern, he pointed to the GOP's resistance to the RTAA as a symbol of the party's bankruptcy. "Our foreign policy and the European recovery program, and everything else, is based on that trade treaty agreement," he stressed, but protectionists "amending to death" the bill as it worked its way through Congress reminded Truman of Hawley-Smoot and the road to World War II.[40] General George Marshall's Plan had just passed Congress a month before the RTAA hearings, Truman pointed out, and crippling amendments to the RTAA threatened this cornerstone of Cold War aid programs as well.[41]

The minority Democrats, calling this scaled-back RTAA bill a "sham and typical protectionist device," played the Cold War card. They read a statement from Cordell Hull, who, as the leader of the Citizen's Committee for Reciprocal

World Trade, focused on the diplomatic reasons for trade liberalization, even under this meager, one-year bill that called for a halt in tariff cuts. The secretary of defense, James Forrestal, then asked the National Military Establishment's Munitions Board to analyze the need for trade expansion. Tariffs were certainly important to protect certain industries, the board concluded, but the nation's security required a general reduction of barriers to allow in strategic materials to replace dwindling stocks. The auto, radio, and machine-tool industries, to name just three with potential as wartime manufacturers, also depended on export markets to maintain their stability. Like Alger Hiss, recently charged with communist subversion, who testified on behalf of Hull's citizen committee, supporters backed the bill, however emasculated, because it was essential to the Marshall Plan's liberalization and integrationist objectives.[42]

Because Congress extended the RTAA for only one year rather than three as the president had requested, the president lashed out that its short duration

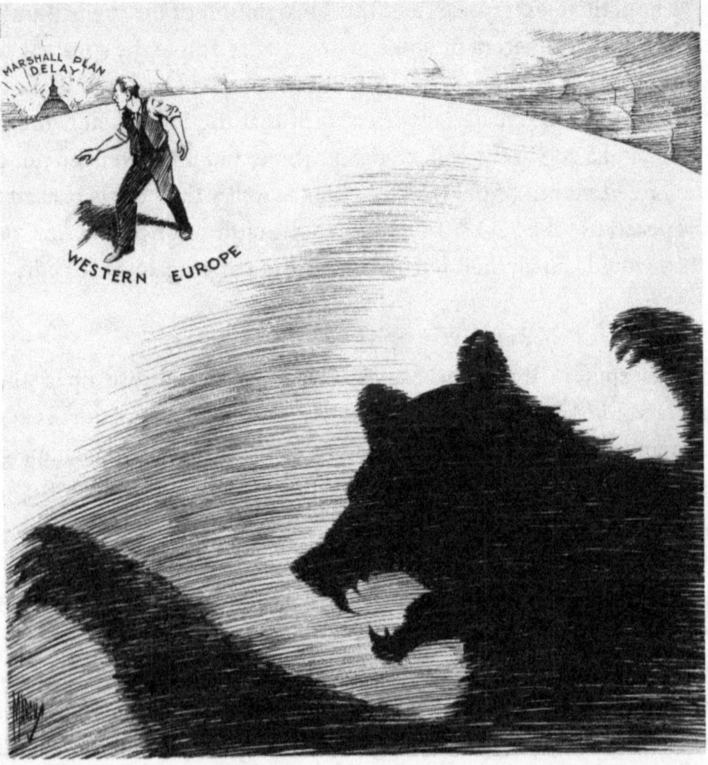

Fig. 4.1 An apprehensive "Western Europe" man looks toward the US Capitol that has the Marshall Plan under consideration, while the shadow of the Soviet bear looms. Congress finally approved the aid in April 1948 in hopes that trade liberalization would save Europe from communist domination. Edwin Marcus, *New York Times*, March 14, 1948, Library of Congress Prints & Photographs Division, LC-USZ62-123456.

raised doubts about American intentions in foreign policy. So did the time-consuming peril point procedure that would "obstruct the negotiation of new agreements" and impinge on US leadership, he added.[43] Ironically, by amending the program, Republicans had cast their lot with it. They would have to prove that their vitiated tariff-reduction authority worked, even if it pursued somewhat weakened free-trade internationalism—but internationalism all the same. Arch-protectionist Bertrand Gearhart's House version of the bill sought congressional veto power over any trade agreement that granted concessions the Tariff Commission deemed too large, which would have denied the State Department its supposedly "unrestricted and autocratic power to raise and lower tariffs without adequate study."[44] The measure was beaten back in the Senate. Republicans also took issue with the notion that they opposed the capitalist peace doctrine. Congressman Gearhart despised being called an "isolationist" by the Democrats. Besides, Republicans who strongly backed the Marshall Plan and favored the ITO, like Arthur Vandenberg, spoke out against Gearhart's veto amendment. Such courage was ill-advised because it took Vandenberg out of the running for president in 1948, smirked observers. Like Truman, Senator Vandenberg reluctantly signed on to the one-year bill so that tariff authority would not lapse and deal a serious blow to American prestige.[45]

A part of Truman's reelection bid in 1948 depended on defending the RTAA and the ITO Charter as components of the Cold War capitalist peace paradigm. On the campaign trail in Texas, for instance, the president accused the GOP of election-year politics in the one-year RTAA, charging that the desire to kill the program entirely should be "a matter of concern to every man, woman, and child in the United States, because it vitally affects our prospects for world peace" by chipping away at world prosperity. By their actions, Republicans threatened the foundation of American foreign policy, the notion that "prosperity is fundamental to peace and security." Worse, he added at a stop in New York, they were stepping back to isolationism just as America was rebuilding war-torn nations and "strengthening the free nations against communism" by aid to Turkey and Greece under the Truman Doctrine and the Marshall Plan. Truman also denounced such obstructionism by resorting to Red Scare tactics. "The Communists would like to see" a Republican in the White House so that the United States would pull out of Europe and Asia, he brazenly noted, and then rather hyperbolically added that the "fate of mankind" depended on US foreign policy, including whether to "continue our reciprocal trade policy or abolish it."[46] But just as he had taken Vandenberg's advice when lobbying for the Truman Doctrine by scaring the hell out of the American people regarding the communist threat, Truman dramatized the utmost necessity of, at long last, casting aside isolationism for free-trade internationalism.

Harry Truman achieved a stunning electoral win in 1948, but the upset helped him little on the RTAA renewal and not at all on the International Trade Organization. When the ITO Charter exited Havana on March 24, it headed to the US Senate for ratification. There, the business purists, in an unholy alliance with protectionists, lay in wait. By 1949, erstwhile free-trade allies like the National Foreign Trade Council had abandoned the ITO. They believed it would not achieve capitalist peace but foment discord instead. Secretary of State Dean Acheson brandished Cold War arguments in defense of the code that, in his words, helped contain "the aggressive conspiracy of the Communists of all countries." He even called the purists self-righteous idealists who unrealistically sought the total abolition of trade and investment barriers. At the Senate hearings, he persisted. "As freedom is hanging in the balance in many parts of the world, and millions of people are looking in our direction for assurance that we really mean what we say," the United States must send the right signal "in the basic field of trade."[47]

With a new Democratic Congress, the administration thought the chances for the ITO had improved and that the RTAA could be fully restored as well. In his inaugural address on January 20, 1949, Truman reminded Americans that at stake was "economic security—for the security and abundance that men in free societies can enjoy" against the "false philosophy" of communism through trade expansion.[48] Such language fed the Cold War consensus that the Big Three—the ITO, the RTAA, and the Marshall Plan—pursued trade initiatives critical to defending against communism. Thus, while Marshall Planners crowed that the recovery program had knocked back the Soviets, Truman asked for a three-year extension, retroactive to 1948, of the RTAA—"the indispensable other half of the Marshall Plan," declared the *New York Times*—and urged the House to approve the Charter "as essential to American bipartisan foreign policy."[49] But the business community bided its time. There was no rush on the Charter; after all, it was the GATT, to convene for a second "round" (as the tariff negotiations were called) in Annecy, France, that depended on authority under the RTAA. The turnover in parties in Congress worked wonders for the capitalist peace concept, at least for the Reciprocal Trade Agreements Act. Eliminating the peril point provision, it blew through the Ways and Means Committee in six days. The full House passed the RTAA renewal in early February, 319–69.[50]

Despite the overwhelming vote, protectionists put up a fight. They tried again to empower the Tariff Commission to hold up trade agreements and referred to the national security argument for vital industries and commodities, scoffing at trade's linkage to foreign policy and demanding high tariffs instead. According to the American Tariff League, the only relationship the RTAA and the ITO had to the Marshall Plan lay in their "common commitment . . . to reduce tariffs to the vanishing point."[51] Conspiracy theory took a darker turn. Congressman Reed called out internationalists like Alger Hiss (then under investigation by the House Committee on Un-American Activities) for "peddling our information to foreign countries, to our enemies" that businessmen had secretly entrusted to diplomats regarding imports. He accused Clayton's 110–person delegation at the GATT talks in Geneva of having harbored nine communist sympathizers because they had granted so many tariff concessions to foreigners.[52] This was outlandish, yet two weeks of Senate Finance Committee hearings yielded, on March 11, a partisan 7–6 vote in favor of the House bill. A narrow veto, 43–38, of the peril point provision offered by Senator Eugene Milliken, former chairman of the Finance Committee, scared the administration. Southerners, in particular, began protesting that textile imports undermined national security, a complaint heard increasingly in the years to come. Due to lobbying for the North Atlantic Treaty Organization (NATO), which only drove home the importance of the capitalist peace, the bill did not make it to the Senate floor until September. Truman eagerly signed it on September 25, 1949.

In April 1949, as the RTAA campaign continued, the GATT convened for its second round. Lasting until August, this Annecy round was less contentious than the Geneva talks, but disagreements arose nonetheless. Tightening export controls toward communist satellites was one issue. Czechoslovakia had imported coal mine drills from the West for re-export to the Soviet Union, which could use them to extract uranium for atomic bombs. (In September, the USSR would successfully test a nuclear weapon, another reminder that the Free World needed to unify as a prosperous bloc.) Furthermore, controversy arose over most-favored-nation status for Japan. Washington confronted resistance by the British Commonwealth, which recalled Tokyo's prewar predatory trade and currency policies. Once the US occupation ended, Japan might return to such punishing practices. The Americans countered by elevating the Cold War above trade. They reversed course on democratization in Japan and set out to rebuild an ally deemed critical to containing communism in Asia, of special import as China headed for a revolutionary victory by October. Truman also argued that since western Germany (in 1949 named the Federal Republic after the end of a dangerous superpower standoff in Berlin) got equal trade treatment, so should Japan. This would honor GATT principles and insulate it from communist influence. Truman's team lost this battle at Annecy; Japan remained outside of the GATT. The Americans also failed, again, to eliminate British preferences. As a result, Annecy brought only moderate tariff concessions. At least it continued momentum for the GATT and for an anti-communist foreign policy in general.[53]

That was important because the ITO was on the chopping block in Congress by late April 1949, just as the Annecy round began. Whatever imperfections the business purists considered the Havana Charter to possess were temporary. Its rejection would send the same isolationist signal that the Senate's refusal to join Woodrow Wilson's League of Nations had after World War I. The ITO would become the permanent trade arm to replace the Marshall Plan, due to expire in 1952—sort of the economic equivalent of NATO, wrote William Batt, director of the Committee for the ITO lobby. It also confirmed "to those people throughout the world who look to us for leadership and those beyond the Iron Curtain who would destroy it, that we are determined to continue our drive for international cooperation and peace."[54] But the Charter languished for months until House hearings in 1950, irritating the administration because most other nations made their acceptance of the ITO contingent on Senate ratification. The three-week hearings witnessed a display of support for the Charter from the media and movie industries; women's, veterans, peace, and other civic groups; religious leaders; importers, exporters, and shippers; unions, and the American Farm Bureau Federation Committee. Their support rang hollow in the depths of the Cold War, however.[55]

That is, the Cold War spotlighted capitalist peace principles with such intensity that it may have ultimately doomed the Charter. In June 1950, a war in Korea drew Truman's attention, giving him cold feet on other, less pressing matters. The NATO pact, mutual aid bills, and the Point IV program of development assistance to poor nations still awaited implementation, as did the various elements of the National Security Act that created the Central Intelligence Agency, Department of Defense, the National Security Council, and unified the armed forces. Economic security depended on these initiatives, reported special advisor Gordon Gray late in the year. A sweeping foreign policy review under NSC-68 was also on the president's desk. Furthermore, he faced severe political fallout from the victory of the Chinese communists and the emergence of Senator Joe McCarthy, who criticized the administration for being soft on communism. Liberal domestic legislation also was on the docket.[56]

These crises and confrontations detracted from Truman's ability to connect the dots of national security to the Havana Charter. Warnings about isolationism fell flat. Even most Republicans had joined in the internationalist Cold War consensus. Neither Congress nor business associations and planning groups saw the ITO as essential to this new, dangerous phase in the Cold War. In fact, the security appeal backfired as skeptics looked at the trade code as a socialistic invention that threatened the very democratic capitalist system that NATO and the GATT/RTAA free-trade regime defended. Corporate liberals, like the Committee for Economic Development, the National Planning Association, and the Twentieth Century Fund, were in accord, giving lukewarm support at best for the ITO from the moderate New Deal business wing. In addition, the idea that the Charter might bring peace seemed farfetched. After all, neither the Soviets nor Eastern Europe by extension would join a capitalist multilateral trade order, no matter how much they considered it in their interests to do so. The ITO had simply outlived its universal appeal.[57]

The American public, including businessmen, followed this logic. When asked, in October 1950, whether the United States should trade with the Soviets, fully three-quarters of the press and public replied no, even if that meant shortages of key minerals and other goods. That was a sizable increase from the 60 percent who had wanted to restrict trade with the communists two years before at the height of the Berlin airlift. Others also wanted to stop imports, such as dried eggs, from "Red China" as well.[58] Tellingly, usually staunch capitalist peace allies like the US Council of the International Chamber of Commerce and the National Foreign Trade Council added that the Havana Charter was infected by a Soviet-style "cartelist philosophy" contrary to the American way of life.[59] From the American perspective, it had the further defect of compelling the United States to extend most-favored-nation status to all members of the ITO while it did not receive equal treatment in return. Washington would not be able to protest because it would be a minority nation, owing to the Charter's one-vote, one-country rule. The Chamber advocated drafting a new code under the ECOSOC, while the United States should develop a "bold program" of bilateral negotiations with a nucleus of countries aimed at returning the world to a multilateral trade regime.[60] Not even Truman's fellow Democrats on Capitol Hill, like Senate committee chairmen Walter George (Finance) and Tom Connally (Foreign Relations), could muster much enthusiasm. They balked when capitalism became a handmaiden to the state.[61]

That tepid political reception, when added to the vitriol of the business purists, doomed the grand, half-decade-long effort to write the ITO code. Neoliberals turned the Cold War and capitalist peace ideology on their heads. Philip Cortney himself censured the ITO in a book pointedly called *The Economic Munich*, an allusion to free enterprise's appeasement of statism. Organized labor derided him as anti-worker and anti-development, but even the massive national campaign by Will Clayton and a committee of 124 businessmen, educators, and publishers could not change business sentiment that the Charter made the world safe for socialism. Neither could fifteen days of hearings, ending on May 12, 1950. The next month, the North Korean invasion of South Korea turned the Cold War into a hot war. Furthermore, Clayton (who turned his attention to an Atlantic Union) had aged, and there was nobody with the gravity of Cordell Hull left to press the case. Under withering attack by the Republican Right, Dean Acheson was forced to make the argument for the ITO. The Cold War wreaked havoc on the Charter.[62]

All of these factors—military, ideological, and security—conspired with domestic politics to reshape the capitalist peace agenda and, with it, the fate of the ITO. With McCarthyism in full rage and the US position in Korea deteriorating, the Democrats suffered losses in Congress in the midterm elections of November 1950 that reduced their edge in both houses to a minuscule margin. Protectionists in Congress remained unified against the Charter out of the usual fears of import competition, but they also endorsed the American Bar Association's view that the ITO would unconstitutionally usurp power over commerce from Congress. The protectionists did not concern Truman as much as the defection of the business community. In addition, politically, Senator Vandenberg's retirement due to a losing battle with lung cancer lost the administration a Republican ally. With the RTAA up for renewal in 1951, and the GOP clamoring for reinstatement of the peril point provision, the challenges on the trade policy horizon looked daunting. Truman could get import and export expansion through the RTAA, the GATT, and a vigorous campaign of trade promotion at home and abroad, rather than by a controversial trade code. In August 1950, John Kee, chairman of the House Committee on Foreign Affairs, asked Truman to defer the ITO legislation until the next session. Urgent security demands in Korea and elsewhere suggested a postponement.[63]

On November 20, 1950, Acheson sent a secret memo to Truman that recommended saving the RTAA by quietly jettisoning the ITO and conceiving of the GATT, a non-doctrinaire tariff-negotiating forum of thirty-three nations backed by business, as the key world trade organization. The Charter was "no longer a practical possibility," wrote Acheson. Anyway, many of its divisive provisions, such as on investments, were no longer necessary, and other measures, such as Point IV aid to the global South, had replaced them. Reintroducing the ITO in Congress would fruitlessly end in defeat or indefinite delay, either of which "would be damaging to our foreign policy." The GATT and the RTAA allowed the administration to avoid a needless confrontation in Congress. A decision was needed promptly; a third GATT round of tariff negotiations, at Torquay, England, was imminent. The delegation there needed clarity on which organization would govern world trade.[64]

The president's cabinet and advisors mostly agreed or had no comment, Truman assented to Acheson's reasoning, and diplomats at the Torquay Round were notified that trade authority rested in the Reciprocal Trade Agreements Act. Allies accepted the decision without surprise. Within a few days, Canada introduced a proposal for the next GATT session that gave the forum a permanent secretariat and standing committees to discharge international trade policy. The ITO's development and reconstruction chapters would be incorporated into the GATT or other institutions. The United Nation's ECOSOC absorbed the full-employment provisions. Truman quietly withdrew the Havana Charter from Capitol Hill at the end of December.[65]

The grand experiment of a trade code had crashed on the rocks of the very capitalist peace argument that had birthed it in the first place. Free trade in the Free World meant the subordination of the regulatory state to the national security state. Ushering in an era of world peace through a universal trade code was passé. Free-trade internationalism persisted, but it bent toward the Free World, not toward the United Nations. Over forty years would pass before a comprehensive world trade institution would be considered again, when universal capitalist peace ideology emerged from its Cold War straitjacket. Cordell Hull's trade idealism was officially dead, a victim of anti-communist ideology and containment's strategic realities. It was time for capitalist peace to focus on the Free World rather than the world as a whole.

5

Containment, 1951–1954

The stillborn International Trade Organization ended one era in US trade policy and began another. Since 1933, policymakers had clashed with Congress over protecting domestic industry. Nonetheless, they had sustained momentum toward liberalizing trade barriers. They won their objectives of renewing the Reciprocal Trade Agreements Act and participating in the General Agreement on Tariffs and Trade. The heroic pursuit of peace and a vision of extending New Deal liberal oversight to the trade order had shaped this initial phase, but the demise of the Havana Charter terminated the attempt to forge a regulatory state at the international level. That loss embedded a second, solidifying period of policy, one fixed on implementing a capitalist peace paradigm to serve a NATO/GATT security alliance of Western nations.

Stimulated by the Marshall Plan, Western Europeans in 1950 were on the brink of establishing the European Coal and Steel Community, and a half decade later, they would harmonize tariffs under a common system of duties to establish a customs union, the European Economic Community or the Common Market. Such integration also meant potential discrimination against outsiders, yet Washington tolerated this deviation from free trade because it promoted unity among these fractious capitalist nations in the Cold War. Still, the United States hoped to minimize unfair protectionism by facing one, rather than several, external tariff walls. In September 1950, thirty-three nations (including six acceding ones) convened at the seaside British town of Torquay to begin a third round of GATT negotiations at which the Europeans called a special session to deliberate over a common tariff. In the negotiations with the United States, duty levels also fell, though the Americans bore the brunt of the concessions, once again. France and Britain maintained their protectionism, including imperial preferences, as they tried to plug the "dollar gap" of debilitating payment deficits. To do so, they insisted on unilaterally lowering US tariff rates before discrimination ended in Europe. The United States acquiesced. They did not make a "broadside attack on preferences," wrote Winthrop Brown, alternate

Capitalist Peace. Thomas W. Zeiler, Oxford University Press. © Oxford University Press 2022.
DOI: 10.1093/oso/9780197621363.003.0006

chairman of the American delegation in Torquay. Rather, they only asked for some reductions in specific cases and adequate compensation where barriers were substantial. They also pledged to live up to their obligations as a creditor nation and moderate their tariffs so allies could export to fill the dollar gap.[1] The Cold War required sacrifices for freedom, democracy, and prosperity—the capitalist peace.

This leniency exposed the State Department to such criticism at home that a crisis arose at Torquay Round by mid-March 1951. Washington cast the predicament in broad terms. Secretary of State Dean Acheson informed British Prime Minister Clement Attlee that the crisis adversely affected Anglo-American solidarity well out of proportion to its importance and gave an advantage to those in both countries who had long opposed trade cooperation. Because of domestic irritation over Commonwealth intransigeance, Brown withdrew tariff offers to Britain and canceled a cut in the American wool duty, which prompted Australia, New Zealand, and South Africa to refuse any agreement with the United States at Torquay. The Commonwealth believed that Truman, a poker player, was bluffing and would fold. Instead, he called the British side. Washington hoped Canada might cobble together a decent offer from the Dominions. Truman, however, feared that a collapse at Torquay might sour Canada, its closest trade partner, on cooperation under the terms of the Hyde Park Agreement, reaffirmed in October 1950, which called for a joint defense program to integrate the economic resources of North America. The two eventually signed a bilateral tariff deal, but the US loss on preferences was the "outstanding failure" of the conference. Torquay ended in April as a "one-sided trade arrangement to the whole world—a plain betrayal of American industry and labor," charged the *San Diego Union*, though it conceded the outcome did preserve internationalism and the capitalist peace.[2]

Still, the newspaper had issued a troubling accusation just as the campaign to renew the RTAA got under way in spring 1951. The retreat on preferences was especially bothersome to Acheson because the stalemate gave the impression that the Commonwealth had aligned as a bloc against the United States. Britain had then actually tried to secure a waiver for preferences in the GATT. Washington rejected the request, but London's intention confirmed for protectionists GATT's leniency toward discrimination, especially to the detriment of America. Sure enough, domestic opposition to the RTAA flared again, initially due to the rough going in Torquay. Congressman Theodore Green of Rhode Island, a Democrat, offered a resolution to suspend the round until the unsettled conditions due to the Korean War abated. Acheson deflected this potentially ruinous provision to the GATT and US foreign policy, arguing that Korea showed ever more the need for freer trade to unify the Free World. Green withdrew after getting Truman's promise that domestic interests, including textile manufacturers from his state, would receive fair treatment at Torquay. He also invoked the escape clause for the first time, in December 1950, by withdrawing tariff concessions on women's fur felt hats and hat bodies. Belgium, however, quickly retaliated against US industrial wax. Truman listened to domestic concerns and compromised to ensure a modicum of progress in the GATT talks and win approval of the RTAA. He clearly understood the embedded liberalism in trade during this difficult time.[3] The second phase of the capitalist peace trade agenda did not start well at all.

Nevertheless, capitalist *security* was in force when it came to East-West trade. Czechoslovakia had recently confiscated the property of American nationals, harassed their firms, and criminalized commercial dealings with the West. On short notice, the Czechs ordered a substantial reduction of US embassy personnel in Prague and imprisoned Americans without justification. When it came to trade, they announced concessions solely to benefit the Soviet bloc, guaranteeing special positions to communist corporations and retaliating against imports from the West. Such moves mocked standards of cooperation in the GATT. To protect the forum's integrity, Truman dissolved GATT obligations to Czechoslovakia on November 1, 1950. Other nations, like France, which had substantial trade with Prague, might protest the loss of third-party benefits under the most-favored-nation rule, but the trust so essential to commercial ties was already "rendered a nullity by political events," wrote Acheson.[4]

The administration added to sanctions against the communist nations. Truman suspended GATT concessions with Poland, the People's Republic of China, North Vietnam, and the Soviet Union by the end of 1951. Beijing had already withdrawn from the GATT in 1950, as Mao refused to honor commitments the former Chinese government had undertaken after January 1946. A majority of Americans, moreover, approved of discouraging trade with the communists, including restricting Western European exchanges under the tightening system of export controls and embargoed goods that the Western bloc's Coordinating Committee for Multilateral Export Controls (COCOM) established in 1949. Such an approach hindered efforts to close the dollar gap, for European allies relied on East-West trade and thus chafed at the long list of banned COCOM goods propagated by the United States. A National Intelligence Estimate seemed to side with their cause, conceding that restrictive licensing, blacklisting, and the like had little effect on the "aggressive foreign policy of the USSR." Nonetheless, experts concluded that "a high degree of cooperation from the Western Powers would, if well coordinated and well enforced, seriously retard and limit the development of the Soviet bloc war potential."[5]

Export controls were one of Washington's ways to safeguard the capitalist trade system. In January 1951, Truman spoke of "the community of free nations," including in underdeveloped areas, that must increase the supply of strategic raw materials. Extending the system of trade restrictions (due to expire on June 30,

1951) to communist nations, as well as renewing the RTAA, would further this "common defense objective" by reducing trade barriers.[6] He included the same message in the annual presidential message proclaiming World Trade Week, an event traditionally focused on trade expansion and education, further proving that the capitalist peace was directed at containing communism.[7]

The renewal battle over the RTAA also fully entered the Cold War arena, from the free trade and protectionist sides. By now, the Cold War, together with the hot war in Korea, would presumably make Free World unity through the trade agreements program an easy sell in Congress, but this was not the case. In log-rolling, Hawley-Smoot fashion, legislators led a charge to exempt their manufactures from tariff concessions. That they failed owed much to Truman's acceptance of the escape clause and peril point procedures and his tough stance in Torquay against the communist bloc. The Korean War, the Japanese Peace Treaty of 1951 that ended the American occupation, NATO rearmament, and McCarthyism also focused the RTAA debate on the dangers of communism. Additionally, there was solid backing from business, farm associations, and labor, as well as ordinary citizens who sought lower costs for consumers by decreasing taxes, including tariffs. They understood that Europeans could not pay back their loans without access to the American market. As chairman of the US Council of the International Chamber, George Sloan, told Ways and Means Committee chairman Robert Doughton, the "free world needs assurance at this time that the United States as the major economic power will continue to seek a high level of world trade." Protectionists begged to differ, even though they drew on the Cold War in their arguments as well.[8]

Acheson made direct connections to foreign policy to parry the protectionists. At the House Ways and Means Committee hearings, the secretary of state declared that the challenge was "not only the threat of military aggression. It is also the threat of subversion, of stirring up class strife, of exploiting discontent, of preventing economic improvement." To meet these dangers "we must do everything possible to build up the strength of the free world and to give its people a real stake in its future." This included the less-developed world, where people must "look forward to better living conditions and have a democratic alternative to the promises of the Kremlin" by increasing their production. There were safeguards in place to protect threatened domestic industries, and no large-scale tariff negotiations were planned for the next three years or so that might make protectionists anxious, he added.[9]

But many in Congress remained skeptical about the RTAA's urgency and of the capitalist peace argument, however skewed toward security, and they repeated past jabs against the free trade/peace formula. Republican Thomas

Jenkins scoffed that it had not prevented fascist aggression nor the Cold War. In fact, added Scott King, a Democrat from California, the United States had been in a constant state of war for most of the RTAA's duration. Furthermore, tariff negotiations would bring no understanding with the Soviets. Just as there had been no trade agreement with Hitler, there would be none with Stalin. Congressman Jenkins told Richard Wood of the Friends Committee on National Legislation, which advocated peace through free trade, that altruism was fine "but we live in a pretty sordid world." Wood's church had sent missions to China for decades, but the Chinese turned communist. "Now, do you think we could trust this fine theory that you give us and reasonably expect anything from it, in view of the present situation?"[10]

Protectionists easily argued that trade restrictions, not free trade, ensured defense preparedness by insulating industries exposed to harmful foreign competition. They also pointed out the hypocrisy in the fact that even with exports banned, imports entered from communist and imperialist nations, which rendered the intentions of the capitalist peace doctrine suspect. Security—indeed, survival—depended on protecting the domestic market, defying the hoax of reciprocity. In reality, the diplomats gifted one-way concessions to foreigners of all stripes. With Europe and Japan clearly on the way to recovery, reducing tariff levels was not so pressing anyway. They were already low; the RTAA had, unfortunately, worked too well. Foreign competition—the product of the successful Marshall Plan and RTAA/GATT—hurt industries that produced hats, shoes, bicycles, wire, pottery (dinnerware) and ceramics, furs, fish and seafood, synthetic chemicals, optical equipment (microscopes and binoculars), mechanical pencils and fountain pens, watches, textiles, wool, dairy and beef, pulp and paper, sugar, fruits (Florida tomatoes, northwestern cherries, pears, nuts, and apples) and vegetables (mushrooms), clothespins, oil, coal, and a host of minerals. They all pleaded their cases at the House and Senate hearings, often in desperation or anger over imports from Cold War allies in Europe, Asia, and Latin America. The Korean War added to their arguments, connecting the balance sheet to national security.[11]

Anticipating this logic, Truman sent up a bill designed to mollify the protectionists. It actually provoked opposition from the capitalist peace free traders when it exited the House—from a majority of Democrats, no less—and even Secretary of State Acheson questioned it. The full House agreed to renew the bill for three years, not for two, but it included mandatory escape clauses in trade agreements, the peril point that triggered escape clause action, severe limits on trade with communist nations, and quotas on foreign agriculture imports. Just four of 187 Republicans opposed the peril point clause and forty-two Democrats backed it. Protectionism was resurgent, despite surveys showing that two-thirds of Americans favored lowering tariffs on a reciprocal basis and just 14 percent opposed any duty cuts. Disappointed commentators saw the House version as a "set-back" for the trade agreements program.[12]

In the Senate, all of the protectionist measures remained, albeit with limitations. Under a revised peril point procedure, the Tariff Commission would hold hearings and report to the president within 120 days of its determination of the tariff level below which they considered a concession to imperil an industry. No trade agreement could be concluded until the president received the report, and then he had to tell Congress if a concession went below the peril point. Acheson despised the amendment. Eugene Millikin countered that it guarded the nation's security by providing more oversight in trade deals, particularly with the communists. The measures were slightly modified when the Finance Committee reported out the bill to the full Senate in April, issuing two blows to free-trade internationalism. One meaninglessly disavowed support for the GATT and another reduced the RTAA's shelf life to two years. These won Senate approval by a resounding 72–2 vote in late May. Truman signed the renewal on June 16, stressing his dislike of the "cumbersome and superfluous" peril point provision that returned the RTAA to its Republican version of 1948. But it was better than having no negotiating authority; in whatever form, the law would help Free World unity.[13] Congress might have punished him by rejecting the RTAA when he relieved the outspoken General Douglas MacArthur from his command in Korea. Or the Republicans might have simply balked, not wishing to give the opposition Democrats a win as the GOP eyed a likely return to the White House in 1952.[14]

Protectionism was the real winner. Even Democrats, like the rising stars Lyndon Johnson of Texas and John F. Kennedy of Massachusetts, announced that tariff cuts had gone far enough. Domestic industry was under stress from imports. As one historian has noted, the 1951 RTAA signified a "historic shift in the political economy of U.S. trade policy."[15] The American South, for two centuries a force for low tariffs to boost traditional cotton and tobacco exports, began to turn toward restrictions as it focused on textile and oil imports. The North also shifted, blaming cheap labor imports from Asia (as well as cheap labor in the non-unionized South) for losses in its manufacturing sector. Republicans split between conservative nationalists who sought protectionism and "true reciprocity," and moderate internationalists who saw the RTAA as a weapon against communism and high consumer prices. The tension shaped the Republican Party platform of July 1952.[16] Dwight Eisenhower, a free trader, would have to wade through these waters of protectionism in his own party with caution.

"The old-time religion of reducing America's tariff walls and stimulating free trade has lost the momentum of Cordell Hull's day," wrote an editor for the

Washington Post in February 1951. "The trend, in fact, is in the other direction, with results in some cases too ridiculous to laugh at." The United States gave aid to allies with one hand but then closed the door to their efforts to earn their own way through exports. Affecting everything from Italian garlic to Danish cheese to Icelandic frozen fish fillets, the revocation of GATT concessions worsened the dollar gap, denying allies revenue, while consumers were denied cheap foreign products. This was not the proper behavior for a creditor nation both enjoying full employment and burdened by overstrained finances. Worse, peril points and escape clauses came "at the expense of American defense policy and at the expense of its foreign policy objectives."[17]

In 1952, protectionists saw an opportunity to impose more import restrictions. One called for imports of materials prioritized in government allocation to be cut in half. Another required half of Mutual Security goods to travel in American ships. Others demanded tariff hikes on several products or lowered the duty-free allowance for tourists on the chinaware they brought in from abroad, regardless of the fact that the United States had run an annual trade surplus, exports over imports, averaging $5 billion since World War II. The protectionists looked like selfish crybabies and they stood in the way of the nation's foreign policy agenda. Yet they also had voters on their side. Surveys showed a majority believed the government made it too easy for foreign nations to sell goods in the United States and only a fifth thought it wise to buy more products from abroad. In 1952, upwards of two-thirds believed the government should help businessmen, farmers, and workers hurt by competitive imports.[18]

Truman took up the fight against protectionism on behalf of the capitalist peace doctrine in 1952, his final year in office. There were sixteen applications to the Tariff Commission for escape clause relief. For instance, wielding the RTAA, motorcycle manufacturers asked the Tariff Commission to use the clause and impose higher duties on British motorbikes. The commission refused the appeal, noting that there was no basis for protection because the competition was not unfair—it was simply competition. The British were targets of many Tariff Commission applications—on bicycles and parts, chinaware, and tobacco pipes. The State Department assured allies that despite these frequent attempts to invoke the escape clause, Washington would rebuff protectionists and minimize trade barriers in the interests of mutual security.[19]

Truman continued to confront protectionism. In July 1952, a majority of the Tariff Commission recommended the escape clause to establish a restrictive quota on garlic from Italy and increase the duty to protect some sixty domestic growers. The president refused, informing Congress that he did not find the producers to be suffering from import injury. Indeed, almost all American garlic came from California, from three of the richest agricultural counties in the United States. Four garlic tycoons grew nearly half of the herb but they had diversified so garlic accounted for just 10 percent of their revenue. Truman warned that if nations were to earn their dollars, rather than receive them as aid, then they must be able to trade. Imports must become a substitute for foreign assistance, addressed as an issue of national security.[20]

The Cold War continued to shape his approach to the Tariff Commission. To be sure, he agreed with a ruling that Greek dried figs could be restricted, but only because of an abnormally high crop yield in 1952. He also allowed additional fees on almond imports but denied quotas on shelled filbert nuts. The cost would fall almost entirely on Turkey, reducing that nation's dollar earnings by over $1 million, in addition to its losses incurred because of the higher tariff on figs. Like Greece, Turkey had just joined NATO, but the Tariff Commission was undermining the containment doctrine. Truman also refused to impose higher tariffs on Swiss watches, seeking to keep Switzerland in the Western camp despite its neutrality. According to a report in August by William Draper, the

Fig. 5.1 A European worker shrugs while Stalin is pleased that his Cold War aim of causing tensions among the capitalist nations is proceeding: America seems to prefer sending costly aid rather than engaging in free trade by lowering their high tariffs to let Europe revive. Library of Congress, Prints & Photographs Division, LC-DIG-ds-14544.

American representative to the North Atlantic Council and special representative in Europe, it was also time, as the Marshall Plan era ended, for the West to follow a "trade not aid" policy. That is, Europe had to survive by exporting more to close the dollar gap and doing so would reduce the sizable American trade surplus.[21] At the end of the year, Congress tacked on a rider—Section 104—to the Defense Production Act to impose import quotas on dairy products from five allies, including Canada. Truman denounced this "cheese amendment" as a violation of the capitalist peace, "the kind of law which makes the job of the Kremlin's propaganda experts a great deal easier" by hurting Free World economies.[22]

Big business welcomed Truman's effort but looked forward to Eisenhower's first term to promote free enterprise, access to critical goods, and leadership abroad. The National Foreign Trade Council explained that economic policies "should support diplomacy and military strategy" by acknowledging that the United States depended on global sources of raw materials. "Growing economic interdependence of free nations" depended on a "wider system of multilateral non-discriminatory trade" at the heart of the NATO/GATT bond.[23] The chairman of the New York World Trade Week Committee, banker Nelson Rockefeller, believed that trade growth fought communism at its source—"in the minds and hearts of underprivileged individuals in underdeveloped areas of the world, where the most formidable menace appears."[24] But the poor were very suspicious of the industrial nations. They griped about being denied markets by the very protectionist practices the rich countries accused them of following. Containment in the developing world had turned into a top priority.[25]

This concern about instability led Truman to financier Daniel Bell, chairman of the bipartisan US Public Advisory Board for Mutual Security, to investigate ways of building up the military and economic strength of free-world allies. Following up on the Gray Report's advice to eliminate tariffs on scarce commodities, the Bell Report, issued in March 1953, privileged imports over narrow domestic industry interests. Bell reaffirmed capitalist peace theory at the outset of the Eisenhower years. Industries that could not compete against imports should turn to unemployment insurance, retraining, or conversion to other types of production. Bell's "national interest" test demanded free-trade internationalism.[26]

The protectionist-containment battle greeted Eisenhower as he took office in January 1953. Politically, he had straddled internationalist and nationalist Republicans during the campaign. He was a clear adherent to the capitalist peace, though, especially when combating communism in the developing world through aid and trade. Eisenhower pushed for trade liberalization with allies, many of whom he had worked with closely during the war. The new president cited Stalin's last public political speech in October 1952, in which the aging dictator predicted a breakup of the Western alliance due to, among other things, American restrictions on European and Asian trade. Britain, France, West Germany, and several South Asian nations had inked trade deals with communist countries over the past two years; Bonn and London even exchanged goods with the People's Republic of China. Eisenhower advocated more imports from friends abroad in order to counter the lure of communist markets. A strong believer in market capitalism under the "trade not aid" banner that he lofted over his new administration, he also deplored Republican protectionists. His chief rival for the Republican nomination had been isolationist Robert Taft of Ohio, whom the new president considered to be among the small-minded protectionists whose opposition to international trade risked peace and Free World security. To his new secretary of state, John Foster Dulles, a religiously fervent free-trade internationalist, as well as the rest of his cabinet of free-enterprise purists, Eisenhower emphasized that the capitalist peace paradigm would bury parochialism.[27]

The new administration's contribution to the capitalist peace was pivotal. Roosevelt had reversed protectionism and launched the postwar trade order. Truman had introduced trade liberalism to the security structure of the Cold War. Eisenhower solidified free trade with military policies as a servant of national security for the next four decades. The historian of his foreign economic policy, Burton Kaufman, notes that Eisenhower's "strident anticommunism" actually "circumscribed much of the dialogue on foreign economic policy," particularly toward the developing world. As a fiscal conservative dedicated to minimizing public expenditures, the president dedicated his administration to trade as a means of enhancing Free World prosperity through small government and free enterprise.[28] He activated the containment doctrine in trade policy by reading reports by industrialist Clarence Randall, who was soon appointed to head a special commission that made recommendations on the foreign economic agenda. The administration was also the beneficiary of several investigations undertaken late in the Truman years, such as the Gray, Bell, and Paley Commission Reports. The Paley document, for instance, linked dependable flows of raw materials into NATO alliance nations to military and security policies. Imports of energy and other strategic commodities interrupted by altered trading patterns, market instability, and the industrialization efforts of less-developed nations must grow by more American investment abroad, more development loans to increase extraction, and more effort to solve distribution problems. To accomplish these ends, the Paley Commission urged reductions in trade barriers to further the grand strategy of containment.[29]

For the president, the anti-communist mission relied on internationalism. In his inaugural address, he firmly rejected the "economic solitude" of isolationism because "no free people can for long cling to any privilege or enjoy any safety" without adhering to the "basic law of interdependence, so manifest in the commerce of peace" necessary for prosecuting the Cold War.[30] This meant removing obstacles to goods, capital, and services and ending exchange controls to make currencies freely convertible to facilitate the flow of trade and investments. He thus warned of "the terrific importance this business of trade and partial self-sufficiency, at least in the industrial field, has for national security." Eisenhower intended to confront the protectionist headwinds in his own party by extending the RTAA for another three years.[31]

Confronting isolationism was one thing; asserting the capitalist peace was quite another. Eisenhower and his free-trade allies vigorously did so because he believed quite simply that a failure in trade policy meant "we may fail in all."[32] Automobile industry king Henry Ford II also viewed high tariffs as meaningless without a healthy and free global economic foundation. If the United States did not open its markets to those nations "not yet caught in the spider's web of Soviet Russia," they would "be drawn into the web, one way or another." Japan was an example. Congress had spent hundreds of millions of dollars on this bulwark against communism in Asia. Tokyo could only exist if it expanded trade with the Free World, continued to be subsidized by US taxpayers, or tied its economy to the Soviet bloc. Because the Tariff Commission and the British Commonwealth severely restricted Japan's exports, lucrative trade with communist enemy China remained in play unless Tokyo acceded to the GATT and traded with the Free World. In short, Ford believed "we should buy even more foreign military goods, both for NATO and our own defense setup—and I mean motor vehicles, too—where it is sound economy to do so. This is a healthy, competitive way of strengthening our friends."[33]

Convincing animated protectionists to heed this warning, however, proved impossible. Not willing to contest Republican majorities in Congress that sympathized with protectionism early in his administration, Eisenhower opted for a one-year extension of the RTAA with no additional tariff-cutting authority and a pledge not to negotiate major trade deals in 1953. The escape clause and peril point provisions remained. This was politically astute. Ways and Means hearings in April and May produced over 2,000 pages of testimony, mostly complaints from import-competing producers. The first critic to appear was the influential O. R. Strackbein, a former union organizer who enlisted dozens of labor and business organizations under his newly formed protectionist lobby, the Nationwide Committee on Industry, Agriculture, and Labor on Import-Export Policy. He reminded Congress that these industries were basic both to the national economy and to national security. They dealt in practical realities, he pointedly argued, so different from "a mere theoretical, idealistic, or doctrinaire contact with the import problem" because of the con job diplomats perpetrated through capitalist peace ideology.[34]

Eisenhower's support of the protectionist provisions also gave him breathing room to formulate a comprehensive policy approach to push for free-trade internationalism under a new commission. He had help in his campaign. John Coleman, who assembled a Committee for a National Trade Policy as a counterpart to Strackbein's lobby, talked less about pacifying the world through tariff reductions and more about American leadership to prevent communist inroads. He wished for allies to stand on their own feet through trade expansion. The heaviest hitter was Secretary of State Dulles, who appeared on the sixth day of the Ways and Means hearings for the RTAA. "There exists in the world a vast and powerful conspiracy directed against the United States," he warned, a conspiracy that attracted the despairing masses with the false hope of revolution. One-third of the world had fallen under the sway of communism. More were likely to unless capitalists turned away from using imperialism and protectionism to conduct trade wars for resources, tussles that gave comfort to Soviet leaders, and united in a common front that "is influenced by our own economic policies, including our tariff policy." Dulles asked Congress to renew the RTAA for a year while the president appointed Clarence Randall, of Inland Steel, to head a Commission on Foreign Economic Policy and conduct a comprehensive review.[35]

Because Eisenhower had let the protectionists have their way, the RTAA renewal zipped through Congress, passing the House 363–34 in May and by a mere voice vote in the Senate. Extremists nearly ruined the deal, however, when Senator George Malone tried to terminate the bill entirely and then offered another amendment to give Republicans a majority of votes on the Tariff Commission, thereby upsetting nearly four decades of bipartisan precedent. Both attempts failed. The administration got Congress to authorize the Randall Commission to study trade policy "within the framework of our foreign policy and our global defense plans," announced Eisenhower.[36] His words were in line with efforts to ensure that the Randall Commission was pointed toward trade expansion and internationalism to bolster the containment doctrine.[37]

Awaiting Randall's report, Eisenhower issued a call to arms to the business community. Coleman's Committee for a National Trade Policy, officially established in September 1953, pounded away on Stalin's deathbed prediction of free-world disintegration due to trade friction and continued problems recovering from World War II. His presumed successors, Georgy Malenkov and associates, continued to divide and disrupt the West. Only the United States could doom the prediction by allowing friendly nations to earn dollars to spend on American goods, said Coleman. "The keystone of our security is the building of a free world coalition. We cannot draw the free peoples together militarily if we divide them economically."[38] Businessmen implored the Randall Commission to issue a statement on broad objectives, within a context of the Cold War and the threat of real war that necessitated trade policies conversant with the realist foreign policy of containment.[39]

The Randall Commission's work was part of a major overhaul of the federal bureaucracy with a more efficient and less costly administrative structure. Its specific goal was to expand trade, not aid, to please fiscal conservatives like Eisenhower. Thus, on his insistence, the commission consisted of a bipartisan group of ten congressmen (split between the House and Senate) and seven public members of his choosing. Nobody should be "tarred with either the stick of protectionism or extreme free trade," noted the president's assistant on economic affairs, Gabriel Hauge. That was wishful thinking. Vociferous protectionist legislators Eugene Millikin, Daniel Reed, and Richard Simpson of Pennsylvania signed on.[40] Reed agreed with a constituent who had moaned that officials were brainwashed by capitalist peace thinking. Indeed, the New York congressman reminded Randall of Eisenhower's parting words of advice at the commission's initial White House meeting: "Above all, I urge you to follow one guiding principle—what is best in the national interest." For Reed, that meant exposing all the "neat and easy gimmicks" of the free traders of the past two decades, including loans, the Bretton Woods institutions, the Marshall Plan, and, of course, trade agreements. The "national interest" meant protecting the domestic economy from wayward internationalism.[41]

But Eisenhower's appointees bent the Randall Commission toward the capitalist peace. On the public side, just one member, Cola Parker of Kimberly-Clark, was closely affiliated with protectionists in the National Association of Manufacturers. Randall, a consultant to the Marshall Plan and an ardent free trader, led the commission. He determined to issue a report no later than January 1954 to give Congress time to legislate before the midterm elections crimped efforts to liberalize trade. Randall confessed in his diary that many of the protectionist arguments bordered on the ludicrous; he oftentimes wisecracked with witnesses, such as noting that bubble gum was not a strategic product when a witness claimed everything was related to defense. Yet he also understood the stakes in the Cold War, asking commission members to consider, above all, "the international alignments in the world contest between the creeds of state-servant-of-man and man-servant-of-state." Taxpayers could not foot the Cold War aid bill indefinitely. The commission needed to devise ways for nations to be self-supporting by, in part, export-driven production.[42] Wrote Senator Prescott Bush of Connecticut, a Republican on the commission, closing the gap between American exports and imports to allow allies "to bear their fair share of the

Fig. 5.2 Clarence Randall's Commission on Foreign Economic Policy—with the chairman shown facing the president in September 1953—ended up with a tepid report on free trade because of protectionist pressures. In the second row behind Randall and Eisenhower are John Vorys (second from left) and Prescott Bush just above the president. David McDonald, the labor representative who pushed for adjustment assistance for workers, is in the third row, middle. The fourth row included heavyweights, from left to right, Jere Cooper, Walter George, and protectionist Eugene Millikin. The last row features protectionist and author of the Report's tariff section, Cola Parker, second from left, and compatriot Daniel Reed next to him. Getty Images, Bettmann.

common defense" through freer trade "will have forged a major weapon for winning the cold war."[43] As the president noted, freer flows of trade were imperative "if we are going to have a free world really hang together."[44]

The Randall Commission scheduled hearings in the United States and Europe in October and November 1953 and asked for written statements from over 1,500 organizations and individuals in place of oral testimony. The farm sector supported trade liberalization not just to dispose of surpluses but as a common-sense approach to world leadership, freedom, and peace. Allan Kline of the American Farm Bureau Federation, representing 1.5 million families in every state and Puerto Rico, proclaimed that the "greatest collective effort" must focus foreign economic policy entirely on "our national security." America spent nearly $60 billion annually on armaments, atomic bombs, and military aid. That was not enough. Security "also depends on strong allies" who could expand productivity only if the United States liberalized its trade policies.[45] George Meany, of the American Federation of Labor (AFL), added that without "free world trade, the only way left for us to go would be down." The "self-reliance of free people are powerful weapons against Communist penetration—they are even more important than guns in building the strength of our allies."[46]

The capitalist peace boiled down to the intangibles of faith and conviction, added to hard military and economic factors. The trade system was "held together with the trust and allegiance of our allies across the globe," Brooklyn Democrat Emanuel Cellar told the Randall Commission.[47] In other words, allies recovering from the world war or worried about export markets after the stimulus of the Korean War must have confidence in America's willingness to accept their goods. Indeed, Special Assistant C. D. Jackson, an expert on psychological warfare, added that Europeans were so much more fearful of an American recession than the threat of the hydrogen bomb that a potential downturn paralyzed their thinking. Reinforced by Soviet propaganda, they were convinced that the United States would collapse either by war or depression. That notion must be dispelled by opening markets through free-trade internationalism.[48] Thus, reliably low tariffs were a "politico-psychological" issue for friends abroad, summed up the Committee for Economic Development.[49] Randall stressed this factor as the essence of the Cold War struggle. "Not only can our acts affect the material strength of other countries of the free world, but possibly more important, they can affect the dependability and willingness of our major allies to fight," he reasoned at the hearings in Paris. Economic nationalism resulted from inconsistent trade policy. France, for instance, had expressed anger at American customs procedures that reclassified glass instruments as optical equipment so that higher tariffs could be imposed. Such deceptiveness had a "larger psychological impact" on countries, which sought remedies in protectionism or expanded East-West trade. Randall urged capitalist peace principles to win over hearts and minds.[50]

An understanding of psychology came with a huge dose of containment strategy in the administration's free-trade argument. Edwin Martin, deputy chief of the United States Mission to NATO, was no expert on tariffs, but as a specialist in national security he perceived "certain fundamental principles" that must control trade decisions. Because the Kremlin unscrupulously schemed to fill power vacuums, Washington must be ready not only for armed attack but also for political and economic subversion. The United States must defend its way of life, freeing the West from totalitarian domination. Adequate military strength derived from economic stability and prosperity. As well, the United States could not go it alone against the Soviets without creating a militarized, regimented state. It needed strong allies to preserve democracy and liberty. NATO served this purpose, but only if it could pay for military hardware through open and expanded trade and financial exchanges.[51]

In December 1953, Randall tapped the director of research for the commission, Alfred Neal, to undertake a series of investigative studies as background for the final report. Neal included one on the economic and political role of US trade policy in the service of the containment doctrine. Tracing America's "dominant role" in alliances, the United Nations, and bilateral security links to nations like Japan, he concluded that economic strength underlay these arrangements. Indeed, trade "disputes can weaken or destroy military alliances." For instance, Washington wished to arm West Germany without alienating France and the three Benelux countries by merging Europe into a larger political and economic complex, but American trade barriers armed European producers with a powerful argument for resisting their governments' efforts to reduce their own trade restrictions and sell strategic goods to the Soviet bloc when denied access to Free World markets. The world stood on the threshold of enormous change in production and trade, wrote Neal. Some 600 million industrializing people of Southeast Asia and 185 million people in Latin America and Canada were in the midst of expansion, and Africa and the Middle East were close behind. "The fundamental choice we face in our foreign economic policy is a reflection of the choice we face in our foreign policy as a whole," he concluded. That is, the United States must decide whether to link its economy to the Free World, a grand strategic choice embedded in capitalist peace ideology.[52]

Randall divided the report into sections and put commission members in charge of each one. In the case of tariffs, the protectionist Cola Parker got the lead, naturally opening the door to protectionist witnesses. Although the majority of testimony favored free trade, leaks to the press resulted in a public battle over policy. Reed and Simpson blasted away with diatribes, insisting that the commission compromise its internationalist leanings. Seeking unanimity in the final report, Randall agonized over this dilemma. In intense deliberations that lasted past Christmas, he struggled to get the commission's endorsement of his policies, with mixed results. Unanimous assent arose on foreign aid and there was consensus on commodity agreements. Then Parker, whom Randall respected, rattled the commission with his tariff section by demanding a deal on trade liberalization.[53]

Bolstered by over three hundred submissions at the hearings, oftentimes accompanied by emotional appeals for tariff protection, Parker acknowledged that Eisenhower's phrase "consistent with a sound domestic economy" tempered the charge for free-trade internationalism. National security might be a priority for diplomats, but not one industry witness believed that. Market conditions simply did not exist at present; every nation was steered by government safeguards like social programs and subsidies, not to mention tariffs. To be sure, these statist measures needed modification, but Parker's tariff subcommittee recommended retention of the "much criticized peril point and escape clause provisions" to promote a sound economy. National security depended on protecting domestic economic interests. Mocking capitalist peace notions, he questioned whether developing nations would go communist if they could not expand their exports. Even if tariffs disappeared, said Parker, there would still be "ills" in world trade. O. R. Strackbein, the protectionist lobbyist, accused Randall of being so biased toward free trade, particularly after the Randall Commission chief published a tome called *Freedom's Faith*, that he should resign from his leadership post. Strackbein ridiculed the internationalists who sought "world economic unification by opening the valves between the nations of the world" even if doing so bankrupted industries.[54]

Damn the capitalist peace; protectionism was a necessity. Stunningly, protectionist members on the commission were not convinced even by Parker's hedging, much to Eisenhower's frustration. Congressmen Millikin, Reed, and Simpson stubbornly held to the belief that tariffs, plain and simple, were the most equitable way to guard the economy and Cold War diplomatic objectives. They were not selfish isolationists, existing on the fringe of the national security state but rather patriots with a duty to urge a minority report. The three legislators issued a dissenting view to the final Randall Commission recommendations.[55]

The pressure worked; the report of the Commission on Foreign Economic Policy reflected the tension with protectionism by offering very little in the way of bold new measures toward trade liberalization despite its clear enunciation of capitalist peace principles. The commission advised simplification of tariff schedules and rate structures, weakening the Buy American Act so that foreign nations could fairly bid on government contracts, and GATT multilateral bargains and mediation over trade disputes. The Reciprocal Trade Agreement Act should be renewed for at least three years, preferably longer. Still, tariff cuts must be limited to 5 percent for each of the first three years. And, by retaining the peril point and escape clause provisions, Congress would have a say over GATT agreements. There would also be no special aid for workers displaced by tariff cuts, aid a commission labor representative, David McDonald of the United Steelworkers Union, had asked for. That is, tariffs remained the main way to protect jobs. Additionally, while encouraging a bit more trade between the Soviet bloc and Western Europe, the Randall Commission banned exports to the People's Republic of China and North Korea. The final report, in sum, moderated trade liberalization and lacked innovation in cutting tariffs, solving the dollar gap, and stimulating development. There was consensus on aid cutbacks, private investment, and currency convertibility, but trade internationalism had so divided the commission that protectionist obstacles remained in the document.[56]

Accepting that moderate protectionism was the best he could get at the moment for his "trade not aid" agenda, the president made the commission report the basis of his foreign economic policy. He even appointed Randall as a special White House consultant. To be sure, Eisenhower had little knowledge of the intricacies of trade policy, like the most-favored-nation principle. But his stature and political shrewdness were enough, liberal traders hoped, to get the Randall recommendations through Congress. They were initially optimistic, until protectionists geared up for a fight. The Strackbein message that the capitalist peace was driven by missionary goodwill, by "free trade pacifism—with no grounding in reality," appealed to average Americans who knew little about foreign affairs but a lot about economic survival.[57] Eisenhower sent the commission report to Congress, convinced that it would help contain communism. Protectionists warned him that it would divide the Republicans.[58]

In his special message to Congress on March 30, 1954, Eisenhower repeated that the Randall Commission report ensured a good standard of living and solidarity of the Free World against communism. Not only would the United States have more essential materials critical for its defense, said Eisenhower, but freer trade would "aid in the development of a world for all of us and our children."[59] Randall had asked for a three-year renewal of the Reciprocal Trade Agreements Acts and larger tariff cuts than an annual 5 percent reduction. Congress gave only another one-year renewal of the RTAA and retained the tiny duty reductions in a bill that unanimously passed in the Ways and Means Committee in June. Legislators were in no mood to go out on a free-trade limb in an election year and with the country in recession to boot. Senator Albert Gore Sr. attempted to amend the House bill with a three-year extension just to make the point that the Democrats were on board with Eisenhower's "trade not aid" policy to combat communism. But that approach was shelved for the time being.[60] Randall's report seemed to satisfy no one.

Critics labeled the commission product ineffectual. The British called it "an innocuous little mouse" rather than a document supposed "to have revolutionized world trade." The Soviets gleefully went much further. *Izvestia,* a Soviet newspaper, claimed that protectionist "American monopolies in the domestic market" had prevailed; disillusionment among free traders showed that the "ruling classes" could not deny the economic difficulties in the capitalist world.[61] Business purists also reared up, carping that the commission did not go far enough in an anti-socialist direction. Columnist Walter Lippmann, who balanced a Keynesian faith in government reform with market policies, complained that Randall himself had "sacrificed most of the lucidity and effectiveness of his own case" by compromising in the trade section. That had heartened the remnant of isolationists, who had already backed the Bricker amendment to limit the power of the Executive branch in foreign policy. Most commentators were not so alarmed, though. They believed that Eisenhower should continue the fight against the economic parochialists, even risking a "showdown" in his own party.[62]

The president coddled the protectionists, likely because of their leverage in the upcoming midterm elections. In summer 1954, he considered two Tariff Commission recommendations to increase tariffs: on imports of watches and on lead and zinc. The former industry had long lobbied for protection, claiming its skills were a critical wartime necessity. Despite skepticism by importers of Swiss watches about the national defense argument, Eisenhower sided with the Preparedness Subcommittee in July. He jacked tariffs as much as 50 percent on certain types of watch movements.[63] Lead and zinc producers had more clout because they stretched across several states and their commodities fed into the government's emergency stockpile program. Prices had fallen since the Korean War and import competition was stiff. Dulles warned against imposing higher tariffs that might damage foreign affairs. Eleven nations, all close allies of the United States, had bound (that is, fixed) tariff rates on lead and zinc through GATT accords. Canada, Mexico, and Bolivia would be particularly hard hit, so import restrictions would send shock waves through the hemisphere and undermine efforts to "eliminate the communist problem in Guatemala" (a CIA-led coup began ten days later) by inter-American cooperation, wrote Dulles. In regard to Mexico, Eisenhower was aware of the fraught history of misunderstandings between the two neighbors as well as their differences in culture and language, and he said that in that context a trade war might upset the bilateral relationship by exacerbating the "leftist trend" in the country. On his secretary of state's advice, the president rejected the Tariff Commission's recommendation despite intense pressure from mineral-state Republicans. He opted instead for voluntary export restraints in place of tariffs and later took the same tactic with oil imports.[64]

As historian Burton Kaufman concludes, defense considerations guided Eisenhower's responses to the Tariff Commission, responses that worried capitalist peace advocates. To be sure, the advocates welcomed his refusal to raise tariffs on Belgian hand-blown glass later in the year, after the commission split evenly along party lines. But free traders fretted that the trend toward protectionism sowed distrust. Paul Hoffman called it "suicide by tariff," in which Congress risked separating "us from our overseas friends and allies."[65] State Department officials "shudder to think what will result in our foreign relations with friendly countries if the United States refuses to become a participant and a partner in a multilateral trade agreement." This alluded to the Randall report's allowance for the GATT to be subject to congressional protectionist pressure and to stalled talks over Japan's entry into the GATT.[66]

Former ambassador to the Soviet Union and commerce secretary, Averell Harriman, analyzed the foreign policy dilemma protectionism created. The Free World had united over European recovery and rolling back communism in South Korea, but today "our policies are confusing and uncertain, our leadership is questioned, our alliances are creaking, and American prestige in the world has suffered a major eclipse." The United States also lacked an enthusiastic following in the global South, with even independent nations convinced that they were still held in a form of colonial status because the West controlled markets for their raw materials. The communists may have been turned back in Guatemala, but unfair economic and social conditions persisted to embolden leftists, supported by a Kremlin engaged in an all-out economic competition with the United States as well as a nuclear arms race. Meanwhile, the United States had not fully committed to using its huge resources to promote a better life. In short, chided Harriman, "if we expect other countries to break down trade barriers, we must take the lead" or the Cold War would be lost.[67]

As the year 1955 approached, free traders were on the defensive. At a legislative leadership meeting of Republicans and Democrats in December 1954, the president recognized differences in opinion on trade policy. But all the billions of dollars spent on security would go for naught "unless we do something to enable some of our allies to make a living; and we could do that without ruining our own country." The Randall report took an embedded liberal, moderate protectionist approach, which disappointed his free-trade allies. Senator Lyndon Johnson, the new majority leader, had hoped the commission would have been a "landmark in the history" but had gotten "indigestion" by taking "huge bites and didn't spend very much time chewing over the facts." Johnson asked Eisenhower if he would "drive forward" to reduce trade barriers, and the president assured him that he would. Despite the modesty of the current one-year RTAA renewal bill, he affirmed that it was "the best program that could possibly be devised by the Administration" and vital to the containment doctrine.[68]

6

Offensive, 1955–1958

By 1955, protectionism had roared back to life, despite the Randall Commission's recommendations, a Republican president firmly in the free-trade camp, the return of the low-tariff Democrats to the majority on Capitol Hill, and hope that the Cold War might end under new leadership in Moscow. Ominously, though, the Soviets under their new premier, Nikita Khrushchev, issued a stiff economic and propaganda challenge to the West, and that made trade liberalization even more urgent for Dwight Eisenhower. His agenda included two difficult renewals of the Reciprocal Trade Agreements Act, a controversial fourth round of GATT negotiations, and a rocky try at formalizing a new international trade body. Hovering over these trade issues was the Soviet economic offensive across the globe, a communist response to American containment. Moscow tested capitalist peace internationalism and Washington responded, rebooting Cold War tensions and ideological rivalry.

President Eisenhower began the year with a multi-pronged appeal for free trade: extension of the RTAA; increased investment, technical cooperation, trade fairs, and travel to expand exports; commodity agreements to boost agricultural prosperity; the facilitation of currency convertibility; and a new organizational framework for the GATT. Each would contribute to American and allied growth, he promised; thus each "advances our national security by bringing added strength and self-sufficiency to our allies," particularly those in the undeveloped areas of the world under pressure from the Soviet economic offensive.[1] On the latter, the United States had been negligent. After World War II, Washington viewed the threat from Moscow primarily in military terms. From 1954 to 1956, however, Soviet trade with the global South boomed from $850 million to $1.44 billion, and credits and technical aid grew even more. Khrushchev targeted the decolonizing and neutral nations—visiting India and Burma, for example—to cultivate communism in the developing world.

Capitalist Peace. Thomas W. Zeiler, Oxford University Press. © Oxford University Press 2022.
DOI: 10.1093/oso/9780197621363.003.0007

Advisor Milo Perkins believed the Soviets could "out-promise" America's performance on raising living standards, thereby winning the Cold War because the United States encouraged "false hopes in the hearts of our friends" by turning to protectionism.[2]

The administration knew it had been caught out. C. D. Jackson, the president's assistant on information, wrote that the United States had downplayed Moscow's shift from "the military to the economic weapon." Instead of offering imaginative programs, Washington had responded to the occasional "economic fire alarms" on an ad hoc basis. All of a sudden, "the Soviets had executed a brilliant series of economic forward passes, while we are still in our huddle trying to work out some elementary signals." As a result, the Soviets penetrated the Middle East, for example, with close ties to Yemen, Libya, and Egypt that got these countries arms and heavy equipment from Eastern Europe. The "pistol is at our heads in India, Burma, Japan, and portions of Southeast Asia" as well, lamented Jackson. Jawaharlal Nehru in India, who had first approached the United States for aid, instead made "googoo eyes at Moscow" to plug a billion-dollar gap in his second five-year plan. The Russians happily bought his rice. To be sure, some nations in the developing world were lost causes to socialism, but many, like India, were not. That terrified Jackson. Americans had long assumed that they dominated the economic chessboard of the Cold War, yet Khrushchev "was also muscling in on Santa Claus as well, which puts us in a terribly dangerous position." Jackson counseled trade liberalization to make permanent the impact from aid programs.[3] Saluting the success of Europe's recovery and integration, Eisenhower logically switched assistance to the developing world. Meanwhile, aid appropriations soon exceeded military spending.[4]

The president understood that the Cold War had changed to a battle for hearts and minds rather than solely a superpower military face-off. For that reason, the capitalist peace concept was all the more valuable. The crass, clever, and boastful Khrushchev reinforced the linkage of free-trade internationalism to foreign policy. In the developing world, the United States had reasoned that hopes for freedom and independence would overwhelm regimentation, but the economic offensive revealed that the developing world was more receptive to rubles than ideas. Although the capitalist peace rationalized world economic competition, it deepened trade-military ties without providing new ideas in the post-Stalinist Cold War. Democracy, led by the United States, Eisenhower believed, must "rob the Soviets of the initiative" by its own economic offensive in planning, cooperative initiatives, and inducements like aid, investments, and open markets.[5] Such thinking drew in liberals, such as the anti-communist group Americans for Democratic Action (ADA), and addressed "the grey zone in the cold war, an area largely uncommitted" to the Free World but stymied by the United States' neglect and protectionism.[6]

In 1955, Eisenhower returned from a summit with Khrushchev in Geneva, optimistic about easing tensions in the Cold War. Congress, though, was not in a conciliatory mood. It discussed more spending on aid but refused to do as European allies wanted and lift the restrictions on East-West trade. The spirit of Geneva relaxed tensions between the superpowers for a few years, but they returned in the face of the Soviet offensive and hardening US policies—and were finally dashed when the Russians shot down an American spy plane in 1960. In 1956, Eisenhower withdrew support for the Aswan High Dam from Egypt, with the story playing out in the Suez Crisis later in the year that drove the dynamic Egyptian leader, Gamel Abdel Nasser, into the arms of the Soviets. Communism threatened Latin America too, by 1958, in Fidel Castro's revolutionary Cuba. In Southeast Asia, Dulles signed a military pact with several nations and then took over the French effort in Indochina in 1954, sending aid and advisors to build a pro-Western South Vietnam divided from its communist sister to the north. While it despised the USSR, Beijing also began to assert its interests through economic statecraft in African and Asian nations, in addition to eying trade ties to Japan. In reality, the Soviet offensive made economics more prominent in world affairs than at any time since the Great Depression.[7]

The non-military battle escalated, especially toward developing nations. At the famous Moscow "kitchen debate" with Khrushchev at the opening of the American National Exhibition in 1959, Vice President Richard Nixon expressed faith that the United States excelled in the competition over consumer contentment and technological innovations. Americans were scared of the Soviet Premier's expansionist vision and tough words, however. Still, they knew that Free World trade with rich and poor nations accounted for 95 percent of commerce in the undeveloped nations and territories, which greatly overshadowed the Soviet bloc's 3 percent. Besides, the Russians themselves were desperate for American machinery. Nonetheless, to adjust the capitalist peace paradigm to the Soviet offensive, Clarence Randall, head of the White House's Council for Foreign Economic Policy, established the Subcommittee on Soviet Economic Penetration as a counterweight to Russia and Red China.[8]

It was time to redress trade with the Soviets and its allies. The Mutual Defense Assistance Control Act of 1951, known as the Battle Act, controlled exports of strategic goods to the communist bloc and also punished nations trading such materials by terminating aid to them. Overseen by the Commerce Department, the Battle Act added items to several lists of embargoed goods that had existed since 1947 under the Export Control Act. This legislation allowed exports of goods in short supply but regulated products deemed essential to American national security. A third list developed within the NATO bloc by COCOM—the

Fig. 6.1 Eisenhower has answers in free trade, export expansion, and European integration to the Soviet economic offensive, as he meets with Premier Nikita Khrushchev at Camp David in 1959. National Archives, Eisenhower Presidential Library, Abilene, Kansas.

Coordinating Committee for Multilateral Export Controls—restricted or embargoed other critical goods. Allies chafed at this, especially after the Korean War had subsided. Both Truman and Eisenhower, as well as the Randall Commission, had pledged to ease the controls as a means of boosting Europe's recovery and reducing US aid. The three lists were revised in 1954, though strict sanctions remained on the People's Republic of China.[9]

In 1955, with tensions temporarily eased between the superpowers, farm groups lobbied for relaxation of trade controls. Exporting "soft" goods like food might stimulate communist demand for more consumer products, the thinking went, and trade in less war-related goods might deepen the spirit of Geneva. This turned out to be sheer fantasy. The Russians and their satellites would trade to build their own prosperity, but they would not become dependent on the capitalist nations, preferring to earn foreign exchange for capital goods to help their industrialization. Not surprisingly, East-West trade had declined in recent years as Moscow focused on commerce within its own bloc, which boomed in the 1950s. Thus, there was much symbolism, and fewer real exchanges of goods, between the superpowers, but maybe that was enough to advance peaceful relations. In any case, Secretary of Defense Charles Wilson wished to go no further, while Eisenhower wanted to expand East-West trade to cultivate the favorable climate created at Geneva. He discussed these ideas with Khrushchev, he reported, "particularly we talked about peaceful trade."[10]

The administration highlighted the virtues of the free-enterprise system as part of the outreach to communists. For instance, the Department of Commerce's enhanced trade fair program, in tandem with the U.S. Information Agency, aimed to show the "captive" world that the United States stood for "human dignity and freedom in all its aspects" as well as being the "greatest producer of peaceful goods for the service of mankind." Trade fairs were a reaction to the Soviet economic offensive but also a pitch for more two-way trade with the communists.[11] A meeting of foreign ministers in October 1955 resulted in an agreement with the United States, France, and Britain to remove barriers to Soviet trade and promote travel and cultural exchanges. A few days later, the Commerce Department announced a relaxation of export controls, beginning January 1, 1956.[12]

Congress stepped in, however. Anti-communist Democrats and Republicans listened to the Defense Department's concern that weakening export controls undermined national security. What if the allies sent machine tools to the East bloc and most of them ended up being pirated for Soviet arms production? Congress erupted, moreover, when Eisenhower considered a British request for a revision toward China. The president backed away, though he remained skeptical that "the natural currents of trade" between, say, Japan and Red China, could be denied if Tokyo had nowhere else to turn. In July 1956, the Senate Permanent Investigations Subcommittee found the administration in violation of the Battle Act. Eisenhower retreated until 1958, after another renewal of the Export Control Act. When allies lobbied for relaxing sanctions, the United States joined an international agreement that cut the embargo lists by half. Sales could go forth to Eastern Europe (but not to extremist rogues China, North Korea, and North Vietnam) of civil aircraft, machine tools, ball and roller bearings, and aluminum and copper.[13] Eisenhower manipulated the capitalist peace paradigm in a realist direction to loosen up restrictions on East-West trade, but with modest success. Congress blocked him by casting the capitalist peace in the strictest, most ideological light.

Eisenhower also had his hands full with protectionists, who wanted to combat the Soviet economic offensive by obstructing imports and exports in the General Agreement on Tariffs and Trade, under authorization from the Reciprocal Trade Agreements Act. He hoped to reignite the stalled drive for trade expansion with a three-year renewal of the RTAA in 1955 that would lower tariffs 5 percent in each of those years, plus cut duties in excess of 50 percent. The reductions would be gradual, to appease moderate protectionists. He also sent a list of concessions to be granted to Japan once it acceded to the GATT that year, knowing that his own Republicans anxiously eyed that nation's imports into the domestic market. His plans did not impress the GOP or Democratic opponents; leaders warned of major opposition to the RTAA. Indeed, once House Ways and Means Committee hearings began on January 7, a majority of Democrats and Republicans alike exploded in what observers called the most intense pressure campaign since the RTAA's birth in 1934. Even though Republican bosses assured Eisenhower in private that the bill would pass, it would likely split the party, to the delight of the Democrats. The president appreciated the candor but foreign policy considerations came first. He felt that "all problems of local industry pale into insignificance in relation to the world crisis."[14]

For the administration, that is, the renewal went beyond domestic prosperity to the capitalist peace. Secretary of State Dulles rolled out all of the prior arguments: security meant more than military treaties, goodwill was essential to allied relations, collaboration was a strength of the Free World. Americans might represent just 7 percent of the global population, but their behavior was critical. Friends could be quickly alienated "if we followed trade policies which cut across their vital needs." He could hear Moscow's thunderous applause for protectionism. Confronting a "terrible menace," the United States must sacrifice by buying more imports and "hold together a free world partnership which is indispensable to the peace and security of each of the parties."[15] Secretary of Defense Wilson agreed. The United States could not go it alone. Prescient about the end of the Cold War, Wilson calculated that the "final showdown between the free world and the Communist world may not be a military one. We all hope not. It could very well be in the economic, political and propaganda areas." People would choose the system that best improved their standard of living. This was why the Soviets had launched their economic offensive, he explained. "We, of course, firmly believe that our free system is the best and will ultimately prevail."[16]

Moscow's economic offensive figured decisively in the RTAA. The director of the Foreign Operations Administration, Harold Stassen, displayed a "dramatic" map entitled "The Soviet Bloc Intensifies Economic Warfare." It showed locations of worldwide communist trade fairs, agreements, and offers of capital and technical assistance. He warned of the USSR's rapid penetration into areas with vast populations whose suffering from low living standards made them targets of "a tremendous struggle for the allegiance of mankind." The United States must respond likewise, releasing "forces of private initiative" by moving "in a constructive mutually beneficial trade approach to the world" to counter Moscow. James Schramm of the Committee for a National Trade Policy warned that military bases throughout the world would be "less than useless to us unless the people who live in those areas are convinced that they have a stake in preserving our kind of world." If they perceived more promise in the Soviet system, then a domino effect would occur, rolling back America's defensive boundaries "from Pakistan to Seattle, and from the Oder to Sandy Hook." In short, "the reciprocal trade agreements program has come to be a weathervane of American economic intentions" in the world.[17]

Japan was singled out as well. Free traders welcomed Japan as an example of how the capitalist peace model deterred the Soviet offensive. "I cannot, for the life of me, understand the callousness with which some of us approach the problems of trading with Japan," complained the State Department's Charles Taft in remarks apparently so critical of the protectionists that Senators Robert Kerr and Millikin left the RTAA hearings in a huff. Congress had just authorized military appropriations to protect Taiwan from communist attack in the first Formosa Straits crisis. But, Taft warned, should Japan decide "that she has to play economic ball with both sides of the Iron Curtain in order to live—we will have lost an outpost more important than Formosa." Protectionists foolishly risked national security so domestic producers could make handkerchiefs or gloves in textile mills, but Taft doubted those industries would disappear due to Japanese competition. Nonetheless, "even if they did disappear, the plain fact is that it would be far better to lose them than to lose Japan."[18] Witnesses from peak industries like petroleum, which urged more oil imports, as well as the usual associations of women's clubs, church groups, veterans, and academics, joined farm, labor (port workers, for example), and corporate organizations to testify that Free World nations like Japan had to trade.[19]

Protectionists were incredulous when it came to Japan. Barely hiding his contempt for the "Japs," as he derogatorily called them, Congressman Richard Simpson told Dulles that Tokyo's natural trading partner was China, not the United States, and revised export control lists allowed Japan to trade with Beijing. Nations like Japan not only did not depend on the American market but shopped for the best deal, just like the French, Belgians, and Scandinavians bought the cheapest coal from communist Poland. If Eisenhower really wanted to prosecute the Cold War, all of this trade should halt. But in the last analysis, American economic health was the critical base for national security. For instance, with its shoddy but cheap products, Japan was hollowing out the domestic cotton textile industry. Who would make uniforms for the US Armed Forces in the event of war? Southern and New England textile industries were essential to the nation's defense.[20]

For the protectionists, the campaign against the Soviet economic offensive through freer trade was just another internationalist excuse for the capitalist peace theory. O. R. Strackbein, of the umbrella organization the Nationwide Committee of Industry, Agriculture, and Labor on Import-Export Policy, sighed at the RTAA hearings that "liberalized trade has been tapped as the best way to fight communism. Gentlemen, if it were only that easy." West Virginia Democratic congressman Cleveland Bailey, concerned for coal and glass interests, warned that the low-tariff view "has within it all the seeds of self-deception, pollyanna welfarism, fear of Communist and unsound economic planning necessary to destroy our present standard of living." Legislators cleverly referred to the national security argument to boost protection, rather than reduce it.[21]

Ultimately, the opponents of the RTAA lost, though they did provoke some scares. The Ways and Means Committee witnessed an onslaught of attempts by individual industries to obtain protection. An effort to silence these special interests with a cloture vote failed, which prompted the new Speaker, Sam Rayburn, to leave his chair dramatically and demand a halt to amendments from the House floor. All remaining amendments were then prohibited and the RTAA cleared the House by a single vote, after just two days of floor debate. After that close call, the Senate proved an even bigger obstacle in its three weeks of hearings in March. Senator Millikin repeated his demand to bring the GATT to Congress for approval and also warned that no Republicans were willing to approve the bill that came out of the House without a pet amendment, or more. Eisenhower responded that he wished that "Members of Congress who were opposing the bill would come here and have to deal with these foreign problems and see what we are up against" with Moscow's economic offensive.[22] Anticipating the resistance, no State Department official appeared before the Finance Committee. Senators Malone and Millikin hinted at a major fight once the bill reached the Senate floor.[23]

Informed by the Senate majority leader that the bill was in deep trouble, Eisenhower bent, accepting several amendments. One pressed for congressional approval of each trade agreement, and another sought to bind the president to Tariff Commission rulings except for cases of national defense. Some strengthened the peril point, escape clause, and national security provisions to protect domestic industries even if, in some cases, only part of an industry was suffering from import competition. The president also received (unrequested) authority to impose quotas on imports deemed vital to the national defense. The Democrats were furious. In protest, many refused to take part in the Senate debate, urging the president to stand by his principles. Eisenhower shied away from log-rolling politics, however. He felt lucky to get a 15 percent tariff-cut extension over three years, especially as the Senate considered a spate of last-minute amendments. In conference, the House accepted the protectionist provisions, though not these latecomers, and the bill passed Congress in June. Eisenhower signed on, hearing criticism about his spinelessness but calling the compromise a "tremendous victory" for peace and security. The Democrats were correct to call the RTAA of 1955 a most moderate liberal trade law, at best.[24]

At least the State Department could take the new authority to the next round of the GATT. The major initiative related to these negotiations in Geneva was the accession of Japan to the forum. This was controversial. At home, domestic industries (textiles, glassware, autos, optical goods, crabmeat) feared cheap imports from the country, and allies abroad who had experienced Japan's trade predations before World War II resisted the accession. Commerce Secretary Sinclair Weeks expressed reservations about granting a big list of concessions to Japan, especially in a wide range of textiles. He asked Eisenhower to keep the escape clause under consideration. Capitalist peace ideology, though, guided policy. Washington overcame European opposition and ushered Japan into the GATT in August 1955. Stabilizing the Japanese economy by offering ample export opportunities in Western and Asian markets would turn the nation away from Red China. An economically powerful Japan was also essential to security in Asia and the Pacific. The Department of State affirmed that "the overriding interest of the United States is to strengthen our national security by taking the first step toward binding Japan to the Free World" through free-trade internationalism in the GATT forum.[25]

Trouble surfaced at the negotiations, however, when the United States orchestrated concessions on 40 percent of Japanese exports and sought to generalize them to third countries under the unconditional most-favored-nation principle. The British Commonwealth and European countries balked by invoking the GATT escape clause under Article 35, citing unfair and unusual competition. In short, they refused to grant concessions to Japan, whose unfair labor costs would apparently remain low for years. The only effective answer to this economic argument was the capitalist peace. Japanese diplomats hinted that they would turn to communist nations if their exports were denied access to Western markets, and when it came to Western exports, they refused to back down by offering to decrease duties on American petrochemicals, heavy machinery, electronics, boots and shoes, and autos. In the end, the Geneva Round of negotiations yielded direct US concessions to Japan valued at nearly $395 million on 84 percent of its exports, while Tokyo granted tariff cuts on merely 1.6 percent of US exports. American negotiators conceded in an unbalanced deal, but President Eisenhower took a broader view. He later told reporters that to "keep Japan, our friend, on this side of the Iron Curtain," the United States had to sacrifice on import competition.[26]

Over the next several decades, the 1955 GATT accord opened America's markets to Japanese low-wage manufactured goods that directly hurt industries. As a result, the cotton textile industry got much attention over the next few years. Although the administration questioned its claims of injury, the sector won a voluntary export control agreement that Japan announced in 1957, and more relief followed in a bilateral deal in the early 1960s after imports skyrocketed. There was also strong reaction in Congress. Regardless of the capitalist peace rationale of strengthening a Cold War ally, textile-state legislators called for import restrictions against Japan. The European Article 35 dispute was also not resolved for a decade, when Japan established formal GATT relations with the major contracting parties. By then, it was clear that Tokyo was in the West's camp, though only closely aligned with the United States.[27]

Besides the Japanese issue, agriculture and administration were top items at the fourth round of the GATT in Geneva. The United States received a waiver from obligations not to restrict imports because of its domestic farm subsidies, and others followed with their own protectionism. Agriculture became a constant bone of contention in the GATT from that point forward. The contracting parties also sought to create an organization to administer the rules of the General Agreement on Tariffs and Trade. Because the forum was an executive agreement and not a formal international organization, protectionists repeatedly tried to block negotiations on the constitutional grounds that Congress oversaw commerce and had never ratified the GATT. The contracting parties countered by trying to set up an Organization for Trade Cooperation (OTC) in March 1955, with a secretariat, an executive committee of seventeen members, and an assembly representing GATT members. Unlike the aborted International Trade Organization, the OTC would not have authority over national trade policies. This more modest body would be submitted to legislatures for ratification, including Congress, simply to strengthen the GATT's consultative mechanisms. Because the GATT had weighted voting, the OTC could not be created without American membership.[28]

Basically an administrative matter, the OTC was cast, rather hyperbolically, in the capitalist peace mold because it lacked enthusiastic support. Eisenhower sent it to Congress on April 14, 1955, explaining the need for a mechanism to discuss mutual trade problems when no negotiating rounds or annual sessions were under way. If the United States did not join, he exaggerated, then there may be a "regional re-alignment of nations" that "would play directly into the hands of the Communists" and their economic offensive.[29] Dulles saw it as part of the front line of the Cold War, as did the retired Will Clayton, who warned that repudiation of the Organization for Trade Cooperation by Congress would be a "slap in the face" to friends abroad. The effect "on our partners in NATO will be extremely unfortunate."[30]

Perhaps, but free traders feared that presenting the OTC alongside the RTAA renewal would either delay it or, worse, let protectionists marry the two bills, to the detriment of both. They thought that Congress had too much on its agenda to get to the OTC, and it turned out that Eisenhower did as well. His heart attack in August slowed down everything on Capitol Hill. Business purists, moreover, were wary of the OTC, though not as intensely as they had been of the ITO. Still, the National Foreign Trade Council announced its opposition to the GATT's reorganization if the Organization for Trade Cooperation projected "into a field of activities which have no proper place in the operations of an international trade organization," such as full employment, investments, and development.[31] Neoliberals, like the old ITO opponent Philip Cortney, understood the OTC's importance in the Cold War. Like the protectionists who derided it as an undemocratic super-bureaucracy that did an end run around the Constitution, however, the free-enterprise purists were on guard. Another unholy alliance regarding global trade institutions emerged, with purists applauding protectionists in Congress when they managed to defer hearings on the OTC to 1956.[32]

Recovered from his illness and eyeing his reelection in 1956, Eisenhower plugged membership in the OTC as enlightened self-interest steeped in the capitalist peace. It was imperative because it came "at a time when the Soviet Union is stepping up its foreign economic efforts."[33] Along with NATO, the Organization for Economic Cooperation and Development, the Coal and Steel Community, and the Council for Europe, the OTC was part of a freshly conceived cooperative venture called the Atlantic Community. In October, the president spoke of two exciting additions to the interdependent Atlantic Community. One was a common market of six nations, a European Economic Community, that would eliminate all internal trade barriers. The other entailed a free-trade area around that common market, called the European Free Trade Association. From 1956 onward, Western leaders placed economic interdependence on nearly equal footing with military planning. They believed in an increasingly co-equal Europe as the linchpin of a strong and united Western community. The OTC linked to a grand strategy to join this "international family" through free-trade internationalism.[34]

Digesting this capitalist peace message, labor, farm, civic, and some business groups gave their blessings to the OTC in the Ways and Means hearings. Surveys of the overseas press revealed upward of 85 percent of journalists—and over 90 percent of citizens polled—were aware that the OTC's passage would counter the Soviets by strengthening the West's economies. Some, like pharmaceutical exporters, echoed that the Russian offensive was "the most dangerous weapon" Moscow had in the Cold War. Congressional delay of the OTC, "the symbol of our entire foreign economic policy, can only spur the Russians on to even greater effort."[35] Indeed, the Council on Foreign Relation's academic and business study group on foreign economic policy found the new policy of technical aid, commodity agreements, and trade fairs for the developing world highly effective against communist economic strategy. The group implied that the Free World must coalesce in every way possible, including administratively under the Organization for Trade Cooperation; NATO was at risk unless its members coordinated their economic policies.[36]

The OTC exited the Ways and Means Committee with amendments, but approval. The full House did not act in the summer of 1956 because leaders predicted the bill's failure. GOP opposition ran two-to-one against it and a number of Democrats, led by southern and New England textile forces, joined them. Eisenhower tried to intimidate Republican minority leader Joseph Martin Jr. by pledging to withhold endorsements from OTC opponents in his 1956 reelection campaign. When Congress stalled again, he also determined to renew his request in 1957 after the voters returned him to the White House. But other matters proved more pressing, including crises in the Middle East and Hungary, and Eisenhower postponed the OTC campaign. Frustrated free traders understood his desire for a breather, but they reminded him that "there is no evidence that Russia plans to forget about its economic offensive until next year."[37]

The Organization for Trade Cooperation standoff became enmeshed in mounting protectionist pressure on issues affecting allies that confounded Eisenhower's capitalist peace campaign. In 1955, adhering to a Tariff Commission recommendation, he raised tariffs on bicycles from England. This alarmed free traders. British prime minister Anthony Eden warned that bicycles were "a crucial test of the whole idea of 'trade not aid'" because unlike other escape clause actions, such as on watches, there were no defense considerations. The possibility of stimulating "adverse political and psychological effects among our Allies" is "far out of proportion to the grievances claimed by the United States industry," added Dulles. Secretary of Agriculture Ezra Benson lamented that Britain and West Germany, which had also developed a bicycle niche market in the United States, could respond by retaliating against American farm exports. The action undermined "the fabric of our political and security alliance," concluded Benson.[38] The Europeans wondered whether American leaders could contain protectionists at home; it appeared that free-trade rhetoric was just that, words. With the American bicycle industry deteriorating, a perplexed Eisenhower did not see how he could avoid tariffs. The very point that there were "no security interests involved" rendered his decision just a minor tariff hike—with only economic consequences—that would not destroy the Western alliance.[39]

London faced more trouble. Wielding the Buy American Act, the Pentagon rejected a British bid to export heavy generating equipment to the United States even though the American bidder came in at a much higher cost. The Randall report had advised exemptions for foreigners in some cases, but Eisenhower retained the act, though he lowered the price differential of 25 percent to 6–10 percent (the British actually bid below 6 percent). Grumbling about retaliation, London did not buy his lame argument about concerns for unemployment. Quite simply, renewed Tariff Commission cases to raise duties on watches and zinc, the failure of the OTC, and the bicycle and Buy American cases, as well as retention of the peril point and escape clauses, put in doubt the continued implementation of free-trade internationalism on America's part.[40]

Eisenhower's protectionist headaches persisted as the oil industry started lobbying for restrictions after foreign oil imports had skyrocketed (since 1951) to the point of glutting the market. Imports rose from 6 percent of overall production in 1951 to over 19 percent five years later. The upward trend indicated that the country had developed a dangerous dependency on foreign supplies that threatened its national security. Sharing this fear, Eisenhower was open to voluntary export quotas from Venezuela, Mexico, and Middle Eastern nations, to the delight of powerful coal- and oil-state politicians, but the State Department warned that protectionism raised fuel costs, quotas were hard to administer, and these nations would be hurt. But when figures for 1957 showed imports climbing and the Office of Defense Mobilization notified him of the threat to security, Eisenhower invoked the national security amendment under the RTAA that allowed an escape from trade agreements. He acquiesced to a regime of voluntary quotas that artificially preserved the market positions of domestic producers. By 1959, voluntarism was so ineffective that, bowing to political pressure, the administration imposed mandatory quotas.[41]

To be sure, the administration labored on its trade not aid strategy. Dulles leaned increasingly toward more aid because trade policies came up short in the face of protectionism. Due to the Soviet economic offensive, the Mutual Security Act grew enormously. Defense was the biggest item, but development assistance, technical cooperation, and other programs were infused with hundreds of millions of dollars, adding to more Export-Import and World Bank loans for the global South. Eisenhower's trade not aid program had given way to trade and aid by 1957. Despite asking for increases in development assistance, which Congress refused, he turned to the RTAA more than ever as a legislative priority.[42]

As protectionist forces mustered, Eisenhower sought a five-year extension and more tariff-cutting authority for the RTAA of 1958, as well as acceptance of the OTC, because of a new dimension in foreign policy that compelled trade liberalization: the European Economic Community (EEC or Common Market). This six-nation, 165-million-people trade bloc had emerged from the Marshall Plan. As Eisenhower told French premier Guy Mollet, integration treaties, including the creation of an atomic community, obliged the United States to bargain down tariffs to ensure that the EEC's common external tariff wall remained low. A revitalized RTAA assured that, through the GATT and, hopefully, the OTC, Europe would not discriminate against nations beyond the common external tariff.[43] The 1957 launch of the Sputnik satellite, highlighting a Soviet technological offensive alongside the economic one, made this plan perhaps an easier sell than before because national security policy was at stake. At the opening of NATO meetings in Paris in December 1957, peace was on Eisenhower's mind, a peace in which "mankind can produce freely, trade freely, travel freely, think freely, pray freely."[44]

Democrats and Republican moderates followed his lead. In 1956, the House Ways and Means Committee established a joint subcommittee to study the tariff's impact on foreign and domestic economic policies. It recommended lowering trade barriers, joining the Organization for Trade Cooperation, easing East-West trade restrictions, and addressing the Soviet threat in the developing world. The goals were already embedded in the capitalist peace model; as the subcommittee reported, "If freer trade strengthens the non-Soviet world as it should, the likelihood of war will be reduced." But Senator Ralph Flanders, a Republican internationalist, saw a risk to the capitalist peace position because defense industries were in danger of bankruptcy by foreign competition.[45] Heading into the RTAA campaign, skepticism toward and fervor about free trade competed as well in Congress.

The free traders did not sit by idly. The US Council of the International Chamber of Commerce enlisted dozens of private sector groups to form "Americans for the OTC," which joined with the Department of State for ratification of the body. The allied National Foreign Trade Council, under Charles Taft, sloughed off its earlier concerns about OTC statism and blasted away at Congress for the delay in ratification, wondering how, given the "precarious state of our foreign relations," there could still be opposition to it. The Sunday *New York Times* headlined that the "O.T.C. May Decide U.S. Fate Abroad."[46] Nonetheless, Congress refused even to talk about participation, though the new EEC intensified the need for oversight over a changed trading world, and the GATT contracting parties, in November 1957, demanded approval of the OTC. The Democratic majority in both the House and Senate argued that until GOP approval was clear—and it was not—they would not budge on the OTC. In December, a Subcommittee on Foreign Trade Policy, under Congressman Hale Boggs, investigated the nation's tariff laws and recommended more aid and more trade. When just a handful of dissenting industries appeared at ten days of hearings, the Boggs Committee concluded that trade liberalization and the OTC made sense in terms of the capitalist peace because they prevented disputes that resulted in disunity, impoverishment, and penetration by extreme ideologies. The alphabet of trade forums—the RTAA, the GATT, and the OTC—were essential to the livelihoods of the entire Free World. The Boggs Committee ended up with one big idea to back up this agenda, calling for a ten-year renewal of basic trade law.[47]

The president asked for half of that. While he appreciated Boggs's efforts, he compromised with protectionists before sending his bill to Congress. Allies there predicted the biggest battle over the Reciprocal Trade Agreements Act in its quarter century. Opponents were angry that Eisenhower had approved only four of fifteen Tariff Commission recommendations to invoke the escape clause or raise duties, demanding presidential tariff hikes of up to 50 percent in escape clause cases. Eisenhower agreed and also conceded on a proposal for automatic resort to the escape clause when peril point investigations found tariffs insufficient to protect an industry. He and Dulles calculated that these concessions would facilitate a five-year renewal of the RTAA, with 25 percent tariff-cut authority, and then earn a victory on the Organization for Trade Cooperation. But free traders also thought he had caved to protectionism. Will Clayton angrily wrote Adlai Stevenson, care of Dulles, that "the prostitution of national policy to serve the selfish interests of these minorities" had to end.[48] Dulles ordered another study of the Soviet economic offensive, which had been greatly augmented by loans and trade agreements, because he feared that Moscow's agenda would be even more effective if Congress weakened free-trade internationalism.[49]

Eisenhower also raised the alarms, but he did so by gently prodding the protectionists with capitalist peace missives. When a reporter for the *Chicago Daily News* asked whether he had packed the Tariff Commission with anti–free traders, he countered that he had not appointed any "high protectionist" to that body but was merely trying to be "more flexible" in meeting the complaints of those who sought import protection.[50] In the State of the Union address in January 1958, he cast the RTAA as a means to "wage total peace" in the Cold War, chiding protectionists with President William McKinley's admonition over a half century earlier that America's place on the global stage made isolationism impossible, that the "period of exclusiveness is past."[51] A few weeks later, lauding the administration's accomplishments at a breakfast with the Republican National Committee, he reminded his party that "even the most elaborate military buildup may well prove but an expensive illusion of security" without liberal trade agreements.[52] Eisenhower put the Cold War front and center. He was willing to extend the olive branch to protectionists but demonstrated his backbone when it came to national security.

When he sent the Reciprocal Trade Agreements Act to Capitol Hill on January 30, he led off with the argument that freer trade meant domestic growth but then turned to foreign policy. The bill was crucial "to our national security and for our entire foreign policy," especially in meeting the economic challenge issued by "the Communist imperialists." The Soviets sought to detach free world nations, one by one, from the Western alliance and "swing them into the orbit of Communist influence." Washington must recognize Moscow's capacity both to export and import as means to "exploit trade difficulties of the free world" and divide those nations. The issue was whether democracy and the "system of free competitive enterprise for which we stand will meet successfully in the international economic arena the challenge hurled by the Soviet leaders."[53]

Democrats reported trouble with the trade bill by the end of the Ways and Means hearings in late March due to an emerging recession, but Eisenhower pushed forward with his capitalist peace argument. Freer trade was, simply, "one of the iron imperatives of security and peace."[54] The president also hammered away within his own party with the internationalist rejoinder to the Soviet economic offensive. He told the Republican Women's National Conference, for example, that the Soviets could be countered in the developing world by reducing tariffs and quotas to help developing nations build up diversified economies, fueled by American exports from farms and factories. This would also curb revolutionary frustrations and encourage millions to acquire a stake in the capitalist way of life, with a flourishing peace as a result.[55] Joining almost every cabinet member, along with several top legislators, officials, and business activists, at a Washington, DC, conference on international trade policy on March 27, he warned that it was "the Communist system that the Kremlin is determined to export. It is the system of economic freedom that the Kremlin is determined to destroy." Only by trade growth among Free World nations could freedom win out. That is, "to live they must trade. It is simple as that."[56] Cordell Hull could not have said it better.

The administration turned to a massive lobbying initiative on the basis that the Cold War had transformed. The Committee for a National Trade Policy mobilized funding, explaining that the "declaration of economic war upon us by the Communists" was a crisis that protectionists abetted. "We declare war upon you—excuse me for using such an expression—in the peaceful field of trade," Khrushchev had declared. "The threat to the United States is not the ICBM, but in the field of peaceful production. We declare a war we will win over the United States."[57] To be sure, Eisenhower told the Soviets that he welcomed "peaceful co-operation" between the superpowers; he approved of "trade that carries no political or warlike implications."[58] He was also confident that while the "Sino-Soviet economic offensive" was serious, it "was perfectly capable of being successfully countered if the combined strengths of free government and free enterprise were fully applied to the achievement of this objective" through, among other initiatives, trade expansion.[59] Echoed Prime Minister Harold MacMillan, more trade would prove Karl Marx wrong and show that the West could avoid poverty and slumps. Not only that, but Vice President Nixon warned that by emasculating aid, information, and reciprocal trade agreements, "the billions we spend for missiles and submarines and aircraft will be going right down a rat hole."[60] Despite "all of the current hysteria about missiles," said Nixon, the markets of Asia, Latin America, and Africa were the "real targets of the Soviets."[61]

Free-trade advocates warmed to this capitalist peace/security message in hundreds of venues, in tune with Eisenhower's appeal to bolster the free-enterprise system and a foreign policy backed by freer trade. Business leaders at home and abroad recognized that the 1958 bill came amidst conditions in the world that differed from the times of previous renewals. The growing propaganda power of the Soviet bloc, the potential strength of the Common Market, and greater dependence on trade in the domestic economy at large had been transformative in forging an interdependence among nations and capitalists alike. Congressman Emanuel Celler of New York noted that the flight time between Moscow and the American Midwest was just nine hours by the polar route. This showed "not only the narrowing of the world as we knew it only some short twenty-five years ago but stresses the interdependence of all nations. No man, no country, can live as an island unto himself, or itself."[62]

Protectionists scoffed at and reversed the foreign policy arguments. Richard Simpson questioned whether the common worker should shoulder the burden of defense by losing his or her job to import competition, even from nations that did not have a trade agreement with the United States. They also played the national security gambit on oil and other essential goods that supposedly were under duress from imports. Strackbein's Nationwide Committee, and the dozens of sons and daughters of liberty from all the states who populated the American Coalition of Patriotic Societies, contested each rationale behind the legislation. Speaker Rayburn grew fearful of the bill's prospects because Ways and Means approved of provisions to allow Congress to override presidential decisions if counter to Tariff Commission recommendations, lengthened the period for the commission's peril point investigations, and decreased the time for escape clause reviews. Simpson then tried to gut the entire bill on the House floor by proposing a two-year extension with no tariff-cutting authority and more power for the Tariff Commission, all of which angered Eisenhower. The Simpson amendment was defeated, but not by a large margin. The full House then approved the RTAA bill even as Daniel Reed's motion to recommit the entire bill and strengthen the national security amendment made headway before the vote. The president was relieved once the legislation exited the House.[63]

But Senate hostility was even stronger. Eisenhower faced troublemakers in his own party, such as the Republican minority leader, California's William Knowland. Another prominent Republican, Styles Bridges of New Hampshire, insisted on just a three-year extension. Sure enough, amendments reduced both the tariff-cutting authority and period of the extension, while the Finance Committee added to the House's new national security clause by requiring the president to raise duties on imports if they threatened American defenses. Moderate Republican Ralph Flanders would head a nine-member commission to investigate the RTAA program's aims and report to Congress by June 30, 1960. The most bothersome amendment, though, came from conservative Democrats Strom Thurmond and Robert Kerr and compelled the president to accept a Tariff Commission ruling or face a congressional override. The Oklahoman Kerr guarded the oil industry, while Thurmond, a southerner, protected textile producers. Both also cherished the constitutional prerogatives of Congress over trade, asking why the executive branch disregarded the Tariff Commission. To counter the Kerr-Thurmond amendment, Eisenhower offered to shorten the RTAA extension to three years if the Senate voted it down, and Majority Leader Johnson orchestrated the deal. Other senators backed the RTAA to fund mutual security appropriations or were swayed to the capitalist peace as Marines went ashore in Iraq, Jordan, and Lebanon as part of the Eisenhower Doctrine to stop communism in the Middle East.[64]

After House-Senate conferees trimmed the RTAA's duration to four years and its authority to reduce tariffs by 20 percent, rejected the Flanders committee, and accepted the congressional override amendment, the RTAA went through. Republican support was actually higher than in the previous renewal in 1955, likely because of bipartisan agreement on amendments and the appeal to foreign policy objectives. After eight months of deliberation in Congress, the president signed the renewal on August 20, 1958, proclaiming that the United States had stood by its vow to protect its allies by free trade.[65]

Larger foreign policy motivations aside, however, Eisenhower's enthusiasm disguised the reality that his compromises essentially froze tariff rates for four years, which meant the United States could not offer deep tariff concessions to the Common Market or buy more imports from the global South. The Committee for a National Trade Policy proclaimed this RTAA "the most highly protectionist measure ever passed by Congress in all the Reciprocal Trade renewals since 1934."[66] The real agents of change were located in the developing world, Western Europe, and Moscow. Recent anti-American demonstrations in Lebanon, North Africa, Burma, Indonesia, Japan, and throughout South America showed the United States to be falling short in meeting the aspirations for better and higher living standards. The European Economic Community also grabbed headlines as a dynamic entity; Latin Americans followed the European integrationist model with their own ideas for common markets. The United States seemed to be standing pat, talking about interdependence but leaving others to set the agenda. Considering the rejection, again, of the Organization for Trade Cooperation, the Reciprocal Trade Agreements Act of 1958 was simply inadequate for its times.[67]

The failure to meet the rising hopes of the developing world spoke directly to the dangers implicit in the Soviet economic offensive. The GATT, for starters, glaringly ignored the poor nations. A panel led by Harvard's Gottfried Haberler concluded, in November 1958, that declining prices for export commodities and rising prices for manufacturers from the rich nations—unfavorable "terms of trade"—were the cardinal problem. Even Haberler, though, turned to traditional arguments about boosting imports from the developing nations by growing demand in the advanced industrial North rather than by overhauling the system through preferential trade treatment to favor producers and merchants in the global South. A huge split on trade was imminent; the Cold War would be won or lost in undeveloped areas. Free traders recognized this reality, at least in principle, but they could not address it until fresh policies aligned with expectations.[68]

As the year ended, there was mounting unease in foreign trade policy circles about problems and prospects facing the United States. The problems had to be taken up by the GATT, itself still unwieldy because it lacked a continuing organization and conducted business through a single annual session of the contracting parties. Washington faced tough prospects, particularly because mounting protectionism vitiated bold foreign economic policies. The Organization for Trade Cooperation could be tried again but had no urgency in Congress. Slow growth rates of primary commodity exports and fluctuating prices in the South; the advent of the Common Market, European Free Trade Area, and Latin American preferential blocs; and the decline in US exports and overall world trade had to be addressed. Behind all of these "family" issues, wrote Sidney Swensrud of the Committee for a National Trade Policy in December 1958, was the "massive Soviet economic offensive" that exposed the numerous possibilities that prospects for "trade warfare among the free nations are more real than they have been for many years."[69] At least the trade agreements program, however diminished, could be applied at a fifth round of the GATT, in Geneva. The obstacles to the capitalist peace, however, were clear as America headed into a new decade of change, challenges, and Cold War.

7

Competition, 1959–1963

The Cold War reached its most dangerous point in 1962 when the United States and the Soviet Union engaged in a nuclear standoff over Cuba. A year before, a crisis over control of Berlin ended with the communists building a wall to prevent citizens from fleeing to the West. Nikita Khrushchev sought to test the young president, John F. Kennedy, and heightened tensions as a result. Thankfully, a period of superpower détente by the mid-1960s followed these flare-ups, but America's commitment in Vietnam showed that the Cold War was in full swing. Anti-communism remained the context for trade policy, but ironically, capitalist peace strategy seemed secondary to tussles with friends. In this new era, competitive threats emerged from within the Free World alliance that rivaled those from outside of it.

The advent of the European Economic Community posed a direct challenge to American trade policy. These six nations privileged their internal trade over that of outsiders and wielded considerable power as a bloc of exporters to eat into global markets. Export competition and discriminatory protectionism also exacerbated a looming threat: a growing US balance-of-payments deficit. At the moment, trade actually did not cause this international payments shortfall—a higher outflow of spending abroad than the United States took in. The country ran a healthy trade surplus (more exports over imports) of $3.3 billion in 1958. Rather, $2.6 billion in foreign aid programs, overseas military spending of $3.4 billion, and private investment of $2.8 billion explained the payments gap, and all three were trending higher. All three, though, could be ameliorated by encouraging other nations to accept more American exports, and they would lean in that direction only if the United States reciprocated with trade liberalization on a grand scale that recognized the new economic power alignment created by the Common Market.

Capitalist Peace. Thomas W. Zeiler, Oxford University Press. © Oxford University Press 2022.
DOI: 10.1093/oso/9780197621363.003.0008

Gold reflected the payments deficit crisis. Allies had absorbed American spending by holding dollars in reserve, but they cashed those in for bullion at ever-higher rates because the last exchange controls from the early postwar period had been lifted by the late 1950s. (At the time, the dollar was tied to the price of gold.) They could then convert the gold into their own currencies, effecting a currency conversion that was a goal of the Bretton Woods monetary system and an indication of capitalism's return to normalcy and European economic health with it. The demand for gold—the basis of confidence in the dollar—caused an outflow of US stocks of $2.3 billion. This "gold drain" might prompt disquieting adjustments in foreign relations. Aid and military outlays, and political leverage, would decline as Washington reined in spending to stem the depletion of gold. Eisenhower devised remedies, trying to shift more of the defense and development burden to Europe by approaching the deficit as an issue in the Atlantic Community partnership. That effort fell flat. Allies counted on Washington to continue to foot the bill and, in truth, American hegemony depended on this sacrifice. Yet the payments deficit showed that the era of the United States' outright predominance was ending; the intensifying financial pressure directly related to claims on Washington's leadership of the Free World.[1]

Thus, the payments crisis affected the Cold War. Moscow's obsession with technology, development, and trade, said Secretary of State Christian Herter, provided a competitive threat by the "single starkly monolithic way of communism." Meanwhile, the United States enjoyed the good life of prosperity in suburbia, believing that the defensive curtain of nuclear security and traditional trade and aid networks were sufficient to protect the Free World.[2] But allies were draining American coffers, thereby testing the capitalist peace effort. Eisenhower believed that growing world trade through the GATT and easing trade controls would expand American exports, help pay down the deficit, and allow the United States to meet challenges abroad. These included those close to home from a revolutionary Fidel Castro in Cuba as well as containment of communist power in the global South and Europe, especially in Berlin. The Russians, though, allocated a far larger percentage of their total output to poor nations than the United States, and these countries noticed. Moscow committed to winning the Cold War by buying influence and security—whatever deficits the Soviets ran were irrelevant in a state-trading country.[3]

Even East-West trade had to be reconsidered in light of the deficit because allies sought to ease export controls on the communist nations. In 1959, the British sought special consideration for Poland and Yugoslavia through the GATT, although whether either could comply with the obligation for reciprocity was in question. The administration predicted that expanding trade with the communist bloc, which had fallen off in the past few years, would amount to a meager $150 million gain in exports if controls were totally removed. Still, foreign policy advisors pushed for liberalization to prevent the Soviet bloc from playing NATO allies off one another as they clamored for markets. Some saw East-West trade as a means of prying apart the Warsaw Pact. Military leaders disagreed. They believed that Moscow saw only a propaganda purpose in trade deals while China sought to boost its undeveloped military potential through them. The Department of Commerce, which licensed products in East-West trade, brandished the capitalist peace concept as a weapon, claiming that the Berlin crisis made peaceful trade toward the bloc incompatible with American foreign policy.[4] Cold Warriors warned against sending more strategic commodities to the communist bloc because state monopolies still compelled capitalists to violate GATT non-discrimination and veer from market pricing. Principles were at stake. The "whole structure of spiritual and moral values on which Western civilization is based," wrote Governor Nelson Rockefeller of New York, was at risk by trade with the communists. Eisenhower shelved the issue in September 1960, leaving it for the next administration.[5]

However, he could not postpone dealing with competitive friends, however, who were the very cause of the payment deficit. As Eisenhower said, the "soundness of the dollar is as important to the world and to us as any other factor I can think of" because "much of world stability and world peace hangs" on a confidence in the dollar and gold.[6] Protectionism ran counter to interdependence, a term he used frequently. That interdependence was now reality, but it also worsened the deficit and pressured him to raise tariffs for revenue to offset outlays abroad. Such was the case with higher duties on imports of British turbines, which provoked an outcry by this close ally. An anchor of the Free World's Pacific defense perimeter, Australia, also railed against American lead and zinc quotas, while Canada chafed at restrictions on agricultural exports to the United States, and Japan, a democratic outpost in East Asia, faced increasing protectionism to its exports.[7]

The same was true, with equally daunting prospects, in the developing world. The United States was the major trade partner of many nations of the global South. Most depended on one or two commodities—Chilean copper, Indonesian rubber, Bolivian tin, Brazilian coffee, Venezuelan oil, and Mexican and Peruvian lead and zinc—for export to the United States. Denied that market, they would suffer economic and political instability, thus making their allegiance in the Cold War questionable. Import quotas had, for example, caused violent anti-American protests in Venezuela and Peru and prompted sharp criticism in Mexico. The head of the Central Intelligence Agency, Allen Dulles, believed that "the most serious challenge that this country has ever faced in times of peace" came from Soviet economic programs in the global South. That contest required a counter-offensive of expanded and liberalized trade that put private sector capital, technology, and experience to work in foreign policy.[8] Free-trade policy could also point trade blocs in Latin America outward to prevent regional self-sufficiency damaging to the US payments balance.[9]

The need to think harder about the developing world was clear. After Vice President Nixon encountered riots in Venezuela in 1958, the president's brother, Milton, an expert on Latin America, added "a note of urgency" that Washington re-examine relations with a region in demographic ferment.[10] Poor countries chafed at the capitalist system, some turning to bilateral deals with communists as protectionism rose in the West. George Meany of the AFL-CIO, the American envoy to the UN General Assembly, suggested more political rights for workers to offset the Soviets' appeal. Will Clayton preferred commercial integration as a remedy to Free World fissures. A sure way to stop communism, "an economic federation of the free world, with 1 ¾ billion people" producing at comparative advantage and free of trade restrictions would mimic the forty-eight states of the United States, he explained.[11] Such a federation might seem to idealistically harness the capitalist peace paradigm to the new era of competition, but Cold War realism shaped his view, for if the wealth gap between North and South widened through trade inequity, then Khrushchev "will bury us as he has boasted," Clayton reckoned.[12]

This fear led Congress and the administration to place aid and trade in more multilateral and regional contexts. Cold War spending would continue, of course, but the payments deficit altered Washington's capacity to pay so there must be no backsliding toward protectionism. To be sure, the Common Market must meet its responsibilities to share the burdens of the Free World, too. When gold reserves dropped by $2 billion in 1958 and another $1 billion in the first three quarters of 1959, the effect was felt across the government. Partly political in terms of leverage, partly psychological as a bellwether of fiscal responsibility and national strength, gold affected the entire foreign policy program throughout the free and uncommitted worlds.[13]

The competition among friends that so affected the integrity of the dollar motivated the Eisenhower administration to increase the trade surplus. That excess surged in 1957 to $6 billion due to sales prompted by the Suez Crisis of late 1956. But recovery from the recession in 1959 raised imports to the point that the surplus fell to just $835 million, though it boomed again in 1960. Still, the gold drain persisted, prompting Eisenhower to turn to a concerted export expansion program as a remedy. Such an effort had long existed; promotion of commercial interests was a major function of consulates before World War II. For the past decade, however, these activities were downgraded, as meeting demand at home took precedence. The payments crisis fueled an all-encompassing export effort that continued into the next decades. On March 17, 1960, Eisenhower asked Congress for millions of dollars to launch a massive campaign to boost sales abroad. It was time for the United States to "sizzle or fizzle" in export growth, explained a Department of Commerce official.[14] Five business leaders ran a National Export Expansion Committee under the Department of Commerce, while some thirty-three regional committees and several states appointed advisory groups to educate the public. More trade fairs and consular missions, additional credits and export insurance, improved transportation facilities, small-business engagement—and, of course, reducing trade barriers—targeted what the Export Expansion Committee termed "exportunities" for business abroad.[15]

The continuing battle against protectionism went hand in hand with the export drive. In the election year of 1960, protectionists hoped to wring concessions from those on the stump. Even a free trader like Congressman Hale Boggs of Louisiana could turn around and rail against a Tariff Commission decision not to recommend duties on imported shrimp. When Senator Kenneth Keating proposed legislation to equalize the labor cost differential between "sweatshop" nations and advanced countries with new tariffs, the administration reacted in horror. Clarence Randall warned that if this throwback to Hawley-Smoot passed, all international trade would cease. He was disturbed, however, that several free-trade internationalists, such as Prescott Bush of Connecticut, had signed on to the measure even when faced with Eisenhower's promise to veto it—though it never reached his desk.[16]

Eisenhower also refreshed the idea of partnership with Europe, predicating the Atlantic Community on freer trade and defense burden-sharing with NATO allies to solve the payments crisis. Thus, part of his endorsement of the Common Market and Free Trade Association rested on raising Western Europe's aid and military spending. He also endorsed the twenty-nation Organization for Economic Co-operation and Development (OECD), which enlarged the Marshall Plan–era Organization for European Economic Cooperation. Sending the OECD to Congress for ratification, Eisenhower saw it as a consultative body to channel aid from the North to the global South and as another initiative to promote liberalization with Atlantic partners. Maintaining Western unity in trade in the face of protectionist headwinds, the ultimate objective of the capitalist peace in the Cold War, would also be pursued in a new round of international tariff negotiations. Stimulated by GATT director Eric Wyndham-White's "Trade Expansion Program," the GATT addressed the new Europe and, perhaps, aspirations of the global South.[17]

The United States had long backed economic integration, not shying away from combining the Free Trade Association and the EEC into a conglomerate even if they temporarily discriminated against American exports. The British sought fusion to get access to the Common Market, but France, led by the theatrical continentalist Charles de Gaulle, viewed London as a Trojan Horse for US interests in Europe. Washington feared Gaullist antagonism might prompt a trade war, dividing NATO. Eisenhower also worried about the height of the EEC's planned external tariff on outsiders and duty levels of the Free Trade Area countries that maintained their own national tariffs. Integration as a tool of containment was no solace if protectionism mounted against American goods and investments. Regardless, European integration augured an assertive trade policy. The Inner Six (the founding nations of the EEC) and the Outer Seven (the nations of the European Free Trade Association) embodied the "beginnings of a movement which will force all non-Communist industrial nations to join," noted Will Clayton, who dreamed that Canada and America would link to them, and then merge the British Commonwealth, GATT, the OECD, and outliers like Spain into a "Free World Common Market," a "giant step" toward winning the Cold War.[18]

Heading for a Western summit meeting in early 1960 in Paris, Eisenhower determined to encourage integration, burden-sharing on defense and aid, and trade expansion to dent the payments deficit. Overall, business cycles rather than trade competition hurt exports though discrimination remained in Japan and Europe. While traditionally protectionist Japanese interests resisted liberalization, the prospects were better in Europe as long as regional tariffs stayed low and non-discriminatory.[19] But in the end, Eisenhower bequeathed to John F. Kennedy a payments crisis that imperiled the entire capitalist peace agenda.

Alarmed by the balance of payments, Senator Kennedy endorsed a fresh look at trade policy, as Eisenhower had, for foreign policy reasons. Campaigning in 1960, he linked free trade to correcting the deficit, even though this position could spark voter anger. But he had an idea to quell dissent while aiding works. Representing Massachusetts textiles, fishing, and other industries affected by imports, Kennedy had a moderate record of protectionism. Yet, while he backed the peril point provision, he stressed the idea of adjustment assistance, or job retraining and other vocational help for workers displaced by imports. He urged caution on Tariff Commission rulings because protectionism generally hurt allies and undermined national security. His opponent, Richard Nixon, took the same capitalist peace line but, unlike the Republican, the liberal Kennedy scared business. Thus, he advocated balancing the international payments account by arguing that trade restrictions generally must fall. The GOP admitted that "the Democratic platform has a more liberal 'free trade' outlook" than the Republican one.[20]

In the transition between administrations, the president-elect commissioned a task force to look into solving the payments crisis. The deficit was "not a joke," he told a banker; it demanded "serious consideration" if the United States were to remain the leader of the Free World. His conservative father also needled him about the gold crisis, maintaining that a sound dollar was fundamental to American values. Kennedy did not opt for the viable option of reforming the international monetary order because that required devaluing the dollar, perhaps toppling the currency from its dominant position. The task force advocated instead more burden-sharing in NATO, discouraging capital outflows, and interest rate manipulation to encourage investment at home. And, by magnifying free-trade internationalism, the new administration turned to an even more dynamic approach to the deficit. A Task Force on Foreign Economic Policy, chaired by avowed free-trade integrationist George Ball, nicknamed "Mr. Europe," sought to marshal "political, social, cultural, and economic" resources in the service of "the security, freedom, and prosperity of the United States within a strong Free World."[21] An open, competitive, and growing global capitalist economy was essential to this vision, one that Kennedy's predecessors had held but that now seemed stale and feeble. Ball had his eye on Europe. Washington had lost the initiative in trade liberalization, with a bankrupt Reciprocal Trade Agreements Act so "encrusted with restrictive devices in repeated legislative struggles" that it could not meet the challenge from European blocs. As "only the strongest of the strong," the United States must persuade other "industrial giants" to reassert the capitalist peace in the face of protectionism through vigorous and creative free-trade internationalist policies. A sweeping transformation was in order. The new president certainly embraced a reinvigorated approach to trade.[22]

Kennedy tapped Ball as under secretary of state for economic affairs to keep the administration trained on the capitalist peace strategy. He viewed Ball as his trade guru, like Randall, Clayton, and Hull had been for his predecessors. Ball recommended a brand new RTAA to prevent the dissolution of the Atlantic community into discriminatory trade blocs and lure the EEC to accept Britain into its ranks. He also advocated easing East-West trade controls, ending preferential trade blocs (such as the EEC-African regime), and maximizing access for the developing nations into the markets of advanced countries, but only under the most-favored-nation principle. These were fairly traditional aims that Eisenhower had voiced, but Kennedy was an activist at least in addressing the global South, as his most dynamic initiatives like the Peace Corps and Alliance for Progress demonstrated. When it came to Europe, Kennedy welcomed Ball's boldness because his foreign policy agenda was at risk without a solution to the payments deficit. Thus, he bolstered Eisenhower's export expansion program, establishing at the end of his first year, "E" (Export) awards as incentives for Americans to sell more abroad. "If we're not able to export substantially more than we import," he warned, then "we're going to either cut all assistance to countries abroad or draw our troops home."[23] Protectionism had "disastrous effects to the dollar" abroad; nothing less than national security was at stake.[24]

His first test of protectionist strength arose when he sent the Organization for Economic Cooperation and Development treaty to the Senate for ratification, in March 1961. It had a Code of Liberalization attached to it that Eisenhower had downplayed to sneak in a new administrative trade structure. Kennedy prudently detached the code entirely from the treaty after congressional protectionists protested it as unconstitutional and an underhanded attempt to revisit the ITO and OTC and bypass Congress. Ball assured the legislators that the OECD had no role in tariff negotiations. Instead, it was purely an economic coordinating body for the United Nations and NATO, facilitating development plans and perhaps mediating between the European Six and Seven. The OECD could also help with the payments deficit, added Treasury Secretary Douglas Dillon, by countering the Soviet economic offensive with non-American aid. The removal of the trade code smoothed the way for ratification of the OECD. Anyway, Kennedy had a grander strategy in mind for trade expansion.[25]

In fact, renovation of the RTAA became the top legislative priority of the administration in 1962. Due to his weak leverage in Congress, as well as protectionist strength, the president gave the impression of limiting Ball's outright free-trade influence by running the trade bill from a special White House task force under a Republican banker, Howard Petersen. An internationalist free trader, Petersen nonetheless had a reputation for fairness. Having spent a half decade in the nation's capital under Dulles's supervision, he accepted the task force position due to the potential for dynamism in trade policy. Like Ball, he sought sweeping authority for the president to cut tariffs over at least a five-year period. Petersen agreed, however, that certain provisions of trade law, such as the peril point, must remain. Ball was more radical, seeking to junk these protectionist measures as a capitalist peace purist. The politically cunning Petersen and Kennedy prevailed.[26]

Compromise allowed the administration to attack the core problem for the American trade agenda: the Common Market's unified external tariff. The GATT permitted customs unions, despite their inherent discriminatory nature, if their external tariff was not higher than individual national duties. The imperative was to keep the EEC's tariff level as low as possible because the Six were such a huge potential export market for the United States. In September 1960, at the initial stages of the Dillon Round of the General Agreement on Tariffs and Trade, named in the Treasury Secretary's honor, the Americans zeroed in on the external tariff. The Six determined to defend the common market, however; they threw down the gauntlet, demanding strict reciprocity for any concessions, meaning high US tariffs must fall. Finding a balance between trade expansion and softening the blow from rising imports was the challenge, but without a deal, the North would turn to protectionism and the resentful South might bolt from the Free World. Japan straddled both sides of the issue but was offended by

European and American protectionism. Washington needed hard concessions on the EEC external tariff and the Free Trade Association's individual duties at the Dillon Round. Limiting market disruption for political reasons was critical, but trade expansion for foreign policy reasons was paramount.[27]

At the two-year GATT Dillon Round, however, the Europeans showed up the Americans. The European Economic Community offered general and steep "linear" 20 percent tariff cuts, that is, cuts across their entire sector of industrial goods, but the United States offered only 5 percent reductions a year on select items. The Six would also not consider any cuts on farm imports until their Common Agricultural Policy (CAP) was fully formulated, a delay that showed their capability to resist American demands for more market access in the sector. In short, Washington was stuck at this fifth round of GATT negotiations. Unless Brussels sacrificed, the common external tariff would not drop to the lowest possible level, Secretary of State Christian Herter warned Eisenhower during his transition out of office in late 1960.[28]

American trade options, in short, were idled. Washington had spent some $80 billion dollars since 1948 on European recovery and productivity. Now France, West Germany, and Belgium, which guarded the EEC's tariff ramparts, needed to give back by, among other policies, allowing US food exports into Europe at a robust rate. If not, the United States might retreat from commitments abroad, mimicking the doomed London Economic Conference when Franklin Roosevelt had unilaterally devalued the dollar. If something similar happened again, NATO could blow apart, downgrading the Cold War internationalist and security apparatus constructed to effect the capitalist peace. All sides at the Dillon Round needed to refrain from autarchic trade policies. But Eisenhower's staff predicted that the talks would be the toughest ever because of entrenched European agricultural protectionism and the inadequate authority of the RTAA to bargain down the Six's external tariff, as well as the peril point procedure, which could prevent offers to match the Common Market. The requirement of negotiating product-by-product, rather than by the Common Market's across-the-board authorization, also handcuffed meaningful American offers.[29] Kennedy needed some creative solutions.

In his first year, he dealt with the protectionist devils at home to clear the way for a bold response to Europe on tariffs by skillfully negotiating political side deals with resistant and powerful legislators. Kennedy accepted some escape clause recommendations from the Tariff Commission, for example, imposing more restrictions on carpets and glass imports from Belgium. This not only provoked retaliation from an ally but complicated his foreign policy. The restrictions on Belgian goods made it harder on the president to broker the humiliating Belgian withdrawal from the Congo and to rally European support for his stubborn stance on Berlin, especially after the Berlin Wall was erected in August 1961. Kennedy, though, looked to the larger picture of trade liberalization with a new trade bill and thus exchanged protectionism for votes in Congress. Limits on cotton textiles from Asia, furthermore, quelled protests from powerful textile-state legislators. That one worried Kennedy and Ball because a fee on imports peeved the Japanese, who had so protested American security policies that Eisenhower had canceled his state visit to Tokyo just fifteen months earlier. Kennedy had repaired the damage by assuring Prime Minister Hayato Ikeda that he fully understood Japan's need to trade to survive. He had to quell a rebellion from textile protectionists, however. Furthermore, a request (denied) to Canada to limit its lumber exports followed on the heels of Kennedy's promise to look into a Tariff Commission investigation of foreign lumber sales. He also opted for caps on oil imports, striking a deal with Robert Kerr of Oklahoma that yielded this influential senator's help in corralling votes for the upcoming trade legislation.[30] Kennedy made short-term protectionist deals to revolutionize the RTAA and save the capitalist peace over the long run.

But he could not save the Dillon Round, which ended just before the RTAA of 1958 had expired in June 1962 by yielding tariff cuts of only 4 percent on average. Kennedy tried to ameliorate the situation by waiving restrictions on key import-sensitive items like steel products, tableware, and fabrics, but to no avail. The EEC refused to unbind, or roll back, its tariff rates on crops, which affected a third of America's total exports to Europe. The Department of Agriculture complained, as exports of wheat and corn would stagnate. State Department negotiators advised tossing in the towel and looking toward new tariff-reduction authority to take to the next round of the General Agreement on Tariffs and Trade. If not, the trade forum itself might fold. Legislators grew so irate over the Dillon Round that they demanded a special trade negotiator to operate out of the White House rather than from the free-trading State Department, a negotiator more amenable to domestic interests. The president gave the negotiations one last gasp, permitting concessions on an additional $76 million of non-sensitive imports. The Six brushed him off again, withdrawing dozens of offers from the table in response.[31]

In early March 1962, the Dillon Round limped to a conclusion. Kennedy gave a positive spin, declaring that the United States got more than it gave in industrial tariffs and lamely told reporters that at least the round showed that the United States and the Six could bargain together. As Ball added, this was the first time Europe had spoken "with one voice," thereby advancing the idea of an Atlantic partnership. Nonetheless, the reality was that negotiators fell "grievously short of bargaining power," lamented the president. The RTAA was inadequate to the task of helping "to mold the EEC's external trade policy along liberal lines."[32]

The outlook was bleak for the capitalist peace: the balance-of-payments deficit would worsen without trade expansion with the Six and the Outer Seven, and development in the global South would stall if Europe became inaccessible to outsiders. If the Common Market turned inward, warned Ball, "free men everywhere"—from Laos to Iran—would turn from Lincoln to Lenin.[33] The Atlantic Community would evolve into "strictly a rich man's club which would eventually be isolated in the world and finally completely surrounded" by communism, warned Kennedy.[34]

Prospects in the Cold War had dimmed, regardless of the dynamism of a young president and his vibrant New Frontier aimed at transforming a world of friends and foes alike. Thus, Kennedy dramatically cast the trade problem in a wider context. Building on Truman's notion that the collective defense of NATO depended on economic as well as military strength, he drew on Eisenhower's idea of interdependence. Kennedy announced an ambitious "Grand Design" for an Atlantic Community to remake the Free World alliance. Some considered this community a cultural expression to unify the West through the pursuit of freedom, liberty, justice, democracy, and human rights. Its sources derived from ancient Greek thought, Roman law, the Judeo-Christian tradition of the dignity of the individual, and parliamentary rule—the same elements in capitalist peace ideology. To be sure, there was little consciousness of such a profound transatlantic identity among average citizens, but harnessed to the capitalist peace, it innovatively and energetically responded to communist ideology. The Grand Design must expand cooperation "on every front," said Kennedy. This included "cooperation to include common problems of trade and money, and by uniting in the effort to construct a sound, growing economy for the entire non-Communist world."[35] On his trip to Europe in June 1961, where he met De Gaulle and Khrushchev, the president spoke of transatlantic unity as a basis of human freedom. As a step toward unity, in mid-August, he endorsed Britain's entry into the EEC. Continued economic integration, he said, "can bring new vitality to the Atlantic Community, and mounting strength to the free world."[36] Success depended on the United States; behind the Grand Design's objective to ease the payments deficit was his legislative gem: the Trade Expansion Act.

The bill was not an easy sell because the 87th Congress was the most conservative since 1954, run by a coalition of southern Democrats and Republicans who did not like free trade. Kennedy could not rely on the guidance of so-called whales of influence in the Senate, like Lyndon Johnson, who had left the Senate to become his vice president, nor the skills of House Speaker Sam Rayburn, who had just died. Ways and Means Chairman Wilbur Mills liked Kennedy but not imports nor, necessarily, free-trade internationalism. He confessed his disgust "about how the State Department had been trading away our economic advantages for political advantages."[37] At hearings in 1961, protectionists had come out in force. A Subcommittee on the Impact of Imports and Exports, under Pennsylvania's John Dent, led off months of hearings divided into eight parts by products hit by imports. Dent quoted Kennedy's own words that domestic producers must be protected.[38] This was a context for the political side deals on carpets and glass, textiles, lumber, and oil that enabled the president to send out a trade bill reflecting the dynamism necessary to meet US foreign policy goals and domestic competitive challenges.

The campaign began in earnest in late 1961 as the administration rounded up believers in the capitalist peace. Hearings under Congressman Hale Boggs, like those he ran in years past, supported trade liberalization but also exposed the defects of the RTAA. Former Secretary of State Acheson, an unofficial advisor, reminded the Boggs Committee that only by unity could the Atlantic Community win the Cold War. Present at the creation of Europe's integration when he worked alongside Robert Schuman and Jean Monnet, Acheson warned that the Common Market must not become an exclusive bloc surrounded by high tariffs. A "decisive decision" to split or cooperate awaited Europe and the United States.[39] Former secretary of state Christian Herter joined Will Clayton in stealing the limelight at the next set of hearings under the Joint Economic Committee with an essay titled "A New Look at Foreign Economic Policy in Light of the Cold War and the Extension of the Common Market in Europe." It warned of the drift toward protectionism on both sides of the Atlantic. "Western security, in short, was under duress," threatened because America lacked substantial authority to negotiate with the Six.[40] George Ball added that the alliance stood on "the threshold of a new trading world," a powerful antidote to Soviet penetration. It was time to update three-decade-old reciprocal trade law into a free-trade weapon appropriate for the 1960s and beyond.[41]

Relations with Atlantic partners grabbed the most attention, especially from the business community. A group from the private sector advised "throwing open our doors" to competitors on a reciprocal basis, giving friends and neutrals in the West and South a chance to earn their way and avoid "commercial warfare amongst ourselves" that would please only the Soviets. Opening markets by lowering tariffs would "knit together the free world in its pursuit of freedom as no other single move could possibly do, while simultaneously strengthening the non-Communist world by underpinning its basic viability." The year 1962 was "a turning point in history" in the new, competitive trading world shaped by free-trade internationalism.[42]

Top-level meetings at the presidential compound in Hyannis Port and in Washington, DC, convinced Kennedy to proceed. He certainly took a political gamble if he hewed too closely to George Ball's doctrinaire free-trade line. Ball

Fig. 7.1 Former State Department brass Dean Acheson and Will Clayton, before the Boggs Committee in December 1961, urge cooperation with the European Common Market through an Atlantic partnership of free-trade internationalism. Library of Congress, Prints and Photographs Division, NYWT&S Collection, LC-USZ62-90145.

himself recognized the risk, so he advised a delay in the trade bill until 1963, after midterm elections, which would also give time for EEC policies and institutions to emerge. Having made the political side deals, though, Kennedy preferred a direct appeal based on the capitalist peace rather than be steered by inward-looking electoral politics and the whims of the exclusionary Six. A call to arms was more in his nature.[43] Philip Trezise, Ball's deputy, believed that the United States operated in "an environment of hypercaution and negativism about trade policy" that only an unflinchingly forward-looking law could overcome, and the president agreed.[44]

The first public inkling of the trade bill came at a press conference on November 8, 1961, when Kennedy let on that recommendations would be forthcoming in early 1962. Republican Barry Goldwater accused the administration of trying to join the EEC, but Kennedy dismissed that notion. He did stress that the payments imbalance had to be corrected by boosting the trade surplus ever higher by opening up the Common Market. Another option was for American business to jump tariff walls by investments, yet that would hurt the domestic economy and cause a larger gold outflow. In back-to-back speeches, one to industry and the other to organized labor, he tipped his hand. He was not asking for a renewal of the RTAA, but for its replacement. The Trade Expansion Act (TEA) let the two great capitalist markets of America and Europe "be harnessed together in a team capable of pulling the full weight of our common military, economic and political aspirations." Military policy defended against the communist drive to impose its way of life. "But there is one area, in particular, where the initiative can and has been ours—an area of strategic importance in which we have the capacity for a still greater effort—and that is in the area of economic policy," Kennedy told the National Association of Manufacturers.[45] The next day, before the AFL-CIO convention, a crowd firmly in his camp, he asked Big Labor to endorse his trade plans as it had done for Roosevelt's and Truman's by trusting in liberal adjustment assistance to offset import competition. Yet there was also "a chance to move the United States forward in the 1960s, not only in the economic sphere but also to make a contribution to the cause of freedom."[46] Ultimately, the argument came down to capitalist peace.

Although opinion polls showed less support for lower tariffs than in the past, they gave overwhelming support for the Trade Expansion Act across partisan political lines. Presidents Hoover, Truman, and Eisenhower backed the bill, joining Nixon and two dozen governors. Journalists called the Common Market and TEA historic initiatives, though they warned of an uphill struggle in Congress; the *Saturday Evening Post* predicted the "greatest debate of the century." Audiences seemed to grasp the capitalist peace perspective. As the *Nashville Tennessean* and the *Toledo Blade* lectured, tariff reductions fused the Atlantic partnership into a global capitalist alliance. "A free world trading area has possibilities so enormous that [it] could put Moscow on the defensive," declared the editorial column of the *New Republic*.[47]

To pique the public's imagination, the Trade Expansion Act offered four ways of cutting tariffs over a five-year period until June 1967. The basic authority called for a huge halving of duties across the board, on a linear basis, and not item by item as before. Tariffs of 5 percent or less would be abolished entirely. Most novel was the "dominant supplier" provision. For products in which the United States and the Common Market accounted for 80 percent of global market share, tariffs could be totally eliminated. At the moment, only aircraft and margarine and shortening amounted to that percentage, but the potential to augment the list of goods was great if Britain joined the Six. Thus, the TEA gave leverage to meet the challenge from the common external tariff and also to persuade the EEC to admit Britain into its ranks. Finally, the TEA was the first major trade law to focus on developing nations. It erased tariffs on tropical commodities and called for curbs on European preferences toward Africa by steering Latin American goods from US markets to Europe. This was self-interested but it also dealt with the old bogey of discriminatory trade regimes. Alongside the bold tariff-cutting provisions came safeguards for domestic producers and workers, though with limits. The TEA required proof that imports directly, and in the main, caused injury to producers, resort to the escape clause would no longer apply to partial injury, and the Tariff Commission would not make peril point determinations but only recommend them. The national security clause remained for defense-related industries to avoid trade agreements, but the burden of proof was high. The president could also raise tariffs, but the biggest safeguard cleverly veered from protectionism. The TEA provided federal aid for unemployment compensation, retraining, retirement benefits, and relocation for those injured by imports. Such adjustment assistance promoted the principle of comparative advantage and, above all, allowed foreign policy, rather than domestic concerns, to guide trade policy.[48]

John Kennedy proposed the most transformative trade legislation since 1934, but it was also a risk. A relatively weak president sent Congress a bill shaped by evangelicals like Ball, who provoked protectionists amid distracting foreign policy crises. He had done his political homework with textiles, oil, and lumber, but he expended limited capital on a bill that could easily lose, calculating that its tremendous scope, as well as the need to get the country moving again after the stalled late Eisenhower years, would win the day. After all, the torch had been passed to a new generation. Under Kennedy's Grand Design of capitalist peace, the Trade Expansion Act promised a concert of Western nations to counter the loss of postwar hegemony. This was his message when he presented the bill to Congress in January 1962, and it remained the logic during the vigorous campaign for votes. Citing the threats of Marxism, the Berlin crisis, radicalism in Latin America, a quagmire in Vietnam, the payments deficit, and "the greatest challenge of all"—the European Common Market—he claimed his trade initiative "could well affect the unity of the West, the course of the Cold War, and the economic growth of our Nation for a generation to come." The West could "either grow together or we grow apart," Kennedy proclaimed, that is, either "trade or fade." Capitalist peace ideology could succeed only by the same firm leadership that had been the rule in the postwar years.[49] "We are among the makers of history. We have a capacity to shape the course of events in front of us," proclaimed Secretary of State Dean Rusk.[50]

The impassioned and shrewd lobbying and the capitalist peace architecture worked. A parade of government officials, followed by industry, agriculture, and labor leaders, trooped to Capitol Hill to warn of the dire consequences if the United States retreated in trade policy. Ways and Means Committee hearings lasted five weeks in March and April, witnessing protectionist protest from dozens of industries. The president's politicking and pronouncements about deepening prosperity and security in the Atlantic Community paid off. The committee reported out the bill in near unanimity. It did strip tariff negotiating

Fig. 7.2 Men representing a public confused by Kennedy's just-announced Trade Expansion Act, designed to negotiate down tariffs with Europe, keep America competitive, and bolster the Free World, worry that US-Common Market trade relations will undermine the American economy. Library of Congress, Prints and Photographs Division, LC-USZ62-90145.

authority from the State Department and gave it to an ambassador-level Special Trade Representative, based in the president's office, which Kennedy did not like because it exposed the White House to politics, but he went along to win the legislation. The House passed the TEA in June by a whopping 298–125 margin.[51]

As the bill reached the Senate, Kennedy hit the peak of his rhetorical skills by brandishing the capitalist peace paradigm. On July 4, he issued a "Declaration of Interdependence" in Philadelphia's Independence Hall, linking the United States and Europe in a "concrete Atlantic partnership" to bring prosperity through freer trade, security by a unified NATO front to deter aggression, and the achievement of "a world of law and free choice, banishing the world of war and coercion" perpetrated by communism.[52] The Finance Committee heard the bill for four weeks in July and August. O. R. Strackbein of the Nationwide Committee on Import-Export Policy called TEA a deviation from the detested Cordell Hull's program because its five-year duration might cross over administrations and added to arbitrary executive powers while gutting the escape clause. Kennedy had spouted puerile free-trade propaganda; Strackbein could not understand why former opponents of the RTAA now backed the Trade Expansion Act, which was, simply, "unilateral economic disarmament." He guessed, correctly, that some had been bought off by Kennedy's side deals and that others were comforted that tariffs could be discarded for adjustment assistance, which Strackbein saw (correctly, as it turned out) as weak.[53] But many were also convinced that the TEA was as much a foreign policy bill as a trade law. Thus, Robert Kerr could say that the Common Market was "a part of the western civilization against communist expansion and aggression," and through the TEA, it would become "a real partner with the United States in the cold war with Communism."[54] Protectionists were simply overwhelmed by free-trade internationalism in the Senate hearings.

The message was effective, although Congress reduced some powers over liberalization. Ball urged the Finance Committee to eliminate the House prohibition on most-favored-nation status for Yugoslavia and Poland. Yugoslavia's had existed under an 1881 treaty with Serbia but had been suspended years before, while Poland had enjoyed equal trade standing until 1951. The senators restored most-favored-nation status for both, though they retained the ban on the USSR, China, and others. Regardless, House and Senate conferees removed the status from the final bill, giving Kennedy his only major defeat in the TEA campaign. There were some other minor modifications to ease passage. For instance, a majority in both houses could veto presidential decisions against escape clause relief. Moreover, two members from each chamber, one from each political party, were appointed to the American delegation to the upcoming GATT negotiations; in the past, legislators served only as observers. Adjustment assistance also had a close call. It survived by just one vote after Chairman Harry Byrd of Virginia wanted to bank on Tariff Commission rulings rather than federal aid to deal with import competition. The Finance Committee reversed its usual position as the more protectionist body of the two houses of Congress and reported out the bill intact, by a unanimous 17–0 vote. Republicans could find little to fault in the TEA, particularly favoring the dominant supplier provision directed at the Common Market. The Senate sent it through, 78–8, with only one Democrat opposed.[55]

Fig. 7.3 Kennedy signs the historic Trade Expansion Act on October 11, 1962. Standing behind the seated president, from left to right, are Secretary of Commerce Luther Hodges, Congressmen John Flynt, Hale Boggs (partially hidden), Wilbur Mills (with glasses, to Kennedy's immediate right), Secretary of Defense Robert McNamara (mostly hidden), Senator Robert Kerr, Congressman John Byrnes, Senators Mike Mansfield, Russell Long, and John Pastore, Secretary of State Dean Rusk (in back), Senator Hubert Humphrey, Congressman Cecil King, Treasury Secretary C. Douglas Dillon (in back, mostly hidden), Congressmen Howard Baker and Eugene Keogh (in back, mostly hidden), Special Assistant Howard C. Petersen, Secretary of Agriculture Orville Freeman, and Under Secretary of State George Ball. Abbie Rowe, White House Photographs, John F. Kennedy Presidential Library and Museum, Boston.

Kennedy signed the bill on October 11, just three days before detecting Soviet missiles in Cuba. Unaware that he was about to enter the most dangerous moment of the Cold War, he explained the strategic import of the Trade Expansion Act. The "most important international piece of legislation, I think, affecting economics since the passage of the Marshall Plan," the TEA enhanced "the prospects of free institutions and free societies everywhere. It aggregated the greatest economic power in the history of the world," providing assurance of a "vital expanding economy in the free world" that would be "a strong counter to the threat of the world Communist movement." Kennedy played the long game of capitalist peace. Gathering together "like-minded nations" turned out to be critical as the world stood on the brink of nuclear catastrophe.[56]

The administration immediately implemented the Trade Expansion Act, readying for negotiations with the Common Market and the rest of the world. A month after signing the legislation, Kennedy appointed respected former secretary of state Christian Herter as the first Special Trade Representative (STR) to represent the United States at the next round of the General Agreement on Tariffs and Trade. He had wanted to go bigger than a mid-level bureaucrat because "somebody of the caliber of Christian Herter" would bring to bear the power of the White House to influence the Atlantic partnership.[57] It would take well into the next year to plan for the GATT round, named after Kennedy himself, as the STR and his delegation held difficult but productive preparatory talks with the Six, especially on agricultural trade. Focused on foreign policy, Herter conceived of his position as "one which ties into our security, because quite obviously unless we're able to meet our balance of payments in time, then we are going to have to find other means of solving it." For the capitalist peace to survive and thrive, it came down to " 'export or die' " for the United States at the GATT negotiations.[58]

Success hinged on forging the Atlantic Community, yet in 1963 a partnership to unify the allies under a common multilateral nuclear shield, insulate the global South from communism, and reverse the payments crisis remained on the drawing board. For one, Kennedy had not consulted allies during the Cuban Missile Crisis, leading the ornery Charles de Gaulle to wonder what "partnership" meant if partners were not kept informed during such momentous decisions. He thus advised Europe to create its own nuclear force to give the region independence from both superpowers. The Grand Design in trade, moreover, was battered as the GATT preparations continued. The administration sought to limit the gold outflow, backing special monetary drawing rights in Europe to stem currency conversion into dollars and intensifying the export drive. Treasury Secretary Dillon confessed, however, that there were no panaceas to the deficit on the horizon. The president asked about the prospect for growth in farm exports to Europe. The only encouraging news in "an otherwise not very encouraging picture of the agricultural scene" was that Japan had committed to buy more American commodities.[59] The brilliant light of the Grand Design dimmed in 1963.

The fact was that, despite the TEA victory and flashy rhetoric, Kennedy also not only faced protectionists at home but obstacles in Europe. The European Economic Community's Council of Ministers considered a potentially "monstrous" influx of American goods, especially through the TEA's dominant supplier provision, and thus carefully determined the Six's common external tariff and the common agricultural policy heading into the Kennedy Round. After all, the EEC suffered a trade deficit with the United States. Then, the hammer fell on the Grand Design. On January 14, 1963, de Gaulle vetoed British membership in the Common Market, claiming that Britain was not really a continental power. Rather, London's close ties to Washington made it an Atlanticist agent for American exports and investments, undermining the Common Market's independence. The other five members opposed de Gaulle but even they were not bowled over by the Grand Design's Atlantic partnership framework. Kennedy could do little to save the dominant supplier provision. Without Britain, few products reached the 80 percent trade threshold that abolished tariffs between the United States and the Six. That hurt the export drive, and thus worsened the payments balance. Protectionists applauded the veto, however, because it vitiated the effort for trade liberalization and internationalism.[60]

The veto was a blow to Kennedy and, at a deeper level, to the capitalist peace. Reporters pondered American influence in Europe as the president reminded them that de Gaulle's rejection threatened the Atlantic partnership and prosecution of the Cold War. In addition, in this "Decade of Development," Europe's help was essential to keep the undeveloped nations on the West's side through mutual aid spending. The Six had to decide what kind of Europe they wanted, said Kennedy, "one looking out or looking in."[61] Lest anyone forget, the United States "went through a very difficult and dangerous experience this fall in Cuba" and he saw "no real evidence that the policy of the Communist world towards us is basically changed. They still do not wish us well." So "it would be a disaster" if the EEC and America divided. But the veto revealed the Grand Design to be a mere pipe dream.[62]

The veto turned out to be the biggest news of the year on the trade front. "Mr. Europe," George Ball, darted between overseas missions in Europe, discovering that while there was no danger of the EEC falling apart, the Common Market could close doors to Washington's influence in trade and nuclear matters. With the threat of war over Berlin dissipated, de Gaulle's insistence on French grandeur, no matter how outlandish in terms of world power, had purchase. Gaullism included the notion that within a few years, there would be no need for Americans to remain in Europe to guarantee security. Meanwhile, the customs union must be protected from US export and investment penetration. Frustrated, Kennedy saw the veto as politically motivated (and de Gaulle vetoed British membership again in 1967). It gave the appearance that "the French have gagged us in a major way, because that just pleases them." It also complicated matters for other EEC members like West Germany. Bonn joined Paris in the historic Elysée Franco-German Treaty of Friendship in May 1963, putting to rest a century of antagonism. Still, the accord depended on American support. Europe would have to decide its fate, and Kennedy had thought that the Trade Expansion Act could help relations by amending the dominant supplier provision. That was not to be, though Ball argued that Britain's exclusion from the EEC should not deter the GATT talks.[63]

Shrugging off Gaullism as part of the growing pains of the Common Market turned out to be a bad bluff. For starters, Congress was not convinced that trade liberalization could overcome the veto. The president's lieutenants had heard from key senators like Kerr and Republican Everett Dirksen of Illinois that the TEA's authority had been gutted, leading the administration to ask Ways and Means chairman Wilbur Mills to issue a formal statement to the contrary. Kennedy feared, however, that the Republicans and protectionists "will say that we should have done something" to predict de Gaulle's move "and that our policy lies in ruins." Perhaps West Germany might be convinced to buy more farm goods and open up to Latin America, but the old specter of retreat from Europe was making the rounds once again.[64] The president accepted a British request to send Herter to London to discuss the GATT negotiations, with the proviso that the STR would talk about trade but listen on security matters. Kennedy also did not want American opinion to react too negatively to Gaullism.[65]

In the end, the Americans and the EEC nations other than France registered their discontent with de Gaulle and then turned to the Kennedy Round preparations. De Gaulle himself would settle down, they guessed, especially because he needed the Friendship Treaty with Bonn to keep West Germany in his trade corner. Faced with the freeing of trade in the GATT, he would also accept the inevitable Atlantic partnership because he needed the EEC to protect French agriculture and provide ample funds for France's African colonies. The father of the Common Market, Jean Monnet, believed the veto was just "a minor interruption" in the ongoing process of European integration.[66] In fact, many in Europe sided with Kennedy; the veto seemed like "a rather irresponsible anti-Americanism and sort of a new European isolationism."[67] Reasoned the president, "If de Gaulle wants to screw us, he can, pretty good here" in trade and security. Still, no other nation would allow the Common Market to "be discriminatory against us," replied Ball, and the GATT Round would prove that, pointing away from de Gaulle's narrow vision for Europe.[68]

By May 1963, the ground rules for the tariff negotiations were set, though under duress. The Commission of the European Economic Community, headed by Walter Hallstein, had bargained hard enough to raise doubts about his desire for trade liberalization. This was especially so in agriculture, in which the EEC's Mansholt Plan raised world wheat prices and asked for an end to US subsidies, thereby protecting farmers (particularly the French) from low-cost American exports. This inflationary policy threatened Kennedy's reelection prospects in the Midwest. Furthermore, the Common Agricultural Policy could stymie imports into the EEC; Ball hoped that the Six would impose reasonable import levies but in private, he knew the administration would lose on the wheat price issue. He would trade that defeat for "a liberal Kennedy Round," or lower tariffs on industrial goods and more access into European markets for specialty commodities like fruit and seed grains. Kennedy let on in public that "we have a long road to hoe, but we have always known that" about a deal with the Six, especially in agriculture. From his capitalist peace standpoint, he was impressed that the Atlantic partnership remained viable during these tough preparatory talks as "both sides realize that the West cannot possibly afford to have a breakdown in trade relations."[69]

Yet reality boded ill for prospects at the GATT round. Economist John Kenneth Galbraith warned in August that the trade surplus had declined for three years and would sink further as the EEC raised tariffs. Some claimed that "muscular and masculine bargaining during the Kennedy round" would offset the obstacles to American exports but this was "self-delusion," alleged Galbraith. Tariffs were rising against the United States; they would decline only if Herter offered equal concessions. The payments deficit weakened Herter's hand, yet worse, tariffs would be cut on EEC consumer goods, which were responsive to lower prices and high incomes at home, as well as on capital goods like machinery that Europe bought because of its technological superiority. In sum, what had been a liberal trade policy born from a reaction against Hawley-Smoot and postwar creditor status faced a reversed situation. Tariffs were low but the United States ran a deficit. History showed that to correct a payments deficit, raising tariffs and domestic prices were necessary evils. Galbraith, albeit a free trader, thus counseled against automatic liberalization of trade. With European tariffs going up, Kennedy should apply a temporary offsetting surcharge on manufactured goods from the Common Market. In short, he could halt free trade or he could limit the freedom of travel and redeploy troops to slow the gold outflow. For Galbraith, free-trade internationalism was unraveling, though an unpalatable protectionist surcharge could save it.[70] Tradition won out and the idea was set aside, but such a remedy awaited the Nixon years a half decade later when America's international accounts had sunk to even lower depths.

Wary and uncertain, the administration reached an eventual deal for proceeding with the Kennedy Round that seemed good for the United States. It included agriculture, though the Six pondered excluding crops because their common policy was not yet complete. The Americans won on reducing tariffs on an across-the-board basis, in which all nations would cut by the same percentage. The Six had proposed reducing tariffs on an adjusted, pre-determined basis, which would leave them relatively high, but they lost the argument. Ball was ecstatic and told Kennedy that the process was "completely on our terms" because it asserted the principle of linear cuts for all. To be sure, EEC agricultural import levies loomed, but those restrictions could be muted. Kennedy wanted economic gains, not just principles, and Ball assured him that STR's team could "go forward and get substantial cuts out of the Common Market" to defy de Gaulle, who hoped for failure at the GATT negotiations. "Fortunately, we had practically the whole Free World on our side at the end," wrote Ball, though Kennedy should not "crow too much about it" because the "Europeans were really dug in on" protecting their farm sector.[71]

Kennedy fully agreed. In Frankfurt, West Germany, on June 25, 1963, a day before his famous speech at the Berlin Wall, he spoke of the "great economic challenge" in the upcoming trade negotiations. Because it involved industry and agriculture, and the "trading needs and aspirations of other free world countries, including Japan," the Kennedy Round would be "a test of our unity." Truly, a "rising tide lifts all the boats," as they said in his native Cape Cod, and the United States and Europe "could be partners in prosperity" just as they had been in the adversity of war and recovery.[72] This message of conciliation was particularly germane. A trade war had erupted over the sale of American poultry in Europe—the infamous "chicken war"—that de Gaulle relished as a way to sour West Germany (the top chicken producer on the continent) on the Atlantic partnership. This was an ominous signal of how tough the Six would be on agricultural trade, protecting their inefficient producers even while risking US retaliation, a course Lyndon Johnson took in the chicken war in his first month as president.[73]

Storm clouds were on the horizon in 1963, tempests that roiled the capitalist peace. The export drive itself must take off, Kennedy urged in September, for the GATT talks would "determine the climate in which American exporters will operate for years to come" in Western Europe and also with the ninety or so developing nations in need of US goods. Trade policy and private export expansion could be meshed with aid programs to boost the trade surplus, payments balance, and friends around the world.[74] The message that the rich must help the poor and that all would benefit from freer trade came just a few weeks before Kennedy's death. The GATT round, he was convinced, would help toward that goal. To facilitate that outcome, he informed Ball on November 20 that he planned to offer, when he returned from Dallas, a simple deal to West German Chancellor Ludwig Erhard in which the United States would buy more German industrial goods if Europe imported more American agriculture.[75]

Kennedy would never speak to Erhard, of course. In trade, the tragedy of his death was multiplied by rising barriers from competitive friends, revolts against US policies, and changes in American power in the international arena. At home, dissent was also on the rise. All of these trends had implications for the Cold War, and all molded the trade agenda as a continuing catalyst for peace and security.

8

Revolt, 1964–1970

Like his predecessors, Lyndon Johnson believed in the capitalist peace. In his folksy way, he noted that the United States "must trade with the rest of the world, because people that you meet and you work with and that you talk with and you trade with you get along better with."[1] Just as the Vietnam War sapped American power, however, trade policy also hit headwinds of protectionism, challenges from the global South, and pressure to improve relations with the communist bloc. Up until the late 1950s, US foreign policy had been heroic, remaking the world after a horrible conflict and containing the communist threat. By the 1960s, with recovery complete, the hero sought the status quo as anti-communist fervor in foreign policy gave way to economic concerns at home and abroad. In an age of restiveness, rebellion, and détente, the capitalist peace argument was tougher to make than it ever had been.

From the mid-1960s onward, policymakers focused more on business than ever before, taking for granted that trade served the cause of internationalism and security. Johnson's true interest lay in alleviating poverty and advancing civil rights under his Great Society social programs at home. The Vietnam War undermined this war on poverty, along with liberalism. Abroad, the Grand Design lay in tatters in French hands. Britain did not enter the European Economic Community, the Kennedy Round of GATT struggled, and in 1966, de Gaulle kicked NATO facilities out of his country. The president sought "the dream of a partnership across the Atlantic—and across the Pacific," he said in his first speech to Congress, through the export drive to reverse the payments deficit and aiding poor nations.[2] Washington and Bonn, in particular, talked about Europeans footing more of the NATO bill and ideas percolated to prop up the dollar by easing trade controls through "bridge-building" in Eastern Europe. Imposing limits on capital movements, monetary reform, and even a joint venture by automakers to manufacture an economy car that competed with the popular

Capitalist Peace. Thomas W. Zeiler, Oxford University Press. © Oxford University Press 2022.
DOI: 10.1093/oso/9780197621363.003.0009

German Volkswagen also arose; a Task Force on Foreign Economic Policy advocated more exports, trade liberalization, and attention to the deficit. Despite these measures, spending on Vietnam and poverty overheated the economy and the world financial system.[3]

Financing foreign policy hinged on, of course, freer trade. Days after Kennedy's assassination, Special Trade Representative Herter asked National Security Advisor McGeorge Bundy to remind Johnson that the General Agreement on Tariff and Trade talks were critical to "the future strength and cohesiveness of the free world." The world could not be both prosperous and protectionist.[4] He did not need to convince the president who, on the last day of 1963, vetoed yet another protectionist bill, this one an attempt to mark products with the country of origin to encourage consumers to buy American goods. In addition to being costly, such restrictive measures, warned Johnson, would "invite retaliation against our exports at a time when we are trying to expand our trade and improve Western unity."[5]

A growing crisis in trade with the developing South complicated Johnson's thinking. Moscow attracted poor nations by investment, trade, and aid, but Washington seemed to retreat, debating, with the payments deficit in mind, how much aid it could afford. Perhaps the United States might bend its free-trade principles by granting preferential access to the American market for developing countries to prevent them from fleeing into the Soviet camp. What was needed was innovation, but the application of free-trade internationalism followed a traditional course based on non-discrimination principles that benefited the North and was not fully responsive to the emerging nations. Thus, these nations began to protest against the American-led free-trade canon of the General Agreement on Tariffs and Trade. As US aid continued to grow under the modernization theories of Kennedy and Johnson experts, moreover, Washington designed development to mesh with the trade order, multinational corporate investments, and the Cold War. That counter-insurgency tactics would bring stability within developing countries (like South Vietnam) to make them liberal and outward-looking, however, strained capitalist peace theory, to say the least. The Green Berets and the Peace Corps in Asia were two sides of the same coin, as were military assistance to dictators and the Alliance for Progress in Latin America.[6] Trade liberalization fed into this double-sided approach that used the military hand in hand with economics to pursue development, but the global South sought to separate security from economics.

Having grown up in rural poverty surrounded by farmers who depended on exports to survive, Johnson likened the aspirations of emerging nations to his youthful quest for prosperity and independence. As a southerner, he also resisted protectionism, but as an effective legislator, he said all the right things at home and was cautious in tariff-cutting because he knew there were few votes in free trade. As a Texan who knew where the money came from, he also stood by protection of the domestic petroleum industry, though due to his ties to oil, he got an undeserved reputation as a most tepid free trader. In actuality, he was a fervent capitalist peace advocate, dismissive of stringent import restrictions. Johnson also fully understood the gold drain crisis, working assiduously during his five years in office to reverse the payments deficit by tax and capital controls, monetary reform, and export expansion through trade liberalization.[7] Traditional in many ways, he also understood the desires of the global South. Summing up the problem, his foreign policy team wrote that "the less developed world looks to be both the greatest challenge to our creative powers and the largest source of cumulating instability in the years ahead."[8]

Emerging nations demanded that a trade system meet their expectations and serve their welfare, just like the GATT focused on the rich, but their rebellion questioned the market theory of comparative advantage that, along with the Soviet economic offensive, had bred radicalism, or so policymakers believed. Stabilizing efforts like the Alliance for Progress and common markets were possible solutions, but the entire trade system needed reconceptualization—and

Fig. 8.1 Seated at the far right, Lyndon Johnson, in September 1965, confers with advisors, including the essential trade advisor, George Ball (to Johnson's immediate right), on the gold outflow and the balance of payments deficit. LBJ Library photo by Yoichi Okamoto.

Johnson knew it. The catalyst came in March 1964, with an uprising at the United Nations Conference on Trade and Development (UNCTAD).[9] Developing countries intended to reshape the trade order by compelling the North to grant preferential treatment for their exports. The UNCTAD regime of, essentially, discrimination, would operate outside of the free-market dogmatism of GATT that, according to nations of the South, stacked the trade deck against them.

Poor nations had hoped for more from the GATT. A Program for the Expansion of Trade in 1961 provided them with some protection from imports and preferences on manufactured exports but the United States and others had dithered on it. An Action Program in late 1962 called for more drastic industrial tariff cuts by the advanced countries and removal of barriers to primary agricultural goods, though this time the EEC balked because France wanted to preserve its preferential trade relationship with its African and Caribbean Associated Overseas Countries, which it did under the Yaounde Convention of 1963. Yaounde contradicted the GATT's most-favored-nation principle, however, besides crimping the export efforts of non-signatories, especially Latin American nations. The United States opposed this preference scheme for the same reason it had opposed Britain's imperial discriminatory preferences regime decades before, and the blow to Latin Americans was doubly galling. With GATT remedies to sputtering development efforts falling short, the global South, at the Kennedy Round, turned to UNCTAD's preferential system, requiring the rich to cut tariffs particularly on manufactures, open their markets, stabilize commodity prices, and forgo requiring full reciprocity by the poor. This time, the United States got cold feet. To be sure, preferences might serve the capitalist peace by attracting the global South to the Free World, but they would also provoke a convulsion of protectionism at home against low-wage imports. Kennedy, and then Johnson, thus fell back on traditional free-trade principles and policies, urging nations to diversify production and exports, integrate on a regional basis, and seek more East-South trade under careful monitoring.[10]

On the eve of the Kennedy Round, in early 1964, the United States offered to halve tariffs to help the poorer South but still denounced preferences. Johnson blandly talked of solving the problems of the periphery on a market-oriented "commercial basis," though he pledged to make the GATT talks more amenable to developing countries. But they denounced the American list of exceptions to tariff concessions because it removed items crucial to their development, despite the efforts of GATT ministers to minimize exemptions. The emerging nations had had enough. Some 2,000 delegates from 120 nations and organizations convened UNCTAD in Geneva in 1964, parallel to the GATT, under Raul Prebisch, an Argentine economist who embraced structuralism, or the notion that a core of rich countries imposed their will on a periphery of developing nations. The North created a system of dependency by terms of trade that favored its expensive goods over the cheaper products and commodities of the South, and the Kennedy Round would only worsen these terms. The GATT presumed a heterogeneity of national interests, North and South alike, based on the classical theory of comparative advantage, but that was not the case. Prebisch pushed a dramatic increase of exports of manufactures to the advanced countries, which he deemed responsible for correcting the deteriorating terms of trade and for stabilizing commodity prices as well. Unequal trade relationships must end through sacrifices on the part of the free-trading North.[11]

This economic rationale fed into fears that intensifying protest would undermine the capitalist peace. Indeed, communists applauded UNCTAD because the capitalists would ostensibly foot the bill for aid, trade, and development, and the Soviet bloc could join the chorus of boos against Western imperialism. The CIA reported that the GATT was so unpopular that communist propaganda found purchase in claiming that the rich capitalists would always exploit the poor through free enterprise. This logic angered the United States because, for starters, communism could offer nothing better. Soviet trade with the developing nations was meager, the products were shoddy (a steel mill in India failed to meet Western standards), and deals, like the one on cotton sales from Egypt, favored the Russians. Worse, financing through non-convertible rubles tied these countries to the bloc. Regardless, the South unified behind two positions: the Kennedy Round would not help them and UNCTAD would by institutionalizing their grievances. Not only were the Americans on the wrong side, but they were largely alone. The Common Market, backed by Britain, endorsed a Belgian scheme called the Brasseur Plan, that mimicked UNCTAD by calling for a system of preferences generalized to apply to the entire developing world. A generalized regime would thus adhere to the most-favored-nation rule in which all countries received and gave equal treatment.[12] Washington opposed the idea.

Johnson's representative to UNCTAD, George Ball, was annoyed. If the United States gave way to UNCTAD's demands in an election year, Republicans could pillory Johnson for allowing in harmful imports and hurting the payments deficit. UNCTAD also threatened the GATT, a pillar of American foreign policy, and gifted the Soviets undue influence. Ball offered a compromise—some commodity stabilization agreements, exemption from reciprocal tariff cuts at the Kennedy Round, and funding for a permanent secretariat for UNCTAD. He stuck by his opposition to preferences, however, because they trashed the entire nondiscriminatory trade "theology" of the United States and the GATT. Ball labeled UNCTAD a mere sideshow to the main event in Geneva: American-European tariff negotiations. He also made such a bad impression with Prebisch and company that McGeorge Bundy, the national security advisor, counseled accepting generalized preferences to remove the target of recrimination from Washington's back. This squabble could spill into Cold War security issues, Bundy warned. The president went so far as to pledge cooperation with UNCTAD and dodged a bullet when the 1964 meeting established a secretariat but postponed, under pressure from Washington, the controversial preferences issue.[13]

The reprieve was temporary. The United States had a preferential trade arrangement with the Philippines and was negotiating one on auto parts with Canada, so it was hardly an innocent. Thus, Herter accepted preferences as long as they were non-discriminatory and if the EEC junked its arrangements with African nations. It took the appointment of a new under secretary of state for economic affairs, Anthony Solomon, to reverse nearly two hundred years of upholding the most-favored-nation rule. A specialist in Latin American development, Solomon conceded that the issue was favored by too many nations to disappear. Besides, generalizing preferences would deter the Six from blocking access to their market. In 1965, when Australia sought a waiver from the GATT to grant preferential trade treatment, the contracting parties voted 51–1 in favor of generalized preferences. Ball was the lone dissenter. By August 1966, as he prepared to retire in protest over the Vietnam War, even he knew that Washington had lost the initiative in trade policy, at least on this issue.[14]

Momentum carried the Generalized System of Preferences to fruition. Hoping Congress would back it on humanitarian and security grounds, Solomon suggested waiting until after the 1968 elections to endorse the new order. The global South would not wait, however, and Latin Americans had already lobbied for a temporary regional preferential system with the United States. The United Nations General Assembly, dominated by the developing world, jumped on board. Queried by the president, business and labor organizations cautiously supported the generalized system as long as there were safeguards for domestic industry and workers, and if they truly applied to all so as not to contradict the rule of non-discriminatory treatment. Satisfied on the home front, Johnson expressed a willingness to explore temporary preferences at a summit of the Organization of American States in April 1967.[15]

The following year, at the second UNCTAD meeting in New Delhi, the United States came around to the generalized preferences regime largely to compensate for a weak showing at the Kennedy Round. By this time, the Vietnam conflict had deteriorated, the Six-Day War had soured the Arab world on America, and black South Africans were revolting against the apartheid regime. American protectionism had exempted key products, like textiles, steel, and minerals, from tariff reductions, so poor countries came out of Geneva empty-handed. In 1968, the National Council of Churches called protectionism, the lack of investment in the South, and congressional bickering over aid shameful offenses against humanity, especially considering the United States had done so much for the recovery of wealthy advanced nations after World War II. At the

Kennedy Round, Washington did give sizable tariff cuts on tropical products, with a focus on Latin America, but it still resisted preferences, to the detriment of regional producers. In the eyes of the poor, Kennedy's concern that his namesake GATT round would be viewed as a "rich man's deal" that offered "apologetic" concessions had come to pass.[16]

UNCTAD II did not give the South all it wanted, either. The generalized system did not appear until 1976, when it even exempted some imports and was temporary to boot. Critics blamed emerging nations for their worsening terms of trade and trade deficits; their own political, social, and economic systems were so rife with corruption and inefficiencies that development stagnated. Above all, because the United States needed to maintain its trade surplus to pay for Cold War commitments, the developing world's revolt was a threat to security. In short, the diplomatic interests came first, although when applied to the global South, that stance was inimical to the spirit of the capitalist peace. Still, because the UNCTAD revolt also menaced Free World cohesion, the Nixon administration later explained that preferences had become such a major symbol of American intentions toward the global South that they could not be discarded. Thus, with big business tolerant of UNCTAD, the Johnson administration ended up approving generalized preferences because they paid "some political dividends" in relations with emerging nations. That was important in the Cold War.[17]

There was another revolt against American foreign policy and the capitalist peace, this one at home, against liberalization of East-West trade. In the early 1960s, Kennedy had not shirked from confronting Soviet and Chinese ambitions; nevertheless, he had preferred "peaceful competition—for prestige, for markets, for scientific achievement, even for men's minds" in relations with the communist world. Toward this end, he had sought "increased discretion to use economic tools" such as easing export controls and unfreezing the assets of nations that tipped toward the West, like Poland and Yugoslavia.[18] After the harrowing Cuban Missile crisis, European allies asked for a moderation of trade restrictions as a step toward preventing another nuclear near-miss by superpower détente. Cold Warriors blocked this path, however, and as a result, despite the thaw in relations with Moscow, Kennedy just marginally liberalized controls. Ending embargoes with Cuba, the People's Republic of China (PRC), North Vietnam, and North Korea was off limits because these countries were deemed regional aggressors. There was also a question of whether expanding trade would even effect much change in behavior. More likely, internal transformations and defections, coupled with the current economic crisis facing Moscow and Eastern Europe, would lead the communists to lift travel restrictions, allow unrestricted religious worship, and end international subversion. The heady days of the Soviet economic offensive had given way to declining industrial output, agricultural failures, and a sharp increase in defense outlays, so both the psychological and economic effects of the Cold War bore on the issue of East-West trade. That is, as Walt Rostow had explained in a report to Kennedy in July 1963, denying trade "has come to be an important symbol of our cold war resolve and purpose and of our moral disapproval of the USSR."[19]

In other words, during the Kennedy and then Johnson years, capitalist peace ideology had penetrated into public views of communism but from two opposing directions. One was a call for tough, inflexible trade policies toward the communists, while the other sought engagement to change and separate the bloc. The administration itself had internally debated, with Rostow and Commerce Department officials seeking to harden controls while they waited on Moscow to make peaceful moves. The departments of State and Defense pursued easing trade restrictions, especially toward the more pliable Eastern European satellites. Rather than wait on the enemy, Dean Rusk and Robert McNamara thought that the president should initiate concessions to coax along the Soviets. Kennedy had agreed with them. He had accepted increased trade by allies, particularly Britain and West Germany, with East Germany, and in October 1963, he announced a big sale of wheat to the Russians. When public opinion seemed favorable, and after an amicable visit by Yugoslav leader, Josef Tito, he considered relaxing the trade embargoes. Yet Kennedy did not want to go overboard in détente, which might provoke anti-communists in Congress. The issue passed to Lyndon Johnson.[20]

President Johnson looked on East-West trade as part of his "bridge-building" to Eastern Europe rather than solely as an instrument of national security, which put him in the Kennedy-Rusk-McNamara camp. While he knew that fearful Americans focused more on capitalist security than capitalist peace, business was on his side. The National Foreign Trade Council, for instance, leaned toward liberalization as a national interest and rejected moral or political arguments against trade expansion with communists. They preferred to "make economic rapprochement appear as a logical sequel" to the Cold War. East-West trade policy should allow business "to compete more freely with other countries now engaged in this trade" for profit but also to narrow areas of conflict by adding items to the list of goods eligible for commerce.[21] Toward this end, Johnson won renewal from a suspicious Congress for most-favored-nation treatment for Yugoslavia and Poland, sold more wheat and extended credits to Eastern European nations, and signed a commercial agreement with Romania to drive a wedge between the feuding Bucharest and Moscow. The Department of Commerce came around to liberalizing sales of lucrative agricultural machinery because American manufacturers lost when the Soviets bought them elsewhere. The president was a realist, however, demanding a quid pro quo rather than giveaways. Timing was also a factor; Johnson did not need to excite anti-communists by easing restrictions before the 1964 presidential election.[22]

The administration labored over the issue. When the Export Control Review Board considered the sale of six beet harvesters to the Soviets in March 1964, for instance, Secretary of Agriculture Orville Freeman was circumspect due to national security considerations. "In a context between ideologies which is being carried out in the sphere of economic development," he wrote, "any measure that strengthens the economic potential of the opponent would seem unjustified unless accompanied by at least a corresponding strengthening of our own potential." Improving superpower relations was a laudable goal, but Moscow was still a totalitarian power, even if the "cold war between ideologies and ways of life is to be fought on an economic basis instead of a military basis." The departments of State and Commerce concurred because the Russians had not abandoned their aim of burying the West. Still, not all consumer products were strategic. Luther Hodges in Commerce quipped that the United States could sell the communists "anything they can 'eat, drink, or smoke'"—and even advanced beet harvesters. Freeman estimated that in any case, it would take the Soviets five years to develop comparable technology. The administration advocated "constant surveillance" of the impact of non-strategic goods on communist economies as it approved the harvester sale.[23]

Johnson sought liberalization because increasing exports potentially had a positive effect on the payments deficit, and Congress seemed to agree. In the 1965 State of the Union address, he pointed to the "aggressive face" of communism in Asia, yet he welcomed the new Soviet leader, Leonid Brezhnev, urging the Eastern European countries to "assert their identity" through independent trade deals with the West.[24] A few days later, the president encouraged a group of business leaders recently returned from Moscow to explore expanding trade with the Soviets. He noted that the Senate Foreign Relations Committee had sent out a questionnaire asking for their views, and then he laid on the capitalist peace argument. Trade offered "no better way to come to know each other than to engage in peaceful and profitable commerce together" as well as attain national interests.[25] A month later, he appointed industrialist J. Irwin Miller to head a Special Committee on US Trade and Relations with Eastern European Countries and the Soviet Union to explore growing non-strategic East-West trade with the communists, excluding North Korea, the PRC, Cuba, and North Vietnam.

The Miller Committee reported on April 29, 1965, confirming the capitalist peace's softer application to East-West trade. With the assent of national security policymakers, a consensus on liberalization emerged even as Congress balked at the committee's recommendations. Miller found that trade restraints had not undermined Soviet military capabilities nor stopped its economic offensive. In fact, little had been gained by the COCOM regime and embargoes; the Soviets had not changed, and Western Europe, Japan, and even Eastern Europeans had stepped into the vacuum the United States left. The committee recommended a more flexible trade policy and an easing of embargoes, with the concurrence of the CIA and the departments of State and Commerce. The United States must engage and compete rather than withdraw and protect. Profits were at stake but so was the possibility of prying open the closed Soviet society with consumer goods. And "when tensions mount," wrote the State Department's Thomas Mann, trade contacts might ease them.[26]

Capitalist peace was the crux of the argument. Noted George Kennan, the overriding values were "political rather than economic," and the Miller Committee confirmed that notion by reporting that East-West trade "is politics in the broadest sense" in that "this intimate engagement of men and nations will in time be altered by the engagement itself."[27] Moscow might be persuaded to ease persecution of the second largest Jewish population in the world, for instance. As the political advisor Myer Feldman well knew, 5.5 million American Jews fixated on letting Soviet Jews unite with families abroad. Exchanging people for exports might change Soviet policy, convince Congress to trade with the communists, and earn electoral votes, thus showing the value of the capitalist peace approach. The Miller Report clearly pushed the primacy of security, yet a shift in American trade policies could even rebuild Russia's "historical ties with the West" as well as exploit the Sino-Soviet split and ferment in Eastern Europe. Concluded Miller, a properly conceived liberalization of East-West trade "could become a significant and useful device in the pursuit of our national security and welfare and of world peace."[28]

Congress resisted, though, once an East-West Trade Relations Act arrived on Capitol Hill in May 1966. Conservatives were skeptical, for CIA analyses revealed the continued Soviet (and more aggressive Chinese) economic offensives to "enhance total communist power relative to that of the United States and its allies" through trade. Those efforts built communist prestige in the less-developed world. In short, détente was an illusion. The chairman of the Council on Foreign Relations, banker John McCloy, observed, "The Soviet Union has not given any evidence as yet of having made the deep choice between the Chinese ideology and a real attachment to the West." Moscow promoted wars of liberation, not peaceful co-existence or disarmament supported by normal trade, and sought to undermine the American political and social systems.[29] Indeed, a long paper commissioned by the National Association of Manufacturers in 1966 also warned that the tiger had the same stripes. Soviet specialist Mose L. Harvey of the University of Miami wrote that having not changed their ideology or intentions in pursuing "a struggle in which our national survival is at stake," the

Soviets had shown that friendly relations were only theoretically linked to trade liberalization. Trade denial was the safest course in the Cold War.[30]

The administration conceded that this view, which much of Congress held, permitted only piecemeal steps in trade. Congress blocked presidential discretionary power in the East-West Trade Relations bill, on which hearings finally occurred in 1968 after a year's delay. The junior senator from Minnesota, Democrat Walter Mondale, proposed a resolution to ease constraints on trade with Eastern European satellites. When the matter went to the Banking and Currency Committee with widespread endorsement, powerful Senator Strom Thurmond, who had joined the GOP in 1964, immediately jumped on it. In a devastating critique of capitalist peace thinking, he expressed irritation that those who opposed trade liberalization of any sort were always characterized as warmakers and those in favor as embracing peace. The "facts of international politics and economics are that such trade does two things: First, it provides no incentive for peace for the Communist nations," which continued to aid North Vietnam against the United States. Second, "it increases the probability of war" because these nations acquired goods on the cheap that cost millions of dollars to research and develop, thereby allowing them to divert scarce resources to arms. Helping the payments balance did not hold water with him either, for East-West trade had a marginal effect on outlays compared to monetary and fiscal policies. Arguments for expanding trade "assumes something which I believe to be false, namely that the bonds of nationalism are stronger than those of communism." The Mondale resolution set a "dangerous precedent," concluded Thurmond, based on a wrong-headed assumption—namely, capitalist peace.[31]

Congress tempered the bill, but the administration, opposed to Thurmond's brand of protectionist realism, did not give up on trade liberalization as part of its grand strategy toward international communism. By 1968, over seven hundred items from the COCOM export control list, including four hundred in October 1966 alone, were cleared for trade with the enemy. Computers, machine tools, and export credit guarantees flowed to Poland, Bulgaria, Czechoslovakia, and Hungary while Fiat-Vaz began building an auto plant in the USSR. This was part of bridge-building to the East and Johnson's cordiality with Brezhnev, whom he had met at the Glassboro Summit in New Jersey in June 1967. After the disastrous Tet Offensive in Vietnam in January 1968, the president tightened export constraints on nations that aided North Vietnam, but when the Czechs tried to liberalize their economy in the face of Soviet intimidation, Congress responded with a trade accord. The Soviet invasion of Prague in August nixed that, though trade with Eastern Europe nonetheless continued on an upward trajectory. East-West trade liberalization was increasingly embedded within the capitalist peace paradigm, promoting detente while not abandoning the Cold War. So-called rogue nations like Mao's revolutionary China aside, the dangers of trade with most of the communist bloc seemed diminished.[32]

Because Richard Nixon and Henry Kissinger based their foreign policy on détente with the PRC and Soviet Union, strategic trade relations adhered to the Kennedy-Johnson liberalization plans until Congress hardened once again. Laying out his worldview on February 18, 1970, President Nixon acknowledged a world order transformed by the recovery of vital allies, new nations with identities distinct from imperial and Cold War constructs, and a communist bloc fractured by the bitter Beijing-Moscow rivalry and Eastern European nationalism. Floating over all was the erosion of American superiority in nuclear weapons to the USSR and China. His Nixon Doctrine reflected this new world of equals, as he believed that foreign economic policy should always be discussed in a political context, and thus, because trade problems had become so intense at home and abroad, the National Security Council should be involved. To ensure that allies shared the costs of internationalism, he wanted to end the era in which Washington was asked to unilaterally "conceive all the plans, design all the programs, execute all the decisions and undertake all the defense of the free nations of the world." Drawing on the capitalist peace, he declared that "peace has an economic dimension" even when dealing with enemies.[33]

The new era of global pluralism required, in National Security Advisor Henry Kissinger's words, a "stable structure of peace" based, in part, on freer trade. In its details, foreign policy aimed at peace in Vietnam, balance between China and the Soviet Union, cultivation of closer relations between Eastern and Western Europe, reductions in nuclear arms with the USSR, peace in the Middle East, fixing the rapidly deteriorating payments imbalance, and reform of the disintegrating system of international monetary exchange under Bretton Woods. However he framed it, Nixon looked on East-West trade "essentially for political reasons."[34] As his chief foreign economic advisor, Peter Flanigan, put it in 1970 in a talk with an official in the Soviet embassy, easing export controls blended into the notion that "trade was only part of the broader fabric of international relations" that aimed for security and world peace. The Soviet official added that "Marx had said that economics was the fundamental of all international relations" but Flanigan countered that "political considerations would be the major determinant in any economic decisions" as well.[35] Trade was embedded in diplomacy, so caution was imperative. More trade might strengthen ruling groups in the communist world or raise superpower tensions if satellites tried to break away from Moscow. At home, the administration could expect strong conservative and liberal reactions to either a soft or a hard approach. Options ran from liberalizing to standing pat, concluded a National Security Council paper, and

Nixon must know, above all, that there was "no simple cause-and-effect relations between the level of our trade with the Communist countries and the state of our political relations with them."[36] In other words, there was no certainty that free-trade internationalism, however modified for dealing with the communist world, would ease or end the Cold War or enhance American influence with those nations.

Nevertheless, East-West trade involved diplomacy at its highest level. Just after entering office, Nixon hinted at accommodation with China by relaxing minor controls and predicting more progress should the PRC bring North Vietnam to the peace table. In August 1969, he became the first American president to visit a communist nation, Romania, where he pledged fewer controls and more trade. By December, Congress replaced the Export Control Act with the Export Administration Act, for the first time in the Cold War leading the way in trade liberalization with the communists. Nixon authorized his secretary of commerce, Maurice Stans, to look for additional ways to liberalize East-West trade though he refused to grant the USSR most-favored-nation status, which he thought premature. He did engage in selective trade reforms to bring Moscow to the arms control table. When asked about his reluctance to grant Russia equal treatment, he replied, "I do not accept the philosophy that increased trade results in improved political relations. In fact, just the converse is true. Better political relations lead to improved trade."[37] This seems to turn capitalist peace doctrine on its head. In basic philosophy, though, whether economics preceded politics or vice versa, like all presidents in the twentieth century, Nixon linked economics to politics, security, and, ultimately, to peace.

In April 1964, days before the opening of the Kennedy Round of GATT, six dozen congressional leaders from thirty-eight states gathered to protest imports. They suggested so many protectionist measures to slow the inflow that Herter worried about an uprising against the General Agreement on Tariffs and Trade itself. He darkly pondered the possibilities: Would this be a year of retraction in trade, as *The Economist* warned? To keep the negotiations on track, Johnson refused to add more products to the list of exceptions the United States presented in Geneva, but the EEC's list stirred outrage. The French designated numerous products ineligible for concessions, and other Europeans flexed their external tariff muscle so much that the Americans feared that the Kennedy Round might end in a whimper. Harvard's John Kenneth Galbraith thought that the Round had been oversold anyway, because the European Economic Community was set on protectionism and winning at America's expense. Any failure, meanwhile, would damage US foreign policy. The National Security Council's McGeorge Bundy told White House advisor Bill Moyers that the president should not "tie his own prestige too tightly to the negotiations" but instead gather his "group of fat cats" in the Advisory Committee on Trade Negotiations, a free-trade lobby, to guard his political flank.[38] Indeed, Johnson called a meeting to pledge trade liberalization, however unpopular, as essential to "a much better world, a world where peace endures, and where prosperity is present."[39] The business leaders appreciated the morale boost of capitalist peace internationalism in the onslaught of protectionism.[40]

Under cloudy political skies, forty-six nations began the Kennedy Round in May 1964, launching months of haggling over the exceptions lists. No nation wanted to pare down its list because doing so would open up home markets to more competition. The United States sought to minimize the Common Agricultural Policy and external tariff to assure more access into the EEC while the Europeans railed against high spikes in US tariffs, the escape clause, and nontariff barriers like the Buy American Act. GATT Director Eric Wyndham White came up with a reprieve by dividing the key industrial tariffs into five sectors so that they could be addressed on technical rather than political grounds. Deals in these sectors—in import-sensitive pulp and paper, aluminum, cotton textiles, steel, and chemicals—took shape late in 1966, but anger and disappointment had only begun regarding EEC agricultural offers. The Kennedy Round, which grew to over seventy contracting parties, was larger than any previous GATT round. It also dragged out for three and a half years, losing its energy and luster.[41]

Like all trade negotiations, the Kennedy Round boiled down to a tough give-and-take among business rivals. In 1964, it was clear that the rebels were in Europe, as the Six cautioned against exaggerating the possibility of large tariff cuts while they squabbled among themselves over trade, integration, and agricultural policy. Gaullism underlay the contention, so much so that the Common Market itself suspended operations altogether in 1965. This EEC crisis only added to protectionist applause for obstacles to trade liberalization; the presidential election of 1964 had leveraged that sentiment. Republicans had criticized Johnson for making the United States look like a self-sacrificing free-trading rube at the hands of clever allies. Republican candidate Barry Goldwater shifted his position according to the political winds by embracing protectionism, then accusing Johnson of caving to protectionists who threatened stability abroad by demanding voluntary export constraints from allies in Europe and Asia. Secure in his election bid, the president stayed the course and won handily. Yet Republicans had served notice that EEC levies on American farm exports were unacceptable—as well as criticizing the Kennedy Round by 1965 and the Atlantic partnership with it.[42]

The United States was trapped in its own Cold War conundrum. Washington paid a lot for security in Europe, funded in part by exports, especially of agriculture. But Europe protected itself from outsiders, and the more reliant the United

States was on exports, the more susceptible it was to pressure from the Common Market. While cutting barriers remained the goal at the Kennedy Round, all parties tied trade to domestic politics in an embedded liberal approach that caused clashes in Geneva. As a result, a gloom descended over the talks. The CIA noted the likelihood of a prolonged stalemate over agriculture within the Common Market, and between the United States and the Six once the EEC crisis was resolved, that would allow protectionism to "do incalculable harm to the unity and strength of the Free World" by returning the Atlantic powers to nationalism and trade wars.[43] Secretary of State Rusk lamented that Washington could no longer compel and cajole its allies, even if 1965 was the International Cooperation Year. Europe needed to avoid drifting inward; but the Six did not seem to listen, nor did protectionists at home. Rusk deflatingly stated that "the Kennedy Round, like all great enterprises, could come to nothing."[44]

STR Herter asked the Common Market—America's biggest agricultural customer—to give way. The EEC saw the United States as unrealistic regarding commodity protectionism in Europe; the Six could barely agree among themselves about fixing unified internal costs for commodities, much less take a common stance toward outsiders. A proposed special agreement on grains that granted low-priced US exports more access to Europe might discourage relatively inefficient European production and prod Western Europe to send more food aid to the developing world to ease the American burden. The grains accord provided a glimmer of hope in the farm sector before de Gaulle shut down Common Market operations in protest over weakening the common agricultural policy by such arrangements and threw the Kennedy Round into a quandary. In August 1965, Agriculture's Orville Freeman counseled postponing the tariff negotiations until the Six were ready; however, Herter overruled him because he did not wish to anger domestic producers by granting concessions on manufactures and giving in on farm goods. But he proceeded to table agricultural offers in the hopes of wresting concessions from importers in Europe, Canada, and Japan, though he withheld items of interest to the Six until their crisis ended. That was it. By the end of 1965, the Kennedy Round was lifeless.[45]

Only nationalists and protectionists on both sides of the Atlantic rejoiced at the EEC shutdown before de Gaulle relented in 1966. His five partners granted French farmers a subsidy and acquiesced to budget and voting procedures that lessened the power of the bureaucrats in Brussels and gave nationalist voices, like his, more clout. The eleven-month delay worried all parties because in June 20, 1967, Johnson's tariff-negotiating authority expired under the TEA. At the swearing in of the new Special Trade Representative, William Roth, in March 1967, Johnson warned against "narrow special interests" prevailing in Geneva and damaging "the economic and political fabric of the world community."[46] That was still the case in the agricultural sector. Under pressure from legislators, the Department of Agriculture was positively frantic over EEC import levies but realized that beating the Common Market with a stick was not going to work. Regardless of the enormous pressures on EEC policymakers, the Common Market had come of age as the new powerhouse in the Western trading world. The Six might adhere to the capitalist peace yet prized their economic power. Thus, as expected, except for grains, their tariff offers in agriculture were weak. Roth gave up; American farmers lost out.[47]

In the industrial sectors, various schemes quieted protectionism by regulatory measures. Even in the difficult chemical sector, Roth hammered out a deal by offering up the American Selling Price that mandated imports priced at the higher US cost. In the Kennedy Round "crisis" period of April–June 1967, before the TEA elapsed, the Common Market reciprocated on chemicals with decent concessions. Industrial tariffs overall fell across the board to a paltry 9 percent level, a gain for the United States and its export drive. Francis Bator, the National Security Council advisor on trade policy, told Johnson that the outcome promoted the capitalist peace campaign by guaranteeing, for the Atlantic Community, "our economic strength and vitality in the cause of freedom." On the whole, the GATT talks were "an important test" for the Free World, he added, as "we and our friends" looked past economics to the security interests of 200 million people in the Western alliance.[48]

The press applauded the Kennedy Round as the pinnacle of cooperation in international trade talks. Indeed, the tariff reductions applied to a whopping three-quarters of all world trade, with average cuts of 35–39 percent applied to $40 billion worth of goods. Japan was the only country that got more concessions from the United States than it gave, foreshadowing impending conflict over the next few decades, though accords with Europe and Canada favored the Americans. Roth's team granted $6.4 billion in concessions on manufactured goods and got $6.7 billion in return over the next five years. The GATT's Wyndham White had effused before the final deal that the Kennedy Round resulted in "a substantial measure of tariff disarmament" to set the stage for such growth in trade for the industrialized and developing nations alike that it would fuse nations in an "era of interdependence" of prosperity, development, and peace.[49] Consumed by the Vietnam War and unrest at home, Johnson welcomed the results as a bit of good news in an otherwise bleak foreign policy landscape, alluding to the capitalist peace by claiming that the agreement reinforced American "strength and vitality in the cause of freedom."[50]

Like Wyndham White's hyperbole, this turned out to be boosterism. There were disappointments in the Kennedy Round for the United States, as not all industrial sector deals netted a gain. Furthermore, non-tariff barriers were largely neglected, so they became the new problem in trade as tariffs dwindled to next to nothing. Exporters got some, but not enough, advantages from the Kennedy Round, which posed dire consequences for America's balance-of-payments account. Despite the good face Orville Freeman put on agriculture, farmers knew a loss when they saw one. The United States won no assurances of future access to the Common Market. The politics of trade were already having an impact. Rusk instructed Johnson to ask for just a two-year renewal of the TEA because Congress would balk at another sweeping bill after the showing in Geneva in the farm sector. Perhaps a blue-ribbon panel could flesh out a grander trade strategy that demanded more free trade among the industrialized nations and the mitigation of protectionism toward poor countries. In truth, though, the European rebels had won; Rusk noted that a "continental trade wall" had been constructed. Washington "could, like Joshua, trumpet against such a wall and perhaps it would crumble. But prudence dictates that we arm ourselves with other tools" such as a focus on the global South. Even then, the restoration of Washington's historic hegemony and leadership in the trade field was in doubt.[51]

Without a major change in trade, as well as reform of the monetary system, a new wave of protectionism and isolationism seemed imminent. The payments deficit and gold drain had temporarily shrunk, only to resurface by 1967 as Great Society and Vietnam spending raised inflation and the overheated economy stimulated a demand for imports. Washington still funded the lion's share of NATO defense expenditures despite its intense pressure on West Germany and Britain to offset American payments. A new reserve currency, Special Drawing Rights, let the United States continue to spend, yet the dollar and the Bretton Woods system itself came under great stress. Even the elaborate bureaucracy created under the export expansion drive stopped meeting in 1967, though the following year, the president established an Export Expansion Advisory Committee to provide guidance. Ominously, the trade surplus dipped as a rising chorus of criticism against the Trade Expansion Act and the Kennedy Round rang out. Farmers and legislators were livid that Johnson had accepted Common Market discrimination.[52] Financial deficits, declining trade balances, inflation, and competition from abroad—and the Vietnam War—made it easy to turn away from the capitalist peace concept.

The Common Market had made its mark. Charles De Gaulle continued to fight with his partners in the EEC while focusing his wrath on Washington, while a new cultural front opened as the supposed "Americanization" of Europe rankled the French. In military affairs, Paris began its troop withdrawal from NATO in March 1966, rocking the alliance and the idea of an Atlantic partnership. Except for West Germany, the other Europeans derided Johnson's deteriorating war in Vietnam; with Erhard's removal from office, even that friend disappeared. The United States still hoped for British entry into the EEC to point Europe in an outward-looking direction, but with Gaullism prevalent, this seemed far-fetched. The European Economic Community itself refused to halt protectionism in the farm arena and the consequences for the American trade surplus were dire. The amount of exports over imports plunged from a high of $6.8 billion in 1964 to $3.8 billion two years later, with much of the decline attributable to the EEC because the bilateral surplus with the Six was halved by 1967.[53] The European rebellion compelled Washington to pay a steep price for its capitalist peace foreign and free-trade internationalist policies.

Policymakers paid a price at home as well. The big business community applauded the Geneva results, calling for further reductions in barriers toward the West, the South, and the East, but there was general disgust. Many saw the Kennedy Round as a loss on the balance sheet, and scholarship has borne out their assessment. Senator Everett Dirksen and Congressman Gerald Ford, both moderate Republicans, had issued critical statements in March 1967, even before the Round ended; they claimed that foreign goods prospered in the American market but exporters did not receive the same reciprocity abroad. Theirs was the opening congressional salvo. Senator Russell Long, chairman of the Finance Committee, had begun oversight hearings to hold trade negotiators' feet to the fire, but he took them for suckers. So did Democrat George Smathers, who beseeched STR Roth not to "trade off a horse and accept a rabbit." Worried about labor, Indiana Republican Vance Hartke voiced a frequently heard line that the "economy cannot be dismantled to make the rest of the world happy."[54] That is, for the critics, capitalist peace had been the driver of trade policy for too long and had gone too far. "We realize that we must maintain our friendship with different countries throughout the world," wrote the American Apparel Industry, but the obsession with internationalism "is seriously hurting our own economy, is threatening the future of our own workers and is contributing greatly to the imbalance of payments"—a vital matter in the foreign policy that the capitalist peace purported to protect.[55]

A rash of quota bills, organized labor's defection on free trade, and the elevation of economics over diplomacy followed as a result of these broadsides and sent Johnson to war against protectionism. In December 1967, he repeated that the GATT talks had reinforced a strong NATO alliance by preventing "a chain reaction of counter-protection and retaliation that would put in jeopardy our ability to work together and to prosper together." Critics were simply being "shortsighted" by pushing against a policy road first traveled over thirty years ago under Cordell Hull.[56] "Protectionism is no answer to our balance-of-payments problem," he reiterated in early 1968. The solution lay with expanded trade, he argued, even as statistics in May revealed that the trade surplus had its poorest quarterly showing since 1959.[57] By year's end, the House had proposed to attach 729 quota bills, and the Senate 19, onto the TEA extension as a direct reaction to the Kennedy Round.[58]

The protectionists knew the Kennedy Round had not done its job of boosting the domestic economy as advertised, and they erupted across the political spectrum. Their erstwhile spokesman, O. R. Strackbein, lashed out at the sectoral deals at the Kennedy Round that loosed bombs against the economy. Senator Abraham Ribicoff, a liberal Democrat, miffed that the United States-Canada Auto Agreement of 1965 gave unfettered access into the home market, correctly

Fig. 8.2 By the end of the Kennedy Round in 1967, protectionism, in the guise of import quotas, was a disturbing concern for free traders and the Johnson administration. Cartoonist Herb Block portrays foreign trade interests as a large angry bear. A 1967 Herblock Cartoon, © The Herb Block Foundation.

predicted that Detroit would suffer trade deficits in car parts for decades. Johnson had allowed a deal that "screwed" Americans, he railed. At Ways and Means hearings in summer 1968 for a two-year extension of the Trade Expansion Act, Congress initially refused to honor Johnson's request to end the American Selling Price, and then textile, footwear, steel, and oil interests caught fire with demands for import quotas. In the election campaign of 1968, moreover, Democrats trumpeted liberalization as a boon for cooperation while Republicans turned on the capitalist peace and even the business sector perceived shrinking export opportunities abroad. In general, the GOP pushed for fair, not free, trade, to restrict low-cost imports. Senator Vance Hartke summed up, that because the Kennedy Round resulted in "unilateral disarmament," Congress must step in to "insure [*sic*] that trade is fair" in the future.[59]

Even internationalists like Richard Nixon embraced the fairness doctrine as the volatile year of 1968 wore on. They particularly feared Congress would impose quotas that would trigger a trade war that no nation would win. Quotas were ludicrous, claimed free traders, for an export-surplus nation like the United States. Such "an economic cold war where nobody trusts anybody and everybody stagnates," warned trade advisor Francis Bator, was simply "a matter of international politics as well as economics."[60] But with an economy in trouble and American society in an upheaval in the late 1960s, few were listening to expressions of the capitalist peace, and even the administration used consumer rather than diplomatic arguments at trade hearings on Capitol Hill. For instance, Dean Rusk barely mentioned the broader foreign policy objectives behind trade liberalization, focusing instead on the threat of the quota bills, access to the EEC, the threat from Japan, and the impact of trade on the domestic economy. In other words, the protectionist rebels shaped the debate.[61]

Indeed, in his final months in office, Johnson rallied against the quota bills but he had to exchange their defeat for retention of other barriers, such as the American Selling Price. He might have inadvertently encouraged the revolt when he announced the TEA of 1968 by fixating on imports and exports, thereby playing into the hands of those who also focused on the bottom line. The president titled his announcement "Greater Prosperity Through Expanded World Trade." It fell flat, and the extension bill failed as key allies, namely Big Labor, shockingly deserted the free-trade internationalist cause for the first time in decades.[62]

Lyndon Johnson left a legacy of rebellions everywhere in the trading world, including at home. The thirty-year era of capitalist peace dogma was waning, and in the tumultuous year of assassinations, Vietnam, and Democratic Party infighting, trade policy seemed to follow the trend of deterioration. In his last State of the Union address, in January 1969, Johnson linked peace to liberal trade policies and leadership, but that seemed mere lip service.[63] His successor also embedded trade in foreign policy, but he took a different tack. Richard Nixon unabashedly calculated his internationalist trade agenda according to domestic politics.

Nixon sensed the political fallout from the emphasis on capitalist peace. As historian Alfred Eckes Jr. has noted, a generation of administrations had embraced largely one-sided trade liberalization to promote world peace and security. The 1968 election campaign had discouraged that approach. The American Independent candidate, George Wallace, attracted blue-collar workers by pledging to stem imports from low-wage nations, while Nixon demanded tough bargaining to lower non-tariff barriers to exports and prevent imports from capturing excessive shares of the American market. Even the Democrat, Hubert Humphrey, sought to curb destructive imports. Although he had scant interest in trade policy, Nixon did see it as a diplomatic bargaining chip. For instance, he linked granting most-favored-nation status to détente, the Vietnam War, cooperation in the Middle East, and resolving outstanding Berlin issues. But Nixon accepted protectionism, not just export expansion, as the answer to economic distress, and his secretary of commerce, Maurice Stans, led the way. Even though he abhorred protectionism, Stans enforced the escape clause to deal with the payments crisis, an approach that tolerated a nationalistic diversion in trade policy. The Tariff Commission, with new appointees schooled in business or in Congress, also moved to protect certain industries much more vigorously than previous commissions had done. With the Kennedy Round in mind, Nixon, like his allies in Congress, downplayed further multilateral negotiations and looked instead to targeted bilateral deals, with Japan as a main target. He called for fair competition in trade, grasping, above all, the politics of trade.[64] Nixon was, fittingly, a rebellious president in an era of revolt.

It took two years for Nixon's neo-mercantilist, fair-trade approach to develop. The balance-of-payments account actually turned into a surplus in 1969, the only year after World War II it did so, as Lyndon Johnson's fiscal austerity measures took effect. Nixon adhered to them out of an obsession over the performance of the domestic economy and its political ramifications. Faced with rising debt and unemployment, Nixon focused on the 1970 midterm elections. He needed to reinflate the economy by appealing to a blue-collar base, the "Silent Majority" of union labor that was reshaping the Republican Party, and protectionism offered a way. Unions did not buy into his vision yet, and though the GOP added two Senate seats in 1970, the Democrats added to their House majority. At the same time, Nixon laid the groundwork for détente through a dramatic arms control agreement with the Soviets and plans to open relations with the People's Republic of China. This was a tricky strategy because he also needed to stimulate the sagging economy to head off extreme protectionism. Nixon held to capitalist peace ideology, but the domestic front demanded attention to make internationalism possible. Thus, he hoped for export constraints by allies rather than congressional quotas; if that failed, he would play tougher.[65]

Trade policy for the two years was tough but balanced. In March 1969, Nixon submitted trade legislation, calling for retaliation against unfair trade practices and more import relief at home. He also requested authority to reduce tariffs up by 20 percent and to end the American Selling Price. A task force on trade policy, under counselor Alan Greenspan, urged caution because the quotas bills carried over from the Johnson years, and Nixon's coddling of protectionists, alarmed allies that a third of a century of trade liberalization might be abandoned. In sum, the term "fair competition" conjured up fears. Greenspan recommended against a "grand design for a new trade policy," but he asked for a strong statement in favor of liberalization. Nixon could open markets abroad by reciprocal deals, assist workers through adjustment assistance, link East-West trade to foreign policy initiatives, and endorse generalized preferences to encourage independence from former colonial masters on behalf of emerging nations. Trade policy also had to be pursued with monetary and development reforms in a comprehensive package addressing the new realities of a competitive world. Henry Kissinger preferred this approach, reasoning that "foreign policy should not be the primary determinant of U.S. trade policy"—a stunning challenge to the capitalist peace paradigm from a national security advisor. The more traditional secretary of state, William Rogers, urged Nixon to "cast off the pall of protectionism that is enveloping international economic relations" by reasserting leadership over the trade regime.[66] As Nixon announced in his "New Strategy for Peace" in February 1970, such a role was essential. "Peace has an economic dimension: In a world of independent states and interdependent economies, the price of a failure of collaborative effort is high—in both political and economic terms."[67]

Acknowledging to European allies the enormous pressure for quotas, Nixon informed them not to anticipate another big round of reductions of tariff barriers. To be sure, he continued to stress European unity, British accession to the Common Market, and consultations over trade problems, such as the Six's harmful proposal to tax American soybeans. The EEC and the United States, he said, had a "joint responsibility" of "promoting a liberal international trade system through outward-looking policy and in future multilateral trade negotiations."[68] To his advisors, however, Nixon "linked NATO to soybeans" and said his support for the military alliance "would be seriously jeopardized if the Europeans took restrictive action against U.S. exports because mid-western Congressmen, who he can now control on security matters, would shift their views if European trade restrictions hurt them directly."[69] Above all, a transformation in policy was in order. In a special message on trade policy in November

1969, Nixon made "clear that the trade problems of the 1970s will differ significantly from those of the past."[70]

Interdependence was a fact, but so was domestic politics. Multinational corporations, satellite communications, and free trade had internationalized the world economy. Nations now competed effectively with the United States. He welcomed them; liberal non-discriminatory trade must prevail. Yet a healthy trade surplus needed to be restored, not least to reverse the payments imbalance and answer protectionism. New trade legislation addressed these concerns.[71] A free trader, Nixon divided peace and security from domestic economics and politics.

An enormous fight with a close ally, Japan, over its textile exports illustrates Nixon's fixation on the politics of trade. In November 1969, he and Prime Minister Eisaku Sato secretly agreed to return occupied Okinawa to Japanese control in exchange for tight restrictions on textile exports. The textile side of the deal provoked consternation, confusion, and hostility. Nixon needed to deal with a $1 billion trade deficit—and counting—with Japan that would quadruple by 1972. Japan also had penetrated American markets, accounting for over 15 percent of total US imports, but the same was not true for America's exports across the Pacific, which met inaccessible, protected markets orchestrated by a government/industrial nexus. Along with an undervalued yen, this dribble of exports accounted for the trade deficit. Nixon had long sided with the Cold War notion that the United States must sacrifice its home market to stabilize Japan, a base of Free World security in Asia, yet the outcries at home were intensifying. He turned out to be a pitiless, strong-armed negotiator and also nearly ruined the world trade system through the textile wrangle.[72]

Nixon's show of force consumed two summit conferences, two ministerial meetings, and nine separate negotiations over three years. Significant mismanagement allowed domestic politics to poison international affairs, as his Silent Majority strategy rallied white southerners in textile states, led by Strom Thurmond, who pledged a confrontation with Japan. In return for his endorsement of Nixon in the 1968 election, the senator wanted a slowdown on both civil rights legislation (which he got) and textile quotas to protect South Carolina producers. Meanwhile, Japanese business criticized the tough tactics, resentful of the "voluntary" export restraints their own government requested. Nationalists in Tokyo, like those in America, wanted to be heard. That the two nations faced off was a product of a quarter-century of knotted security and economics that had begun to unravel. Japan chafed at its secondary position as a client state, while the United States questioned its benevolence to an increasingly effective competitor. The Cold War consensus had faded. When once presidents were disinclined to pressure Tokyo, by Nixon's time, Japan was deemed a threat to the very order Washington had built and defended. Even Kissinger, never much interested in trade, realized the textile wrangle had entered his realm of foreign policy in a worrisome way. The president's national security team welcomed the Trade Act of 1969, wrote Kissinger's economic advisor, C. Fred Bergsten, because it demonstrated the administration's general commitment to trade liberalization. Nixon zeroed in on politics, though, pressuring Sato to impose quotas. Kissinger followed with insults, referring to the Japanese as "little Sony salesmen" focused only on money and not the larger picture of the Cold War. Sato countered, accurately, that American textile policy was "contrary to free trade principles."[73]

By hammering at a close ally, the textile issue directly threatened the capitalist peace model. Secretary of State Rogers warned that protracted negotiations over textiles "are weakening the U.S.-Japanese relationship, giving impetus to unwholesome aspects of Japanese nationalism, and affecting the stability of the Sato government."[74] In his reflective moments, Nixon agreed, telling Sato that peace and harmony were his overall goals. A CIA National Intelligence Estimate concluded that over the next decade, Japan would expand its role in the world due to its dynamic economy and burst of national power. Tokyo had a key part in improving relations with China, easing America's withdrawal from South Vietnam, and dealing with threats to Cambodia and Taiwan. Nixon knew protectionism at home risked upsetting Japanese politics and, equally as bad, trade barriers would undermine Tokyo's newfound international status as a helpful Asian power that had overcome its World War II legacy and championed the United Nations, tolerated an American military presence, and aided developing regional nations.[75]

For Nixon, though, textiles equated to politics. The trade bill allowed Wilbur Mills to deploy his Ways and Means Committee in a campaign for quotas, and that rankled Nixon. An improbable candidate for president in 1972, this powerful southerner held hearings in which seemingly every industry suffering from imports testified. He then proposed adding to the Trade Act of 1970 (renamed from 1969) his Mills Bill that triggered quotas on any imported item that captured over 15 percent of the domestic market. Business groups, administration officials, and Japan saw an imminent trade war and thought the Mills Bill was a bridge too far. He opposed it as a nominal free trader, to stifle a political rival, and for foreign policy reasons, and promised a veto of the entire Trade Act because the textile quarrel could spill over into broad political relations with Japan and the alliance and even hinder a withdrawal from the Vietnam War. Even Mills got cold feet. He and Nixon welcomed consideration of the Mills Bill in the Senate Finance Committee in October, but the simmering domestic pressure on textiles indicated that the quota issue had spun out of control. Fortunately, mandatory quotas died on Congress's adjournment in December, before the Senate could act, preventing what the Federal Reserve's Arthur Burns warned "would be the most important backward step in post–World War II international policy."[76]

The textile issue prompted the administration to launch a major reexamination of liberal trade policy and principles, actually the first time such a reconsideration had occurred in the capitalist peace era since the 1930s. In response to the shift by Big Labor and Congress toward protectionism, in April 1970, Nixon appointed a Commission on Trade and Investment, under IBM executive Albert Williams, to study the crisis in United States trade policy. The Williams Commission would report in 1971, the same year that Nixon turned up the heat on Japan in dramatic fashion by stunningly threatening to invoke the Trading with the Enemy Act—toward a friend—if Sato did not restrain textile exports. Bilateral relations hit bottom, but Nixon's arm-twisting, dictated by short-term electoral politics, forced Sato to place voluntary restraints on textile exports and get Okinawa in return. His muscle-flexing signaled that Americans would no longer robotically embrace the capitalist peace; a postwar phase of automatic internationalism in trade had ended.[77]

Foreign policy had changed, but the capitalist peace was not so much jettisoned as lowered in priority. The United States began to lean more toward economics rather than just security interests as before. As trade expert Ernest Preeg wrote in January 1971, the time had arrived for new initiatives in foreign economic policy because economic "problems will assume a greater place in the totality of our foreign relations in the years ahead."[78] The need for a vigorous response to challenges with the communists, with the developing world, with allies in Europe and Asia, and toward protectionists at home was evident. This was especially so in light of the bitter talks with Japan over textiles and threats by Congress to impose quotas on hundreds of imported products. Nixon had surprises waiting, however, challenging the capitalist peace order in ways not seen since the Great Depression. In the end, perhaps the president was the greatest trade rebel of them all.

9

Shock, 1971–1979

On August 15, 1971, President Nixon announced on national television a unilateral decision to remedy America's diminished global position due to the ailing dollar. Developed in secret, his plan prevented allies from exchanging their dollars for gold and imposed a 10 percent surcharge on imports to compel exporting countries to revalue their currencies. To tame inflation, he imposed wage and price controls—a stunning policy for a conservative—under his New Economic Policy (ironically, the same name as Lenin's economic agenda in the 1920s). This second of three so-called Nixon Shocks was, simply, shocking. His intention to visit Beijing to discuss diplomatic relations after a twenty-two-year hiatus represented the first shock; the third came when he hit Japan with the Trading with the Enemy Act over textile exports. The second Nixon Shock induced monetary negotiations that doomed the gold-based Bretton Woods system and punished free-trading friends. Treasury Secretary John Connally, who engineered it, crowed, "Foreigners are out to screw us. Our job is to screw them first."[1] Such neo-mercantilism did not honor the capitalist peace paradigm; the 1970s was a time of transformation.

Grand strategy and ideology—liberal internationalism itself—came under fire in the mean decade of the 1970s. The second Nixon Shock led Connally to gloat that Americans could no longer be called "patsies"; nonetheless, Nixon grew uneasy over the diplomatic implications of his jarring move.[2] He spoke constantly about the transformations of parity in the United States' relative strength vis-à-vis the rest of the world that the Nixon Doctrine recognized. Soviet nuclear capabilities had altered the balance of power; no longer was the United States predominant in security affairs. Friends, moreover, had revitalized as trade competitors, and a new approach was necessary to address that change. The "central issue" in trade persisted: did liberalization still serve American interests? Protectionists, who had risen in strength, did not think so, but Nixon labored to

Capitalist Peace. Thomas W. Zeiler, Oxford University Press. © Oxford University Press 2022.
DOI: 10.1093/oso/9780197621363.003.0010

fend them off, though delicately. "Our trade policy problem is not ours alone," he said. "It is truly international in scope. We and other countries shall all move toward freer trade together or we shall all retreat to protectionism together."[3]

Nixon's new Council on International Economic Policy prioritized a fresh agenda for trade policy. As the Commission on International Trade and Investment, chaired by Albert Williams, readied its report, the Council on International Economic Policy, under investment banker Peter Peterson, toed the internationalist, capitalist peace line. This did not always translate upward; the buzzword was still "partnership," but interdependence, Nixon-style, meant real, concrete measures to correct the deteriorating domestic economy. It was time for hard diplomacy and politics, not theory, but the hint of mercantilism worried free-trade advocates. The National Foreign Trade Council could stomach short-term deviations from liberalization, but "realism requires recognition that a number of critical problems may be even less amenable to quick resolution."[4]

The difficult and changing economic environment, overlaid by benign rhetoric urging cooperation, was the underlying theme of the Williams Commission. The commission reported to Nixon in July 1971, a month before the second shock. Predicting that the United States would run its first merchandise trade deficit since the middle of the Great Depression that year, Williams gave the president ammunition for his audacious moves in the world economy. To be sure, the commission endorsed liberal trade and even suggested intensive negotiations to lower existing barriers (especially to commodities from the developing South), eliminate most tariffs in a decade, and abolish the rest within twenty-five years. In addition, monetary reform was needed for greater exchange rate flexibility. There were also recommendations to reduce the payments deficit that conflicted with this liberal posture, including orderly marketing arrangements—essentially, export restraint agreements. If these remedies failed, the report endorsed Wilbur Mills's plan for a temporary blanket surcharge on imports. This contravention of GATT obligations, which Johnson had considered in 1968, represented "a protectionist move with severe foreign policy consequences," warned the National Security Council.[5] In terms of sheer gall, however, a surcharge's possible dramatic impact at home and abroad captured Nixon's attention.

Paul McCracken, chairman of the Council of Economic Advisors, warned about drastic action that protectionists would use as evidence that the economy was floundering from imports. "We must keep our cool here and maintain our perspective" because the trade position "is part of a much larger ball game" based on a weak dollar, he admonished Nixon.[6] Radical change was in order under an economy-first ideology, countered nationalists in the administration, led by Connally. As the Williams Commission echoed, there is "increasing concern that the foreign economic policy of our government has given insufficient weight to our economic interests and too much weight to our foreign policy relations, that it is still influenced by a 'Marshall Plan psychology' appropriate for an earlier period."[7] Nixon tipped toward that view.

The surcharge became reality when the president declared the second Nixon Shock. This was about stemming inflation, which was about politics as well as the domestic economy, as much as the need to boost the dollar and curb the payments deficit. Nixon slammed shut the gold window and imposed a 10 percent surcharge on imports, pledging to remove it if Japan, West Germany, and others revalued their currencies against the dollar to make US exports more attractive, and theirs less so. Nixon noted in his evening announcement that he sought two of the nation's "greatest ideals" with his policies: "to bring about a full generation of peace, and to create a new prosperity without war." That perfectly expressed the capitalist peace but he really sought to rekindle the nation's ability to compete in the world economy by a draconian, politicized action.[8] Essentially, he put America first. Nixon could have negotiated to suit his internationalist leaning, but instead, as a politician frustrated by criticism from protectionists and a bad economy, he chose the big, audacious play. The move elicited stunned headlines around the world. There were appreciative ones at home, though, where the economy consistently polled ahead of other issues, including the Vietnam War, as the nation's top problem.[9]

Beyond politics, the Nixon Shock sought to reassert American power. In trade, the temporary import surcharge spurred on devaluation by allies and set a warrior tone that Nixon cultivated as a tough negotiator. An even bigger issue was at stake, though, as the Shock addressed a central premise of the capitalist peace model. In the words of C. Fred Bergsten, the National Security Council's economic advisor, "foreign economic policy has been the handmaiden of overall U.S. foreign policy through the post-war period," but pressure and circumstances necessitated a switch in that relationship. Whereas the great initiatives—Bretton Woods, the General Agreement on Tariffs and Trade, the Marshall Plan, the Alliance for Progress—were based on "foreign policy considerations," Nixon had decided to "increase the 'economic' content of foreign economic policy—for the same reasons that we are now seeking to share our global role in political and security matters." Free-trade internationalism still underlay the capitalist peace, but the key was to find a balance between economic and foreign policy components. This meant the elevation of economics, as Nixon sought Cold War unity behind a renovated trade system.[10] To combat inroads on American hegemony, the administration called for capitalist reform as well as peace, and this approach remained a fixation during the decade—and has done so ever since.

Fig. 9.1 Richard Nixon's economic shock of August 15, 1971, included a 10% import surcharge on foreign goods to correct the US payments imbalance, representing the first turn toward nationalistic mercantilism by a president since the Great Depression. The president, shown seated middle, joins his advisors at Camp David before his announcement. To his right is Treasury Secretary John Connally, the architect of the draconian measure, which included wage and price controls. George Schultz of the Budget Office is to Nixon's left, and Paul McCracken of the Council of Economic Advisors (CEA) and Arthur Burns, chair of the Federal Reserve System, are on either end, as CEA member Herbert Stein walks by. The Richard Nixon Presidential Library and Museum (National Archives and Records Administration).

The Nixon Shock signaled a faith in competition but with such a nationalistic thrust that allies came decidedly second to the domestic economy. Regardless of the lofty rhetoric about shared values in world affairs, this was a stark message to friends abroad. The surcharge in particular served as an ultimatum; either trade partners assume a greater burden in economic affairs or risk a backlash by American voters who would ruin the internationalist economic order. Supporters called it a "Pearl Harbor in reverse" to Japan, the primary target of the Nixon Shock.[11] Nixon reasoned that others should start paying the piper. The United States used to hold "all the chips" in the poker game of world trade, and "we had to spread them around so that others could play," but that "is no longer true today," he informed Congress.[12] His advisor, H. R. Haldeman, instructed speechwriters to reinforce the notion "that we have too long acted as Uncle Sugar and now we've got to be Uncle Sam."[13] The Treasury's Connally added that "it's time to put the country first; we're coming into a new era."[14]

In sum, the Nixon Shock jolted friends to help build a new system of trade and finance to prevent recurring crises, quiet protectionism, and maintain a strong alliance—to reform and preserve the capitalist peace. The Federal Reserve's Paul Volcker argued that the August 15 moves, including the import surcharge, aimed not to restrict trade but quite the reverse. Allies needed adjustments to improve America's position in the world economy. Nixon confessed that some might view his approach as self-interested nationalism, though he saw it as thwarting isolationism. "An America that is unable to maintain its military strength—and, incidentally, in the whole free world the United States pays two-thirds of the military bill today—a weak America that is unable to have its economic policies abroad, our economic, our foreign aid programs, the rest," he said, "inevitably will withdraw into itself."[15] He did not seek "to declare war on the other great trading nations" but rather prod them into paying their fair share to build "a permanent foundation for fair, free-international trade in the future."[16]

Trade partners got the revised capitalist peace message, which they understood even if they despised the import surcharge spanking. Latin Americans were furious, and even Poland and Yugoslavia issued rebukes. Canada and Asian allies expressed their dismay, fearing that the temporary tax on imports would extend for some time, and the European Economic Community protested through the GATT that the surcharge was inimical to free-trade doctrine. It was, and it triggered diplomatic dissent as a result. Kissinger met with European officials who, like Ralf Dahrendorf, commissioner for trade of the European Communities (the renamed EEC), informed him that changing the exchange parity of the dollar with their currencies was acceptable but the "overriding feeling within Europe is that no unilateral concessions on trade should be made to the United States." After all, the American deficit was not Europe's fault, nor did the Common Market want a trade war. Whether Washington wanted one was another matter; the import tax, feared Europeans, might be "a de facto and unilateral annulment" of the Kennedy Round results.[17] Reporting from abroad, economic czar Peter Peterson told Nixon that the allies accused the United States "of everything from 'indifference' to 'intransigence,' to being 'bullies' and 'bludgeoning' our partners." They also considered calling Nixon's bluff, perhaps retaliating because they suspected the surcharge was imposed only for domestic political reasons.[18]

The Japanese, reported the American embassy in Tokyo, though charmed by Connally when he visited Tokyo in November 1971 to pursue currency revaluation, were stunned into "self-reflection" about their economic policies, which is what Nixon had hoped. Connally claimed that the Nixon Shock had not singled out Japan, but he was being disingenuous. Japan, the third biggest economic power on earth, limited import penetration while its goods seized American markets. He knew the import surcharge and revaluation of currencies would hit

Japan harder than any nation and, after all, the country had undergone substantial Nixonian arm-twisting on textiles. Once again, Japan was a scapegoat for America's inability to deal with its self-imposed unemployment and inflation. Nonetheless, Tokyo dutifully revalued the yen and over the next year of meetings with Kissinger, Japan agreed to reduce the country's bilateral trade surplus with the United States by two-thirds, to close to $1 billion. The good ally fell in line.[19]

Nixon, too, was disingenuous toward Japan. He cringed at racist talk of a "'yellow peril' threat" because the Japanese were good suppliers of autos and electronics, and good customers as well. Textiles in particular, regretted Kissinger, had reached a "high plane" of foreign policy, well out of proportion to their importance, including threats to use the Trading with the Enemy Act in September if Tokyo did not assent to export restraints.[20] But in private, the president showed his political colors, and personal contempt, complaining that he should have held back on the return of Okinawa "'til we got the bastards on the line" regarding textiles. He got Japanese acquiescence on currency revaluation and a textile deal that fall.[21]

Yet his contempt toward Japanese trade competition set an unsavory tone, even adding to Tokyo's overall feelings of inferiority to, and racial rejection by, the West. Despite its new economic power status and desire to end its subservience to the United States, Japan seemed more a client than an independent state. Nixon's opening to the People's Republic of China (the first Nixon Shock), though welcomed as a means of reducing world tensions, was also unsettling because it might shift Washington's attention away from its erstwhile ally, though Tokyo and Beijing agreed to normalize relations in late September 1972. Still, the economic and textile shocks added to psychological insecurity and stirred the kind of belligerent nationalism in Japan that reminded observers of the 1930s. Prime Minister Sato in 1972 revealed a sense of gratification that the "series of rough jolts" of the past six months, including the three Nixon Shocks as well as Taiwan being unseated from the United Nations, were over. Nonetheless, uncertainty about future bilateral relations and Japan's role in the world would remain for decades, as Japan's growing $3.5 billion trade surplus with the United States provoked more disputes.[22]

At home, Democrats hammered at most aspects of the August 15 plan while supporters welcomed the bold approach. Most Republicans thought of Nixon, according to radio commentator Paul Harvey, as a "gutsy quarterback" who had tried to defeat inflation by traditional runs into the line. After losing yardage, he had gambled on the fourth down with a big play that risked his reelection. Organized labor also mostly applauded the strong message, though not so much the wage controls, but Democratic National Chairman Larry O'Brien smirked that it was "no wonder the President wants to run off to China. Faced with that kind of an economic mess, who wouldn't?"[23] If trade partners retaliated over the surcharge, Nixon would have nobody to blame but himself, bristled Wilbur Mills. While most of the business community backed the wage and price freeze to tame inflation, they were lukewarm over the gold and import tax measures. The surcharge was so tough, warned one, that it "could set off a trade war."[24] Floating exchange rates might make exports more competitive, but the import tax was a protectionist overreaction to the payments deficit. "If the real purpose of the surcharge is psychological warfare with the Japanese and the West Europeans," stated the Committee for a National Trade Policy, "this is a very risky gamble." It raised doubts about American intentions that have "at best been drifting" backward of late. Better to restore confidence through free-trade internationalism, backstopped by a coherent adjustment strategy at home.[25]

The use of trade and monetary weapons to wrest changes from allies and satisfy the clamor in Congress saved the dollar. The trade balance, however, continued to stagnate. The surcharge had to end, Kissinger noted by late November 1971, before it poisoned relations with Europeans and damaged their economies beyond repair. Indeed, officials rushed to Europe and Japan, expressing concern over a spirit of "turning-inward on both sides of the Atlantic which, if left unchecked, could drift toward a new kind of dangerous political isolationism which neither could afford," wrote advisor Peter Flanigan in June 1972.[26] Nixon held the line. As he informed British Prime Minister Edward Heath, he did not fear being branded a nationalist who deviated from freer trade. Thus, Connally eventually pressured the allies into revaluing their currencies and creating new exchange rate parities under the Smithsonian Agreement of December 1972, and Nixon responded by ending the import surcharge. In 1973, a floating exchange regime replaced the dollar parities that had, once again, collapsed, and along with Japan and the European Community, Washington promoted renewed efforts for trade liberalism through the GATT. Nonetheless, confirmed Nixon, more import competition was a "political loser" in the United States.[27] Such cynicism questioned the relevance of the capitalist peace paradigm.

Assaulting the traditional capitalist peace concept came back to haunt Nixon, ironically, when he tried to ease relations with the Soviet Union. Congress cast trade with the communists in economic terms or as a bludgeon on human rights rather than as a tool of détente, wedging apart the bloc, or winning the Cold War. The administration sought to link economics to improving overall relations, and Nixon started by easing trade and credit restrictions with the Soviet Union (and Poland) to facilitate commercial arrangements as part of an agreement reached during his historic visit to Moscow and Warsaw in May 1972. Trade talks paved the way for the superpowers to co-exist peacefully through cooperative endeavors, such as the joint Apollo-Soyuz space missions launched in 1975, but Nixon faced dissent against détente that ultimately led to its breakdown.[28]

China also served as a good example of détente through trade, guided by the capitalist peace. Of course, Washington guarded against Red Chinese aggression in Asia as the nation recovered from its frenetic Cultural Revolution, but normalization of relations might serve American interests by extricating the country from the Vietnam War through pressure on Hanoi. Talking to China might leverage relations with the Soviets, who split ideologically with the PRC and sought arms control agreements with Nixon. Beijing itself was emerging from isolation; the United Nations seated the PRC, for instance. Although a subsidiary issue to security considerations for Taiwan, Japan, and Indochina, trade could nonetheless facilitate China's improved standing in the world. As a result of these calculations, on "broad foreign policy grounds," in July 1969, Nixon quietly ordered a relaxation of trade controls, removing China from the strict embargo list and permitting purchases of non-strategic goods such as food, pharmaceuticals, and fertilizer. Tourists and overseas residents could buy up to $100 of Chinese goods for non-commercial purposes, and companies and foreign subsidiaries got authorization to sell non-strategic products on the same basis, though they could not import directly from China.[29]

Liberalization quickened as the administration perceived exchanges with China had political purposes, even if they didn't yield immediate profits. In 1970, the Commerce Department authorized oil companies to ship to and from the PRC, and the following year, Nixon announced expedited visas for PRC visitors and relaxation of currency controls on dollars. Merchant vessels were cleared to call at Chinese ports as the two-decades-old trade embargo ended, lifting restrictions on imports from China and boosting American exports. Kissinger's visits to China throughout 1971 yielded cautious optimism that trade and travel agreements were aiding the cause of détente. By early 1972, the State Department and National Security Council discussed affording the PRC licensing treatment equal to the Soviet Union's in respect to commodities and technology available for export, and over Defense Department objections, Nixon approved the move. The administration knew China could get most of these goods elsewhere anyway, and Beijing had expected such liberalization. Readying for Nixon's trip to Beijing in February 1972, State also proposed trade missions, centers, and fairs in China to help exporters. During the visit, trade was discussed between foreign ministers, though both sides knew this was mostly theatrics to warm up general relations. Secretary of State Rogers turned back a request from his counterpart, Chi P'eng-fei, for most-favored-nation treatment because there were so few exports from China and the differential in tariff rates was minimal. Nonetheless, the Shanghai Communiqué of February 28, 1972, noted the desire to facilitate expanded trade on a basis of equality and mutual benefit.[30]

Diplomacy toward China provoked protests by Cold Warriors worried about Taiwan's independence and by the hard-right fringe at home. For the latter, Mao was still a gangster, mass murderer, and illegitimate leader who aimed to destroy God and family as part of a worldwide conspiracy to spread a "new order" of communist "absolute, atheistic, amoral, and merciless tyranny."[31] Supporters of Taiwan, like the World Chinese Traders Convention, representing 20 million people of Chinese descent outside the mainland, viewed this violator of a free society and a free-enterprise system as a real threat to the capitalist peace. There were less ideological but legitimate concerns about China's behavior, including memories of its aggression in Korea, its support of African rebellions, and its aggressive actions in India, Tibet, and Southeast Asia. Opponents bombarded Democratic Oklahoma congressman Fred Harris on his introduction of an amendment to the trade bill of 1971 to grant China most-favored-nation status. Most Republicans viewed China as permanently and implacably hostile to America.[32]

Liberals and realists, on the other hand, sought engagement, and the Nixon visit was a step toward resolution of outstanding issues, like the PRC-Taiwan standoff. Besides, once the PRC joined the United Nations in 1971, the world community considered Beijing part of the future. For the foreign policy establishment, the Chinese seemed more bent on development than on aggression. Missionaries urged normalization to reduce tensions, deal constructively with war in Asia, and nurture mutual understanding. Thus, Nixon's gradualism toward the PRC was proper and realistic. Although China was unlikely to rush to consumerism any time soon—the vaunted China Market of centuries past still animated investors—it could buy technology as well as goods like musical instruments and sports equipment. China was needy, but not naive; granting most-favored-nation status down the road would show sincerity. Americans might hate Red China, wrote Republican Page Belcher, but it "represents nearly one fourth of the world's population [and] I think it would be very unrealistic to treat them as if they no longer exist."[33]

Thus, Nixon moved thoughtfully in the trade arena. Foreign Minister P'eng-fei had pledged to allow American companies into the Chinese market, initially inviting a small number to attend the Canton Fair in spring 1972. Appreciative of the gesture, the administration still proceeded slowly because of Chinese mercantilism; Beijing sought only imports essential to its economy and exports for hard currency. Rogers reminded the Chinese that expanding trade was desirable but not critical to the United States, but that the important point was that such trade had "political and economic significance." That is, trade under capitalist peace guidelines, Nixon believed, was "important as evidence of the improvement in our relationship."[34]

A foreign policy shocker, the China opening contrasted to the tough sell for freer trade at home as an assertive Congress demanded fair trade—managed trade as it was called—including import quotas. In late 1971, two Democrats, Representative James Burke of Massachusetts and Senator Vance Hartke of Illinois, introduced legislation to return imports, on a product-by-product basis, to the level reached in 1965, which would decrease the volume of imports by one-third, and then freeze them there. Furthermore, the Burke-Hartke bill created a new agency to administer quotas, exemptions, and the escape clause if imports undermined domestic production. Unions backed the measure to stem unemployment, blaming job losses on imports and the relocation abroad of low-wage industries like textiles and electronics. Burke himself had supported the Trade Expansion Act as a job creator, yet a decade later, he reversed himself and sided with the AFL-CIO on worker protection. Burke-Hartke so trashed GATT principles and rules that Nixon, big business, and exporters abhorred it. Like the import surcharge of the Nixon Shock, the president developed qualms about economic nationalism, but he also prepared for his re-election campaign in which he counted on the Silent Majority of blue-collar support. His image as a tough, but internationalist, trader would help him against the fervently peace-minded and universalist George McGovern in the 1972 election. Nixon wanted to put the shocks behind him because, at heart, he was a capitalist peace and security advocate. But he also needed to attract those who backed Burke-Hartke. He split the difference, leaning toward liberalization by arguing for a "fair trade policy, not an insulation from trade" in Fortress America mode.[35]

The protectionist surge did not deter his return to the fold; perhaps his August 15 policy had scared him a bit, and he realized his foreign policy agenda was vitiated by protectionism and that his Nixon Shocks had done enough to assuage Congress. In any case, Burke-Hartke, which he would have vetoed anyway, was so radical that it was never reported out of committee. His trade policies also worked in the election, in which he was the overwhelming favorite due to his peace plan in Vietnam. Despite continued economic turmoil and his own brewing catastrophe, Watergate, the re-elected Nixon leveraged the risky unilateral protectionist approach of his first term to reassert capitalist peace liberalization. In April 1973, he introduced a trade bill that asked for five years of authority to reduce tariffs by up to 60 percent over ten years and eliminate all tariffs under 5 percent. Negotiators would take this comprehensive Trade Reform Act to a new GATT round; its goal, wrote Kissinger's economic advisor, Robert Hormats, was to head off "extremely divisive" legislation like Burke-Hartke that "would surely touch off a disastrous trade war" among the allies and "deal a lethal blow to any Presidential initiatives with Europe and Japan next year."[36]

European Community enlargement, and protectionism abroad, partly motivated the bill as well. New trade authority could attack non-tariff barriers in Europe, which was about to add Britain (at long last), Denmark, Ireland, and Norway. As an economic superpower itself, noted Peter Flanigan of the administration's Council on International Economic Policy, the EC presented uncertainties about the role of Western Europe in the world economy. The United States could either take a confrontational stance or approach Europe on multilateral terms to reduce worldwide trade barriers and reform the monetary system, and the administration chose the latter option. Dealing with Europe would not be easy, however, because the EC was still unyielding on agricultural import levies and on restricting preferential trade agreements with former colonies, which the European Community explained away as foreign policy concerns separate from trade talks. Flanigan learned that the Italians, British, and Germans understood the need to keep the EC outward looking and avoid an Atlantic split, but without decisive authority for trade liberalization, Washington could encounter trouble with its closest allies, who enjoyed growing power and confidence. After being pushed around on monetary affairs, in the calm after the Smithsonian Agreement, Europeans were ready for a major round of trade negotiations. The administration geared up for an overhaul in trade strategy to meet their wish.[37]

The trade bill was critical to workers, consumers, and trade partners—the latter especially because, Nixon stressed, it mitigated economic conflict that bred political tensions and weakened security ties. He talked of peace, ironically, as the Yom Kippur war erupted in the Middle East in October 1973. Ever the realist as he reconnected to the capitalist peace tradition, the president did not believe that trade automatically led to peace. The roads to World Wars I and II had shown that trade partners would fight each other as well as the enemy; thus, it "is grave illusion ever to think" that "trade by itself" leads to peace. On the other hand, the United States was at peace everywhere for the first time in twelve years. The superpowers might be far apart in their ideals and values, but trade played a part in the détente between them. So, Nixon remarked, "let's understand the positive point that can be made about trade and how it can help in building a structure of peace" by enhancing contacts that convinced prosperous people to discuss differences rather than fight over them. Summing up, he said, as nations had "a greater stake in trade, they have less incentive to wage war."[38]

He directed his internationalist thoughts at protectionists and those struggling against import competition because the Trade Reform Act faced an uphill struggle as the first oil crisis made recession fears flare, wages stagnated, prices rose, and unions continued to rebel against free trade. Nixon's bill had help for the unions and for exporters, most notably allowing import restrictions against countries that unfairly shut out American products by denying most-favored-nation treatment—restrictions that would violate GATT obligations, but so be it because inaccessible overseas markets frustrated exporters. On the moderate protectionist side, he proposed a novel "fast-track" provision that allowed Congress to vote on any trade agreement the president submitted within ninety days. This meant bypassing cumbersome non-tariff barrier procedures, which liberal traders applauded, but compelled the executive branch to consult with Congress before accepting a trade deal, thus reasserting the legislative branch's constitutional prerogative over commerce after having lost it forty years earlier. The novel provisions seemed secondary at the House Ways and Means Committee hearings, however, where even Democrats backed mandatory import quotas, though all of them failed to pass. Still, hundreds of producers came out against liberalization, piling up 5,000 pages of testimony that included skepticism about embedding trade in foreign policy. Congressman Burke captured the moment. Some economics professors reasoned that industries must adjust to competition, that Japan was a model of such adaptation, and that protectionism skewed trade. Burke, a Bostonian, frowned on this argument from these Harvard pundits, blaming imports for killing off textile, shoe, and fishing producers from New England as well as tens of thousands of jobs. Entire cities, like Fall River, had collapsed as a result. It was time for protection, he asserted, as did many other protectionists, liberal and conservative alike.[39]

Nixon accepted most changes to his bill, but he protested the version that exited the Ways and Means Committee because the attached Jackson-Vanik amendment denied most-favored-nation treatment to the Soviet Union unless Moscow permitted its Jews to emigrate to freedom. Sponsored by two Democrats, the powerful senator Henry "Scoop" Jackson of Washington and the chair of the Ways and Means Subcommittee on Trade, Charles Vanik of Illinois, the provision held up the Trade Reform Act. By December 1973, after the American delegation had left for Tokyo to begin the GATT round without new authority, the House passed the legislation by a decisive vote of 272–140, with Democrats split but southerners carrying it through because of the tough textile deals. Liberals approved the bill for including Jackson-Vanik, among other reasons, but in the Senate, the measure didn't pass for most of 1974. The very efforts of diplomatic masters Kissinger and Nixon to activate the capitalist peace by promoting détente ignited this major controversy.[40]

Back in October 1972, months after the summit meeting in Moscow where Nixon and Leonid Brezhnev signed the Strategic Arms Limitation (SALT I) agreement, the two had also reached a trade agreement granting most-favored-nation status to the USSR in exchange for Moscow's repayment of its Lend-Lease debt of $722 million from World War II. Equal treatment had been in the works for some time, and Brezhnev and Kissinger had also discussed "large-scale point ventures" to appeal to businessmen, though the Soviets made few goods desired by Americans. The summit set up a Joint Commercial Commission to facilitate exchanges in a new era of peaceful competition.[41] Most-favored-nation status stewed until the end of 1972, delayed by election politics. When Jackson and Vanik introduced their measure in January 1973, the battle was joined with Nixon, who saw it as a direct attack on his détente strategy.

Because 60 percent of the House (over 250 members) and nearly three-quarters of the Senate signed on as co-sponsors, Congress laid down the gauntlet as Wilbur Mills tied Jackson-Vanik to the trade bill. By then, there had been continuous demonstrations by Jewish and human rights activists on behalf of "prisoners of conscience" in the Soviet Union, with every crackdown on repatriation precipitating "emergency sessions" of the National Conference on Soviet Jewry that comprised hundreds of agencies and Jewish communities.[42] There were attempts to mediate between Congress and the administration. Two California congressmen, Republican Jerry Pettis and Democrat James Corman, introduced a milder version of Jackson-Vanik that gave most-favored-nation status but based any extension afterward on Soviet progress in human rights. There were also concerns among GOP leaders that a hard-line measure might upset fragile peace talks in the Middle East by provoking Arab dissent over the inflow of Jews to Israel. But Mills preferred the tougher Jackson-Vanik amendment that made Democrats "heroes in American synagogues."[43] Jackson insisted on repeal of legal restrictions on Jews while Moscow preferred exemptions in Soviet rules, such as waiving reimbursement for educational expenses before exiting. As Brezhnev's visit to Washington, DC, in June 1973 loomed, the National Security Council worried that Jewish groups would initiate massive anti-Soviet protests, disrupting the summit and the trend toward liberalization of Soviet emigration policy.[44]

This pressure and the adept efforts of Jackson, who planned to seek the Democratic presidential nomination in 1976, bogged down the administration's efforts to get the trade bill through the House. The emigration issue rose far above a deal for equal trade treatment; the amendment interfered with grand diplomatic strategy. As Kissinger, Treasury Secretary George Schultz, and Peter Flanigan told Nixon, two presidential initiatives were at risk should Jackson-Vanik pass: Soviet cooperation in Middle East peace talks and reform of the international economic system. Jackson-Vanik struck at the capitalist peace because the "significance of both sides of the issue lies in the foreign policy area," namely, détente. If the amendment stood, Nixon would veto the trade bill, thereby denying a congressional mandate at the GATT's Tokyo Round. In sum, they warned, "the fabric of our economic and to some extent, our political and security relations with Europe, Japan, and much of the rest of the world could be damaged to the long-term advantage of the Soviets."[45]

Clearly, there was no good solution to the controversy. Congress would balk if the trade bill were delayed into 1974, a midterm election year, particularly if the economy slowed due to the oil crisis. Moving the bill out of the House with Jackson-Vanik attached, but quietly assuring Moscow that it could be weakened, was an option; another was to veto the Trade Reform Act itself. When Jackson refused a compromise, all of Nixon's counselors except Kissinger favored the first option. For Kissinger, Jackson-Vanik needlessly infected superpower diplomacy with the delicate issues of human rights and American politics. Because Nixon needed the Trade Reform Act promptly to take it to the Tokyo Round that opened in November 1973, he let it reach the House floor. He then threatened a veto if the Senate version included Jackson-Vanik.[46]

As the Senate considered the trade bill, other problems surfaced. Russell Long, chairman of the Finance Committee, knew the Trade Act ("Reform" was discarded) was destined to pass, but he was determined to censure European protectionism. He and Georgian Herman Talmadge, chairman of the Senate Subcommittee on International Trade, were skeptical of capitalist peace motivations behind the bill because their constituent farmers had seen their exports restricted in EC markets despite promises of better access by the special trade representative. When the trade bill went to the House, Kissinger proclaimed it a "New Atlantic Charter" that would link trade to a continued military presence in Europe, but Long mocked the trade/foreign policy connection. He declared that the "bloom is off the rose of 'Atlantic partnership'" because the United States is now the "least favored nation" in a system full of discrimination.[47] The Senate did pass the Trade Act, but the Finance Committee's report reflected Long's rebuke of the capitalist peace when it proclaimed that "no U.S. industry which has suffered serious injury should be cut from relief for foreign policy reasons."[48]

Many witnesses at the Finance Committee hearings agreed with Long. Big Labor, for instance, firmly opposed freer trade, even with the communist world. The AFL-CIO chief George Meany claimed that the United States got "the short end of the stick" when it came to the SALT I agreement, which had brought a "phoney [*sic*] détente" and a deal in commercial relations that favored the Soviets. It was time to place American interests above foreign policy objectives. "Every other nation on this Earth puts the self-interest of its own people first. We think that is a sound policy for the United States of America," Meany said. This was music to the ears of many Democrats as well as old-timer O. R. Strackbein, who still supported the protectionist cause and who, of course, welcomed import quotas and criticized giving the president too much authority to lower trade barriers. Like Meany, he leveled his ire at the capitalist peace, denouncing the "political considerations" that always seemed to come before economics.

It was time to end this elitist foreign policy obsession and focus on America's well-being.[49]

Nixon thought American interests did, indeed, lie with the capitalist peace. In his State of the Union address in January 1974, he blamed the Jackson-Vanik amendment for the Trade Act having stalled in the Senate. Because the provision upset the Soviet Union, it hindered cooperation in initiatives that were important to the American economy. Moscow could help bring oil exporting nations to the negotiating table, for example, to end the Arab embargo, lower oil prices, and, he hoped, put the United States on the road to energy independence. Not having the Trade Act to open markets abroad also raised consumer prices, while its delay jeopardized development for poor nations that relied on trade expansion.[50] On August 8, a day before his resignation, he reminded Congress that the world was waiting at the Tokyo Round for the United States to act on its capitalist peace ideology, for without the Trade Act, the "temptations of short-sighted unilateral actions could also seriously jeopardize gains we have made in the diplomatic and security fields."[51]

Others worried over the capitalist peace as well. The Trilateral Commission, a forum of North American, Japanese, and European private elites, formed in July 1973 to explore shared concerns between the industrialized nations, including the trade arena. Academic Zbigniew Brzezinski urged an end to the current trade regime that was so rife with unilateralism, crises, parochialism, protectionism, and frustrated ambitions on the part of Japan and the global South. That General Agreement on Tariffs and Trade could be replaced by an international pact that subordinated national policies and domestic politics to global initiatives that promoted growth through trade liberalization.[52] Former counselors Edward Fried and C. Fred Bergsten added that because interdependence was a fact, protectionism affected all nations. Since "the economic stakes in foreign economic policy go hand in hand with compelling political considerations," they noted, such unilateral measures as the Nixon Shocks or the Jackson-Vanik amendment precipitated "adverse consequences on political and security relations" that had nothing to do with the tariff law or negotiations.[53]

Jackson-Vanik remained a thorn, however, and the drumbeat from activists grew louder. Kissinger and other officials, including STR William Eberle, figured that the best hope for its elimination would come when Kissinger testified before the Senate Finance Committee. Congressional intrusion in trade policy had just gone too far. For example, one amendment referred to the Finance Committee required the USSR to express outrage at North Vietnam's failure to account for missing American soldiers before receiving trade benefits from the United States. The administration agreed that Hanoi needed to account for these men under the ceasefire terms of January 27, 1973, but Congress had overreached in foreign policy.[54]

In his appearance before the committee on March 7, 1974, Kissinger cut quickly to Jackson-Vanik. Like Congress, he confirmed, the administration did not condone communist immorality. The problem was not about right or wrong but in choosing between alternatives, within the capitalist peace framework that left nations free to decide their own system of government. That is, we "cannot accept the principle that our entire foreign policy . . . should be made dependent on the transformation of the Soviet domestic structure." Détente basically recognized the differences between communists and capitalists that could be placed within a workable structure of peace, but Jackson-Vanik risked upsetting that aim. When it came to Moscow, the administration preferred to focus on nuclear war and trade, not emigration. The issue was how "best to move from our present situation to a safer, freer, more humane world, while at the same time bringing important economic and political benefits to the United States." Kissinger counseled a veto of the Trade Act should the Senate adopt Jackson-Vanik in its present form. He did pledge to seek a compromise with Jackson, however, that both helped the Jews and preserved détente.[55]

A few weeks later, Kissinger met Brezhnev at the Kremlin to prepare for the summit. Pleased that bilateral trade had doubled, the general secretary looked forward to a deal on oil and gas, a new American trade center in Moscow, and more credits once Export-Import Bank restrictions were lifted. Most-favored-nation status lingered as the outstanding issue of the 1972 Moscow accord, however. Kissinger stressed that there was movement toward a solution. Brezhnev should focus on "the general improvement in our political relations" that economic ties encouraged, and once the Trade Act passed, more benefits would flow. Brezhnev listened uneasily, acknowledging Nixon's difficulties with Jackson's amendment that by "linking this matter with something that bears no relation to this entire matter" (emigration) was "tantamount to interference in our internal affairs." The Soviets would not tolerate such insults.[56]

The Jewish community and Jackson got their wish, however, after negotiations with Nixon's administration, and then Gerald Ford's, resulted in a deal. Jackson insisted that Jewish emigration from Russia increase to 100,000 people per year. The Soviets were willing to raise the number to 45,000 in 1974 and not interfere in the outflow, but Jackson stood firm, conceding on a waiver if the Soviets were in full compliance with harassment policies. He told Ford that Brezhnev's position on most-favored-nation status was simply about saving face; what he really wanted were the commercial credits. Regardless, Jackson insisted on Soviet concessions on emigration, and Jewish leaders kept up the pressure for them. After hosting Kissinger again for a one-day hearing, the Senate approved a version of Jackson-Vanik before passing the trade bill by a convincing margin in December 1974, a full year after the House. Under the Agreement on Trade and Emigration, the president granted the Soviets equal trade treatment on a

Fig. 9.2 Henry "Scoop" Jackson, left, confers with Senators Jacob Javits and Abraham Ribicoff, and President Gerald R. Ford, on the Jackson-Vanik amendment to the 1974 trade bill. University of Washington Libraries, Special Collections, Negative Number UW 41099.

temporary basis after Moscow assured that the process of granting freedom of emigration to its Jewish citizens was under way. Ford signed the Trade Act, but then Brezhnev refused these terms, as well the terms of the 1972 trade agreement, in which Moscow had promised repayment of its Lend-Lease obligations.[57] The Soviets did not buy into the capitalist peace.

Nonetheless, the Jackson-Vanik amendment continued to shape policy, remaining on the books for decades. In 1975, human rights, including religious freedom, were a prominent part of the thirty-five-nation Helsinki Accords that formalized post–World War II territorial boundaries. When Jimmy Carter made human rights a basis of his foreign policy, he tended to ignore them for Beijing because he wanted to get in on the trade action that other nations enjoyed there and also to use trade to liberalize the PRC. The most-favored-nation issue with communists persisted, becoming a relic of the Cold War until the Jackson-Vanik amendment was repealed in 2012.[58]

With Jackson-Vanik passed, Gerald Ford decided to sign the Trade Act of 1974. A stronger dollar alongside constraints on exports of steel and textiles had temporarily eased the trade deficit and therefore muted protectionism for the time being. The OPEC oil embargo sent the deficit roaring back, though, as petroleum imports tripled in value in 1974 and threw the United States back into recession. A traditional free trader, Ford disliked the Jackson-Vanik amendment for the same reasons Nixon and Kissinger detested it: It was discriminatory, a threat to executive authority at trade negotiations, and a rash entrance of politics into the trade arena. But the GATT beckoned. Four days after taking office, Ford urged passage of the Trade Act because 105 nations awaited in Tokyo. As the months passed, he grew more agitated. By November, with still no word from the Senate, he alluded to the capitalist peace, warning that without trade liberalization, the "unacceptable alternative is economic warfare from which no winners would emerge."[59] The Senate finally voted for the bill on December 14, putting the United States, said Ford, "in a position to launch a trade program that will strengthen our economy and further our efforts for peace."[60] Jackson-Vanik made him somewhat reluctant to sign the Trade Act in January 1975, but he knew his veto would be overridden.[61]

The Trade Act was a sweeping measure that bent to political winds, representing a third overhaul of legislation since the Reciprocal Trade Agreements Act of 1934 and the Trade Expansion Act of 1962, reflecting the economic straits of the 1970s but pushing forward with negotiating authority to lower trade barriers at the Tokyo Round. Participation in the Generalized System of Preferences, which Japan and Europe had ratified in 1971, became law. In general, Congress opened American markets, but the Trade Act assuaged protectionists with side deals, more adjustment assistance (that never materialized for workers), fast-track authority to give Congress a greater say over agreements, and an expansive reading of the escape clause, allowing industries to show that imports caused substantial, not major, injury. As well, temporary import relief measures could last up to five years, and firms got more relief from dumping, when foreign producers sold exports below the home-market price. Significantly, Section 301 authorized the Special Trade Representative to retaliate if nations restricted American exports, which took aim at EC agricultural protectionism and Japan's closed markets. Institutionally, the United States Trade Representative (USTR) replaced the STR as the official negotiating arm of the executive branch, and the Tariff Commission, renamed the International Trade Commission, was converted into an independent agency to make it more responsive to Congress. In sum, the Trade Act liberalized policy but also protected American interests more, at home and abroad. The debate revealed a Democratic shift away from a traditional free-trade stance, while many Republicans retreated from protectionism. To be sure, the capitalist peace concept remained in the background, though internationalism competed much more with economics in these hard times.[62]

The United States could now jump into the GATT round in Tokyo. These Multilateral Trade Negotiations (MTN), which concluded in 1979, aimed to dismantle trade barriers among the industrial nations, developing countries, and even the communist bloc. Tariffs, which dropped by a third at the Tokyo Round, were already minimal coming out of the Kennedy Round, so there was more emphasis on the clutter of national non-tariff barriers. They were so ubiquitous that the MTN dealt with them in six codes covering government procurement, technical barriers, subsidies and countervailing duties, customs valuations, import licensing, and anti-dumping. Although adhering to the codes was optional, they were the first attempt to extend GATT doctrine beyond tariffs, even though they were not very strict, as protectionism in the United States, Europe, and Japan attested.[63]

Nations of the global South also showed up at the GATT and, for the first time, assumed an active role, even though they looked past the forum to UNCTAD IV, which convened in Nairobi in 1976. They received special treatment under the generalized system of preferences, in which they put much stock. The North would rather have them in General Agreement on Tariffs and Trade than UNCTAD, for the latter could devolve into confrontation once again. UNCTAD might even elevate the radical New International Economic Order that sought an overhaul of traditional trade and investment policies by promoting self-reliance and debt-forgiveness in the South. But more and more emerging nations sought admission to the American-led capitalist order—the People's Republic of China was a key example—that showed these alternatives to be less appealing than integrating with the Free World.[64]

Reflecting the pressures of the interdependent world economy, the rich industrial powers comprising the Group of Six (West Germany, France, Italy, the United Kingdom, Japan, and the United States, which later added Canada to become the G7) began informal economic summit meetings. They met at Rambouillet, France, in November 1975 to discuss problems outside of the formal structures of the IMF and the GATT. Leaders hoped to project confidence and willpower, wrote Kissinger's office, in a time of recession and energy uncertainty. The United States was the only superpower present; it was also the geographical link between North and South, and Atlantic and Pacific, thus giving Washington a leadership role in world economic matters. Representing nearly three-quarters of world trade, the G6 noted that the interdependence of open, democratic societies demanded joint decisions based on cooperation that transcended differences, resources, and political and social systems. Focused on recovery and growth, it urged the reduction of trade barriers, particularly those that were rising precipitously in the United States, at the MTN in Tokyo. Rambouillet reinforced commitments to the capitalist peace paradigm. According to Ford's foreign policy advisors, the G6 showed that "the destinies of the industrial democracies are intertwined on economic issues in much the same way as they are in the sphere of defense and mutual security, and that differences must be subordinated to their paramount interest in their common well-being."[65]

As the worldwide economic recovery stalled and protectionism rose in the United States, the administration made strong statements in favor of the multilateral trade talks. An OECD Trade Pledge aimed at avoiding restrictive measures and a Tokyo Declaration adopted at the outset of the MTN vowed to liberalize, expand, and reform trade. Overlaying these agendas was diplomacy and politics. "International trade is, to a large extent, the glue which cements relations amongst the Western nations," wrote the Department of State in a background paper to the meetings. "It is also fundamental to Western efforts to establish more stable and beneficial relations between North and South and between East and West." In broad economic terms, the summit was critical to the capitalist peace, which was a foundation of US foreign policy.[66] Nonetheless, public opinion among allies showed a healthy skepticism toward American commitments to open its markets through free-trade internationalism, and as the presidential election season got under way, Democratic candidate Jimmy Carter piled on. In May 1975, he declared in Tokyo that the Nixon/Ford team was weak on trade liberalization. Indeed, Ford struggled in 1976 against such broad attacks on its foreign policy. When the Senate Finance Committee held four days of hearings on foreign trade policy early in the election year, witnesses referred to interdependence by harping on unemployment, which linked all nations. The fixation on the economy worried free traders, the guardians of foreign policy interests.[67]

They fought a rearguard action against protectionism. Five years before, Nixon had refused an escape clause recommendation to raise duties on leather footwear from Spain and Italy, promising Spanish dictator Francisco Franco not to impose them in return for a lease extension on American military bases. The International Trade Commission advised protectionism, though, and under the Trade Act of 1974, Congress could override a presidential rejection of the ruling with quotas or higher tariffs. Choosing adjustment assistance to aid the footwear firms, Ford told a manufacturing group in April 1976 that "several foreign countries would be hurt the most if we impose either quotas or any of the other remedies[;] our trade with them would suffer, and of course you know it is Spain, it is Italy, it is Brazil."[68]

The fact of the matter, as National Security Advisor Zbigniew Brzezinski warned President Carter in 1977, was that shoes were "a test case" of foreign economic policy, commitments to allies, and the effort to wean poor nations from Soviet influence. While the domestic shoe industry employed 170,000 workers in thirty-six states and accounted for 1.4% of the Consumer Price Index, shoe imports amounted to $1.4 billion from seventy-five countries. Footwear was the biggest case in history to be considered for restrictions. To be sure, imports were a problem, but so was protectionism's effect on foreign policy. Shoe quotas would strengthen the Eurocommunist movement in Italy and worsen an economic crisis in Spain, a country embracing a fragile democracy after Franco. Import restraints also added another issue to Brazil's rejection of military aid, non-proliferation of nuclear weapons, and human rights reforms; panicked a South Korea already anxious over American troop withdrawals; further upset Taiwan, which was already miffed by normalization with the PRC; and exacerbated Mexico's rising unemployment rate, which drove people across the border. These foreign policy considerations—problems confronting the capitalist peace—led Carter to negotiate orderly marketing agreements rather than harsh quotas, against the advice of the Trade Commission, as protectionists desired.[69]

Myriad industry complaints grew only more acute as presidents trained their efforts on trade liberalization, hoping to boost exports as a result of the MTN in Tokyo. The G7 summit in Puerto Rico in June 1976 presented an opportunity to emphasize interdependence through expansive trade, finance, energy, and aid policies but protectionist storm warnings clouded a cautiously upbeat assessment. All leaders at the summit except for Chancellor Helmut Schmidt of West Germany were in weak leadership positions due to the recession. Democrats on the Joint Economic Committee pointed out to Ford that inflation and unemployment must be his focus at the summit, and that he should not be fooled by OECD predictions for strong growth. The president, however, stayed positive, and the joint declaration at the Puerto Rico meetings pledged to fight protectionism, further develop East-West trade ties, and conclude the Tokyo Round by the end of 1977. The administration even considered that the North vow "complete or substantial free trade" with the global South by 2000 at the MTN. In San Juan, Kissinger lauded "the solidarity of the Western democracies," which guaranteed peace as well as prosperity.[70]

Ford's brave defense of the capitalist peace continued on the campaign trail, but in foreign policy, he stumbled. In a debate in October 1976 in which Carter came out swinging, the sitting president implied that Eastern Europe was free from Soviet tyranny. The gaffe also did not help win over voters to expand East-West trade. In any case, the country was sick of Republicans after Watergate, and it was in no mood for trade liberalization. Politics overrode foreign policy in an election year, particularly among voting blocs affected by imports of shoes and steel.[71] Ford was a sitting duck for the critics, and Jimmy Carter took advantage.

Carter took office after the worst economic downturn in postwar history, though by 1977, the economy was in recovery until fears of recession became nightmares by the end of his term as interest rates skyrocketed along with joblessness. This so-called stagflation crisis shaped his trade agenda as high interest rates led to a strong dollar, at the expense of the industrial export sector. Along with the Soviet invasion of Afghanistan and the disastrous hostage crisis in Iran, the economy wrecked his presidency. Nevertheless, Carter remained a firm trade internationalist, a stance bolstered by his advocacy for human rights, cultivation of North-South relations, and moderation toward the new trading power on the block, Japan. "Our desire for justice, stability, and peace finds practical expression in world trade," he proclaimed after a few months, with capitalist peace rhetoric.[72]

When it came to the foreign policy of trade, Carter focused on the global South by seeking to reverse the Kissinger era of "confrontation politics" dividing the emerging nations. Carter was genuinely repentant about Washington's history of intervention in the developing world. America had also become dependent on raw materials like oil, nickel, lead, and tin, so confrontation was counterproductive. For its part, inspired by OPEC's effectiveness in raising oil prices, the global South sought help for booming populations and yawning poverty through growth, managing natural resources, dealing with terrorism, stabilizing food prices, gaining technology, and for some, joining the nuclear club. Carter vowed a new global order of equity and hope—a new progressive take on the capitalist peace—centered on "basic human needs" (food/nutrition, health services, and education) to attack dire poverty. He shifted the focus to poor people, rather than poor nations, experimenting with creative development strategies. This all amounted to a try at a more systematic foreign assistance program than before, but it failed because the developing world saw it as patronizing and Americans as too interventionist. Even having a North-South policy was questioned; like Kissinger before him, Carter failed to construct a compelling concept of development. The eruption of superpower tensions midway through his term also shifted his priorities. Besides, his coddling of dictators, like the Philippines' Ferdinand Marcos and the Shah of Iran, belied his intentions to an extent.[73]

Regardless, reform of institutions (including the GATT), cooperation with UNCTAD (with a hope of phasing out preferences), and increasing market access for poor nations at the Tokyo Round (without poking the protectionist bears at home) shaped the agenda. The caveats reflected traditional policies because the administration sought long-term adjustments to problems rather than quick fixes for political reasons. Kennedy, another reformer, had paid attention to development, but in an era of prosperity. Facing hardship at home and abroad, Carter prioritized the "North-South dialogue" at a time not conducive to reform.[74]

A task force warned of inroads on the capitalist peace regime. While protectionism could hurt the US economy, it cautioned that trade conflicts "could also have a seriously adverse effect on *U.S. foreign policy*" because economic issues were so central to both rich and developing nations. Consumer pressures had built a new constituency for freer trade at home, and there was also widespread recognition that liberalization "is the most meaningful step which the richer countries can take to help the poor." The task force suggested ample resort to adjustment assistance and consultations with Congress, interest groups, and key countries (like France) on agriculture to deal with protectionism. It also proposed a "mini-MTN" in Tokyo by the end of the year with specific industries to jumpstart the stalled GATT talks and "head off a real threat of international trade war." The administration should look toward 1979 to conclude the round with a modicum of liberalization and, in the interim, call for a G7 summit in 1977 to illustrate Carter's innovative approach to development and trade.[75] Sent to Europe and Asia after the inauguration, Vice President Walter Mondale urged multilateral management of the trade system rather than the "dangerous precedent of bilateral solutions" that fed into unilateral protectionist pressures and weakened the GATT cooperative framework.[76]

Was there room for the capitalist peace in these hard times? Perhaps not. Mondale got a warm reception in Japan, which suffered from inflation, but a cooler one in West Germany, which did not. Clayton Yeutter, the outgoing USTR, noted that the trade climate soured as deficits worsened due to oil import prices and slow recovery in Europe. Progress at the Tokyo Round had been painfully slow as well. Japan's trade surplus and its concentration on certain goods, like autos, consumer electronics, and steel, had generated "near hysteria" in Europe and the United States. Heading into the London economic summit in early May 1977, Carter told reporters that he opposed protectionism but with unemployment the highest among the G7, at 7 percent, export restraints might just be the most politically feasible course. He got one with Japan on color televisions after the International Trade Commission recommended tariff protection, restricting exports by nearly 41 percent over a three-year period. In London, however, Carter met resistance on his stimulus package that privileged jobs over price stability.[77]

The seven nations determined to fight protectionism, but America's trade imbalance was not helping. The deficit tripled that of 1976, driven by high oil prices, the fact that G7 nations had failed to sustain expansion of their economies, and a rapidly devalued dollar, which sparked acrimony about the unfair advantage US exports had over weakened trade partners. Bad economies meant little generosity toward expanding imports from the global South, which set up clashes with the developing nations' own economic summit groupings, the G19 and G77. Prime Minister Takeo Fukuda of Japan reminded his counterparts that failure to deal with trade problems in a time of economic distress smacked of the 1930s, when "the situation instead became a backdrop to World War II."[78] But in his State of the Union address in January 1978, Carter spoke exclusively about the domestic economy when it came to trade. In a return to the turn inward under Nixon, Carter insisted that "free trade must also be fair trade."[79]

Carter intervened to prop up the dollar, which stabilized in summer 1978, but the hits kept coming, this time from oil markets. The G8 (adding the European Commission) had turned to their next summit in Bonn to do something about the cost of oil, and all eyes turned to Washington to see if it would reduce oil to control inflation. Carter understood his obligations, so he agreed to decontrol oil prices—that is, raise them to the world price level by 1980—though consumers punished him at the polls. The decreasing value of the dollar was directly linked to the United States' spending roughly $2 billion a year to import oil, which worsened the trade deficit by raising the price of imports—and inflationary prices with them. One way or another, Carter told audiences, oil imports must be reduced. There were storm clouds over the Tokyo Round. The G8 devised growth targets, retained the anti-protectionist pledge of earlier summits, and focused on expanding exports and investments in the emerging nations. They applauded progress at the MTN, which they planned to conclude by the end of the year after it had crawled along for three years, provoking the derisive label the "Long Round." The MTN sped up by late 1977, aided by mini-trade agreements that overcame European Community and American protectionism, thereby setting up a big close. Recessionary factors dashed hopes of a sweeping package of liberalization, however, as protectionism arose again. As USTR Robert Strauss wrote Carter, the administration must persevere. A failure in Tokyo would lower living standards and "weaken the international cooperation on which everyone's security depends," added Henry Owen, the ambassador at large for economic summits.[80]

Halfway through his term, Carter understood that regardless of such foreign policy victories as ratification of the Panama Canal treaties, Middle East peace, progress in SALT II arms control with the Soviets, formal relations with China, and a NATO buildup in Europe, his reelection depended on reversing economic stagnation (inflation and unemployment) at home, and expanding exports was critical to that task. Thus, the Multilateral Trade Negotiations had to be completed. Just after the 1979 New Year, the president had announced the progress made on the six non-tariff barrier codes and organizational reforms in the GATT. Strauss also pressed on agricultural trade but assured the European Community that he had no intention of assailing its import levy structure; rather, the United States simply wanted to get "our nose a little bit more under the tent" to liberalize the sector a bit more.[81] Carter's determination paid off, as the Tokyo Round ended in April 1979 without much controversy—and with limited results. Tariffs dropped, but they were already low; the global South got some concessions, though they demanded more. The industrial codes were a start toward addressing, however vaguely, non-tariff barriers. But agricultural trade controversies intensified ever more. Announcing the accord, Carter said that the new rules created more "equitable conditions" and that through "such fair and open trade, we strengthen peace and trust in the world and make more efficient use of the world's human and material resources."[82]

The fair-trade doctrine circumscribed this reference to capitalist peace foreign policy. Managed trade deviated from grand gestures of free trade because of intensifying protectionist pressures around the world that threatened to disrupt the GATT. As Henry Owens informed Carter, "British World War II infantry manuals advised troops that the best way to avoid mortar fire was by going forward, and somewhat the same principle applies in trade" in the face of protectionist barrages. The symbolic importance of the Tokyo Round might not be enough, though, to prevent a downward spiral of retaliation against free trade-internationalism.[83]

Because the MTN results were so unthreatening, the Trade Agreements Act of 1979 went through Congress easily despite an economy in shambles from the second oil shock and rising unemployment. The Trade Act of 1974's fast-track process required Carter to submit Tokyo Round enabling legislation to Congress. Skilled leadership by USTR Strauss, the only administration witness at the mere two days of Senate hearings in July, helped smooth things in Congress so there were no tantrums over imports or agricultural exports. Strauss noted that by insisting on more access to the EC, the Round might have dragged out another two years, and in the end, farmers accepted marginal improvements in the levies. The bill passed, and Carter exulted about the new trade law, in part because he needed good news since OPEC had just decided to jack up oil prices. Perhaps the capitalist peace could provide a distraction to the economic woes. Thus, he argued that trade liberalization "opens up thousands of unpublicized avenues of consultation and cooperation and the sharing of responsibility which quite often can help to alleviate political tensions and eliminate divisions," with the expansion of human rights and an increase in "productive interdependence" as the byproducts.[84] His signature on the Trade Agreements Act was a highpoint in an otherwise gritty year of recession.

What should have been a solid accomplishment on Capitol Hill got lost in the maelstrom of events in 1979, both economic and political. Inflation roared ahead, even in sober West Germany, which suffered its first trade deficit since 1965. If the German engine was sputtering, then the rest of the industrialized world was in trouble. That was certainly the case for the United States, where joblessness rose, production fell, and inflation rocketed upward with no remedies in sight except for the vigorous action of Federal Reserve chair, Paul Volcker, who stepped in with dramatically high interest rates and consumer credit controls. Those measures, however prudent, cratered Carter's public opinion ratings, because higher interest rates made exports less appealing but stimulated imports, which rocked manufacturers and industrial labor. He tried to remain constructive by talking of harmonious patterns of trade and payments, but his words paled in comparison to the crumpling economy and subsequent public outcry. The recession gave Carter's critics the upper hand. Former Treasury Secretary John Connally pointedly remarked to the press that if he were president, he would tell the Japanese prime minister that unless Japan bought more American goods and services, then its televisions and cars destined for the United States would rot on the docks in Yokohama.[85] That idea for managed, neo-mercantilist trade captured the gloomy atmosphere.

In fact, Carter's supporters noted that he had gone on the defensive in international economic policy. Oil prices and interdependence had revealed vulnerability to competition from a global community of economic equals, and the shocks of the past decade—and most recently, the fall of the Shah of Iran—showed that Washington no longer controlled the course of world events. The tendency was to withdraw, mope, or lash out at the competition through fair-trade policies rather than engage as an internationalist through free trade. The country seemed to shrink from challenges, its political will for capitalist peace absent. Carter recognized this so-called malaise, as he infamously told a national television audience.[86]

Most ominously, major achievements in foreign policy, including even SALT II nuclear arms reductions, looked like weaknesses when the Iranian Revolution culminated in the hostage crisis beginning in November 1979. The next month, the Soviets moved into Afghanistan, as events completely turned against Carter. His commitment to human rights seemed hollow as he focused increasingly on security and stability. When he mentioned trade, it was in the context of employment, low interest rates, and surpluses.[87] Chaos and uncertainty choked initiatives as the country headed into the election year of 1980. The decade ended as it had begun, with a nation shocked by transformations in the international arena and with capitalist peace ideology seemingly on the wane.

10

Victory, 1980–1990

In 1979, Cold War détente ended, but a decade later, the superpower conflict itself was all but over as the Berlin Wall fell and the Soviet Union headed toward oblivion. Historians debate who and what were responsible for the end of the Cold War, but it was clear that the United States had "won" it, even though competition in the world economy grew ever fiercer. Ideas and ideology, as well as policies, had mattered immensely; Soviet leadership changed with the realization that the country was bankrupted by Western liberalism. The capitalist peace paradigm played a major role in this battle during the 1980s for the hearts and souls in the communist, and capitalist, worlds.

While Jimmy Carter faced a disastrous combination of domestic economic and foreign policy crises in 1980, Republican Ronald Reagan had a clear solution: attack the evils of big government at home and Soviet imperialism abroad. Free trade supported both campaigns. An adherent of the Chicago and Mont Pelerin schools of free market conservatism, Reagan had no qualms about calling out Japan, America's top trade threat, as an unfair, regulatory competitor. Carter stuck to his script of promoting exports through a reorganization of policy under the Trade Agreements Act and hoping for more commercial exchanges with China as well as with partners who met at the Venice G8 summit in June to voice support for interdependence, development, economic stimulation, and limits to oil imports. But protectionism and monetary disorder persisted, as did the protests of the developing nations toward a system they believed was skewed against them. The United States operated in "an era of constraint and limitation," concluded the Report of the President's Commission for a National Agenda for the Eighties, published by a diverse forty-five-member panel. Every initiative in the world economy demanded a cost and had a direct bearing on international politics. Perhaps Washington could calm a fragile world community by

Capitalist Peace. Thomas W. Zeiler, Oxford University Press. © Oxford University Press 2022.
DOI: 10.1093/oso/9780197621363.003.0011

improving the economic performance at home, thereby blurring the lines between domestic and foreign policy.[1]

Such linkage opened the way for the Reagan revolution at home, which placed America first and reoriented away from government stimulus to accomplish this. The National Foreign Trade Council sought "to bring about a favorable climate for restoring American supremacy in world trade and investment" by elevating "market forces" over statist initiatives. This meant reducing trade barriers, including export controls in East-West trade for the benefit of American producers and consumers, and blocking protectionism. The big issue was fiscal reform; Reagan was consumed with reducing government spending and cutting taxes to stimulate productivity and savings. For his part, Carter lauded the export ledger, as overseas sales reached a record $180 billion in 1979. Imports slowed a bit due to limits on oil, but he focused on exports because they provided some 3 million jobs in manufacturing, or one out of every seven jobs in that sector.[2] The president staked his reelection on the economy, and trade was critical to his calculations.

Carter also took aim at the Soviet Union as the Cold War reignited. Observers backed an embargo on trade with the Soviet Union for its incursion into Afghanistan, but business feared that a total shutdown would hurt the economy. Non-military options to Soviet chaos in the Middle East were limited. Grain and technology embargoes did not change Moscow's policies, while the Russians increased imports to record highs by deals with Argentina, Brazil, India, and Canada. Embargoes weakened the unstable dollar and the trade balance, leading to job losses, and they might even kindle a "rally-around-the flag mentality" in the Soviet bloc while dividing NATO allies. Washington simply lacked economic leverage to induce concessions from Moscow; sanctions were inimical to free trade internationalism and the capitalist peace ethic, and they were particularly useless in the immediacy of aggression. "Trade curbs cannot in our view substitute for the tougher steps that are urgently called for in response to the Soviet invasion of Afghanistan," noted the National Foreign Trade Council, "namely a rapid improvement in this Country's [*sic*] military capabilities, a credible strategy for protecting our Middle East oil supply lines, and a firm, consistent and purposefully implemented foreign policy."[3]

Carter actually tried all of these elements—an Olympic boycott, deployment of forces to the Middle East, and a grain embargo—with little to show for it because the United States could not assert its will. When Carter shied from direct confrontation, Reagan pounded on him for supposedly making America Number 2 in the world, including in the trade sphere. On the campaign trail, the president warned against a trade war with Japan, which was reasonable but irked workers and producers. In St. Louis, Carter responded to a question about why citizens found mostly imported goods in stores that "it's very important for us not to build a wall around our country and isolate ourselves from the rest of the world" because Americans must buy from abroad in order to sell abroad.[4] But even his own administration believed that the Japanese "may be pulling a major negotiating coup on us in autos." That sector was, of course, critical to key electoral states like Michigan, yet Tokyo resisted voluntary limits on its auto exports due to bureaucratic red tape, inflated pricing gimmicks, and industry pressures. Senator Donald Riegle, a Michigan Democrat, commandeered a joint resolution against Japan's exports even as the International Trade Commission found, in November 1980, that they were not the cause of serious injury to the Big Three automakers. Critically, though, the White House staff director, Al McDonald, railed against capitalist peace idealism. This former deputy trade representative noted that trade "is a commercial negotiation, not a nebulous foreign policy adjunct." Voters would renounce Carter if he took the high road of internationalism because they embedded capitalist peace in the context of domestic economic stability. Carter did, too, but he was locked into his foreign policy principles, and Reagan made him pay at the ballot box.[5]

Perception of decline generated a reaffirmation of American primacy. Ronald Reagan escalated the fight against Moscow with an assertive security policy, including massive defense spending, deployment and development of nuclear missiles and weapons systems, and military support for "freedom fighters" in global hotspots. He also hoped to squeeze the Soviets economically by outproducing them in weapons and forcing them to the negotiating table. Peace through strength was Reagan's mantra, and some argued that it perverted the capitalist peace. East-West trade exemplified this contradictory policy, as the new administration ended some Carter sanctions but demanded that allies tighten up on their controls.

The problem was that interdependence precluded Reagan's preferred option of direct confrontation. He knew allies and American farmers wanted to ease up on the grain embargo, for instance, but he feared sending the wrong message. "Trade was supposed to make [the] Soviets moderate, instead it has allowed them to build armaments instead of consumer products," he wrote. As their socialist system struggled, he asked, "Wouldn't we be doing more for their people if we let their system fail instead of constantly bailing it out?"[6] This view shifted the Nixon-Ford-Carter approach, in which liberalized East-West trade encouraged political change, to the opposite tack of using controls as punitive measures to dent the USSR's military power.[7] Not surprisingly, the administration introduced the topic of Soviet behavior at the G8 economic summit in Ottawa, in 1981, politicizing this gathering for the first time ever. Reagan hoped for capitalist unity in the renewed Cold War, rather than capitalist peace. The

G8 members were concerned about Moscow's military buildup and its aggressive policies abroad, and they confessed that East-West relations had "not developed as had been hoped a decade ago." Yet casting such trade in terms of politics and security, rather than internationalism and economics, dismayed European friends. Even anti-socialist Margaret Thatcher of Britain resisted restraints on trade with the communists, and rigid controls worried officials like Vice President George Bush.[8]

Reagan followed a strategy of public toughness toward Moscow by stalling disarmament negotiations and issuing combative statements. He might be eager to sell grain to the East bloc but in 1983, he famously called the USSR an evil empire. When export restraints, particularly opposition to an oil pipeline from Russia to Europe, continued, Cold War hawks backed him. That year was a turning point, however, after war games frightened Reagan into moderation. Besides, the United States was no longer the sole dispenser of technology, and the Soviets got around embargoes by trading with many nations. Shedding the rogue tough-guy image, Reagan increasingly drew on capitalist peace thinking by holding out carrots rather than slapping with sticks to coax cooperation from Moscow.[9] To be sure, he demurred until the arrival of the dynamic Soviet reformer Mikhail Gorbachev in March 1985, and then he agreed to the first superpower summit in six years, starting a process that wound down the Cold War. Export restraints eased as a result. Hard-line anti-communists, like Caspar Weinberger and Richard Perle in the Pentagon, were marginalized, replaced by capitalist peace advocates like Secretary of State George Shultz who believed that the COCOM regime—and staunch anti-communism—were obsolete.[10]

Deficits, both foreign and domestic, ran alongside recovery in the Reagan Revolution due to massive tax cuts and military spending that generated huge debts. The trade imbalance, for one, widened as consumers bought more from abroad. The president welcomed investors, especially from Japan, to keep the budget afloat, but that strategy provoked a crisis of confidence because the Japanese started buying up seemingly every landmark in the United States. A longtime target of protectionists, Japan became a dangerous foe in the eyes of the public. To be sure, Tokyo recycled dollars earned from exports into the American economy (though, ironically, Congress demanded voluntary restraints), but it also limited access to its own markets. Reagan took aim at Japan's political-economic structure as a means to pry open the country, compel reciprocity, and ease the trade deficit. Yet Tokyo did not just erect formal barriers but also engaged in complex and historic networks of formal and unstated private-government collusion such as cartels, exclusive distribution relationships, and Buy Japan attitudes that warded off foreign merchants. Coupled with a "Chinese water treatment" of unflappable negotiating tactics, the Japanese veered toward neo-mercantilism. Still, as a key security asset in Asia, the Japanese benefited from the capitalist peace formula; this reliable ally weathered criticism from the United States and Europe. In truth, Japan was simply a better competitor, having adapted to the oil crises, recessions, and Washington's strong-arming on currency revaluation and export restraints, while Americans scapegoated the nation for their own failings. Nonetheless, an assistant secretary of commerce, Clyde Prestowitz, pushed for managed trade in corralling Japan, even suggesting that Tokyo stick to a modest level of imports on specific products.[11]

This was the embedded protectionist fair-trade agenda, designed to save manufacturers and appeal to voters, and it led to a third Multifiber Arrangement to limit imports of apparel, reductions in steel imports, and restraints on Japanese auto exports to 1.8 million cars a year. The new semiconductor industry also got protection in 1986, though consumer groups and the computer industry protested because they feared losing access to low-cost Japanese suppliers. The next year, however, Reagan slapped sanctions on Japan for violating the agreement. As a free trade, free market acolyte, he disavowed protectionism, so he focused on the bilateral partnership in security and economics. During his visit to Tokyo in November 1983, the president pledged that trade conflict would not interfere in relations or the drive for peace, but Congress was antagonistic toward Japan. When Toshima sold submarine tools to the Soviets, legislators smashed radios and televisions on the steps of the Capitol, and resolutions for import quotas flourished. Reagan's reading of Capitol Hill accurately predicted that the sheer size of the Japanese trade surplus, of over $35 billion, would spur protectionism, and he was right. Yet he also was frustrated when trying to open Japan's markets to exports from the United States. In 1988, Congress legislated that the United States Trade Representative identify nations, implicitly Japan, that discriminated against US products and retaliate by limiting access to the American market.[12]

The administration tried to inject capitalist peace ideology into its approach to Japan, but facts were facts: after years of decline, the dollar's rise made exports more expensive and let Japan sell its goods more cheaply. The Plaza Accord of 1985, signed by the United States, Japan, Germany, France, and Britain, required currency revaluation, but as the dollar dropped, Japanese exports still flooded in. The shopping spree to purchase marquee assets, including companies such as Firestone Tire and Rubber company and Cray Computers, as well as Rockefeller Center, Columbia Pictures, Westin Hotels and the Biltmore in Los Angeles, and the trademark for the Indianapolis Motor Speedway to host a race near Tokyo exacerbated anxieties; after the Japanese snapped up condominiums, houses, ranches, ski resorts, and golf clubs (including the prestigious Pebble Beach course), "the World Series or mom" seemed the next targets. Protectionists scrambled to contain the Asian predator, convincing Toyota, Honda, and Nissan to build auto plants in the United States to bypass export limits and boost domestic employment and growth. To be sure, Reagan encouraged consumer rights and investments, and he resisted extensive sanctions on Japan, especially because rival Democrats demanded them. Yet statistics did not lie. Manufacturing employment rose by only 4 percent from 1983 to 1989, due mostly to restructuring of the economy by technology and the rise in service jobs. The merchandise trade deficit also grew to record heights during this period.[13] At least politically, protectionist fair trade, not free-trade internationalism, was more viable.

Reagan did believe, with an ideological fervor, in free markets and in enlisting free trade to serve his anti-communist foreign policy. In short, he championed the capitalist peace, even as the 1980s witnessed the golden era of fair-trade law enforcement. The paradox arose from the Trade Agreements Act for a quasi-judicial process to impose anti-dumping and countervailing duties, mostly against Japan, using a procedure removed from the executive branch and beyond foreign policy considerations. Nonetheless, Reagan was a principled free-trade internationalist. For example, at the only North-South summit meeting in history, at Cancun in October 1981, twenty-two nations from five continents welcomed his push to open the American market in a recommitment to free trade. Concerns arose about China's exports of nuclear materials to Argentina and South Africa, but the overall tenor at Cancun was one of assurances to the global South that its export access problems in the North would be addressed at GATT ministerial meetings. Reagan determined to exercise personal diplomacy for "maintaining a multilateral dialogue with developing countries" in the GATT and the United Nations regarding open markets. In addition, even in the face of domestic opposition, he granted unilateral trade concessions through the Caribbean Basin Initiative with Latin America in 1983–1984.[14]

Prosperity and ultimate victory in the Cold War rested with market openness rather than protectionism in Reagan's view. Free trade could take the shape of a "loose confederation of shopping centers," a depiction of the intimate United States-Canada relationship during a visit to Ottawa in March 1981, an allusion to the free-trade area between the two nations that took root four years later, but freedom of markets—from governments—was his mantra.[15] The GATT remained a pillar of such freedom. Citing Dwight Eisenhower's message in 1957 that international commerce fostered community and peace, Reagan added that "maybe that's even more true today. We see free and expanded trade between people and nations because this form of human activity is beneficial to everyone."[16] On the radio, in August 1983, he focused on jobs and earnings, but trade also meant "cooperation over confrontation."[17]

Dealing with the People's Republic of China, as trade ties had developed over the past decade, was a case in point. More economic exchanges to improve relations and develop that country along market principles was a goal, and Beijing was certainly receptive. Once he dispensed with the Taiwan issue, Reagan visited Beijing in April 1984 to assure the Chinese that "America's door is open to you, and when you walk through, we'll welcome you as our neighbors and our friends." He also accepted China's invitation to trade and invest in its four Special Economic Zones. The economy simply "crackles with the dynamics of change," he exulted.[18] These were remarkable words from a Cold Warrior who had despised Nixon's opening to China the decade before, but they reflected the application of the capitalist peace paradigm to encourage market practices in the communist world. In China, Reagan, and future presidents, found a willing student.[19]

Not since the Eisenhower years had the capitalist peace been a bedrock of trade policy, and it had become so due to Reagan's reverence for the free-market's influence on liberty itself. "It's a question of freedom versus compulsion," because a free international economy trusted in the people.[20] Even by tightening controls on strategic goods to the Soviet bloc, Reagan engaged with notions of liberty. He planned for such intervention to be fleeting until Moscow, as he liked to say, cried uncle, and the free market became the conquering hero over communist tyranny. The "neoconservative revolution" opposed "the sugar-coated poison of protectionism," the sort of statism that stifled freedom.[21] History showed that trade must promote free enterprise as the basis of democracy—truly the American creed—by removing artificial barriers to exports and imports. That "the free way, free trade, democracy—are so far ahead in standard of living and the happiness of their people than the others that have chosen the other, the controlled, the authoritarian way," Reagan noted upon Brezhnev's death in 1982, gave credence to Abraham Lincoln's words that the United States was "the last best hope of man on Earth."[22] Referring to his life in the 1930s, when "the world experienced the ugly specter—protectionism and trade wars and, eventually, real wars and unprecedented suffering and loss of life," Reagan noted that free trade opened markets to avoid the mistakes of the past.[23] In line with the conservative American Enterprise Institute, which held its first forum on international trade in August 1982, he claimed that government's role in trade was to block state power on behalf of protectionism that violated freedom.[24]

Reagan was also realistic about the capitalist peace. "It would be wonderful if we could secure peace through trade alone, but you and I know we can't," he confided to the US Chamber of Commerce, but free-trade internationalism could defeat communist evil by "promoting market-oriented solutions to international economic problems" and thus assuring equity, security, and the American way of life.[25] In Reaganesque metaphorical rhetoric, he reminded listeners that trade partners "are in the same boat. If one partner shoots a hole in the boat, it makes no sense for the other partner to shoot another hole in the boat," he joked. "That's not getting tough. It's getting wet. And eventually it means sinking the boat that's headed for greater growth and prosperity." The "dead-end policies" of protectionism, that is, created conditions in which "the economic pie would shrink and political tensions would multiply."[26]

With recovery evident, a G8 summit convened in June 1984 in London, where Reagan stressed free enterprise as the way to capitalist peace. Secretary of State George Shultz moderated the optimism, briefing him about "Europessimism" regarding the recovery and the obstacles to free trade that would impinge on a proposed GATT round. Reagan visited Normandy for the fortieth anniversary of the D-Day landings to reaffirm America's commitment to NATO, and he reminded listeners of a related commemoration highlighting the half century anniversary of the Reciprocal Trade Agreements Act. NATO and the RTAA—security and trade—were two halves of the West's "peace movement."[27]

Regardless of history, protectionists stood ready as the specter of recession haunted the world economy in the early 1980s, the first truly globalized downturn in which most nations suffered. Restrictive measures to protect jobs strained relations among the Western allies and impinged on the North-South dialogue, which a GATT meeting in November 1982 and consecutive G8 summits addressed. The protectionist clamoring, both by those with genuine grievances and by crackpots, continued to demand non-tariff barriers of fees, taxes, origins rules, and the like. Former STR Robert Strauss warned that this strain of "neo-protectionism" appeared more virulent than in the past, with widespread support from interest groups in politics, labor, agriculture, business, and intellectual communities. "Talk and philosophy" would not do the job; there must be concrete solutions resulting from GATT negotiations.[28]

But politics compelled resort to fair-trade rhetoric. The administration noted that the "political coalition that has supported an open U.S. trade policy has eroded substantially as a result of our inability to solve key trade issues" with Japan and others.[29] Fielding a question about how to keep overseas markets open to American exports, Reagan obfuscated by declaring in favor of free trade "but it has to be fair trade, also."[30] Talking out of both sides of his mouth for political reasons, Reagan said fair trade to nod toward protectionism but embraced free enterprise in a patriotic rendition of the capitalist peace. "We do not seek an America that is closed to the world," Reagan explained in 1985, but rather "a world that is open" through fair, and then freer, trade for prosperity, progress, and peace.[31] For example, in February 1983, Reagan invoked the escape clause by slapping higher tariffs on finished motorcycles after the International

Fig. 10.1 A recession in the early 1980s led to heightened demands for protectionism at home, even as Ronald Reagan pushed for open markets. A 1982 Herblock Cartoon, © The Herb Block Foundation.

Trade Commission had found damage to the domestic industry due to Japanese imports. But the measure was temporary; Harley-Davidson, which filed the grievance, suffered acutely at that point and tariffs would give the company a breather to become more competitive. The approach worked, as Harley enjoyed a resurgence a few years later. On the other hand, the president refused import quotas for the steel industry because he saw them as a political gesture to gain votes by his Democratic rival, Walter Mondale. Thus, protectionism was sometimes necessary to level the playing field to open the way for freer trade in general. To this end, he established a Trade Strike Force in October 1985, chaired by Secretary of Commerce Malcolm Baldrige, to expose unfair trade practices, such as Japan's obstacles to semi-conductors or dumping in the United States.[32]

Fair trade was also at the center of the Trade and Tariff Act of 1984, which Reagan signed a week before his reelection. This update of trade legislation authorized negotiations with emerging nations—a first in the reciprocal trade tradition—as well as the first free-trade agreement (with Israel). It also cleared the way for a new GATT round that had been discussed in 1982 but which took four years of consultation to be launched. The Tariff and Trade Act was initially stuffed with protectionist measures, most of which were excised, except to restrain steel imports. As Reagan stressed, the bill "insists on something just as important—fair trade," by incorporating Senator John Danforth's reciprocity proposal to lower foreign trade barriers, particularly in the dynamic new trade sectors of services, investment, and high technology. The G8 welcomed the bill as a spark for a new GATT round.[33]

By late summer 1985, the administration had resolved to push for liberalization once fair trade and economic recovery ostensibly smoothed the way for free trade. In September 1986, ministers convened at Punta del Este to announce the Uruguay Round of the General Agreement on Tariffs and Trade multilateral negotiations. They would cover every outstanding trade policy issue; extend the trade system into services, intellectual property, and agricultural reforms; and review GATT articles, rules, and regulations. This was the biggest mandate ever for a trade round, but more than that, it was a vision for interdependence through free trade areas, North-South dialogue, European integration, and the capitalist peace—perhaps even of the end to the Cold War.[34]

Washington began talking about a free trade agreement with Canada—for instance, the genesis of the North American Free Trade Agreement (NAFTA). Broached in Quebec in March 1985, the accord reflected the high volume of trade and investment between the two nations (the highest in the world) that might serve as an example to others to reject protectionism. "We are not interested in building a North American island," Reagan wrote; "rather, we would like to establish a trend toward trade liberalization that others can emulate."[35] The Canada-United States joint declaration to lower barriers to trade, halt protectionism in cross-border exchanges, and undertake a series of measures to reduce impediments to the free market fed directly into the Reagan agenda of free-market capitalism. Consultations led by USTR Clayton Yeutter proceeded with legislators and the private sector as Canadian Prime Minister Brian Mulroney brought the agreement to the parliament in Ottawa. This put pressure on Reagan to move quickly on the initiative to block, in Mulroney's words, "the door of protectionism that is closing on us."[36] Reagan formally notified Congress in December 1985 of his intention to enter into negotiations on the bilateral free-trade arrangement. Both leaders embraced capitalist peace, linking the trade area to the United States-Canada security relationship through consultation, a strengthening of mutual defense, reduction of nuclear arms, maintenance of the Atlantic alliance, and broader international cooperation.[37]

Still, in a sign of the Cold War's dissipation, Reagan's second term turned even more to economics because a fixation on capitalist peace and security seemed less pressing. He repeated that fair trade meant more exports, which resonated with trading dynamos in the global South, such as export champions in the Association of Southeast Asian Nations (ASEAN)—Indonesia, Malaysia, Singapore, Thailand, the Philippines, and Brunei. The usual allusions to capitalist peace were also absent in proclamations of World Trade Week, as Reagan spoke of jobs, exports, competition, and unfair trade practices but not internationalism, and referred often to his Strike Force that identified unfair practices. Perhaps he was tired of the intractable protectionist onslaught, fueled by the skyrocketing trade deficit. Congress even held up the Canadian-United States Free Trade Agreement, as import-competing producers and workers protested, and Reagan told Japanese reporters before the Tokyo G8 summit in May 1986 of his high hopes for the Uruguay Round but that he would not hesitate to protect Americans injured by foreign trade barriers.[38]

He could not fight off protectionists forever. The House considered a Comprehensive Trade Policy Reform Act that attacked traditional trade policy because of the huge trade deficit, which had quadrupled since 1982. When Reagan took office, the current accounts balance ran a $6 billion surplus; by 1985, it was $110 billion in the red. If that trend continued, the United States—now a debtor nation—would suffer a net external loss of over $500 billion. The alarming figures were due to flush consumers buying more imports, but also because American trade policy was the laughingstock of the Free World, accused Democrats running the Ways and Means Committee in 1986. A "slavish" reliance on the outmoded GATT negotiation process, enfeebled enforcement against unfair import competition, little resort to meaningful adjustment assistance, and a lack of a systematic response by a single voice in the government to trade problems punished labor and business. "We still trade commercial advantages for military or foreign policy objectives, even where it is clear that such actions weaken us badly," concluded the committee, assailing the capitalist peace model as well.[39]

Reagan labored against this attempt by congressional Democrats to seize the trade agenda. He labeled the Reform Act a "less trade" bill because it called for opening markets abroad through protectionism at home. Still, the pressure mounted, particularly as the legislation took aim at highly competitive Japan and the four Asian "tigers" of Hong Kong, Singapore, Taiwan, and South Korea, imposing mandatory quotas on Japan, Taiwan, and West Germany in a violation of GATT commitments. Such thinking represented "the worst spirit of Smoot-Hawley [*sic*]," said Reagan, because rather than acquiesce, "nations would engage in trade wars to nobody's benefit" in a cycle of economic nationalism.[40] Reagan despised the defeatist protectionist pessimists because of his latent optimism that America's best days were still ahead. In the spirit of the Statue of Liberty, for instance, as he re-lit its torch on July 4, 1986, the president urged Americans to recall that their "forefathers knew that if you bind up a man's economic life with taxes, tariffs, and regulations, you deprive him of some of his most basic civil rights."[41] He privileged freedom; protectionists believed in economic security.

The overwhelming tide of protectionism swept over him. Protectionism, he pointedly joshed, was like one of "those pie fights in the old Hollywood comedies: Everything and everyone just gets messier and messier."[42] The House's attempt to heighten fair trade ran aground in 1986, but the following year saw the start of a successful campaign in the Omnibus Foreign Trade and Competitiveness Act, which Reagan moderated then reluctantly signed in 1988. First proposed as an amendment by Richard Gephardt, a Missouri Democrat with presidential ambitions who made a name as a pro-labor fair trader, the Omnibus Act became law even though Reagan opposed it. Weeks before House hearings in February 1987, he expressed hope for a bipartisan consensus to limit trade restrictions, taking heart that House Speaker Jim Wright sought access abroad by opening markets at home to foreign goods. Yet the real intention of the trade bill was to ease the struggles of Americans against foreign competition and correct the massive trade deficit, and less about the export drive or consumer desires for cheap goods.[43]

In fact, the Democrats, who controlled Congress, were intensely focused on Japan, the target of controversy and tension when it came to trade politics. Reagan resisted Japan-bashing, but journalists picked up on the constant barrage of complaints from Congress, curious about a possible showdown with Tokyo even though Prime Minister Yasuhiro Nakasone had allowed in more American goods and curbed exports. To deflate Gephardt and company, the administration imposed $300 million worth of new tariffs to punish Tokyo for not fully implementing the restraint agreement on semi-conductor imports. But Reagan viewed protectionism as congressional meddling with a close friend like Japan, so capitalist peace entered the picture. The fruit from the trading tree with Japan fell not just in semi-conductor trade but in the entire bilateral relationship—a "major construction project" of the postwar years that built "a bridge across the Pacific uniting our nations" under the "pillars of a common dedication to freedom and democracy, broad economic relations, and a sharing of defense burdens." The two nations had become true partners in the security of the Western Pacific, fueled by trade revenue. Until markets were fully open, however, the bridge could not be completed.[44]

With the Soviets on the ropes, the capitalist peace argument, rather than economics and petty politics, should be paramount. Preparing for the G8 economic

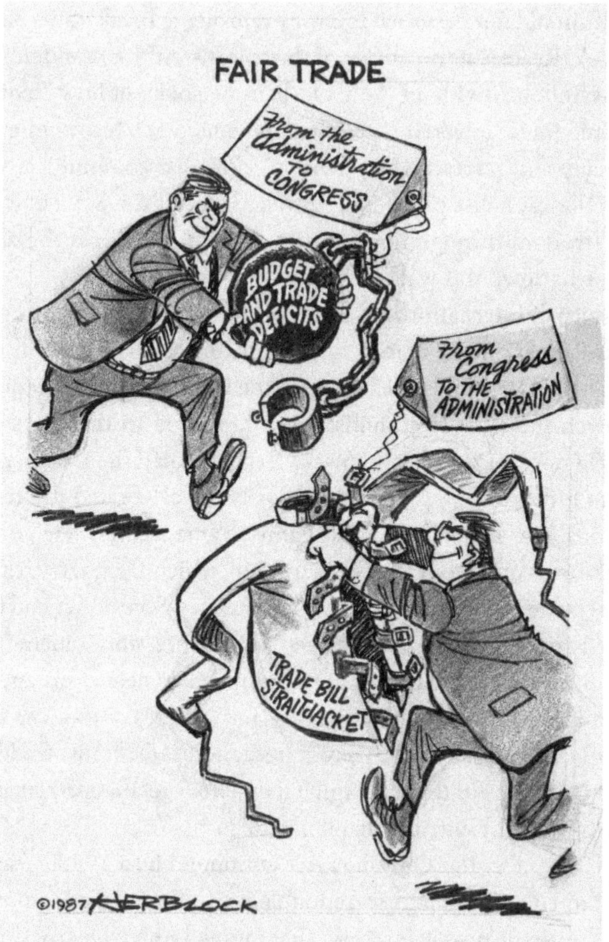

Fig. 10.2 Calls for fair trade disguised the protectionist intention behind liberal opposition to free trade due to economic dislocation at home and federal budget deficits. A 1987 Herblock Cartoon, © The Herb Block Foundation.

summit in Venice in June 1987, the administration pondered two challenges facing the West. The Free World needed to maintain economic vitality despite dislocations, and it had to prevent the appealing Gorbachev from undermining Western unity. Ironically, Reagan's advisors told him, both challenges arose from the success of his anti-communist, free-enterprise policies, though they also depended on confidence in basic principles held by the West, under the gun due to flagging economies. Moscow talked of openness, and freer trade could reinforce Gorbachev, replacing the Cold War with an era of democratic progress. The Marshall Plan and the GATT had been launched forty years earlier to build a new age of freedom through prosperity. The West had shared the largesse back then; it should not pass on it today by refusing to break down barriers.[45] On June 12, 1987, Reagan stood at one of those walls. At the Brandenburg Gate in Berlin, the symbolic divide of the Cold War, he spoke of how "reduced tariffs, expanded free trade, lowered taxes" had generated the "economic miracle" of West Germany and refuted Khrushchev's claim that communism would bury capitalism. The capitalist peace had prevailed, and if the Soviets wanted prosperity and freedom through liberalization, then Reagan had the answer. "Mr. Gorbachev, tear down this wall!"[46]

That inspiring, internationalist message did not resonate at home, though. The Gephardt amendment, demanding mandatory retaliation against trade partners, passed the House on April 29, 1987. The Democrats had few qualms about fair trade even though the administration protested to the Ways and Means chairman, Democrat Dan Rostenkowski. Reagan called the Democrats cowards who tried to hide from foreign competition as he celebrated the resurgence of Harley-Davidson at its plant in York, Pennsylvania, in May. He confessed that "my temperature's up" about the Gephardt bill, which Democrats called "one of the toughest trade bills of this century." The Hawley-Smoot Act had been tough, too, especially on Americans during the Great Depression—including a young and struggling Ronald Reagan.[47] The current bill reflected an agenda of "pit bull economics" in that it looked harmless but "it'll tear America's future apart with higher taxes, new and costly programs, and protectionist trade policies."[48] Reagan promised to veto the trade bill if mandatory retaliation remained, which persuaded thirty-eight senators that it had to go.[49]

As the debate over the Omnibus Act continued into 1988, Reagan wanted to mollify the Democrats and so redoubled his efforts to gain more access in Japan for domestic producers. He championed the construction industry, which had been shut out of bidding for Kansai Airport, targeted obstacles to semi-conductors, rice, and other farm products, and urged the new prime minister, Noboru Takeshita, to ease restrictions. The administration also relied on his foreign policy team. General Colin Powell, for instance, reminded both the National Security Council and the Economic Policy Council of the capitalist peace concept, stressing that "the economic relationship is not something separate from our strategic and security relationship with Japan." Trade should not be linked to defense cooperation, "but the sum of the outcomes of these problems is very much a part of the same thing."[50] Likewise, the president stood firm against Congress. As a vote on the trade bill neared in the House-Senate conference committee, he vowed a veto again because the mandatory retaliation provision required him to start a trade war. Getting some laughs from business leaders, Reagan pointedly added that congressional sponsors "talk about learning from the Japanese, but why did they have to take their lesson from Kamikaze pilots?"[51] Free trade meant peace through competition, not war.

Attention turned to the conference committee in March, when Reagan welcomed the news that House and Senate leaders had eliminated some troublesome protectionist measures, but not enough of them. The "fearmongers had their heyday" the previous October, when the stock market plummeted 508 points in a day, charged Reagan. These same "doomsayers" predicted ruin through freer trade, even though the trade deficit had narrowed and exports were booming.[52] The United States must be a better example to the world, especially as negotiations loomed regarding the Uruguay Round and a North American free-trade zone that had added Mexico to its grand plan.[53]

The arguments did not work. In April, both chambers of Congress passed the conference report, including the mandatory retaliation rider Reagan found so offensive. It required advance notice of layoffs or plant closings due to import competition, thus striking directly at private enterprise principles by allowing the kind of bureaucratic interference he so detested. There were elements of the Omnibus law that he liked, such as giving new authority to negotiators to open markets abroad and more adjustment assistance for worker training, education, and job placement. Yet he disliked limits on energy exports from Alaska and expanded ethanol imports, debt forgiveness, and industrial central planning under a Council on Competitiveness. He eked out a half-baked victory when the Senate's vote fell three votes short of the two-thirds majority needed to override his veto of May 24.[54]

In the end, though, the Omnibus Trade Act satisfied the protectionists more than Reagan, who grudgingly signed it on August 23, 1988. He sniped at language that required negotiations on specific trade topics and allowed easier access to International Trade Commission investigations for Congress. The legislation reformed export promotion and export control laws, and it ventured into new territory, addressing exchange rate policies and debt problems in the global South. Most critical for Reagan was the bolstered Section 301, which enforced sanctions against unfair foreign trade practices. Still, Congress would have a larger role in the multilateral negotiating process, which enhanced protectionist influence. He disguised his disappointment by resting on capitalist peace ideology. The Omnibus Trade Act boosted "the condition called freedom—the freedom of the human soul to the freedom of choice that is the hallmark of our democracy to, yes, the freedom we speak of today, the freedom to exchange goods, services, and ideas in the world market."[55] The act had a three-year lifespan, so it was short enough, and it cleared the way for the GATT Uruguay Round.

At least the legislation provided for authority to engage in trade negotiations in the emerging, expansive, globalized, and peaceful international arena, all products of the waning Cold War as the world stood at the threshold of a new era. Following the Intermediate-Range Nuclear Forces Treaty (INF) in December 1987, the superpowers signed a framework for a joint United States-USSR

Commercial Commission to expand trade relations through business missions, centers, and tourism reminiscent of the foregone agreement in 1972 during the era of détente. Some five hundred American businessmen arrived in Moscow to talk trade, offer advice, and build excitement about Reagan's visit to the capital in May 1988, a historic event for a staunch Cold Warrior. In Moscow, he linked freedom to free trade, even though he remained skeptical about Gorbachev's reforms. But the trend toward the demise of the USSR was clear.[56] Indeed, the incipient withdrawal of Soviet forces from Afghanistan and the fall of the Berlin Wall in November 1988 indicated the end of the Cold War was in sight and, with it, Soviet communism.

Reagan drew on the G8 summits, as well as the successful negotiations for the Canadian-United States Free Trade Agreement (FTA), as models for multilateral cooperation at the Uruguay Round. He signed the FTA on July 25, 1988, creating the largest free-trade area in the world. A pioneering effort, it went beyond a typical trade agreement and covered investment, services, technology, and agriculture, which the GATT was also addressing. He had already planted the seeds for a North American free-trade zone by informing Congress in January that he would travel to Mexico to discuss that country's accession to the United States-Canada accord. He envisioned "a day when the free flow of trade, from the tip of Tierra del Fuego to the Arctic Circle, united people of the Western Hemisphere in a bond of mutually beneficial exchange, when all borders become what the U.S.-Canadian border so long has been: a meeting place rather than a dividing line"—like a united Berlin, Germany, and Europe.[57] At the Toronto summit in June, the G8 supported GATT rules to facilitate the Uruguay Round. Most exciting, though, was the integration of the American and Canadian economies and the path toward European Community unity, to be completed by 1992, truly the culmination of capitalist peace dreams.[58]

George H. W. Bush did not deviate from the Reagan free market approach until he raised taxes as part of a budget deal with Congress in 1990, as he oversaw the demise of the Soviet Union and a new phase of globalization that complicated the trade arena. Only about a fifth of world trade was governed by GATT rules by this point; many sectors—steel, textiles, autos—were exempt from the trade regime or operated under bilateral arrangements. Thus, the Uruguay Round targeted non-tariff barriers and, despite strong opposition in Europe, Washington wanted to add agriculture and services into the discussions. Furthermore, the less-developed nations were wary of easing investment oversight, and because they enjoyed increased leverage at trade negotiations (roughly 40 percent of US exports went to them), they sought more reciprocity through an improved Generalized System of Preferences. The emergence, moreover, of

Fig. 10.3 The Canada-United States Free Trade Agreement was completed in the months after this meeting between Reagan and Prime Minister Brian Mulroney, and signed in January 1988, as a cornerstone of capitalist peace integration. In 1994, with the addition of Mexico, the accord was replaced by the North American Free Trade Agreement (NAFTA), which itself was superseded by the US-Canada-Mexico Agreement in 2020. Courtesy Ronald Reagan Library, C41189-7A.

China and India as major economic powers, with two-fifths of the world's population and awesome market and production potential, added to the pressures from the emerging nations. As well, the relationship of the United States-Canada (and possibly Mexico) Free Trade Agreement and other integrative institutions to the GATT proved exigent, particularly as outsiders worried about their impact. European Community plans for a large common market of 320 million people, with no internal trade and investment barriers, a single currency, and uniform external and regulatory systems, added to the complexities of interdependence. Throw in controversies over sanctions, including provocative ones to end apartheid in South Africa, controls on strategic goods, and access to cheaper oil, and the clash between national security goals and economic growth daunted the GATT contracting parties and challenged capitalist peace thinking. The Bush team also confronted the Senate Finance Committee's new power under the Omnibus Trade Act that permitted investigation, and implied protectionist safeguards, into any trade-related matter.[59]

Bush understood the pitfall of domestic politics, but he was as much on the side of free trade as his predecessor. In February 1989, a month into his presidency, he talked about the "fool's gold" of protectionism, which may "seem like the easy way out," he told the South Korean National Assembly, "but it is really the quickest way down." Bush insisted that work still lay ahead for Korea, Japan, and others to rid the trade system of obstacles so they could continue their remarkable growth.[60] The president would both pester and help them, refusing to roll over to foreign or domestic protectionism. For instance, he named Japan as a Super 301 priority, activating the Omnibus Trade Act's authority to retaliate against unfair restraints on American exports. Congress did not wish to pick on Japan alone, but the country was unavoidable; after all, bilateral trade represented over a third of the trade deficit. Bush agreed that Japanese discrimination—Japan bought cheap logs but not more expensive lumber, for example—was to blame, but repeated efforts to negotiate away unfair treatment of American goods usually failed. He determined to keep combating such economic nationalism, which was incongruous in an era "when the global marketplace has become a fact of life" in Asia, Eastern Europe, and the global South.[61]

His presidency began as the protectionist spotlight shone most intensely on Japan. Dealing with Tokyo rendered the capitalist peace argument moot for many legislators because Congress saw Japan as the chief obstacle to remedying the trade deficit and forging a multilateral deal in Uruguay. In preparation for a meeting with the new Japanese Prime Minister, Toshiki Kaifu, in early March 1990, Bush's Economic Council noted that Japan's Ministry of International Trade and Industry (MITI), had announced a four-part import promotion program, including tax incentives, tariff cuts, and spending increases. The council confessed, however, that the measures would "yield only modest results" and they "should not be viewed as a substitute for significant actions" under Super 301 or in the Structural Impediment Initiative talks in Tokyo. The prediction was correct; these efforts brought scant progress. "Cosmetic actions will not be sufficient to assuage congressional critics," the advisors warned, but platitudes prevailed as Bush and Kaifu merely pledged to continue to build a "broad partnership for the future" to deal with trade issues.[62]

Congress took note, denouncing the Bush-Kaifu summit in hearings before a subcommittee on international trade of the Senate Finance Committee. Chairman Max Baucus gave credit to Bush for addressing Japan's unfair practices more than Reagan had, but he still got the typical Japanese promises with little carry-through. Baucus warned that his patience was not infinite; Japan must either open its markets or face retaliation. Senator Danforth then cast the argument in terms of capitalist peace. A week before, the Nicaraguan election had overthrown the leftist Sandinistas and installed the Chamorro government, which sought aid from the United States, as did most of Eastern Europe. These emerging democracies looked to Washington but there was simply not enough money to go around. "If freedom is to work throughout the world, if the world economic system is to prosper, it must be propelled, not by gifts, but by growth," said the Missouri Democrat, and Japan, as the second biggest economy in the world, was essential to the market's success. The European Community was not going to step in because its EC-92 schedule of integration portended less, not more, access to Europe. Japan had a "responsibility for freedom" because it had been the beneficiary of Washington's generous policies since World War II. It must reform "structural or systematic barriers" in its market or the world economy would be impaired. Tokyo did not budge.[63]

The administration balanced between toughness and internationalist accommodation in this waning Cold War period. Bush believed that the dawn of globalization confirmed that the capitalist peace framework had succeeded. In fact, the framework was all the more relevant after the Cold War. In swearing in the new US Trade Representative, Carla Hills, in February 1989, he noted that "our trade relationships are a vital factor in America's international alliances that help secure freedom and stability for so much of the world." After all, trade partners were allies, not enemies. Beyond diplomacy, he noted that "we seek open trade because that goal is as morally correct as it is economically beneficial."[64] Even as the economy softened by 1990, and protectionism reignited, the administration held to capitalist peace theology. Bush would "avoid bashing some trading partner—popular though that might be in the political arena. I think it's bad foreign policy."[65] In May, he told exporters that boosting trade with the former communist nations and staying on guard against protectionism were the keys to security. Export "E" awards had first begun during conflict, in World War II, and with peace after the Cold War, he noted, it seemed "a very appropriate time to confer these awards."[66] Even Iraq's incursion into Kuwait in August 1990 triggered his capitalist peace instincts. Bush asked Congress to reject a bill restricting imports of textiles, apparel, and footwear from indispensable Middle Eastern allies like Turkey and Egypt, who, "despite economic hardship for them, have stood firm with us against Saddam Hussein's brutal aggression."[67]

The GATT talks gave a concrete rationale to such thinking as well. In April 1988, the Trade Negotiations Committee of the Uruguay Round completed its mid-term review, which gave a framework for negotiations, including those in the troublesome agricultural sector. The G8 determined in Paris the next year to resist "the tendency towards unilateralism, bilateralism, sectoralism, and managed trade which threatens to undermine the multilateral system and the Uruguay Round negotiations," but time was running out.[68] Thus, USTR Hill submitted a proposal in October 1990 calling for ambitious reductions in farm protectionism. Secretary of Agriculture Clayton Yeutter noted that obsolete and inefficient government intervention in the sector had bogged down trade long enough, and while the Uruguay Round would not bring utopia, some progress was necessary as the agricultural sector was holding things up. As his top priority in trade, Bush aimed for December 1990 to complete the negotiations, but the impasse on agriculture dragged on for the next few years, with a bleak prognosis for success.[69]

On a separate but related track, Bush and the president of Mexico, Carlos Salinas de Gortari, agreed to consultations for a Mexico-United States Free Trade Agreement in June 1990. Mexico had entered the GATT in 1988, the year its bilateral trade with the United States had soared by $17 billion, to $50 billion. Like the United States-Canada accord, this FTA covered a range of issues, from trade to investment to services, and hopes ran strong that it might be the first step in converting the entire hemisphere into a job-creating economic juggernaut. The FTA kicked off Bush's Enterprise for the Americas Initiative, which sought to liberalize trade and promote democracy, ultimately through a free-trade zone among North, Central, and South America and the Caribbean nations.[70]

While discussions continued regarding NAFTA, the administration also deliberated over the integration of former communist nations into the globalizing capitalist economy. In June 1990, Jimmy Carter, among others, urged most-favored-nation status for the Soviet Union, merited because of Gorbachev's liberal Jewish emigration policy, withdrawal from Afghanistan, and other actions. More taxing was dealing with China after the world responded in horror to the massacre of pro-democracy protesters in Tiananmen Square in June 1989. Analysts had had great hopes for China's modernization and integration into global trade networks, but debate justifiably intensified over how to treat what some called a rogue nation, others labeled an economic predator, and still others saw as a rising superpower to be welcomed into the world economy. In Tiananmen, stated the Treasury's Sydney Jones a year after the bloodbath, "we see China perhaps taking one step forward and one step back. But at least they recognize that they need to make many changes."[71] That was Bush's view, though it was out of sync with human rights advocates, who had the ear of many in Congress.

Activists bristled at the president's decision in May 1990 to renew most-favored-nation status for China. In 1989, Bush had issued an executive order that halted the deportation of Chinese nationals, especially students. Nonetheless, as Democratic Speaker Tom Foley noted, both parties wanted to revoke most-favored-nation status because, as New York Republican senator Alphonse D'Amato summed up, "trade concessions should not be given to the butchers of Beijing." He introduced a bipartisan resolution to rescind equal trade treatment until China reformed. For the Democrats, the Senate majority leader, George Mitchell, judged the president's decision to be "profoundly wrong" because it was "inconsistent with American values," including capitalist peace ideology. The United States was trying to convince the Chinese to support individual rights, added Wisconsin congressman David Obey, and then "Bush sends them a message 'Don't worry, we really don't mean it.'" Lloyd Bentsen, chair of the Senate Finance Committee and a recent vice-presidential candidate, was willing to listen to the administration's explanation. But like Alan Cranston, a California Democrat and majority whip who promised hearings in the Senate Foreign Relations Committee, he wished to probe China's "abominable" human rights record that "shows no signs of improving."[72] Regarding the PRC and human rights, both sides could—and did—use the capitalist peace to support their arguments.

Bush, who had served as the de facto American ambassador to China in 1974, carried through, however, talking economic benefits as the business community and much of the press applauded. The administration did impose a list of sanctions on Beijing to appease the critics, such as stopping high-level official visits to China, Chinese naval visits to American ports, and commercial sales of weapons and helicopters. Furthermore, Washington persuaded the World Bank to freeze $1 billion in loans and shelved talk of liberalizing export controls under COCOM, and then postponed the Science and Technology Agreement's extension, refused insurance for investors in China, and gave asylum to refugees. Nonetheless, the foremost lobbying group for most-favored-nation treatment, the National Council for United States-China Trade, linked bilateral trade to market considerations. First off, the economic significance of withdrawing equal status was dire. Some $4 billion in investments and nearly $6 billion in exports to China were at risk, including wheat, aircraft and aerospace equipment, fertilizer, cotton, timber and paper, computers, and acid. Consumers would also suffer, for Chinese apparel, footwear, and toys faced a 40 percent increase in American tariffs. In sum, the two nations were increasingly tied by exports; the United States had become China's largest market. Hong Kong would be an innocent victim as well, losing up to 20,000 jobs. The British colony, to be turned over to China in 1999, was already shaken by the Tiananmen Square massacre and other hard-line policies from Beijing. And trade partners, who agreed at the 1989 G8 summit to maintain sanctions on China, would not follow America's lead should it deny most-favored-nation status, holding that equal status in trade was critical to prodding political and economic reforms. Business leaders knew that allies would simply fill the gaps if the United States vacated Chinese markets.[73] The risk of a collapse on the Western consensus was one reason, moreover, that Bush twisted the capitalist peace paradigm to fit a difficult situation.

That is, the capitalist peace applied quite literally as a quid pro quo was based on the notion that commercial engagement would moderate Chinese behavior. Legally, China met the requirements of the Jackson-Vanik amendment on emigration, and some 17,000 nationals, mainly students, had gotten immigration visas. Above all, denial of most-favored-nation status would undermine democratic reformers, giving "geriatric" hard-line communists, who had spent decades building their revolution, a reason to halt liberal reforms and make their own people suffer as a result. Sanctions remained in place, anyway, and Beijing had taken some steps to meet human rights demands, such as freeing 211 prisoners, engaging in talks to resume the Fulbright and Peace Corps programs in the country, and lifting martial law in January 1990. But engagement would pay off mostly in the long run. After all, Western involvement in China had helped produce the social changes behind the Tiananmen demonstrations. Opening to the West "gave further impetus to market-oriented economic reforms, created expanded opportunities for people-to-people contacts, and justified the sending of thousands of China's best and brightest students to the US for higher education where they were exposed to Western values and democratic ideals," argued the National Security Council.[74] Denying most-favored-nation status would not only damage American commercial interests but would also "fail to achieve our foreign policy objectives," concluded the US Chamber of Commerce. Because renewal would be undertaken on an annual basis, persecution could be closely monitored.[75]

Capitalist peace had become a simple deal for China: reform and receive economic benefits. That was not free trade internationalism—or internationalism in any sense—but a workable approach based on a realism toward the PRC, on what was possible within the confines of Chinese nationalism, American politics, and Western foreign policy objectives. The conflict also epitomized the trade challenges of the post–Cold War world that had inspired idealistic hopes of globalized prosperity and peace for all but, in reality, would result in as many disappointments as resolutions. Such was the case with reform in China.

So instrumental to defeating communism, the capitalist peace paradigm did not necessarily bring universal acclaim for liberal trade. Conflict between the GATT contracting parties—the United States and Japan (and Europe and Japan) in access talks, and the executive branch and Congress—remained the rule, and protectionism continued to reshape the trade agenda. The North American and European integration processes provided positive signs of progress, but soon NAFTA sparked tensions at home. The new era of globalization, witness to the triumph of American foreign policy with the so-called Washington Consensus of free market principles, also stirred opposition that simmered and then boiled over in the years to come. Capitalist peace itself remained a dubious proposition for many observers, though the concept drove the globalization ethos in American diplomacy regardless of the skeptics and potential for backlash.

11

Globalization, 1991–2000

The end of the Cold War birthed a resurgence in capitalist peace belief, which supported the process of globalization—an ideology in its own right. America, the sole superpower, integrated globalization into its foreign policy, shaping the international economy through free-trade internationalism that embedded market capitalism in the world economic system. Pressured by protectionism, the multilateral trade system had been in disarray for two decades; now the hope of peace and prosperity through open free trade seemed possible, nourished by a relaxation of security imperatives and the integrative force of the free market. In the 1990s, a positivism about openness, interdependence, and connectedness drove diplomats, thereby vindicating the capitalist peace. That faith would be tested at home and abroad, even as it triumphed.

Transitioning the Soviet Union and its satellites into a new world order was a priority of American foreign policy, and as much as defense, economics shaped this effort. George Bush's grand vision for peace hinged on a stable and prosperous world economy, one with no place for narrow protectionist thinking and practices but one that embraced "a free-enterprise view of the human community," he proclaimed in May 1991.[1] When the Soviet Union passed into a history at the end of the year, such capitalist openness and interdependence seemed logical. As part of comprehensive aid packages to promote democracy, the administration extended most-favored-nation status to all former Soviet satellites and territories, including Latvia, Lithuania, and Estonia, new republics like Kazakhstan, and old ones like Albania and Romania, though the latter was suspended until 1996 to protest the vicious Ceausescu regime. At G8 meetings, Bush also challenged the European Community, Eastern Europe's largest buyer, to open its markets to agriculture and liberalize free-trade area agreements with former communist states. Visiting Moscow, Bush came closer than any president before him to directly referencing the capitalist peace by linking "free markets

Capitalist Peace. Thomas W. Zeiler, Oxford University Press. © Oxford University Press 2022.
DOI: 10.1093/oso/9780197621363.003.0012

and free people" in the "joint venture between political and economic liberty," which was "the spirit of democratic capitalism."[2]

The good feelings about, and upward trends in, globalized integration combined with nagging problems with old friends like Japan, the contracting parties of the Uruguay Round, and North American trade partners. Albeit distracted by the Persian Gulf War, on February 5, 1991, Bush announced that he and the leaders of Mexico and Canada intended to enter into negotiations for a comprehensive agreement to integrate their economies, expanding trade and investment covering their 360 million people and $6 trillion in output. Bush lauded the effort as part of the free-market system that would "build a new, peaceful world order" by converting the "democratic triumphs of the past year" in the communist world "to free societies and free market economies." The North American free-trade zone had such a dynamic potential for generating prosperity that lobbies like the Hispanic Alliance for Free Trade cropped up to sponsor the capitalist peace with free-trade internationalism.[3]

Indeed, NAFTA pivoted on the historically charged United States-Mexico relationship. A ninety-member blue-ribbon panel of hemispheric leaders called the Inter-American Dialogue noted that by value, US exports to the region exceeded those to Japan. Mexico doubled its imports from its neighbor from $12 billion to $27 billion over the previous four years, yet its bad working conditions, environmental degradation, and violations of the democratic process and human rights troubled relations. Some progressives wanted these issues included in a "social charter" to be addressed by all North Americans. In addition, the Hispanic Alliance for Free Trade denounced the AFL-CIO for a "tinge of racism" in its opposition to the free-trade zone. Unions oftentimes characterized Mexicans as dirty people who would spread disease through freer exchanges of goods. Congressman Gephardt accused Bush himself of playing the race card and told an all-black university that opponents of NAFTA had resorted to slurs against Mexicans. Gephardt provided no evidence, and Bush denied the charge.[4]

Advocates of NAFTA were motivated, in part, by seeking to counter the paternalism and condescension in traditional US responses to Mexico. Congressman Bill Richardson of New Mexico, a Democrat whose mother was Spanish, noted that most of the Congressional Hispanic Caucus supported NAFTA, but he also heard the "Mexico bashing" surrounding fast-track authority in trade law. Curiously, there had been no mention of cultural differences when the free-trade agreement with Canada was being negotiated, though Quebec separatism had flared up around the same time as the trade negotiations. But Mexico was a target, as were "many of us with Latin blood," added Richardson, who were "sensitive to being pictured as products of Banana Republics—Latins that cannot manage cannot do things." He did not believe such views were racist, but "if you are Hispanic, you know what I am talking about." In any case, NAFTA would be good for Hispanics, who comprised 10 percent of the population of the United States, he said. They would benefit in terms of jobs, investment, and relations with Mexico.[5] Others were less circumspect about denouncing discrimination. The Coalition for Open Markets and Expanded Trade, a grassroots lobby against trade barriers founded in 1985, had no patience for NAFTA critics. "Let the xenophobes stand on the sidelines wringing their hands and chanting their now familiar litany of woe-woe-isms," wrote member Patricia de Stacy Harrison. The claim that "Mexicans run away with our labor force" and undermine environmental and labor standards was just protectionism and prejudice. The debate was not about trade but was grounded in fear, despair, and intolerance that had no place in capitalist peace ideology.[6]

There was hefty opposition to NAFTA, however. Legislators like Ronald Coleman, a Texas Democrat, sought a deal that paid attention to health, environmental, and labor conditions, as well as diplomacy before he voted for NAFTA negotiation authorizing legislation under a fast-track renewal law. Opponents argued that NAFTA bypassed US regulations and the democratic process, and in March 1991, several House members asked the Ways and Means Committee to withdraw the fast-track procedure and thereby prevent negotiation of NAFTA. Fast-track, which enabled Congress to vote up or down on trade accords but not amend them, had been around for seventeen years but drew dissent from protectionists like Senator Ernest Hollings, who mustered thirty-seven colleagues against the renewal (fast track had lapsed in 1991). One advertisement blared "Beware! Fast Track Could Be Hazardous to Your Health" because it did not safeguard water and food quality according to US standards.[7] The pact, they claimed, allowed low-wage Mexico, with its lax standards, to shift jobs and production southward. Third-party presidential candidate Ross Perot memorably warned, as well, against the "giant sucking sound" from Mexico as jobs drained over the southern border. The face of the anti-NAFTA movement during the 1992 election, the wealthy, populist-sounding businessman Perot helped draw 19 percent of the vote from Bush. The president defended the agreement as a jobs-creator, while the centrist "New Democrat," Bill Clinton, sat on the fence. The Arkansas governor nodded approval but derided trade deficits in general and lax oversight in NAFTA of labor and environmental regulations specifically. Denouncing the scare tactics, big business, farmers, and Republicans lobbied for fast track because they wanted NAFTA established.[8]

The foreign response exposed opposition, too. Prime Minister Mulroney backed the trilateral arrangement, but few Canadians thought much of a free-trade deal with Mexico; over half of those polled sought the abrogation of the United States-Canada deal should NAFTA come into being. Some of this sentiment arose from opportunistic nationalists looking to withdraw from any internationalist arrangement, though automakers and other producers feared

Fig. 11.1 In the 1992 presidential election campaign, independent Ross Perot became the hero of protectionists when he denounced NAFTA as a curse on American jobs. The Republican, George H. W. Bush, and the Democrat, Bill Clinton, scrambled to explain their support for free trade internationalism. Pat Oliphant, 1992 Universal Press Syndicate

competition from cheap Mexican products, a sentiment so prevalent that there were fears Ottawa would drop out of the NAFTA talks. For the European Community, a hemispheric free-trade zone "scares the hell out of them," Mulroney told Bush, because, like their customs union, it too would privilege members over outsiders in trade. Bush cleverly used this fear as a means to prod Europe toward concessions at the Uruguay Round.[9]

In the end, Congress approved the fast-track extension, which enabled both negotiations over NAFTA and at the Uruguay Round of the GATT. Although they still had qualms about the free-trade area, most legislators did not want to jeopardize the GATT round, so they backed fast-track renewal. In the meantime, NAFTA got mired in two rounds of electoral politics. In the 1992 presidential contest, Bush claimed that Democrats wanted to slap tariffs on new trade coming across the border, but when it came to domestic politics, Bill Clinton had the upper hand. His campaign blamed the current recession on Bush, reciting the now famous quip by advisor James Carville, "It's the economy, stupid." The Bush team struck back with the accusation that Clinton "paid lip service to free trade in the abstract" and showed its low enthusiasm for NAFTA by issuing a "sourpuss, three sentence statement" hedged with caveats about protections for workers, the environment, and farmers.[10] Most Democrats agreed with Clinton, however, and even clearer opposition to NAFTA emanated from organized labor, including the United Auto Workers, the Teamsters, and the AFL-CIO.

Bush juggled between internationalism and fair trade, but the end of the Cold War had weakened his capitalist peace and security argument for freer trade.[11]

Nonetheless, Bush lauded the historic trilateral agreement as a model of capitalist peace ideology. With the Cold War over, he explained, the principal challenge for the United States was "to compete in a rapidly changing, expanding global marketplace." NAFTA leveled the playing field by allowing companies to sell goods "from Alaska to the Yucatan," and he hoped one day that a free-trade zone would stretch to the very bottom tip of South America.[12] Bush put stock in a "new generation of democratic leaders" under whom "a tide of economic reform and trade liberalization is transforming the hemisphere," just as designed by the capitalist peace. NAFTA boosted its prospects. The "hemisphere can be as well a zone of peace, where trade flows freely, prosperity is shared, the rule of law is respected, and the gifts of human knowledge are harnessed for all." The three nations signed the agreement on December 17, 1992, sending it to their legislatures for ratification.[13]

Fast track again came into play because it had been renewed for only two years, and not only NAFTA but the Uruguay Round hinged on Washington's having negotiating authority. Like Senator Joseph Biden of Delaware, some claimed that "the question of whether to extend fast track goes beyond an agreement with Mexico." Stressing that his vote "does not mean that I have cast my lot with the pure free traders," Biden explained that the reason to extend fast track "was to permit the Uruguay Round of the GATT to go forward." Even if NAFTA had grabbed the spotlight, Uruguay must be the focus to "cement the world's commitment to multilateral free trade."[14] In December 1991, the director-general of the General Agreement on Tariffs and Trade, Arthur Dunkel, orchestrated a legal agreement that compiled all the technical work into a final accord. The "Dunkel draft" included issues from the initial Uruguay Round mandate of 1986, except for commitments to cut import duties and open service markets. Bush insisted on a conclusion of the Round in 1992 to promote growth, give him a pre-election victory, and ultimately demonstrate that the "passing of the cold war must not mark the beginning a new age of isolationism."[15] It was not until November 1992 that the United States and the single-market European Union (EU)—formerly the European Community—settled their differences on agriculture. This Blair House accord permitted the Uruguay Round to continue as the Clinton administration took office.

Like NAFTA, Japan also generated electoral sparks. Few linked exports to job growth, and the push for market access and diplomacy did not gain Bush many votes except from corporate interests, but average Americans certainly blamed imports for job losses. In what seemed to be an annual trek of Japanese prime ministers, Toshiki Kaifu paid yet another visit to the United States, this time to the Bush compound at Kennebunkport, Maine, in July 1991. With the bilateral trade deficit again on the rise, the US-Japan Business Council and big corporations urged Tokyo to open up. They reached a fair-trade agreement on computers in January 1992, though enforcement was still at issue. Bush admitted, however, that the neoliberal critics were right about America's slacking competitiveness, including declining educational standards that undermined the workforce and quality control systems. Such remarks were not well received in Congress or by voters, no matter how true they were, and the clamor against Japan grew noisier. Michael Crichton's racist book and film, *Rising Sun*, which appeared in movie theaters in 1992, presented a barely fictionalized account of the sinister Japan Inc., a corporate/government juggernaut that abused Americans, including women. The fiftieth anniversary of the attack on Pearl Harbor the previous year had triggered commentary implying that Tokyo had replaced bombs with buying power to assail American interests. And when the Cold War ended, the struggling United States asked who had really triumphed; the cynics declared for Japan. Right-wing GOP presidential challenger Patrick Buchanan ran on this xenophobic message, vowing to be "a blocking back for Detroit" and "play hardball" with the Japanese (though he hypocritically drove a foreign car). Buchanan accused "Japan Inc." of benefiting from "its battle for economic supremacy with the United States" by supposedly recruiting "a fifth column of mercenaries, ex-Cabinet officers, former White House aides, and U.S. Senators" sent into the halls of Congress to advocate for "the new Empire of the Rising Sun."[16] Optics did not help matters when, at a banquet in his honor in Tokyo in January, Bush vomited on Prime Minister Kiichi Miyazawa and then fainted. This proved highly symbolic of America's plight. The two leaders lauded capitalist peace, or the historic, harmonious partnership between the United States and Japan that brought peace, stability, and mutual profits, but there was a sickness in the bilateral trade deficit that poisoned diplomacy and politics.[17]

Bill Clinton basically followed Bush's stance toward Japan, the only difference being that by Clinton's second term, the Japanese economy nosedived, so protectionist pressure dissipated as talk of the mighty competitor faded. Before that came to pass, however, deputy USTR Charlene Barshevsky lamented that Washington always seemed on the defensive. The Japanese were clever negotiators, and while they knew they could not avoid Super 301 punishment, which sanctioned them for limiting market access, they waited out American tantrums and then backed off slightly by letting in more exports, though falling short of hitting benchmarks. Clinton's team decided on a new approach: get the domestic economic house in order by recognizing the linkage between macroeconomic, structural, and sectoral policies. That meant, explained Laura Tyson of the National Economic Council, reducing the budget deficit and enhancing

Fig. 11.2 Cynicism abounded toward the trade threat from Japan, a nation that always seemed to better America at trade negotiations as it free-rode under America's security umbrella even as the Cold War ended. A 1992 Herblock Cartoon, © The Herb Block Foundation.

competitiveness rather than blaming Japan and looking tough to Congress.[18] Her tactics guarded the capitalist peace.

This shift, though, revealed Japan as a threat to the trade system and a support for internationalism due to its surpluses with many countries rather than just the United States. Protectionism and retaliation, warned Tyson, "will actually make it more difficult to use our national trade laws effectively by undermining our reputation as the champion of the multilateral system and our credibility as a reliable trading partner." That would also jeopardize progress on trade liberalization through the multination Asia-Pacific Economic Cooperation (APEC) forum, in Latin America toward a regional free-trade area, and among the rich nations at G8 meetings. She suggested targeting Super 301 actions only for clear cases like Japanese cellular telephone restraints and establishing an independent commission on autos and auto parts. Above all, Clinton should visibly diversify imports to convince the Japanese to open up or see their biggest market diminished.[19] Washington's role as the lead exponent of the capitalist peace was at stake, for America should prevent "this valued friend and ally and a bulwark of peace, stability, and democracy" from provoking a trade war that could sour relations, counseled the next US Trade Representative, Mickey Kantor.[20]

Globalization became Bill Clinton's mantra in this uniquely unipolar moment of American predominance. Although he also faced all the challenges Bush had been dealt, because of Clinton's focus on the world economy, these challenges and his initiatives coalesced into the busiest and the most transformative agenda in the trade history of the United States, save for World War II. Clinton had to conceptualize a new world economic order as globalization accelerated, causing tremendous growth and profits but also recurrent crises that undermined stability and confidence. He also dealt with the transition to a post-industrial service economy, though the new president believed Americans could adjust as long as they adhered to a national strategy to develop the skills and support needed for the structures, trends, and competition. Clinton acknowledged a future of insecurity, as globalization brought change at rocket speed, but this did not mean the state should abandon public welfare. For him, in the conceptual tradition of the capitalist peace, domestic and foreign policies were indivisible.[21]

As columnist Joe Klein aptly noted, Clinton was the first "globalist" president in history, giving primacy to world economic affairs and technology. Like his predecessors, he was a free-trade internationalist, but in the post–Cold War environment, he reshaped the capitalist peace paradigm away from strategic foreign policy to embrace the broader process of globalization. Al From, founder of the Democratic Leadership Council that had backed the centrist Clinton in the election, identified the three elements of this New Democrat growth strategy, in which fiscal discipline to encourage private entrepreneurs joined expanded trade and opening markets abroad. In short, Clinton had an abstract faith in free trade that he put into practice by elevating "soft power" in foreign policy. He rearranged traditional priorities to place economics at the same level as military and security calculations, though he ended up expending substantial political capital doing so.[22]

The Clinton blueprint kept the huge transition from the Cold War at the center of the trade agenda, which presumed, rather than justified, the capitalist peace. The post–Cold War period was filled with opportunity but also turned calamitous at times. A series of crises in the Clinton era—over the Mexican peso in 1994, Asian currency in 1997–1998, and the 2000 dot.com bubble and beyond—raised questions about the democratic-capitalist governments that endorsed globalization and the process of integrating the world economy into unified markets. The upsides—innovation, streamlined and more extensive transportation and communications networks, higher rates of migration, enormous profits in finance and trade, impressive growth in the global South, and cultural integration—became overwhelmed by politics, and thus by the negatives. Dissent emerged against institutions like the GATT; its successor, the World Trade Organization; and the International Monetary Fund, an anger that confronted capitalist peace thinking and even capitalism and democracy themselves.[23]

Part of the challenge came from Clinton's own Democratic Party, which shied from free-market neo-liberalism. Constituents in the labor, consumer, environmental, and civil rights movements saw free trade as a tool of selfish corporations and harmful to the poor; and consumer advocates labeled integrative global bodies like NAFTA undemocratic, beyond the reach of legislatures because of bureaucratic dominance or fast-track procedures that made their amendment impossible and inaccessible to courts. While Big Agriculture exporters, business, and economists defended the free-trade zone by accusing unions of outmoded protectionism, small vegetable and fruit growers feared an influx of cheap imports from Mexico, and labor predicted the flight of manufacturing across the border. Democrats in Congress rallied against NAFTA throughout 1993, worsening its prospects for ratification. The president had to stand for his centrist, internationalist economic blueprint.[24]

At congressional hearings, opponents rang a wake-up call for Clinton. Ways and Means chairman Dan Rostenkowski, a friend to the administration, lauded NAFTA, particularly after three supplemental agreements enhanced labor and environmental standards and protected against import surges. He also invoked the specter of Hawley-Smoot, warning that "what we seem to learn from history is that we never seem to learn from history. And so we must relive it." But Carl Levin, a fellow Democrat from the Rust Belt, shot back that the deal with Mexico would unfairly hurt workers just as much as imports from Japan did. USTR Kantor submitted a brief devoted almost entirely to the economic benefits of NAFTA, adding that friendly relations with Mexico, after decades of conflict, were at stake.[25] Before the Senate Finance Committee, though, many scoffed at this capitalist peace argument. When progressive Bill Bradley of New Jersey invoked scholar Samuel Huntington's theory of a clash of civilizations by urging "building bridges with other people and not holding ourselves apart from them" as protectionists hoped to do, Ernest Hollings rose in defiance. NAFTA opponents were portrayed as demagogues who supposedly lacked the greater vision of globalization, he protested, and stood in the way of anti-poverty and democratic agendas. "Not so. Huh-uh," he mocked. "Go, please, to this year's State Department record on human rights in Mexico." The government of Carlo Salinas was so rife with political corruption that Clinton sent Jimmy Carter to oversee elections there. Democracy and free markets meant suppression of wages and rights, not capitalist peace, Hollings concluded.[26] Democrat Sam Gejdenson of Connecticut captured the essence of Clinton's globalization centrism by asking whether "we gain or lose from NAFTA? In all likelihood, both will occur."[27]

Clinton actually agreed with this argument. He promised to negotiate deals to strengthen environmental and labor standards but also to appeal to Republican free marketeers for votes and win over enough undecided Democrats by proving that exports would raise employment. The inevitability of globalization drove his reasoning, for Americans, he said, must produce "in ways that will be rewarded in the hard glare of international economic competition."[28] That meant adaptation by preventing the European Union and Japan from sweetheart deals with Mexico and Canada. Capitalist peace ideology came into play as well. For "decades, we have preached and preached and preached great democracy, greater respect for human rights, and more open markets to Latin America," noted Clinton. The North American Free Trade Agreement helped attain those foreign policy objectives.[29] Fresh from dictatorship, for instance, Chile hoped to join NAFTA one day to safeguard its democracy. Rife with drug lords, Colombia looked to free trade to diversify its markets in the way NAFTA would do. Mexico violated human rights and could be more open, but if the United States shut it out, Clinton believed, this neighbor would likely "become less democratic."[30]

Capitalist peace history undergirded his argument. Clinton used the dedication of the Kennedy Library in October 1993 to sound like his predecessor, who would have endorsed NAFTA. America's "national destiny depends upon our continuing to reach out" rather than turning "our backs on our neighbors and the rest of the world." The end of the Cold War was "our decisive moment" to "continue on the journey" of building internationalism, security, and prosperity by courage and vigor.[31] Sending NAFTA to Congress on November 3, he urged a "commitment to more free and more fair world trade [that] encouraged democracy and human rights in nations that trade with us."[32] On Veterans Day, moreover, in a capitalist peace flourish, Clinton relayed the words of the former chairman of the Joint Chiefs of Staff, Admiral William Crowe. "Well, if you've ever been in uniform and been around the world, you know what it means to have the opportunity to live in peace with your two biggest neighbors and to have commerce and friendly cooperation and competition and what it means to live and grow together."[33]

Yet Clinton acknowledged opponents' fears because working-class Americans were under stress. To be sure, NAFTA was both "good policy and bad politics," he confessed. The capitalist peace view was sound, but "the substance of NAFTA consistently lost to raw politics," he told his chief of staff, Mack McLarty, and it cost him votes from traditional Democratic allies in the labor and environmental movements. Not having NAFTA would not solve their issues, but the insecurities were also not going to disappear.[34] The NAFTA campaign tested his considerable political skills. Clinton calculated that majority leader Richard Gephardt, the second most powerful Democrat in the House, opposed the agreement because he sought labor support for a presidential run against Clinton in 1996 or Vice President Al Gore four years later. Congressman David Bonior of Michigan gave an emotional speech in the eleven hours of debate on the House floor on November 17, denouncing NAFTA as a threat to US living standards. He also turned around the capitalist peace argument, countering that it allowed Mexico to continue to exploit its people and deny them political and economic rights. Gephardt, too, later explained that trade policy went hand in hand with moral leadership and the obligation to boost democracy and human rights, not just revenue and profits. Such universal interests were also the United States' national interests; Washington must fight for living conditions through a globalist trade policy that was a force for progress. Liberals clearly took an internationalist position, but they turned to fear-mongering as well. As a result, by September 1993, over eighty House members remained uncommitted, putting NAFTA twenty votes short of passage.[35]

Clinton personally lobbied for votes among these party members, launching a major public campaign that included gathering former presidents at the White House to sing NAFTA's praises. Clinton also showed letters of support from economists projecting a net gain in jobs while he highlighted the side agreements that improved labor and environmental standards. His efforts paid off, as some House members started to treat the pact more favorably when they realized that it was better to have Mexico inside the tent under regulations than outside of it with no restraints on low-wage goods. They also welcomed a cooperative endeavor among 400 million people in this vast NAFTA market. But in reality, Clinton's fate was in the hands of Newt Gingrich's Republicans. After a nasty fight that, in trade historian and economist Douglas Irwin's words, became "the most epic trade-policy battle in Congress since the end of World War II," the House passed the bill, 234–200. A majority of Democrats voted against NAFTA but a minority joined a strong showing by the Republicans to put it over the top. Clinton called it the Lazarus Act, for NAFTA had been resurrected from the dead. The Senate approved it days later, 61–38, with only ten Republicans against and Democrats evenly split.[36]

Fig. 11.3 Bill Clinton's campaign for NAFTA involved multiple lobbying groups and also enlisted the public support of three former presidents, Jimmy Carter, George Bush, and Gerald Ford, to counter staunch opposition from populists and from progressives within Clinton's own Democratic Party. Clinton Presidential Library, Photographer: Ralph Alswang.

An ecstatic Clinton left the next day for an APEC meeting in Seattle, envisioning his globalized version of the capitalist peace victorious. More than ever, he said, "our security is tied to economics." To be sure, military threats remained, "but increasingly, our place in the world will be determined as much by the skills of our workers as by the strength of our weapons, as much by our ability to pull down foreign trade barriers as our ability to breach distant ramparts."[37] He relished signing NAFTA on December 8, 1993, in the same room that Harry Truman had signed the NATO accord over four decades earlier. That institution, like the General Agreement on Tariffs and Trade and others built by "Truman and Acheson, by Marshall and Vandenberg," had helped win the Cold War, and now that grim contest had "been replaced by the exuberant uncertainty of international economic competition" that required attention.[38] The Clinton center, occupied by capitalist peace internationalists, had held. NAFTA took effect on January 1, 1994.[39]

The NAFTA battle had political repercussions, for the president had demoralized the Democratic base with the victory as well as by his ineptitude in failing to pass universal health care. Progressives would also oppose his bailout loan to rescue the Mexican peso in 1994, believing it a deal for bankers, and some opposed the upcoming renewal of fast-track authority in 1994, which passed anyway.[40] Still, the progressives had registered their disdain for globalization fever. Al Gore would also shy from free trade as he tried to shore up support for his presidential bid in 2000. Clinton was proud that the House had ultimately sided with globalization, but the NAFTA vote highlighted the drift away from free trade within his own party. Democrats embraced the capitalist peace, to be sure, as well as internationalism, but not the free-trade means of getting there.[41]

Clinton moved on immediately to the Uruguay Round, which ended in December 1993, the same month he initialed the North American Free Trade Agreement. In July, the United States, the European Union, Japan, and Canada (the Quad) had announced deals on tariffs and market access, but resolving each one was not accomplished until December 15. The seven-year Round among 117 nations encompassed a sweeping set of agreements that included rules in new areas such as services. These guarded intellectual property rights, improved dispute settlement mechanisms, reformed agricultural trade, abolished the protectionist Multifiber Arrangement in textiles, and created the World Trade Organization (WTO) to replace the more modest GATT. There was even planning for a new round of negotiations. Like his advisors, Clinton correctly called the result "the largest, most comprehensive set of trade agreements in history." Congress easily ratified the Uruguay Round in November 1994 after uneventful hearings. Even though environmentalists and labor soon rallied against the WTO, they were initially muted because that 128-member organization (by 2015, it had 160 members) promoted exports of agricultural goods, technology, and services rather than low-wage imports, like NAFTA did. Facilitating globalization following the Cold War, the WTO confirmed that capitalism and cooperation marched together.[42]

Thus, the capitalist peace figured into Clinton's campaign for ratification of the Uruguay Round and of the WTO that emerged from it. Sandy Berger, the deputy national security advisor, explained that the trade agreement reflected "two fundamental principles" of free-trade internationalism. First was "the need to elevate international economics to the top echelon of American foreign policy," the aim of the capitalist peace model. The second principle was "the disappearing walls between domestic and foreign policy," the essence of globalization.[43] Such a position was in keeping with how the WTO envisioned its role. In 1994, the director-general of the GATT, Peter Sutherland, stated that opening up trade opportunities in the troubled hotspots of the Middle East and Africa was one of the most important ways for the WTO to help the peace process. While the effect of the capitalist peace should not be exaggerated, the history of the 1930s showed it did have an effect, and as Renato Ruggiero, the director-general of the WTO, said further, postwar history showed that through lowering trade barriers and opening economies, "historic enemies have been transformed into inseparable partners." He hoped to see the same trend, especially in the global South. Sounding like Cordell Hull, Ruggiero explained that the road to peace lay with an interdependent trading world in which "goods, services, and investment . . . cross borders—not missiles and soldiers."[44]

Clinton told his audiences that this was no time to gloat. "In many ways, it would be easy to offer you only a message of simple celebration," he told young listeners in Brussels in January 1994, "to trumpet our common heritage, to rejoice that our labors for peace have been rewarded, to cheer on the economic progress that is occurring." But obstacles remained to building a lasting peace. These included reforming NATO and promoting "greater economic vitality" through "vibrant and open market economies" that fueled prosperity in the West.[45] Integration of Europe, reaching out to the former communist nations, convincing Japan and dynamic Asia to take a leadership role in trade and development, and otherwise "building on the momentum generated by the GATT agreement" on the environment, anti-trust policies, and labor standards were all components of his foreign policy for the globalization era.[46] He placed economics on an equal footing with the promotion of defense and democracy.

Uruguay and the WTO were building blocks of democracy, the objective of capitalist peace ideology. They were part of an overall strategy of moving the foreign policy framework from containment to enlargement of the "world's free community of market democracies," in the words of National Security Advisor Anthony Lake. This meant more than fostering new democracies among former communist nations and integrating them into the world capitalist system. The GATT talks also helped with "renewal at home" and "strengthening the democratic core" among allies, as well as promoting the "humanitarian agenda" that could "stimulate democratic and market development in many areas of the world." For Lake, like Clinton, the GATT/WTO negotiations came down to deciding on "active American engagement abroad on behalf of democracy and expanded trade" in a world of diffuse threats.[47]

Democracy (including human rights) promotion constituted one leg of Clinton's foreign policy triad, with security and trade being the other two. Together, they reconceptualized the capitalist peace for the new millennium. As Congress considered the Uruguay Round/WTO treaty in November 1994, Clinton talked of the prosperity, human rights, and democracy shared by the rich and the most destitute nations alike. "Experience shows us over and over again that commerce can promote cooperation, that more prosperity helps to open societies in the world, and that the more societies are open the more they understand that maximizing freedom and prosperity can go hand-in-hand."[48] The triad pointed to plans for a Free Trade Area of the Americas (FTAA) to spread NAFTA to the entire region. The Summit of the Americas Declaration of Principles announced in December that "the Americas are a community of democratic societies" for the first time in history, boosted by free-trade internationalism that furthered regional integration and deepened domestic prosperity. These, in turn, fostered political stability, democracy, labor, and environmental reforms—all elements of the refreshed capitalist peace paradigm.[49]

The only curveball in this grand game came from the domestic political arena. In September 1994, Clinton sent the Uruguay Agreement and the WTO to Congress, which considered it two months later in unmodified form under fast-track rules. The Ways and Means Committee had reported out the WTO favorably in a day but the final vote awaited a seismic political shift after the midterm elections, when Republicans took both houses of Congress for the first time in forty years. Speaker Newt Gingrich turned out not to be the problem, however. Like Arthur Vandenberg who had defied his party and supported the GATT, Gingrich noted that partisanship on trade matters must stop "at the water's edge" and, thus, Congress approved the Uruguay Round/WTO accord, which the president signed on December 8.[50] The political fallout from his own party haunted Clinton until he left office in 2001, however. Democratic defection from NAFTA, and then the WTO, revealed deep ideological fissures. Willie Rudd of the AFL-CIO, for example, asked Clinton when he had last shopped for a stuffed animal, a pair of gloves, a radio, or a camera. Had he "found one made in America" rather than in Asia? Since the president liked to jog, "I'm sure you get a lot of exercise trying to find American-made running shoes and jogging suits," Rudd quipped, arguing that free-trade globalization was slaughtering domestic manufacturers. The "GATT is no good for America, the Democratic Party, or your re-election as President of this great country." When it came to trade, warned Big Labor's Rudd, the "most important job you save may be your own."[51]

Such remarks boded ill for the extension of the fast-track process in 1994, before the GOP seizure of Congress. With the passage of the GATT and WTO treaties, labor Democrats were not convinced of the need for renewal at this time. The House Committee on International Relations held hearings for just two days before the WTO/Uruguay Round vote, titling its proceedings "Fast Track: On Course or Derailed? Necessary or Not?" Republican Ileana Ros-Lehtinen of Florida defended the administration. Opponents claimed that over the eight months NAFTA had existed, the promises on labor, environment, and safety were not being kept, she explained. Furthermore, export expansion under the terms of the Uruguay Round was also supposedly doubtful. And worse, fast track held legislators hostage to foreign policy concerns. Ros-Lehtinen jumped on this latter critique. By promoting foreign retaliation against protectionism in the United States, should fast track not pass, Washington would lose the ability to shape economic and political agendas in the Americas and beyond. Added Secretary of State Madeleine Albright, fast track was "a foreign policy imperative" serving US interests and ideals. It had "great symbolic importance" for reformers in Eastern Europe, Africa, and Asia by committing the United States to the democratic and economic changes they sought.[52]

Progressives' rebellion against this stance, though, was leveled at the seeming disregard for jobs. The goal of fast track was to promote access for exports into foreign markets. While trade agreements seemingly gave away the domestic market, though, a suffering working class wondered about the export growth. As Democrat Brad Sherman of California jibed, Washington's approach to the world, and especially "our richer friends," had long indicated "that we would like the honor of defending their trade routes, territorial integrity and sovereignty." In return, unfortunately, "we would like to make massive trade concessions."[53] Because of the momentum for the WTO, fast track passed this time around, yet three years later, the extension suffered a different fate. By 1997, the economy had soared and unemployment was dropping, but Clinton had to call on Republicans, once again, to bail him out. In terms of capitalist peace, he explained that "this is about more than economics. By expanding trade, we can advance the cause of freedom and democracy around the world."[54]

The Democrats would have none of it, as just four members of the party supported fast track in the Ways and Means Committee, with twelve against. Minority Leader Gephardt and the Democratic Whip, David Bonior, were among the biggest critics. An internationalist, Bonior backed a free-trade area with Mexico. "There was no question," he said on the House floor, "that our future is linked with the future of Mexico and the good people of Mexico." But he wanted to stand up for working people in the United States, democracy in Mexico, and human rights the world over with a good NAFTA accord, not one that only benefited Fortune 500 companies at the expense of workers.[55] Clinton asked Gingrich to delay the vote, which the Speaker did until the following year, when the Republicans exposed Democratic divisions by holding the vote. Clinton lost, 243–180, at the hands of his own party. He considered the rejection, cringed an advisor, "as a massive and very personal 'Fuck you, Bill Clinton.'"[56]

The administration understandably rested after the massive coalescence of the NAFTA, WTO, and fast-track programs and focused on a message of integration, growth, and partnership. In Mexico, a devalued peso and inflation immediately caused a crisis with America's third biggest trade partner. Offering a $50 billion loan package in January 1995, Clinton preserved a key export market, supported jobs, slowed illegal immigration, and served the capitalist peace by giving "countries all around the world confidence that open markets and democracy are the best guarantees for peace and prosperity."[57] Imagine, he told the Canadian parliament in February 1995, the result if nations had not united to stop Iraqi aggression in Kuwait, or the genocide in Rwanda had been even worse, or if "we hadn't worked together over such a long period of time from the end of World War II" to lower trade barriers that "plague[d] the world trading system."[58] Some envisioned a huge transatlantic free-trade area, which Speaker Gingrich labeled one of the "projects large enough to hold us all together," rather than allow globalization to crumble under the weight of nostalgic protectionism. Even AFL-CIO president Lane Kirkland endorsed that plan.[59] In May 1998, a Transatlantic Economic Partnership, linked to the WTO, emerged "to further market opening and strengthening of links between the U.S. and EU economies to support further multilateral liberalization, while benefiting our peoples."[60]

Still, protectionist pressures grew inexorably, especially in the election year of 1996. Progressives chafed at Clinton's hymn of globalization and his announcement of the nation's first proclaimed National Export Strategy, which seemed less about capitalist peace and more about neo-conservative free-market policies. With discontent rising, the president pushed hard on freer trade as the salve for economic woes, though he understood that change was unsettling. Thus, as he converted into campaign mode, he played both sides, offering compassion that smacked of fair trade but staying grounded in capitalist peace through globalization. Standing on a wharf in New Orleans, he recalled John F. Kennedy's words at the same place over three decades earlier, about the choice facing the nation either "to trade or fade." That meant neither building walls around the country nor completely knocking them down, that is, "trade that is both free and fair, truly open, two-way open trade."[61]

An Eisenhower Republican who had long supported free trade, GOP nominee Bob Dole had trouble distancing himself from Clinton on trade because he backed the barrage of free-trade measures that the administration had passed. To be sure, the Senate majority leader accused Clinton of ineptitude, lacking fortitude toward Japan, and adding to the huge trade deficit. From Kansas, Dole supported export expansion for big farmers; as a good politician, he promised fair trade for all Americans. As well, he supported most-favored-nation status for China, though he savored Clinton's discomfort with his Democratic base on the matter. In the end, Dole merely attacked around the edges, ineffectively politicizing the trade debate during the campaign. Clinton handily beat him by tying the senator to the protectionist Republican provocateur Patrick Buchanan, while progressives held their noses on globalization and voted his way.[62]

Despite the victory, Clinton had trouble on his hands. Observers on the left and among iconoclastic conservatives like Irving Kristol and Buchanan were uncomfortable with globalization, regardless of its rationalization by capitalist peace logic, because the process eschewed domestic priorities. Of course, peace in Bosnia and between the PLO and Israelis, and prospects of a permanent cease-fire in Northern Ireland—all Clinton accomplishments in foreign policy—were welcome. But Americans excluded from capital-intensive, export-oriented, and high-profit service industries struggled, so the more officials insisted that foreign policy touched lives at home, the more average Americans complained that a foreign policy with free trade at its center overwhelmed them. Neoconservatism, or the "commercialization of foreign policy," privileged wealthy investors and diminished government's role at home; this "new mercantilism" of a networked world economy was run by and for elites.[63] There were also worries that the insistence on open markets and democracy in the global South incited resentment that undercut multilateral cooperation. That Clinton believed democracies rarely made war on one another did not end repression. In fact, linking trade to democracy and human rights often bred anger—in China but also with APEC and ASEAN allies like Japan, Taiwan, and South Korea.[64]

Such judgments seeded a rebellion against the World Trade Organization, presaged by the aborted fast-track renewal in 1997. Under WTO rules, protecting the home market was difficult because export restraints were prohibited, as were import quotas, even if approved by Congress and part of its constitutional prerogative to oversee commerce. In addition, the administration sought to build on the Uruguay Round by opening discussions to liberalize trade in e-commerce, agriculture, and services, though most WTO members were unenthusiastic about a new round of negotiations. Furthermore, emerging nations now had a strong voice in trade forums; pursuing more regulations over labor and the environment met opposition from the global South seeking to expand exports to rich countries. Revealingly, at the five-year renewals of the WTO in 2000 and 2005, liberals called for Washington's withdrawal from the organization.[65]

Clinton maintained his faith in globalization with trade initiatives around the world, from Central America to Africa, that connected open markets to peace. Perhaps emboldened by his reelection, he became an even more assertive free trader, telling protectionists that their approach was "simply not an option because globalization is irreversible."[66] The defeat of fast track in 1997 didn't alter his conviction that global integration was "a great tide, inexorably wearing away the established order of things."[67] National security advisor Sandy Berger paraphrased the old musical song, "Stop the Global Economy, I Want to Get Off," for an audience at Dartmouth College in October 1998. Economic integration was neither good nor bad, "but it is almost certainly a fact. Countries that try to turn back will find that the road has disappeared behind them."[68] Perhaps the time had come to elevate the National Economic Council to the stature of the National Security Council, joining trade and foreign policy formally at long last. Despite the globalization mantra, a large majority, and an even higher percentage of unions, blamed unemployment on trade deals, NAFTA, and fast track.[69]

Inviting WTO ministers to Seattle for their next meeting, Clinton picked up on the negative vibes by proposing revised rules in May 1998 to address some of the issues that rallied opponents. He urged more transparency to make the trade system accountable to environmental concerns, changes wrought by the information age, voices of ordinary people, and effective governance. He did admit to business leaders that corralling "the forces of globalization to work for all of our citizens is literally a challenge for every nation in the world." He remained convinced, however, that adaptation was the key to success in a globalized world, especially after he visited Latin America and Africa and proposed free-trade zones in these regions.[70] Then came the Seattle ministerial of the WTO in December 1999.

Opposition to the WTO, free trade, and NAFTA aligned into an unusual coalition of labor, environmental, human, and religious rights activists, joined by revolutionary groups and anti-bureaucratic conservatives like the purists who had lobbied against the ITO in the 1940s. They inspired a massive protest in the streets that destroyed property and led to mass arrests, a "Battle in Seattle" exhibiting the deep and widening fissures over globalization and freer trade. Treasury Secretary Lawrence Summers later crowed that tariff reductions during the Clinton years "amounted to the largest tax cut in the history of the world," but his exuberance missed the point. Actually, for the critics, that was the point they objected to. The WTO-led economic regime seemed rigged against the poor, instead favoring the bankers, investors, and other profiteers who jetted around the globe making deals.[71] Clinton's come-to-Jesus moderation on globalization was too late. In fairness, he recognized the downsides. Yet he also had been awed by the phenomena of massive transporting of airline passengers, transmissions of email messages, and completion of investments across borders. Watching the Seattle protests, he admitted there were real problems with globalization, particularly that more people were being left behind, even entire regions like sub-Saharan Africa. "So, the question is, how can we create a global economy with a human face, one that rewards work everywhere, one that gives all people a chance to improve their lot and still raise their families in dignity and support communities that are coming together, not being torn apart?"[72] That reference to compassionate globalization became his new defense of what opponents called the hyper-capitalist peace ideology.

In revealing remarks in October 1999, weeks before Seattle, Clinton showed that he knew which way the wind was blowing for progressives. Laying out his agenda to the centrist Democratic Leadership Council, he noted that the positive effects of the new market economy had not been felt "from Appalachia to the Mississippi Delta to the Indian reservations to the inner cities." He asked for WTO rules that would follow American standards in health, safety, and the environment rather than lower international benchmarks, rules that would guard human rights, outlaw child labor, and maintain decent living standards. Unions wanted even more protections but Clinton demurred. After all, labor issues had not even been discussed at the last ministerial meeting in 1996; that they were now on the agenda showed remarkable progress. The president concluded with a unifying message, seeking to "expand the family of nations that benefit from trade and play by the rules," yet he invoked Franklin D. Roosevelt's vision that "a basic essential to a permanent peace is a decent standard of living for all individual men and women and children in the world." That spoke to average people, giving globalization a human face and invoking the capitalist peace to spread the benefits of freer trade across the planet and to provide "a chance to move the world closer to genuine interdependence rooted in shared commitments to peace and reconciliation."[73]

For the protesters this was simply lip service, and that reaction put Clinton on the defensive. In the midst of the Seattle rally, he urged building "a much deeper consensus for global trade to carry it forward," which was why he insisted on discussion of tougher standards.[74] Yet when he showed up in the city, he delivered a mixed message. Clinton knew that people "within my own party" were upset but he did "not see how we can have the country and the future we want unless America continues to be a leading force for expanding trade, expanding markets for goods and services, expanding the reach of international commerce" under the WTO as an agent of globalization. After all, talk of labor or the environment "could be twisted to be an excuse for protectionism" by uncompetitive interests.[75] Long skilled at hedging, Clinton knew the capitalist peace chicken of elevating globalization as his foreign policy framework had come home to roost, but he would soldier on amid the disgruntlement.

In the months to come, Clinton flip-flopped on globalization but generally stayed the course of free trade. At the World Economic Forum in Davos, Switzerland, in January 2000, he indicted the entrepreneurial friends of hypercapitalism, the "multinational corporations and their political supporters" who had created a "global economy that served their needs, believing that growth resulting from trade would create wealth and jobs everywhere." He assured poor countries and workforces dislocated by imports and technology that the WTO was not captive to the wealthy, but on reflection, he toed the free-trade internationalist line. "I thought the anti-trade, anti-globalization forces were wrong in believing that trade had increased poverty." There was a "third way" beyond unregulated trade or protectionism that would bring both growth and social justice, and thus "persuade the twenty-first-century world to walk away from the modern horrors of terrorism and weapons of mass destruction and the old conflicts rooted in racial, religious, and tribal hatreds."[76] At the millennium, peace on earth reigned, though politicians wondered if it was capitalist peace.[77]

The dissenters also made it troublesome to extend most-favored-nation status, now called Permanent Normal Trade Relations (PNTR), to the People's Republic of China. Beijing was a specter in Seattle, seeking to join the World Trade Organization to further its booming economy with more trade and investments. The West saw China in transition, so the promotion of global norms in trade was welcome, yet Chinese human rights violations and ambitions for proliferating weapons of mass destruction were stumbling blocks to WTO membership. Congress, for one, had noted for several years that China needed to adjust its economy as Taiwan had done before it acceded to the WTO in 2002. Permanent Normal Trade Relations encapsulated the struggle between pure economic considerations and capitalist peace. Market policies of the 1990s transformed China from one of the world's poorest countries, representing just 5 percent of global exports in 1980, to a juggernaut, and by 2014, it held 12 percent of world exports. But criticism of Chinese behavior was prevalent.[78]

In truth, Washington had long spoken in a divided voice on the matter. Policymakers denounced human rights abuses but then renewed trade benefits. The issue of Permanent Normal Trade Relations for China epitomized the tensions between free traders and protectionists, liberals and conservatives, and foreign policy realists and idealists. Advocates of PNTR, such as importers and exporters of toys, hoped that China would not persecute its people but they looked beyond morality to their profits. Like most of the big-city press, they believed that revoking most-favored-nation status was the wrong tool to effect change. Bush had shrewdly proposed to advance Taiwan's membership in the GATT and he also cleverly played the morality card. By pursuing "a policy that cultivates contacts with the Chinese people, promotes commerce to our benefit, we can help create a climate of democratic change."[79] Business advocates, like the National Foreign Trade Council, naturally cared more about being denied access to Chinese markets and looked the other way at Beijing's repressive tactics. Not surprisingly, the council applauded Bush's veto of a most-favored-nation bill linking trade to human rights, and clapped again, though uneasily, when, in 1994, Clinton talked about decoupling PNTR from Chinese behavior.[80]

The economic side of the ledger was an easier sell. Big business and agriculture feared losing the vast and dynamic China dream market to Asian and European competitors if Congress rejected PNTR. The dozens of companies affiliated with the United States-China Business Council welcomed Clinton's "dedicated efforts to sustain the economic bases of U.S.-China relations and the pursuit of PNTR," as well as entrance into the WTO. Sorely humiliated when refused entry into the WTO in 1994, Beijing's elite had grown disenchanted with America, warned business interests. Thus, "China's increasingly brittle response to perceived US insults and pressures is difficult to define or measure."[81]

However, usually supportive of big business, conservatives put up a fight due to foreign policy and capitalist peace factors. They worried that technology transfers might make China a national security threat with advanced weaponry and surveillance capabilities. After all, Beijing conducted underground nuclear tests. Defense concerns led many usually reliable free-trading Republicans to seek annual most-favored-nation reviews instead of permanent status for China.[82] There was also the issue of democracy and human rights. As Assistant Secretary of State Winston Lord explained, "Americans have not forgotten Tiananmen Square."[83]

On the other side, protectionist labor Democrats opposed permanent trade relations on the same grounds as NAFTA because they sought safeguards for American workers. As economist Robert Gordon has argued, tariffs had been relatively substantial from the 1930s to the mid-1960s compared to this globalized era. Such protectionism had brought higher wages and more union organization and less outsourcing abroad of jobs by manufacturers, but times had changed.[84] Free trade seemed to hurt workers. Sherrod Brown, progressive congressman from Ohio, wrote an entire book, *Myths of Free Trade*, in 2004 that made this argument as well as obliterating the capitalist peace perspective. According to Brown, the WTO gave elite bureaucrats the power to make secretive decisions, insulated from electorates, in favor of private interests that cared more about foreign policy than American workers, and through their actions accommodate Japan and later China through free trade. Sounding like protectionist O. R. Strackbein from decades past, Brown ridiculed the notion that free trade conveyed human rights and freedom from authoritarianism. "They say it over and over" on Capitol Hill "that the best way to promote democracy around the world is to engage in free trade with totalitarian countries" like China. But the United States often fell on the wrong side of history by propping up dictators and making the world safe for business. Constructive engagement of dictators like Augusto Pinochet in Chile or the communists in Beijing was an illusion because their systems lacked fundamental freedoms to begin with. The United States may grant PNTR but Chinese scholars and dissidents were still imprisoned, and so-called criminals—in actuality, political prisoners—were executed and their organs harvested. Free trade promoted such gruesome persecution as well as corruption, and not capitalist peace, concluded the congressman.[85]

China's application to the World Trade Organization hinged on opening markets, adhering to international financial and legal standards, and earning PNTR by progress in human rights. In touch with the Chinese leadership, Jimmy Carter thought Beijing was in an untenable position. Seeking to open the "Middle Kingdom," China tried to reform politically but faced such a steady stream of condemnation that its resentment swelled. The United States must understand that like most emerging nations, the PRC defined human rights in terms of shelter, food, health care, employment, and education. Protecting basic economic rights differed from the West's focus on political freedoms, such as speech and worship. In March 1994, Carter counseled Clinton to back off or else a "decision you make this year on trade with China may well be irreversible, and a great loss to American business and also to ordinary Chinese citizens."[86]

Clinton absorbed Carter's argument. While he criticized China's human rights record, he saw PNTR as the way to move Beijing in the right direction, recalling in his memoirs that "we needed to stay involved with, not isolate, China."[87] Clinton had been critical of Bush's willingness to grant most-favored-nation status, so he asked Secretary of State Warren Christopher to investigate human rights issues. In May 1993, Christopher reported that prison reforms were under way, emigration cases had been resolved, and for the first time, China promised to adhere to the Universal Declaration of Human Rights, though abuses such as arrests of political dissidents and repression of Tibet's religious and cultural traditions persisted. The administration understood Beijing's sensitivity to interference in its domestic affairs. Its leaders had their hands full managing the country's transition to a modern economy and the associated huge shift of its population from rural to coastal cities to work in factories. In the end, Clinton agreed with his economic and foreign policy advisors, most commentators, and Jimmy Carter. Separating human rights from trade, hoping to get to the capitalist peace in a compromised fashion, he granted most-favored-nation status to China. "Greater trade and involvement would bring more prosperity to Chinese citizens; more contacts with the outside world; more cooperation on problems like North Korea, where we needed it; great adherence to the rules of international law; and, we hoped, the advance of personal freedom and human rights," he explained.[88] Free trade would encourage a Chinese middle class to moderate the government's harsh policies, though in hindsight, putting such trust in Beijing turned out to be folly.

Nonetheless, China would still be constantly scolded for its human rights record. Speaking with PRC president Jiang Zemin in 1995, Clinton criticized him for slowing progress on human rights, though Jiang brushed such remarks aside, as usual. As a biographer recorded, Clinton "renewed his anthem of friendship, distinguishing between disputed issues and hostility. He listed many things to fix about the relationship, from pirated CDs and movies to persecution in Tibet, but he insisted that the United States wanted to be China's friend" and supported its membership in the WTO. His caveat was environmental concerns; Clinton warned Jiang not to "ruin the planet" as China grew wealthier.[89] Organized labor added to the human rights critique because China prohibited independent trade unions that might improve wages and working conditions, and thus raise labor costs and the price of competitive exports. Wrote a textile union official, apparel imports made by forced labor at so-called Labor Reeducation camps, or jails, were illegal. Beijing ignored the nagging.[90]

By 1998, Clinton believed that Beijing had progressed on human rights. Jiang confessed the government's mistakes at Tiananmen Square, though he warned off Washington from making human rights its central concern toward China. The administration took that warning to heart, deciding not to let the one issue of persecution, however huge, define relations between two major players in Asia. After all, revoking most-favored-nation status would, believed Sandy Berger, "cut off our contact with the Chinese people, not strengthen the

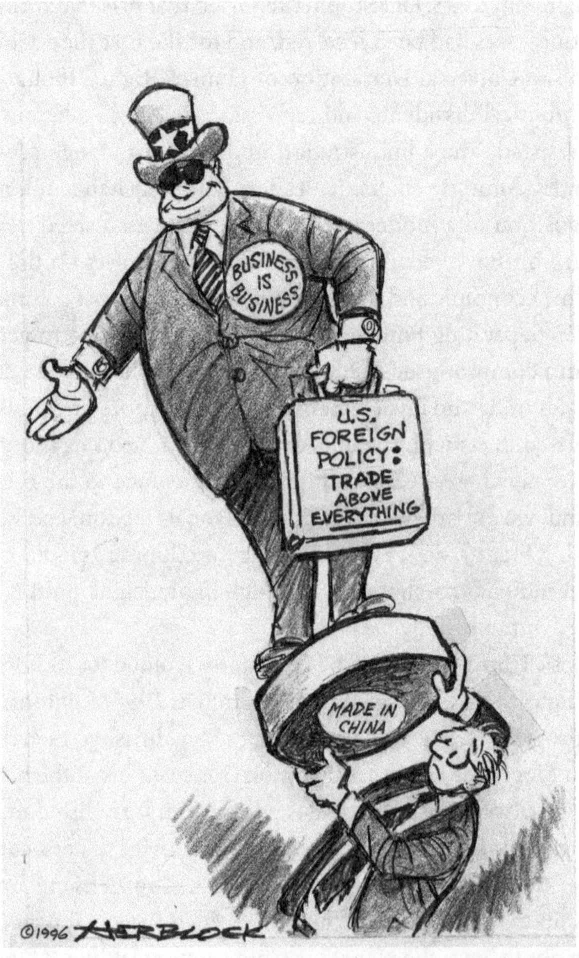

Fig. 11.4 The annual battle over most-favored-nation treatment for the People's Republic of China proved tricky for supporters of the capitalist peace paradigm; they advocated engagement through freer trade relations, while opponents wanted Beijing to improve its human rights record. A 1996 Herblock Cartoon, © The Herb Block Foundation.

forces for human rights."[91] In June, Clinton actually debated Jiang in China on religious liberty, claiming it was the first time people saw their leader engage on the issue. Besides, there were other worries about China, such as the growing bilateral trade deficit, reports of espionage in the United States, and stolen intellectual property. A military solution over Taiwan always loomed as well. And then there was impeachment, which Clinton dodged in February 1999. Perhaps thankful to protectionist Democrats who had voted to save his presidency, he reversed course and refused permanent trade relations as Jiang readied to travel to Washington. A visit to China by Secretary of State Albright and Larry Summers of the Treasury, and then intensive negotiations through the summer, redirected the wind. By fall, the two nations agreed to resume negotiations on the WTO and PNTR in preparation for the Seattle meetings.[92]

The campaign for Permanent Normal Trade Relations followed mostly along the lines of NAFTA, as both sides dug in. Most Americans did not follow the issue closely, though half of union members promised to vote against any congressional candidate who backed PNTR. The House set the tone. Benjamin Gilman, chairman of the Committee on International Relations, opened hearings by criticizing China for not living up to a myriad of promises and mocked the administration's view that PNTR would attain American interests without giving anything away. Rather, Beijing would win something very dear: "relief from the spotlight on its human rights record." The ranking minority member, Sam Gejdenson, added that the Chinese regime was even more repressive than the Soviet Union, but the United States had withheld equal trade treatment with Moscow for decades based on the single issue of Jewish emigration.[93] Eventually, side deals smoothed the way in Congress, and enough legislators were convinced that engagement would open up China's economy and promote human rights that they cast votes for PNTR. The first report of the Commission on International Religious Freedom on China paralleled the State Department's conclusions: The monitoring spotlight must stay trained on Beijing but its entry into the World Trade Organization would improve conditions. The vote was close in the House, though more decisive in the Senate, and Clinton signed the PNTR legislation on October 10, 2000.[94]

Permanent Normal Trade Relations got China admitted into the World Trade Organization. Tariffs on Chinese goods did not change much since the country had received equal treatment in trade for years, but entry did mean that China's growth of the past few decades would multiply exponentially, as the nation found numerous trade outlets through multilateral integration. As a result, from 2001 to 2003, China's exports surged. Over the next few years, imports into the United States led to the loss of nearly a million labor-intensive jobs, on top of over a half million that disappeared in the 1990s. The apparel and furniture industries in the South and Midwest were particularly hard hit by cheap imports from China. Except in those sectors, however, there were few voices of dissent at the time because recessions led to declines in domestic employment in the first two-thirds of the 2000s, and consumers benefited from cheap Chinese goods. The trade deficit with China began to grow, but specialists blamed China's undervalued currency, in which manipulation of the renminbi made its exports very cheap. The Chinese import shock, unlike Japan's two decades before, did not lead to a surge in protectionism at the time.[95]

In any case, by the new millennium, the world had changed dramatically, with capitalist peace notions weighed down by globalization's discontents. Opponents questioned the liberal trade order, disillusioned by the neo-liberal Washington Consensus that had shaped the post–Cold War era—at least so far. Globalization still needed a human face so "that spirited economic competition does not become a race to the bottom" and a "pretext for protectionism" that might lead to violence and an upheaval in the social order, Clinton explained at the University of Warwick in Britain a month before leaving office.[96] "I think my successor and his successor will be struggling with this whole issue of a global capitalist system and how you create the kind of underpinnings to make people believe it can be a more just society," he told a journalist just after the disputed 2000 presidential election. "And I think the resentment against the United States is altogether predictable; we seem to be doing well, and they're not."[97] Terrorists certainly agreed.

12

Crisis, 2001–2021

On September 11, 2001 (9/11), terrorists attacked the World Trade Center in New York City and the Pentagon in Washington, DC, transforming the domestic and foreign policy landscape. Change and challenge seemed constants, straight through the Great Recession of 2008–2009, populist uprisings, and the coronavirus pandemic that began in late 2019. The capitalist peace was clearly under duress in this long era of crises. Leaders had two possible responses. They could look forward, wielding the capitalist peace paradigm, or they could ignore the lessons of history in a nationalistic throwback to the Great Depression. Over these two decades, Washington engaged in both strategies. A conservative, George W. Bush, fiercely defended the capitalist peace as a neo-liberal free trader. A progressive, Barack Obama, moderated trade liberalization but nonetheless defended the capitalist peace. Donald Trump issued a personalized attack on free-trade internationalism, dissolving the capitalist peace. Then Joe Biden aimed to restore it. The twenty-year crisis witnessed a full circle of capitalist peace dogma, nihilism, and moderation.

George W. Bush worshipped at the capitalist peace altar, sanctified by free trade, during his eight years in office. For starters, he got a batch of free-trade agreements through Congress when only four had previously existed—NAFTA and bilaterals with Israel, Canada, and Jordan—and he negotiated the Free Trade Area for the Americas (FTAA) and a similar regional zone with Middle Eastern countries. As well, Bush saw China join the WTO, followed by Taiwan the following day, and then former enemy Vietnam a half decade later. Deals fell short with a group of southern African nations, Malaysia, Thailand, and the United Arab Emirates, and he engaged in fruitless years of negotiations at the WTO's Doha Round. Nonetheless, Bush had campaigned on a platform of free-trade internationalism, and he largely made good on his promises. He had announced his presidential run by declaring that he would "break down barriers

Capitalist Peace. Thomas W. Zeiler, Oxford University Press. © Oxford University Press 2022.
DOI: 10.1093/oso/9780197621363.003.0013

everywhere, entirely, so the whole world trades in freedom. The fearful build walls. The confident demolish them."[1] Considering his belligerence in a foreign policy based on a war against terrorism, including two hot wars, he covered his tracks by injecting capitalist peace thought into every decision he made, including cabinet appointments. But Bush was a true believer. For instance, he pledged to Colin Powell, the secretary of state, to "promote a fully democratic western hemisphere bound together by free trade." Robert Zoellick, named United States Trade Representative (USTR), recalled Bush saying that "free trade is about freedom. It's important for our economy but also for America's other interests and values throughout the world."[2]

He hardly deviated from this message, but like his predecessors over the previous two decades, Bush spoke the language of fair trade because domestic politics dictated it. For instance, Bush became the first president to initiate an escape clause action on imports, targeting the practices of the European Union and Asian nations in dumping steel. His rationale was that steel imports had surged four years before during the Asian financial crisis, even though they had returned to normal by the time he took office. The tariffs violated WTO safeguards, prompting the EU to mount a successful challenge, but by the time the WTO ruled against him, in December 2003, he had lifted the tariffs. They had garnered votes for Republicans in the 2002 midterm elections, so they were of little further use.[3]

The focus of his trade policy, however, was clearly in the liberal direction—and almost fanatically so. In what Zoellick called "competitive liberalization," Washington pursued bilateral and regional agreements to pressure Japan, the EU, and China—all of which enjoyed big trade surpluses with the United States—to reduce trade barriers through the WTO. The administration renamed fast track "trade promotion authority" to kickstart stalled bilateral talks, which, it strategized, would seed sweeping multilateral agreements. The problem lay with Congress, which balked at Bush's ambitions in 2001 even though his own party had control. The Battle in Seattle was just too fresh in congressional memories, so the president stuck to a simple capitalist peace message that grounded foreign policy in his die-hard free-trade position. He followed a most extreme form of market capitalism, even if it caused distress through what Federal Reserve chairman Alan Greenspan called "creative destruction." As Greenspan explained, "Unfettered markets create a degree of wealth that fosters a more civilized existence" that advanced the well-being of Americans and their trade partners.[4] Bush unabashedly agreed, not just for economic reasons but for philosophical reasons as well: free trade would turn "American influence into generations of democratic peace."[5] This capitalist peace advocate signaled that "I've rejected isolationism, as you know, and protectionism" as a result.[6]

Thus, Bush voiced free-trade internationalist goals in the most simplistic mix of capitalist peace rhetoric any president had since Dwight Eisenhower. The administration, he pledged, would "be a force for good and a champion of freedom. We will work for free markets, free trade, and freedom from oppression," delivering on "the promise of market-oriented systems." Change was not easy but "trade lifts lives, and trade furthers political freedom around the world."[7] In short, trade brought democracy, resulting in capitalist peace. "Democracies don't fight each other," Bush announced as one of his "universal truths," though he did not acknowledge that there had been conflict among democracies. The Yugoslav Wars of the 1990s, Turkey's invasion of Cyprus, and fighting between India and Pakistan over Kashmir were examples but he really meant relations between the Western capitalist nations.[8] In his eyes, societies "that open to commerce across their borders will open to democracy within their borders, not always immediately and not always smoothly, but in good time."[9] Free trade made diplomatic sense; for Bush, it was a moral imperative.

To further his crusade, in May 2001, Bush asked for the power to drive a comprehensive internationalist free-trade agenda. Trade promotion authority would allow the United States to address labor standards, environmental regulations, transparency in the World Trade Oganization, and new issues like e-commerce and intellectual property rights. It was also critical to a new round of trade barrier negotiations, the Free Trade Agreement for the Americas, and a number of bilateral and regional accords with Jordan, Vietnam, Laos, Andean nations, and southeast Europe. The president also sought reauthorization of the Generalized System of Preferences to promote the integration of developing nations into the global economy and end their dependency on foreign aid. His was a massive ask to Congress, an attempt to address globalization by elevating discussion above the protectionism-liberal trade debate that had so bogged down initiatives.[10]

Bush first focused attention on smaller agreements because the multilateral WTO round was still being planned. In June 2001, he submitted to Congress a bilateral trade agreement with Vietnam that the Clinton administration had worked on in the hopes of opening that country to exports and investment in return for Hanoi liberalizing its emigration statutes. Bush extended the Jackson-Vanik waiver for another year to encourage this change in a nation isolated and ravaged by the long war with the United States and one that seemed headed for disaster due to its state-run economy. Hanoi was open to change, having normalized relations with the EU and the United States in the 1990s through the termination of the wartime trade embargo and diplomatic recognition. American business interests were eager to enter this emerging market. The National Foreign Trade Council's Coalition for United States-Vietnam Trade had publicized commercial opportunities after the country began assisting in the location of American soldiers missing in action, and in 2000, after insistence that Hanoi focus on human rights, a historic bilateral agreement followed that granted Vietnam most-favored-nation treatment. The Senate ratified the deal the next year, adding in Laos and Cambodia for regional coverage, and then Congress endorsed Vietnam's application to the WTO, welcoming Hanoi's successful admission bid in 2007.[11] This blending of foreign policy and trade was a quintessential application of the capitalist peace paradigm.

Capitalist peace soon revolved around the transformative attacks on September 11, 2001. This was no time for protectionism, argued Bush, but an opportunity to shore up alliances and friendships. Liberals like Charles Rangel of New York, the senior Democrat on the Ways and Means Committee, chafed at the administration's effort to pass trade authority and agreements by wrapping them in the flag with an "appeal to patriotism" based on the need "to fight terrorism." The administration, accused Rangel, tried to cover its neo-conservative agenda of deregulation, trickle-down economics, and free trade by capitalizing on fear and foreign policy imperatives. "Fast Track will not find the perpetrators" of 9/11, echoed Leo Gerard of the United Steelworkers.[12] Yet the War on Terror was a powerful argument for freer trade, just as the Cold War had been, even as it shoved Bush's military agenda to the fore. Reflective of a newfound interest in the Middle East, the administration announced two weeks after 9/11 that the bilateral trade agreement with Jordan—the first with an Arab nation—would take effect. Cooperation with old enemies, such as the Russians under Vladimir Putin's iron rule, became desirable as terrorism and security overrode all other concerns. Bush later told ranchers in South Dakota that free and fair trade meant standing "squarely in the face of evil" with sound, reciprocal policies, showing that, above all, Americans "could love our neighbor like we'd like to be loved ourself" in perilous times.[13]

In mid-October, Bush attended the Asia-Pacific Economic Cooperation summit in Shanghai to thank Asian leaders for their sympathy for the 9/11 victims and vowed to fight for common values shared by the West, Asia, and Islam. Among them was "the power and appeal of markets and trade" because, from China to Chile, nations had benefited from lower trade barriers. Indonesia had lowered infant mortality rates, and Malaysia had cut illiteracy by a third due in part to free-trade internationalism. The upcoming WTO ministerial meetings in Doha, Qatar, where China and Taiwan would be officially admitted into the trade organization, would further boost the twenty-one nation APEC through multilateral liberalization. Bush was in Shanghai "to assure our friends and to inform our foes that the progress of trade and freedom will continue. The ties of culture and commerce will grow stronger" after the tragedy of 9/11.[14]

The WTO ministerial meeting in November launched the Doha Development Round of negotiations, despite the reluctance of many developing nations because they had never gotten promised access to the North. They insisted on attention to their interests, thus the word "Development" in the Round's title. Anticipating China's participation in the WTO, Washington removed the last hurdle in December by terminating the Jackson-Vanik provisions. This did not mean ignoring China's violations of human rights, but the administration hedged on the issue even more than Clinton had. US Trade Rrepresentative Zoellick preferred to separate trade from politics, believing that China's membership would open Beijing up to new ideas. In short, Chinese persecution was old news once the PRC was in the World Trade Organization; it was time to negotiate on free trade at Doha.[15] As Bush banged the drum of free-trade internationalism, nobody imagined that the announcement of the Doha Round would actually be its highpoint and that it would devolve into stalemates over principles and practices.

Regardless, Bush persevered in his quest for free market, globalized internationalism. At one level, he pursued Western unity, telling French president Jacques Chirac that "globalization in trade has to go hand in hand with globalization of solidarity."[16] At another, he saw democracy in the Middle East, aided by free markets, as the answer to the poverty that bred religious fanaticism. He took the Reagan Revolution to new heights in a self-conscious effort to show terrorists that they could not defeat neo-liberalism. In fact, Bush determined to spread market capitalism. As he noted in May 2003, free trade, human rights, and the rule of law were "ideals in the reconstruction of Afghanistan and Iraq" once the United States went to war in both nations.[17]

The Doha Round stimulated the campaign for trade promotion authority under the Bipartisan Trade Promotion Authority Act. Fast track had lapsed since 1997, but Bush's foreign policy team argued for its return to promote the capitalist peace. Condoleezza Rice, the national security advisor, noted that trade promotion "is not just an economic issue" but "also a tool for democracy." For instance, many current Latin American leaders, who had served jail time under military juntas in the 1980s, faced "crushing problems" that threatened their new democracies. Washington had "to deliver on the promise of trade" to help them out of poverty and protect them from terrorism. "We seek not merely to leave the world safer," concluded Rice, "but to leave it better; to leave it a world that makes it possible for all men and women to experience the exhilaration and the challenges of freedom."[18]

The renewal of trade promotion authority came after an uprising by Democrats who still sat on the fence about free trade. In Senate Finance Committee hearings, both sides talked about bipartisanship, but the battle ended up pitting Republicans against a fairly unified Democratic front of centrists and progressives who balked at the glaring market orientation of trade policy. "Globalization is here to stay," said one, Sander Levin. "The question is whether we should blindly embrace it" or ensure that it helped American workers and producers. John Kerry and Charles Rangel pleaded for true bipartisanship through a reassessment of the deleterious effects of trade integration on the environment and labor market, welcoming fast track but also a "new consensus" that the head of the National Wildlife Federation said included "the values and interests of all Americans."[19] The Republicans countered with warnings about protectionism and lost export opportunities without trade promotion power. "Trade barriers are a lot like the barnacles that get encrusted on the hull of a ship," Senator Charles Grassley of Iowa explained. "They build up over time, they slow down the ship, they are hard to scrape off." Over eight rounds of global trade negotiations and successive renewals of liberal trade legislation during the previous seventy years, the United States had led the way toward an open and prosperous trading world, and allies expected it to uphold that commitment.[20]

But partisanship, not compromise, reigned. In control of Congress, the Republicans rammed through trade promotion authority without provisions for environmental and labor requirements, which was not surprising since they cared little for unions, and even less for the environment, having withdrawn the United States from the Kyoto Protocol that aimed to cut greenhouse gas emissions. The tactic worked—barely. The House passed the renewal by just one vote, 215–214, with the GOP polling 194–24 in favor, while Democrats voted 188–20 against it.[21] Bush signed the restoration of trade promotion authority in early August 2002 for a four-year period, praising the law's impact on "freedom throughout the world," though he really meant freedom for big investors and corporations to profit from globalization.[22] Washington was back in business at the WTO's Doha Round, but free trade hung over politics like a plague.

Partisan politics also influenced bilateral trade agreements. Republicans approved eight bilaterals under Bush, and three more—with Panama, Colombia, and the Republic of Korea—under a GOP Congress in 2011 in the Obama years. Republicans from southern textile states and manufacturing areas in the Midwest, however, diverged from the party line due to import damage from China. Likewise, some Democrats veered to the free-trade side on deals with unthreatening trade partners, like Australia, Morocco, and Bahrain. On the whole, though, progressives opposed bilaterals with Chile (the first free-trade accord with a South American nation) and Singapore (the first with an Asia-Pacific country) in 2003, the Central American Free Trade Agreement and Dominican Republic (CAFTA-DR) in 2005, Oman the following year, and the three Obama-era deals. Their opposition forced Republicans into near unanimity, and when Bush's Iraq war caused the GOP majority to disappear in the 2006 midterm election, so did support for bilaterals for the remainder of his term. Even the Republicans fought among themselves, as a rising chorus of right-wing populists advocated protectionism. Talk of regional integration, liberalization, and internationalism quieted down.[23]

Domestic interests like the sugar industry, for example, brushed aside foreign policy concerns and zeroed in on the harm CAFTA and other bilaterals had done. They turned around the administration's argument, taking issue with the claim that free-trade agreements would lift Latin America out of poverty by raising wages. Richard Trumka of the AFL-CIO pointed out that, after eleven years of NAFTA, Mexican pay scales were still low. During hearings on each bilateral, progressives and populists chanted for more protection for labor, the environment, intellectual property rights, health, safety, and transparency. Dianne Feinstein, Democrat from California, added at Senate Judiciary hearings that employers could sneak around immigration law by reissuing temporary work visas to foreign nationals under the terms of the accords.[24] Bilaterals must consider domestic law, demanded the skeptics.

To be sure, the commercial benefits were minuscule, so the administration played up the capitalist peace angle. All the CAFTA countries together, for instance, comprised an economy the size of metropolitan Denver, but as Bush told regional foreign policy experts in 2002, the effort by American nations to prevent a return to the oppression of two decades earlier and to combat terrorism and drug trafficking of the present day pivoted on free markets and commerce. "Some question the fairness of free and open trade, while holding out the false promise of protectionism. And there's even greater danger, that some may come to doubt democracy itself." CAFTA reinforced the will toward social and political reform.[25] Joe Barton, chairman of the House Committee on Energy and Commerce that held hearings on CAFTA, drove home this point. "More than just the economic advantages, passing this agreement does more than a thousand speeches to tell the developing world about the benefits of democracy and the rule of law."[26] Bush also asked for an extension of the Andean Trade Preference Act on these grounds, and outside of the hemisphere, he endorsed Clinton's African Growth and Opportunity Act through an Africa Action Plan at a G8 summit. Additional support arose for a bilateral agreement with the Southern African Customs Union in 2003, as Bush declared that nations open to trade beyond their borders were also open to democracy within them.[27]

Some bilaterals were uncontroversial, clear in both their economic and especially security benefits. The July 2004 deal with Australia, for example, sailed through Congress. This was only the third free-trade agreement in history between industrial nations, the others being Australia's with New Zealand and the United States-Canada accord of 1988. The accord between the two close partners gave a one-two punch in the Doha Round and, said Bush, "adds an important dimension to our bilateral relationship with a steadfast ally in the global economic and strategic arena."[28] The signing of the United States-Singapore Free Trade Agreement, the president said, also linked trade to capitalist peace ideals and defense, noting that Prime Minister Goh Chok Tong had committed "to a world that trades in freedom" as "a vital and steadfast friend in the fight against global terror."[29] Congressman Pete Sessions noted that Singapore, a good market for exports, had also participated in joint military training exercises, shared its bases since 1992, and provided logistical support to the United States Navy and Air Force. Argued Judy Biggert, Republican from Illinois, FTAs were "not gifts that we dispense to favored allies in exchange for their vote in international bodies." Rather, they were "mutually beneficial arrangements that serve the national economic interests of both parties," and without them, security would be at risk.[30]

In the Middle East, applying free-trade internationalism to security was paramount as well, especially with the ongoing wars in Iraq and Afghanistan. The 9/11 Commission had recommended bilateral trade agreements, specifically with Bahrain and Morocco, as means of absorbing these "under-integrated" nations into the global economy and inspiring them to overcome poverty. Bahrain was a longtime strategic ally, going back to 1949 when it hosted the US Navy's Middle East Fleet and then the Fifth Fleet's expansive headquarters. It had been recently designated a Major Non-NATO Ally and a bilateral agreement would strengthen these ties as well as those of the Arab region. After all, Bahrain served as an economic gateway to the Arab Gulf, an island model, like Singapore in the Pacific, of modernization, reform, and high-quality living standards. The bilateral (passed in 2006) advanced the "shared goals of peace and stability" in the Arab world, said Rear Admiral Harold Bernsen.[31] The same logic applied to Oman, though a trade agreement dragged into the Obama years. Said David Hamod of the National US-Arab Chamber of Commerce in 2006, Oman "has been a reliable partner in the war on terrorism" by allowing access to strategic ports and air bases. Vital to the coalition's success, a bilateral accord would solidify its allegiance to the West.[32]

This was the vision for the United States-Middle East Free Trade Area (MEFTA), which was in negotiation for ten years before it was established in 2013. Senators Max Baucus and John McCain, and Congressmen Adam Smith and Calvin Dooley, introduced a bipartisan bill to give the sixteen countries of the Middle East (including North Africa) short-term trade preferences as stepping stones to the final free-trade accord. Although the preferences covered no more than 5 percent of American trade, business interests saw opportunities in the region. They pushed for full engagement for export and investment coalitions through bilateral negotiations, as well as by promoting the Saudi

Arabia's accession to the World Trade Organization.[33] This effort also filled a "blank spot" in the trade agenda for the Muslim world, analyst Edward Gesser noted in 2003, one that risked "undermining rather than supporting the war on terrorism." The western Muslim states had suffered trade and investment stagnation for a quarter century. The "social consequences of unemployment, political tension, and rising appeal for religious extremism" were the results.[34] So, Bush trained the capitalist peace lens on the region, as did Barack Obama. In his historic speech in Cairo in June 2009, Obama lauded a "partnership between America and Islam" through MEFTA, which supported the notion that "all of us share common aspirations to live in peace and security, to get an education and to work with dignity."[35] The Arab Spring of 2010–2011, sweeping an anti-poverty and pro-democracy message across the region, added urgency to trade expansion.

A bilateral deal with Colombia in 2007 exhibited Bush's strategic concerns, though they did not always convince Congress to act. One of Washington's closest friends in the hemisphere, Bogota saw its democracy at risk because of a potent network of terrorists and drug traffickers. While President Alvaro Uribe was not perfect, Bush believed that the country was headed in the right direction in terms of democratic reform. A rejection of the agreement, however, would hurt Colombia and, worse, "damage America's credibility in the region and make other countries less willing to cooperate in the future." If Washington did so, Venezuelan dictator Hugo Chavez would gain by further spreading his "false populism" that mocked democracy.[36] Bush was outraged when House Speaker Nancy Pelosi stopped the clock on congressional consideration in April 2008, questioning Bush's analysis. She claimed that workers would suffer from import competition and that Uribe still exposed labor organizers to violence. Bush lashed out that it was not in American interests to "stiff an ally" like Colombia, but ratification would have to await a new administration.[37]

The Doha Round proved just as troubling for Bush's free-trade dogma as progressive opposition to the bilaterals. Agricultural issues unsurprisingly bogged down negotiations, so the G8 tried to jumpstart them. This effort included a 2004 discussion of a United States-European Union free-trade area that might prod Doha participants into action by dealing with regulatory and financial issues between the transatlantic powers. The administration and the EU plugged away in Bush's second term, as German Chancellor Angela Merkel reminded Bush that good relations did not rest solely on fighting terrorism but on shared interests like compelling competitors like China to abide by international rules. At the end of April 2007, both sides announced a Transatlantic Economic Council to oversee progress on the framework for economic integration, though formal agreement awaited the Obama years as the idea morphed into the Trans-Atlantic Trade and Investment Partnership.[38] The Doha Round did not enjoy

Fig. 12.1 A doctrinaire free trader, George W. Bush signed numerous bilateral accords to further prosperity and bind nations into a democratic, security, and capitalist alliance. Here, he meets with President Alvaro Uribe of Colombia at the White House in 2008, when Colombia ratified the deal. However, the US Congress, under pressure from labor and human rights advocates in the Democratic Party, held up the agreement until 2011. George W. Bush Presidential Library and Museum.

such success, however. By 2008, the United States and India were at an impasse over how much the North could raise tariffs in the event of an import surge. That conflict, and the financial crisis that shook the entire world, shut down negotiations for years.[39]

Barack Obama was ambivalent about free trade. He hailed from the northern progressive wing of the Democratic Party that was hostile to agreements like NAFTA and CAFTA. Neither a centrist on trade like Clinton nor a purist like Bush, he accepted globalization but warned that increasingly insecure workers believed that the government was not on their side and would turn to protectionism as a result. Washington, advised Obama, must pay attention "to the losers from free trade."[40] Beginning his run for the White House in late 2007, the senator looked for balance, knowing that "we can't go back to yesterday or wall off our economy from everyone else." But the problem "is not that the world is flat," as Bush neo-liberals believed, but "that our playing field isn't level." Bush's policies of free-market capitalism had accelerated trends of income inequality. "Like all of you, I believe in free trade," said Obama. "But we have to acknowledge that for millions of Americans, its burdens outweigh its benefits."[41] He hoped to revise NAFTA and other deals to make them more responsive to the plight of average Americans. "I won't stand here and tell you that we can—or should—stop free trade," but job losses due to government idleness were unacceptable. He took aim at his primary opponent, Hillary Clinton, who had supported her husband's NAFTA, though she cynically called for a "time-out on trade" to appeal to voters. Clearly, countered Obama, "decades of trade deals like NAFTA and China have been signed with plenty of protections for corporations and their profits but none for our environment or our workers who've seen factories shut their doors and millions of jobs disappear" in the Bush years.[42]

As a progressive internationalist, Obama cared for the laboring class; capitalist peace meant, for him, open trade to promote human rights, including those for workers. The new president thus wrestled with the Bush bilaterals, insisting that trade "must be part of the solution" but opposing CAFTA because, like Central America's bishops, he worried that "the needs of workers were not adequately addressed." He backed the bilateral with Peru, with its binding labor and environmental provisions, but opposed the one with Bogota, as had Speaker Pelosi, "because the violence against unions in Colombia would make a mockery of the very labor protections that we have insisted be included in these kinds of agreements."[43] Indeed, it took the Republican takeover of Congress in 2011 to resurrect the Colombia, Korea, and Panama deals, though Obama backed them only after they wrote in trade adjustment assistance for labor. Doing so then cleared the way to larger political, foreign policy, and social issues. In October 2011, for instance, Obama explained that the Panama agreement "further reflects a commitment on the part of the United States to sustained engagement in support of democracy, economic growth, and opportunity" in the region as a whole.[44] He and President Lee Myung-bak also welcomed a close relationship with Korea, strengthened by the FTA that, said the Korean leader, "signals the beginning of an economic alliance" that would "strengthen and elevate our military and political alliance to a whole new level."[45]

So, Obama grasped the capitalist peace, but when compared to Bush (and Clinton), he elevated jobs to the level of peace and security through free-trade internationalism. This fixation irked conservative Republicans who criticized Obama for supposedly abandoning the capitalist peace paradigm and congressional bipartisanship when considering the bilaterals. In 2011, these Republicans renewed the linkage of foreign policy to trade. For instance, the House Subcommittee on the Western Hemisphere of the Committee on Foreign Affairs, under Florida GOP Chairman Connie Mack, called its hearings "National Security and Foreign Policy Priorities" when it deliberated on the Colombia and Panama deals. At Mack's hearings, free traders attacked the obsession with labor unions; Obama ignored Colombia's progress in reforming drug-trafficking centers, like the city of Medellin, that depended on revenue from trade. When the president bypassed Colombia and Panama in his first trip to the region, Mack accused him of failing to "fight back against the promotion of lawlessness in nations like Venezuela" or against drug and terrorist flows. While Obama dithered, the United States lost a fifth of its market share in Colombia, as China tripled its business in the country, and the EU and Canada also signed lucrative bilaterals. Washington was missing the very economic boat that would help float workers, Republicans charged, while Obama also undermined foreign policy.[46]

The critics mistook his reticence about tying trade to security for a neglect of capitalist peace principles. Obama simply was more vocal on human rights than, say, Bill Clinton, and certainly more than George W. Bush, and he focused capitalist peace thinking more sharply on the average citizen. He facilitated the Colombia bilateral, for instance, when Juan Manuel Santos Calderon—who won the Nobel Peace Prize for negotiating an end to the country's leftist FARC (Revolutionary Armed Forces of Colombia) rebellion—took over in 2010. Obama also linked killings of labor leaders with progress on the Colombia bilateral during talks with President Uribe in 2009, though he was not initially too happy with Santos's record, either. Because activists were killed in Santos's first ten months in office, Obama held his feet to the fire by writing into the agreement an "Action Plan Related to Labor Rights" that required specific steps, with timelines, to protect union members. The pressure led to the creation of a Colombian Labor Ministry tasked with oversight, criminal code reform, and specific protections. Even then, with the addition of follow-up mechanisms to check on progress, many unions in Colombia joined progressives in the United States to resist the bilateral. The Confederation of Workers of Colombia and the Central Union of Workers refused to sign on, and while the General Labor Confederation and the Colombian Pensioners Confederation did support the accord, it did so only because it strengthened worker rights. The Action Plan set Colombia on a more stable road to democracy, announced Santos, and the free-trade agreement "establishes stronger defense of workers—physical defense of workers." That was enough for Obama to sign, though progressives continued grumbling about the targeted violence against unions and inadequate efforts to bring the perpetrators to justice.[47]

By undercutting world trade in 2009 by 12 percent, the largest drop since World War II, the Great Recession forced Obama to privilege the economy over diplomacy, through fiscal stimulus and not protectionism. Still, he had to answer to the Occupy Movement of progressive protesters who had emerged in the wake of the financial crisis. They blamed Wall Street and free-market policies that had enriched the so-called 1 percent at the expense of everyone else. Although the movement faded, Bernie Sanders's protectionist platform a few years later resuscitated it. Obama imposed new duties on car and truck tires against China in 2009 in a minor move that addressed the growing trade deficit with that nation. Trade was not a priority in his recovery plans, however. Nevertheless, Congress compelled inclusion of some Buy America provisions in the massive stimulus package in early 2009, though Obama judged that they violated WTO rules. Anyway, protectionism "would be a mistake right now," he feared. "That is a potential source of trade wars that we can't afford at a time when trade is sinking all across the globe."[48] The next year, he earned some breathing room from the recession, so he turned to a new five-step National Export Initiative aimed at creating 2 million jobs, which placed him in a long line of presidential advocates of export promotion programs stretching back to the 1950s. Overseen by an Export Council chaired by the heads of Boeing and Xerox, the initiative included financial support for exporters, insisted on fair access to markets abroad, and reformed the export control system to end burdensome decades-old licensing regulations on consumer goods.[49]

That economics took center stage did not mean that Obama shirked his responsibility to promote the capitalist peace, for he still embraced human rights. NAFTA, for example, needed to strengthen labor protections, but protectionism itself was not the answer. "If we stop tapping the water in international trade," he explained, "it's like taking a fish out of water, and then we'll lack water."[50] At the G20 summit in London in April 2009, he urged listeners to "keep in mind some historical context" of the 1930s when the world "was slow to act, and people paid an enormous price." That also occurred in the 1980s when the debt crisis deepened in Latin America and "pushed millions into poverty." Even his recent approval of a "surge" of troops in Afghanistan to stabilize the war effort there were related to trade, though somewhat idealistically, because the military effort would indirectly make the world safe for globalization, which helped that nation "in terms of improving living standards, reducing the cost of goods, and bringing the world closer together."[51] He also welcomed Russia into the WTO in late 2011 because the country complied with rules on legal transparency and trade behavior. Membership came alongside Moscow's cooperation with American forces in Afghanistan and securing nuclear materials, although when Vladimir Putin invaded Crimea in 2014, the G8 members kicked Russia out of the organization.[52]

Obama increasingly wielded free-trade internationalism as the world moved further from the Great Recession. He criticized the "knee-jerk suspicion of multilateral institutions" that was nonsensical because "it is a force-multiplier for us. It is a way for us through peaceful means to expand our influence and our power and to make sure that the international rules of the road are working for us and working for everybody who's following basic international norms."[53] An improving economy and a foreign policy "pivot" to Asia to address the dynamic APEC nations and the trade threat from Beijing highlighted the capitalist peace agenda. In trips to Asia (three in his first twenty-two months in office), the president targeted both business and diplomacy. In Mumbai in November 2010, for instance, he claimed that the two-way commercial and investment partnership with India, heavily weighted in technology and services, was critical to the future of the world economy and to Indian democracy. Perhaps electoral politics was on his mind as well when he learned in New Delhi that the Republicans had swept back into power in Congress. "As the world's two largest democracies, as large and growing free market economies, as diverse, multiethnic societies with strong traditions of pluralism and tolerance, we have not only an opportunity, but also a responsibility to lead" the pursuit of prosperity, peace, and security, he told reporters as he stood with Prime Minister Manmohan Singh.[54]

There was good reason for Obama to travel to Asia, because his pivot drove much of the administration's trade policy, particularly to counter Chinese influence. In November 2011, the United States joined Asian nations to launch the Trans-Pacific Partnership (TPP), its name evoking a foreign policy. The TPP owed its existence as much to stalemate at the Doha Round as it did to a shift in foreign policy priorities; by 2007, it became clear that the WTO negotiations faced numbing obstacles. Thus, Bush had turned to a plurilateral trade strategy similar to the MEFTA approach in the Middle East, identifying four nations—Chile, New Zealand, Singapore, and Brunei—to forge a Pacific free-trade zone. Ultimately, twelve nations joined what became the TPP, in an effort to build the largest single trade agreement ever. Home to 40 percent of the world's population, the TPP twelve produced about 60 percent of global gross domestic product and hosted the fastest growing economies in the world. The Asia-Pacific region bought 62 percent of American goods traded in 2012, with the TPP (including Mexico, Canada, and Japan) accounting for 40 percent of that exchange. The United States already had free-trade accords with six Trans-Pacific Partnership nations, Japan being the largest without a free-trade agreement, and other partners' extensive free-trade networks through ASEAN and APEC offered more opportunities. The TPP projected beyond tariffs by regulating all sorts of service, digital, government procurement, intellectual property, and other regulatory standards. And it also addressed diplomacy, namely, a unified response to the People's Republic of China.[55]

The Trans-Pacific Partnership attracted bipartisan support because of the export possibilities but mainly due to the strategy behind it. There was dissent from the AFL-CIO, which worried that labor rights violators like Burma and China might join, and some criticized rules of origin that allowed Vietnam to export goods made with Chinese labor. Most free traders focused on what was excluded, actually; they wanted more out of the agreement. To the ire of legislators from Kentucky like Senators Rand Paul and Mitch McConnell, for instance, tobacco would not be part of the agreement because of its health dangers. With $414 billion in sales in 2011 and a 1.2-million-person workforce in 28 nations, Walmart also sought assurances that new nations could easily accede to the TPP so that the company could expand its supply chains. Others lamented the lack of trade promotion authority that handcuffed negotiations with the TPP partners or chafed at restrictions on registered lobbies to shape legislation in Congress.[56]

Foreign policy undergirded the profit seeking. Beginning negotiations with the TTP countries in 2009, Obama noted that the region had welcomed reengagement with Washington ten years after 9/11, when the focus had been security in the Middle East. Strategically, the TPP represented a multilateral response to assertive China, which Obama had long targeted as a trade problem. He sought better enforcement of trade agreements, which is why he had acted on Chinese tire imports. Americans needed a level playing field, including a halt to currency manipulation that inflated the cost of American exports and made China's cheaper. Yet there were deeper problems, complacency when it came to the innovative and brash People's Republic being the main one. Years before, China sold low-skill assembly-line goods with little impact on the United States' economy, but then it advanced from producing toys to computers and soon cars as it moved up the value stream of the global economy. Secretary of State Hillary Clinton convened a business roundtable in Shanghai in 2010, reflecting China's status as one of America's biggest markets. "For us to close ourselves off from that market would be a mistake," warned Obama, but Beijing must play by the rules by ceasing intellectual property piracy and curbing state procurement so that foreigners could get fair treatment when bidding for contracts. The president swore to protect Americans from China's challenges to the status quo.[57]

The approach to the Trans-Pacific Partnership had more to it than a strategic trade component, however; it was motivated by grand strategy. Obama confirmed his hope for a constructive relationship with China at a press conference with PRC president Hu Jintao in 2011, and at the United Nations, he welcomed China's willingness to impose sanctions on Iran's nuclear program, reduce tensions on the Korean peninsula, and back the referendum creating Southern Sudan. He was clear, though, that regional security depended on Chinese recognition of Washington's support for an independent Taiwan, freedom of navigation and unimpeded commerce, and international law. Furthermore, he and Hu discussed human rights, including for Tibet, and both agreed to increase the number of students crossing the Pacific, which was critical to personal diplomacy, engagement, and Chinese modernization. Hu believed that both nations were headed in the right direction, as they respected each other's interests and ultimately pursued growth and peace together. But there was no doubt that China was the geo-political target of the TPP, especially because the entrance requirements were loaded with qualifications for labor, environmental, and human rights protections that China could not meet.[58]

The fake invitation hinted that China was decidedly out of favor. In 2012, an election year, Obama vowed to confront Beijing's violations of trade rules, though his Republican opponent, Mitt Romney, countered that the president was not strong enough. In an October 2012 debate, Romney charged that the administration's defense cuts, along with its permissive policy on currency manipulation, called into question its commitment to projecting global strength against China. Surely, Beijing did not want war or protectionism, but because it did not adhere to norms and rules in trade and finance, Obama alluded to "organizing trade relations with countries other than China so that China starts feeling more pressure about meeting basic international standards" and stressed the "very clear signal that America is a Pacific power, that we are going to have a presence there."[59] In the Trans-Pacific Partnership, he had an effective answer to China.

Reporters jumped on the security and ideological conflicts that made the TPP essential, especially as an agent of capitalist peace. In June 2013, as a reelected Obama stood next to the new Chinese president, Xi Jinping, Obama interrogated him about cyber-hacking of intellectual property, financial accounts, and infrastructure. Xi explained these away as the work of non-state criminals, but cybersecurity, trade conflict, and an intense Sino-Japanese dispute over Beijing's militarization of the Senkaku Islands rendered dubious his remarks that patience would forge mutual benefits for all Asians. America preferred not to wait but to signal its commitment to security and democratic values in the region through the TPP. In late 2014, Obama met with TPP members at APEC with a simple message, said the USTR Mike Froman. Washington will be "very clear when we believe that China's actions are actually pushing outside the boundaries of what we believe to be the necessary international norms that govern the relations between nations and the way we resolve disputes," such as in cybersecurity. The national security deputy advisor, Ben Rhodes, echoed that when it came to "rebalance" in the Asia-Pacific area, Obama sought "the security of our allies and the civility of the region" including "certain things that are universal, the right to, again, speak your mind, access information, to freedom of assembly." Ratification of the TPP would ensure these rights and compel Beijing to as well.[60]

As the administration sought congressional passage of the TPP in 2015, backers hoped for fast action on Capitol Hill because China would take advantage of America's absence. In 2013, Beijing had proposed an alternative, the Regional Comprehensive Economic Partnership, that not only excluded the United States but also permitted such low standards that many poor ASEAN nations might be attracted to it. In contrast, stressed Matt Salmon of the House Subcommittee on Asia and the Pacific, the TPP let Washington "shape the rules and introduce practices" that protected human rights, labor, the environment, and intellectual property—issues not addressed in China's project. Above all, while the pivot to Asia focused on "military outcomes," the TPP moved beyond to acknowledge that "the United States has been, and will continue to be, a Pacific power." Sitting on the sidelines, awaiting China's next move, would doom that effort. Despite the "rebalance" of American forces, the defense budget had declined by 60 percent, and political stalemate in Washington had paralyzed decision-making. Add in the distraction of crises elsewhere, such as between Ukraine and Russia, and ISIS in Iraq and Syria, and the capitalist peace seemed muted. "The strategic and security situation in East Asia has become ever more fraught," declared a spokesman for the American Enterprise Institute, to the point that "there has been growing concern among allies and trading partners regarding US steadfastness and staying power in the region." The TPP could remedy that image.[61]

Leaders in the Asia-Pacific region knew that free-trade internationalism, under the TPP, supported their security and principles. Quarrels with neighbors over maritime jurisdiction—such as China stationing an oil rig near the Paracel Islands that Vietnam claimed, or its unilateral declaration of an Air Defense Identification Zone in the East China Sea that required nations to notify Beijing of flights across the area (Washington refused)—gave the lie to Beijing's purported peaceful intentions. To Singapore's prime minister, Lee Hsien Loong, failure to join the TPP would undermine Obama's pivot to Asia. "If you don't finish the TPP you are just giving the game away [to China]." After all, when the United States said it promoted trade, "what are you promoting" in fact? "What does it mean when you say you are a Pacific power? That just does not make sense."[62] Obama said that if American partners were left "waiting at the altar [and] the bride doesn't arrive, I think there are people who are going to be very hurt, not just emotionally but really damaged for a long time to come."[63] The Japanese prime minister, Shinzo Abe, added that the agreement solidified "freedom, democracy, basic human rights, and rule of law" in the region, "universal values" that TPP members shared.[64] After all, said Australia's prime minister Malcolm Turnbull in 2016, the TPP was "much more than a trade deal." Global prosperity and security have "been founded on the peace and order in the Asia-Pacific" that the United States and its allies underwrote and must continue to do in the face of Chinese assertiveness.[65] In short, the capitalist peace was at stake.

The Obama administration understood the logic that American must defend against Chinese bullying by joining the Trans-Pacific Partnership. Secretary of Defense Ash Carter later explained that the Partnership projected strategic interests. "In fact, you may not expect to hear this from a Secretary of Defense, but in terms of our rebalance in the broadest sense, passing TPP is as important to me as another aircraft carrier," Carter declared in April 2015.[66] Obama vowed to defend Asia from Beijing's trying to use its size as "the 800-pound gorilla" to set the trade rules and disadvantage the United States as well.[67] In November 2015, he asked national security experts Henry Kissinger, Joint Chiefs of Staff chairman Michael Mullen, James Baker, and Colin Powell to plug the TPP, driving home the capitalist peace point that "our economic prosperity and our national security" could not be separated when it came to China.[68]

The broader implications of the TPP even stretched beyond China to Obama's cherished fight for human rights. An ASEAN business summit in Kuala Lumpur, Malaysia, in late fall 2015 gave him a platform to declare that the Trans-Pacific Partnership was "a long-term investment in our shared security and in universal human rights." Trade by itself did not bring social justice, but when "done right it can help fuel progress in other areas." This meant that American leadership could improve working conditions bordering on slavery, raise living standards and food security, end political corruption that stole dreams, and protect labor rights. The TPP, reiterated Obama, "sends a powerful message" that "Americans and people across this region stand together for a shared vision of a future that is more peaceful and more secure and that upholds the universal rights of every human being."[69]

But in a more realistic vein, Obama returned to the notion that the TPP fostered capitalist peace and security through cooperation. The Cold War had proven that case. The United States "helped fashion the international institutions and global trading system that have stitched our economies together and helped prevent another war between major powers," noted the president. The TPP would do the same in Asia. Even more, the accord would bind the United States to the region, just as the General Agreement on Tariffs and Trade and the North Atlantic Treaty Organization had done in Europe. "There's a virtuous circle: Our alliances are the foundation for our security, which becomes the foundation of our prosperity, which allows us to invest in the source of our strength, including our alliances." By forging "deeper partnerships" with fast-growing nations like Malaysia and Vietnam, the United States encouraged these countries to make greater contributions to regional security. In short, concluded Obama, with the Trans-Pacific Partnership conceptualized in the capitalist peace's image, the belief "that economic disagreements should be resolved peacefully through dialogue, not through bullying or coercion" would prevail.[70]

Elements of the capitalist peace depended on the nuts and bolts of trade policy, so trade promotion authority activated grand strategy. Always a challenge to pass, the fast-track negotiating mandate had expired in 2006 and Democrats refused to renew it when they took over Congress three years later. Multinational corporate voices, among others, lobbied hard for its return, but progressives remained ambivalent or hostile. Thus, like his predecessors, Obama turned to the Republicans—a painful choice for a progressive like him. They gave their support to trade promotion authority, as well as the TPP, under the Bipartisan Congressional Trade Priorities and Accountability Act of 2015, which passed the Senate by a vote of 62–38 in May, with thirty Democrats opposed, and sneaked by in the House, 212–208. The right-wing House removed the one solace to Democrats—adjustment assistance—from the measure, though Congress wrote a separate law, the Trade Preference Extension Act, that included retraining and compensation aid to soften the blow of trade liberalization for workers. The Trans-Pacific Partnership came into existence later that year.[71]

That success was a contrast to the Doha Round. Trade tensions between India and the United States and disagreements with the European Union over regulations and agriculture simmered in the WTO for the entire Obama run, until the end of 2015, despite an interim agreement at the December 2014 Bali Ministerial meeting. The so-called Bali Package streamlined trade, improved tariff rate quotas, and allowed the emerging nations more options for food security, but India led a small group of developing countries that demanded more WTO regulations to aid poor farmers and blocked the Bali deal until Washington and New Delhi reached a tentative agreement in November 2014. But by then, many developing nations had, ironically, soured on this so-called Development Round. Still stalemated at a meeting in Nairobi in 2016, WTO ministers buried the Doha Round forever; it was the first failed round in the GATT's history.[72]

Obama had pushed a separate trade agenda for the global South as a way of lubricating the Doha talks. For instance, he campaigned for investment and trade in Africa, among the world's fastest growing regions, seeking a ten-year renewal of the African Growth and Opportunity Act (AGOA), which Congress passed in 2015. That year, in a dramatic reversal and initially in secret, the administration also began to normalize relations with Cuba, eventually lifting travel and financial restrictions, reopening the American embassy in Havana that had closed over a half century earlier, and taking Cuba off the terrorist watch list. Donald Trump blustered that he would cancel these Obama agreements if elected, even though during his term, the trade relationship remained intact as diplomatic objectives won out.[73]

Facing European resistance at Doha and encouraged by the TPP talks, the administration also turned to a plurilateral trade strategy with the European Union under a Transatlantic Trade and Investment Partnership (TTIP) that fulfilled a dream of Atlanticists going back to the 1940s. Obama announced the Partnership at his State of the Union address in 2013 in the context of jobs, but he embraced the capitalist peace by asking Congress to remember "that today's world presents not just dangers, not just threats, it presents opportunities," and "fair and free" trade with Europe was one of them.[74] The TTIP was an impressive association, comprising nearly half of the world's gross national product, a trillion dollars in trade in goods and services, $3.7 trillion in investments, and 13 million jobs on both sides of the Atlantic. This represented the largest free-trade agreement in history. At the G8 summit in Northern Ireland in June 2013, a month before the first round of TTIP negotiations, the president urged trade partners to "stay focused on the big picture—the economic and strategic importance of this partnership"—and reinvigorate the trade system. His words did nothing for the Doha Round, but they did stimulate enthusiasm for the Transatlantic Trade and Investment Partnership.[75] Stopping in Berlin, Obama stood with Angela Merkel to proclaim that the Atlantic community's "enduring bonds based on common values and common ideals very much remains."[76]

Negotiations over the TTIP proceeded slowly, as the Doha Round faded, because at the new partnership's core lay the elimination of barriers to trade and investment to enhance market access in America and Europe. That goal dealt with European Union, national, and local regulations, which included, complained American farm interests, the EU's "bagful of scary tricks" in agriculture.[77] The partnership also addressed digital trade, environmental policies, intellectual property, labor standards, and health, such as genetically grown food, all of which arose after decades of disputes that had held up previous GATT rounds and bogged down the Doha talks. To facilitate agreement, the TTIP became more about harmonizing policies than reducing barriers. In Brussels alongside EU officials in March 2014, Obama insisted on protections for consumers, human rights, and the environment to demonstrate that trade agreements could be done the right, democratic, way by being subject to scrutiny.[78]

Even if the negotiations centered on economic regulations, the Transatlantic Trade and Investment Partnership directly related to capitalist peace ideology. The "extensive and mature nature of the U.S.-EU economic relationship distinguishes the dynamics of the TTIP negotiations," noted a congressional report in 2014, and those dynamics extended beyond traditional trade issues to the very conduct of negotiations between two trading partners of relatively equal size. The transatlantic political relationship would be changed, for instance, especially in the context of the rebalancing toward the Asia-Pacific region and the TPP. When allies worried about a "'pivot away' from Europe and key institutions," such as NATO and the EU itself, the administration stressed that the Trans-Pacific Partnership did not come at the expense of Europe. And the TTIP "could reinforce the United States' commitment to Europe in general and especially to the European Union's role as a critical U.S. partner in the international community."[79] At a basic level, said a senior administration official, the TTIP underscored "the geo-strategic interests of both the United States and Europe" by planting a firm stake in European integration to convince Europeans themselves that Washington would always be a close partner.[80] Donald Tusk, president of the European Council, noted in a visit to Washington that he and Obama talked about Russia's aggression in Ukraine, ISIS terrorism, and the Transatlantic Trade and Investment Partnership. These involved "three different—very different—challenges [that] have a common denominator, I think. It's a need, maybe greater than ever before, for unity of Europe and the United States. We are witnessing today calling into question, and even attacking . . . our fundamental values, like freedom, liberal democracy, prosperity, and for sure, geopolitical order."[81]

The TTIP answered those voices with a rounding chorus of democratic capitalist unity. For former ambassador to the European Union, Stuart Eizenstadt, the "geopolitical importance to this agreement" sent "an important signal" to Europeans, who "share our core values of democracy, free speech, respect for human rights and the rule of law." Moreover, there were "two competing models of governance in the world: One is the free market democratic model, and the other is the autocratic state-controlled, state-dominated model." A successful TTIP, facilitated by free-trade internationalism, would show the world that democracy was "the best model to meet the challenges of the twenty-first century."[82]

The TTIP negotiations unfortunately dragged into the 2016 election year, and ultimately, events overtook the negotiations, including the announcement by the British prime minister that London intended to leave the European Union. Obama opposed Brexit because EU membership strengthened Britain's economy, security, and democracy, though he recognized that populism revealed, once again, that globalization and integration did not work well for everyone. Still, the kind of "crude populism that is often divisive" was not the political answer, he admonished.[83] The presidential election results then doomed the Transatlantic Trade and Investment Partnership. In the primaries, Democratic challenger Bernie Sanders criticized Hillary Clinton, the secretary of state who had helped negotiate both the TTIP and the TTP. His message that both trade arrangements hurt workers forced Clinton to back off from her own creations. Donald Trump then made headway against her during the general election campaign by blasting away at such "disastrous" trade deals, including both trade partnerships. Obama stiffened his defense of the TTIP, indirectly criticizing the Republican candidate for believing that "building walls" or "disparaging Muslims" would boost the economy and security.[84] When Trump won by promising to put America first in trade relations, the TTIP was an early casualty, as Trump raised tariffs on European goods beginning in 2017. The two sides calmed down the trade conflict, but in 2019, the European Union declared the

Fig. 12.2 In Brisbane, Australia, President Barack Obama met with G20 European leaders, including (from Obama's left) British Prime Minister David Cameron, German Chancellor Angela Merkel, the EU's Herman Van Rompuy and Jean-Claude Juncker, Prime Ministers Mariano Rajoy Brey (Spain) and Matteo Renzi (Italy), and President Francois Hollande of France, to discuss the ambitious Transatlantic Trade and Investment Partnership (TTIP), the largest multilateral trade agreement in history and the culmination of globalized capitalist peace efforts. Barack Obama Presidential Library, November 16, 2015, Photo Number P111614PS-0387. Pete Souza, Photographer.

TTIP negotiations "obsolete and no longer relevant."[85] The first strategic transatlantic trade alliance died on the vine.

Unlike George W. Bush and Barack Obama—or any other resident of the White House since the mid-nineteenth century, for that matter—Donald Trump disparaged the capitalist peace idea. In reversing three-quarters of a century of support for multilateral liberalization and free-trade internationalism, he made clear he did not conceive of trade as a foreign policy tool to promote democracy, shared prosperity, peace, and security. Rather, Trump characterized trade partners and closest friends as thieves out to steal copyrights, jobs, and companies, ravaging the domestic economy with their cut-rate exports and lure of cheap labor. That is, he had a wholly economic zero-sum, some called it transactional, approach to trade. And he got elected, in part, by vowing to reverse trade deficits and job losses, not to mention integration, by unilaterally shifting from free trade to protectionism by jacking up tariffs against China, Canada, Mexico, and

Western Europe; renegotiating the North American Free Trade Agreement; and withdrawing from the Trans-Pacific Partnership. He made good on these promises, though after four years in office he had little to show for his mercantilist policies other than larger trade deficits, the same stresses as before on the workforce and new ones on farmers, and distrust from allies. Never before had an administration spoken out so forcefully in favor of protectionism, not even Herbert Hoover's, though to his credit Hoover had believed in internationalism.[86]

Considering Trump's views on foreign policy, his speeches were not surprising. He admired the historic crusades against fascism and communism but complained that, from the 1990s onward, the pursuit of global prosperity and democracy had relegated American interests to the back burner. He would reverse course with a contradiction: isolationism combined with a muscular Christian mission abroad. "Instead of trying to spread universal values that not everybody shares or wants, we should understand that strengthening and promoting Western civilization and its accomplishments will do more to inspire positive reforms around the world than military interventions," he claimed. This stance deviated from internationalism, and certainly from capitalist peace, because it required both a unilateral and a non-inclusive approach to other nations. Trump demanded the right to police borders, halt immigration, and stop trade deals, putting American interests first. Of course, in reality, all administrations stretching back to Roosevelt's put America first. The difference was that Trump's foreign and trade agendas were inherently negative, even nihilistic; regardless of his rhetorical grandstanding, his policies fled from world leadership. "We will no longer surrender this country or its people to the false song of globalism," he declared on the campaign trail in 2016.[87] In reality, it was Trump's questioning of globalism—of internationalism rather than globalization that rankled progressives—that exposed this supposed billionaire, with his overseas assets, as fake as well as a hypocrite. His approach was also self-defeating, for it represented outmoded isolationism and incendiary nationalism designed to stir up discontent rather than solve real problems.

Trump's was a peculiar, idiosyncratic brand of populism. Historically, populism endorsed freer trade, as low tariffs benefited farmers, workers, and consumers and overcame high-cost protection of manufactured goods. Ostensibly to correct trade deficits, Trump recklessly raised tariffs that prompted foreign retaliation and thus hurt the people the tariffs were designed to help: food producers, factory workers, and average consumers. This simplistic and certainly loud approach defied the establishment, which populists liked because they viewed themselves (in part, correctly) as victims of industries that had departed America for offshore production, but they were vulnerable to Trump's words that undermined decades of capitalist peace that had built prosperity around the world; maintained national security interests; and addressed problems of poverty, human rights, health, climate change, and labor standards. Trump tended to ignore these realities.

Although he voiced the domestic frustration over years of globalization and free trade that reached a crescendo in the 2016 election, he was also out of step with most of the world on trade issues. At the end of his first year in office, the WTO launched a Trade for Peace Initiative under the G7 + WTO Accessions Group to recruit new countries, many of them troubling problems for American foreign policy, like Afghanistan, Yemen, and South Sudan. The initiative aimed to promote good governance, build peace through stability and growth, and deepen the "intersections among multilateral trade, peace and security."[88] As the World Trade Organization's deputy director general Alan Wolff explained, the project's founders, joined by peace and economic organizations, were well aware of how hard it was to prevent war, the same ones that peacemakers had encountered after World War I. Woodrow Wilson had asked for the removal of economic barriers and the establishment of trade equality as a principle. Nations had not listened then but they did after the Second World War. The WTO's Wolff wrote. "History teaches us that trade does not guarantee peace. However, it does give peace a better chance."[89] For instance, at the Horn of Africa, Sudan and Ethiopia had prioritized trade liberalization as the way to end war. Freer trade built "business relationships based on trust" to promote peace, security, democracy, and human rights.[90] Such internationalist rhetoric confronted Trump's goading nationalist populism.[91]

For Trump, who seemed to eschew an accurate reading of history, trade was pure business dealing, and it focused on Trump himself on the grand global stage. It did not allude to national interests gained from longtime foreign policies or to friends abroad. To be sure, he had an audience among a desperate, oftentimes angry, electorate who had either actually felt the brunt of imports or perceived imports to be their economic undoing, even though technology, automation, and personal failings were more likely culprits. His supporters (most of whom were solidly middle class rather than workers) also despised internationalist cosmopolitans and educated leaders, whom they believed to be elitist, condescending, and unpatriotic.

Trump was certainly damaging to international relations. He denounced NATO allies as financial slackers; fought over trade with Canada and Europe; embraced autocrats in Russia, the Philippines, and elsewhere; and discriminated against immigrants. These positions—with protectionism added—were elements of his America First agenda, with which he intended to jolt the global community. For their part, Americans still supported trade opportunities, but farmers, a Trump constituency, saw their exports collapse when China retaliated against his tariff hikes by cutting purchases of soybeans and other products. Trump's largely conservative supporters were so hurt by his trade policy that they had to rely on bailouts—government handouts—from the Treasury. In short, this was not the business or diplomatic leadership expected from the United States. It certainly did not strengthen the response of the democracies to illegal Chinese behavior in the world economy or to the successful grand strategy of capitalist peace.[92]

Trump and his advisors, like Stephen Bannon and Stephen Miller, looked at the global arena as a place to dominate, though in reality, that view was anachronistic. The administration pushed a strategy of "great-power competition" to intensify the rivalry with China and place NATO allies in service to the American military hegemon. Yet years of war in Iraq and Afghanistan, a defiant Russia, and a rising China joined with Trump's trashing of the liberal internationalist NATO/GATT coalition, compelled multilateral adaptation on Washington's part. To be sure, the United States was still a giant and, like Obama, Trump swore to promote freedom and democracy. But he engaged in news-grabbing crusades like trying to negotiate peace with the dictator in North Korea, Kim Jong-un, or withdrawing from useful engagement with Iran and Syria. This unrestrained unilateralist could not make America great again; indeed, it was great, but its hegemony was long gone, as other nations competed effectively with the United States in a globalized community. Post–Cold War presidents had understood that change, regardless of their party affiliation, temperament, or dreams.[93] Trump seemed oblivious to this truth or purposefully vindictive so he could profit politically at home.

On the North American Free Trade Agreement, Trump alienated Mexico and undermined goodwill on trade with Canada with his tariff hikes. He was not inclined to conceive of NAFTA within the capitalist peace paradigm, as a development tool for Mexico, or as a way to solidify the hemisphere in a democratic and rights-based alliance. To be sure, the FTA needed updating; Congress and the private sector, including labor, had long referred to the needed "modernization" of NAFTA. That is, it needed fresh legal and regulatory provisions, especially because the North American supply chain had more fully developed since NAFTA's birth. E-commerce had not existed in 1993, for instance, and customs procedures had grown burdensome. Legislators, moreover, wanted cheaper access for farm goods into both neighbors' markets (dairy products to Canada, fruit to Mexico) as well as maintenance of high standards in trade. Democrats accurately noted that Trump's vaunted overhaul of NAFTA—the United States-Mexico-Canada Agreement (USMCA), signed on November 30, 2018—merely updated policies for the digital age. The basic NAFTA framework remained, with a sunset clause that limited the agreement to sixteen years.[94] Trump's steel and aluminum tariffs held up the USMCA in both Mexican and Canadian parliaments, another example of the administration's working at cross purposes with friends. Nevertheless, the Democratic House resoundingly passed the

USMCA a day after impeaching Trump in mid-December 2019, and the Senate overwhelmingly ratified it in January 2020, three weeks before acquitting him of his alleged meddling in Ukraine.

In the global economy and trade sphere, Trump's blinkered views led him to see the nation's biggest trade challenge, China, in terms of a dog-eat-dog world. The world's second biggest importer and largest exporter and trade partner to every major East Asian country, including American allies, the PRC was a juggernaut of production, technology, military spending, and trade presence—and showed no sign of flattening its upward trajectory in those categories. This was the imperative behind the TPP: as a counterweight to Beijing's power.[95] Trump stacked his administration with protectionist, anti-Chinese officials such as trade advisor Peter Navarro and USTR Robert Lighthizer, so it quickly became evident that trade deficits and politics, rather than foreign policy, guided decision-making on China. Lighthizer focused trade policy on workers, a bit dubious coming from an international lawyer who had negotiated several bilateral free-trade accords, but essential for the Trump reelection game plan.[96]

There was no mention of national security, offsetting Chinese power and plans in the Asian-Pacific region, cooperating with like-minded allies, or building on the tradition of multilateral negotiations when Trump withdrew the United States from the TPP just three days after entering office in January 2017. Instead, the notice mentioned protecting workers from trade deals by negotiating "one-on-one" bilateral agreements that supposedly benefited the United States.[97] One-on-one meant that Trump occupied the limelight, but pulling out of the TPP did not make any sense geopolitically and made his trade agenda more incoherent.

The confrontation with China and anti-internationalism did not bear much fruit except for endearing him to his parochial base, old-guard protectionists, and Sinophobes. At subcommittee hearings hosted by the House Committee on Ways and Means in October 2017, legislators on both sides of the aisle shook their heads in dismay at the administration's trade record over its first year. Republicans wanted improvements in agreements with the Asia-Pacific nations but welcomed reductions in barriers and cooperation in the TPP, while Democrats ridiculed Trump's policy of initiating investigations into steel and aluminum imports, then backing off only to discover that consumers and producers bought madly from abroad before the tariffs went into effect. This frenzy led to skyrocketing imports and worsening deficits, a defeat for his protectionist intentions. Exiting the Trans-Pacific Partnership also elevated China's regional Comprehensive Economic Partnership. In any case, the eleven remaining TPP nations carried on without Washington's involvement, and Japan and the European Union considered a bilateral accord, marginalizing the United States. Trump threatened to withdraw from the bilateral accord with Korea because of the deficit with this close ally, oblivious that doing so might harm national security, not to mention that quitting deals, combined with protectionism, threatened rules that protected American interests. Beyond trade, the Asian nations were considering infrastructure investment across the Eurasian supercontinent, such as China's Belt and Road Initiative, that could reorder trade patterns and affect Washington's strategic position.[98] This was no time for unilateral, isolationist thinking.

Like Trump himself, his trade philosophy never evolved with the office or circumstances. Like Japan in the 1980s, China now "screwed" and "beat" the United States, stealing trade secrets and jobs, but this time around, the art of the deal would go America's way, he claimed. In fact, this sent exactly the wrong signal to China. As international relations specialist Julian Gewirtz has written, Xi believed Trump wanted a good deal rather than reform of China's illiberal state-run economic system, like Obama, the Bushes, and Clinton had sought. His confrontation with China brought Xi to the table but with the unfortunate result that Beijing became all the more determined to reject liberalization, despite the trade war. Members of both parties appreciated that Trump took "China head-on," said Texas Congressman Kevin Brady, ranking Republican on the Ways and Means Committee. While a majority of 115,000 voters surveyed by AP VoteCast near the November 2018 midterm elections disapproved of Trump's severe trade policy, of those who approved of his job overall, 88 percent liked his toughness toward China. "I beat China all the time" he had declared when entering the presidential race in 2015, and this bragging sounded good to slim majorities in import-competing Pennsylvania, Ohio, Wisconsin, and Michigan during the election.[99] These voters might be excused for anti-China feeling because they had lost jobs, but Trump was supposed to care about foreign policy.

Trump's bark was louder than his bite. He reveled in his tariff war with China, scoring points with his political base of frustrated fanatics but barely moving the needle in the bilateral relationship. That is, the trade deficit with China in 2019 mimicked the gap before he took office and grew larger the following year. To be sure, China's incomplete transition to a free-market economy, its state-directed policies that distorted trade and investment, and its cyber espionage and currency manipulation needed attention, if not sanction. The US Trade Representative noted in its annual report on the World Trade Organization that the United States had mistakenly backed China's entry into that organization because Beijing had never fully embraced an open market trade regime. China remained nonplussed, filing a grievance against Trump's solar panel tariffs in the WTO in August 2018. Trump had pledged a more aggressive stance against the trade deficit and worked out a deal with Xi in April 2017—the "100-day plan on trade"—that got market access commitments by China. Nothing much came of the efforts except purchase of American soybeans, though not at the promised amount, despite Trump's visit to Beijing to insist that the deficit be reduced. Still, he blamed the deficit on the laxity of previous administrations toward China.

Relations became ever more strained. With dubious national security justification, Trump imposed additional tariffs on steel and aluminum, China being the world's biggest producer of these commodities. Xi retaliated. In June 2018, Trump announced a two-stage plan to increase tariffs by $36 and $16 billion, and China responded with its own two-stage program of tariff hikes. This tit-for-tat action threatened not only bilateral commercial ties but a disruption of global supply chains, higher consumer prices, and diminished growth in the United States. Such a "one-dimensional" unilateral approach through tariffs would not stop a mighty predator like China. Rather than join with allies to shape Chinese behavior in the TPP, however, Trump's policies were haphazard and weak, lacking the united power of allies, the driving idea of the capitalist peace, and the thrust of free-trade internationalism behind them.[100]

Beginning his final year in office, Trump imposed new tariffs on almost $450 million of steel and aluminum products, not only hitting China but allies Taiwan, Japan, and the EU as well. In February 2020, Xi and Trump agreed to phased-in decreases and exemptions for tariffs, but the damage was done. By mid-March, the ominous effects of the trade war were apparent when the novel coronavirus pandemic started sweeping the world. Because of tariff hikes on medical products, American buyers had reduced purchases from China and did not replace them with imports from other nations. Dangerous shortages ensued. As the pandemic caused a worldwide economic crisis and a temporary end to decades of robust Chinese growth, the trade war became moot as commerce shut down. The sum total of tariff hikes, real or threatened, not to mention the cruelty and futility of protectionism in the face of the pandemic, pulled back the curtain on Trump's illogical failure in dealing with China.[101]

Trump also abandoned capitalist peace ideology in dealing with other countries, an approach that backfired there, too. He hurt Americans when Europe, Canada, and China retaliated against his tariffs by raising their own against American goods—soybean farmers, boat-makers, and spirits producers were caught in the crossfire. Even in the COVID-19 pandemic, he inappropriately pursued a vengeful trade policy when, in August 2020, he raised tariffs on Canadian aluminum. In late October, the WTO ruled that the European Union was entitled to levy tariffs on $4 billion worth of American exports.[102] Populist protectionism had not paid off.

Trump and his enablers in Congress and the executive branch had not only burdened the world economy but endangered the United States as the election loomed. He crowed in 2020 that he had gotten results—farmers and manufacturers loved him for this confrontation with China and Beijing itself had caved to the pressure. Before denouncing his political enemies, he claimed to a roused American Farm Bureau Federation in Austin, Texas, in January that "we now perhaps have the best relationship that we've had with China in many, many years." The deals with China supposedly enhanced the domestic economy and national security, though he did not say how. "We're taking care of our country. It's 'Make America Great Again.' It's 'Keep America Great.' It's whatever you want to call it. We're in the greatest country anywhere in the world, and we're taking care of you."[103] But actually, it was China that seemed great again. The PRC began to recover from the recession by fall 2020, while the United States remained mired in it. For all Trump's sound and fury, only the pandemic-induced recession narrowed the bilateral trade gap in 2020; Americans were simply not buying. Indeed, as recovery from the global recession took hold, the trade deficit with China hit record levels by spring 2021.

In trade and foreign policy, in a nutshell, Trump held out false, but patriotic, prophesies to willing listeners, but he ultimately met defeat. Trump exposed his arbitrary approach to foreign and commercial affairs as he threatened to shut down all immigration and foreign work visas in the United States and, at the end of May 2020, denounced Beijing's security crackdown on Hong Kong while he issued dubious statements about cures for the coronavirus and downplayed its death toll. Perhaps finally fearful of the economic repercussions, he did not deviate from the first phase of tariff reductions made earlier in the year, but once again, Trump went back and forth on trade and protectionism as the economy tanked. Old friends abroad refused to let Americans travel to their countries, perhaps in an implicit questioning of the electorate's sanity under such an unruly leader.

Indeed, many allies got their wish when former vice president, Joe Biden, ousted Trump in the November elections, even though the victory provoked a debate between the mainstream liberals and the progressives over trade. On March 3, 2021, the new secretary of state, Antony J. Blinken, gave his first major address, which clearly demonstrated progressive influence, noting that domestic economic health would be closely tied to foreign policy. That seemed like an ominous sign for free traders, who heard that agreements might even be junked if they served only those at the top and threatened workers, businesses, and the middle class. But crucially, *internationalists* issued that statement. Biden would not stand by and let the capitalist peace paradigm continue to wither. Take China, for example. America might never rejoin the Trans-Pacific Partnership, but a philosophical shift—or return—was in order, he made clear. The key, as it had always been before Trump, was negotiating "from a position of strength," which required "working with allies and partners, not denigrating them, because our combined weight is much harder for China to ignore." Diplomacy and engaging international organizations were also essential, he said, "because where we have pulled back, China has filled in." And America must stand "up for our values when human rights are abused in Xinjiang or when democracy is trampled in Hong Kong, because if we don't, China will act with even greater impunity."[104]

In short, the world needed and required internationalism on the part of the United States, even if free trade was somewhat moderated from the George W. Bush years. Free-trade internationalism had cycled back; the Biden administration moved to end transatlantic and hemispheric tariff wars in 2021 even as it embraced a worker-oriented policy, caution toward China, and renewed zeal for climate-driven and innovative trade agreements. To be sure, he shared many objectives with his predecessor, especially toughness toward Beijing and a trade agenda for the middle class. In addition, like Trump, he struggled to meet the challenges of the COVID pandemic, including strains in global supply chains that prompted shortages and drove up inflation. But Biden's tactics—of multilateralism and cooperation—were polar opposites of Trump's. Americans in both parties, as well as observers abroad, applauded the steps toward restoration of the capitalist peace to the core of American foreign policy.

Conclusion

A Near-Century of Capitalist Peace

Donald Trump was not the catalyst for this book but he certainly provided further motivation to write this history of internationalism, commerce, and diplomacy, as he sparked interest in trade issues not witnessed since the early Clinton years. Thus, he became a foil for my premise: free-trade internationalism undergirded the capitalist peace, which proved generally beneficial to the United States and the world. Trump's notion of America First flew in the face of this conclusion by exaggerating the consequences of past policies, privileging protectionism despite its historical record, and ultimately, betraying America itself. His approach was redundant because, as this book has shown, protectionists had long put America first by opposing the linkage of trade to foreign policy. The Red Scare conspiracy theorists of the late 1940s took an extreme view of this thinking when they attacked imports as products of supposedly traitorous State Department negotiators who supposedly undermined the economy and democracy. But protectionism was ever present in American politics and had intensified enough by the time of Trump's election to make it politically worthwhile for him to champion it. His rhetoric on trade capitalized on longtime protectionist undercurrents that served his misconceived and failed nationalist-populist trade policy.

Trump is instructive for this book's argument because he reflected three unhealthy and dangerous shifts in trade decision-making. First, the Republican Party had long supported free trade, ever since it threw off isolationism during the Second World War. Republican critics since then had complained that trade was not free enough—the business purists who rejected both the International Trade Organization and the Organization for Trade Cooperation and the neo-liberal globalizers being two cases. Trump was out of step with his own Republican Party, most of which still adhered to free-trade internationalism but was now

Capitalist Peace. Thomas W. Zeiler, Oxford University Press. © Oxford University Press 2022.
DOI: 10.1093/oso/9780197621363.003.0014

chained to populist rage. Second, the executive branch had never expressed such a politicized version of protectionism that played to the anger, rather than the better angels, of the electorate. Richard Nixon's economic shock of 1971, which rivaled Trump's nationalist reversal of traditional American policy and played to electoral politics as well, was an intense but brief move that could even be rationalized by the circumstances of times—a disintegrated American monetary position, the demise of the Bretton Woods system, and the first trade deficits in nearly a century. Nixon was tough, but he also returned to internationalism and regretted what he later viewed as a mistake. Trump never retreated nor did he learn. The result was not surprising: a counter-productive policy to which other nations responded by retaliating with tariff wars.

Third, the executive branch had for decades championed internationalism (the brief diversion in the early Nixon years being the exception), including free trade. Unlike Trump, policymakers knew history, understood the dangers of economic nationalism, and were convinced of the logic of capitalist peace ideology. They saw that free-trade internationalism promoted cooperation, not conflict, among capitalist nations, and developed stronger democracies that united against fascism, communism, terrorism, and human rights violators. Trump, never a team player, did not comprehend that the capitalist peace, transmitted by free-trade internationalism rather than unilateral economic nationalism, embodied the true American interest.

Protectionism stretched back to the country's beginning and forward to the present. After all, Franklin Roosevelt—focused on his domestic New Deal—had privileged America first in his early years in office by undermining the London Economic conference and allowing only careful, reciprocal tariff cuts under his trade agreements program. The British Commonwealth and Empire, of course, had its imperial preference system, strengthened by the Ottawa regime in the early 1930s, which defied the most-favored-nation principle. To be sure, the Cold War largely muffled protectionism as an impractical approach, though it did not disappear—as Dwight Eisenhower experienced persistent trouble with protectionists within his own Republican Party. The progressive revolt against market capitalism and free trade after the Kennedy Round accelerated after the Cold War in the Democratic Party and reshaped liberalism as a result. Anti-globalizers in the 1990s, and then Occupy and Bernie Sanders and Tea Party populist activists in the 2010s, all denounced free-trade deals, the diplomats who negotiated them, and the corporations that profited.

The free-trade/protectionist debate will continue to rage on. It persistently pushed the low-key capitalist peace into the background and will continue to do so. Trump's views were nothing new except that he displayed a frustrating ignorance about history. That is, the world had been down this road before during the Great Depression, and protectionism had helped bring about a second world war.

While protectionism was, and remains, attractive because it provides a simple, patriotic-sounding answer to economic dislocations that Americans suffer, the fact remains that all but the most rabid protectionists since the 1930s still endorsed some form of involvement in the world. In other words, most Americans wanted more, not less, engagement through aid, alliances, and trade. There was always an outcry when traditional producers could not compete with imports or were shut out of markets abroad, but turning inward to abandon multilateral agreements for prosperity, development, security, human rights, and later environmental protection was not their preferred course. Liberals might seek to modify trade deals in the interests of average Americans, but they did not turn their backs on the responsibility to take part in internationalist endeavors around the world. Conservatives (and liberals) woke up to a dangerous international arena in the postwar years, turning to free-trade internationalism as a means of shoring up the Free World.

Most liberals and progressives knew that freer trade was logical because it coaxed nations to open their markets to American exports, and that redounded in Washington's projection of power overseas. The very criticism by liberals that administrations did not do enough for the global South in trade, for example, showed that they wanted fuller engagement in the world economy, even if it meant sacrificing markets at home. Decades later, progressives—to the left of liberals—did not stress profits through free trade, as conservatives did. Rather, they believed the world trading system must foster democracy and human rights, and that the United States could use its commercial leverage toward those ends. That was, in short, an internationalist argument that conservatives agreed with as well. Liberals criticized when market-led globalization seemed to excuse human rights violations overseas but they were not nihilists. Progressives sought international cooperation to improve the lot of people.

For their part, conservatives backed fair trade to open up markets to American exports and investments. Since the Reciprocal Trade Agreements Act of 1958, presidents have resorted to numerous safeguards to protect workers and industry from imports, such as the national security and escape clauses and various peril point provisions included in agreements. Congress clearly put America first; and parochial Republicans in the heartland, who still dominated the party, backed such measures even if presidents opposed them. The modern wave of the GOP, beginning in the 1980s and led by neo-liberal free marketeers, then joined with the executive branch against any trade restrictions as globalization took root. They also abandoned any pretense of helping heartland workers, but they convinced the blue-collar laborers that the cause of their struggles lay abroad and not at home. Neo-liberals deregulated, privatized, and mobilized capital by investments and tax cuts that benefited high earners and the wealthy. They cleverly blamed unemployment and factory closings on import competition (from the EU, Japan, and then China) rather than on extreme market capitalist policies. Thus, they opened the way for nationalist-populists to make the same argument and also to seize control of the Republican Party and turn it toward America first.

Like liberals, however, the neo-liberal conservatives approached foreign relations by embracing friendship toward allies abroad. In this, they deviated from the nationalist-populists, even though many neo-liberals backed Trump, at least at first, because they despised the liberal and progressive alternatives. In short, though, conservatives and liberals devised multilateral ways to confront rivals and enemies through soft power, trade included. Capitalist peace, like the theory of comparative advantage, was not an either/or—not a zero-sum—proposition. Free-trade policy worked economically, though it always needed attention to reform, and conservatives and liberals agreed that free-trade internationalism succeeded in the diplomatic arena as a bastion of security, peace, and democracy.

The capitalist peace doctrine that emerged from the Great Depression did not bring a perfect world, prosperity for all, or eternal peace. It was an instrument of foreign policy that converted trade policy from narrow nationalism based on protectionism into a force for mutual aid, security, and political reform abroad. The figures who surrounded presidents, like the presidents themselves, appreciated the appeal, and the need on occasion, for protectionism, but they recast trade policy for foreign policy reasons. The alternatives to the capitalist peace, as they saw them, of hyper-nationalism, fascism, militarism, and communism represented unacceptable threats to democracy.

These crusaders started with Cordell Hull, surely the American father of the capitalist peace idea, backed up by Francis Sayre and Harry Hawkins, and the next generation in the 1940s centered on Will Clayton, with Winthrop Brown, Clair Wilcox, and others in support. John Foster Dulles and Clarence Randall led the charge for free-trade internationalism in the following decade, and George Ball, with a boost from Christian Herter, advised two presidents in the 1960s. In the meaner next half-century, notables did not stand out. These times of economic struggle were best expressed by fair-trade policies and protectionism in a context of relative decline, regeneration through free-market policies and globalization, and a series of crises. The capitalist peace paradigm was assumed, altered, and subsumed at times by politicians and bureaucrats. But whatever the change in the global arena—from depression and war to Cold War, from unipolarity to a war on terror and repeated crises—internationalist principles nonetheless persisted. The capitalist peace endured, connecting trade to foreign policy. Although he tried, even Trump could not sever that relationship.

Until 2017, Washington took the initiative in foreign affairs, and free-trade internationalism funneled that activism toward engagement with the world. Instead of looking for monsters to destroy in reactive ways, leaders hoped to shore up the world economy as a means of defending the United States and its allies. Even when the domestic economy emerged as a fixation in the 1970s, the government and business sectors projected foreign policy in trade affairs. Free traders did not wait for other nations to act. Rather, capitalist peacemakers encouraged liberalism and frowned on anti-democratic and dangerous ideologies, trying to persuade nations to cooperate under liberal rules and norms.

Franklin Roosevelt built the liberal, internationalist order, his successors strengthened it, and all elevated American leadership to the fore. It was based on the promotion of free markets and private property, human rights, representative democracy, and multilateral cooperation among nations. Achieving and preserving these elements of liberalism hinged on the leadership of the United States; America was central to the global pursuit of political, economic, and social freedoms, and the security and peace they would bring.[1] Even deviations like the Nixon Shock of August 15, 1971, did not push the United States from its internationalist course, conceptualized and maintained on the basis of capitalist peace ideology. Even in the era of globalization and economic crisis, despite the naysayers, Americans still adhered to that internationalist vision of free trade. Sometimes that vision clashed with the interests of other nations or granted America profits at their expense. Some pointed to forms of imperial domination. But American foreign policy remained grounded in the capitalist peace vision, seeking to join trade liberalization to political liberalization through an interventionist approach to the world.[2]

Again, the results were not perfect, by any means, but the benefits were monumental. Producers and workers struggled to adapt to import competition or met resistance abroad to exports, and many failed. The successes outweighed the losses, especially in terms of an overall grand strategy designed to bring prosperity, peace, and security to a conflicted global arena. Applying the capitalist peace was a process, with steps forward and back, that generally encouraged cooperation, built alliances of like-minded people and nations, and helped unite nations during and after World War II. In fact, the capitalist peace worked so effectively that business and politicians applied pressure to ease trade restrictions even with enemies and anti-democratic forces, such as the Soviet Union and later the People's Republic of China.

Leaders sought to shape world economic structures, development, and finance through liberal trade policies, and diplomatic, political, and social designs followed closely behind. The United States envisioned freer trade as a means of injecting its values, principles, and practices into the world economy and into other nations. This meant that capitalist peace thinking required economic sacrifices at home so that friends and allies could become prosperous, and, thus, stable and secure democratic partners in the international community. Admittedly, opening domestic markets on behalf of grand strategic objectives brought hardships, but so did automation and inadequate fiscal expenditures to adjust to a modern global economy. Trade was often a scapegoat for economic problems. Sometimes the accusations were true, but in the bigger picture, trade boosted the American way of life and the free, democratic world itself.

The United States pursued trade liberalization because it could, as a hegemon, exercising its dominance under a supposed consensus of free enterprise. Some, like Harry Truman, Dwight Eisenhower, Ronald Reagan, and George W. Bush, were perfectly comfortable with that approach. Others, like John F. Kennedy, Richard Nixon, Lyndon Johnson, George H. W. Bush, and Bill Clinton, championed it but grew uneasy as times changed around them. Jimmy Carter and Barack Obama and, at times, Roosevelt, became critics when the system overlooked the poor and struggling masses at home and abroad. Yet all, like most of the private sector and voters, endorsed a basic trade internationalism that enhanced American power and projected a foreign policy that made sense for the world. The United States was surely guilty of propagating conflict and inequality beyond its shores, but even so-called free-trade imperialism, one of the labels critics applied to capitalist peace dogma and free-trade internationalism, was a better alternative than debilitating isolationism, protectionism, and war.

The capitalist peace was the *only* option to prevent a recurrence of the Great Depression and the war it wrought, the *only* way to keep Americans turned toward commitments overseas, and the *only* means to provide security, development, and mutual prosperity—and ultimately peace—for a world that had torn itself apart and stood on the brink of nuclear conflict afterward. The paradigm turned out to be flexible as well. Free-trade internationalism turned from promoting universal values to encouraging democratic capitalist nations to confront communism, terrorism, and modern-day China. The capitalist peace also demanded fair treatment for those struggling for profits, both overseas and at home, offering opportunities to trade in the American market so they remained tied to America. Like the Wilsonian internationalist blueprint, capitalist peace made sense as a grand strategy.

Free trade was an element in that foreign policy, though a critical one as the United States built postwar institutions and consolidated allies in the Cold War. The capitalist peace also helped lay to rest nonsensical isolationism as a viable policy, a position wholly inappropriate for the leader of the free, globalized world during times of crisis. Isolationism and its cousin, unilateralism, were, and are, the constant siren songs for those who lack knowledge of this quite alarming history and who erroneously believe they can insulate themselves from the rest of the globe. Roosevelt, guided by Cordell Hull, envisioned a transformation in thinking: to harness America's massive economic power to a new world order based on democratic capitalism, multilateral agreement, and human rights. The United States could have easily turned to protectionism, though at a steep price. Certainly, the world would have been worse off, as fascism, communism, and nationalism crept forward to fill the vacuum left by the isolated United States. The capitalist peace, then, was self-interested and made sense in the long game of promoting and protecting democratic values. That is why Roosevelt welcomed careful trade liberalization, postwar planning, and the projection of American principles in a world that had gone wrong. His successors followed his lead. The world can always go wrong again unless we continue to acknowledge that trade and foreign policy are intimately connected, and that wielding both in wise, prudent ways is essential to security and peace.

Trade liberalization, derived from the capitalist peace paradigm, built economies, integrated nations, provided security through military pacts, and, ultimately, brought peace. If reductions in tariffs could help foster cooperation, democracy, and peace, then free-trade internationalism was an effective, safe, and rather cheap way to pay for global security and comity. Challenges remained, and still do, including the fight for global equity, democratic stability, and rights and opportunities for all. In the Trump years and beyond, internationalists lamented the illiberal turn in many countries, including the United States.

But in the end, capitalist liberalism won the Second World War and the Cold War, enriched the North, and helped develop much of the global South with material goods. Capitalist peace, though not without its faults and deviations from this mission, also boosted democracy and promoted and maintained human rights. It answered, with internationalism, to the uncertain period of globalization, terrorism, populist nationalism, and shifts in world power relationships that followed. This remains quite an impressive record that derived from the complex, rather arcane set of rules, regulations, and norms that comprised American trade policy. They became the blueprint for the international commercial order; since the mid-twentieth century, the United States oversaw the development of a remarkably stable, prosperous, and mutually beneficial system for itself and its allies. There were deviations; conflicts erupted and inequalities emerged in the world. Poverty was not eliminated, and neither were grudges, quarrels, and outright clashes. Politics in many countries, including the United States, became more brutish, ugly, and polarized, even descending into civil schisms. But on the larger scale of grand strategy, trade boosted security, global peace prevailed, and a third world war did not occur. In large part, goods rather than soldiers crossed borders in the capitalist alliance of free trade. A welcome sight across continents riven by war, the long-standing ambition of philosophers, merchants, and politicians had come to pass. Capitalist peace had reshaped the world for the better.

NOTES

Archives Abbreviations

AC	Carl Albert Congressional Research Center
BIO	Bureau of International Operations, Record Group 151, NARA
CDL	Clinton Digital Library, William J. Clinton Library
CFR	Council on Foreign Relations, Princeton University Library
CEA	Staff Office, Council on Economic Advisors, Jimmy Carter Library
CFEP	U.S. Council on Foreign Economic Policy, Dwight D. Eisenhower Library
DDEL	Dwight D. Eisenhower Library
FDRL	Franklin D. Roosevelt Library
FRUS	*Foreign Relations of the United States*
GBL	George H.W. Bush Library
GRFL	Gerald R. Ford Library
HHPL	Herbert Hoover Presidential Library
HKOF	Henry Kissinger Office Files, Richard M. Nixon Library
HL	Hagley Museum and Library
HSTL	Harry S Truman Library
IEA	International Economic Affairs Staff, Gerald R. Ford Library
JCL	Jimmy Carter Library
JFKL	John F. Kennedy Library
LBJL	Lyndon B. Johnson Library
LC	Library of Congress
MRC	Modern Records Center Warwick
NARA	National Archives and Records Administration
NFTC	National Foreign Trade Council, Hagley Library
NCJW	National Council of Jewish Women, Library of Congress
NORC	National Opinion Research Center
NSC	National Security Council Files, various archives
NSF	National Security Files, various archives
OIRE	Office of International Regional Economics, Record Group 489, NARA
OPA	Office of Public Affairs, National Archives and Records Administration
PA	Parliamentary Archives
POF	President's Official File, various archives
PPF	President's Personal File, various archives
PUL	Princeton University Library
RAC	Rockefeller Archives Center
RG	Record Group, various archives
RMNL	Richard M. Nixon Library

RRL	Ronald Reagan Library
SMOF	Staff Member and Office Files, various archives
SVP	Senate and Vice-Presidential Papers, Harry S Truman Library
WHCF	White House Central Files, various archives
WHORM	White House Office of Records Management, various archives
WHOS	White House Office of Speechwriting, various archives
WHPO	White House Press Office, various archives
WJCL	William J. Clinton Library

Introduction

1. See Bibliography for complete bibliographic information. Abbreviations in notes refer to libraries, archives, and files listed in the Bibliography, and a list of these abbreviations appears there. Unless otherwise noted, all Internet sources were accessed September 1, 2021. For the new left, see Gardner, LaFeber, and McCormick, *Creation of the American Empire*; Williams, *Tragedy of American Diplomacy*. For the history of capitalism, see Konczal, *Freedom from the Market*; Slobodian, *Globalists*; Treu, Schmelzer, and Burkhart, *Degrowth in Movements.*
2. See Sluga and Clavin, eds., *Internationalisms.*
3. Kupchan, *Isolationism;* Wertheim, *Tomorrow the World.*
4. Ruggie, "International Regimes, Transactions, and Change"; Ruggie, "Globalization and the Embedded Liberalism Compromise."
5. Strange, "Protectionism and World Politics."
6. See, for instance, Kuttner, *The End of Laissez-Faire*, 116–122.
7. For comprehensive trade histories, see Eckes, *Opening America's Market*; Irwin, *Clashing over Commerce;* Johnson, *Wealth of a Nation*; McKenzie, *GATT and Global Order.*
8. See Clausing, "The Progressive Case Against Protectionism"; Irwin, *Free Trade Under Fire.*
9. Neff, *Friends but No Allies*, 42. For free-trade orthodoxy and history, see Gomes, *Economics and Ideology of Free Trade*; Irwin, *Against the Tide*; Palen, *"Conspiracy" of Free Trade*; Viner, *Studies in the Theory of International Trade.*
10. On the substantial literature on democratic peace theory, see Egan, "Democracy, the State, and Global Capitalism," 84–94; Russett, *Grasping the Democratic Peace.* For a skeptic, see Braumoeller, *Only the Dead*, 219–221. For an excellent summary, and a conclusion that the notion that trade means peace must be considered on a case-by-case basis, see Barbieri, *Liberal Illusion.*
11. Quoted in Pinker, *Better Angels*, 285.
12. Pinker, *Better Angels*, 287. See also Rosenberg, *Financial Missionaries to the World*; Mazower, *Governing the World*, 39.
13. Leffler, *Preponderance of Power*, 14.
14. Choi, "Re-Evaluating Capitalist and Democratic Peace Models," 767.
15. Neff, *Friends but No Allies*, 159–177. See also McKenzie, *GATT and Global Order*, 31–33, 62–103.
16. Mandelbaum, *Ideas that Conquered the World*, 266.
17. Domke, *War and the Changing Global System*, 107, 137–139. See also MacDonald, *Invisible Hand of Peace.* For the influence of trade (and security concerns) on the domestic arena, see Katznelson and Shefter, eds, *Shaped by War and Trade.*
18. For neoliberal regime theory, see Keohane, *After Hegemony*; Ikenberry, Lake, and Mastanduno, eds., *The State and American Foreign Economic Policy.* For a summary of capitalist peace and classical-liberal theories over time, see Dorussen and Ward, "Trade Networks and the Kantian Peace," 29–32. For proponents, see Hegre, Oneal, and Russett, "Trade Does Promote Peace," 763–772; Oneal and Russett, "The Classical Liberals Were Right," 267–289; Polachek, "Conflict and Trade." For a new left view of the general "peace and prosperity" thesis in US foreign policy, see the old but relevant Paterson, "The Economic Cold War," iv, 56–75.
19. Gartzke, "The Capitalist Peace," 166–182; Mousseau, "The Democratic Peace Unraveled," 186–196.
20. Blainey, *Causes of War*, 20.
21. Quoted in Sobek, *Causes of War*, 107–116.

22. Quoted in Mazower, *Governing the World*, 43. See also McKenzie, *GATT and Global Order*, 27.
23. Russett and Oneal, *Triangulating Peace*, 129, italics in original. See also Braumoeller, *Only the Dead*, 58.
24. Mazower, *Governing the World*, 39.
25. Barbieri, *Liberal Illusion*, 1–2, 6–7.
26. Angell, *Great Illusion*. See also Cortright, *Peace*, 239, 251–252; McKenzie, *GATT and Global Order*, 28–30.
27. On commercial activism without grand strategy, see Kupchan, *Isolationism*, 6–7, 217–222, 242–244, 253–254.
28. On Wilsonian economics, see Ninkovich, *Wilsonian Century*, 66–77; Ambrosius, *Woodrow Wilson and American Internationalism*; Smith, *Why Wilson Matters*, 1–140. On postwar globalism, see Rosenboim, *Emergence of Globalism*.
29. On the postwar trade system, see Clavin and Dungy, "Trade, Law, and the Global Order of 1919," 555–558, 563.
30. Irwin, *Clashing over Commerce*, 330–371; Eckes, *Opening America's Market*, 90–93; Johnson, *Wealth of a Nation*, 170.
31. Kupchan, *Isolationism*, 271–275, 306–308.

Chapter 1

1. Nicholas Murray Butler, "A Call to Action," January 13, 1933, folder Foreign Affairs Misc. Subjects, box 397, Democratic Party: National Committee Papers, FDRL.
2. Free traders and Democrats propagate that legend. See Pastor, *Congress and the Politics*, 8; Johnson, *Wealth of a Nation*, 202; Irwin, *Clashing over Commerce*, 394–340; Phalan, Yazegi, and Rustici, "The Hawley-Smoot Tariff and the Great Depression."
3. "Why Other Nations Protest," *The* (Portland) *Oregonian*, June 4, 1929, folder Tariff Commission-Press Analysis July 24–August 24, box 334, Presidential Subject Files, HHPL. See also "1,028 Economists Ask Hoover to Veto Pending Tariff Bill," *New York Times*, May 5, 1930, 1.
4. Eckes, *Opening America's Market*, 112–139; digests of so-called foreign "protests" against the Hawley-Smoot Bill, October 29, 1932, folder Tariff Commission-Correspondence 1932 October 21–31, box 319, Presidential Subject Files, HHPL. In fact, fifty-nine countries protested the legislation before its passage. See also Pastor, *Congress and the Politics*, 81, 95.
5. Leffler, "1921–1932," 232.
6. J. E. Sitterley and V. D'Aquila to A. A. Dacco, August 6, 1929, folder Tariff Commission-Correspondence August 1–15, 1929box 317, Presidential Subject Files, HHPL.
7. Leffler, "1921–1932," 248, also 253.
8. The Beaverbrook-Rothermere-Baldwin Quarrel and the Position of Free Trade, June 30, 1929, ref. no. LG/G/26/1, Correspondence between Lloyd George and Gareth Jones, The Lloyd George Papers [LG-GJ], PA; "Empire Ever: Nazi-ism Never," reprinted from the *Daily Express*, January 17, 1934, ref. no. BBK/G/12/38, Henry Graham White Papers, box 5, PA; Empire Free Trade, gramophone record, May 27, 1934, Notes of Speeches, ref. no. BBK/F/25-29, Beaverbrook Papers, PA. See also Leffler, "1921–1932," 258.
9. Lloyd George, The American Tariff, June 27, 1930, LG/G/1, LG-GJ, PA.
10. Irwin, *Clashing over Commerce*, 408, also 400–407. See also Pastor, *Congress and the Politics*, 79.
11. The Tariff and International Relations, [1932], box 33, Rexford Tugwell Papers, FDRL. See also Reflections of Popular Sentiment on the Tariff Bill, [undated], folder Hawley-Smoot Tariff Bill, 1930, box 3, Edward Dana Durand Papers, HHPL.
12. Herbert H. Walther to the President, May 20, 1930, folder Tariff Commission-Veto 1930 May 20, box 335, Presidential Subject Files, HHPL.
13. John Barrett memorandum, July 17, 1929, folder Tariff Commission July 16–31, box 335, Presidential Subject Files, HHPL.
14. "War, Peace, and the Tariff," *The Churchman*, [1930], folder Tariff Commission-Veto 1930 May 24, box 335, Presidential Subject Files, HHPL.

15. Irving Fisher to the President, June 2, 1930, folder Tariff Commission-Veto 1930 June 2, box 335, Presidential Subject Files, HHPL.
16. W. Y. Elliott, Debts and Credits: An Economic Balance Sheet Drawn Up to Meet Political Necessities, [undated], folder Tariff, box 39, Tugwell Papers, FDRL.
17. Warren Dupre Smith to President Herbert Hoover, August 28, 1930, folder Tariff 1929–1933, box 211, PPF, HHPL.
18. Address of Governor Franklin D. Roosevelt, February 2, 1932, folder Tariff, box 465, Henry Morgenthau Jr. Papers, FDRL.
19. Dallek, *Franklin D. Roosevelt and American Foreign Policy,* 20; Speech by Hoover, [1932], folder Campaign Speech Data-Tariff, Miscellaneous (2), 1932, box 286, Presidential Subject Files, HHPL. See also Julius Klein to Theodore Joslin, October 1, 1932, folder Campaign Speech Data-Tariff, Correspondence 1930–1932, box 286, Presidential Subject Files, HHPL.
20. Mrs. J. J. C. Harvey to Herbert Hoover, August 15, 1932, folder Tariff Commission-Correspondence 1932 June–August, box 319, Presidential Subject Files, HHPL.
21. Tariff Revision by International Log-Rolling, [1932], folder Tariff, Miscellaneous (1), 1932, box 286; Republican Tariff Has Saved Agriculture, Industry and Labor, folder Republican Party-Campaign Literature, 1932, box 309, Presidential Subject Files, HHPL.
22. Campaign Book of the Democratic Party: Candidates and Issues, 1932, Part 1, box 1, Series V: Subject Files, President's Secretary's Files (digital), FDRL.
23. Inaugural Address, March 4, 1933, *The American Presidency Project* (Santa Barbara, CA: University of California-Santa Barbara), http://www.presidency.ucsb.edu/ws/index.php?pid=14473&st=Inaugural&st1=.
24. Tugwell, "The New Course of International Trade," 1933, folder "The New Course . . . ," box 30, Tugwell Papers, FDRL. See also Tugwell's Preliminary Draft of a World Constitution, Draft III, folder World Constitution: Draft, box 39, Tugwell Papers, FDRL; Gardner, *Economic Aspects of New Deal Diplomacy*, 12–14; Schmitz, *Sailor*, chapter 1.
25. Second Joint Statement, April 28, 1933, http://www.presidency.ucsb.edu/ws/index.php?pid=14632&st=&st1=.
26. Joint Statement by the President, Viscount Kikujiro Ishii, and Mr. Nigo Fukai, May 27, 1933, folder State Department, 1933–1937, box 8, Series II: Confidential Files, President's Secretary's Files, FDRL.
27. Joint Statement, May 12, 1933, http://www.presidency.ucsb.edu/ws/index.php?pid=14640&st=&st1=.
28. Hull, *Memoirs, Vol. I*, 81–82, 84.
29. Butler, *Cautious Visionary*, 7–9, also 10.
30. Hull, *Memoirs, Vol.* 1, 84–86.
31. Hathaway, "1933–1945," 281, also 282.
32. League of Nations, Monetary and Economic Conference, Draft Annotated Agenda, January 20, 1933, box 1, folder Diplomatic Files: Department of State, 1933–1934: World Economic Conference, Jon Cooper Wiley Papers, FDRL. See also League of Nations International Institute of Intellectual Co-Operation, "The State and Economic Live [LIVES?]," May 29–June 2, 1933, Part I: The Most-Favoured Nation Clause, 2–3; Professor Gregory and Aylmer Vallance, Free Trade and the World Economic Crisis: A Manifesto, May 20, 1933, WH1/5/11, Free Trade 1933, Henry Graham White Papers, PA.
33. Hull, *Memoirs, Vol. I*, 170–171, 286. See also Gardner, *Economic Aspects*, 28–30; *FRUS 1933*, Vol. 1, General (1950): 524, 535, 554; The Roosevelt Administration and the London Conference of 1933, from Raymond Moley, *After Seven Years*, September 30, 1944, reel 46, box 80–81, Cordell Hull Papers, LC. See also Rexford Tugwell diary, February 26, 1933, folder Monetary Preliminaries and Diary, 12/20/32–2/27/33, box 30, Tugwell Papers, FDRL.
34. Bernard Child, Interruption or Recovery of World Trade: The European Panorama, June 1934, Final Report, State, 1933–1934, Pt. II, box 69, Series IV: Departmental Correspondence, President's Secretary's Files, FDRL.
35. Hull to the President, Summary of Work of the Monetary and Economic Conference, August 5, 1933, State Department, 1933–1937, box 8, Series II: Confidential Files, President's Secretary's Files, FDRL.
36. Butler, *Cautious Visionary*, 37.

37. Johnson, *Wealth of a Nation*, 246–254.
38. Appendix, Agenda for Delegates to the Conference at Montevideo, November 4, 1933, folder State, 1933–1934, Part 1, box 69, Series IV: Departmental Correspondence, President's Secretary's Files, FDRL.
39. Hull, *Memoirs, Vol. 1*, 355.
40. Chorev, *Remaking U.S. Trade Policy*, 45–65.
41. Johnson, *Wealth of a Nation*, 258–262; Message to Congress, March 2, 1934, http://www.presidency.ucsb.edu/ws/index.php?pid=14817&st=&st1=; Arthur H. Vandenberg, No Tariff Dictatorship, May 18, 1934, *Congressional Record*, June 8, 1935. See also Butler, *Cautious Visionary*, 82–96: Address of the Chairman of the National Foreign Trade Council, 21st Annual Meeting, March 4, 1935, folder 12, box 24, NFTC, HL; U.S. Congress, House Committee on Ways and Means, *Reciprocal Trade Agreements Hearings*, 73rd Cong., 2d sess., 1934, Sayre, 303–320; Crowther, 480; U.S. Congress, Senate Committee on Finance, *Reciprocal Trade Agreements Hearings*, 73rd Cong., 2d sess., 1934, Sayre and senators, 64–70; American Tariffs League, 378–82.
42. Sayre, The United States Trade Agreements Program and Most-Favored-Nation Treatment, November 28, 1934, State, 1933–1934, Pt. II, Series IV: Departmental Correspondence, box 69, President's Secretary's Files, FDRL.
43. Gardner, *Economic Aspects*, 44.
44. Memorandum of Conversation between German Ambassador Hans Luther and Secretary of State Hull, September 20, 1934, reel 29, box 58, Hull Papers, LC.
45. George N. Peek to the President, December 31, 1934, folder Report of Special Advisor to the President on Foreign Trade, box 150, Key Pittman Papers, LC. See also Butler, *Cautious Visionary*, 97–120.
46. George N. Peek to the President, July 16, 1935, box 53, file Agriculture-Peek, Series IV: Departmental Correspondence, President's Secretary's Files, FDRL.
47. Dallek, *Franklin D. Roosevelt*, 92; Gardner, *Economic Aspects*, 100–104.
48. Hull, *Memoirs, Vol. I*, 390–392.
49. *FRUS 1934*, Vol. I, British Commonwealth (1951), 646, 685; Butler, *Cautious Visionary*, 121–137. See also Howe, "Free Trade and Global Order," 26–46.
50. Hull, *Memoirs, Vol. 1*, 363–365.
51. Hull to the President, February 14, 1935, container 10, PPF 1820, folder Foreign Trade Agreements, PPF, FDRL. See also Hathaway, "1933–1945," 298.
52. Excerpts from Charles Crowell, "Recovery Unlimited," [1935], container 10, PPF 1820, folder Foreign Trade Agreements, PPF, FDRL.
53. Address of the Chairman of the NFTC, "Great Prosperity through Greater Foreign Trade," February 7, 1934, folder 12, box 24, Corporate Records, NFTC, HL.
54. Watson to the President, July 6, 1935, and attached speech, box 1, folder OF 614a: Foreign Trade 1935, Franklin D. Roosevelt Papers, POF, FDRL.
55. Radio Address of Gerard Swope, April 25, 1935, box 1, folder OF 614a: Foreign Trade 1935, POF, FDRL.
56. Hull, *Memoirs, Vol. I*, 377. See also Irwin, *Clashing over Commerce*, 427–429.
57. Hull to the President, February 15, 1935, box 69, File State, 1935, Part I, Series IV: Departmental Correspondence, President's Secretary's Files, FDRL. See also *FRUS 1935*, Vol. I, General (1953): 406.
58. Roosevelt to Thomas, November 13, 1935, folder PPF 1908, box 1892 (1940–45)–1908, PPF, FDRL.

Chapter 2

1. "Trade Pacts Power Flayed," February 2, 1937, *Los Angeles Times*, 7. See also "Hull Assailed and Endorsed on Trade Pact," February 5, 1937, (Toronto) *Globe and Mail*, 1.
2. Johnson, *Wealth of a Nation*, 275, also 272–274.
3. Johnson, *Wealth of a Nation*, 276.
4. Butler, *Cautious Visionary*, 163. See also U.S. Congress, House Ways and Means, *Extending*, 1937, U.S. Chamber of Commerce, 78; Johnson, *Wealth of a Nation*, 277. The Nobel

nomination extended back to 1937 and Hull won the award in 1945: see Newton Baker to Walton Moore, January 13, 1937, folder State-Moore, R. Walton, 1937–1939, box 75, Series IV: Departmental Correspondence, President's Secretary's Files (digital), FDRL.

5. Hull address, Minneapolis, October 7, 1936, State-Hull, Cordell, 1933–1937, box 73, Series IV: Departmental Correspondence, President's Secretary's Files (digital), FDRL.
6. Address at Chautauqua, August 14, 1936, https://www.presidency.ucsb.edu/documents/address-chautauqua-ny.
7. Roosevelt to James A. Farrell, NFTC, November 13, 1936, folder NFTC, file 1892-1908, PPF, FDRL.
8. Hull, *Memoirs, Vol. I*, 463; Address of the Chairman, NFTC, January 29, 1936, folder 12, box 24, NFTC, HL. See also Gardner, *Economic Aspects*, 93.
9. League of Nations, Economic Committee, Remarks of the Present Phase of International Economic Relations, September 1936, reel 51, box 88, Hull Papers, LC.
10. Sayre, "America Must Act," December 1935, World Affairs Pamphlets No. 13, 1936, folder 1820 Speech Material, Container 10, PPF, FDRL; Address by Sayre, Trade Policies and Peace, January 20, 1936, *Department of State Pub. No. 837* (Washington, DC: USGPO, 1936), 14.
11. Butler, *Cautious Visionary*, 159. See also *FRUS 1936*, Vol. 1, General (1953): 411, 412.
12. Moser notes for the Secretary, November 22, 1937, folder State-Hull, Cordell, 1933–1937, box 73, Series IV: Departmental Correspondence, President's Secretary's Files (digital), FDRL. See also Hull, *Memoirs, Vol. I*, 455, also 449–454; Butler, *Cautious Visionary*, 161–162.
13. Hull, *Memoirs, Vol. I*, 493, also 487. See also Gardner, *Economic Aspects*, 14–15.
14. Address before the Inter-American Conference for the Maintenance of Peace, December 1, 1936, https://www.presidency.ucsb.edu/documents/address-before-the-inter-american-conference-for-the-maintenance-peace-buenos-aires. See also Memorandum for the President, January 8, 1938, folder State-Hull, Cordell 1938, box 74, Series IV: Departmental Correspondence, President's Secretary's Files (digital), FDRL.
15. Hull, *Memoirs, Vol. I*, 498.
16. *FRUS 1936*, Vol. 1: 513. Address of the Chairman, NFTC, February 24, 1937, folder 12, box 24, NFTC, HL; Notes for film speech, July 13, 1934; notes of speech to Empire Crusade Club, October 2, 1935, and January 15, 1936; broadcast to Australia, December 20, 1935; folder 1935–1936, BBK/F/25–29, Notes of Speeches, Beaverbrook Papers, PA; Butler, *Cautious Visionary*, 137–138.
17. *FRUS 1936*, Vol. 1: 406.
18. *FRUS 1936*, Vol. 1: 544, also 552, 524.
19. *FRUS 1936*, Vol. 1: 549. See also Butler, *Cautious Visionary*, 140–144; *FRUS 1936*, Vol. 1: 546, 548.
20. *FRUS 1936*, Vol. 1: 532, 553.
21. *FRUS 1936*, Vol. 1: 607, also *FRUS 1936*, Vol. 1: 586, 588, 606.
22. *FRUS 1936*, Vol. 1: 626, also *FRUS 1936*, Vol. 1: 625.
23. Butler, *Cautious Visionary*, 153, also 145–152. See also *FRUS 1937*, Vol. I, General (1954): 5.
24. Hull, *Memoirs, Vol. I*, 518, also 460. See also Johnson, *Wealth of a Nation*, 278–279.
25. U.S. Congress, House Ways and Means, *Extending*, 1937, Roosevelt to Chairman Robert Doughton, 2.
26. Sayre to the President [1937]; Report of the Committee on Peace, National Peace Conference and Walter W. Van Kirk, Director, Explanatory Note; Report of the Committee on Economics and Peace, January 15, 1937, box 1908, PPF, FDRL.
27. Sayre, The Winning of Peace, May 19, 1937, folder Foreign Trade Week, box 1533, PPF, FDRL. See also U.S. Congress, House Ways and Means, *Extending*, 1937, Hull, 13, 23, 26–27.
28. "Hull Is Attacked over Trade Pacts," February 5, 1937, *New York Times*, 2.
29. U.S. Congress, House Ways and Means, *Extending*, 1937, Woodruff, 32.
30. "House Democrats Favor Trade Pact," February 3, 1937, *Baltimore Sun*, 6.
31. U.S. Congress, Senate Finance, *Extending*, 1937, Hull to Harrison, 3–4.
32. U.S. Congress, Senate Finance, *Extending*, 1937, Douglas, 513, also skeptic Francis Garvan, 226–227.
33. Hull, *Memoirs, Vol. I*, 520.

34. Berle, Business Can Safeguard World Peace, July 9, 1937, folder Speeches-1937 (July–December), box 141, Adolf A. Berle Papers, FDRL. See also Fireside Chat, October 12, 1937, https://www.presidency.ucsb.edu/people/president/franklin-d-roosevelt; Schwartz, *Liberal*, 59–62, 104–113; Report of the Foreign Trade Committee, Business Advisory Council, November 22, 1937, folder Foreign Trade Committee 1936–1940, box 146, W. Averell Harriman Papers, LC; Lichtenstein, "Market Triumphalism and the Wishful Liberals," 109–110.
35. Hull, *Memoirs, Vol. I*, 523–524.
36. Davis to Secretary of State, 740.00/154, May 18, 1937, folder Dispatches Great Britain, March 8, 1937–May 23, 1938, box 20, Series II: Confidential File, President's Secretary's Files (digital), FDRL.
37. Hull, *Memoirs, Vol. I*, 524–525.
38. Dulles, The Problem of Peace in a Dynamic World, Christianity and International Order, Spring 1937, folder Article: speech title, box 281, John Foster Dulles Papers, PUL. See also Thompson, *For God and Globe*, 167–189.
39. Address by Buell before the Foreign Policy Association, January 22, 1938, folder Reciprocal Trade, box 55, James Roosevelt Papers, FDRL.
40. Raymond Leslie Buell, The Hull Trade Program and the American System, World Affairs Pamphlet No. 2, April 1938, folder Trade Agreements, box 151, Key Pittman Papers, LC.
41. Hull, *Memoirs, Vol. I*, 528.
42. *FRUS 1937*, Vol. II, British Commonwealth (1954): 27, 32, 36.
43. *FRUS 1938*, Vol. II, British Commonwealth (1954): 36, 45. See also *FRUS 1937*, Vol. II: 45; Memorandum of Conversation, Hull and Lindsay, August 19, 1937, box 58, reel 29, Hull Papers, LC.
44. Memorandum of Conversation, Hull and Lindsay, September 3, 1938, box 58, reel 29, Hull Papers, LC.
45. *FRUS 1938*, Vol. II: 62; Gardner, *Economic Aspects*, 107; Panitch and Gindin, *The Making of Global Capitalism*, 67–71.
46. Lippman in Digest of dinner discussion, American Foreign Trade Group, The Hull Program vs. Totalitarian Trade Policy, November 16, 1938, Council on Foreign Relations, folder 1, box 132, Volume 9, 1938–1939, Series 3, Studies Department, CFR, PUL.
47. Hull, *Memoirs, Vol. I*, 529–530.
48. Hull, *Memoirs, Vol. I*, 612. See also Hull to James Farrell, October 29, 1939, folder National Foreign Trade Council, file 1908, PPF, FDRL.
49. Message to Hitler and Mussolini, April 14, 1939, https://www.presidency.ucsb.edu/documents/message-adolf-hitler-and-benito-mussolini.
50. Hugh R. Wilson to Francis Sayre, November 10 and 14, 1938; Secretary of State for the Economics Ministry Rudolf Brinkmann to Wilson, October 31, 1938, folder Sayre, Francis B., box 3, Hugh R. Wilson Papers, HHPL; Mooney to the President, March 12, 1940 and March 14, 1940, folder 02, box 262, Welles Papers, FDRL. Rudolf Brinkmann, an official whom Göring trusted on economic policy, suggested an "American Mark" to facilitate commercial exchanges. Nothing came of the idea, but it showed an unease with the West's drift away from Germany.
51. International Consultative Group for Peace and Disarmament in Geneva, Economics of the Peace Failure 1919–1939, Surveys and Reports No. 2, December 1939, folder Causes of the Peace Failure, box 17, Arthur Sweetser Papers, LC; [British] Political and Economic Planning, European Order and World Order, October 10, 1939, to Council on Foreign Relations, Economic and Financial Group, folder 3, box 45, Jacob Viner Papers, PUL; Department of State, Advisory Committee on Problems of Foreign Relations, World Order, January 22, 1940, folder 07, box 191, Sumner Welles Papers, FDRL.
52. Hull to the President, December 4, 1939, folder State-Hull, Cordell October 1939–1940, box 74, Series IV: Departmental Correspondence, President's Secretary's Files (digital), FDRL.
53. Hull, *Memoirs, Vol. I*, 747.
54. Business Advisory Council, Report on Reciprocal Trade Agreements Program, January 12, 1940, folder Foreign Trade Committee 1936–1940, box 146, Harriman Papers, LC. See also Brockway, *Battles Without Bullets*, 14–15, 85, 90–93.

55. Mark Sullivan, "New Tariff Battle: The 'Reciprocal Trade Pacts,'" *Washington Post*, January 11, 1940, 9. See also Streit, *Union Now*, 163.
56. Annual Message, January 3, 1940, https://www.presidency.ucsb.edu/documents/annual-message-the-congress.
57. Radio Address, March 8, 1940, https://www.presidency.ucsb.edu/documents/radio-address-anniversary-farm-dinners. See also Edwin James to Arthur Sulzberger, April 4, 1940, folder Treasury-Morgenthau, Henry, January–April 1940, box 79, Series IV: Departmental Correspondence, President's Secretary's Files (digital), FDRL.
58. Hull, *Memoirs, Vol. I*, 748; U.S. Congress, House Ways and Means, *Extending*, 1937, Hull, 11, 32–33.
59. Grady, "How Shall America Trade?" *Christian Science Monitor*, January 20, 1940, 15.
60. U.S. Congress, Senate Finance, *Extending*, 1937, Lodge, 81. See also U.S. Congress, House Ways and Means, *Extending*, 1937, Treadway, 988.
61. U.S. Congress, Senate Finance, *Extending*, 1937, Wallace, 80; Grady, 149–140.
62. U.S. Congress, Senate Finance, *Extending*, 1937, Hull, 25–26. See also "Congress Report Backs Trade Pacts," *New York Times*, February 15, 1940, 5.
63. Statement on Signing the RTAA, April 12, 1940, https://www.presidency.ucsb.edu/documents/statement-signing-the-reciprocal-trade-agreements-bill.
64. Excerpts from Press Conference, July 5, 1940, https://www.presidency.ucsb.edu/documents/excerpts-from-the-press-conference-hyde-park-new-york.
65. *FRUS 1940*, Vol. III, British Commonwealth (1958): 307.
66. Planks on Foreign Relations, folder Drafts July 1940, box 65, Berle Papers, FDRL. See also Extracts from Utterances by Wendell Willkie with Reference to Foreign Trade, Tariffs and Trade Agreements, April 1940, reel 51, box 88, Hull Papers, LC.
67. *FRUS 1940*, Vol. I, General (1959): 30. See also *FRUS 1940*, Vol. IV, Far East (1955): 665; *FRUS 1940*, Vol. III: 669, 672.

Chapter 3

1. Radio Address, May 27, 1941, https://www.presidency.ucsb.edu/documents/radio-address-announcing-unlimited-national-emergency, accessed April 17, 2019. See also Johnstone, *Against Immediate Evil*, 9.
2. Final Declaration of the Twenty-Eighth National Foreign Trade Convention, October 6–8, 1941, box 1908, PPF, FDRL. See also Hull, *Memoirs, Vol. II*, 920–923.
3. Federal Council of the Churches of Christ in America, Commission to Study the Bases of a Just and Durable Peace, Data Material and Discussion Questions, April 15, 1941, and Pamphlet, May 7, 1941, Dulles Papers, PUL. See also Cooperative League, Commission to Study the Organization of Peace, Report of Economic Section, Economic Organization of Welfare, November 1943, folder Peace-Commission, box 140, Cooperative League of the USA Papers, HSTL.
4. Committee on International Organization, Report of the Twenty-Fifth Special Meeting, July 19, 1941, folder Visit to England July 1941, box 3, Whitney Shepardson Papers, FDRL.
5. W. H. Shepardson, America and the War II, July 15, 1941, folder Visit to England July 1941, box 3, Shepardson Papers, FDRL.
6. Hathaway, "1933–1945," 316. See also Woods, *Changing of the Guard*, 9–61; Johnson, *Wealth of a Nation*, 284–290; Gardner, *Economic Aspects*, 276.
7. *FRUS 1941*, Vol. III, British Commonwealth (1959): 9.
8. Official Statements of Postwar Policy, Equal Access, January 3, 1942, folder 02, box 190, Welles Papers, FDRL.
9. Johnson, *Wealth of a Nation*, 292. See also Some Confidential Notes on Questions Relating to Article VII of the Mutual Aid Agreement, [undated], folder 08, box 191; National Foreign Trade Council, Consensus of Opinion Re Federation of British Industries, September 15, 1942, folder 01, box 82, Welles Papers, FDRL; Report of the FBI International Trade Policy Committee, February, 1944, MS 200/F/3/D2/2/7, Federation of British Industries Collection, MRC.

10. *FRUS 1941,* Vol. III: 11.
11. *FRUS 1941,* Vol. III: 13.
12. Johnson, *Wealth of a Nation,* 293–294; Irwin, *Clashing over Commerce,* 458; Gardner, *Economic Aspects,* 277.
13. Johnson, *Wealth of a Nation,* 295.
14. Hawkins to Acheson, Welles, and Hull, August 4, 1941; Hull to the President, August 18, 1941, folder State April–December 1941, box 71, Series IV: Departmental Correspondence, President's Secretary's Files (digital), FDRL.
15. Pollard, *Economic Security and the Origins,* 67.
16. Johnson, *Wealth of a Nation,* 298–299. See also FDR to the Secretary of State, September 29, 1944, folder State-Hull, Cordell September–December 1944, box 75, Series IV: Departmental Correspondence, President's Secretary's Files (digital), FDRL; Rosenboim, *Emergence of Globalism,* 138.
17. Gardner, *Economic Aspects,* 279. See also Mallery, *Economic Union and Durable Peace,* 4, 12–13, 24–27; A Policy for Peace, series from the *Daily Express,* March 1945, BBK/G/12/38, Beaverbrook Papers, PA.
18. Leebaert, *Grand Improvisation,* 15, 29–30.
19. Johnstone, *Against Immediate Evil,* 148; *FRUS 1941,* Vol. III: 33, 36.
20. Roosevelt to James Farrell, October 3, 1942, box 1908, PPF, FDRL. See also J. B. Condliffe, *Agenda for a Postwar World,* quoted in Mallery, *Economic Union,* 72; James Shotwell, Preliminary Memorandum on International Organization, July 28, 1942, folder 08, box 192, Welles Papers; *FRUS 1942,* Vol. I, General (1960): 452.
21. Percy W. Bidwell, ed., Council on Foreign Relations, *Our Foreign Policy in War and Peace: Some Regional Views,* pp. 53–69, 1942, folder 03, box 191, Welles Papers, FDRL; Office of War Information, Special Intelligence Report, America and the Post-War World, December 16, 1942, folder Post-War–Foreign, box 100, Oscar Cox Papers, FDRL; Department of State, Division of Special Research, Summary of Opinion and Ideas on International Post-War Problems, July 15, 1942, September 23, 1942, and October 7, 1942, folder 01, box 190, Welles Papers, FDRL.
22. Hull, *Memoirs, Vol. II,* 953. See also *FRUS 1942,* Vol. I: 456, 458.
23. Johnson, *Wealth of a Nation,* 299–304.
24. *FRUS 1942,* Vol. I: 143. See also Hull, *Memoirs, Vol. II,* 1280.
25. *FRUS 1942,* Vol. I: 159.
26. War Cabinet, Discussions on Agenda Under Article VII, UK Delegation, September 9, 1943, L. P. Thompson-McCausland Papers, Bank of England.
27. Irwin, *Clashing over Commerce,* 461–462.
28. Acheson Address to Commonwealth Club of California, The Place of Bretton Woods in Economic Collective Security, March 23, 1945; Morgenthau, Bretton Woods and International Cooperation, reprint from *Foreign Affairs,* January 1945, July 1945, folder Bretton Woods-Printed Monographs, box 129, Cox Papers, FDRL. See also E. M. Bernstein address to Export Managers Club of New York, Bretton Woods Agreements and American Foreign Trade, August 25, 1944, folder Bretton Woods Conference, box 2, Louis Bean Papers, FDRL.
29. Address by Leo Pasvolsky, The Problem of Economic Peace After the War, March 4, 1942; Sumner Welles, Trade Realities and Peace draft, December 31, 1942, folder 8, box 94, Viner Papers, PUL. See also Hathaway, "1933–1945," 320.
30. *FRUS 1944,* Vol. II, General: Economic and Social Matters (1967): 5, 8, 45, 51.
31. *FRUS 1944,* Vol. II: 10, 20, 23, 30, 35, 44.
32. U.S. Congress, House Ways and Means, *Extension,* 1943, Sayre, 166; Chamber of Commerce, 926. See also *Business Week,* April 3, 1943, 1050.
33. Clare Booth Luce, address on Reciprocal Trade Treaties, May 11, 1943, folder 16, box 672, Clare Booth Luce Papers, LC. See also U.S. Congress, House Ways and Means, *Extension,* 1943, Rockefeller, 100.
34. "The 'Isolation' Myth," *New York Evening Sun,* April 25, 1943, 619; U.S. Congress, House Ways and Means, *Extension,* 1943, Knutson, 192, Linder, 376.

35. Vandenberg statement, May 20, 1943, roll 7, Arthur H. Vandenberg Papers, Bentley Historical Library. See also U.S. Congress, Senate Committee on Finance, *Extension*, 1943, 7–10, 27; Meijer, *Arthur Vandenberg*, 191–192.
36. Irwin, *Clashing over Commerce*, 453, also 454.
37. Office of War Information, Attitudes Toward Peace Planning, March 6, 1943; Special Memorandum No. 96, Attitudes Toward the Moscow Conference and International Cooperation, December 11, 1943, folder Peace (1), box 99; Special Services Division Report No. 102, Looking Forward to a Global Peace, January 13, 1943, folder Peace (2), box 96, Cox Papers, FDRL.
38. Roosevelt to Eugene Thomas, October 3, 1944, box 1908, PPF, FDRL. See also Committee for Economic Development, A Twelve Point Framework for the American Postwar Economy, August 7, 1944, folder 3, box 29, Will Clayton Papers, HSTL.
39. Mallery, *Economic Union*, 67. An economist who made his name in recreation facilities in Philadelphia, Mallery joined economist John Condliffe and Clarence Streit, among others, in calling for an Atlantic Union to offset discriminatory trade blocs and to unify the Western democracies. See Condliffe, "The Foreign Economic Policy of the United States," Memorandum Number 11, September 25, 1944, folder Research: Tariffs, 1944, 1950, box 82, Clarence Streit Papers, LC; Rosenbloom, *Emergence*, 146–148; Hull, *Memoirs, Vol. II*, 1476–1479.
40. *FRUS 1945*, Vol. VI, British Commonwealth (1969): 2; Johnson, *Wealth of a Nation*, 322–342.
41. Percy W. Bidwell, Proposal for an International Trade Commission, January 1944, folder Post War Trade, box 210, Harry L. Hopkins Papers, FDRL.
42. Mordecai Ezekiel address before Women's Action Committee for Victory and Lasting Peace, May 2, 1945, folder Economic and Social Aspects, May 1945, box 39, Mordecai Ezekiel Papers, FDRL.
43. Criticism of CED Statement on Foreign Policy, [1945], folder International Trade (1), box 30, Series IV, Gardiner Means Papers, FDRL. See also Department of State, Radio Bulletin No. 137, June 8, 1945, Aldrich speech to Canadian Manufacturers Association, folder June 1945, box 86, President's Secretary's Files, HSTL.
44. Johnson, *Wealth of a Nation*, 310–313; Pollard, *Economic Security*, 12; Hathaway, "1933–1945," 328.
45. Hull, *Memoirs, Vol. II*, 1735, 1737.
46. Irwin, *Clashing over Commerce*, 464.
47. Clayton address to Chamber of Commerce of the United States, May 5, 1938, folder Speeches 1937–1938, box 17, Clayton Papers, HSTL. On Clayton and protectionists, see B. E. Pinkerton to Clayton, June 21, 1938, folder Tariffs 1937–1938, box 17; John Napier Dyer to Albert Thomas, February 14, 1940, folder Reciprocal Trade Agreements, 1940, box 14, Clayton Papers, HSTL.
48. Pollard, *Economic Security*, 40; Johnson, *Wealth of a Nation*, 314–317. On Truman, see speech in Kansas City, April 19, 1937, box 285, SVP: Speech File; Truman Campaign Committee, press release, July 5, 1940, folder Senatorial Election, 1940, box 28, Family, Business, and Personal Affairs Collection, Harry S. Truman Papers, HSTL.
49. Sanchez-Sibony, *Red Globalization*, 57–59.
50. Pollard, *Economic Security*, 13. See also Dobson, *US Economic Statecraft for Survival*, 44, 70–112.
51. Message to Congress, February 12, 1945, https://www.presidency.ucsb.edu/documents/message-congress-the-bretton-woods-agreements. See also Irwin, *Clashing over Commerce*, 466.
52. Message to Congress, March 26, 1945, https://www.presidency.ucsb.edu/documents/message-congress-the-trade-agreements-act.
53. U.S. Congress, House Ways and Means, *1945 Extension*, 11–12. See also Department of State radio, World Trade and World Peace, March 10, 1945 (Washington, DC: USGPO, 1945), 16–17; Wendell Willkie, "Tariff and International Trade," June 17, 1944, folder Wendell Willkie article, box 21, Irita Van Doren Papers, LC; Zipp, *The Idealist*, 260–261.
54. U.S. Congress, House Ways and Means, *1945 Extension*, Clayton, 15–16 and 22.

55. Irwin, *Clashing over Commerce*, 467. See also U.S. Congress, House Ways and Means, *1945 Extension*, Knutson, 26–30, 36–37, also 5–6. Stettinius begged off appearing because of diplomatic commitments, including preparations for the United Nations. See also *Chicago Sun*, May 22, 1945, Department of State, Radio Bulletin No. 124, folder May 1945, box 86, President's Secretary's Files, HSTL.
56. Irwin, *Clashing over Commerce*, 468, also 469.
57. Irwin, *Clashing over Commerce*, 471. See also Johnson, *Wealth of a Nation*, 317–321; U.S. Congress, Senate Committee on Finance, *1945 Extension*, Taft, 331–332, 456–458; "Senator Taft's Brother Backs Trade Bill as Hearings End," *The* [Baltimore] *Sun*, June 6, 1945, 1.
58. Acting Secretary Grew, June 23, 1945, Department of State Radio Bulletin No. 150, June 20, 1945; *New York Times*, June 20, 1945, Department of State Radio Bulletin No. 147, June 20, 1945, folder June 1945, box 86, President's Secretary's Files, HSTL.
59. Charles H. Olmsted Jr., "A Soldier Speaks," *Hartford Courant*, June 7, 1945, 10.
60. *FRUS 1945*, Vol. II, General: Political and Economic Matters (1967): 667. See also Executive Committee on Economic Foreign Policy, D-108/45, July 21, 1945, folder [1 of 3], box 37, Confidential Files, HSTL; Clayton to the Secretary of State, November 1, 1945, folder November 8, 1945, box 8, NFTC, HL.
61. *FRUS 1945*, Vol. II: 668, also 670.
62. Coppock to Wilcox, Some General Factors Which Bear on Our International Economic Program, October 8, 1945; Joseph D. Coppock, Economics of Peace, November 15, 1945, folder Office of International Trade Policy, box 2, Joseph Coppock Papers, HSTL. See also *FRUS 1945*, Vol. VI: 46, 63; *FRUS 1945*, Vol. II: 675.
63. Hathaway, "1933–1945," 325. See also Sanchez-Sibony, *Red Globalization*, 61–66.
64. *FRUS 1945*, Vol. II: 671, 678.
65. Eckes, *Opening America's Market*, 157; Pollard and Wells, "1945–1960," 333–334; Kunz, *Butter and Guns*, 27–28.
66. U.S. Congress, House Ways and Means, *1945 Extension*, American Watch Manufacturing Industry in Opposition to H.R. 2652, 976–977; U.S. Congress, Senate Finance, *1945 Extension*, American Watchmakers Union, 284–285, American Glassware Association, 1478–1479.
67. Leffler, *Preponderance of Power*, 191.

Chapter 4

1. State of the Union, January 21, 1946, https://www.presidency.ucsb.edu/documents/message-the-congress-the-state-the-union-and-the-budget-for-1947.
2. Gardner, *Economic Aspects*, 293–325; Zeiler, *Free Trade, Free World*, 61–62.
3. *FRUS 1946*, Vol. I, General (1972): 645.
4. Pollard, *Economic Security*, 35, 182–209; Dobson, *US Economic*, 82–112.
5. *FRUS 1946*, Vol. I: 640; Zeiler, *Free Trade, Free World*, 64.
6. Mallery, *More Than Conquerors*, ix, 44, 139, also 49, 90–92, 115–131.
7. Citizens Conference on International Economic Union, Urgency of an International Trade Organization, September 16, 1946; Robert L. Gulick Jr., International Trade Organization: Teamwork for World Prosperity, [1946], folder International Trade Organization, box 245, John Winant Papers, FDRL.
8. Summary of Eugene P. Thomas to Truman, October 3, 1946, folder [proposed], box 528, Official File, Truman Papers, HSTL; China-America Council of Commerce and Industry and China Division-Far East Committee of the National Foreign Trade Council, State Control of Industry and Trade in China, [August 1946], folder September 26, 1946, box 8, NFTC, HL.
9. L. P. Thompson-McCausland, I.T.O. Charter, November 21, 1946, OV170/1 cop = 38, Governor's Files, Bank of England. See also *FRUS 1946*, Vol. I: 663, 650, 704; John Abbink, Notes on Havana, December 13, 1947, folder December 19, 1947, box 8, NFTC, HL.
10. Final Declaration of the Thirty-Fourth National Foreign Trade Convention, October 20–33, 1947, America's Stake in the World Economy, folder October 10, 1947, box 8, NFTC, HL.
11. Wilcox, *A Charter for World Trade*, 214, also 215–218. See also Clayton to Henry Wallace, March 25, 1946, folder (Tariffs), box 2, Coppock Papers, HSTL.

12. Johnson, *Wealth of a Nation*, 386. See also Dexter Fergie, "Geopolitics Turned Inwards: The Princeton Military Studies Group and the National Security Imagination," *Diplomatic History* 43:4 (September 2019), 645, 668–669.
13. Address in Chicago, April 6, 1946, https://www.presidency.ucsb.edu/documents/address-chicago-army-day.
14. Morris S. Rosenthal address to thirty-fourth National Foreign Trade Convention, October 21, 1947, folder Marshall Plan Press Releases (1 of 2), box 4, Dean Acheson Papers, HSTL. See also World Trade Foundation of America, Operation New Brunswick, June 6, 1946; First Annual Report of the World Trade Foundation of America, [1946], folder World Trade Foundation, box 59, Clayton Papers, HSTL.
15. Special Message to the Congress, January 8, 1947, https://www.presidency.ucsb.edu/documents/special-message-the-congress-the-presidents-first-economic-report.
16. Zeiler, *Free Trade, Free World*, 83–84.
17. Memorandum of conversation, Roland Wilson, Australian Embassy and US officials, April 1, 1948, folder MemCons January–December 1948, box 15, Official File, HSTL. See also James T. Patterson to the President, March 24, 1948, folder 275-A (January–May 1948), box 899, Official File, HSTL.
18. Mont Pelerin Conference, April 1–10, 1947, folder 15, box 5, Mont Pelerin Society Records, Hoover Institution Library and Archives, Stanford University, Palo Alto, California. See also Burgin, *Great Persuasion*, 55–151; Mirowski and Plehwe, *Road from Mont Pelerin*.
19. Quoted in Caldwell, ed., *Collected Works of F.A. Hayek, Vol. II*, 224, also 223.
20. Statement by the President, February 25, 1947, https://www.presidency.ucsb.edu/documents/statement-the-president-upon-issuing-order-the-administration-the-reciprocal-trade. See also Thompson-McCausland to R. W. B. Clarke, February 27, 1947, OV170/1/cop = 38, Governor's Files; *London Times* in Department of State, Foreign Press Summary, March 20, 1947, folder March 20, 1946–April 16, 1947, box 4, Staff Member and Office Files (SMOF), Rose Conway Files, HSTL.
21. Zeiler, *Free Trade, Free World*, 78. See also Johnson, *Wealth of a Nation*, 343–353.
22. Address on Foreign Economic Policy, March 6, 1947, https://www.presidency.ucsb.edu/documents/address-foreign-economic-policy-delivered-baylor-university.
23. Address Before the Canadian Parliament, June 11, 1947, https://www.presidency.ucsb.edu/documents/address-before-the-canadian-parliament-ottawa-0.
24. ADA, Toward Total Peace: A Liberal Foreign Policy for the United States, [1947], folder Marshall Plan Press Releases (1 of 2), box 4, Acheson Papers, HSTL. See also Irwin, *Clashing over Commerce*, 491.
25. G. L. F. Bolton to Thompson-McCausland, May 21, 1947, OV170/1, cop = 38, Governor's Files. See also President of the Board of Trade, The Trade Negotiations at Geneva, July 22, 1947, ADM 14/21 cop = 11, Thompson-McCausland Papers; *FRUS 1947*, Vol. I, General (1973): 460, 464, 463.
26. *FRUS 1947*, Vol. I: 466, 483; Veto of the Wool Act, June 26, 1947, https://www.presidency.ucsb.edu/documents/veto-the-wool-act; Zeiler, *Free Trade, Free World*, 89–102.
27. *FRUS 1947*, Vol. I: 503. See also *FRUS 1947*, Vol. I: 486, 490, 495; Irwin, *Clashing over Commerce*, 472.
28. Statement by the President, October 29, 1947, https://www.presidency.ucsb.edu/documents/statement-the-president-the-general-agreement-tariffs-and-trade. See also *FRUS 1947*, Vol. I: 504, 508, 515; Preliminary Report of the National Foreign Trade Council, United Kingdom Committee, August 25, 1947, folder September 12, 1947, 18, box 8, NFTC, HL; Zeiler, *Free Trade, Free World*, 108–126.
29. *FRUS 1947*, Vol. I: 518.
30. Irwin, Mavroidis, and Sykes, *Genesis of the GATT*, 80–119; Special Message to the Congress, December 19, 1947, https://www.presidency.ucsb.edu/documents/special-message-the-congress-the-marshall-plan; Berle, "The Marshall Plan in the European Struggle," New School for Social Research, December 16, 1947, folder Articles 1945–1947, box 166, Berle Papers, FDRL.
31. Joseph Coppock, U.S. Foreign Economic Policy Reconsidered, September 1947, folder Economic Policy-Foreign Trade, box 1, Coppock Papers, HSTL.

32. Statement by the President, March 24, 1948, https://www.presidency.ucsb.edu/documents/statement-the-president-the-signing-the-charter-the-international-trade-organization; Special Message to the Congress, March 1, 1948, https://www.presidency.ucsb.edu/documents/special-message-the-congress-requesting-extension-the-reciprocal-trade-act.
33. *FRUS 1948*, Vol. I, Pt. 2, General (1976): 132.
34. Executive Committee of the U.S. Council of the International Chamber of Commerce, Statement of Position on the Havana Charter for an International Trade Organization, May 9, 1950, folder Correspondence 16, box 161, NFTC, HL.
35. John E. Lockwood to Rockefeller, March 28, 1949, folder 919, box 96, Series L, RG Projects, Rockefeller Personal Papers, RAC, Sleepy Hollow, New York.
36. Final Declaration of the 35th National Foreign Trade Convention, Private Enterprise Is the World's Best Hope, November 10, 1948, folder June 10, 1949, box 9, NFTC, HL; Johnson, *Wealth of a Nation*, 412–420, 424–434; NAM's Statement on the I.T.O. Charter, March 30, 1949, folder 19, box 161, NFTC, HL; Zeiler, *Free Trade, Free World*, 151, 152.
37. *FRUS 1948*, Vol. I, Pt. 2: 147, also 135.
38. Minutes of Executive Committee Meeting, Committee for the Marshall Plan, November 13, 1947, box 4, Acheson Papers, HSTL. See also Dulles, "Can We Guarantee a Free Europe?" June 12, 1948, folder Article from Collier's, box 284, Dulles Papers, PUL.
39. Robert F. Loree, Statement on European Recovery Program, January 29, 1948, folder February 20, 1948, box 9, NFTC, HL.
40. The President's News Conference, April 29, 1948, https://www.presidency.ucsb.edu/documents/the-presidents-news-conference-660. See also Address in Omaha, June 5, 1948, https://www.presidency.ucsb.edu/documents/address-omaha-the-reunion-the-35th-division.
41. Johnson, *Wealth of a Nation*, 408.
42. U.S. Congress, Senate Finance, *Extending*, 1948, Democrats, 9; Hull, 14; Forrestal to Milliken, 105; Hiss, 194.
43. Statement by the President, June 26, 1948, https://www.presidency.ucsb.edu/documents/statement-the-president-upon-signing-the-trade-agreements-extension-act-1.
44. John D. Morris, "House Body Votes Tariff Act Curbs," *New York Times*, May 15, 1948, 8.
45. U.S. Congress, Senate Finance, *Extending*, June 4, 1948, Gearhart, 239; Memorandum for Mr. Clifford, June 16, 1948, folder Reciprocal Trade Agreements, box 11, Clark Clifford Files, HSTL; Richard L. Strout, "Vandenberg Defies Party on Trade Agreements: Congress Abdicated," *Christian Science Monitor*, May 28, 1948, 3; Johnson, *Wealth of a Nation*, 411.
46. Address at Bonham, Texas, September 27, 1948, https://www.presidency.ucsb.edu/documents/address-bonham-texas; Rear Platform and Other Informal Remarks, October 8, 1948, https://www.presidency.ucsb.edu/documents/rear-platform-and-other-informal-remarks-new-york; Address at the Brooklyn Academy of Music, October 29, 1948, https://www.presidency.ucsb.edu/documents/address-the-brooklyn-academy-music-new-york-city.
47. Zeiler, *Free Trade, Free World*, 156. See also Wilcox, *Charter for World Trade*, 219.
48. Inaugural Address, January 20, 1949, https://www.presidency.ucsb.edu/documents/inaugural-address-4.
49. Zeiler, *Free Trade, Free World*, 166.
50. Johnson, *Wealth of a Nation*, 408–412.
51. U.S. Congress, House Ways and Means, *1949 Extension*, American Tariff League, 328; also Statement on Antimony, Quicksilver, Tungsten, Manganese, and Chrome, 420–422.
52. U.S. Congress, House Ways and Means, *1949 Extension*, Reed, 13, 14, also 20.
53. *FRUS 1949*, Vol. I, National Security Policy (1976): 268, 274, 280, 287; Zeiler, *Free Trade, Free World*, 170–178.
54. Batt to James Tanham, March 18, 1949, folder 1, box 72, Clayton Papers. See also William Batt address, The Importance of the ITO to America's Position in World Affairs, April 14, 1949, folder Reciprocal Trade Agreement, box 67, Clayton Papers, HSTL.
55. *FRUS 1949*, Vol. I: 275; Eric Johnson, Motion Picture Association of America Statement on the International Trade Organization, April 27, 1950, folder International Trade Organization, box 99, Clayton Papers, HSTL; "The ITO Charter Should Be Ratified," *Business Week*, February 25, 1950, folder [2 of 2], box 527, Official File, HSTL; U.S. Congress, House

Foreign Affairs, *Membership and Participation*, 1950. The hearings stretched over three weeks and included 150 pages of letters, mostly supportive of the Charter.

56. Leffler, *Preponderance of Power*, 333–418.
57. Philip W. Bonsal to Harriman and Katz, ECE Meeting at Geneva, June 16, 1950, and attached memorandum, Discrimination in Eastern Europe, undated, folder 4, box 271, Harriman Papers, LC; Whitham, *Post-War Business Planners in the United States*, 2, 4–8, 131–148; Sanchez-Sibony, *Red Globalization*, 66–80.
58. Department of State, Monthly Survey of American Opinion on International Affairs, Survey No, 114, October 1950, folder 1950, box 12, Office of Public Affairs [OPA], Record Group 59 [RG 59], Department of State Records, NARA.
59. Executive Committee of the U.S. Council of the ICC, [1950], folder [2 of 2], box 527, Official File, HSTL.
60. Final Declaration of the Thirty-Seventh National Foreign Trade Convention, October 27, 1950, folder 6, box 10, NFTC, HL.
61. Zeiler, *Free Trade, Free World*, 166.
62. Johnson, *Wealth of a Nation*, 412–420, 424–434; Cortney to Clayton, March 3, 1949, folder 2, box 76, Clayton Papers, HSTL; Slobodian, *Globalists*, 233–234, 134, also 124–122; U.S. Congress, House Foreign Affairs, *Membership and Participation*, 1950, Acheson, 10; Committee for the International Trade Organization, The Committee Believes, January 12, 1950, folder 15, box 161, NFTC, HL. For the Atlantic Union, brainchild of Clarence Streit and other idealists, see Editorial, Freedom and Union, December 5, 1950, folder 2, box 97, Clayton Papers, HSTL; Talbot Imlay, "Clarence Streit, Federalist Frameworks, and Wartime American Internationalism," *Diplomatic History* 44:5 (November 2020): 831.
63. U.S. Congress, House Foreign Affairs, *Membership and Participation*, 1950, Congs. Frances Bolton and Donald Jackson, 77; Walter Judd, 142; American Bar Association, 486–492; John D. Hartigan to Wayne G. Taylor, June 20, 1950, folder Economic Cooperation Administration, box 16, Gordon Gray Files; Kee to the President, August 10, 1950, folder [2 of 2], box 527, Official File, HSTL. The administration embarked in 1950 on a multifaceted program of trade fairs in several America cities, along with special exhibits in department stores to display foreign wares and other efforts to promote consumption of foreign goods. The private sector cooperated. For example, IBM's chairman, Thomas Watson, and Lieutenant General Walter Bedell Smith of the First Army presented to the National Association of Manufacturers (NAM) a project to erect a World Trade Center in New York City to exhibit American products and house major trade and industrial organizations. This would also display US productive might and link trade to peace, as the Center would be adjacent to the UN. NAM turned down the idea because current Cold War tensions elevated the likelihood of the United Nations' demise, and thus the location would be pointless. See Report of the Special Committee of the NAM Board of Directors to Consider Proposal for World Trade Center, June 7–8, 1950, folder Special Committee World Trade Fair & Headquarters Project, box 59, Series I, NAM, HL.
64. *FRUS 1950*, Vol. I, National Security Affairs (1977): 272, also 271. See also Johnson, *Wealth of a Nation*, 435–438; Zeiler, *Free Trade, Free World*, 153–164.
65. *FRUS 1950*, Vol. I: 276.

Chapter 5

1. *FRUS 1951*: Vol. 1, National Security Affairs (1979): 463, 468.
2. Monthly Survey of American Opinion on International Affairs, Survey No. 120, Developments of April 1951, folder 1951, box 12, OPA, NARA. See also *FRUS 1951*: Vol. 1: 477, 481, 484; For a summary of the Torquay Round, see *FRUS 1951*: Vol. 1: 460.
3. *FRUS 1951*: Vol. 1: 505, 676, 697, 700, 702; Commonwealth Economic Conference, UK Delegation, E. A. Cohen on discussion with Deutsch, October 9, 1952, C.E.C.(o)(Z)(52)18, ADM14/33, Thompson-McCausland Papers, Bank of England; Zeiler, *Free Trade, Free World*, 180–185.
4. *FRUS 1951*, Vol. I: 562, also 567, 688. See also McKenzie, *GATT*, 72–74.

5. *FRUS 1951*, Vol. I: 360, also 347, 358; "U.S. Suspends Trade Concessions on Imports from U.S.S.R, Poland," *Department of State Bulletin* 25: 649, December 3, 1951, 913–914; Circular Telegram, January 26, 1950, 394.31/1-2650, box 1426, Decimal Files, RG 59; Survey No. 323, April 22, 1952, NORC.
6. Annual Message, https://www.presidency.ucsb.edu/documents/annual-message-the-congress-the-presidents-economic-report-2, January 12, 1951. See also *FRUS 1951*, Vol. I: 362, 368.
7. Proclamation 2927, May 8, 1951, https://www.presidency.ucsb.edu/documents/proclamation-2927-world-trade-week-1951.
8. "Extension of Reciprocal Trade Agreements Act Urged," *Wall Street Journal*, January 22, 1951, 6. On the free traders, see John E. Metcalf to Senator Robert Taft, May 21, 1951; Mrs. Lowell W. Raymond to Taft, April 6, 1951, folder Reciprocal Trade Agreements, box 1058, Robert A. Taft Papers, LC.
9. U.S. Congress, House Ways and Means, *Extension*, 1951, Acheson, 2–3.
10. U.S. Congress, House Ways and Means, *Extension*, 1951, Jenkins, 180, King, 31.
11. U.S. Congress, House Ways and Means, *Extension*, 1951, American Tariff League, 277; Richard Simpson, 27; U.S. Congress, Senate Finance, *Trade Agreements*, 1951, Forstmann, 235.
12. Monthly Survey of American Opinion on International Affairs, Survey No. 118, Developments of February 1951, folder 1951, box 12, OPA, NARA.
13. Statement by the President, June 16, 1951, https://www.presidency.ucsb.edu/documents/statement-the-president-upon-signing-the-trade-agreements-extension-act-2. See also U.S. Congress, Senate Finance, *Trade Agreements*, 1951, Acheson, 8; Millikin, 412, 415; "Two Year Extension of Trade Pacts Law Voted by Senate Unit," April 27, 1951, *Boston Globe*, 9.
14. Zeiler, *Free Trade, Free World*, 188.
15. Irwin, *Clashing over Commerce*, 510, also 511.
16. Republican Party Platform, July 7, 1952, https://www.presidency.ucsb.edu/documents/republican-party-platform-1952.
17. Alfred Friendly, "Climbing Tariffs Counteracting Our Foreign Aid: Tariffs Nullify U.S. Aid," *Washington Post*, February 24, 1952, B1.
18. Zeiler, *Free Trade, Free World*, 189–190; Surveys, No. 332, October 15, 1952; No. 325, May 28, 1952; No. 333, November 17, 1952, NORC; Monthly Survey of American Opinion on International Affairs, Survey No. 139, Developments of November 1952, folder 1952, box 12; Opinion Polling Results on Tariff Topics, January 9, 1953, folder Foreign Policy 1953, box 1, OPA, NARA. Business, rather than labor, was seen as the primary victim of imports. Not surprisingly, the more educated the audience, the more it favored tariff cuts, though reciprocal and not unilateral reductions. The same percentage of Democrats as Republicans and Independents—over a third—backed reductions in duties, and there was also little difference in regional support—about a third polled—for freer trade.
19. "Test Case on Tariffs," *Washington Post*, June 18, 1952, 14. See also "U.S. Note to Britain Affirms Aim Is Still to Ease Tariffs," *New York Times*, May 13, 1952, 1.
20. Alfred Friendly, "Truman Scolds Tariff Unit for Urging Curbs on Garlic," *Washington Post*, July 22, 1952, 11. See also Monthly Survey of American Opinion on International Affairs, Survey No. 134, Developments of June 1952, folder 1952, box 12, OPA, NARA.
21. William H. Draper Jr., Report to the President, August 22, 1952, folder Trade, box 198, President's Secretary's Files, HSTL. See also Monthly Survey of American Opinion on International Affairs, Survey No. 136, Developments of August 1952, folder 1952, box 12, OPA, NARA; Statement by the President, October 20, 1952, https://www.presidency.ucsb.edu/documents/statement-the-president-concerning-the-import-quota-shelled-filberts.
22. Zeiler, *Free Trade, Free World*, 189.
23. A Statement on Foreign Economic Policy by the National Foreign Trade Council, September 1951, folder September 14, 1957, box 10, NFTC, HL.
24. Press release, New York World Trade Week Committee, May 2, 1951, folder 328, box 37, RG 4, Nelson A. Rockefeller Papers, RAC.
25. Willard Thorp, "Basic Policy Issues in Economic Development," *Department of State Bulletin* 24:602 (January 15, 1951): 98; League of Women Voters, The Citizen and International Trade, Publication No. 191, February 1952, folder CNTP-Exhibit Material-10/25–29/53, box 10, U.S. Randall Series, U.S. Council on Foreign Economic Policy Records, DDEL.

26. Eckes, *Opening America's Market*, 166; Letter to Members of the Public Advisory Board, July 13, 1952, https://www.presidency.ucsb.edu/documents/letter-members-the-public-advisory-board-for-mutual-security-requesting-study-foreign.
27. Zeiler, *Free Trade, Free World*, 191–192. See also Bevan Sewell, "Pragmatism, Religion, and John Foster Dulles' Embrace of Christian Internationalism in the 1930s," *Diplomatic History* 41:4 (September 2017): 806–810, 819–820.
28. Kaufman, *Trade and Aid*, 9, also 12–13.
29. Digest of Report of President's Materials Policy [Paley] Commission, January 23, 1953, folder September 11, 1948, box 9, NFTC, HL.
30. Inaugural Address, January 20, 1953, https://www.presidency.ucsb.edu/people/president/dwight-d-eisenhower.
31. The President's New Conference, February 25, 1953, https://www.presidency.ucsb.edu/documents/the-presidents-news-conference-484.
32. The President's Program to Expand World Trade [1953], Committee for a National Trade Policy, folder Pamphlets-Randall Commission, box 14, Cellar Papers, LC. See also Kaufman, *Trade and Aid*, 15, 16.
33. Ford address at annual winter meeting of the Inland Daily Press Association, February 17, 1953, folder Trade, box 1280, Robert A. Taft Sr. Papers, LC. On Japan, see also *FRUS 1952–1954*, Vol. I, Pt. 1, General: Economic and Political Matters (1983): 32.
34. U.S. Congress, House Ways and Means, *Trade Agreements Extension*, 1953, Strackbein, 9, also 12, 16. See also Kaufman, *Trade and Aid*, 16–17; Dick Furland to Mr. Reed, The Reciprocal Trade Program: Did It Contribute to World War II, May 13, 1953, folder 1953 Commission on Foreign Economic Policy, box 5, Daniel Reed Papers, Cornell University Library.
35. U.S. Congress, House Ways and Means, *Trade Agreements Extension*, 1953, Dulles, 588–589, also 591. See also John S. Coleman to Carl Albert, May 29, 1953, folder 5, box 20, Carl Albert Papers, AC; Paul G. Hoffman Address, University of Notre Dame, Freer Trade for a Stronger Free World, May 12, 1953, folder Committee on Foreign Trade Education 1953–1958, box 71, Paul G. Hoffman Papers, HSTL.
36. Letter to the President of the Senate, May 2, 1953, https://www.presidency.ucsb.edu/documents/letter-the-president-the-senate-and-the-speaker-the-house-representatives-recommending. See also U.S. Congress, Senate Finance, *Trade Agreements Extension*, 1953; Edward F. Ryan, "Senate Votes Extension of Trade Pacts," *Washington Post*, July 3, 1953.
37. Radio Report, August 5, 1953, https://www.presidency.ucsb.edu/documents/radio-report-the-american-people-the-achievements-the-administration-and-the-83d-congress. See also Memorandum for the President, Recommendation of European Ambassadors on Trade Policies, September 26, 1953, folder September 1953, box 1, Ann C. Whitman Papers, DDEL; Summary of Meeting, October 13, 1953, Department of Commerce, Export Advisory Committee, Samuel Anderson, folder October 13, 1953, box 2, BIO, RG 151, NARA.
38. Press release, September 21, 1953, folder 298 (1), box 927, Official File, WHCF, DDEL. See also Draft of Proposed Preamble, NFTC Board of Directors, September 18, 1953, box 11, NFTC, HL.
39. Jesse Tapp to Clarence Randall, September 30, 1953, folder Notebook 43, box 109, Reed Papers, Cornell University Library.
40. Hauge to the Secretary of Commerce, May 12, 1953, folder Foreign Economic Policy, Commission, box 34, Sinclair Weeks Papers, Dartmouth College Library.
41. Reed to Randall, September 28, 1953, folder Notebook 43, box 109, Reed Papers, Cornell University Library. See also James P. Selvage to Reed, September 9, 1953; Reed to Selvage, September 15, 1953, folder 1953 Commission, box 4, Reed Papers, Cornell University Library.
42. Lamar Fleming to Mr. Randall, October 9, 1953, folder Correspondence October 1953, box 38, Bourke B. Hickenlooper Papers, HHL. See also CFEP, Volume 1, folder August–October 1953, Randall journal entry for October 29, 1953, Clarence B. Randall Journals, DDEL.
43. Press release, Bush, October 6, 1953, box 3, Series IV, Prescott Bush Papers, University of Connecticut.
44. The President's News Conference, November 18, 1953, https://www.presidency.ucsb.edu/documents/the-presidents-news-conference-490.

45. Kline before the CFEP, October 28, 1953, folder 595, box 50, MS 73/327, American Cotton Manufacturers Institute Collection, Museum of American Textile History; George W. Dewey to Charles Dake, November 24, 1953, folder Agriculture (1), box 29, CFEP, DDEL.
46. Meany to the CFEP, American Trade Policy in the Free World, October 28, 1953, folder Foreign Trade Printed Material, box 11, Celler papers, LC.
47. Statement of Emanuel Celler to the Commission on Foreign Economic Policy, [1953], folder Foreign Trade Printed Material, box 11, Celler papers, LC.
48. Jackson to Randall, October 19, 1953, folder 1953 Commission, box 5, Reed Papers, Cornell University Library.
49. H. van B. Cleveland, United States Tariff Policy, April 15, 1954; U.S. Tariff Policy, May 3, 1954, folder International Trade (2), box 30, Series IV, Means Papers, FDRL. See also Edward C. Cale, Maintaining Mutually Advantageous Trade with Latin America, *Department of State Bulletin* 28:725, May 18, 1954, 717; CFEP Hearings, William Batt, October 21, 1953, folder 10/21/53-(2), box 7, CFEP, DDEL.
50. Randall in Dillon testimony, CFEP Hearings, Paris, November 12, 1953, folder 11/12/53, box 9, CFEP, DDEL.
51. Martin to CFEP, November 11, 1953, folder 11/11/53, box 9, CFEP, DDEL. See also Randall journal entry, October 29, 1953, folder 10/29-11/18/53, box 1, Randall Journals, DDEL.
52. Neal to the CFEP, Staff Report: Area 3-No.7, Transmitting Staff Report, *The Economic and Political Role of United States Trade Policy*, December 4, 1953, folder Drafts (1), box 41, CFEP, DDEL.
53. Randall journal entry, November 20, 1953, folder 11/20-12/23/53, box 1, Randall Journals, DDEL; Kaufman, *Trade and Aid*, 21.
54. Strackbein, October 28, 1953, CFEP Hearings, folder (10/28/53-(1), box 7, CFEP, DDEL. See also Parker to the CFEP, December 10, 1953 and December 19, 1953, folder Parker: Summary of Tariffs and Trade Policy, box 39, CFEP, DDEL; Randall journal entry, November 18, 1953, folder 10/29–11/18/53, box 1, Randall Journals, DDEL; Strackbein to Vorys, November 20, 1953, folder FEPC-1953, box 68, John M. Vorys Papers, Ohio Historical Society.
55. Randall journal entry, November 20, 1953, folder 11/20–12/23/53, box 1, Randall Journals, DDEL; American Tariff League, CFEP Hearing, October 29, 1953, folder October 29, 1953 (1), box 8, CFEP, DDEL; William Davidson to Randall, November 4, 1953, folder Foreign Economic Policy Commission, box 68, Vorys Papers, Ohio Historical Society.
56. Alfred C. Neal to CFEP, Transmitting Staff Report, How Restrictive Are United States Tariffs? November 18, 1953, folder Drafts (1), box 41, CFEP, DDEL.
57. Nation-Wide Committee of Industry, Agriculture, and Labor on Import-Export Policy, Free Trade: A Form of Economic Pacifism [1953–1954], folder CFEP-Correspondence November 1953–November 1959, box 11, Celler papers, LC. See also Randall journal entry, January 14, 1954, folder 1/6–26/54, box 1, Randall Journals, DDEL.
58. State of the Union, January 7, 1954, https://www.presidency.ucsb.edu/documents/annual-message-the-congress-the-state-the-union-13. See also *FRUS 1952–1954*, Vol. I, Pt. 1: 66.
59. Special Message to the Congress, March 30, 1954, https://www.presidency.ucsb.edu/documents/special-message-the-congress-foreign-economic-policy.
60. Kaufman, *Trade and Aid*, 18–26, 37–39; Randall journal entry, November 20, 1953, folder 11/20–12/23/53, box 1, Randall Journals, DDEL; Sinclair Weeks to the President, March 12, 1954, folder Council on Foreign Economic Policy, box 31, Weeks Papers, Dartmouth College.
61. M. Mikhailov, Illusions and Reality Regarding the Publication in the United States of the "Randall Commission" Report, *Izvestia*, January 27, 1954, folder Correspondence February–March 1954, box 40, Hickenlooper Papers, HHPL.
62. Goodwin, *Walter Lippmann*, 316–350. See also Press Intelligence, Newspaper Coverage of the Randall Report, January 24–March 1, 1954, folder 149-B-2 January–June 1954, box 768, WHCF, DDEL.
63. The President's News Conference, July 28, 1954, https://www.presidency.ucsb.edu/documents/the-presidents-news-conference-467; Council on Foreign Relations, Study Group on

What the Tariff Means to American Industries, Watch Industry, May 4, 1954, Vol. LV 1954/55, CFR, PUL.
64. *FRUS 1952-1954*, Vol. I, Pt. 1: 57, 59.
65. B. A. Rittersporn Jr. to the Editors, *LOOK Magazine*, February 10, 1954, folder Committee on Foreign Trade Education, 1953–1958, box 71, Hoffman Papers, HSTL. See also Kaufman, *Trade and Aid*, 39. On glass, see Council on Foreign Relations, Study Group on What the Tariff Means to American Industries, Working Paper No. 7, Glassware Industry [1955], Vol. LV 1954/55, CFR, PUL.
66. Samuel C. Waugh to Randall, August 26, 1954, 3594.41/8-2654, box 1448, Decimal File, RG 59, NARA.
67. Harriman address at Sixth Annual Foreign Policy Conference, Colgate University, How Realistic Is Our Economic Policy, July 14, 1954, folder 7, box 375, Adlai E. Stevenson Papers, PUL.
68. Legislative Meeting, December 13, 1954, folder 1954 (5), box 1, Legislative Meeting Series, Ann C. Whitman Files, Whitman Papers, DDEL.

Chapter 6

1. Special Message to the Congress, January 10, 1955, https://www.presidency.ucsb.edu/documents/special-message-the-congress-the-foreign-economic-policy-the-united-states.
2. Perkins to Joseph Dodge, March 8, 1955, folder 596, box 77, Rockefeller Papers, RG 54, RAC. See also Pollard and Wells, "Era of American Economic Hegemony," 360.
3. *FRUS 1955–1957*, Vol. IX, Foreign Economic Policy (1987): 2.
4. Pollard and Wells, "Era of American Economic Hegemony," 363.
5. *FRUS 1955–1957*, Vol. IX: 5.
6. ADA, Partnership for Freedom: Proposals for World Economic Growth [1955], folder 3, box 3, Stevenson Papers, PUL. See also *FRUS 1955–1957*, Vol. IX: 7.
7. Kaufman, *Trade and Aid*, 58–60; Zhang, *Beijing's Economic Statecraft*, 97–168.
8. U.S. Embassy Moscow, Mikoyan calls for increased trade with the United States, July 23, 1955, folder 596, box 77, Rockefeller Papers, RG 53; *FRUS 1955–1957*, Vol. IX: 9; *FRUS 1955–1957*, Vol. IX: 10.
9. Dobson, *US Economic*, 134–141.
10. Radio and Television Address, July 25, 1955, https://www.presidency.ucsb.edu/documents/radio-and-television-address-the-american-people-the-geneva-conference. See also Department of State, Intelligence Report: No. 6890, Soviet Foreign Trade: Policies, Performance, Prospects, April 11, 1955, folder 597, box 77, Rockefeller Papers, RG 54; Dobson, *US Economic*, 117–134; Sanchez-Sibony, *Red Globalization*, 81–94.
11. Agreed Policy Guide Lines for International Trade Fair Program, April 25, 1955, folder Bureau of Foreign Commerce, box 27, Weeks Papers, Dartmouth College.
12. Kaufman, *Trade and Aid*, 60–63.
13. Kaufman, *Trade and Aid*, 130–131; *FRUS 195--1957*, Vol. IX: 8.
14. L. A. Minnich Jr., Legislative Leadership Meeting, February 8, 1955, folder 1955(1), box 1, Legislative Meeting Files, Whitman Files. See also Raymond Wilcove, "Permanent Tariff Act Aim of Key House Democrats," *Washington Post and Times-Herald*, November 27, 1954, 11.
15. U.S. Congress, House Ways and Means, *Trade Agreements Extension*, 1955, Dulles, 43–47.
16. U.S. Congress, House Ways and Means, *Trade Agreements Extension*, 1955, Wilson, 186–188.
17. U.S. Congress, House Ways and Means, *Trade Agreements Extension*, 1955, Stassen, 217, 220, 222, Schramm, 281–282.
18. Allen Drury, "Attack on Tariff Act Foes by C. P. Taft Stirs Dispute," *New York Times*, March 19, 2019, 1; U.S. Congress, House Ways and Means, *Trade Agreements Extension*, 1955, Taft, 2467.
19. Final Declaration of the Forty-Second National Foreign Trade Convention, November 14–16, 1955, folder 22, box 79, NFTC, HL; U.S. Congress, House Ways and Means, *Trade Agreements Extension*, 1955, Standard Oil Co., 426–427; Federation of Women's Clubs, 479; Cong. John Moss, 491; The Friends Committee on National Legislation, 546–548; North Atlantic Ports Association, 689–693; Japanese Chamber of Commerce of New York, 709–711.

20. U.S. Congress, House Ways and Means, *Trade Agreements Extension*, 1955, Cong. Robert Hale, 1586–1588; Congs. Henderson Lanham, Kenneth Roberts, and Hugh Alexander, 1595–1607; Simpson, 2509; Cong. Charles Vursell, 1520.
21. U.S. Congress, House Ways and Means, *Trade Agreements Extension*, 1955, Strackbein, 973, Bailey, 1364, also Wickersham, 1829.
22. L. A. Minnich Jr., Legislative Leadership Meeting, March 22, 1955, folder 1955(2), box 1,, Legislative Meeting Series, Whitman Files.
23. U.S. Congress, Senate Finance, *Trade Agreements Extension*, 1955.
24. "He Compromises—And Gets His Trade Agreements Program," May 6, 1955, *Baltimore Sun*, 22. See also Kaufman, *Trade and Aid*, 41–43; Irwin, *Clashing over Commerce*, 514–515; Johnson, *Wealth of a Nation*, 449–450.
25. Eckes, *Opening America's Market*, 170.
26. The President's News Conference, April 10, 1957, https://www.presidency.ucsb.edu/documents/the-presidents-news-conference-269.
27. *FRUS 1955–1957*, Vol. IX: 61, 68, 99; Kaufman, *Trade and Aid*, 39–41; Eckes, *Opening America's Market*, 173–175.
28. *FRUS 1955–1957*, Vol. IX: 26; Irwin, *Clashing over Commerce*, 516; Kaufman, *Trade and Aid*, 44.
29. Special Message to the Congress, April 14, 1955, https://www.presidency.ucsb.edu/documents/special-message-the-congress-united-states-membership-the-proposed-organization-for-trade.
30. Clayton to Cooper, March 2, 1956, folder CNTP, box 117, Clayton Papers, HSTL. See also Johnson, *Wealth of a Nation*, 450.
31. Statement by the National Foreign Trade Council Concerning the Revised GATT and Proposed Organization for Trade Cooperation, May 13, 1955, folder Conference Room May 20, 1955, box 12, NFTC, HL. See also Samuel Waugh to Randall, April 15, 1955, folder 299, box 972, WHCF, DDEL; Raymond Vernon, "America's Foreign Trade Policy and the GATT," *Essays in International Finance* 21 (October 1954): 19–24.
32. Johnson, *Wealth of a Nation*, 450, 451; Proposed Preamble to Final Declaration of Forty-Third National Foreign Trade Convention, Foreign Trade and Investment Promote Security and Prosperity, folder September 26, 1956, box 12, NFTC, HL; Cortney to Paul Hoffman, May 28, 1957, folder Americans for the OTC, box 79, Hoffman Papers, HSTL; U.S. Congress, House Ways and Means, *Organization for Trade Cooperation Hearings*, 1956, International Chamber of Commerce, 670–672.
33. The President's News Conference, May 4, 1956, https://www.presidency.ucsb.edu/documents/the-presidents-news-conference-301.
34. Address and Remarks at Baylor University, May 25, 1956, https://www.presidency.ucsb.edu/documents/address-and-remarks-the-baylor-university-commencement-ceremonies-waco-texas. On interdependence, see Denis Healey, Nationalism and Neutralism in the Western Community; Lincoln Gordon, Political and Economic Institutions of the Western Community; Raymond Aron, The Actual Causes of Tension between Europe and the United States, Bilderberg Conference, St. Simons Island, Georgia, February 1957, folder Bilderberg Conference (3 of 4), box 6, Lincoln Gordon Papers, JFKL.
35. B. A. Rittersporn Jr. to the President, June 26, 1955, folder Committee on Foreign Trade Education, box 71, Hoffman Papers, HSTL. See also Committee on Foreign Trade Education, The Returns Are In, folder Committee on Foreign Trade Education, box 71, Hoffman Papers, HSTL.
36. CFR, Study Group on United States Foreign Economic Policy, First Meeting, November 14, 1956; Working Paper Number 2, The Problem for the West, October 25, 1956, folder 5, box 162, CFR Records; U.S. Congress, House Ways and Means, *Organization for Trade Cooperation Hearings*, 1956, Dulles, 10–11.
37. Newsletter of the Committee on Foreign Trade Education, Winning the Tariff Battle, [1956], folder Reciprocal Trade-GATT-OTC, box D, Albert Gore Sr. Senate Papers, Middle Tennessee State University. See also *FRUS 1955–1957*, Vol. IX: 74; Johnson, *Wealth of a Nation*, 451–452; Jacob Javits to Henry Latham, July 17, 1956, folder Organization for Trade Cooperation 1956, box 5, Series 8, Jacob Javits Papers, SUNY-Stony Brook.

38. *FRUS 1955–1957*, Vol. IX: 27, 28, 36, also 35.
39. *FRUS 1955–1957*, Vol. IX: 37, also 31, 47.
40. *FRUS 1955–1957*, Vol. IX: 91.
41. Kaufman, *Trade and Aid*, 88–91.
42. Kaufman, *Trade and Aid*, 45–56; Message to the Congress, February 11, 1957, https://www.presidency.ucsb.edu/documents/message-the-congress-transmitting-annual-report-the-operation-the-trade-agreements-program.
43. Joint Statement, February 28, 1957, https://www.presidency.ucsb.edu/documents/joint-statement-following-discussions-with-the-premier-the-republic-france; Kaufman, *Trade and Aid*, 113. The original six were France, West Germany, Italy, Belgium, the Netherlands, and Luxembourg.
44. Remarks at the Opening of the NATO Meetings, December 16, 1957, https://www.presidency.ucsb.edu/documents/remarks-the-opening-the-nato-meetings-paris.
45. U.S. Congress, House Subcommittee on Foreign Economic Policy, *Foreign Economic Policy*, 1956, 24.
46. Brendan Jones, "O.T.C. May Decide U.S. Fate Abroad," *New York Times*, April 28, 1957, F1. See also Lamar Fleming Jr. to Philip D. Reed, May 31, 1957, folder CED, 1/57–1/68, box 15, Philip D. Reed Papers, HL.
47. Council on Foreign Economic Policy, Foreign Economic Policy and the Trade Agreements Program, September 13, 1957, folder Boggs Subcommittee (1), box 2, CFEP-Chairman Files, Papers Series, DDEL; *FRUS 1955–1957*, Vol. IX: 13; U.S. Congress, House Ways and Means, *Foreign Trade Policy*, 1957, Lincoln Gordon, 13–15; Thomas Schelling, 23–25.
48. Clayton to Stevenson, December 2, 1957, folder 8, box 19, Stevenson Papers, PUL. See also Kaufman, *Trade and Aid*, 121–122.
49. Kaufman, *Trade and Aid*, 122–124.
50. The President's News Conference, February 5, 1958, https://www.presidency.ucsb.edu/documents/the-presidents-news-conference-249.
51. State of the Union, January 9, 1958, https://www.presidency.ucsb.edu/documents/annual-message-the-congress-the-state-the-union-10.
52. Excerpts from Remarks, January 31, 1958, https://www.presidency.ucsb.edu/documents/excerpts-from-remarks-republican-national-committee-breakfast.
53. Special Message to the Congress, January 30, 1958, https://www.presidency.ucsb.edu/documents/special-message-the-congress-the-reciprocal-trade-agreements-program.
54. The President's News Conference, April 9, 1958, https://www.presidency.ucsb.edu/documents/the-presidents-news-conference-261.
55. Remarks at Sixth Annual Republican Women's National Conference, March 18, 1958, https://www.presidency.ucsb.edu/documents/remarks-sixth-annual-republican-womens-national-conference.
56. Address at the National Conference of International Trade Policy, March 27, 1958, https://www.presidency.ucsb.edu/documents/address-the-national-conference-international-trade-policy. See also *FRUS 1958–1960*, Vol. IV: 64.
57. Charles D. Hilles Jr. and S. A. Swensrud to J. D. Rockefeller, December 19, 1957, folder 234A, box 27, RG 2, Series F, Office of Mssrs. Rockefeller: Economic Interests, RAC.
58. Letter to Nikolai Bulganin, January 13, 1958, https://www.presidency.ucsb.edu/documents/letter-nikolai-bulganin-chairman-council-ministers-ussr.
59. *FRUS 1958–1960*, Vol. IV, Foreign Economic Policy (1992): 11.
60. Charles D. Hilles Jr. and S. A. Swensrud to J. D. Rockefeller, December 19, 1957, folder 234A, box 27, RG 2, Series F, RAC. See also *FRUS 1958–1960*, Vol. IV: 12.
61. *FRUS 1958–1960*, Vol. IV: 3.
62. Celler statement, Strength Through Trade and Aid, March 14, 1958, folder International Trade #1, box 250, Celler Papers, LC. See also Proposed Preamble to Final Declaration of Forty-Fifth National Foreign Trade Convention, International Trade and Investment Liberate Man's Creative Power and Foster World Understanding, September 30, 1958, folder September 30, 1958, box 13, NFTC, HL.

63. Kaufman, *Trade and Aid*, 124–126; U.S. Congress, House Ways and Means, *Renewal of Trade Agreements*, 1958, McElroy, 72; Simpson, 80; American Coalition of Patriotic Societies, 2149–2155.
64. Kaufman, *Trade and Aid*, 126–128; U.S. Congress, Senate Finance, *Trade Agreements Act Extension*, 1958, Dulles-Kerr exchange, 8–120.
65. Remarks at the National Corn Picking Contest, October 17, 1958, https://www.presidency.ucsb.edu/documents/remarks-the-national-corn-picking-contest-cedar-rapids-iowa,.
66. Kaufman, *Trade and Aid*, 126, also 129.
67. Greenwald to Frank, Regional Markets in Latin America, March 18, 1958, 394.41/3–1858, box 1391, Decimal File, NARA; Robert Murphy before the Senate Foreign Relations Committee, May 19, 1958, *Department of State Bulletin* 38:989 (June 9, 1958): 952–961.
68. C. Edward Galbreath to Randall, November 21, 1958, folder GATT (5), box 5, Randall Series, Chairman's Files, CFEP; Roy R. Rubottom Jr. address, Basic Principles Governing United States Relations with Latin America, *Department of State Bulletin* 38:981 (April 14, 1958): 608–614; Kaufman, *Trade and Aid*, 129–132.
69. Swensrud to Randall, December 3, 1958, folder OTC, box 9, Randall Series, Chairman's Files CFEP. See also *FRUS 1958–1960*, Vol. IV: 80.

Chapter 7

1. *FRUS 1958–1960*, Vol. IV: 22, 23; Pollard and Wells, "Era of American Economic Hegemony," 379–381.
2. Herter address to the NFTC, November 16, 1959, box 16, Christian A. Herter Papers, DDEL.
3. Gilbert statement for the Joint Economic Committee, Economics for Cold War, folder 1959 no. 2, box 273, Joseph C. O'Mahoney Papers, American Heritage Center; *FRUS 1958–1960*, Vol. IV: 26.
4. *FRUS 1958–1960*, Vol. IV: 340, 341, 342.
5. Remarks by Governor Rockefeller to the New York Board of Trade, October 8, 1959, folder 1892, box 91, Rockefeller Gubernatorial Records, RAC. See also Dulles to U.S. Embassy Warsaw, July 3, 1958, 394.41/5-158; Herter to U.S. Embassy Belgrade, April 22, 1959, 394.41/4-2159, box 1392, Decimal Files, NARA; Stacy May, A Proposal for Applying GATT Trading Principles to Communist-Bloc Trade with the Free World, June 5, 1959, folder 341, box 59, Stacy May Papers, RAC; *FRUS 1958–1960*, Vol. IV: 350.
6. Remarks at the Annual Meeting of the U.S. Chamber of Commerce, May 2, 1960, https://www.presidency.ucsb.edu/documents/remarks-the-annual-meeting-the-us-chamber-commerce.
7. Address at the Gettysburg College Convocation, April 4, 1959, https://www.presidency.ucsb.edu/documents/address-the-gettysburg-college-convocation-the-importance-understanding; *FRUS 1958–1960*, Vol. IV: 101.
8. Dulles quoted in Boggs Address before the U.S. Council of the International Chamber of Commerce, The Need to Encourage American Trade and Investment Abroad, April 23, 1959, box 1, Speaking Engagement Series, Hale Boggs Papers, Howard-Tilton Memorial Library.
9. *FRUS 1958–1960*, Vol. IV: 101.
10. Milton Eisenhower, United States-Latin American Relations, 1953–1958, December 27, 1958, *Department of State Bulletin* 40: 1021 (January 19, 1959): 89–105.
11. Clayton to J. W. Fulbright, May 20, 1959; Clayton Memorandum, May 20, 1959, folder Common Market, Clayton Papers, HSTL. See also Meany in Committee II of United Nations General Assembly, November 5, 1959, *Department of State Bulletin* 41:1068 (December 14, 1959): 878–887.
12. Will Clayton, Discussion of Economic and Political Aspects of the European Common Market: Its Relationship to the Cold War, and Its Probable Effect on the United States World Trading Position, August 14, 1961, folder 2, box 266, Atlantic Council of the United States Records, Hoover Institution.
13. *FRUS 1958–1960*, Vol. IV: 28; Kaufman, *Trade and Aid*, 152–179.

14. Bradley Fisk address before the Greater Miami Manufacturers' Association, March 17, 1960, folder Speeches, box 1, Office of International Trade, National and Regional Export Council, BIO, NARA. See also Digest of Final Declarations of National Foreign Trade Conventions, Foreign Economic Policy, box 73, NFTC, HL; C. Douglas Dillon to Chiefs of Mission, January 4, 1960, folder (3), box 3, Chairman's Files, CFEP.
15. Paul H. Brent, National Export Expansion Committee to Regional Export Expansion Committee Chairmen, November 4, 1960, folder Exportunities Film Strip 1960, box 4, BIO, NARA. See also Special Message to the Congress, March 17, 1960, https://www.presidency.ucsb.edu/documents/special-message-the-congress-concerning-the-administrations-program-promote-the-growth; Export Expansion, *Congressional Quarterly-Almanac* (1960): 709–711; Secretary Mueller Appoints 5-Member Export Expansion Committee, March 31, 1960, folders Export Promotion(1) and (2), box 4, Chairman's Files, CFEP; Secretary Mueller Announces 33 Regional Export Expansion Committees, May 19, 1960, folder International Affairs-Export Sales, box 1, BIO, NARA; Minutes of the Colorado Export Expansion Committee Meeting, August 9, 1960, folder Trade, box 40, Series III, Gordon L. Allott Papers, University of Colorado Boulder Libraries.
16. Boggs Address to the Fifteenth Annual Cleveland World Trade Conference, Foreign Trade and Investment: The Challenge of the Sixties, April 7, 1960, box 1, Press Releases File, Boggs Papers, Howard-Tilton Memorial Library; C. Edward Galbreath to Randall, January 6, 1960; Randall to General Persons, January 7, 1960, folder January (2), box 1, Chairman's Records, CFEP; Joel Broyhill, Export Program Wrong Medicine, April 27, 1960, *Congressional Record*, vol. 3 86:2, A3603–3604.
17. C. Edward Galbreath to Randall, April 21, 1959, box 1, Chronological Files, Chairman's Files, CFEP; *FRUS 1958–1960*, Vol. IV: 109.
18. Clayton to Samuel W. Anderson, August 14, 1959; Clayton to Judge St. John Garwood, June 3, 1959, folder Correspondence [2 of 2], box 1, Ellen Clayton Garwood Papers, HSTL; Clayton, A Free World Common Market, November 24, 1959, folder International Trade-Common Market, box 126, Clayton Papers, HSTL. See also *FRUS 1958–1960*, Vol. VII, Pt. 1, Western European Integration (1993): 63, 71, 72, 79; Kaufman, *Trade and Aid*, 178–188; John Heinz II, The Challenge of Atlantic Trade Liberalization, April 25, 1959, folder Trade Policy (1 of 2), box 90, Gordon Papers, JFKL.
19. Interagency Steering Group for the Promotion of Export Sales, Working Group I, Over-All Factors Which Influence Prospects of Increased U.S. Exports [January 1960]; Area Market Evaluation Country Report, Japan, January 23, 1960, and EEC and EFTA, January 27, 1960; Trade Fairs, Trade Missions, and Trade Centers, January 26, 1960; Working Group II, Content of Commercial Activity of the Foreign Service, Office of International Regional Economics, Bureau of International Commerce Records, Record Group 489, Records of International Trade Administration, NARA; National Export Expansion Committee, Year-End Report, January 6, 1961, folder NEEC Meeting 4/25/61, box 3, BIO, NARA; *FRUS 1958–1960*, Vol. IV: 121.
20. Statement by Senator John. F. Kennedy, October 31, 1960, https://www.presidency.ucsb.edu/documents/statement-senator-john-f-kennedy-balance-payments-philadelphia-pa; Senator Kennedy, October 18, 1960, https://www.presidency.ucsb.edu/documents/senator-kennedy-why-should-the-american-businessman-support-the-democratic-party-new-york; Press Conference of Vice President Richard M. Nixon, August 3, 1960, https://www.presidency.ucsb.edu/documents/tv-press-conference-vice-president-richard-m-nixon-honolulu-hi. Comparison of Republican and Democratic Platforms, September 9, 1960, folder 74, box 13, Rockefeller Gubernatorial Papers, RAC.
21. Ball to Rusk and Bowles, January 1, 1961, folder 4, box 91, George W. Ball Papers, PUL. See also Zeiler, *American Trade*, 48.
22. The Task Force on Foreign Economic Policy, December 31, 1960, box 51A, C. Douglas Dillon Papers, JFKL.
23. The President's News Conference, November 29, 1961, https://www.presidency.ucsb.edu/documents/the-presidents-news-conference-199. See also Zeiler, *American Trade*, 53.
24. The President's News Conference, March 8, 1961, https://www.presidency.ucsb.edu/documents/the-presidents-news-conference-195. See also Telcon, Ball and Boggs, October

20, 1961, folder Commercial Policy 1961, box 2, Ball Papers, JFKL; The Working Group on Foreign Trade and Investment, Righting the US Balance of Payments, January 30, 1961, folder Balance of Payments, 1961, box 1, Jack N. Behrman Papers, JFKL.

25. U.S. Congress, Senate Foreign Relations, *Organization for Cooperation and Development*, 1961, Ball, 5–6; Dillon, 8–10, 47–49.
26. Telcon, Ball, and Petersen, June 16, 1961, folder Commercial Policy 1961, box 2, Ball Papers, JFKL; Zeiler, *American Trade*, 56.
27. Dillon address before the Foreign Traders Association of Philadelphia, September 15, 1960, *Department of State Bulletin* 43:1111 (October 10, 1960): 563–567; Irwin, *Clashing over Commerce*, 521; U.S. Delegation, 16th Session of the Contracting Parties, Avoidance of Market Disruption, May 2, 1960, folder [GATT], box 6, Don Paarlberg Records, DDEL.
28. *FRUS 1958–1960*, Vol. IV: 140, 141, 143; *FRUS 1961–1963*, Vol. IX, Foreign Economic Policy (1995): 224; Zeiler, *American Trade*, 75–127.
29. *FRUS 1958–1960*, Vol. IV: 133, 134.
30. *FRUS 1961–1963*, Vol. IX: 211, 218, 226, 245; Telcon, Feldman, and Ball, January 23, 1962, folder Commercial Policy 1962–1963, box 2, Ball Papers, JFKL, 245.
31. *FRUS 1961–1963*, Vol. IX: 237; Eckes, *Opening America's Market*, 180–184.
32. Special Messages to the Congress, March 7, 1962, https://www.presidency.ucsb.edu/documents/special-messages-the-congress-the-trade-agreements-concluded-the-geneva-tariff-conference; Telcon, Reston, and Ball, July 25, 1962, folder US and Europe, 3/2/61–7/10/63, box 8, Ball Papers, JFKL.
33. Ball address before the Eighth Annual Conference on International Affairs of the Cincinnati Council on World Affairs, February 16, 1962, folder Under Secretary Ball's Speeches [folder 1 of 2], box 288, National Security Files, Presidential Files, JFKL.
34. Telcon, Ball to the President, February 20, 1962, folder Common Market, box 2, Ball Papers, JFKL.
35. Message to the Permanent Council, February 15, 1961, https://www.presidency.ucsb.edu/documents/message-the-permanent-council-the-north-atlantic-treaty-organization. See also Francis S. Hutchins, Cultural Needs of the Atlantic Community [1961], folder 5, box 268, Atlantic Council of the United States Records, Hoover Institution; Irwin, *Clashing over Commerce*, 521; Telcon, Ball, and Reston, July 25, 1962, folder US and Europe, 3/2/61–7/10/63, box 8, Ball Papers, JFKL.
36. The President's News Conference, August 10, 1961, https://www.presidency.ucsb.edu/documents/the-presidents-news-conference-205. See also Zeiler, *American Trade*, 64.
37. Johnson, *Wealth of a Nation*, 458.
38. U.S. Congress, House Education and Labor, *Impact of Imports and Exports on Employment*, 1961–1962, Dent, 2.
39. Corrected Acheson statement before the Subcommittee on Foreign Economic Policy of the Joint Economic Committee, December 5, 1961, folder 51, box 135, Acheson Papers, HSTL.
40. U.S. Congress, House Joint Economic Committee, *Foreign Economic Policy*, 1961, Herter and Clayton, 1, also 2–10.
41. Zeiler, *American Trade*, 65.
42. A Statement on United States Foreign Trade Policy by a Working Group of the Business Community, [1961], folder Trade General, box 20, White House Files, Arthur M. Schlesinger Jr. Papers, JFKL.
43. Department of State, 1962 Trade Agreements Legislation, October 12, 1961, folder Reciprocal Trade (1), box 24, White House Staff Files–Myer Feldman Files, JFKL. See also *FRUS 1961–1963*, Vol. IX: 230.
44. *FRUS 1961–1963*, Vol. IX: 228.
45. Address in New York City, December 6, 1961, https://www.presidency.ucsb.edu/documents/address-new-york-city-the-national-association-manufacturers. See also The President's News Conference, November 8, 1961, https://www.presidency.ucsb.edu/documents/the-presidents-news-conference-198.
46. Address in Miami, December 7, 1961, https://www.presidency.ucsb.edu/documents/address-miami-the-opening-the-afl-cio-convention.

47. Joe Alex Morris, "The Great Tariff Battle," *Saturday Evening Post* [1962], folder Trade Expansion Act 1962, box 248, Charles P. Taft Papers, LC; Department of State, Public Comment on U.S. Trade Policy, December 6, 1961–January 10, 1962; Temple Wanamaker to Department of State, January 16, 1962, folder FO 3-3, 1-16-62-1-25-62, box 565, Pre-Presidential Files: Senate Files-Holburn, JFKL. See also Peter T. Jones to the Secretary, Public Support for the Trade Expansion Act, March 7, 1962; Trade Bill Supported by Governors of 20 States [1962], folder 27, Howard G. Petersen Papers, JFKL; Coordinating Council of Organizations on International Trade Policy to Editorial Writers, Columnists and Commentators, May 18, 1962, folder Trade Expansion Act, box 41, Post-Presidential Papers, HSTL.
48. Telcon, Ball, and Gudeman, November 6, 1961, folder Common Market, box 2, Ball Papers, JFKL; *FRUS 1961–1963*, Vol. IX: 240; Zeiler, *American Trade*, 67–69. On adjustment assistance, see Frank, *Foreign Trade and Domestic Aid*, 40–44.
49. Special Message to the Congress, January 25, 1962, https://www.presidency.ucsb.edu/documents/special-message-the-congress-foreign-trade-policy.
50. Address by Dean Rusk before the Treasury Department Conference, U.S. Trade Policy—Challenge and Opportunity, January 19, 1962, folder Public Statements on Trade Legislation, Petersen Papers, JFKL.
51. U.S. Congress, House Ways and Means, *Trade Expansion Act of 1962*; Irwin, *Clashing over Commerce*, 523–526; Address before the Conference on Trade Policy, May 17, 1962, https://www.presidency.ucsb.edu/documents/address-before-the-conference-trade-policy.
52. Address at Independence Hall, July 4, 1962, https://www.presidency.ucsb.edu/documents/address-independence-hall-philadelphia.
53. U.S. Congress, Senate Finance, *Trade Expansion Act of 1962*, Strackbein, 410, 411, 420.
54. Interview on KOCO-TV Oklahoma City [1962], folder Radio-Television Appearance, box 3, Petersen Papers, JFKL.
55. Irwin, *Clashing over Commerce*, 526–527. Strom Thurmond was the Democratic dissenter. On Yugoslavia and Poland, see Telcon, Kaysen, and Ball, September 27, 1962; the President and Ball, September 28, 1962; Hartke and Ball, October 8, 1962, folder Trade Legislation, 7/62–12/62, box 8, Ball Papers, JFKL. For the GOP, see Current Positions Notebook, Foreign Trade, October 5, 1962, folder 74, box 13, Rockefeller Gubernatorial Records, RAC.
56. Remarks upon Signing the Trade Expansion Act, October 11, 1962, https://www.presidency.ucsb.edu/documents/remarks-upon-signing-the-trade-expansion-act; Message to the Prime Minister of Canada, October 19, 1962, https://www.presidency.ucsb.edu/documents/message-the-prime-minister-canada-international-trade.
57. Telcon, Sharon, and Ball, November 8, 1962, folder Trade Legislation, 7/62–12/62, box 8, Ball Papers, JFKL. See also Telcon, Arthur Dean and Ball, September 26, 1962, folder Trade Legislation, 7/62–12/62, box 8, Ball Papers, JFKL.
58. Address and Question and Answer Period, December 14, 1962, https://www.presidency.ucsb.edu/documents/address-and-question-and-answer-period-the-economic-club-new-york.
59. *FRUS 1961–1963*, Vol. IX: 24. See also Jackson, *De Gaulle*, 582; Max Frankel, "Administration's 'Grand Design" Is Again Being Redefined," *New York Times*, February 18, 1963: 13.
60. Zeiler, *American Trade*, 159–162; McKenzie, *GATT and Global Order*, 88–93.
61. The President's News Conference, January 24, 1963, https://www.presidency.ucsb.edu/documents/the-presidents-news-conference-163.
62. The President's News Conference, February 7, 1963, https://www.presidency.ucsb.edu/documents/the-presidents-news-conference-157. See also Jackson, *De Gaulle*, 592–596, 652, 679.
63. Telcon, The President and Ball, January 29, 1963, also Schaetzel and Ball, January 17, 1963; Bundy and Ball, January 29, 1963; The President and Ball, January 29, 1963, folder Common Market, 1/17/63–11/21/63, box 2, Ball Papers, JFKL.
64. Telcon, The President and Ball, January 29, 1963, folder Common Market, 1/17/63–11/21/63, box 2, Ball Papers, JFKL.
65. Telcon, The President and Ball, January 30, 1963, folder Common Market, 1/17/63–11/21/63, box 2, Ball Papers, JFKL.

66. Telcons, Childs, and Ball, January 30, 1963; Kaysen and Ball, February 26, 1963, also Herter and Ball, April 24, 1963, folder Common Market, 1/17/63–11/21/63, box 2, Ball Papers, JFKL.
67. Telcon, Arthur Schlesinger and Ball, February 8, 1963, folder Common Market, 1/17/63–11/21/63, box 2, Ball Papers, JFKL.
68. Telcon, The President and Ball, February 13, 1963, folder Common Market, 1/17/63–11/21/63, box 2, Ball Papers, JFKL.
69. The President's News Conference, May 22, 1963, https://www.presidency.ucsb.edu/documents/the-presidents-news-conference-167. See also Telcon, Kaysen, and Ball, February 26, 1963, and June 7, 1963, folder Common Market, 1/17/6–11/21/63, box 2, Ball Papers, JFKL; *FRUS 1961–1963*, Vol. IX: 279.
70. *FRUS 1961–1963*, Vol. IX: 32.
71. Telcon, The President and Ball, May 21, 1963, folder Trade Legislation 6/63–11/63, box 8, Ball Papers, JFKL.
72. Address in the Assembly Hall, June 25, 1963, https://www.presidency.ucsb.edu/documents/address-the-assembly-hall-the-paulskirche-frankfurt.
73. Telcon, Marquis Childs, and Ball, August 14, 1963, folder Trade Legislation 5/63–11/63, box 8, Ball Papers, JFKL; Zeiler, *American Trade*, 134–138.
74. Address before the White House Conference on Exports, September 17, 1963, https://www.presidency.ucsb.edu/documents/address-before-the-white-house-conference-exports.
75. Telcon, The President and Ball, November 20, 1963, folder Common Market, 1/17/63–11/21/63, box 2, Ball Papers, JFKL.

Chapter 8

1. Remarks at Lindbergh Field, October 28, 1964, https://www.presidency.ucsb.edu/documents/remarks-lindbergh-field-san-diego.
2. Address before a Joint Session of the Congress, November 27, 1963, https://www.presidency.ucsb.edu/documents/address-before-joint-session-the-congress-0.
3. Kunz, *Butter and Guns*, 108–119, 149–179; Joint Statement, December 29, 1963, https://www.presidency.ucsb.edu/documents/joint-statement-following-discussions-with-chancellor-erhard; Merlyn Trued to G. Griffith Johnson, Task Force Report, November 25, 1964; Dillon, Ball, and Bundy to the President, December 11, 1964, folder Moyers's "Brief"-Task Force, box 31, Francis M. Bator Papers, LBJL. Automakers rejected the economy car idea, refusing to work jointly out of competitive instincts, to avoid violating anti-monopoly laws, and also because of the projected low profit margin. See *FRUS 1964–1968*, Vol. VIII, International Monetary and Trade Policy (1998): 291.
4. Draft Statement re: Trade Negotiations, November 26, 1963, folder Trade-General Vol. 1 [3 of 4], box 47, NSF, LBJL.
5. Memorandum of Disapproval, December 31, 1963, https://www.presidency.ucsb.edu/documents/memorandum-disapproval-bill-relating-the-marking-imported-articles.
6. Calleo, "Since 1961," 407–409; Lawrence, *The End of Ambition*, 79–105.
7. Presidential Statement No. 3, October 26, 1964, https://www.presidency.ucsb.edu/documents/presidential-statement-no-3-economic-issues-strengthening-our-balance-payments; Zeiler, *American Trade*, 177–180.
8. Report on the President's Task Force on Foreign Economic Policy, November 25, 1964, box 31, Bator Papers, LBJL.
9. Statement by the President, November 13, 1964, https://www.presidency.ucsb.edu/documents/statement-the-president-response-report-the-inter-american-committee-the-alliance-for.
10. *FRUS 1964–1968*, Vol. IX, International Development and Defense Policy (1997): 90; *FRUS 1961–1963*, Vol. IX: 290.
11. *FRUS 1964–1968*, Vol. IX: 92; Vol. VIII: 286.
12. CIA, GATT, and the Kennedy Round, April 24, 1964; The Trade Negotiations [May 1964], folder (GATT) 5/4/64 [2 of 2], box 48, NSF, LBJL.

13. Zeiler, *American Trade*, 190–203.
14. Zeiler, *American Trade*, 204–206.
15. *FRUS 1964–1968*, Vol. IX: 133, 140; Declaration of the 55th National Foreign Trade Convention, November 18–20, 1968, folder Board Room, box 17, NFTC, HL.
16. Zeiler, *American Trade*, 213. See also "World Poverty and the Demands of Justice," adopted by the General Board, February 29, 1969, National Council of Churches Archive, https://nationalcouncilofchurches.us/common-witness-ncc/world-poverty-and-the-demands-of-justice/.
17. NSC-U/SM 38, Tariff Preferences for Less Developed Countries, August 14, 1969; NSSM-48, Preferences for the Less Developed Countries (LDCs), Issues for Decision, August 11, 1969, folder Trade-Tariff Preference [3 of 4], box 48, Hendrik S. Houthakker Files, CEA, SMOF, WHCF, RMNL. See also Zeiler, *American Trade*, 213–216.
18. State of the Union, January 30, 1961, https://www.presidency.ucsb.edu/documents/annual-message-the-congress-the-state-the-union-5.
19. Policy Planning Council, U.S. Policy on Trade with the European Soviet Bloc, July 8, 1963, box 310, National Security Files, JFKL. See also *FRUS 1961–1963*, Vol. IX: 298; CIA, Soviet Economic Problems Multiply, January 9, 1964, folder Briefing Book East-West Trade [folder 2 of 3], box 53, Dillon Papers, JFKL; Dobson, *U.S. Economic*, 168; Andreas Lowenfeld, East-West Trade [1964], Abram Chayes Papers, JFKL.
20. *FRUS 1961–1963*, Vol. IX: 304, 309, 312, 313, 324, 327, 332; Dobson, *US Economic*, 170–171; Telcon, Harriman, and Ball, October 18, 1963, folder East-West Trade 9/26/63–10/18/63, box 3, Ball Papers, JFKL.
21. Tino Peretz speech before the American Management Association, May 20–22, 1964, folder East-West Trade Reports, box 6, Behrman Papers, JFKL. See also Declaration of the 51st National Foreign Trade Convention, November 16–18, 1964, folder September 15, 1965, box 15, NFTC, HL; Calleo, "Since 1961," 407.
22. *FRUS 1964–1968*, Vol. IX: 154, also 150, 153.
23. Freeman to the President, Special Report on Licensing of Exports to Soviet Bloc Nations, March 4, 1964; Freeman conversation with Miller Committee, March 3, 1965, folder Miller Conversations-Rusk, box 23; Memorandum for McGeorge Bundy, Export of Beet Harvesters to the Soviet Union, March 3, 1964; Export Control Review Board, Summary of Arguments on Three Questions Considered at the Meeting of January 20, 1964 [undated], folder East-West, Volume 1 [2 of 2], box 49, NSF, LBJL.
24. State of the Union, January 4, 1965, https://www.presidency.ucsb.edu/documents/annual-message-the-congress-the-state-the-union-26. See also *FRUS 1964–1968*, Vol. IX: 161, 162; Bundy to the President, April 14, 1964, folder East-West, Volume 1 [2 of 2], box 49, NSF, LBJL.
25. Remarks to a Group of Business Leaders, January 7, 1965, https://www.presidency.ucsb.edu/documents/remarks-group-business-leaders-upon-their-return-from-visit-moscow.
26. *FRUS 1964–1968*, Vol. IX: 173, also 175. See also Dobson, *US Economic*, 174–177.
27. Dobson, *US Economic*, 176.
28. Report to the President of the Special Committee on U.S. Trade Relations with Eastern European Countries and the Soviet Union, April 29, 1965, folder East-West Trade Reports, box 6, Behrman Papers, JFKL. See also Myer Feldman, The Jews of the Soviet Union [1964], folder Russian anti-semitism, box 74, Feldman papers, JFKL; Record of Committee Meetings, March 4 and 5, 1965, folder Miller Committee Meetings [1][1 of 2], box 49, NSF, LBJL.
29. CIA, Thomas L. Hughes to the Secretary, The Communist Economic Offensive Through 1963, June 18, 1964, folder Miller Committee [1][1 of 3], box 19; McCloy to Eugene Black, March 29, 1965, box 23, NSF, LBJL.
30. Mose L. Harvey, East-West Trade and United States Policy, 1966, pp. 246, 247, 249, 250, folder International Affairs (General), box 27, NAM, HL.
31. U.S. Congress, Senate Banking and Currency, *East-West Trade*, 1968, 4, 6. See also Summary Notes of 569th NSC Meeting, May 3, 1967, folder NSC Meetings, Vol. 4 Tab 51, 5/3/67, box 2, NSF, LBJL; *FRUS 1964–1968*, Vol. IX: 185.
32. Dobson, *US Economic*, 176–180; Notes of the President's Interview with Nicholas Carroll, *London Sunday Times*, October 6, 1967, folder October 1967 Meetings, box 3, Meeting Notes File, LBJL; C. Stewart Baeder before the International Economic Affairs Committee,

The NAM and the East-West Trade Question, April 26, 1966, folder 100-0 1966, box 93, NAM, HL.

33. First Annual Report, February 18, 1970, https://www.presidency.ucsb.edu/documents/first-annual-report-the-congress-united-states-foreign-policy-for-the-1970s. See also *FRUS 1969–1976*, Vol. III, Foreign Economic Policy (2001): 19, 26.
34. *FRUS 1969–1976*, Vol. III: 19.
35. Flanigan to Kissinger, April 21, 1970, folder EX TA Trade [3 of 57, January–June 1970], box 1, Subject Files, WHCF, RMNL.
36. NSMM 35, U.S. Trade Policy Toward Communist Countries (Excluding China, Cuba, and Yugoslavia), from Jeanne W. Davis, May 12, 1969, folder Trade-East-West NSSM 35, box 48, Houthakker Files. See also Anthony Jurich to Bryce Harlow, East-West Trade, May 14, 1969, folder Ex TA Trade [1 of 57], box 1, Subject Files, WHCF, RMNL.
37. Dobson, *US Economic*, 199, also 183–190, 195–200.
38. McGeorge Bundy to Bill Moyers, March 18, 1964; Galbraith to President Johnson, March 11, 1964, folder Trade-General Vol. 1 [4 of 4], box 47, NSF, LBJL. See also Telcon, Herter, and Ball, October 21, 1964, folder Kennedy Round [4/30/64–8/3/66], box 4, Ball Papers, LBJL; *FRUS 1964–1968*, Vol. VIII: 262.
39. Remarks to the Members of the Public Advisory Committee, April 21, 1964, https://www.presidency.ucsb.edu/documents/remarks-the-members-the-public-advisory-committee-trade-negotiations.
40. Declaration of the Fifty-First National Foreign Trade Convention, November 16–18, 1964, folder September 15, 1965, box 15, NFTC, HL.
41. *FRUS 1964–1968*, Vol. VIII: 268, 270; Irwin, *Clashing over Commerce*, 528.
42. *FRUS 1964–1968*, Vol. VIII: 227, 243, 250, 297; Platform Planks, World Trade, June 5, 1964, folder 13, box 76, Issue Books, Rockefeller Gubernatorial; Bill Roth to Francis Bator and Myer Feldman, September 25, 1964; Rusk and Ball to White House Message Center, September 26, 1964, folder Trade-General Vol. 2 [4 of 4], box 47, NSF, LBJL.
43. CIA, Special Report, GATT and the Kennedy Round, April 24, 1964, folder (GATT) 5/4/64 [2 of 2], box 48, NSF, LBJL.
44. Zeiler, *American Trade*, 189. See also Benjamin Read to McGeorge Bundy, March 26, 1965, folder Trade-General Vol. 2 [3 of 4], box 47, NSF, LBJL.
45. *FRUS 1964–1968*, Vol. VIII: 272, 290; Memorandum of Conversation, German and U.S. officials, December 21, 1965, folder Erhard Visit, box 21, Bator Papers, LBJL.
46. Statement by the President, March 24, 1967, https://www.presidency.ucsb.edu/documents/statement-the-president-the-swearing-william-roth-special-representative-for-trade. See also *FRUS 1964–1968*, Vol. VIII: 304.
47. *FRUS 1964–1968*, Vol. VIII: 315, 317, 344; Coppolaro, *Making of a World Trading Power*, 147–148, 168–176.
48. *FRUS 19641968*, Vol. VIII: 360, also 351.
49. Eckes, *Opening America's Market*, 192.
50. Statement by the President, May 16, 1967, https://www.presidency.ucsb.edu/documents/statement-the-president-the-general-agreement-reached-the-kennedy-round-trade-negotiations.
51. Johnson, *Wealth of a Nation*, 461; Eckes, *Opening America's Market*, 192; *FRUS 1964–1968*, Vol. VIII: 330, 333.
52. Bator to the President, Important Points for Kiesinger, Wilson, and Moro, April 22, 1967, folder Trade-Kennedy Round [1/67-6/68], box 48, NSF, LBJL; Kunz, *Butter and Guns*, 170–179; Statement by the President, July 31, 1968, https://www.presidency.ucsb.edu/documents/statement-the-president-upon-signing-order-establishing-the-export-expansion-advisory; *FRUS 1964–1968*, Vol. VIII: 324.
53. Summary Notes of 569th NSC Meeting, May 3, 1967, folder NSC Meetings, Vol. 4 Tab 51, 5/3/67, box 2, NSF, LBJL; Douglas Dillon, Some Thoughts on U.S. Policy and Gaullist France, [1967], folder Europe [2 of 2], box 25, Bator Papers, LBJL; Zeiler, *American Trade*, 217–239.
54. Eckes, *Opening America's Market*, 193. See also Declaration of the Fifty-Fourth National Foreign Trade Convention, Strengthening the World Economy–A Reassessment of Responsibilities and Policies, October 19, 1967, box 16, NFTC, HL.

55. AAI to U.S. Tariff Commission, February 6, 1967, folder 1967 Trade, box 196, Edward W. Brooke Papers, LC.
56. Special Message to the Congress, November 27, 1967, https://www.presidency.ucsb.edu/documents/special-message-the-congress-transmitting-multilateral-trade-agreement-concluding-the.
57. Annual Message, February 1, 1968, https://www.presidency.ucsb.edu/documents/annual-message-the-congress-the-economic-report-the-president-16.
58. Zeiler, *American Trade*, 240.
59. Zeiler, *American Trade*, 240. See also Irwin, *Clashing over Commerce*, 530–531; Eckes, *Opening America's Market*, 192–194.
60. Zeiler, *American Trade*, 240.
61. U.S. Congress, House Ways and Means, *Foreign Trade and Tariff Proposals*, 1968, Rusk, 650.
62. Special Message to the Congress, May 28, 1968, https://www.presidency.ucsb.edu/documents/special-message-the-congress-greater-prosperity-through-expanded-world-trade; Declaration of the 55th National Foreign Trade Convention, November 18–20, 1968, folder October 30, 1968, box 17, NFTC, HL.
63. State of the Union, January 14, 1969, https://www.presidency.ucsb.edu/documents/annual-message-the-congress-the-state-the-union-30.
64. Eckes, *Opening America's Market*, 211–213; Secretary Stans before the Williams Commission, August 6, 1970, folder EX TA Trade [5 of 57], box 1, WHCF, Subject Files, RMNL.
65. Matusow, *Nixon's Economy*, 80–83; Pastor, *Congress*, 123–134.
66. Arthur Burns to Henry Kissinger, February 7, 1969, Report of the Task Force on Foreign Trade Policy, folder Trade General Vol. 1 [June '69–January '70], box 401, NSC Subject Files, RMNL; Rogers to the President, March 24, 1969, folder VIII-4, box 3, Arthur Burns, SMOF, RMNL. See also William Roth to the President, Future United States Foreign Trade Policy, January 14, 1969, folder Trade-IA-ECOSOC, box 48, Houthakker Files, CEA, SMOF, WHCF, RMNL; Irwin, *Clashing over Commerce*, 532.
67. Nixon to Congress, United States Foreign Policy for the 1970s: A New Strategy for Peace, February 18, 1970, folder Vol. 1 [3 of 3], box 325, Subject Files, NSC, RMNL.
68. Memorandum for the President, Your Meeting with Jean Rey on June 16, 1969, folder Vol. 1 [1 of 1], box 322, NSC, RMNL.
69. *FRUS 1969–1976*, Vol. III: 19.
70. Special Message to the Congress, November 18, 1969, https://www.presidency.ucsb.edu/documents/special-message-the-congress-united-states-trade-policy.
71. *FRUS 1969–1976*, Vol. III: 3.
72. Zeiler, "Nixon Shocks Japan, Inc.," 292–294; Matusow, *Nixon's Economy*, 119.
73. Zeiler, "Nixon Shocks Japan, Inc.," 295. See also *FRUS 1969–1976*, Vol. XIX, Pt. 2, Japan (2018): 40; Destler, Fukui, and Sato, *Textile Wrangle*, 26, 320; Barnhart, "From Hershey Bars to Motor Cars," 207–215; C. Fred Bergsten to Kissinger, U.S. Trade Legislation for 1969, August 7, 1969, folder Trade General Vol. 1, box 401, Subject Files, NSC, RMNL.
74. *FRUS 1969–1976*, Vol. XIX, Pt. 2: 64.
75. *FRUS 1969–1976*, Vol. XIX, Pt. 2: 45, 46, 47.
76. Matusow, *Nixon's Economy*, 122. See also U.S. Congress, House Ways and Means, *Tariff and Trade Proposals*, 1970; CNTP statement, August 19, 1970, folder CNTP 1969–1970, box 18, Lynn R. Edminister Papers, HSTL; *FRUS 1969–1976*, Vol. XIX, Pt. 2: 56, 58; The President's News Conference, July 20, 1970, https://www.presidency.ucsb.edu/documents/the-presidents-news-conference-145.
77. Johnson, *Wealth of a Nation*, 469; Irwin, *Clashing over Commerce*, 533; Matusow, *Nixon's Economy*, 123; Bergsten to Kissinger, Need for a Position on Trade Legislation for 1971, December 29, 1970; Memorandum of Conversation with the President, Williams, and Bergsten, Launching the President's Commission on Trade and Investment, April 6, 1970, folder Trade General Vol. II [2 of 2], box 401, Subject Files, NSC, RMNL; *FRUS 1969–1976*, Vol. XIX, Pt. 2: 71; Zeiler, "Nixon Shocks Japan, Inc.," 295–296.
78. Preeg, Taking the Initiative in Foreign Economic Policy, January 18, 1971, folder EX TA Trade [9 of 57], box 2, Subject Files, WHCF, RMNL.

Chapter 9

1. Zeiler, "Nixon Shocks," 298. See also John Ehrlichman Notes at Meeting with the President, August 3, 1971, folder (1 of 5), John D. Ehrlichman Papers, SMOF, WHSF, RMNL.
2. Zeiler, "Requiem for the Common Man," 13. See also Statement by Secretary of the Treasury John B. Connally at the Opening of a News Conference, August 16, 1971, folder 23, box 94, AC.
3. Marina Whitman to Peter G. Peterson, May 7, 1971, folder International Economic Policy Council, box 23, Houthakker Files, SMOF, WHCF, RMNL.
4. NFTC, Forward: Imperatives for World Economic Progress, October 23, 1971, box 18, NFTC, HL.
5. Ernest Johnston to Kissinger, August 2, 1971, folder Vol IV July–December 1971 [1 of 2], box 402, Subject Files, NSC, RMNL; Irwin, *Clashing over Commerce*, 538–539.
6. McCracken to the President, July 27, 1971, folder EX TA TRADE [17 of 57], box 3, Subject Files, WHCF, RMNL.
7. Irwin, *Clashing over Commerce*, 539.
8. Address to the Nation, August 15, 1971, https://www.presidency.ucsb.edu/documents/address-the-nation-outlining-new-economic-policy-the-challenge-peace.
9. *Time* Magazine, August 30, 1971; Harris Poll, October 1971, folder file #11 (2 of 2), Box 355, H. R. Haldeman Papers, SMOF, WHCF, RMNL; Harold Gulliver, *Atlanta Constitution* and Cruise Palmer, *The Kansas City Times and Star*, [1971], folder President's Handwriting August 1–15, 1971, box 13, PPF, RMNL.
10. *FRUS 1969–1976*, Vol. III: 64. See also Matusow, *Nixon's Economy*, 149–180; Stein, *Pivotal Decade*, xii.
11. "Thought for Today" [1971], folder 2, box 145, AC.
12. Address to the Congress, September 9, 1971, https://www.presidency.ucsb.edu/documents/address-the-congress-stabilization-the-economy.
13. Haldeman to Ray Price and Bill Safire, August 30, 1971, folder August 15 speech 1971, box 150, Haldeman Papers, RMNL.
14. Haldeman, Connally Notes, August 30, 1971, folder Chron August 1971 A-I, box 197, Haldeman Papers, RMNL.
15. The President's News Conference, September 15, 1971, https://www.presidency.ucsb.edu/documents/the-presidents-news-conference-139. See also Volcker remarks at the second meeting of the World Economy Study Group, Adlai Stevenson Institute of International Affairs, November 11, 1971, folder [4 of 4], box 8, Paul W. McCracken Papers, SMOF, WHCF, RMNL; *FRUS 1969–1976*, Vol. III: 76.
16. Remarks at a Question-and-Answer Session, September 23, 1971, https://www.presidency.ucsb.edu/documents/remarks-question-and-answer-session-with-10-member-panel-the-economic-club-detroit.
17. Robert Hormats to Kissinger, October 6, 1971, folder Vol II 1971–1972, box 322, Subject Files, NSC, RMNL. See also *FRUS 1969–1976*, Vol. III: 174.
18. Peterson to the President, The Quadriad Meeting—Politics and Policy, November 6, 1971, folder Presidential Suspension; Peterson, Foreign Reactions to the Trade Measures in the New Economic Policy, October 29, 1971, folder Presidential Suspension, June–December 1971 #2, box 53, Staff Secretary Memoranda Files, SMOF, WHSF, RMNL; *FRUS 1969–1976*, Vol. III: 188.
19. *FRUS 1969–1976*, Vol. III: 77; Embassy Tokyo to Secretary of State, November 7, 1971, folder 4 of 4, box 8; Peter G. Peterson, August 24, 1971, The Approach to Japan-Next Steps, August 24, 1971, folder September 1971, 2 of 2, box 11, McCracken Papers; Kissinger to the President, Highlights of My Second Visit to Japan, August 19, 1972, folder HAK's Secret Paris Trip, box 22, HKOF, NSC, RMNL.
20. *FRUS 1969–1976*, Vol. XIX, Pt. 2: 73, also 94.
21. *FRUS 1969–1976*, Vol. XIX, Pt. 2: 100.
22. *FRUS 1969–1976*, Vol. XIX, Pt. 2: 109, also *FRUS 1969–1976*, Vol. XIX, Pt. 2: 90, 101, 111, 112, 115, 130, 136; Hormats to Kissinger, Japanese/U.S. Cooperation in World Economy,

June 8, 1972, folder JUSEC Luncheon [1 of 7]; Kissinger to the President, My Trip to Japan, June 19, 1972, folder JUSEC Luncheon [2 of 7], box 21, HKOF, RMNL.

23. Paul Harvey News, President Nixon: A Gutsy Quarterback, August 1971, folder Ehrlichman-1971, box 3, Patrick Buchanan Papers, SMOF, WHSF, RMNL; Remarks by Lawrence F. O'Brien at Harry S. Truman Awards Dinner, September 25, 1971, folder 40, box 61, AC. On labor, see Haldeman to Buchanan, ORC Economic Poll, August 26, 1971, folder Haldeman 2 of 2, box 3, Buchanan Papers, RMNL.
24. NBC remarks, [August 1971]; Roger Johnson to Haldeman, Telephone Reactions to the President's Economic Message, folder August 15 speech 1971, box 150, Haldeman Papers, RMNL. See also Mills before the National Shoe Fair National Industry Luncheon, September 12, 1971, folder 14, box 417, Wilbur D. Mills Archive; "A system torn down must be rebuilt" and "World Trade," *Business Week* (August 21, 1971): 26–28.
25. David J. Steinberg, CNTP, August 23, 1971, folder 5, box 258, Fred Harris Collection, AC. See also Haldeman to Buchanan, ORC Economic Poll, August 26, 1971, folder Haldeman 2 of 2, box 3, Buchanan Papers, RMNL.
26. *FRUS 1969–1976*, Vol. III: 91, also 94, 98, 100, 104, 108; Kunz, *Butter and Guns*, 209.
27. Memorandum of conversation with Ortoli, Nixon, and Kissinger, October 1, 1973, folder EC Vol. IV [1 of 1], box 322, Subject Files, NSC, RMNL. See also Sargent, *Superpower Transformed*, 116–130.
28. Joint Communiqué, May 29, 1972, https://www.presidency.ucsb.edu/documents/joint-communique-following-discussions-with-soviet-leaders; Dobson, *US Economic*, 203.
29. *FRUS 1969–1976*, Vol. XVII, China (2006):14, 95.
30. *FRUS 1969–1976*, Vol. XVII: 10, 116, 127, 164, 185, 198; Attachment A, Chronology of US Moves Toward Relaxation of Controls on Trade with the PRC [1972], box 93; Joint Communiqué, February 28, 1972, folder China-President's Trip [1 of 3]; Holdridge/Lord to Kissinger, China Trip Meeting with the State Department, February 3, 1972, folder China-President's Trip [3 of 4], box 88, HKOF, RMNL; Zhang, *Beijing's Economic Statecraft*, 241–275.
31. A Protest to the President from Patriotic Americans, August 19, 1971, folder 20, box 133, AC.
32. Yao Shiong Shio to Nixon, May 25, 1971, folder EX TA TRADE [15 of 57], box 3, Subject Files, WHCF, RMNL; Louis Loeffler Jr. to Harris, June 18, 1971, folder 3, box 258, Harris Collection, AC; Buchanan to the President, Notes on Republican Leadership Meeting on July 20, 1971, August 7, 1971, folder August 1971, box 1, Buchanan Papers, RMNL.
33. Belcher to John Shelton, October 18, 1971, folder 10, box 164, Page Belcher Collection, AC. See also Background Paper on United States Policy Towards China and the Responsibility of the Church, May 4, 1971, folder 20, box 133, AC; *FRUS 1969–1976*, Vol. XVII: 105; Harris statement before the Committee for New China Policy, June 14, 1971, folder 14, box 256, Harris Collection, AC.
34. Counterpart Meetings between the Secretary of State and the Foreign Minister of the People's Republic of China, February 22, 1972, folder China-President's Talks [4 of 4], box 88, HKOF, RMNL; *FRUS 1969–1976*, Vol. XVII: 211; T. D. Jones to Nixon, March 28, 1973, folder EX TA Trade [42 of 57], box 6, Subject Files, WHCF, RMNL.
35. K. E. Miller to Page Belcher, March 21, 1972, folder 10, box 164, Belcher Collection, AC. For Burke-Hartke, see Ira P. Taylor to Russell Long, October 26, 1971, folder 14, box 130; J. H. Morris to Long, March 7, 1972, folder 43, box 142, Russell B. Long Papers, Louisiana State University; A. Lowenfeld, An International Economic Policy for the United States, [1972], folder McGovern International Economics 3, box 6, Chayes Papers, JFKL.
36. Hormats to Kissinger, European Strategy and Trade Legislation, December 14, 1972, folder Trade Vol. V [1 of 2], box 402, Subject Files, NSC, RMNL. See also Irwin, *Clashing over Commerce*, 540–542.
37. CIEPSM #19, U.S. Economic Relations with the European Community [1972], folder EC-CIEP [1 of 2], box 9, Marina V. N. Whitman File, CEA: Office Files, RMNL; Report of Visit to Western Europe by Peter M. Flanigan, May 30–June 10, 1972, folder CIEP-Flanigan Visit, box 4, Whitman File, RMNL; Office of the Special Representative for Trade Negotiations, A Design for the International Trading System in the 1970's, July 7, 1972, folder EX TA Trade

[26 of 57], box 4; Helmut Sonnenfeldt to Kissinger, October 27, 1972, folder EX TA Trade [52 of 57] to GEN TA Trade [3 of 24], box 8, Subject Files, WHCF, RMNL.

38. Remarks at the Conclusion, October 11, 1973, https://www.presidency.ucsb.edu/documents/remarks-the-conclusion-conference-export-expansion.
39. U.S. Congress, House Ways and Means, *Trade Reform Act of 1973*, Burke and Houthakker, 1137, 1163. See also Hormats to Kissinger, Trade Legislation, March 2, 1973, folder Trade Vol. V [1 of 2], box 402, NSC Files, RMNL; Frank, *Foreign Trade*, 59–71.
40. Johnson, *Wealth of a Nation*, 477; Dobson, *US Economic*, 204–210.
41. Peterson to the President, May 19, 1972, folder Briefing Book for Moscow Meeting, box 73; Memorandum of Conversation with Brezhnev and Kissinger, April 24, 1972; Melvyn Laird to the Assistant to the President for National Security Affairs, Briefing Papers for President's Trip to Moscow, May 13, 1972; Flanigan to the President, Commercial Agreements, May 23, 1972, folder Briefing Book for Moscow Meeting, box 73, HKOF, RMNL; *FRUS 1969–1976*, Vol. XV, Soviet Union (2011): 41.
42. The National Conference on Soviet Jewry, Plenum Meeting, August 15, 1972; Richard Maas, Chairman, NCSJ to Constitutent Organizations, October 2, 1972, folder NCSJ July–December 1972, box 366, NCJW, LC.
43. Barber B. Conable Jr. to Kissinger, March 3, 1973, folder EX TA Trade [38 of 57], box 6, Subject Files, WHCF, RMNL. See also William Pearce to Kissinger and George Schultz, Title V and the Jackson/Vanik Amendment, September 16, 1973, folder Trade Vol. VI [1 of 2], box 403, Subject Files, NSC, RMNL; Joint Statement by Congressmen Wilbur Mills and Charles Vanik and Senator Henry M. Jackson, February 7, 1973, folder National Conference on Soviet Jewry, January–June 1973, box 366, NCJW, LC.
44. *FRUS 1969–1976*, Vol. XV: 92, 96.
45. Kissinger, Schultz, Flanigan to the President, To Move or Not to Move the Trade Bill, November 30, 1973, folder Trade Vol. VI [1 of 2], box 403, NSC Subject Files.
46. Charles Cooper to General Scowcroft, Comments on Trade Bill and Jackson/Vanik, October 23, 1973, folder Trade Vol. VI [1 of 2], box 403, Subject Files, NSC, RMNL.
47. Johnson, *Wealth of a Nation*, 480.
48. Eckes, *Opening America's Market*, 245.
49. U.S. Congress, Senate Finance, *Trade Reform Act of 1973*, Meany, 1143, 1161; Strackbein, 1248–1249.
50. State of the Union, January 30, 1974, https://www.presidency.ucsb.edu/documents/annual-message-the-congress-the-state-the-union.
51. Message to the Congress, August 8, 1974, https://www.presidency.ucsb.edu/documents/message-the-congress-transmitting-annual-report-the-trade-agreements-program-for-1973.
52. Brzezinski, Crisis of the International System: A Strategic Overview, January 28, 1974, folder Correspondence 1/74 Trilateral Commission Files, box 7, Zbigniew Brzezinski Collection, JCL.
53. Fried and Bergsten, United States Foreign Economic Policy: The Stakes and the Issues, April 1974, folder Foreign Policy, 10/73–8/74, box 16, Issues Office-Stuart Eizenstat, 1976 Presidential Campaign, Jimmy Carter Pre-Presidential Papers, JCL.
54. Linwood Holton to Russell B. Long, [February 1973], folder Trade Bill, box 13, Congressional Relations File, O'Donnell and Jenckes Files, GRFL; Eberle to Kissinger, Title IV of the Trade Bill, March 1, 1974, folder Trade January 1, 1974 [1 of 1], box 403, Subject Files, NSC, RMNL.
55. Senate Finance *Trade Reform Act*, Kissinger, 454, 457, also 463.
56. *FRUS 1969–1976*, Vol. XV: 168, also 162. See also Statement by Senator Henry M. Jackson, Announcing Agreement on Trade and Emigration; Stanley Lowell to Members of the Plenum and Member Agencies, December 23, 1974; October 18, 1974, folder NCSJ May 1974–December 1974, box 366, NCJW, LC.
57. *FRUS 1969–1976*, Vol. XXXI, Foreign Economic Policy (2009): 207, also 104, 105, 215; Kissinger to the President, Exchanges with Senator Jackson Regarding His Amendment to the Trade Bill, August 9, 1974; Jackson to the President, September 11, 1974, box 23, PSF, NSA, GRFL; U.S. Congress, Senate Finance, *Emigration Amendment*, 1974, Kissinger, 81, 101, 106, 111; Johnson, *Wealth of a Nation*, 477–479; Secretary of State press conference,

Soviets Reject Trade Agreement, January 14, 1975, folder 2/27/74, box 9, Sidney L. Jones Papers, GRFL.

58. *FRUS 1969–1976*, Vol. XVI, Soviet Union (2012): 119, also 125. For Carter, see Newspaper Farm Editors of America, September 30, 1977, https://www.presidency.ucsb.edu/documents/newspaper-farm-editors-america-interview-with-members-the-organization.
59. Message to the Congress, November 18, 1974, https://www.presidency.ucsb.edu/documents/message-the-congress-legislative-priorities-0. See also Irwin, *Clashing over Commerce*, 546–549.
60. Statement following Senate Action, December 14, 1974, https://www.presidency.ucsb.edu/documents/statement-following-senate-action-the-trade-act-1974.
61. Remarks upon Signing the Trade Act, January 3, 1974, https://www.presidency.ucsb.edu/documents/remarks-upon-signing-the-trade-act-1974.
62. Irwin, *Clashing over Commerce*, 549–555; Sargent, *Superpower Transformed*, 165–197.
63. International Economic Policy Review, Strategy for MTN, [1974]; Rogers Morton, Strategy for MTN, May 1, 1975; STR, Background Paper for Strategy for MTN Strategy Discussion, [May 1975], folder International Economic Policy Review (5), box 112, Institutional Files, NSC, GRFL; *FRUS 1969–1976*, Vol. XXXI: Foreign Economic Policy (2009): 232; NFTC, Policy Declaration, November 1975, box 20, NFTC, HL.
64. *FRUS 1969–1976*, Vol. XXXI: 236, 301, 306. See also Franczak, "Losing the Battle, Winning the War," 885–889. In the end, America failed to get approval at UNCTAD IV for an International Resource Bank but largely beat back the NEIO.
65. *FRUS 1969–1976*, Vol. XXXI: 121, also 112. See also Briefing Paper for Arthur F. Burns, November 15–17, 1975, folder Rambouillet, Briefing Book (1), box B62, Arthur Burns Papers, GRFL; Economic Summit, Second Session, November 16, 1975; Press Conference, Kissinger and Treasury Secretary Simon, Air Force One [November 1975], folder Rambouillet (5), box 4, National Security Advisor, Staff Files, IEA, GRFL.
66. Department of State, Background and Analysis to Support U.S. Position, [1975], folder Rambouillet Briefing Book (2), box B62, Burns Papers, GRFL. See also Frederick Dent to L. William Seidman, International Trade Papers for the Economic Summit, October 21, 1975, folder Rambouillet (General), box B62, Burns Papers, GRFL.
67. USIA, General and Educated Opinion on International Economic Issues in Western Europe and Japan, September 12, 1975, folder Intl. Economic Summit, November 15–17, 1975, box 312, Office of Economic Affairs: L. William Seidman Papers, GRFL; Rich Hutcheson to Governor Carter, Foreign Policy Speech, May 5, 1975, folder Foreign Policy May 5, 1975, box 17, Eizenstat Papers, LC; U.S. Congress, Senate Finance, *Oversight Hearings*, 1976.
68. Remarks and a Question-and-Answer Session, April 2, 1976, https://www.presidency.ucsb.edu/documents/remarks-and-question-and-answer-session-milwaukee-economic-forum-the-wisconsin-association. See also Bergsten to Kissinger, Pending Critical Presidential Decision on Shoe Imports, February 17, 1971, folder Trade Vol. III, [1 of 2], box 402, Subject Files, NSC, RMNL; Robert Ingersoll to the President, Your Meeting with EC President Ortoli, February 23, 1976, folder European Community (1), box 5, Presidential Subject Files, NSC Advisor, GRFL; Dryden, *Trade Warriors*, 198–206.
69. *FRUS 1977–1980*, Vol. III, Foreign Economic Policy (2013): 10, 11. See also Eckes, *Opening America's Markets*, 246–248.
70. *FRUS 1969–1976*, Vol. XXXI: 150. See also Press Conference, Kissinger, William Simon, and Alan Greenspan, June 3, 1976, folder Economic Summit Memoranda and Statements (2), box 319, Seidman Papers, GRFL; Joint Economic Committee to Ford, June 25, 1976, folder FO 6–5, box 33, WHCF, GRFL; Joint Declaration, June 28, 1976, https://www.presidency.ucsb.edu/documents/joint-declaration-following-the-international-summit-conference-puerto-rico.
71. Jimmy Carter's Foreign Affairs Notebook, Points for the Foreign Policy/Defense Debate, October 5, 1976, folder Carter's Foreign Affairs Notebook by Harned Pettus Hoose [1], box 18, Eizenstat Papers, LC; *FRUS 1969–1976*, Vol. XXXI: 238.
72. Proclamation 4496, April 8, 1977, https://www.presidency.ucsb.edu/documents/proclamation-4496-world-trade-week-1977.
73. *FRUS 1977–1980*, Vol. III: 257, 263, 271, 273, 277, 354.

74. *FRUS 1977–1980,* Vol. III: 270, also 295, 308, 310.
75. Carter-Mondale Transition Staff, Foreign Economic and Interdependence Issues, November 2, 1976, box 44, Staff Office: Council of Economic Advisors [Staff Office-CEA]: Charles L. Schultze's Subject Files, Staff Office: Council of Economic Advisors, JCL. Italics in original.
76. *FRUS 1977–1980,* Vol. III: 1.
77. *FRUS 197--1980,* Vol. III: 4, 5, 31; European Newspaper Journalists, April 25, 1977, https://www.presidency.ucsb.edu/documents/european-newspaper-journalists-question-and-answer-session.
78. *FRUS 1977–1980,* Vol. III: 27, also 21; Biven, *Jimmy Carter's Economy,* 28–38, 95–112; CIEC Senior Officials Meeting, Issues, Paper, Trade, [1977], folder Trade 8/77, box 451, International Financial and Economic Developments Subject Files, Staff Office-CEA, JCL.
79. State of the Union, January 19, 1978, https://www.presidency.ucsb.edu/documents/the-state-the-union-address-delivered-before-joint-session-the-congress-1. On fair trade, NFTC Policy Declaration, Unfair Trade Practices, September 1, 1978, box 21, NFTC, HL.
80. *FRUS 1977–1980,* Vol. III: 183, also 61, 125, 133, 138, 159, 163; Notes for presentation to Summit Preparatory Group, May 26, 1978, folder Summit 1978 [2], box 450; Vance, Blumenthal, Schultze, Brzezinski, Owen to the President July 7, 1978, and Tabs A, B, C and Annexes I and II, folder (Venice) Summit, box 90, Schultze's Subject Files, Staff Office, CEA, JCL; Biven, *Jimmy Carter's Economy,* 113–121, 145–183; 159.
81. Eckes, *Revisiting U.S. Trade Policy,* 118, also 144–166. See also International Trade Agreements, January 4, 1979, https://www.presidency.ucsb.edu/documents/memorandum-from-the-president-international-trade-agreements; Dryden, *Trade Warriors,* 231–253; *FRUS 1977–1980,* Vol. III: 184.
82. Multilateral Trade Negotiations Agreements, April 12, 1979, https://www.presidency.ucsb.edu/documents/multilateral-trade-negotiations-agreements-statement-the-president. See also *FRUS 1977–1980,* Vol. III: 330.
83. *FRUS 1977–1980,* Vol. III: 197.
84. Trade Agreements Act of 1979, July 26, 1979, https://www.presidency.ucsb.edu/documents/trade-agreements-act-1979-remarks-signing-hr-4537-into-law. See also U.S. Congress, Senate Finance, *Trade Agreements Act of 1979,* Strauss, 400–429; Irwin, *Clashing over Commerce,* 555–559.
85. Interview with the President, June 20, 1979, https://www.presidency.ucsb.edu/documents/interview-with-the-president-question-and-answer-session-with-members-the-japanese-press.
86. See, for example, Frank A. Weil before the New York Regional Meeting of the White House Conference on Small Business, A Case for an Expanding Mercantilism, April 5, 1979, folder Export Policy (Weil), box 2, Gerald Rafshoon Files, Communications, JCL.
87. National Governors' Association, February 25, 1979, https://www.presidency.ucsb.edu/documents/national-governors-association-remarks-and-question-and-answer-session-with-members-the.

Chapter 10

1. Report of the President's Commission for a National Agenda for the Eighties [1980], box 17, RG 220, Records for the President's Commission for a National Agenda for the Eighties, JCL. See also *FRUS 1977–1980,* Vol. III: 240.
2. NFTC, 1981 Policy Declaration drafts on Protectionism, December 4, 1980; International Trade, December 5, 1980; Exports Controls and East-West Trade, December 5, 1980, folder December 18, 1980, box 22, NFTC, HL; *FRUS 197--1980,* Vol. III: 247; United States Export Promotion Policies, September 9, 1980, https://www.presidency.ucsb.edu/documents/united-states-export-promotion-policies-message-the-congress-reporting-the-administration.
3. NFTC to Senator Adlai E. Stevenson, April 15, 1980, folder 1980 Minutes of Board Meetings, box 7, NFTC, HL. See also Dobson, *US Economic,* 250.
4. Tacoma, Washington Remarks, September 23, 1980, https://www.presidency.ucsb.edu/documents/tacoma-washington-remarks-interview-with-komo-tv; St. Louis, Missouri

Remarks, October 13, 1980, https://www.presidency.ucsb.edu/documents/st-louis-missouri-remarks-and-question-and-answer-session-townhall-meeting.

5. McDonald to Henry Owen, Trade Negotiations with Japan, July 3, 1980, folder 5, box 10, Stuart Eizenstadt Papers, LC. See also *FRUS 1977–1980*, Vol. III: 197.
6. Brinkley, ed., *Reagan Diaries, Vol. I*, 16.
7. William G. Hyland, "U.S.-Soviet Relations: The Long Road Back," *Foreign Affairs* 60:3 (January 1981): 542–544.
8. Briefing paper, Ottawa Economic Summit, July 19–22, 1981, Binder (1), box 7, Trip Files, Executive Secretariat, NSC, RRL. See also Daniel J. Murphy to Counsellor to the President, April 30, 1981, folder (1 of 5), box 7, Jerry Jordan Files, RRL.
9. Lawrence Brady address before the Trans-Atlantic Conference on East-West Trade, East-West Trade: The U.S. Position, August 25, 1983; Marshall Goldman, The Plusses and Minuses of Economic Détente, folder 1, Trans-Atlantic Conference on East-West Trade records, Hoover Institution.
10. Trilateral Commission, Trilateral Economic Relations with the Soviet Union and Eastern Europe, February 18, 1982, folder 1599, box 147, Trilateral Commission Collection, RAC; Dobson, *US Economic*, 266–281.
11. Japan Strategy, EC-Japan relations [1981], Binder (3), box 11, Trip Files, Executive Secretariat, NSC, RRL; Zeiler, "Business Is War," 236, also 226–230; Kemp, *Climax of Capitalism*, 22; Preliminary draft, U.S. Trade Policy toward Japan [December 1981]; Frank Vargo, Trade Strategy, folder U.S.-Japan-Trade Policy (1), box 1, Douglas McGinn Files, RRL.
12. Remarks at a Reception, November 10, 1983, https://www.presidency.ucsb.edu/documents/remarks-reception-for-american-and-japanese-businessmen-tokyo-japan; Zeiler, "Business Is War," 240.
13. Kunz, *Butter and Guns*, 311–315; Irwin, *Clashing over Commerce*, 602–604.
14. Cancun-Trade [1981], folder [3 of 3], box 1, Charles P. Tyson Files, RRL. See also Eckes, *Opening America's Market*, 254, 274–277; Alexander Haig Jr. to the President, Your Meetings with Other Heads of State or Government in Cancun, folder Cancun [1 of 5], box 1, Tyson Files, RRL.
15. Remarks of the President and Prime Minister, March 11, 1981, https://www.presidency.ucsb.edu/documents/remarks-the-president-and-prime-minister-pierre-elliott-trudeau-canada-before-joint.
16. Remarks at the Swearing-in Ceremony, October 15, 1981, https://www.presidency.ucsb.edu/documents/remarks-the-swearing-ceremony-for-members-the-presidents-export-council.
17. Radio Address, August 6, 1983, https://www.presidency.ucsb.edu/documents/radio-address-the-nation-international-trade.
18. Remarks to Chinese Community Leaders, April 27, 1984, https://www.presidency.ucsb.edu/documents/remarks-chinese-community-leaders-beijing-china. See also Zhang, *Beijing's Economic Statecraft*, 263–289.
19. On trade ties, see Talley, *Forgotten Vanguard*; Ingleson, *Making Made in China*.
20. Remarks at a Luncheon, October 15, 1981, https://www.presidency.ucsb.edu/documents/remarks-luncheon-the-world-affairs-council-philadelphia-philadelphia-pennsylvania.
21. Remarks at the National Leadership Forum, April 6, 1984, https://www.presidency.ucsb.edu/documents/remarks-the-national-leadership-forum-the-center-for-international-and-strategic-studies. See also Remarks at Eureka College, February 6, 1984, https://www.presidency.ucsb.edu/documents/remarks-eureka-college-eureka-illinois; Prasad, *Politics of Free Markets*, 43–97.
22. The President's News Conference, November 11, 1982, https://www.presidency.ucsb.edu/documents/the-presidents-news-conference-1003.
23. Radio Address, November 20, 1982, https://www.presidency.ucsb.edu/documents/radio-address-the-nation-international-free-trade.
24. Report of the first AEI World Forum on International Trade Policy, August 13–15, 1982, box 12, Jones Papers, GRFL. See also USTR William Brock to members of the Trade Policy Committee, January 11, 1983, folder TPC (1 of 7), box 3, Geoffrey Carliner Files, RRL.

25. Remarks at the Annual Meeting, April 26, 1981, https://www.presidency.ucsb.edu/documents/remarks-the-annual-meeting-the-united-states-chamber-commerce-4; Message to the Congress, January 31, 1983, https://www.presidency.ucsb.edu/documents/message-the-congress-transmitting-the-fiscal-year-1984-budget.
26. Remarks and a Question-and-Answer Session, May 10, 1983, https://www.presidency.ucsb.edu/documents/remarks-and-question-and-answer-session-during-united-states-chamber-commerce.
27. Radio Address, June 2, 1984, https://www.presidency.ucsb.edu/documents/radio-address-the-nation-the-trip-europe-0. See also Shultz to the President, London Summit Bilaterals, May 14, 1984; Robert McFarlane to the President, London Economic Summit, May 19, 1984, Binder (1), box 8, William P. Clark Files, RRL; Japan Country Paper [May 1984], box 8, Executive Secretariat Files, RRL; Kissinger, First Annual "Mocatta" Lecture, International Economics and World Order, September 24, 1984, folder 3, box I:94, Robert S. McNamara Papers, LC.
28. Trilateral Commission, Intra-Trilateral Trade Tensions and Strengthening the GATT System: Three Presentations, June 23, 1982, folder 3281, box 334, Trilateral Commission Collection, RAC. See also Press Briefing, Shultz and Donald Regan, The Economic Summit at Williamsburg, May 24, 1983, folder 05/28/1983 Radio (2), box 98, WHOS, RRL; A. J. Miranda to George Bush, December 14, 1982, folder Buy America (Pre-1985 only), box 002 (1983), Office of Vice President George Bush, Subject Files, Subseries TA, GBL.
29. Douglas McMinn to William P. Clark, November 6, 1982, folder U.S.-Japan Trade Policy (3), box 1, McMinn Files, RRL.
30. Remarks and a Question-and-Answer Session, January 26, 1983, https://www.presidency.ucsb.edu/documents/remarks-and-question-and-answer-session-with-members-the-massachusetts-high-technology.
31. Radio Address, September 14, 1985, https://www.presidency.ucsb.edu/documents/radio-address-the-nation-the-farm-industry.
32. Question-and-Answer Session, May 27, 1983, https://www.presidency.ucsb.edu/documents/question-and-answer-session-with-reporters-domestic-and-foreign-policy-issues; Eckes, *Opening America's Market*, 252–253; Radio Address, September 22, 1984, https://www.presidency.ucsb.edu/documents/radio-address-the-nation-the-agricultural-and-steel-industries; Minutes, Economic Policy Council, Report of the Strike Force, November 5, 1985, folder 12/05/1985 (11:00 am), box 14, Beryl W. Sprinkel Files, RRL.
33. Remarks on Signing, October 30, 1984, https://www.presidency.ucsb.edu/documents/remarks-signing-the-trade-and-tariff-act-1984. See also Bonn Economic Summit, May 4, 1985, https://www.presidency.ucsb.edu/documents/bonn-economic-summit-declaration-sustained-growth-and-higher-employment.
34. Working Group on General Trade Negotiation Strategy to the Economic Policy Council, Action Plan for Multi-pronged Trade Policy Strategy, August 19, 1985, folder Trade General (1 of 7), box 6, Thomas Moore Files, RRL.
35. Written Responses, March 6, 1985, https://www.presidency.ucsb.edu/documents/written-responses-questions-submitted-macleans-magazine-canada.
36. Mulroney, Notes for an Address to the Nation on the Trade Initiative, June 16, 1986, folder 198 (8), WHOS, RRL.
37. Joint Canada-United States Declarations on Trade and International Security, March 18, 1985, https://www.presidency.ucsb.edu/documents/joint-canada-united-states-declarations-trade-and-international-security; Minutes, Economic Policy Council, December 5, 1985, folder 12/05/1985 (11:00 am), box 14, Sprinkel Files, RRL.
38. Remarks in an Interview, April 10, 1986, https://www.presidency.ucsb.edu/documents/remarks-interview-with-representatives-yomiuri-shimbun-japan-together-with-written. See also Radio Address, May 4, 1986, https://www.presidency.ucsb.edu/documents/radio-address-the-nation-the-presidents-trip-indonesia-and-japan; Remarks at a White House Ceremony, May 19, 1986, https://www.presidency.ucsb.edu/documents/remarks-white-house-ceremony-for-world-trade-week-and-the-e-and-e-star-awards.
39. U.S. Congress, House Ways and Means, *Comprehensive Trade Reform Act of 1986*, 1986, 2–6.

40. Statement by Principal Deputy Press Secretary Speakes, May 22, 1986, https://www.presidency.ucsb.edu/documents/statement-principal-deputy-press-secretary-speakes-house-representatives-approval-the.
41. Radio Address, July 5, 1986, https://www.presidency.ucsb.edu/documents/radio-address-the-nation-independence-day-and-the-centennial-the-statue-liberty.
42. Radio Address, June 28, 1986, https://www.presidency.ucsb.edu/documents/radio-address-the-nation-international-trade-0.
43. Remarks to Business Leaders, February 17, 1987, https://www.presidency.ucsb.edu/documents/remarks-business-leaders-white-house-briefing-economic-competitiveness.
44. Remarks at the 75th Annual Meeting, April 27, 1987, https://www.presidency.ucsb.edu/documents/remarks-the-75th-annual-meeting-the-united-states-chamber-commerce. See also Cong. Frank Horton and Howard Wolpe to George Bush, July 11, 1985, folder TA 3199998VP, Office of Vice President George Bush, Subject Files, Subseries TA, GBL.
45. Address to Western Europe, June 5, 1987, https://www.presidency.ucsb.edu/documents/address-western-europe-from-the-venice-economic-summit. See also Frank Carlucci, Meeting with the National Security Council, May 20, 1987, folder NSC 147, box 9, Executive Secretariat: Meeting Files, RRL; John P. Hardt and Jean F. Boone, A Congressional Guide for Economic Negotiations with the Soviet Union, The U.S.-Soviet Trade Roundtable Series, January 29, 1988, folder 7, box 43, Peter Rodman Papers, LC.
46. Remarks on East-West Relations, June 12, 1987, https://www.presidency.ucsb.edu/documents/remarks-east-west-relations-the-brandenburg-gate-west-berlin.
47. Remarks to Harley-Davidson Company Employees, May 6, 1987, https://www.presidency.ucsb.edu/documents/remarks-harley-davidson-company-employees-york-pennsylvania. See also Secretaries of the Treasury, Commerce, Labor, and Agriculture, USTR, and OMB Director to Rostenkowski, October 10, 1987, folder OA/ID 13239, box 11, Stephen Hart Files, WHPO, GBL.
48. Remarks at the Annual Meeting, September 14, 1987, https://www.presidency.ucsb.edu/documents/remarks-the-annual-meeting-the-national-alliance-business.
49. Remarks on the Observance, November 18, 1987, https://www.presidency.ucsb.edu/documents/remarks-the-observance-the-25th-anniversary-the-office-the-united-states-trade.
50. Colin Powell and Nancy Risque, Meeting with the National Security Council/Economic Policy Council, January 12, 1988, folder NSC 00150 01/12/1988, box 9, Meeting Files, Executive Secretariat, NSC, RRL. See also General Powell's Talking Points for the NSC/PC Meeting on US-Japan Relations: Takeshita Visit, folder NSC 00150 01/12/1988, box 9, Meeting Files, Executive Secretariat, NSC, RRL.
51. Remarks to Business Leaders, March 11, 1988, https://www.presidency.ucsb.edu/documents/remarks-business-leaders-white-house-briefing-international-trade.
52. Radio Address, April 23, 1988, https://www.presidency.ucsb.edu/documents/radio-address-the-nation-the-trade-bill-and-the-persian-gulf-conflict.
53. Remarks at a White House Briefing, March 23, 1988, https://www.presidency.ucsb.edu/documents/remarks-white-house-briefing-for-members-the-american-business-conference-0.
54. Radio Address, May 14, 1988, https://www.presidency.ucsb.edu/documents/radio-address-the-nation-free-and-fair-trade-3.
55. Remarks on Signing, August 23, 1988, https://www.presidency.ucsb.edu/documents/remarks-signing-the-omnibus-trade-and-competitiveness-act-1988-long-beach-california. See also the Congressional Research Service Report for Congress, H.R. 3: The Omnibus Trade and Competitiveness Act of 1988: An Analysis of the Major Trade Provisions, May 24, 1988, 1–2.
56. U.S. Delegation to the US-USSR Working Group of Exports, Concrete Steps to be Taken by the Joint US-USSR Commercial Commission to Expand US-Soviet Trade and Economic Relations, February 18–19, 1988, folder (1 of 5), box 6, Stephen Dezansky Files, RRL; Radio Address, June 4, 1988, https://www.presidency.ucsb.edu/documents/radio-address-the-nation-the-soviet-united-states-summit-meeting-moscow-and-the-toronto. See also "500

businessmen to talk trade with Moscow," April 11, 1988, folder OA/ID 13238, box 10, Hart Files, GBL.

57. State of the Union, January 25, 1988, https://www.presidency.ucsb.edu/documents/address-before-joint-session-congress-the-state-the-union-0. See also James Baker III, Economic Policy Council to the President, October 9, 1987, folder Free Trade Agreement with Canada, box 10, Hart Files, GBL; USTR, Briefing Paper on the U.S.-Canada Free Trade Agreement, May 1988, folder 5/9/88 Canada FTA, box 1, Roger Bolton Files, RRL.
58. Toronto Economic Summit, June 21, 1988, https://www.presidency.ucsb.edu/documents/toronto-economic-summit-conference-economic-declaration.
59. Sidney L. Jones, U.S. Economic Policies in an Integrated World Economy, folder Scholarly Papers 11/9–10/88, box 12, Jones Papers, GRFL; William Maroni to James Baker III, 147th Meeting of the Economic Policy Council, August 5, 1988, folder EPC (1), box 10, Nancy Risque Files, RRL; Collins, *More*, 166–209.
60. Remarks to the National Assembly, February 27, 1989, https://www.presidency.ucsb.edu/documents/remarks-the-national-assembly-seoul.
61. Remarks at the United States Coast Guard Academy, May 24, 1989, https://www.presidency.ucsb.edu/documents/remarks-the-united-states-coast-guard-academy-commencement-ceremony-new-london-connecticut. See also Carl Levin to the President, May 23, 1989, TA [039063], Subject Files, WHORM, GBL.
62. Nicholas Brady to the President, Your Meeting with Japanese Prime Minister Kaifu, March 2, 1980; Baker to the President, Your Meeting with Prime Minister Toshiki Kaifu, March 20, 1990, OA/ID CF01119 [2], White House Office of Policy Development, Stephen Farrar Files, GBL.
63. U.S. Congress, Senate Finance, *United States-Japan Structural Impediments Initiative*, 1990, Danforth, 3–4, also Backus, 1–2.
64. Remarks at the Swearing-in Ceremony, February 6, 1989, https://www.presidency.ucsb.edu/documents/remarks-the-swearing-ceremony-for-carla-hills-united-states-trade-representative.
65. Remarks and a Question-and-Answer Session, December 11, 1989, https://www.presidency.ucsb.edu/documents/remarks-and-question-and-answer-session-with-newspaper-editors.
66. Remarks at the Presentation Ceremony, May 23, 1990, https://www.presidency.ucsb.edu/documents/remarks-the-presentation-ceremony-for-the-e-star-awards.
67. Letter to Congressional Leaders, September 17, 1990, https://www.presidency.ucsb.edu/documents/letter-congressional-leaders-textile-apparel-and-footwear-trade-legislation.
68. Paris Economic Summit, July 16, 1989, https://www.presidency.ucsb.edu/documents/paris-economic-summit-economic-declaration.
69. Statement by Yeutter, October 15, 1990; USTR press release, United States Submits Agriculture Proposal in the Uruguay Round, October 15, 1990, OA/ID 03695-017, Cooper Evans Files, White House Office of Cabinet Affairs, GBL.
70. Mexico-United States Joint Statement, June 11, 1990, https://www.presidency.ucsb.edu/documents/mexico-united-states-joint-statement-negotiation-free-trade-agreement; Remarks Announcing the Enterprise for the Americas Initiative, June 27, 1990, https://www.presidency.ucsb.edu/documents/remarks-announcing-the-enterprise-for-the-americas-initiative.
71. Jones, The U.S. Role in the Economic Transformation of East Central Europe, Alpbach Forum, August 27, 1990, box 13, Jones Papers, GRFL. See also Scowcroft to the President, Carter Letter on MFN, June 7, 1990, TA 147416, Subject Files, WHORM, GBL.
72. John Undeland to Marlin Fitzwater, Congressional Reaction to the President's Announcement on MFN Status for China, May 24, 1990, TA 147416, Subject Files, WHORM, GBL.
73. The United States-China Business Council, The Cost of Removing MFN from China, April 23, 1990; Adi Ignatius, "China Frees 211 Prisoners in Move Seen Aimed at Retaining Most-Favored Nation Trade Status," *Wall Street Journal*, May 11, 1990, folder China-MFN Renewal, Evans Files; Virginia Lampley and Karl Jackson to Scowcroft, China-MFN Informational Material, May 23, 1990, China Sanctions; Fact Sheet on Continuation of MFN for China, TA [124659], Subject Files, WHORM, GBL; Talley, *Forgotten*, 5, 71–79.

74. Virginia Lampley and Karl Jackson, National Security Council to Scowcroft, China-MFN Informational Material, May 23, 1990, MFN Trade Status for China, TA Trade [124659], Subject Files, WHORM, GBL.
75. U.S. Chamber of Commerce to Rostenkowski, July 18, 1990, OA/ID 05805, Farrar Files, GBL.

Chapter 11

1. Remarks at the Hampton University, May 12, 1991, https://www.presidency.ucsb.edu/documents/remarks-the-hampton-university-commencement-ceremony-hampton-virginia.
2. Remarks to Soviet and United States Businessmen, July 31, 1991, https://www.presidency.ucsb.edu/advanced-search?field-keywords=Remarks+to+Soviet+and+United+States+Businessmen+in+Moscow&items_per_page=25. See also Office of the Press Secretary, Fact Sheet: Trade Enhancement Initiative for Central and Eastern Europe, March 20, 1991, OA/ID 07951, box 1, Laura Melillo Files, WHPO, GBL; Twenty Senators to President Bush, October 21, 1991, TA Trade 285581, Subject Files, WHORM, GBL.
3. Remarks and a Question-and-Answer Session, February 6, 1991, https://www.presidency.ucsb.edu/documents/remarks-and-question-and-answer-session-meeting-the-economic-club-new-york-new-york. See also Remarks at a White House Briefing, March 19, 1991, https://www.presidency.ucsb.edu/documents/remarks-white-house-briefing-for-the-national-leadership-the-hispanic-alliance-for-free.
4. Press release, Response by the Hispanic Alliance for Free Trade to AFL-CIO Advertisement Against N.A.F.T.A., May 7, 1991, OA/ID 13267-006, Judy Smith Files, WHPO, GBL; William Welch, Gephardt Blasts Bush on Race, May 13, 1991, OA/ID 12929-0151, box 28, Marlin Fitzwater Files, GBL. See also press release, May 20, 1991, Hemispheric Group Endorses Free Trade among Mexico, Canada, and United States, folder InterAmerican Dialogue NAFTA May–July 1991; Six Mexican professors and writers to Lic. Gonazalo Martinez Corbalo, November 28, 1990, folder InterAmerican Dialogue, NAFTA December 1990–April 1991, box 380, Sol Linowitz Papers, LC.
5. Richardson speech at the Heritage Foundation, May 15, 1991, The U.S.-Mexico Free Trade Agreement: Prospects for Hispanics, OA/ID CF01379 [1 of 3], NSC, Charles A. Gillespie Files, GBL.
6. Harrison, National Women's Economic Alliance, Woe Woe-ist or Winners, May 9, 1991, OA/ID 08647-007, Ron Kaufman Files, White House Office of Political Affairs, GBL.
7. "Beware! Fast Track Could Be Hazardous to Your Health," Roll Call, April 29, 1991, 7, folder Trade-Fast Track, OA/ID 12929-0151, box 28, Fitzwater Files, WHPO, GBL. See also Report to the Congress on the Extension of Fast Track Procedures, March 1, 1991, OA/ID 05805, Farrar Files, GBL; Coleman to Bush, March 14, 1991, Case No. 220890 TA Trade, WHORM Subject Files, GBL; U.S. Congress, House of Representatives, Disapproving the Application of "Fast Track" Procedures to Trade Agreement Implementing Bills: Report 102-63, Part 2, Adverse Report, 103rd Cong., 1st sess., 1991; Irwin, *Clashing over Commerce*, 628.
8. John Undeland and Floyd Jones to Fitzwater, Demarest, Bolten, Lydon, August 13, 1992, TA 261485, Subject Files, WHORM, GBL; Presidential Debate, October 15, 1992, https://www.presidency.ucsb.edu/documents/presidential-debate-the-university-richmond; Clinton, *My Life*, 43; The North American Free Trade Agreement, Myths and Realities, folder NAFTA 12/91, OA/ID 13896-006, Tony Snow Files, WHOS, GBL; Irwin, *Clashing over Commerce*, 631–632; Panitch and Gindin, *Making*, 228.
9. Telephone Conversation with the President and Prime Minister Brian Mulroney, February 5, 1991; American Embassy, Ottawa to Secretary of State, Canadian Participation in a Mexico FTA: The View from Canada, January 1991, OA/ID CF01379 [3 of 3], Farrar Files, GBL; Brent Scowcroft memorandum of meeting with Carla Hills, October 7, 1992, OA.ID CF01771 [1 of 3], Walter H. Kansteiner Files, NSC, GBL.
10. "Inhaling Free Trade, Review & Outlook," [August 1992], OA/ID 12921, box 20, Fitzwater Files, WHPO, GBL.
11. John Undeland and Floyd Jones to Fitzwater, Demarest, Bolten, and Lydon, August 13, 1993, NAFTA Editorials, OA/ID 12921, box 20, Fitzwater Files, WHPO, GBL; Irwin, *Clashing over Commerce*, 628–629.

12. Remarks Announcing the Completion of Negotiations, August 12, 1992, https://www.presidency.ucsb.edu/documents/remarks-announcing-the-completion-negotiations-the-north-american-free-trade-agreement.
13. Remarks on Signing, December 17, 1992, https://www.presidency.ucsb.edu/documents/remarks-signing-the-north-american-free-trade-agreement.
14. Biden to Sol Linowitz, June 12, 1991, folder InterAmerican Dialogue, NAFTA May–July 1991, box 380, Linowitz Papers, LC.
15. Remarks to the Korean National Assembly, January 6, 1992, https://www.presidency.ucsb.edu/documents/remarks-the-korean-national-assembly-seoul.
16. Pat Buchanan on the Issues; Buchanan and Gephardt notes, folder 2, box 1, OA/ID 08647-025, Kaufman Files, GBL. See also Zeiler, "Business," 240; Anne Armstrong to Samuel Skinner, April 9, 1992, folder 321592 Trade, GBL; John Marous and Robert Allen to Bush, October 25, 1991, folder TA 281601, Subject Files, WHORM, GBL; News Conference, July 11, 1991, https://www.presidency.ucsb.edu/documents/news-conference-president-bush-and-prime-minister-toshiki-kaifu-japan-kennebunkport-maine.
17. Text of Remarks, January 9, 1992, https://www.presidency.ucsb.edu/documents/text-remarks-the-japanese-welcoming-committee-luncheon-tokyo; Testimony of Ambassador Carla Hills before the Senate Committee on Finance, January 23, 1992, Japan: Trade [OA/ID 05806][1], Farrar Files, GBL.
18. USTR, Japan Framework, June 18, 1993, folder Japan [2][OA/ID 5059, box 1, Laura D'Andrea Tyson, Alpha Files, WHORM, WJCL. See also Barshevsky to Cutter et al., Observations based on my recent meeting with the Japanese, September 24, 1993, folder Japan [1][OA/ID 5059, box 1, Tyson Files, WHORM, WJCL; Office of the Press Secretary, Background Briefing by Senior Administration Official, April 16, 1993, folder Japan (5), https://clinton.presidentiallibraries.us/items/show/#48455, Philip "P. J." Crowley, Office of Press and Communications, CDL, WJCL.
19. Tyson to the Japan Deputies Group, Reflections on Our Japan Trade Strategy, September 7, 1994, folder [2], OA/ID 505, box 1, Tyson Files, WHORM, WJCL; Remarks on the Japan-United States Trade Agreement, June 28, 1995, https://www.presidency.ucsb.edu/documents/remarks-the-japan-united-states-trade-agreement.
20. Press Briefing, May 10, 1995, https://www.presidency.ucsb.edu/documents/press-briefing-ambassador-mickey-kantor-dr-laura-tyson-secretary-commerce-ron-brown.
21. Eckes and Zeiler, *Globalization and the American Century*, 225–237.
22. Klein, *The Natural*, 57, 78–79, also 12; From, *New Democrats and the Return to Power*, 204.
23. Despite its downsides and the critics, many viewed globalization as inevitable. See Chanda, *Bound Together*, 245–301. For the protesters' views, see Klein, *No Logo*.
24. William Archey to all staff, NAFTA, November 11, 1993; Richard Lesher, Holding America Hostage, folder NAFTA, box 39, Chamber of Commerce of the United States Records, HL; Irwin, *Clashing over Commerce*, 634–638.
25. U.S. Congress, House Ways and Means, *North American Free-Trade Agreement*, 1993, Rostenkowski, 9–10; Levin, 12; Kantor, 30.
26. U.S. Congress, Senate Finance, *NAFTA*, 1993, Bradley, 11; Hollings, 14, 16.
27. U.S. Congress, House Foreign Affairs, *NAFTA and American Jobs*, 1993, Gejdensen, 1.
28. Remarks to the Export-Import Bank Conference, May 6, 1993, https://www.presidency.ucsb.edu/documents/remarks-the-export-import-bank-conference. See also Letter to Congressional Leaders, November 15, 1993, https://www.presidency.ucsb.edu/documents/letter-congressional-leaders-nafta.
29. Irwin, *Clashing over Commerce*, 638. See also Branch, *Clinton Tapes*, 59.
30. Remarks on NAFTA, November 4, 1993, https://www.presidency.ucsb.edu/documents/remarks-nafta-employees-lexmark-international-lexington.
31. Remarks at the Dedication, October 29, 1993, https://www.presidency.ucsb.edu/documents/message-the-congress-transmitting-proposed-legislation-implement-the-north-american-free.
32. Message to the Congress, https://www.presidency.ucsb.edu/documents/message-the-congress-transmitting-proposed-legislation-implement-the-north-american-free, November 3, 1993.

33. Remarks at a Veterans Day Breakfast, November 11, 1993, https://www.presidency.ucsb.edu/documents/remarks-veterans-day-breakfast.
34. Branch, *Clinton Tapes*, 49, 60; Tod Robberson, "Delay Perils NAFTA, Salinas Says," *Washington Post* (October 7, 1993), folder 4, box 103, Mary McGrory Papers, LC.
35. Irwin, *Clashing over Commerce*, 638–641; Clinton, *My Life*, 540. See also Gephardt, The New Internationalism: The Nexus Between American National Interests and Globalism, May 5, 1998, http://www.econstrat.org/images/ESI_Research_Reports_PDF/the%20new%20internationalism%20-%20the%20nexus%20between%20american%20national%20interests%20and%20globalism%20(richard%20a.%20gephardt).pdf.
36. Irwin, *Clashing over Commerce*, 642, also 643; Branch, *Clinton Tapes*, 83, also 50, 219. Clinton, *My Life*, 546–547. See also Office of the Press Secretary, statements issued by former Presidents Bush, Reagan, and Ford endorsing NAFTA, November 2, 1993, https://clinton.presidentiallibraries.us/items/show/#48566; Economists to the President, September 1, 1993, https://clinton.presidentiallibraries.us/items/show/#48569, Crowley Files, CDL, WJCL.
37. Remarks to the Seattle APEC Host Committee, November 19, 1993, https://www.presidency.ucsb.edu/documents/remarks-the-seattle-apec-host-committee.
38. Remarks on Signing, December 8, 1993, https://www.presidency.ucsb.edu/documents/remarks-signing-the-north-american-free-trade-agreement-implementation-act.
39. The President's Radio Address, December 18, 1993, https://www.presidency.ucsb.edu/documents/the-presidents-radio-address-570.
40. U.S. Congress, House Ways and Means, *President's Request for Extension*, 1993.
41. Irwin, *Clashing over Commerce*, 639–643; Branch, *Clinton Tapes*, 85; Clinton, *My Life*, 629, 643, 769.
42. Irwin, *Clashing over Commerce*, 644, also 651, 652, 655. See also U.S. Congress, House Ways and Means, *Trade Agreements*, 1994, 101; Mazower, *Governing the World*, 361.
43. Press Briefing by Robert Rubin et al., December 14, 1993, folder Trade (2), https://clinton.presidentiallibraries.us/items/show/#48620, Crowley Files, CDL, WJCL.
44. Ruggiero address, Trading Towards Peace, MENA III Conference, November 12, 1996, WTO Publication News Archive, https://www.wto.org/english/news_e/pres96_e/pr058_e.htm. See also Sutherland, "Opening up New Opportunities for Trade," October 31, 1994, GATT Digital Library, https://exhibits.stanford.edu/gatt/catalog/jv865sm3537; What is the WTO, Ten Things, April 3, 2018, *World Trade Organization Publications News Archive*, https://www.wto.org/english/thewto_e/whatis_e/10thi_e/10thi09_e.htm.
45. Remarks to Future Leaders, January 9, 1994, https://www.presidency.ucsb.edu/documents/remarks-future-leaders-europe-brussels.
46. The President's News Conference, January 11, 1994, https://www.presidency.ucsb.edu/documents/the-presidents-news-conference-with-european-union-leaders-brussels-0.
47. Remarks of Anthony Lake, From Containment to Enlargement, September 21, 1993, https://clinton.presidentiallibraries.us/items/show/#9013, Anthony Blinken Collection, NSC Speechwriting Office, CDL, WJCL. See also Bennett Freeman and Tom Malinowski to Tom Donilon, August 13, 1994, folder Lake 9194 Speech-Notes, Blinken Collection, CDL, WJCL.
48. Remarks at the Edmund A. Walsh School, November 10, 1994, https://www.presidency.ucsb.edu/documents/remarks-the-edmund-walsh-school-foreign-service-georgetown-university.
49. Summit of the Americas Declaration of Principles, December 3, 1994, 9409729 [OA/ID 484], box 1, NSC and Executive Secretary Files, WJCL.
50. Remarks to the International Business Community, November 16, 1994, https://www.presidency.ucsb.edu/documents/remarks-the-international-business-community-jakarta. See also U.S. Congress, House Ways and Means, *World Trade Organization Hearings*, 1994.
51. Rudd to Clinton, November 17, 1994, folder I T012, 088396 [OA/ID 23360], box 7, Subject Files-General, WHORM, WJCL.
52. U.S. Congress, House International Relations, *Fast Track*, 1994, Ros-Lehtinen, 2, also 42.
53. U.S. Congress, House International Relations, *Fast Track*, Sherman, 20, also 22.
54. Irwin, *Clashing over Commerce*, 657.
55. C-Span, David Bonior on NAFTA, November 17, 1993, https://www.c-span.org/video/?c4541434/user-clip-democratic-whip-david-bonior-nafta.

56. Klein, *The Natural*, 16.
57. The President's Radio Address, January 21, 1995, https://www.presidency.ucsb.edu/documents/the-presidents-radio-address-305.
58. Remarks to the Canadian Parliament, February 23, 1995, https://www.presidency.ucsb.edu/documents/remarks-the-canadian-parliament-ottawa.
59. Quoted in Gabriele Heuser, "America and Europe: Common Challenges in a Changing World," *1995 Working Paper No. 6, Maryland Seminar on U.S. Foreign Policymaking*, University of Maryland, 34, also 35.
60. United States-European Union Statement, December 18, 1998, https://www.presidency.ucsb.edu/documents/united-states-european-union-statement-cooperation-the-global-economy.
61. Remarks at the Dedication, March 18, 1996, https://www.presidency.ucsb.edu/documents/remarks-the-dedication-the-nashville-wharf-new-orleans-louisiana.
62. Dole speech to the American Textile Manufacturers Institute, March 25, 1995, http://dolearchivecollections.ku.edu/collections/speeches/098/c019_098_004_all.pdf, Press Release, China MFN, May 20, 1996, http://dolearchivecollections.ku.edu/collections/press_releases/960520chi.pdf, Robert J. Dole Speeches Collection (Digital), Robert and Elizabeth Dole Archive.
63. See, for example, Michael J. Oppenheimer, "The New Mercantilism: Where Is Business Leading Our Foreign Policy?" *Working Paper in Division of International Studies Special Series, End of the American Century?* Woodrow Wilson Center, September 1996. For conservatives, see Kolozi, *Conservatives Against Capitalism*.
64. Sheldon W. Simon and Donald K. Emmerson, "Security, Democracy, and Economic Liberalization: Competing Priorities in U.S. Asia Policy," National Bureau of Asian Research, Vol. 7:2, September 1996, [OA/ID 13135], box 38, Ira Magaziner Files, Domestic Policy Council, CDL, WJCL; Anthony Lake, American Foreign Policy on the Eve of the Millennium speech, March 28, 1996, https://clinton.presidentiallibraries.us/items/show/#9442, Blinken Collection, Speechwriting Office, National Security, CDL, WJCL.
65. Irwin, *Clashing over Commerce*, 661–662; U.S. Congress, House of Representatives, *Withdrawing the Approval*, 2000; U.S. Congress, House of Representatives, *Withdrawing the Approval*, 2005.
66. Remarks in Littleton, Colorado, June 19, 1997, https://www.presidency.ucsb.edu/documents/remarks-littleton-colorado.
67. Remarks to the 52d Session, September 22, 1997, https://www.presidency.ucsb.edu/documents/remarks-the-52d-session-the-united-nations-general-assembly-new-york-city.
68. Berger, America's Role in the World, October 16, 1998, SRB Dartmouth Speech, https://clinton.presidentiallibraries.us/items/show/#9902, Blinken Collection, Speechwriting Office, National Security, CDL, WJCL.
69. Remarks in the Globalization and Trade Session, November 1, 1997, https://www.presidency.ucsb.edu/documents/remarks-the-globalization-and-trade-session-the-democratic-national-committees-autumn; Peter D. Hart to AFL-CIO, Fast-track Authorization, August 1, 1997, TA 23064355 [OA/ID 23779], Subject Files, WHORM, WJCL.
70. Remarks to Business and Community Leaders, April 16, 1998, https://www.presidency.ucsb.edu/documents/remarks-business-and-community-leaders-santiago. See also Remarks at the World Trade Organization, May 18, 1998, https://www.presidency.ucsb.edu/documents/remarks-the-world-trade-organization-geneva-switzerland.
71. Summers in Klein, *The Natural*, 7. See also Slobodian, *Globalists*, 277–281.
72. Commencement Address, June 12, 1999, https://www.presidency.ucsb.edu/documents/commencement-address-the-university-chicago-chicago-illinois.
73. Remarks at a Democratic Leadership Council Gala, October 13, 1999, https://www.presidency.ucsb.edu/documents/remarks-democratic-leadership-council-gala. See also The Clinton Administration Agenda for Seattle: Putting a Human Face on the Global Economy, November 29, 1999; Meeting with Labor Leaders, https://clinton.presidentiallibraries.us/items/show/#12236, Jeff Shesol Files, WHOS, Office of Communications, White House Staff and Office Collections, CDL, WJCL.

74. Telephone interview, November 30, 1999, https://www.presidency.ucsb.edu/documents/telephone-interview-with-michael-paulson-the-seattle-post-intelligencer-san-francisco.
75. Remarks to the Trade Community, December 1, 1999, https://www.presidency.ucsb.edu/documents/remarks-the-trade-community-seattle-washington.
76. Clinton, *My Life*, 893–894. See also Remarks to the World Economic Forum, January 29, 2000, https://www.presidency.ucsb.edu/documents/remarks-the-world-economic-forum-and-question-and-answer-session-davos-switzerland.
77. Irwin, *Clashing over Commerce*, 662; Harvey, *Brief History of Neoliberalism*, 93.
78. Shesol to Tomasz Malinowski, WTO: Agenda Framework, October 11, 1999, folder OA/ID 19946, https://clinton.presidentiallibraries.us/items/show/#12129, Shesol Files, WHOS, Office of Communications, White House Staff and Office Collections, CDL, WJCL; U.S. Congress, House Ways and Means, *Accession of China and Taiwan*, 1996; Irwin, *Clashing over Commerce*, 663.
79. Remarks at the Yale University Commencement, May 27, 1991, https://www.presidency.ucsb.edu/documents/remarks-the-yale-university-commencement-ceremony-new-haven-connecticut. See also David A. Miller to John Sununu, May 21, 1991, TA 240318 Trade; Senate Finance Committee to the President, June 19, 1991, TA 248968, Subject Files, WHORM, GBL; Robert W. Barnett, "Don't Misread Tiananmen," *Washington Post*, July 17, 1991, OA/ID 08054-027, Paul McNeill Files; Ray Cline, "Bush's Nod to Taiwan," *The Washington Times* July 26, 1991, F3, TA 262254, Subject Files, WHORM, GBL.
80. Stanley Roth and Robert Kyle to Anthony Lake and Robert Rubin, MFN Briefing Book for the President, May 25, 1994, 9404126, [OA/ID 474], box 2, China and MFN, NSC Records, WJCL; Klein, *The Natural*, 81–82. For exporters, see Andreas Dür, *Protection for Exporters*, 187–210.
81. Robert Kapp, "The Road to 'Normalization,'" *China Business Review*, July–August 1996; The US-China Business Council Letter from the President, Berger-US-China Business Council, https://clinton.presidentiallibraries.us/items/show/#9613, Blinken Collection, Speechwriting Office, National Security, CDL, WJCL. See also Donald Stabeli to the President, November 11, 1996, Blinken Collection, Speechwriting Office, National Security, CDL, WJCL.
82. Irwin, *Clashing over Commerce*, 665.
83. Press Briefing, May 28, 1993, https://www.presidency.ucsb.edu/documents/press-briefing-assistant-secretary-winston-lord.
84. Gordon, *The Rise and Fall of American Growth*, 554.
85. Brown, *Myths of Free Trade*, 62, 97, also 20, 58–59, 99, 103, 130. See also Lichtenstein, "Market Triumphalism," 123–126.
86. Carter to Clinton, March 18, 1994, 9402365 [OA/ID 190], box 1, China and MFN, NSC Records, WJCL. See also Irwin, *Clashing over Commerce*, 663–665.
87. Clinton, *My Life*, 758. See also Zhang, *Beijing's Economic Statecraft*, 289–298, 308–312.
88. Clinton, *My Life*, 598. See also Press Briefing by Lake et al., May 26, 1994, folder China [1], https://clinton.presidentiallibraries.us/items/show/#48431, Crowley Files, CDL, WJCL; Department of State, Bureau of Public Affairs, Press Reacts to MFN Status for China, June 11, 1993; Press Briefing by Assistant Secretary Winston Lord, May 28, 1993, China [3] https://clinton.presidentiallibraries.us/items/show/48433, Crowley Files, CDL, WJCL.
89. Branch, *Clinton Tapes*, 305.
90. Jay Mazur to Clinton and Barshefsky, October 28, 1996, TA003 194525 [OA/ID 14055], box 12, AFL/CIO Records, Subject Files, WHORM, WJCL.
91. Remarks by Samuel R. Berger to Council on Foreign Relations, Building a New Consensus on China, June 6, 1997, https://clinton.presidentiallibraries.us/items/show/#9678, Blinken Collection, Speechwriting Office, National Security Council, CDL, WJCL. See also Clinton, *My Life*, 768; Robert Kapp, "Talking Tough," *China Business Review*, November–December 1996, The US-China Business Council Letter from the President, Berger-US-China Business Council, https://clinton.presidentiallibraries.us/items/show/#9613, Blinken Collection, Speechwriting Office, National Security, CDL, WJCL.
92. U.S. Department of State, Office of the Spokesman, Albright and Foreign Minister Tang Jiaxuan, March 1, 1999, Summers/Albright Trip, box 3, National Economic Council,

WJCL: Sperling: Zemin Files, Asian Affairs, Kenneth Lieberthal Files, WJCL; Press Briefing, September 11, 1999, https://www.presidency.ucsb.edu/documents/press-briefing-national-security-advisor-sandy-berger-national-economic-advisor-gene; Clinton, *My Life*, 793.

93. U.S. Congress, House International Relations, *Granting Permanent Normal Trade Relations Status to China*, 2000, Gilman and Gejdenson, 2–3. See also Richard Siewert to Shesol, May 17, 2000, China PNTR-Greenspan, https://clinton.presidentiallibraries.us/items/show/#12208, OA/ID 21461; Peter D. Hart Research Associates, China Trade: Survey Conducted for the AFL-CIO, January 25–27, 2000, China PNTR-Clinton/WTO-Gen, https://clinton.presidentiallibraries.us/items/show/#12163, Shesol Files, WHOS, Office of Communications, White House Staff and Office Collections, CDL, WJCL; Irwin, *Clashing over Commerce*, 666; U.S. Congress, House Banking and Financial Services, *Permanent Normal Trade Relations for China*, 2000.
94. Department of State, Office of the Spokesman, Richard Boucher statement on Response to Commission on International Religious Freedom's First Annual Report, May 1, 2000, folder Levin-Berueter Discussions [2], OA/ID CF 1177, box 8, China WTO Files, National Economic Council, WJCL; Q&A: PNTR and U.S. National Security; Q&As-Human Rights, May 11, 2000, China PNTR, OA/ID 21461, https://clinton.presidentiallibraries.us/items/show/#12215, Shesol Files, WHOS, Office of Communications, White House Staff and Office Collections, CDL, WJCL; The U.S.-China WTO Accession Deal: China's Conduct in International Organizations, April 10, 2000, [Binder 1][2]; Lawrence Summers speech to Dallas Committee on Foreign Relations, The Case for Normal Trade Relations with China, March 21, 2000, [Binder 1][4] [OA/ID 40753, box 1, China Permanent Trade Status Files, WJCL.
95. Irwin, *Clashing over Commerce*, 668–670.
96. Remarks at the University of Warwick, December 14, 2000, https://www.presidency.ucsb.edu/documents/remarks-the-university-warwick-coventry-united-kingdom.
97. Interview with the New York Times, November 30, 2020, https://www.presidency.ucsb.edu/documents/interview-with-the-new-york-times.

Chapter 12

1. Remarks Announcing Candidacy, June 12, 1999, https://www.presidency.ucsb.edu/documents/remarks-announcing-candidacy-for-the-republican-presidential-nomination-1. See also Irwin, *Clashing over Commerce*, 672, 676–677.
2. The President-Elect's News Conference, December 16, 2000, https://www.presidency.ucsb.edu/documents/the-president-elects-news-conference-announcing-the-nomination-colin-l-powell-secretary, and January 11, 2001, https://www.presidency.ucsb.edu/documents/the-president-elects-news-conference-announcing-the-nomination-elaine-chao-secretary-labor.
3. Irwin, *Clashing over Commerce*, 673.
4. Remarks by Chairman Alan Greenspan, September 25, 2002, https://www.federalreserve.gov/boarddocs/speeches/2002/200209252/default.htm.
5. Remarks to State Department Employees, February 15, 2001, https://www.presidency.ucsb.edu/documents/remarks-state-department-employees-0.
6. The President's News Conference, February 16, 2001, https://www.presidency.ucsb.edu/documents/the-presidents-news-conference-with-president-vicente-fox-mexico-san-cristobal-mexico.
7. Remarks at Western Michigan University, March 27, 2001, https://www.presidency.ucsb.edu/documents/remarks-western-michigan-university-kalamazoo-michigan; Address Before a Joint Session, February 27, 2001, https://www.presidency.ucsb.edu/documents/address-before-joint-session-the-congress-administration-goals.
8. Interview, November 1, 2005, https://www.presidency.ucsb.edu/documents/interview-with-foreign-print-journalists-3.
9. Remarks to the Council of the Americas Conference, May 7, 2001, https://www.presidency.ucsb.edu/documents/remarks-the-council-the-americas-conference.
10. Fact Sheet, May 10, 2001, https://www.presidency.ucsb.edu/documents/fact-sheet-the-presidents-2001-international-trade-agenda.

11. Statement on the Trade Agreement, June 8, 2001, https://www.presidency.ucsb.edu/documents/statement-the-trade-agreement-with-vietnam; U.S.-Vietnam Trade Council, U.S.-Vietnam Economic Normalization Conference, April 7, 1997, OI513297-339, 1996 Bilateral Trade Agreement With Vietnam, Subject Files, WHORM, WJCL; U.S. Congress, Senate Finance, *U.S.-Vietnam Trade Relations*, 2006.
12. Quoted in Brown, *Myths*, 31. See also Galbraith, *Predator State*, 70–72, 202–203; Klein, *Fences and Windows*, 163–190.
13. Remarks at the Dakota Ethanol Plant, April 24, 2002, https://www.presidency.ucsb.edu/documents/remarks-the-dakota-ethanol-plant-wentworth-south-dakota. See also U.S.-Jordan FTA, September 28, 2001, https://www.presidency.ucsb.edu/documents/statement-the-press-secretary-overview-us-jordan-free-trade-agreement-fta; Joint Statement, November 13, 2001, https://www.presidency.ucsb.edu/documents/joint-statement-president-george-w-bush-and-president-vladimir-v-putin-russia-the-new.
14. Remarks at the Chief Executive Officers Summit, October 20, 2001, https://www.presidency.ucsb.edu/documents/remarks-the-chief-executive-officers-summit-shanghai. See also Statement on the Ministerial Decision, November 11, 2001, https://www.presidency.ucsb.edu/documents/statement-the-ministerial-decision-admit-the-peoples-republic-china-and-taiwan-into-the.
15. Statement on the World Trade Organization's Decision, November 14, 2001, https://www.presidency.ucsb.edu/documents/statement-the-world-trade-organizations-decision-launch-new-round-global-trade. See also Press Briefing, August 13, 2002, https://www.presidency.ucsb.edu/documents/press-briefing-secretary-agriculture-ann-veneman-and-ustr-ambassador-robert-zoellick; U.S. Congress, U.S.-China Economic and Security Review Commission, *Issues to Be Addressed*, 2005, Robert Lighthizer, 37; Irwin, *Clashing over Commerce*, 675.
16. The President's News Conference, May 26, 2002, https://www.presidency.ucsb.edu/documents/the-presidents-news-conference-with-president-jacques-chirac-france-paris-france-0.
17. Remarks to the People of Poland, May 31, 2003, https://www.presidency.ucsb.edu/documents/remarks-the-people-poland-krakow-poland.
18. Remarks by the National Security Advisor, February 1, 2002, https://www.presidency.ucsb.edu/documents/remarks-the-national-security-advisor-condoleezza-rice-the-conservative-political-action; and April 29, 2002, https://www.presidency.ucsb.edu/documents/remarks-national-security-advisor-condoleezza-rice-terrorism-and-foreign-policy.
19. U.S. Congress, Senate Finance, *Trade Promotion*, 2001, Levin, 9; National Wildlife Federation, 20.
20. U.S. Congress, Senate Finance, *Trade Promotion*, 2001, Grassley, 4.
21. Irwin, *Clashing over Commerce*, 675.
22. Statement on Senate Action, August 1, 2002, https://www.presidency.ucsb.edu/documents/statement-senate-action-trade-promotion-authority-legislation. See also Gamble, *NFTC*, 106–107.
23. Irwin, *Clashing over Commerce*, 674, 677–681; Smil, *Made in the USA*, 146–151.
24. U.S. Congress, House Energy and Commerce, *Dominican Republic-Central America Free Trade Agreement*, 2005, American Sugar Alliance, 91; U.S. Congress, House Ways and Means, *Implementation of the Dominican Republic*, 2005, Trumka, 99; U.S. Congress, Senate Judiciary, *Proposed United States-Chile*, 2003, Feinstein, 4–5.
25. Remarks to the World Affairs Councils, January 16, 2002, https://www.presidency.ucsb.edu/documents/remarks-the-world-affairs-councils-america-conference. See also Hornbeck, *The Dominican-Central America-United States Free Trade Agreement*, 1.
26. U.S. Congress, House Ways and Means, *Implementation of the Dominican Republic*, Barton, 7.
27. Remarks on Trade-Promotion Authority, April 4, 2002, https://www.presidency.ucsb.edu/documents/remarks-trade-promotion-authority-legislation-and-extension-the-andean-trade-preference. See also Fact Sheet, June 27, 2002, https://www.presidency.ucsb.edu/documents/fact-sheet-g-8-africa-action-plan.
28. Message to the Congress, July 6, 2003, https://www.presidency.ucsb.edu/documents/message-the-congress-transmitting-legislation-implement-the-united-states-australia-free. See also U.S. Congress, Senate Finance, *United States-Australia and United States-Morocco*, 2004, Deputy USTR, 7, 9.

29. Remarks at the Signing Ceremony, May 6, 2003, https://www.presidency.ucsb.edu/documents/remarks-the-signing-ceremony-for-the-united-states-singapore-free-trade-agreement.
30. U.S. Congress, House Ways and Means, *Implementation of U.S. Bilateral Free Trade*, 2003, Sessions, 13, Biggers, 17.
31. Statement by the Press Secretary, May 21, 2003, https://www.presidency.ucsb.edu/documents/statement-the-press-secretary-united-states-bahrain-free-trade-agreement. See also U.S. Congress, House Ways and Means, *Implementation of the United States-Bahrain*, 2005, Bernsen, 42–43; U.S. Congress, Senate Finance, *United States-Bahrain*, 2005, Hamod, 17.
32. U.S. Congress, Senate Finance, *United States-Oman*, 2006, Hamod, 17.
33. Gamble, *NFTC*, 105.
34. Bolle, *Middle East Trade Initiatives*, 2.
35. Remarks in Cairo, June 4, 2009, https://www.presidency.ucsb.edu/documents/remarks-cairo.
36. Remarks in Miami, Florida, October 12, 2007, https://www.presidency.ucsb.edu/documents/remarks-miami-florida-6; Address Before a Joint Session, January 28, 2008, https://www.presidency.ucsb.edu/documents/address-before-joint-session-the-congress-the-state-the-union-18.
37. Remarks Following a Cabinet Meeting, April 14, 2008, https://www.presidency.ucsb.edu/documents/remarks-following-cabinet-meeting-14.
38. The United States and the European Union Initiative, June 20, 2005, https://www.presidency.ucsb.edu/documents/the-united-states-and-the-european-union-initiative-enhance-transatlantic-economic; The President's News Conference, January 13, 2006, https://www.presidency.ucsb.edu/documents/the-presidents-news-conference-with-chancellor-angela-merkel-germany-0; Framework, April 30, 2007, https://www.presidency.ucsb.edu/documents/framework-for-advancing-transatlantic-economic-integration-between-the-united-states.
39. Elsig and Dupont, "Persistent Deadlock in Multilateral Trade Negotiations," 588–603.
40. Irwin, *Clashing over Commerce*, 682.
41. Remarks in New York City, September 17, 2007, https://www.presidency.ucsb.edu/documents/remarks-new-york-city-our-common-stake-americas-prosperity.
42. Remarks in Janesville, Wisconsin," February 13, 2008, https://www.presidency.ucsb.edu/documents/remarks-janesville-wisconsin-keeping-americas-promise.
43. Remarks to the Cuban American National Foundation, May 23, 2008, https://www.presidency.ucsb.edu/documents/remarks-the-cuban-american-national-foundation-miami-florida; Remarks to the AFL-CIO, April 2, 2008, https://www.presidency.ucsb.edu/documents/remarks-the-afl-cio-philadelphia.
44. Message to the Congress, October 3, 2011, https://www.presidency.ucsb.edu/documents/message-the-congress-transmitting-legislation-implement-the-united-states-panama-trade. See also Irwin, *Clashing over Commerce*, 684; Hornbeck, *Trade Adjustment Assistance*, 12–15.
45. The President's News Conference, October 13, 2011, https://www.presidency.ucsb.edu/documents/the-presidents-news-conference-with-president-lee-myung-bak-south-korea.
46. U.S. Congress, House Foreign Affairs, *Colombia and Panama Free Trade Agreements*, 2011, Mack, 31. See also U.S. Congress, House Ways and Means, *Pending Free Trade Agreements with Colombia, Panama, and South Korea*, 2011, Dave Camp and Sander Levin, 4–7; U.S. Congress, Senate Finance, *U.S.-Colombia Trade Promotion*, 2011, Baucus, 1–3.
47. Remarks Following a Meeting, April 7, 2011, https://www.presidency.ucsb.edu/documents/remarks-following-meeting-with-president-juan-manuel-santos-calderon-colombia. See also Villereal and Garcia, *U.S.-Colombia Free Trade Agreement*, 18–25.
48. Interview with Charles Gibson, February 3, 2009, https://www.presidency.ucsb.edu/documents/interview-with-charles-gibson-abc-news.
49. Fact Sheet, March 10, 2020, https://www.presidency.ucsb.edu/documents/fact-sheet-president-obama-details-administration-efforts-support-two-million-new-jobs.
50. Remarks Following a Meeting, March 14, 2009, https://www.presidency.ucsb.edu/documents/remarks-following-meeting-with-president-luiz-inacio-lula-da-silva-brazil-and-exchange.
51. The President's News Conference, April 2, 2009, https://www.presidency.ucsb.edu/documents/the-presidents-news-conference-london.

52. Statement on the Progress, November 10, 2011, https://www.presidency.ucsb.edu/documents/statement-the-progress-russias-world-trade-organization-accession-talks.
53. Interview with Gerald Seib, April 27, 2015, https://www.presidency.ucsb.edu/documents/interview-with-gerald-seib-the-wall-street-journal.
54. The President's News Conference, November 8, 2010, https://www.presidency.ucsb.edu/documents/the-presidents-news-conference-with-prime-minister-manmohan-singh-india-new-delhi.
55. Williams, *Trans-Pacific Partnership (TPP) Countries*, 1–7.
56. Gamble, *NFTC*, 114; Irwin, *Clashing over Commerce*, 684–685; U.S. Congress, House Ways and Means, *Trans-Pacific Partnership*, 2011, Walmart, 40–43; Letter from Kentucky tobacco legislators, 72–73; U.S. Congress, House Foreign Affairs, *Trans-Pacific Partnership Agreement*, 2012, Susan Schwab, former USTR, 13; AFL-CIO, 27.
57. Remarks at an Asia-Pacific Economic Cooperation CEO Summit, November 12, 2011, https://www.presidency.ucsb.edu/documents/remarks-asia-pacific-economic-cooperation-ceo-summit-question-and-answer-session-honolulu. See also Remarks During a Meeting, September 16, 2010, https://www.presidency.ucsb.edu/documents/remarks-during-meeting-with-the-presidents-export-council; Movroidis and Sapir, *China and the WTO*, 14–54.
58. The President's News Conference, January 19, 2011, https://www.presidency.ucsb.edu/documents/the-presidents-news-conference-with-president-hu-jintao-china; Cohen, *America's Response to China*, 290.
59. Presidential Debate, October 22, 2012, https://www.presidency.ucsb.edu/documents/presidential-debate-boca-raton-florida.
60. Press Briefing, November 11, 2014, https://www.presidency.ucsb.edu/documents/press-briefing-press-secretary-josh-earnest-deputy-national-security-advisor-for-2. See also Remarks Following a Meeting, June 7, 2013, https://www.presidency.ucsb.edu/documents/remarks-following-meeting-with-president-xi-jinping-china-and-exchange-with-reporters.
61. U.S. Congress, House Foreign Affairs, *Trans-Pacific Partnership*, 2015, Salmon, 2, AIE, 14.
62. U.S. Congress, House Foreign Affairs, *Trans-Pacific Partnership*, 22.
63. The President's News Conference, August 2, 2016, https://www.presidency.ucsb.edu/documents/the-presidents-news-conference-with-prime-minister-lee-hsien-loong-singapore.
64. The President's News Conference, April 28, 2015, https://www.presidency.ucsb.edu/documents/the-presidents-news-conference-with-prime-minister-shinzo-abe-japan-0.
65. Remarks Prior to a Meeting, January 19, 2016, https://www.presidency.ucsb.edu/documents/remarks-prior-meeting-with-prime-minister-malcolm-b-turnbull-australia.
66. Ash Carter Remarks on the Next Phase of the U.S. Rebalance to the Asia-Pacific, April 6, 2015, https://www.defense.gov/Newsroom/Speeches/Speech/Article/606660/remarks-on-the-next-phase-of-the-us-rebalance-to-the-asia-pacific-mccain-instit/.
67. Remarks to the National Governors Association, February 22, 2016, https://www.presidency.ucsb.edu/documents/remarks-the-national-governors-association-and-question-and-answer-session.
68. Remarks During a Meeting, November 13, 2015, https://www.presidency.ucsb.edu/documents/remarks-during-meeting-with-national-security-leaders-the-trans-pacific-partnership.
69. Remarks at the Association of Southeast Asian Nations Business and Investment Summit, November 21, 2015, https://www.presidency.ucsb.edu/documents/remarks-the-association-southeast-asian-nations-business-and-investment-summit-kuala.
70. Remarks at the Association of Southeast Asian Nations Business and Investment Summit, November 21, 2015, https://www.presidency.ucsb.edu/documents/remarks-the-association-southeast-asian-nations-business-and-investment-summit-kuala.
71. Irwin, *Clashing over Commerce*, 685; Gamble, *NFTC*, 107; Statement on House of Representatives Action, June 12, 2015, https://www.presidency.ucsb.edu/documents/statement-house-representatives-action-trade-promotion-authority-and-trade-adjustment.
72. Schnepf, *WTO Doha Round*, 2–13.
73. Fact Sheet, August 4, 2014, https://www.presidency.ucsb.edu/documents/fact-sheet-investing-african-trade-for-our-common-future; State of the Union, January 12, 2016,

https://www.presidency.ucsb.edu/documents/address-before-joint-session-the-congress-the-state-the-union-19.

74. State of the Union, February 12, 2013, https://www.presidency.ucsb.edu/documents/address-before-joint-session-congress-the-state-the-union-2.
75. Remarks with Cameron, Barroso, and Van Rompuy, June 17, 2013, https://www.presidency.ucsb.edu/documents/remarks-with-prime-minister-david-cameron-the-united-kingdom-president-jose-manuel-durao.
76. The President's News Conference, June 19, 2013, https://www.presidency.ucsb.edu/documents/the-presidents-news-conference-with-chancellor-angela-merkel-germany-berlin-germany-0.
77. U.S. Congress, Senate Finance, *Transatlantic Trade and Investment Partnership*, 2013, National Chicken Council, 11.
78. Akhtar and Jones, *Transatlantic Trade and Investment Partnership Negotiations*, 1–4; The President's News Conference, March 26, 2014, https://www.presidency.ucsb.edu/documents/the-presidents-news-conference-with-president-herman-van-rompuy-the-european-council-and.
79. Akhtar and Jones, *Transatlantic Trade and Investment Partnership Negotiations*, 5.
80. Remarks by Senior Administration Officials, February 4, 2015, https://www.presidency.ucsb.edu/documents/remarks-senior-administration-officials-conference-call-the-vice-presidents-trip-belgium.
81. Remarks Prior to a Meeting, March 9, 2015, https://www.presidency.ucsb.edu/documents/remarks-prior-meeting-with-president-donald-f-tusk-the-european-council-and-exchange-with.
82. U.S. Congress, House Ways and Means, *U.S.-EU Trade and Investment Partnership*, 2013, Eizenstadt, 13.
83. Remarks Following a Meeting, July 10, 2016, https://www.presidency.ucsb.edu/documents/remarks-following-meeting-with-prime-minister-mariano-rajoy-brey-spain-and-exchange-with. See also Akhtar and Jones, *Transatlantic Trade and Investment Partnership: In Brief*, 1–2; Remarks Following a Meeting, July 8, 2016, https://www.presidency.ucsb.edu/documents/remarks-following-meeting-with-president-donald-franciszek-tusk-the-european-council-and.
84. Commencement Address, May 15, 2016, https://www.presidency.ucsb.edu/documents/commencement-address-rutgers-university-new-brunswick-piscataway-new-jersey, accessed April 21, 2020.
85. European Commission, The Transatlantic Trade and Investment Partnership (TTIP), https://ec.europa.eu/trade/policy/in-focus/ttip/index_en.htm. See also Irwin, *Clashing over Commerce*, 686.
86. Irwin, *Clashing over Commerce*, 686–687.
87. Remarks on Foreign Policy, April 27, 2016, https://www.presidency.ucsb.edu/documents/remarks-foreign-policy. Neo-liberalism should have been Trump's lodestar, but he did not hold conservative values. See Slobodian, *Globalists*.
88. Trade for Peace Through WTO Accession, July 4, 2019, WTO Publications News Archives, https://www.wto.org/english/thewto_e/acc_e/tradeforpeace_e.htm.
89. DDG Wolff: Acceding Countries, October 9, 2019, WTO Publications News Archives, https://www.wto.org/english/news_e/news19_e/ddgaw_09oct19_e.htm.
90. Wolff: "There Is a Proven Correlation Between Peace and Open Trade," November 13, 2019, WTO Publications News Archives, https://www.wto.org/english/news_e/news19_e/ddgaw_13nov19_e.htm.
91. Wolff: Trade and Foreign Policy, February 5, 2018, WTO Publications News Archives, https://www.wto.org/english/news_e/news18_e/ddgra_09feb18_e.htm.
92. Friedberg, "An Answer to Aggression," 158–159, 163.
93. Lind and Press, "Reality Check," 41, 47; Krasner, "Learning to Live with Despots," 49.
94. Chuck Grassley, "Trump's Tariffs End or His Trade Deal Dies," *Wall Street Journal*, April 29, 2019, A15.
95. Wertheim, "The Price of Primacy," 20, 27; Allison, "The New Spheres of Influence," 34.

96. U.S. Congress, Senate Finance, *2019 Trade Policy Agenda*, Lighthizer, 1–5. See also Lighthizer, "How to Make Trade Work for Workers," 84–92.
97. Memorandum on Withdrawal, January 23, 2017, https://www.presidency.ucsb.edu/documents/memorandum-withdrawal-the-united-states-from-the-trans-pacific-partnership-negotiations.
98. U.S. Congress, House Ways and Means, *Opportunities to Expand*, 2017, CSIS, 7–8.
99. Kevin Freking, "Trump Has Long Seen Previous U.S. Trade Agreements as Losers," *Valley News*, May 12, 2019, 1. See also Gewirtz, "China Thinks America Is Losing," 66.
100. U.S. Congress, House Foreign Affairs, *China's Predatory Trade and Investment Strategy*, 2018, Cong. Brad Sherman, 8.
101. Morrison, *China-U.S. Trade Issues*, April 16, 2018, 2–3, and July 30, 2018, 1, 57–58; Chad P. Bown and Melina Kolb, "Trump's Trade War Timeline," March 13, 2020, https://www.piie.com/blogs/trade-investment-policy-watch/trump-trade-war-china-date-guide?gclid=CjwKCAjw-YT1BRAFEiwAd2WRtjmKXj4UNdAML8M886dNSdICmr05VObbfTG__u9O_2RLC-dHgy4A7hoCMxMQAvD_BwE?gclid=CjwKCAjw-YT1BRAFEiwAd2WRtjmKXj4UNdAML8M886dNSdICmr05VObbfTG__u9O_2RLC-dHgy4A7hoCMxMQAvD_BwE; Rajesh Kumar Singh, "Trump's Tariffs Add to Pandemic-induced Turmoil of U.S. Manufacturers, *Reuters Business News* (April 30, 2020), https://www.reuters.com/article/us-health-coronavirus-tariffs-idUSKBN22C1MY.
102. Liz Alderman and Ana Swanson, "Europe Can Start Taxing $4 Billion in U.S. Goods in a Trans-Atlantic Trade War," *New York Times*, October 26, 2020, https://www.nytimes.com/live/2020/10/26/business/economy-us-coronavirus?action=click&module=Top%20Stories&pgtype=Homepage#europe-can-start-taxing-4-billion-in-us-goods-in-a-trans-atlantic-trade-war.
103. Remarks at the American Farm Bureau Federation Annual Convention, January 19, 2020, https://www.presidency.ucsb.edu/documents/remarks-the-american-farm-bureau-federation-annual-convention-and-trade-show-austin-texas.
104. Antony J. Blinken, A Foreign Policy for the American People, March 3, 2021, https://www.state.gov/a-foreign-policy-for-the-american-people/.

Conclusion

1. Cooley and Nexon, "The Real Crisis of Global Order," 103.
2. Ikenberry, "Next Liberal Order," 137–139, 141–142.

BIBLIOGRAPHY

Archives

Carl Albert Center Archives, University of Oklahoma, Norman, Oklahoma
Carl Albert Collection
Page Belcher Collection
Fred Harris Collection
American Heritage Center, University of Wyoming, Laramie, Wyoming
Joseph C. O'Mahoney Papers
Bank of England, Archive Section, London, England
ADM 14: L.P. Thompson-McCausland Papers
GI: Governors Files
Bentley Historical Library, University of Michigan, Ann Arbor, Michigan
Arthur H. Vandenberg Papers (microfilm)
George H.W. Bush Presidential Library, College Station, Texas
National Security Council
Charles A. Gillespie Files
Walter H. Kansteiner Files
Earl A. Wayne Files
Philip D. Zelikow Files
Office of Vice President George Bush, Subject Files, Subseries Trade Agreements [TA]
White House Office of Cabinet Affairs
Cooper Evans Files
White House Office of Media Affairs
Paul McNeill Files
White House Office of Policy Development
Stephan Farrar Files
White House Office of Political Affairs
Ron Kaufman Files
White House Office of Records Management
White House Press Office
Marlin Fitzwater Files, Subseries: Subject Files: Alpha Files
Stephen Hart Files
Laura Melillo Files
Judy Smith Files
White House Office of Speechwriting
Carol Aarhus Files, Alpha Files

Tony Snow Files, Subject Files
Jimmy Carter Library, Atlanta, Georgia
Jimmy Carter Papers—Pre-Presidential
1976 Presidential Campaign
Stuart Eizenstat Subject Files
Noel Sterret Foreign Clippings
Records for the President's Commission for a National Agenda for the Eighties
Communications
Gerald Rafshoon
National Security Advisor: Brzezinski Material: Schechter/Friendly Files
Speechwriter's Office: Acsah Nesmith's Subject Files
Staff Office: Council of Economic Advisors
Charles L. Schultze's Subject Files
International Financial and Economic Development Files
Office of Anne Wexler
Jane Wales Subject Files
White House Press Office
Media Liaison Office Files
Jim Purk's Subject Files
Zbigniew Brzezinski Collection
William J. Clinton Library, Little Rock, Arkansas
China Permanent Trade Status, 1993–2001, 2010-1026-F
Clinton Digital Library https://clinton.presidentiallibraries.us
National Security Council and Executive Secretary
National Security, Speechwriting Office, Antony Blinken Collection
Office of Press and Communications, Philip "P.J." Crowley
Domestic Policy Council
2012-0259-F: Ira Magaziner
National Economic Council
2010-1024-F: China, WTO
2014-1039-F: Sperling, Gene: Jiang Zemin and Trade Issues 1999
National Security Council Records
2009-0013-F: Asia Pacific Economic Cooperation (APEC) 2000
2014-1037-F: China and MFN
2017-0398-F: Free Trade Area of the Americas (FTAA)
White House Staff and Office Collections, Office of Communications
Office of Speechwriting: Jeff Shesol
White House Office of Records Management
Alpha Files: Laura D. Tyson
Subject Files, General
2014-1062-F: 1996 Bilateral Trade Agreement with Vietnam
2013-0306-F: American Federation of Labor/Congress Industrial Organizations
Cornell University Library, Division of Rare and Manuscript Collections, Ithaca, New York
Daniel A. Reed Papers
Dartmouth College, Rauner Special Collections Library, Hanover, New Hampshire
Sinclair Weeks Papers
Robert J. Dole Institute of Politics, University of Kansas, Lawrence, Kansas
Robert and Elizabeth Dole Archive and Special Collections
Digitized Press Releases, 1961–1996
Speeches Collection (Digital), 1958–1996
Dwight D. Eisenhower Library, Abilene, Kansas
Christian A. Herter Papers

Don Paarlberg Records
Joseph Rand Records
Clarence B. Randall Journals
U.S. Council on Foreign Economic Policy Records
CFEP Papers Series
Chairman's Files
Chronological Files
Randall Series
Agency Subseries
Correspondence Subseries
Subject Subseries
Ann C. Whitman Papers
Ann C. Whitman Files, Legislative Meeting Series
White House Central Files
Official Files
Gerald R. Ford Library, Ann Arbor, Michigan
William J. Baroody, Jr. Files
William J. Baroody, Jr. Papers
Arthur F. Burns Papers
Gerald R. Ford
Congressional Papers: Legislative Files
Vice-Presidential Papers
Robert A. Goldwin Papers
Robert T. Hartmann Files
Robert T. Hartmann Papers
Sydney L. Jones Papers
Marvin Kosters Papers
Melvyn R. Laird Papers
David R. MacDonald Papers
Michael Moskow Papers
National Security Council Advisor
Kissinger-Scowcroft West Wing Office Files
International Economic Affairs Staff: Files
Presidential Agency Files
Presidential Subject Files
Trip Briefing Books and Cables of Henry Kissinger
Trip Briefing Books and Cables of President Ford
Trip Cables of Brent Scowcroft
Ron Nessen Papers
Patrick O'Donnell and Joseph Jenckes Files
L. William Seidman Files
William E. Simon Papers (microfiche)
United States-China Business Council
U.S. Council of Economic Advisors: Records
U.S. National Security Council
Institutional Files
University of Michigan: Law School: Student Case Files of Gerald Ford
White House Central Files
GATT Digital Library 1947–1994, General Agreement on Tariffs and Trade, https://exhibits.stanford.edu/gatt, Stanford University Libraries, California
Hagley Museum and Library, Wilmington, Delaware
National Association of Manufacturers Records
National Foreign Trade Council Records

Philip D. Reed Papers
Chamber of Commerce of the United States Records
Hendrix College, Conway, Arkansas
  Wilbur D. Mills Archive
Herbert Hoover Presidential Library, West Branch, Iowa
Edward Dana Durand Papers
Bourke B. Hickenlooper Papers
Presidential Personal Files
Presidential Subject Files
Hugh R. Wilson Papers
Hoover Institution, Library and Archives, Stanford University, Stanford, California
  Atlantic Council of the United States Records
  Henry F. Grady Typescript (1953)
  F. A. Harper Papers
  Mont Pelerin Society Records
  Trans-Atlantic Conference on East-West Trade Records
Howard-Tilton Memorial Library, Tulane University, New Orleans, Louisiana
  Hale Boggs Papers
Lyndon B. Johnson Library, Austin, Texas
  Administrative History: Department of State
George W. Ball Papers
  Francis M. Bator Papers
  Cabinet Papers
  Clark M. Clifford Papers
  Frederick L. Deming Papers
  Democratic National Committee
  Edward R. Fried Files
  Meetings Notes Files
  National Security Files
Francis Bator Files
McGeorge Bundy Files
Committee Files
Robert Komer Files
Name Files
National Security Action Memorandums
National Security Council Meetings Files
Walt W. Rostow Files
Subject Files
  Bernard Norwood Papers
  Drew Pearson Papers
  William Roth Papers
  Senate Files
  Anthony Solomon Personal Papers
  Task Force Reports
  White House Aides, Office Files
    Advertising Council
    Ceil Bellinger
    Joseph Califano
    James C. Gaither
    Robert N. Goodwin
    Lawrence E. Levinson
    Bill Moyers
    William R. Sparks

Henry Hall Wilson
White House Central Files
Confidential Files
White House Press Office Files
John F. Kennedy Library, Boston, Massachusetts
George Ball Personal Papers
Jack Behrman
Abram Chayes
Harlan Cleveland
C. Douglas Dillon
Myer Feldman
Personal Papers
Staff Files
Lincoln Gordon
Papers of John F. Kennedy
Pre-Presidential Papers
Presidential Campaign Files, 1960: Speeches and the Press (digital), https://www.jfklibrary.org/Asset-Viewer/Archives/JFKCAMP1960-1029-028.aspx
Senate Files: Holburn
Presidential Files
National Security Files
Departments and Agencies
Carl Kaysen
Subjects
White House Central Files: Subject Files
Howard C. Petersen
Arthur M. Schlesinger
Library of Congress, Washington, DC
Carl Ackerman
Joseph/Stewart Alsop
Atlantic Union Committee
Ray Stannard Baker
William Borah
Edward W. Brooke
Vannevar Bush
Emanuel Celler
Edward Clark
Clarence Darrow
Russell W. Davenport
E. G. Draper
Stuart Eizenstadt
W. Averell Harriman
Cordell Hull (microfilm)
Philip C. Jessup
Dudley Wright Knox
James Landis
League of Women Voters
Sol Linowitz
Clare Booth Luce
Henry Luce
Lewis Machen
Mary McGrory
Robert S. McNamara

Patsy T. Mink
Daniel Patrick Moynihan
National Council of Jewish Women
Paul H. Nitze
Key Pittman
Abraham Ribicoff
Peter Rodman
Donald Rumsfeld
Charles E. Russell
St. George L. Sieussat
James Simmons
Clarence Streit
Arthur Sweetser
Charles P. Taft
Robert A. Taft, Sr.
Russell Train
Irita Taylor Van Doren
Louisiana State University, Baton Rouge, Louisiana
Russell B. Long Papers
Massachusetts Historical Society, Boston, Massachusetts
Leverett Saltonstall Papers
George Meany Memorial AFL-CIO Archives, University Libraries, University of Maryland, College Park, Maryland
AFL-CIO, Department of Legislation
Middle Tennessee State University, Albert Gore Research Center, Murfreesboro, Tennessee
Albert Gore, Sr. Senate Papers
Modern Records Centre, University of Warwick, Coventry, Great Britain
Trade Unions Congress Archives
MSS 200/F: Federation of British Industries
MSS 221: Empires Industries Association
MSS 292: Trade Unions Congress
Mont Pelerin Society. https://www.montpelerin.org/
Museum of American Textile History, North Andover, Massachusetts
American Cotton Manufacturers Institute, MS 73/327
National Archives and Records Administration of the United States, College Park, Maryland
Record Group 43: Records of International Conferences, Commissions, and Expositions
International Trade Files
Record Group 59: General Records of the Department of State
Decimal Files
Office of Public Affairs
Record Group 151: Records of the Bureau of Foreign and Domestic Commerce
Bureau of International Operations
Record Group 273: National Security Council
Record Group 306: United States Information Agency
Record Group 489: Records of the International Trade Administration
Bureau of International Commerce
Office of International Regional Economics, Director's Office
National Council of Churches (digital) collection, https://nationalcouncilofchurches.us/
National Opinion Research Center, University of Chicago, Chicago, Illinois
Nebraska State Historical Society, Lincoln, Nebraska
Carl T. Curtis Papers

Richard M. Nixon Library, Yorba Linda, California
H. R. Haldeman Papers
National Security Council Files
Henry A. Kissinger Office Files
Country Files
HAK Trip Files
Subject Files
President's Personal Files: President's Handwriting Files
White House Central Files
Staff Member and Office Files
Patrick J. Buchanan
Arthur Burns
Council of Economic Advisors: Office Files
Hendrik S. Houthakker
Herbert Stein
Marina v. N. Whitman
John. D. Ehrlichman
Peter M. Flanigan
H. R. Haldeman
Paul W. McCracken
Staff Secretary: Memoranda Files
Gordon C. Strachan
Subject Files
(F9) Finance
(TA) Trade
Ohio Historical Society, Columbus, Ohio
John M. Vorys Papers
Parliamentary Archives, London, England
The Beaverbrook Papers
F-Campaign, Propaganda and Speeches
The Lloyd George Papers
G/26-Correspondence between Lloyd-George and Gareth Jones
The Henry Graham White Papers
WHI-Personal/Political Papers
Princeton University, Seeley Mudd Library, Princeton, New Jersey
George W. Ball Papers
Council on Foreign Relations Records
Public Policy Papers
Studies Department, Subseries 3B: Records of Groups
John Foster Dulles Papers
Adlai E. Stevenson Papers
Jacob Viner Papers
Ronald Reagan Library, Simi Valley, California
Roger Bolton Files
Geoffrey O. Carliner Files
William P. Clark Files
Stephen I. Danzansky Files
Executive Secretariat, National Security Council
Meeting Files
Trip Files
Jerry L. Jordan Files
Douglas W. McMinn Files
Thomas G. Moore Files

Nancy J. Risque Files
Beryl W. Sprinkel Files
Charles P. Tyson Files
White House Office of Speechwriting: Research Office
Rockefeller Archives Center, Sleepy Hollow, New York
RG 54, Nelson A. Rockefeller Papers
RG Projects, Nelson A. Rockefeller Personal Papers
Rockefeller Gubernatorial Papers
Series L, Record Groups
Trilateral Commission Collection
Franklin D. Roosevelt Library, Hyde Park, New York
Louis H. Bean Papers
Adolf A. Berle Papers
Oscar Cox Papers
Ernest Cuneo Papers
Democratic Party: National Committee Papers
Mordecail Ezekiel Papers
Harry L. Hopkins Papers
Joseph Lash Papers
Gardner C. Means Papers
Henry Morgenthau, Jr. Papers
Peter H. Odegard Papers
Franklin D. Roosevelt
Family, Business, and Personal Papers:
Writing and Statement Files
President's Official Files
President's Personal Files
President's Secretary's Files
http://www.fdrlibrary.marist.edu/archives/collections/franklin/?p=collections/finding aid&id=502
Series II: Confidential Files
Series III: Diplomatic Correspondence
Series V: Subject Files
James Roosevelt Papers
Whitney Hart Shepardson Papers
Rexford G. Tugwell Diary
Rexford G. Tugwell Papers
Sumner Welles Papers
Claude R. Wickard Papers
John Cooper Wiley Papers
John G. Winant Papers
SUNY Stony Brook Library, Special Collections, Stony Brook, New York
Jacob K. Javits Papers
Harry S Truman Library, Independence, Missouri
Dean Acheson Papers
Eben A. Ayers Papers
Charles F. Brannan Papers
Honore M. Catudel Papers
Will L. Clayton Papers
Clark M. Clifford Files
Clark M. Clifford Papers
Cooperative League of the United States of America Records
Joseph D. Coppock Papers

Lynn R. Edminister Papers
George M. Elsey Papers
Ellen Clayton Garwood Papers
Henry F. Grady Papers
Gordon Gray Files
Dallas C. Halverstadt Papers
Robert E. Hannegan Papers
Paul G. Hoffman Papers
Milton Katz Papers
Leon H. Keyserling Papers
David D. Lloyd Papers
Robert McNaughton Papers
Charles S. Murphy Files
Philleo Nash Papers
George Neal Papers
Edwin G. Nourse Papers
Arthur Paul Papers
Edwin W. Pauley Papers
Paul A. Porter Papers
Robert Rhodes Papers
Melbourne Spector Papers
Staff Member and Office Files
Rose A. Conway Files
Harry S Truman Papers
Family, Business, and Personal Affairs
Post-Presidential Papers
President's Secretary's Files
Senator Vice-President: Correspondence Files
Senator Vice-President: Speech Files
White House Central Files
Confidential Files
Official Files
President's Personal Files
Syracuse University, Special Collections Research Center, Syracuse, New York
Ralph E. Flanders Papers
University of Arizona, Special Collections, Tucson, Arizona
Stewart L. Udall Papers
University of Chicago Library, Chicago, Illinois
Paul H. Douglas Papers
National Opinion Research Center
University of Colorado Boulder Libraries, Boulder, Colorado
Gordon L. Allott Papers, Series III
University of Connecticut, Historical Manuscripts and Archives, Storrs, Connecticut
Prescott Bush Papers
World Trade Organization: News Publications Archives, https://www.wto.org/english/news_e/archive_e/publ_arc_e.htm

Published Primary Sources

* Unless otherwise noted, all Internet sources were accessed September 1, 2021.

American Presidency Project, http://www.presidency.ucsb.edu/

Bonior, David. Democratic Whip David Bonior on NAFTA. November 17, 1993. C-Span. https://www.cspan.org/video/?c4541434/user-clip-democratic-whip-david-bonior-nafta

Gephardt, Richard. The New Internationalism: The Nexus Between American National Interests and Globalism. Economic Strategy Institute. May 5, 1998. http://www.econstrat.org/images/ESI_Research_Reports_PDF/the%20new%20internationalism%20-%20the%20nexus%20between%20american%20national%20interests%20and%20globalism%20(richard%20a.%20gephardt).pdf.

Government Publications

Akhtar, Shayerah Ilias and Vivian C. Jones. *Transatlantic Trade and Investment Partnership (TTIP) Negotiations*. Washington, DC: Congressional Research Service Report for Congress. February 14, 2014.

Akhtar, Shayerah Ilias and Vivian C. Jones. *Transatlantic Trade and Investment Partnership (TTIP): In Brief*. Washington, DC: Congressional Research Service Report for Congress. June 11, 2014.

Bolle, Mary Jane. *Middle East Trade Initiatives: S. 1121/H.R. 2267 and the Administration's Plan*. Washington, DC: Congressional Research Service Report for Congress. April 26, 2004.

Cooper, William H. et al., *H.R. 3: The Omnibus Trade and Competitiveness Act of 1988: An Analysis of the Major Trade Provisions*. Washington, DC: Congressional Research Service Report for Congress. May 24, 1988.

Foreign Relations of the United States. Washington, DC: U.S. Government Printing Office, 1933–1980.

Hornbeck, J. F. *The Dominican-Central America-United States Trade Agreement (CAFTA DR): Developments in Trade and Investment*. Washington, DC: Congressional Research Service. April 9, 2012.

Hornbeck. J. F. *Trade Adjustment Assistance (TAA) and Its Role in U.S. Trade Policy*. Washington, DC: Congressional Research Service. August 5, 2013.

Morrison, Wayne M. *China-U.S. Trade Issues*. Washington, DC: Congressional Research Service. April 16, 2018.

Morrison, Wayne M. *China-U.S. Trade Issues*. Washington, DC: Congressional Research Service. July 30, 2018.

Movroidis, Petros C. and Andre Sapir. *China and the WTO: Why Multilateralism Still Matters* Princeton, NJ: Princeton University Press, 2021.

Schnepf, Randy. *WTO Doha Round: Implications for U.S. Agriculture*. Washington, DC: Congressional Research Service Report for Congress. April 20, 2015.

Villereal, M. Angeles and Edward Y. Garcia. *The U.S.-Colombia Free Trade Agreement: Background and Issues*. Washington, DC: Congressional Research Service Report for Congress. March 28, 2018.

Williams, Brock R. *Trans-Pacific Partnership (TPP) Countries: Comparative Trade and Economic Analysis*. Washington, DC: Congressional Research Service Report for Congress. June 10, 2013.

Congressional Hearings (listed chronologically)

U.S. Congress. Committee on Ways and Means, House of Representatives. *Reciprocal Trade Agreements: Hearings before the Committee on Ways and Means, House of Representatives. H.R. 8430*. 73rd Cong., 2d sess., March 8–14, 1934.

U.S. Congress. Committee on Finance, Senate. *Reciprocal Trade Agreements: Hearings before the Committee on Finance, United States Senate. HR. 8687*. 73rd Cong., 2d sess., April–May, 1934.

U.S. Congress. Committee on Ways and Means, House of Representatives. *Extending Reciprocal Foreign Trade Agreement Act: Hearings before the Committee on Ways and Means, House of Representatives. H.J. Res. 96*. 75th Congress, 1st sess., January 21–26, 1937.

U.S. Congress. Committee on Finance, Senate. *Extending Reciprocal Foreign Trade Agreement Act: Hearings before the Committee on Finance, United States Senate. H.J. Res. 96.* 75th Congress, 1st sess., February 10–15, 1937.

U.S. Congress. Committee on Ways and Means, House of Representatives. *Extension of Reciprocal Trade Agreements Act: Hearings before the Committee on Ways and Means, House of Representatives. H.J. Res. 407.* 76th Congress, 3rd sess., January 11–19, 1940.

U.S. Congress. Committee on Finance, Senate. *Extension of Reciprocal Trade Agreements Act: Hearings before the Committee on Finance, Senate. H.J. Res. 407.* 76th Congress, 3rd sess., February 26-29, March 1–6, 1940.

U.S. Congress. Committee on Ways and Means, House of Representatives. *Extension of Reciprocal Trade Agreement Act: Hearings before the Committee on Ways and Means, House of Representatives. H.J. Res. 111.* 78th Congress, 1st sess., April 12–23, 1943.

U.S. Congress. Committee on Finance, Senate. *Extension of Reciprocal Trade Agreements Act: Hearings before the Committee on Finance, Senate. H.J. Res. 111.* 78th Congress, 1st sess., May 17–22, 1943.

U.S. Congress. Committee on Ways and Means, House of Representatives. *1945 Extension of Reciprocal Trade Agreement Act: Hearings before the Committee on Ways and Means, House of Representatives. H.J. Res. 3240.* 79th Congress, 1st sess., April 18–30, May 1–14, 1945.

U.S. Congress. Committee on Finance, Senate. *1945 Extension of Reciprocal Trade Agreements Act: Hearings before the Committee on Finance, Senate. H.J. Res. 3240.* 79th Congress, 1st sess., May 30–31, June 1–5, 1945.

U.S. Congress. Committee on Finance, Senate. *Extending Authority to Negotiate Trade Agreements: Hearings before the Committee on Finance, Senate. H.R. 6566.* 80th Congress, 2nd sess., June 1–5, 1948.

U.S. Congress. Committee on Ways and Means, House of Representatives. *1949 Extension of Reciprocal Trade Agreement Act: Hearings before the Committee on Ways and Means, House of Representatives. H.R. 1211.* 81st Congress, 1st sess., January 24–31, February 1, 1949.

U.S. Congress. Committee on Finance, Senate. *Extension of the Reciprocal Trade Agreements: Hearings before the Committee on Finance, Senate. H.R. 3240.* 80th Congress, 2nd sess., June 1–5, 1948.

U.S. Congress. Committee on Foreign Affairs, House of Representatives. *Membership and Participation by the United States in the International Trade Organization: Hearings before the Committee on Foreign Affairs, H.J. Res. 236.* 81st Cong., 2nd sess., April 19–27, May 1–12, 1950.

U.S. Congress. Committee on Ways and Means, House of Representatives. *Extension of Reciprocal Trade Agreement Act: Hearings before the Committee on Ways and Means, House of Representatives. H.R. 1612.* 82nd Congress, 1st sess., January 22–26, 1951.

U.S. Congress. Committee on Finance, Senate. *Trade Agreements Extension Act of 1951: Hearings before the Committee on Finance, Senate. H.R. 1612.* 82nd Congress, 1st sess., February 22–28, March 1–13, 1951.

U.S. Congress. Committee on Ways and Means, House of Representatives. *Trade Agreements Extension Act of 1953: Hearings before the Committee on Ways and Means, House of Representatives. H.R. 4294.* 83rd Congress, 1st sess., April 27–30, May 1–19, 1953.

U.S. Congress. Committee on Finance, Senate. *Trade Agreements Extension Act of 1953: Hearings before the Committee on Finance, Senate, Executive Session. H.R. 1612.* 82nd Congress, 1st sess., June 24, 1953.

U.S. Congress. Committee on Ways and Means, House of Representatives. *Trade Agreements Extension: Hearings before the Committee on Ways and Means, House of Representatives. H.R. 1.* 84th Congress, 1st sess., January 7–31, February 1–7, 1955.

U.S. Congress. Committee on Finance, Senate. *Trade Agreements Extension Act: Hearings before the Committee on Finance, Senate, Executive Session. H.R. 1.* 84th Congress, 1st sess., March 2–18, 1955.

U.S. Congress. Joint Committee on the Economic Report. *Subcommittee on Foreign Economic Policy. Foreign Economic Policy, Report of the Joint Committee on the Economic Report. Senate Report No. 1312.* 84th Congress, 2nd sess., January 5, 1956.

U.S. Congress. Committee on Ways and Means, House of Representatives. *Organization for Trade Cooperation: Hearings before the Committee on Ways and Means, House of Representatives. H.R. 5550.* 84th Congress, 2nd sess., March 1–16, 1956.

U.S. Congress. Committee on Ways and Means. *Foreign Trade Policy: Hearings Before the Subcommittee on Foreign Trade Policy of the Committee on Ways and Means. H. Res. 104.* 85th Congress, 1st sess., December 2–18, 1957.

U.S. Congress. Committee on Ways and Means, House of Representatives. *Renewal of Trade Agreements Act: Hearings before the Committee on Ways and Means, House of Representatives.* 85th Congress, 2nd sess., February 17–28, March 3–25, 1958.

U.S. Congress. Committee on Finance, Senate. *Trade Agreements Act Extension: Hearings before the Committee on Finance, Senate, Executive Session.* 85th Congress, 2nd sess., June 20–30, July 1–3, 1958.

U.S. Congress. Committee on Foreign Relations, Senate. *Organization for Cooperation and Development: Hearings before the Committee on Foreign Relations, Senate.* 87th Congress, 1st sess., February 14–15, March 1–6, 1961.

U.S. Congress. Committee on Education and Labor, House of Representatives. *Impact of Imports and Exports on Employment: Hearings before the Subcommittee on the Impact of Imports and Exports on American Employment of the Committee on Education and Labor, House of Representatives.* 87th Congress, 1st sess., Parts I-8, June 1961–January 1962.

U.S. Congress. Joint Economic Committee, House of Representatives. *Foreign Economic Policy: Hearings before the Subcommittee on Foreign Economic Policy, House of Representatives.* 87th Congress, 1st sess., November 1, 1961.

U.S. Congress. Committee on Ways and Means, House of Representatives. *Trade Expansion Act of 1962: Hearings before the Committee on Ways and Means, on HR 11970, House of Representatives.* 85th Congress, 2nd sess., March 12–30, April 2–11, 1962.

U.S. Congress. Committee on Finance, Senate. *Trade Expansion Act of 1962: Hearings before the Committee on Finance, Senate, on HR 11970.* 87th Congress, 2nd sess., July 23–26, 1962.

U.S. Congress. Committee on Ways and Means, House of Representatives. *Foreign Trade and Tariff Proposals: Hearings before the Committee on Ways and Means, on HR 17551, House of Representatives.* 90th Congress, 2nd sess., June 4–July 3, 1968.

U.S. Congress. Committee on Ways and Means, House of Representatives. *Foreign Trade and Tariff Proposals: Hearings before the Committee on Ways and Means, on HR 17551, House of Representatives.* 90th Congress, 2nd sess., June 4–July 3, 1968.

U.S. Congress. Committee on Banking and Currency, Senate. *East-West Trade, Hearings before the Subcommittee on International Finance of the Committee on Banking and Currency, Senate on Senate Joint Resolution 169.* 90th Congress, 2nd sess., June 4–27, July 17–25, 1968.

U.S. Congress. Committee on Finance, Senate. *Trade Act of 1970: Hearings before the Committee on Finance, Senate, on HR 17550.* 91st Congress, 2nd sess., October 9, 12, 1970.

U.S. Congress. Committee on Ways and Means, House of Representatives. *The Trade Reform Act of 1973: Hearings before the Committee on Ways and Means, on HR 6767, House of Representatives.* 93rd Congress, 1st sess., May 9–June 15, 1973.

U.S. Congress. Committee on Finance, Senate. *The Trade Reform Act of 1973: Hearings before the Committee on Finance, Senate, on HR 10710.* 93rd Congress, 2nd sess., March 4–April 10, 1974.

U.S. Congress. Committee on Finance, Senate. *Emigration Amendment to the Trade Reform Act of 1974: Hearing before the Committee on Finance, Senate.* 93rd Congress, 2nd sess., December 8, 1974.

U.S. Congress. Committee on Finance, Senate. *Trade Agreements Act of 1979: Hearing before the Subcommittee on International Trade of the Committee on Finance, Senate.* 96th Congress, 1st sess., July 10–11, 1979.

U.S. Congress. Committee on Finance, Senate. *Oversight Hearings on U.S. Foreign Trade Policy: Hearing before the Committee on Finance, Senate.* 94th Congress, 2nd sess., January 29–February 5, 1976.

U.S. Congress. Committee on Ways and Means, House of Representatives. *Comprehensive Trade Reform Act of 1986: Report together with Dissenting Views of the Committee on Ways and Means, House of Representatives.* 99th Congress, 2nd sess., May 6, 1986.

U.S. Congress. Committee on Foreign Affairs, House of Representatives. *Omnibus Trade and Competitiveness Act of 1988: Hearings before the Subcommittee on International Economic Policy and Trade of the Committee on Foreign Affairs, House of Representatives.* 100th Cong., 1st sess., March 5, 10–12, 1987.

U.S. Congress. Committee on Finance, Senate. *United States-Japan Structural Impediments Initiative (SII): Hearing before the Subcommittee on International Trade of the Committee on Finance, Senate.* 100th Congress, 2nd sess., March 5, 1990.

U.S. Congress. House of Representatives. *Disapproving the Application of "Fast Track" Procedures to Trade Agreement Implementing Bills: Report 102-63, Part 2, Adverse Report. House of Representatives.* 103rd Cong., 1st sess., May 16, 1991.

U.S. Congress. Committee on Ways and Means, House of Representatives. *President's Request for Extension of "Fast Track" Procedures for Uruguay Round Implementation and Possible Administration Requests for Extensions of Expiring Trade Programs: Hearing before the Subcommittee on Trade of the Committee on Ways and Means. House of Representatives.* 103rd Cong., 1st sess., April 27, 1993.

U.S. Congress. Committee on Ways and Means, House of Representatives. *North American Free-Trade Agreement (NAFTA) and Supplemental Agreements to the NAFTA: Hearings before the Committee on Ways and Means and Its Subcommittee on Trade, House of Representatives.* 103rd Cong., 1st sess., September 14–23, 1993.

U.S. Congress. Committee on Finance, Senate. *NAFTA and Related Side Agreements: Hearings before the Committee on Finance, Senate.* 103rd Cong., 1st sess., September 15–28, 1993.

U.S. Congress. Committee on Foreign Affairs, House of Representatives. *NAFTA and American Jobs: Joint Hearings before the Subcommittee on Economic Policy, Trade, and Environment and Western Hemisphere Affairs of the Committee on Foreign Affairs, House of Representatives.* 103rd Cong., 1st sess., October 21, 1993.

U.S. Congress. Committee on Ways and Means, House of Representatives. *Trade Agreements Resulting from the Uruguay Round of Multilateral Trade Negotiations: Hearings before the Committee on Ways and Means and Its Subcommittee on Trade, House of Representatives.* 103rd Cong., 2nd sess., January 26–February 22, 1994.

U.S. Congress. Committee on Ways and Means, House of Representatives. *World Trade Organization: Hearings before the Committee on Ways and Means and Its Subcommittee on Trade, House of Representatives.* 103rd Cong., 2nd sess., June 10, 1994.

U.S. Congress. Committee on Ways and Means, House of Representatives. *Implementation of Uruguay Round Agreements and the World Trade Organization: Hearing before the Subcommittee on Trade of the Committee on Ways and Means, House of Representatives.* 104th Cong., 2nd sess., March 13, 1996.

U.S. Congress. Committee on Ways and Means, House of Representatives. *Accession of China and Taiwan to the World Trade Organization: Hearing before the Subcommittee on Trade of the Committee on Ways and Means. House of Representatives.* 104th Cong., 2nd sess., September 19, 1996.

U.S. Congress. Committee on International Relations, House of Representatives. *Fast Track: On Course or Derailed? Necessary or Not? (Parts II and III: Hearing before the Subcommittee on International Economic Policy and Trade of the Committee on International Relations, House of Representatives.* 105th Cong., 1st sess., September 24 and November 6, 1997.

U.S. Congress. Committee on Finance, Senate. *Managing Global and Regional Trade Policy without Fast Track Negotiating Authority: Hearing before the Subcommittee on International Trade of the Committee on Finance, Senate.* 106th Cong., 1st sess., July 14, 1999.

U.S. Congress. Committee on International Relations, House of Representatives. *Granting Permanent Normal Trade Relations (PNTR) Status to China: Is It in the U.S. National Interest? Hearing before the Committee on International Relations, House of Representatives*. 106th Cong., 2nd sess., May 10, 2000.

U.S. Congress. Committee on Banking and Financial Services, House of Representatives. *Permanent Normal Trade Relations for China (PNTR): Hearing before the Committee on Banking and Financial Services, House of Representatives*. 106th Cong., 2nd sess., May 11, 2000.

U.S. Congress. House of Representatives. *Withdrawing the Approval of the Congress from the Agreement Establishing the World Trade Organization: Report 106-672, Adverse Report together with Additional Views, House of Representatives*. 106th Cong., 2nd sess., June 12, 2000.

U.S. Congress. Committee on Finance, Senate. *Trade Promotion Authority: Hearing before the Committee on Finance, Senate*. 107th Cong., 1st sess., June 20-21, 2001.

U.S. Congress. Committee on Ways and Means, House of Representatives. *Implementation of U.S. Bilateral Free Trade Agreements with Chile and Singapore: Hearing before the Subcommittee on Trade of the Committee on Ways and Means, House of Representatives*. 108th Cong., 1st sess., June 10, 2003.

U.S. Congress. Committee on Judiciary, Senate. *Proposed United States-Chile and United States-Singapore Free Trade Agreements: Hearing before the Committee on the Judiciary, Senate*. 108th Cong., 1st sess., July 14, 2003.

U.S. Congress. Committee on Finance, Senate. *United States-Australia and United States- Morocco Free Trade Agreement: Hearing before the Committee on Finance, Senate*. 108th Cong., 2nd sess., June 15, 2004.

U.S. Congress. Committee on Finance, Senate. *United States-Central America-Dominican Republic Free Trade Agreement: Hearing before the Committee on Finance, Senate*. 109th Cong., 1st sess., April 13, 2005.

U.S. Congress. Committee on Ways and Means, House of Representatives. *Implementation of the Dominican Republic-Central America Free Trade Agreement (DR-CAFTA): Hearing before the Committee on Ways and Means. House of Representatives*. 109th Cong., 1st sess., April 21, 2005.

U.S. Congress. Committee on Energy and Commerce, House of Representatives. *Dominican Republic-Central America Free Trade Agreement: Hearing before the Subcommittee on Commerce, Trade, and Consumer Protection of the Committee on Energy and Commerce, House of Representatives*. 109th Cong., 1st sess., April 28, 2005.

U.S. Congress. House of Representatives. *Withdrawing the Approval of the United States from the Agreement Establishing the World Trade Organization: Report 109-100, Adverse Report together with Additional Views. House of Representatives*. 109th Cong., 1st sess., May 26, 2005.

U.S. Congress. Committee on Ways and Means, House of Representatives. *Implementation of the United States-Bahrain Free Trade Agreement: Hearing before the Committee on Ways and Means. House of Representatives*. 109th Cong., 1st sess., September 29, 2005.

U.S. Congress. Committee on Finance, Senate. *United States-Bahrain Free Trade Agreement: Hearing before the Subcommittee on International Trade of the Committee on Finance, Senate*. 109th Cong., 1st sess., October 6, 2005.

U.S. Congress. U.S.-China Economic and Security Review Commission. *Issues to Be Addressed at the Hong Kong Ministerial Conference of the Doha Round of the World Trade Organization's Trade Expansion Negotiations: Hearing before the U.S.-China Economic and Security Review Commission*. 109th Cong., 1st sess., December 8, 2005.

U.S. Congress. Committee on Finance, Senate. *United States-Oman Free Trade Agreement: Hearing before the Subcommittee on International Trade of the Committee on Finance, Senate*. 109th Cong., 2nd sess., March 6, 2006.

U.S. Congress. Committee on Finance, Senate. *U.S.-Vietnam Trade Relations: Hearing before the Committee on Finance, Senate on S. 3495*. 109th Cong., 2nd sess., July 12, 2006.

U.S. Congress. Committee on Ways and Means, House of Representatives. *The Pending Free Trade Agreements with Colombia, Panama, and South Korea and the Creation of U.S. Jobs: Hearing before the Committee on Ways and Means, House of Representatives*. 112th Cong., 1st sess., January 25, 2011.

U.S. Congress. Committee on Foreign Affairs, House of Representatives. *The Colombia and Panama Free Trade Agreements, National Security and Foreign Policy Priorities: Hearing before the Subcommittee on the Western Hemisphere of the Committee on Foreign Affairs, House of Representatives*. 112th Cong., 1st sess., March 17, 2011.

U.S. Congress. Committee on Finance, Senate. *U.S.-Colombia Trade Promotion Agreement: Hearing before the Committee on Finance, Senate*. 112th Cong., 1st sess., May 11, 2011.

U.S. Congress. Committee on Ways and Means, House of Representatives. *Trans-Pacific Partnership: Hearing before the Subcommittee on Trade of the Committee on Ways and Means*. House of Representatives. 112th Cong., 1st sess., December 14, 2011.

U.S. Congress. Committee on Foreign Affairs, House of Representatives. *The Trans-Pacific Partnership Agreement: Challenges and Potential: Joint Hearing before the Subcommittee on Terrorism, Nonproliferation, and Trade and the Subcommittee on Asia and the Pacific of the Committee on Foreign Affairs, House of Representatives*. 112th Cong., 2nd sess., May 17, 2012.

U.S. Congress. Committee on Ways and Means, House of Representatives. *U.S.-EU Trade and Investment Partnership Negotiations: Hearing before the Subcommittee on Trade of the Committee on Ways and Means, House of Representatives*. 113th Cong., 1st sess., May 16, 2013.

U.S. Congress. Committee on Finance, Senate. *The Transatlantic Trade and Investment Partnership: Achieving the Potential: Hearing before the Committee on Finance, Senate*. 113th Cong., 1st sess., October 30, 2013.

U.S. Congress. Committee on Foreign Affairs, House of Representatives. *The Trans-Pacific Partnership: Prospects for Greater U.S. Trade: Hearing before the Subcommittee on Asia and the Pacific of the Committee on Foreign Affairs, House of Representatives*. 114th Cong., 1st sess., March 4, 2015.

U.S. Congress. Committee on Ways and Means, House of Representatives. *Modernization of the North American Free Trade Agreement (NAFTA): Hearing before the Subcommittee on Trade of the Committee on Ways and Means, House of Representatives*. 115th Cong., 1st sess., July 18, 2017.

U.S. Congress. Committee on Ways and Means, *House of Representatives. Opportunities to Expand U.S. Trade Relationships in the Asia-Pacific Region: Hearing before the Subcommittee on Trade of the Committee on Ways and Means, House of Representatives*. 115th Cong., 1st sess., October 11, 2017.

U.S. Congress. Committee on Foreign Affairs, House of Representatives. *China's Predatory Trade and Investment Strategy: Joint Hearing before the Subcommittee on Terrorism, Nonproliferation, and Trade and the Subcommittee on Asia and the Pacific of the Committee on Foreign Affairs, House of Representatives*. 115th Cong., 2nd sess., July 11, 2018.

U.S. Congress. Committee on Finance, Senate. *The 2019 Trade Policy Agenda/U.S.-Mexico-Canada Agreement: Hearing before the Committee on Finance, Senate*. 116th Cong., 1st sess., June 19, 2019.

Periodicals

American Farm Bureau Federation Official Newsletter
Congressional Quarterly Almanac, 1933–
Department of State Bulletin, 1933–
New York Times, 1930–
Washington Post, 1930–

Secondary Sources

Aaronson, Susan Ariel. *Trade and the American Dream: A Social History of Postwar Trade Policy*. Lexington: University of Kentucky Press, 1996.

Allison, Graham. "The New Spheres of Influence: Sharing the Globe with Other Great Powers." *Foreign Affairs* 99:2 (March–April 2020): 30–40.

Ambrosius, Lloyd. *Woodrow Wilson and American Internationalism*. Cambridge: Cambridge University Press, 2017.

Angell, Norman. *The Great Illusion: A Study of the Relation of Military Power in Nations to Their Economic and Social Advantage*. New York: G. P. Putnam's Sons, 1910.

Alonso, Harriet Hyman. *Peace as a Women's Issue: A History of the U.S. Movement for World Peace and Women's Rights*. Syracuse, NY: Syracuse University Press, 1993.

Barbieri, Katherine. *The Liberal Illusion: Does Trade Promote Peace?* Ann Arbor: University of Michigan Press, 2005.

Barnhart, Michael A. "From Hershey Bars to Motor Cars: America's Economic Policy Toward Japan, 1945–1976." In *Partnership: The United States and Japan, 1951–2001*, ed. Akira Iriye and Robert A. Wampler, 201–222. Tokyo: Kodansha International, 2001.

Becker, William H. and Samuel Wells Jr., eds. *Economics and World Power: An Assessment of American Diplomacy Since 1789*. New York: Columbia University Press, 1984.

Biven, W. Carl. *Jimmy Carter's Economy: Policy in an Age of Limits*. Chapel Hill: University of North Carolina Press, 2002.

Blackwill, Robert D. and Jennifer M. Harris. "The Lost Art of Economic Statecraft: Restoring an American Tradition." *Foreign Affairs* 95:2 (March–April 2016): 99–110.

Blainey, Geoffrey. *The Causes of War*. London: Macmillan, 1973.

Bockman, Johanna. *Markets in the Name of Socialism: The Left-Wing Origins of Neoliberalism*. Stanford: Stanford University Press, 2011.

Bolt, Christine. *The Women's Movements in the United States and Britain from the 1790s to the 1920s*. Amherst: University of Massachusetts Press, 1993.

Branch, Taylor, *The Clinton Tapes: Conversations with a President, 1993–2001*. New York: Simon & Schuster, 2009.

Braumoeller, Bear F. *Only the Dead: The Persistence of War in the Modern Age*. New York: Oxford University Press, 2019.

Brinkley, Douglas, ed. *The Reagan Diaries: Volume I: January 1981–October 1985*. New York: HarperCollins, 2007.

Brockway, Thomas. *Battles Without Bullets: The Story of Economic Warfare*. New York: Foreign Policy Association, 1939.

Brown, Sherrod. *Myths of Free Trade: Why American Trade Policy Has Failed*. New York: Free Press, 2004.

Burgin, Angus. *The Great Persuasion: Reinventing Free Markets Since the Great Depression*. Cambridge, MA: Harvard University Press, 2012.

Burke, Kyle. "Radio Free Enterprise: The Manion Forum and the Making of the Transnational Right in the 1960s. *Diplomatic History* 40:1 (January 2016): 111–139.

Butler, Michael A. *Cautious Visionary: Cordell Hull and Trade Reform, 1933–1937*. Kent, OH: Kent State University Press, 1998.

Caedel, Martin. *Pacifism in Britain, 1914–1945*. New York: Oxford University Press, 1980.

Caedel, Martin. *Semi-Detached Idealists: The British Peace Movement and International Relations*. New York: Oxford University Press, 2000.

Caldwell, Bruce, ed. *The Collected Works of F. A. Hayek*, vol. 2, *The Road to Serfdom: Text and Documents: The Definitive Edition*. Chicago: University of Chicago Press, 2007.

Calleo, David P. "Since 1961: American Power in a New World Economy." In *Economics and World Power: An Assessment of American Diplomacy Since 1789*, ed. William H. Becker and Samuel Wells Jr. New York: Columbia University Press, 1984.

Caryl, Christian. *Strange Rebels: 1979 and the Birth of the 21st Century*. New York: Basic Books, 2013.

Chanda, Nayan. *Bound Together: How Traders, Preachers, Adventurers, and Warriors Shaped Globalization*. New Haven, CT: Yale University Press, 2007.

Chang, Ha-Joon. *Bad Samaritans: The Myth of Free Trade and the Secret History of Capitalism.* London: Bloomsbury Press, 2009.

Choi, Seung-Whan. "Re-Evaluating Capitalist and Democratic Peace Models." *International Studies Quarterly* 55 (2011): 759–769.

Chorev, Nitsan. *Remaking U.S. Trade Policy: From Protectionism to Globalization.* Ithaca, NY: Cornell University Press, 2007.

Clausing, Kimberly. "The Progressive Case Against Protectionism: How Trade and Immigration Help American Workers." *Foreign Affairs* 98:6 (November–December 2019): 109–120.

Clavin, Patricia and Madeleine Dungy. "Trade, Law, and the Global Order of 1919." *Diplomatic History* 44:4 (September 2020): 554–579.

Clinton, Bill. *My Life.* New York: Alfred A. Knopf, 2004.

Cohen, Warren I. *America's Response to China: A History of Sino-American Relations,* 6th ed. New York: Columbia University Press, 2019.

Collins, Robert M. *More: The Politics of Economic Growth in Postwar America.* New York: Oxford University Press, 2000.

Colloque Lippmann. https://www.researchgate.net/publication/346606783_The_Colloque_Walter_Lippmann_How_to_Rebuild_the_Foundations_of_Liberalism.

Cooley, Alexander and Daniel H. Nexon. "The Real Crisis of Global Order: Illiberalism on the Rise." *Foreign Affairs* 101:1 (January–February 2022): 103–118.

Coppolaro, Lucia. *The Making of a World Trading Power: The European Economic Community (EEC) in the GATT Kennedy Round.* London: Routledge, 2013.

Cortright, David. *Peace: A History of Movements and Ideas.* New York: Cambridge University Press, 2008.

Crouch, Colin. *Making Capitalism Fit for Society.* Cambridge: Polity Press, 2013.

Dallek, Robert. *Franklin D. Roosevelt and American Foreign Policy, 1932–1945.* New York: Oxford University Press, 1979.

Destler, I. M., Haruhiro Fukui, and Hideo Sato. *The Textile Wrangle: Conflict in Japanese- American Relations, 1969–1971.* Ithaca, NY: Cornell University Press, 1979.

Dobson, Alan P. *US Economic Statecraft for Survival, 1933–1991.* Abingdon: Routledge, 2002.

Domke, William K. *War and the Changing Global System.* New Haven, CT: Yale University Press, 1988.

Dorussen, Han and Hugh Ward. "Trade Networks and Kantian Peace." *Journal of Peace Research* 47:1 (2010): 29–42.

Dryden, Steve. *Trade Warriors: USTR and the American Crusade for Free Trade.* New York: Oxford University Press, 1995.

Dumas, Lloyd J. "Economics and Alternative Security: Toward a Peacekeeping International Economy." In *Alternative Security: Living Without Nuclear Deterrence,* ed. Burn H. Weston. Boulder, CO: Westview Press, 1990.

Dumenil, Gerard and Dominique Levy. *The Crisis of Neoliberalism.* Cambridge, MA: Harvard University Press, 2011.

Dür, Andreas. *Protection for Exporters: Power and Discrimination in Transatlantic Trade Relations, 1930–2010.* Ithaca, NY: Cornell University Press, 2010.

Eckes, Alfred E. Jr. *Opening America's Market: U.S. Foreign Trade Policy Since 1776.* Chapel Hill: University of North Carolina Press, 1995.

Eckes, Alfred E. Jr. *Revisiting U.S. Trade Policy: Decisions in Perspective.* Athens: Ohio University Press, 2000.

Eckes, Alfred E. Jr. and Thomas W. Zeiler, *Globalization and the American Century.* Cambridge: Cambridge University Press, 2003.

Egan, Daniel. "Democracy, the State, and Global Capitalism." In *Democratic Peace in Theory and Practice,* ed. Steven W. Hook. Kent, OH: Kent University Press, 2010.

Elsig, Manfred and Cedric Dupont. "Persistent Deadlock in Multilateral Trade Negotiations: The Case of Doha." In *The Oxford Handbook on the World Trade Organization,* ed. Amrita Narlikar, Martin Daunton, and Robert M. Stern. Oxford: Oxford University Press, 2012.

Evans, Richard J. *Comrades and Sisters: Feminism, Socialism, and Pacifism in Europe, 1870–1945*. New York: St. Martin's Press, 1987.

Fawcett, Edmund. *Liberalism: The Life of an Idea*. Princeton, NJ: Princeton University Press, 2014.

Fergie, Dexter. "Geopolitics Turned Inwards: The Princeton Military Studies Group and the National Security Imagination." *Diplomatic History* 43:4 (September 2019): 644–670.

Fones-Wolf, Elizabeth. *Selling Free Enterprise: The Business Assault on Labor and Liberalism, 1945–1960*. Urbana: University of Illinois Press, 1994.

Franczak, Michael. "Losing the Battle, Winning the War: Neoconservatives Versus the New International Economic Order, 1974–82." *Diplomatic History* 43:5 (November 2019): 867–889.

Frank, Charles R. Jr. *Foreign Trade and Domestic Aid*. Washington, DC: Brookings Institution, 1977.

Frank, Dana. *Buy American: The Untold Story of Economic Nationalism*. Boston: Beacon Press, 1999.

Friedberg, Aaron L. "An Answer to Aggression: How to Push Back Against Beijing." *Foreign Affairs* 98:5 (September–October 2020): 150–164.

From, Al. *The New Democrats and the Return to Power*. New York: Palgrave Macmillan, 2013.

Gaddis, John L. "The Long Peace: Elements of Stability in the Postwar International System." *International Security* 10:4 (Spring 1989): 99–142.

Galbraith, James K. *The Predator State: How Conservatives Abandoned the Free Market and Why Liberals Should Too*. New York: Free Press, 2008.

Gamble, D. Geoffrey. *The NFTC Story, 1914–2014*. Indianapolis, IN: Dog Ear Publishing, 2014.

Gardner, Lloyd C. *Economic Aspects of New Deal Diplomacy*. Madison: University of Wisconsin Press, 1964.

Gardner, Lloyd C., Walter F. LaFeber, and Thomas J. McCormick. *Creation of the American Empire: U.S. Diplomatic History*. Chicago: Rand McNally, 1973.

Gardner, Richard N. *Sterling-Dollar Diplomacy: The Origins and the Prospects of Our International Economic Order*, exp. ed. New York: McGraw-Hill, 1969.

Gartzke, Eric. "The Capitalist Peace." *American Journal of Political Science* 51:1 (January 2007): 166–191.

Gartzke, Eric. "The Common Origins of Democracy and Peace." in *Democratic Peace in Theory and Practice*, ed. Steven W. Hook. Kent, OH: Kent State University Press, 2010.

Gewirtz, Julian. "China Thinks America Is Losing: Washington Must Show Beijing It's Wrong." *Foreign Affairs* 99:6 (November–December 2020): 62–72.

Gomes, Leonard. *The Economics and Ideology of Free Trade*. Cheltenham, UK: Edward Elgar, 2003.

Goodwin, Crawfurd D. *Walter Lippmann: Public Economist*. Cambridge, MA: Harvard University Press, 2014.

Gordon, Robert J. *The Rise and Fall of American Growth: The U.S. Standard of Living Since the Civil War*. Princeton, NJ: Princeton University Press, 2016.

Harvey, David. *A Brief History of Neoliberalism*. New York: Oxford University Press, 2005.

Hathaway, Robert M. "1933–1945: Economic Diplomacy in a Time of Crisis." In *Economics and World Power: An Assessment of American Diplomacy Since 1789*, ed. William H. Becker and Samuel Wells Jr. New York: Columbia University Press, 1984.

Hazlitt, Henry, *The Foundations of Morality*. Princeton, NJ: Van Nostrand, 1964.

Hegre, Havard, John R. Oneal, and Bruce Russett. "Trade Does Promote Peace: New Simultaneous Estimates of the Reciprocal Effects of Trade and Conflict." *Journal of Peace Research* 47:6 (2010): 763–774.

Herzog, Jonathan, *The Spiritual-Industrial Complex: America's Religious Battle Against Communism in the Early Cold War*. New York: Oxford University Press, 2011.

Hinkelman, Edward G. *Dictionary of International Trade: Handbook of the Global Trade Community*, 10th ed. Petaluma, CA: World Trade Press, 2013.

Hirschman, Albert O. *National Power and the Structure of Foreign Trade*. Berkeley: University of California Press, 1945.

Howe, Anthony. "Free Trade and Global Order: The Rise and Fall of a Victorian Vision." In *Victorian Visions of Global Order: Empire and International Relations in Nineteenth- Century Political Thought*, ed. Duncan Bell. Cambridge: Cambridge University Press, 2008.

Howe, Anthony. *Free Trade and Liberal England, 1846–1946*. Oxford: Oxford University Press, 1997.

Hufbauer, Gary Clyde and Howard F. Rosen. *Trade Policy for Troubled Industries*. Washington, DC: Institute for International Economics, March 1986.

Hull, Cordell. *The Memoirs of Cordell Hull*, vols. 1 and 2. New York: Macmillan, 1948.

Hunt, Michael H. *Ideology and U.S. Foreign Policy*. New Haven, CT: Yale University Press, 1987.

Hyland, William G. "U.S.-Soviet Relations: The Long Road Back." *Foreign Affairs* 60:3 (January 1981): 525–550.

Ikenberry, G. John. "The Next Liberal Order." *Foreign Affairs* 99:4 (July–August 2020): 133–142.

Ikenberry, G. John, David A. Lake, and Michael Mastanduno, eds. *The State and American Foreign Economic Policy*. Ithaca, NY: Cornell University Press, 1988.

Imlay, Talbot. "Clarence Streit, Federalist Frameworks, and Wartime American Internationalism." *Diplomatic History* 44:5 (November 2020): 808–833.

Ingleson, Elizabeth O. *Making Made in China: The Transformation of U.S.-China Trade in the 1970s*. Cambridge, MA: Harvard University Press, forthcoming.

Irwin, Douglas A. *Against the Tide: An Intellectual History of Free Trade*. Princeton, NJ: Princeton University Press, 1996.

Irwin, Douglas A. *Clashing over Commerce: A History of US Trade Policy*. Chicago: University of Chicago Press, 2017.

Irwin, Douglas A. *Free Trade Under Fire*, 3rd ed. Princeton, NJ: Princeton University Press, 2009.

Irwin, Douglas A., Petros C. Mavroidis, and Alan O. Sykes. *The Genesis of the GATT*. New York: Cambridge University Press, 2008.

Jackson, Julian. *De Gaulle*. Cambridge, MA: Harvard University Press, 2018.

Johnson, C. Donald. *The Wealth of a Nation: A History of Trade Politics in America*. New York: Oxford University Press, 2018.

Johnstone, Andrew. *Against Immediate Evil: American Internationalists and the Four Freedoms on the Eve of World War II*. Ithaca, NY: Cornell University Press, 2014.

Katznelson, Ira and Martin Shefter, eds. *Shaped by War and Trade: International Influences on American Political Development*. Princeton, NJ: Princeton University Press, 2002.

Kaufman, Burton I. *Trade and Aid: Eisenhower's Foreign Economic Policy, 1953–1961*. Baltimore, MD: Johns Hopkins University Press, 1982.

Kemp, Tom. *The Climax of Capitalism: The U.S. Economy in the Twentieth Century*. New York: Longman, 1990.

Keohane, Robert. O. *After Hegemony: Cooperation and Discord in the World Political Economy* Princeton, NJ: Princeton University Press, 1984.

Klein, Joe. *The Natural: The Misunderstood Presidency of Bill Clinton*. New York: Broadway Books, 2002.

Klein, Naomi. *Fences and Windows: Dispatches from the Front Lines of the Globalization Debate*. New York: Picador, 2002.

Klein, Naomi. *No Logo*. New York: Picador, 2002.

Kolozi, Peter. *Conservatives Against Capitalism: From the Industrial Revolution to Globalization*. New York: Columbia University Press, 2017.

Konczal, Mike. *Freedom from the Market: America's Fight to Liberate Itself from the Grip of the Invisible Hand*. New York: New Press, 2021.

Krasner, Stephen D. "Learning to Live with Despots: The Limits of Democracy Promotion." *Foreign Affairs* 99:2 (March–April 2020): 49–55.

Kriesberg, Louis. *Constructive Conflicts: From Escalation to Resolution*, 2nd ed. Lanham, MD: Rowman and Littlefield, 2003.

Kunz, Diane B. *Butter and Guns: America's Cold War Economic Diplomacy*. New York: Simon & Schuster, 1997.

Kupchan, Charles A. *Isolationism: A History of America's Efforts to Shield Itself from the World*. New York: Oxford University Press, 2020.

Kuttner, Robert. *The End of Laissez-Faire: National Purpose and the Global Economy after the Cold War*. Philadelphia: University of Pennsylvania Press, 1992.

Lawrence, Mark Atwood. *The End of Ambition: The United States and the Third World in the Vietnam Era*. Princeton, NJ: Princeton University Press, 2021.

Leebaert, Derek. *Grand Improvisation: America Confronts the British Superpower, 1945–1957* New York: Farrar, Straus and Giroux, 2018.

Leffler, Melvyn P. "1921–1932: Expansionist Impulses and Domestic Constraints." In *Economics and World Power: An Assessment of American Diplomacy Since 1789*, ed. William H. Becker and Samuel Wells Jr. New York: Columbia University Press, 1984.

Leffler, Melvyn P. *A Preponderance of Power: National Security, the Truman Administration, and the Cold War*. Stanford, CA: Stanford University Press, 1992.

Lehmann, Fabrice and Jean-Pierre Lehmann. *Peace and Prosperity Through World Trade: Achieving the 2019 Vision*. Cambridge: Cambridge University Press, 2010.

Lichtenstein, Nelson. "Market Triumphalism and the Wishful Liberals." In *Cold War Triumphalism: The Misuse of History After the Fall of Communism*, ed. Ellen Schrecker. New York: New Press, 2004.

Lighthizer, Robert E. "How to Make Trade Work for Workers." *Foreign Affairs* 99:4 (July–August 2020): 78–92.

Lind, Jennifer and Daryl G. Press. "Reality Check: American Power in an Age of Constraints." *Foreign Affairs* 99:2 (March–April 2020): 41–48.

Lynch, Cecilia. *Beyond Appeasement: Interpreting the Interwar Peace Movements*. Ithaca, NY: Cornell University Press, 1999.

MacDonald, Patrick J. *The Invisible Hand of Peace: Capitalism, the War Machine, and International Relations Theory*. Cambridge: Cambridge University Press, 2009.

Mallery, Otto Tod, *Economic Union and Durable Peace*. New York: Harper & Brothers, 1943.

Mallery, Otto Tod. *More than Conquerors: Building Peace on Fair Trade*. New York: Harper & Brothers, 1947.

Mandelbaum, Michael. *The Ideas that Conquered the World: Peace, Democracy, and Free Markets in the Twenty-First Century*. New York: Public Affairs, 2003.

Mansfield, Edward D. and Brian M. Pollins, eds. *Economic Interdependence and International Conflict: New Perspectives on an Enduring Debate*. Ann Arbor: University of Michigan Press, 2003.

Martin, Marty E. *Modern American Religion*, 3 vols. Chicago: University of Chicago Press, 1990s.

Matusow, Allen J. *Nixon's Economy: Booms, Busts, Dollars, and Votes*. Lawrence: University Press of Kansas, 1998.

Mazower, Mark. *Governing the World: The History of an Idea, 1815 to the Present*. New York: Penguin Books, 2012.

McKenzie, Francine. *GATT and Global Order in the Postwar Era*. Cambridge: Cambridge University Press, 2020.

Meijer, Hendrik. *Arthur Vandenberg: The Man in the Middle of the American Century*. Chicago: University of Chicago Press, 2017.

Meyer, Donald B., *The Protestant Search for Political Realism, 1919–1941*. Berkeley: University of California Press, 1960.

Mirowski, Philip and Dieter Plehwe. *The Road from Mont Pelerin: The Making of the Neoliberal Thought Collective*. Cambridge, MA: Harvard University Press, 2009.

Mousseau, Michael. "The Democratic Peace Unraveled: It's the Economy." *International Studies Quarterly* 57 (2013): 186–197.

Moreton, Bethany. *To Serve God and Wal-Mart: The Making of Christian Free Enterprise*. Cambridge, MA: Harvard University Press, 2009.

Morris, Ian. *War! What Is It Good For? Conflict and the Progress of Civilization from Primates to Robots*. New York: Farrar, Straus and Giroux, 2014.

Nash, George H. *The Conservative Intellectual Movement in America Since 1945*. New York: Intercollegiate Studies Institute, 2006.

Neff, Stephen. *Friends but No Allies: Economic Liberalism and the Law of Nations*. New York: Columbia University Press, 1990.

Ninkovich, Frank. *The Wilsonian Century: U.S. Foreign Policy Since 1900*. Chicago: University of Chicago Press, 1999.

Oneal, John R. and Bruce M. Russett. "The Classical Liberals Were Right: Democracy, Interdependence, and Conflict, 1950–1985." *International Studies Quarterly* 41 (1997): 267–294.

Overbeek, Johannes. *Free Trade Versus Protectionism: A Source Book of Essays and Readings*. Cheltenham, UK: Edward Elgar, 1999.

Palen, Marc-William. *The "Conspiracy" of Free Trade: The Anglo-American Struggle over Empire and Economic Globalisation, 1846–1896*. Cambridge: Cambridge University Press, 2016.

Panitch, Leo and Sam Gindin. *The Making of Global Capitalism: The Political Economy of American Empire*. London: Verso, 2012.

Pastor, Robert A. *Congress and the Politics of U.S. Foreign Economic Policy, 1929–1976*. Berkeley: University of California Press, 1980.

Phalan, Theodor, Deema Yazegi, and Thomas Rustici. "The Smoot-Hawley Tariff and the Great Depression." *Foundation for Economic Education*. https://fee.org/articles/the-smoot-hawley-tariff-and-the-great-depression/.

Philips-Fein, Kim. *Invisible Hands: The Businessmen's Crusade Against the New Deal*. New York: W.W. Norton, 2010.

Pinker, Steven. *The Better Angels of Our Nature: Why Violence Has Declined*. New York: Penguin Group, 2012.

Polachek, Solomon W. "Conflict and Trade." *Journal of Conflict Resolution* 24:1 (March 1980): 55–78.

Polachek, Solomon W. and Carlos Seiglie. "Trade, Peace and Democracy: An Analysis of Dyadic Dispute." *IZA (Institute for the Study of Labor) Discussion Paper* No. 2170 (June 2006): 1–93.

Pollard, Robert A. *Economic Security and the Origins of the Cold War, 1945–1950*. New York: Columbia University Press, 1985.

Pollard, Robert A. and Samuel F. Wells Jr. "1945–1960: The Era of American Economic Hegemony." In *Economics and World Power: An Assessment of American Diplomacy Since 1789*, ed. William H. Becker and Samuel Wells Jr. New York: Columbia University Press, 1984.

Prasad, Monica. *The Politics of Free Markets: The Rise of Neoliberal Economic Policies in Britain, France, Germany, and the United States*. Chicago: University of Chicago Press, 2006.

Richardson, Neil R. "International Trade as a Force for Peace." In *Controversies in International Relations Theory: Realism and the Neoliberal Challenge*, ed. Charles W. Kegley Jr. New York: St. Martin's Press, 1995.

Rosecrance, Richard. *The Rise of the Trading State: Commerce and Conquest in the Modern World*. New York: Basic Books, 1986.

Rosenberg, Emily S. *Financial Missionaries to the World: The Politics and Culture of Dollar Diplomacy, 1900–1930*. Cambridge, MA: Harvard University Press, 1999.

Rosenboim, Or. *The Emergence of Globalism: Visions of World Order in Britain and the United States, 1939–1950*. Princeton, NJ: Princeton University Press, 2017.

Ruggie, John Gerard. "Globalization and the Embedded Liberalism Compromise: The End of an Era?" *Max Planck Institute for the Study of Societies Working Paper*, 97/1. January 1997. https://www.researchgate.net/publication/5015525_Globalization_and_the_Embedded_Liberalism_Compromise_The_End_of_an_Era.

Ruggie, John Gerard. "International Regimes, Transactions, and Change: Embedded Liberalism in the Postwar Economic Order." In *International Regimes*, ed. Stephen D. Krasner. Ithaca, NY: Cornell University Press, 1983.

Russett, Bruce. "Capitalism or Democracy? Not So Fast." *International Interactions* 36:2 (April 2010): 198–205.

Russett, Bruce. *Grasping the Democratic Peace: Principles for a Post–Cold War World*. Princeton, NJ: Princeton University Press, 1993.

Russett, Bruce and John R. Oneal. *Triangulating Peace: Democracy, Interdependence, and International Organizations*. New York: W.W. Norton, 2001.

Samuels, Warren J., Jeff E. Biddle, and John B. Davis, eds. *A Companion to the History of Economic Thought*. Malden: Blackwell, 2003.

Sanchez-Sibony, Oscar. *Red Globalization: The Political Economy of the Soviet Cold War from Stalin to Khrushchev*. Cambridge: Cambridge University Press, 2016.

Sargent, Daniel J. *A Superpower Transformed: The Remaking of American Foreign Relations in the 1970s*. New York: Oxford University Press, 2015.

Schattschneider, E. E. *Politics, Pressures and the Tariff: A Study of Free Enterprise in Pressure Politics, as Shown in the 1929–1930 Revision of the Tariff*. New York: Prentice-Hall, 1935.

Schmitz, David F. *The Sailor: Franklin D. Roosevelt and the Transformation of American Foreign Policy, 1933–1945*. Lexington: University Press of Kentucky, 2021.

Schwartz, Jordan A. *Liberal: Adolf A. Berle and the Vision of an American Era*. New York: Free Press, 1987.

Semmel, Bernard. *The Rise of Free Trade Imperialism: Classical Political Economy and the Empire of Free Trade and Imperialism, 1750–1850*. Cambridge: Cambridge University Press, 1970.

Sestanovich, Stephen. *Maximalist: America in the World from Truman to Obama*. New York: Alfred A. Knopf, 2014.

Sewell, Bevan. "Pragmatism, Religion, and John Foster Dulles' Embrace of Christian Internationalism in the 1930s." *Diplomatic History* 41:4 (September 2017): 799–823.

Singh, Rajesh Kumar. "Trump's Tariffs Add to Pandemic-Induced Turmoil of U.S. Manufacturers," *Reuters Business News* (April 30, 2020), https://www.reuters.com/article/us-health-coronavirus-tariffs-idUSKBN22C1MY.

Slobodian, Quinn. *Globalists: The End of Empire and the Birth of Neoliberalism*. Cambridge. MA: Harvard University Press, 2018.

Sluga, Glenda and Patricia Clavin, eds. *Internationalisms: A Twentieth-Century History*. Cambridge, MA: Cambridge University Press, 2017.

Smil, Vaclav. *Made in the USA: The Rise and Retreat of American Manufacturing*. Cambridge, MA: MIT Press, 2013.

Smith, Tony. *Why Wilson Matters: The Origins of American Liberal Internationalism and Its Crisis Today*. Princeton, NJ: Princeton University Press, 2017.

Sobek, David. *The Causes of War*. Cambridge, UK: Polity Press, 2009.

Spiegel, Henry William. *The Growth of Economic Thought*, 3rd ed. Durham, NC: Duke University Press, 1991.

Staley, Charles E. *A History of Economic Thought: From Aristotle to Arrow*. Cambridge: Basil Blackwell, 1989.

Starr, Harvey, "Democratic Peace and Integration: Synergies Across Levels of Analysis." In *Approaches, Levels, and Methods of Analysis in International Politics: Crossing Boundaries*, ed. Harvey Starr. New York: Palgrave Macmillan, 2006.

Stein, Judith. *Pivotal Decade: How the United States Traded Factories for Finance in the Seventies*. New Haven, CT: Yale University Press, 2010.

Steward, Dick. *Trade and Hemisphere: The Good Neighbor Policy and Reciprocal Trade*. Columbia: University of Missouri Press, 1975.

Strange, Susan. "Protectionism and World Politics," *International Organization* 39:2 (Spring 1985): 233–234

Streit, Clarence. K. *Union Now: A Proposal for a Federal Union of the Democracies of the North Atlantic*. New York: Harper & Brothers, 1940.

Szporluk, Roman. *Communism and Nationalism: Karl Marx Versus Friedrich List*. New York: Oxford University Press, 1988.

Talley, Christian. *Forgotten Vanguard: Informal Diplomacy and the Rise of United States-China Trade, 1972–1980*. Notre Dame, IN: University of Notre Dame Press, 2018.

Thompson, Michael G. *For God and Globe: Christian Internationalism in the United States Between the Great War and the Cold War*. Ithaca, NY: Cornell University Press, 2015.

Trentmann, Frank. *Free Trade Nation: Commerce, Consumption, and Civil Society in Modern Britain*. Oxford: Oxford University Press, 2008.

Treu, Nina, Matthias Schmelzer, and Corinna Burkhart, eds. *Degrowth in Movements: Exploring Pathways for Transformation*. London: Zero Books, 2020.

Tribe, Keith. *Strategies of Economic Order: German Economic Discourse, 1750–1950*. Cambridge: Cambridge University Press, 1995.

United States International Trade Commission. *A Centennial History of the United States International Trade Commission*. USITC Publication 4744. Washington, DC: USITC, November 2017.

Vernon, Raymond Vernon. "America's Foreign Trade Policy and the GATT." *Essays in International Finance* 21 (October 1954): 1–25.

Villard, Oswald Garrison. *Free Trade, Free World*. New York: Robert Schalkenbach, 1947.

Viner, Jacob. *Studies in the Theory of International Trade*. New York: Harper and Brothers, 1937.

Waterhouse, Benjamin. *Lobbying America: The Politics of Business from Nixon to NAFTA*. Princeton, NJ: Princeton University Press, 2014.

Wertheim, Stephen. "The Price of Primacy: Why America Shouldn't Dominate the World." *Foreign Affairs* 99:2 (March–April 2020): 19–29.

Wertheim, Stephen. *Tomorrow the World: The Birth of U.S. Global Supremacy*. Cambridge, MA: Belknap Press, 2020.

White, Lawrence. *The Clash of Economic Ideas: The Great Policy Debates and Experiments of the Last Hundred Years*. New York: Cambridge University Press, 2012.

Whitham, Charlie. *Post-War Business Planners in the United States, 1939–48: The Rise of the Corporate Moderates*. London: Bloomsbury Academic, 2016.

Wilcox, Clair. *A Charter for World Trade*. New York: Macmillan, 1949.

Williams, William A. *The Tragedy of American Diplomacy*, 3rd ed. New York: W. W. Norton, 1972.

Woods, Randall B. *A Changing of the Guard: Anglo-American Relations, 1941–1946*. Chapel Hill: University of North Carolina Press, 1990.

Zeiler, Thomas W. *American Trade and Power in the 1960s*. New York: Columbia University Press, 1992.

Zeiler, Thomas W. "Business Is War in U.S.-Japanese Economic Relations, 1977–2001," In *Partnership: The United States and Japan, 1951–2001*, ed. Akira Iriye and Robert A. Wampler, 223–248. Tokyo: Kodansha International, 2001.

Zeiler, Thomas W. *Free Trade, Free World: The Advent of GATT*. Chapel Hill: University of North Carolina Press, 1999.

Zeiler, Thomas W. "Nixon Shocks Japan, Inc." In *Nixon in the World: American Foreign Relations, 1969–1977*, ed. Fredrik Logevall and Andrew Preston. New York: Oxford University Press, 2008.

Zeiler, Thomas. W. "Requiem for the Common Man: Class, the Nixon Economic Shock, and the Perils of Globalization." *Diplomatic History* 37:1 (January 2013): 1–23.

Zhang, Shu Guang. *Beijing's Economic Statecraft During the Cold War, 1949–1991*. Washington, DC: Woodrow Wilson Center Press, 2014.

Zipp, Samuel. *The Idealist: Wendell Willkie's Wartime Quest to Build One World*. Cambridge, MA: Harvard University Press, 2020.

Dissertations

Greco, John F. "A Foundation for Internationalism: The Carnegie Endowment for International Peace, 1931–1941." Syracuse University, 1971.

Kinne, Brandon. "Beyond the Dyad: How Networks of Economic Interdependence and Political Integration Reduce Interstate Conflict." Yale University, 2009.

Paterson, Thomas G. "The Economic Cold War: American Business and Economic Foreign Policy, 1945–1950." University of California, Berkeley, 1968.
Pennar, J. "Richard Cobden and Cordell Hull: A Comparative Study of the Commercial Policies of Nineteenth Century England and Contemporary United States." Princeton University, 1953.
Sedgewick, Augustine Keefe. "The American System in the World Depression, 1932–1941: The Case of the Coffee Trade." Harvard University, 2011.

INDEX

For the benefit of digital users, indexed terms that span two pages (e.g., 52–53) may, on occasion, appear on only one of those pages.